Minding THE SPIRIT

Minding THE SPIRIT

THE STUDY OF CHRISTIAN SPIRITUALITY

Edited by

Elizabeth A. Dreyer & Mark S. Burrows

The Johns Hopkins University Press
Baltimore & London

© 2005 The Johns Hopkins University Press
All rights reserved. Published 2005
Printed in the United States of America on acid-free paper
9 8 7 6 5 4 3 2 1

Acknowledgment of prior publication of chapters in this book will be found on pp. 381–82, which constitutes a continuation of the copyright page.

The Johns Hopkins University Press
2715 North Charles Street
Baltimore, Maryland 21218-4363
www.press.jhu.edu

Library of Congress Cataloging-in-Publication Data
Minding the Spirit : the study of Christian spirituality / edited by Elizabeth A. Dreyer and Mark S. Burrows.
    p. cm.
Includes bibliographical references.
    ISBN 0-8018-8076-9 (hardcover : alk. paper) — ISBN 0-8018-8077-7 (pbk. : alk. paper)
    1. Spirituality.   I. Dreyer, Elizabeth, 1945–   II. Burrows, Mark S., 1955–
BV4501.3.M558 2005
248—dc22   2004013500

A catalog record for this book is available from the British Library.

To our mentors,

to all who seek a deeper Christian life,

and to those whose call is to "mind the Spirit"

CONTENTS

VIII

PREFACE

*I*t is not often that the academy witnesses the birth of a new discipline. But the essays in *Minding the Spirit* provide a historical and substantive overview of just such an event: the study of spirituality as an academic discipline. There are parallels. Just a century and a half ago, no one had ever heard of psychology or sociology, and now they are established fields of inquiry. The journey for the field of spirituality has been from the ground up; its roots are truly "grass" roots. In North America, interest in what we now call popular spirituality is usually traced back to the 1960s, a time of change and upheaval when a significant portion of the population began to experiment with new forms of consciousness and communication that took the inner life seriously.

Many turned to sources unfamiliar in the West. Some looked to the East, experimenting with transcendental meditation, yoga, and apprenticeship with gurus. Others benefited from Native American traditions, participating in sweat lodges and other rituals linked to nature and the earth. Some feminists found liberation in the practice of Wicca, and many people sought out recently retrieved Celtic attitudes and practices. Still others developed novel spiritualities—what we now call "New Age"—that involve practices such as channeling and the use of crystals. A cursory glance at spirituality offerings in bookstores and on the World Wide Web quickly reveals the vastness and diversity of spiritualities and opportunities for spiritual pilgrims of every stripe. The response to this awakening is remarkable not only for its breadth but also for the varieties of religious experience it embraces. Spirituality is fast becoming a household word not only in churches, mosques, synagogues, and other religious communities, but in corporate America, in medicine, in the academy, and in the global marketplace of ideas and practices.

This soul hunger is not limited to North America but is visible across the globe. Tensions between Israelis and Palestinians, Britain and Ireland, Bosnians and Serbs, and the magnitude of recent terrorist events in the United States

(9/11/01) and Spain (3/11/04) cause us to wring our hands and rend our garments. Can we figure out how to live in peace and preserve our ailing planet? With the world in such disarray, humanity spontaneously looks for answers in unexpected or neglected places, one of which involves reconnection with our spiritual traditions. The experience of crisis, in addition to being a temptation to cynicism and self-pity, can become an invitation to new life.

In the North American and European context, some might see in this spiritual hunger a creative response to the seeming distance or even absence of the holy, a constructive alternative to the decline of traditional religious communities. Others might identify its origins in more positive ways: as a longing for the "more" of life beyond work and the futile quest for status and images of success; in the dissatisfaction that ensues from our insatiable desire for material goods; in a desire to have our imagination engaged; in a renewed wonder at the beauty of the world; in delight in reconnecting with the poetry of life and language. Polish poet Adam Zagajewski reminds us to "praise the mutilated world," filled as it is with exiles, the debris of war, refugees, and other contingencies but also with "the gentle light that strays and vanishes and returns" ("Try to Praise the Mutilated World"). What is involved in taking the time to identify and respond to our deepest desires? To what powers will we turn for the ongoing conversion shaped by both realism and hope?

We marvel and rejoice at the energy and creativity of this quest. But it is also the case that this clamor for the spiritual has become a din about which we worry. Is there any order? Where are these movements headed? Are they anchored in any way in venerable traditions of the past? Do we know what we, or others, are doing? Can we tell the difference between spiritualities of life and those that bring death and destruction on personal and social levels? Can we distinguish between spirituality as ego-trip and as genuine transformation? Faced with the "clear ambiguity" of this resurgence of interest in spirituality in the twenty-first century, we can throw up our hands in confusion and despair or view this sea change as an opportunity, a lure to ever-deeper encounters with God and reality.

The future integrity and viability of spiritualities will depend on leaders and scholars committed to the well-being of the many who seek spiritual enlightenment and freedom. Some will attend to the processes of discernment, developing the insight to notice the difference between constructive and destructive paths. Practitioners will nurture the spiritual development of others through the study and mastery of spiritual disciplines, passing them on from one generation to another. Innovators will experiment with new forms of spirituality, crossing or pushing boundaries in thoughtful and productive ways. Historians will work to identify and preserve from the tradition what is beneficial, and carefully discern what needs to be left behind or translated into new forms. Biblical scholars will wrestle with approaches that interpret texts in relevant and meaningful ways. Scholars trained in diverse disciplines will search out connections between spirituality and art, literature, economics, and sociology, to name but a few.

On this large and complex canvas, this volume is concerned with that brand of spirituality that is specifically Christian. As the reader will discover in the pages ahead, definitions of Christian spirituality may contain diverse elements, but they are also bordered by key concepts such as belief in a triune God, commitment to live a gospel life of love with justice and active concern for the world, and the means of self-transcendence that might lead us toward both personal and social transformation. The study of Christian spirituality is an interdisciplinary undertaking that is self-implicating and part of the wider discipline of spirituality seen from the perspectives of other religions as well as the secular realm.

HISTORICAL OVERVIEW

The recovery of spirituality as an academic discipline should be viewed in the context of the history of theological expression in Christianity's two-thousand-year history. In Christianity's earliest formal theological expression during the second century, Christians saw theology—reflection on the Scriptures, ministry, and participation in liturgy—as a seamless whole. Knowledge and love were integral dimensions of a theologian's work, joined in a loving knowledge and an intelligent love we call wisdom. This sapiential approach reached its apogee in the monastic theology of the Middle Ages, which was based on prayerful consideration of the Scriptures and their varying levels of meaning. Bernard of Clairvaux is a model of this type of integral biblical theology.

Bernard's contemporary in twelfth-century France, Abelard, is usually credited with the shift from theology as prayerful meditation on the Scriptures to theology as a reasoned, speculative activity. Abelard's *Sic et Non* noted and examined contradictions in the tradition and attempted to sort them out logically with the help of philosophical categories. With the emergence of the universities in Europe during the early thirteenth century, theologians began to specialize, making distinctions between biblical, doctrinal, and ascetical theology. The perspective in which theologians made no distinction between the practice of the spiritual life and formal, systematic study of it—Bonaventure and Thomas Aquinas are examples—gave way to a theology at once dialectic and dogmatic that distinguished itself from the pastoral and spiritual aspects of the theological task.

In addition to constant assaults from dualistic perspectives that pitted spirit against matter, a number of theological tensions became divisions. Intellect and affect grew apart as their functions were distinguished: the spiritual life engaged the will in pursuit of divine goodness, while the academic life engaged the mind in the pursuit of divine truth. Increasingly the spiritual life was seen as interior and private, no longer linked to the church's liturgy nor to a morality shaped by structures of public accountability. In addition, there was a diminishment of confidence in the power of symbols to reveal the divine. Reason came to be seen as a surer way than the imagination to encounter and speak about God. Furthermore, in fourteenth-century theologians' writings, the distance between an almighty, transcendent, and absolutely free God, and human beings, subject to the vagaries and vicissitudes of history, began to widen.

As the modern period advanced, the theological task was divided into further specialties. Dogmatic or systematic theology among Roman Catholic theologians was divorced from what became ascetic or mystical theology. As a result of the growing authority of the scientific method in intellectual circles of the seventeenth century, the latter type of theology was assigned a second-class place and gradually forced to the margins of academic theological work. Spiritual theology attended to Christian piety and perfection, practices that shaped the practical, everyday spiritual life of Christians. Systematic theology became the "real" theology of the academy, no longer tethered to the messy world of the community's lived faith.

Fortunately, we are now addressing these many separations in order to make way for new forms of unity. From the grass roots, spirituality has now regained a position in the academy, and this volume traces this important story, one that we hope will have a long and prosperous future.

SPIRITUALITY: DEFINITIONS AND DESCRIPTIONS

The reader will encounter a range of definitions and descriptions of spirituality in the pages ahead. This should come as no surprise. While a great deal of progress has been made in identifying its contours and boundaries, the work of definition goes on, as it should. The trick is to use the tensions of definition in responsible and creative, rather than stultifying, ways. Both the practice of spiritualities and the discipline that engages in ordered reflection on them are on the move, creating a flux with which it is difficult to keep up. While we may find the diversity and the momentum exhilarating, this instability makes efforts like *Minding the Spirit* especially important. We need to step back, to reflect carefully on the plethora of developments in spirituality in order to sift the nourishing wheat from the ephemeral chaff—even though we know well that our conclusions are also provisional, part of an on-going harvest from past traditions that will allow us to till the soil of the present and plant seeds for the future.

A general definition of the term "spirituality" encompasses the following: the daily lived aspect of one's faith commitment in terms of values and behaviors; how one appropriates beliefs about God and the world; the process of conscious integration and transformation of one's life; the journey of self-transcendence; the depth dimension of all human existence; a dialectic that moves one from the inauthentic to the authentic and from the individual to the communal; the quest for ultimate value and meaning. This broader focus can include elements that are explicitly religious, such as prayer, spiritual disciplines, sacraments, retreats, worship, and Bible reading. A particularly Christian spirituality is one that involves conscious discipleship, opening oneself to grace in the generosity of the Creator, through the love of God, by the grace of Jesus Christ, and in the power of the Spirit.

The roots of the word "spirituality" can be traced to the letters of Paul, where he uses the Greek term *pneuma* to refer to a life lived in harmony with the Spirit of God. The Latin word *spiritualitas* first appeared in the fifth century. But by the twelfth century, Paul's concept of spirituality as life lived in the power of the Holy Spirit had given way to an opposition between spiritual and material reality. The body, instead of functioning as the primary vehicle for holiness, began to be seen as an obstacle, even the enemy, of the spiritual life. In the seventeenth century, the French began to use *spiritualité* negatively, to refer to a form of the devout life that was seen to be excessively individualistic and passive. But it was not until the twentieth century that "spirituality" began to refer more generally to the interior life, styles of piety, or the life of the soul. By the 1950s the word had entered a broad popular usage that continues, having expanded from its Roman Catholic home to other Christian denominations, to the practices of other world religions, and to a variety of secular forms, resulting in a bewildering array of meanings.

Walter Principe, C.S.B., was one of the first thinkers to reflect more systematically on the meaning and geography of spirituality. He articulated a three-tiered definition that has been helpful in bringing clarity to the ancient yet ever new experience of spirituality. On the first level, he located the actual lived experience of the spiritual life, that is, the attitudes, dispositions, and practices of daily Christian existence. At this level, one's faith becomes visible in the course of an ordinary day. At the second level reside the communal aspects of spirituality, the spirituality experienced in the family, parish, or congregation. The communal spirituality can also be identified by geography or culture—Latin or Eastern forms—and in modernity by denomination, such as Lutheran, Anglican, or Quaker spiritualities. There are also communal forms of lay spirituality and of vowed religious traditions, such as the Augustinian, Carmelite, Franciscan, Dominican, and Jesuit schools of spirituality. The third level, the level addressed in this volume, encompasses formal reflection on the practice and meaning of the spiritual life.

CONTENTS OF THIS VOLUME

The essays presented here document and make available to the public salient aspects of groundbreaking conversations about the academic discipline of spirituality. In the Introduction, "Beginnings," Douglas Burton-Christie, editor of the journals in which these essays were first published, recounts the contours of the study of spirituality during the important decade of the 1990s, which witnessed the founding of the Society for the Study of Christian Spirituality. This society established the *Christian Spirituality Bulletin* (published 1993–2000), as a forum for serious discussion and examination of issues related to the study of spirituality, one that continues in its new incarnation, *Spiritus*. We invite the reader to join in this conversation, to learn about, absorb, add to, and make use of these critical analyses on the substance, methods, and implications of the study of spirituality.

The essays included in this volume were all first published in the *Bulletin* or *Spiritus*. They engage a group of topics, among the much broader spectrum of themes currently being addressed by scholars of spirituality, and offer timely insight into the kinds of questions, methods, and critical approaches employed by scholars in the field. We have arranged the essays under five broad headings, each introduced by an overview. Part I, "Spirituality as an Academic Discipline: Foundations and Methods," addresses the basic intellectual structure, methods, and directions relevant to the academic study of spirituality. Part II, "The Self-Implicating Nature of the Study of Spirituality," probes the importance of subjectivity and participation, as well as the reading of texts (hermeneutics) and contexts (interdisciplinarity) as shaping factors in research on spirituality. Part III, "Interpreting the Tradition: Historical and Theological Perspectives," grounds and links spirituality with its rich two-thousand-year tradition and explores the crucial relationship between theology and spirituality. Part IV, "Spirituality and Healing," reflects on the healing nature of spirituality and underlines the importance of praxis for the discipline by broadening the theoretical orientations of the earlier sections in terms of concrete examples in particular contexts. The last part, "Spirituality and Aesthetics," treats the reader to a feast of images and sounds, presenting them as central to the experience and study of religious experience. The Afterword examines the view ahead for this young discipline that is so full of promise. We observe strengths and weaknesses of what has gone before and note neglected areas, but above all we suggest an imaginative vision of where the discipline may take us in the immediate years ahead. We conclude with suggestions for further reading, in the hope that readers will be moved to continue their study of particular aspects of spirituality to which they are especially drawn.

This volume is intended for a wide audience. Christians engaged in an intentional spiritual journey will be enriched by the organized reflection these essays provide. Clergy, religious, and Christian lay ministers will be aided by the ways in which this material can ground and inform the many streams of Christian service. Scholars working within and beyond the broad boundaries of Christian communities and educational institutions will benefit from the accessibility of essays covering the salient aspects of this new discipline. Students of spirituality or related theological, biblical, and historical fields will find this material invaluable, particularly in terms of key historical developments and methodological questions that advance the boundaries of this and related disciplines in new and constructive ways. Teachers of spirituality and mentors in the spiritual life will rejoice in the help this volume will provide for their own labors and for a focused reading of relevant material with and for their students and fellow seekers. Finally, this volume invites serious practitioners and students of spirituality from other religions or secular perspectives to enter into dialogue with one of the world's great religious traditions.

ACKNOWLEDGMENTS

The production of this volume has been a genuine team effort, and there are many people to thank. The editors received invaluable assistance in the detailed task of re-keying, scanning, and editing the essays from the *Christian Spirituality Bulletin* from Charlene Wallace, Alison Cornish, and David Perrin. The College of Arts and Sciences at Fairfield University provided a grant to help defray expenses related to the preparation of *Minding the Spirit*, as did Andover Newton Theological School in funding a portion of the technical assistance for this project.

We also acknowledge with gratitude the Society for the Study of Christian Spirituality, which for more than a decade has gathered together scholars working in the field of Christian spirituality. The meetings of this society at the annual conventions of the American Academy of Religion and the Society of Biblical Literature have been the occasion for much conversation about the dimensions of this emerging field. Particular thanks are due to all of our authors, whose careful thinking and articulation of so many important aspects of the study of spirituality provide the meat of this historic and important work. Authors were quick to respond to requests for information and encouraged our efforts to produce this volume.

Finally, we are grateful to our editor, Henry Tom, and his assistant, Claire McCabe, at the Johns Hopkins University Press, who provided answers to questions and shepherded the volume to publication with expeditiousness and aplomb.

INTRODUCTION: BEGINNINGS

DOUGLAS BURTON-CHRISTIE

*T*here is a country and western song whose refrain is, "Mamas, don't let your babies grow up to be cowboys." I cannot remember precisely why this stern warning was issued. No doubt it had something to do with the singer's rueful awareness that most cowboys are scoundrels, unable to hold down a steady job, incapable of steadfastness in love, destined to wander endlessly from one part of the range to another stirring up trouble along the way. As far as I know, no one has yet penned the words, "Mamas, don't let your babies grow up to be editors." Nor is it difficult to see why. The image of an editor buried deep in manuscripts, struggling to meet deadlines, worrying over delinquent or unhappy authors, never quite getting to the end of the process (because there is no end), is not completely without pathos; but neither does it grip us imaginatively the way the fate of that lonesome cowboy does. Alas.

This editor never imagined he would grow up to become one. It came about completely by accident. But like many unplanned and unexpected events, it has brought with it many interesting and happy surprises. Not least of these is the opportunity to engage, over a period of more than ten years, an extraordinary community of scholars, teachers, and practitioners of Christian spirituality. If a journal can help community to happen—and I believe this has been true of both the *Christian Spirituality Bulletin* and *Spiritus*—then it is doing its work in the world. If along the way, those participating in the creation of the journal—authors, reviewers, readers, editors—learn valuable things about their field and gain maturity and depth of vision in relation to their own work, then one has to count the whole exercise as utterly worthwhile. In these introductory remarks, I would like to comment on some of what I have learned during these past ten years working as editor of these two journals.

My first observation has to do with the importance of community and conversation and the role a journal can play in helping to cultivate both. There is an undeniably solitary dimension to the work of scholarship. At the same time, most of us long to be in conversation with others, to learn through the give and take of conversation. Not only is there great pleasure to be had in conversation, but it is also necessary to the honing and maturing of any given scholar's work. Often, we only come to know the value of our work (as well its weaknesses) through the process of public dissemination. In the spring of 1993, when the first issue of the *Christian Spirituality Bulletin* appeared, there was already a lively conversation among scholars about the meaning of spirituality. The Paulist Press series Classics of Western Spirituality was well developed by then; Crossroad was publishing its encyclopedia *World Spirituality*. Articles and essays on spirituality appeared from time to time in various journals (whose primary vision was usually *not* spirituality). There was a growing interest in spirituality visible in diverse locales within the academy and within society and culture at large. Still, in a very real sense, scholars committed to the work of reflecting critically on the Christian spiritual traditions had no gathering place where they could meet and discuss their work.

This began to change during the early 1990s, first with the creation of the Society for the Study of Christian Spirituality (SSCS) in 1992 and then with the appearance of the *Christian Spirituality Bulletin* in 1993 as the official publication of the society. The meetings of the SSCS, held in conjunction with the annual convention of the American Academy of Religion and the Society of Biblical Literature, provided a place where scholars in the field could count on engaging their colleagues seriously about matters of shared concern. The *Christian Spirituality Bulletin* offered something comparable, a scholarly journal devoted to critical reflection on an entire range of texts, traditions, and questions relating to Christian spirituality.

From its inception, the journal was conversational and informal in tone. The first issue featured responses to Philip Sheldrake's groundbreaking book *Spirituality and History*, which had provided the focal point for the first gathering of the SSCS in San Francisco in 1992. We conversed, listened, and responded to one another's work, striving continuously to expand the conversation in new directions. And to a great extent, this is how the journal continued to operate for the next eight years. In the process, as we continued working and reflecting together, both in the *Bulletin* and during our annual meetings, a common discourse began to emerge about the field as a whole. Of course, this is not to say that there was always consensus about the key issues or about the appropriate methods for examining them. Not at all. But what did emerge was a growing sense of the range of questions that belonged within the discourse of spirituality and the distinctive methods and approaches that characterized our work. In this sense, it seems clear to me that the spirit of conversation that characterized the work of the *Bulletin* and of the SSCS as a whole has been crucial to the development and maturing of the field during the past ten years.

Engaging in an authentic, open-ended conversation also means allowing the conversation to go where it will. This has been a characteristic feature of the work of the *Bulletin* from its inception and has continued to characterize the work of *Spiritus,* which emerged as the journal of the society in 2001. We have emphasized the need for openness in pursuing almost any question that seems pertinent to the task of understanding better the shape and character of spiritual experience. Many of these questions reflect the state of Christian spirituality as a field of study, a field gradually coming into its own in terms of methods and approaches. Questions of method, for example, have figured prominently in the essays that appeared in the *Bulletin*. Some of these have to do with broad methodological questions regarding the particular shape of the field and its relationship to other fields. This has been particularly challenging given the complex origins of the field of Christian spirituality and its identification at one time or another in its evolution with historical studies and with systematic theology. The question of how to locate the field and what methods are most appropriate and useful becomes even more complex when the relationship between spirituality and a wide range of non-theological or religious disciplines is brought into view. Certainly such questions have a particular interest to scholars, for whom issues of method are bound to figure prominently. Locating spirituality in this way within the context of related disciplines is a tremendous help in elucidating how the interpretation of spiritual experience can be most meaningfully pursued. But the effort to locate spirituality as a discipline has a much wider application, especially given the present cultural climate, in which the language of spirituality is becoming increasingly important as a means of articulating how human beings understand the place and significance of transcendence in their lives. The eclectic and non-religious meanings attached to spirituality require an effort to scrutinize and evaluate the assumptions that govern its usage. The investigation of such questions has become an important part of the work of contemporary scholars of spirituality.

Other challenges involve the discipline's place in the academy. In spite of increasing attention to questions of spirituality in a range of academic disciplines, including sociology, psychology, medicine, ecology, and business, there is a widespread popular perception of spirituality as naïve and intellectually shallow. The marketing of spirituality for mass consumption feeds into such stereotypes. Here, spirituality is often characterized by a dizzying eclecticism, by a focus on the individual spiritual journey (as distinct from its communal and political dimensions), by a lack of any coherent theology, and by a free-floating sense of the Spirit unmoored from historical experience. The widespread popular interest in spirituality is certainly an important phenomenon of our time that ought to be taken seriously. However, when spirituality is identified largely in terms of this popular approach, it becomes immensely challenging to articulate an understanding of spirituality that is critical and intellectually serious. This has always been an important part of the work of the SSCS—to investigate the meaning of spiritual experience both critically and creatively, with the aim of grasping more profoundly what it means for us as persons and as communities.

The precise nature of this critical, creative work varies depending on the particular issues under consideration. If one examines the key issues in both the *Bulletin* and *Spiritus,* several major themes emerge. Some of these pertain to questions of Christian identity, and this is consistent with the primary focus of these journals. However, much of the work transcends the bounds of the Christian tradition, touching on issues of broader concern. A brief review of these themes reveals many of the preoccupations of scholars in the field for the past decade or so.

One of the questions that surfaces persistently is the appropriate relationship between theology and spirituality. This is an old question, dating back to the very origins of Christianity. However, whereas the relationship between religious experience and the articulation of that experience in theological terms was more or less assumed to be integral in the earliest centuries of Christian experience, it has become for us a much more complex question. Part of the difficulty in the modern era has been the tendency in certain quarters to place spirituality at the service of systematic or dogmatic theology, obscuring the particular claims of spirituality as a way of understanding and interpreting spiritual experience. While there has been a sustained effort to free spirituality from unhelpful aspects of its relationship to theology, there has also been a growing recognition of the need to rethink the relationship between them. Part of this work has involved considering what becomes of theology when it fails to pay sufficient attention to the ground of experience that informs meaningful theological discourse. But the exploration has also included asking what happens to spirituality and the understanding of spiritual experience when it becomes detached from coherent theological articulation.

There has been a similar ferment among historians of Christian spirituality. One of the most significant achievements of the past fifty years has been the appearance of many critical editions and translations of classic texts (as well as previously obscure texts) in Christian spirituality. It is impossible to overestimate the significance of this fundamental work, for without it, the creative process of reinterpretation and retrieval would not be possible. Scholars of spirituality have learned to scrutinize the historical record more critically, noticing especially the gaps and silences that reveal patterns of exclusion. The recovery of voices mostly lost to us—the so-called heterodox, women, the socially and politically marginal—has been a significant accomplishment of recent decades. Equally important has been the increasingly wide range of methodologies employed by historians to interpret and critique the historical expression of spirituality. This includes the use of critical social and political theory to unmask systemic patterns of exclusion or exploitation or to illumi-nate larger cultural patterns that more traditional methods of interpretation often miss. It also includes an increasingly refined adaptation of methods developed in other fields, such as the use of papyrological evidence to illumi-nate social reality, or the critical investigation of art, sculpture, and architec-ture as a way of grasping the visual and spacial dimensions of spiritual experi-ence. What is gradually emerging is a more fully realized and complex sense of the spirituality of persons and communities from the historical past, something that has tremendous potential for helping contemporary Christian communi-ties reimagine themselves.

History is not the only arena where new methodologies are creating a fresh way of perceiving spiritual experience. Increasingly, the field of spirituality is benefiting from a vibrant and multifaceted engagement with other disciplines, such as psychology, sociology, political science, and the natural sciences. In some cases, methods and approaches from these fields are being employed to shed light on classic texts and figures from the history of Christian spirituality. However, there are also cognate fields that help interpret a range of contempo-rary issues in spirituality. For those working at developing a deeper and more adequate understanding of spiritual direction, for example, the use of methods and perspectives drawn from psychology has been invaluable. Scholars seeking to retrieve the ecological dimension of Christian spirituality have benefited immensely from conversations among biologists, cosmologists, poets, and natural historians concerning the intricate life of the natural world. The precise means through which one engages these other disciplines and draws upon their methods to articulate a coherent vision of Christian spirituality is still in the process of being fully articulated, but there is no doubt that our understanding of spiritual experience is deepened by a thoughtful, interdisciplinary engage-ment with these fields.

So, too, has work in the field been deepened by an awareness of the inescapably political dimensions of spirituality. Issues of politics, race, class, and gender have come to play an increasingly significant role in our under-standing of how we perceive and interpret spiritual experience. No longer is it possible to ignore these crucial dimensions of human experience as we attempt to understand where and how human beings experience themselves as touched by the Spirit or, alternatively, as degraded by racism, sexism, and classism. Conceptual habits with which the Christian spiritual tradition has long struggled—especially dualistic dichotomies between body and soul, heaven and earth, spirit and matter—have often obscured our capacity to take seriously the embodied, social, and political dimensions of spiritual experience. Increasingly, we are coming to see that unless we reckon with these issues, we will be left with a poor, thin, and ultimately inadequate, vision of Christian life.

A similar concern for depth and wholeness has motivated contemporary scholars in the field to seek out the presence of Spirit in what has often been understood as the margins of the Christian community. From its inception, the Christian community struggled to find conceptual language supple enough to encompass and describe the presence of God experienced by Christians while also taking seriously the authentic insight found within non-Christian spiritual experience. A similar challenge exists today, whether the focus is the emerging dialogue between Christian spirituality and the spiritualities of other major world religions, or the attempt to articulate the meaning of the many emerging secular or non-religious spiritualities. Certainly the differences among such varied expressions of spiritual experience are not to be minimized. Indeed, much of the work of scholarship that attends to the dialogue between and among these traditions must be about noticing the particularities, the differences. However, it is also crucial to discern those places of commonality that enable persons from different traditions to face one another with respect, honesty, and affection, and sometimes to discover in such relationships a kindred sense of spiritual experience. Christians have a huge stake in such questions, especially if we hope to engage and participate in the issues facing the wider human community.

The expansiveness that characterizes such inter-religious dialogue extends to the role of art in expressing and interpreting spiritual experience. Both the *Bulletin* and *Spiritus* have included art and aesthetic interests central to the conversation about the meaning of spirituality. These concerns have affected almost every aspect of the life of these two journals—the careful attention to design, the inclusion of photography and poetry as key parts of the journals' content, the sustained reflection on literature, music, painting, film, and other forms of artistic expression. Inquiring into the spiritual meaning of such artistic expression is, of course, a complex and demanding task. It is yet another arena where sophisticated interdisciplinary tools are required to assess the spirituality suggested or contained in works of art. Without this attention to art and its role in forming the religious imagination, we risk losing touch with a fundamental source of spirituality.

These are but some of the key concerns shaping the emerging field of Christian spirituality, and the list is by no means exhaustive of the interests and questions that occupy scholars in the field. Still, it provides an initial attempt to delineate the kinds of issues that have emerged with some consistency during the past ten years in the *Bulletin* and *Spiritus*. It is impossible to predict where the field will go from here. This is surely a sign of its creativity and vitality. The conversation that has emerged in these journals has contributed to this open-ended exploration of spiritual experience. As we engage one another in conversation, often across significant differences of confessional or disciplinary location, real opportunities have emerged for growth and deepening in our own understanding of how best to interpret the phenomena before us. Humility is necessarily involved in such a process. To learn to hold our own hard-won convictions while also opening ourselves to the insights and discoveries of others requires a capacity to enter into a social process of discovery. Such a communal vision is necessary to the work we are engaged in. *Minding the Spirit* presents the fruit of this conversation among persons who share a common commitment to search out with honesty and integrity the life of the Spirit in its manifold expressions. This volume is testimony to the vibrancy and depth of this commitment among its contributors and, we hope, its readers.

PART ONE

Spirituality as an Academic Discipline

Foundations and Methods

Spirituality is not an invention of modernity, though the modern academy has been the context in which the disciplined study of spirituality has emerged as a field of critical inquiry. This is not to suggest that spirituality has become the sole provenance of scholars. Nothing could be further from the truth. But it is fair to say that spirituality has been a growth industry in the book market of the last several decades. A casual survey of any general bookstore, whether in a large city or a small town, inevitably includes at least one prominent section devoted to spirituality under some rubric, including sections variously entitled "devotional literature," "metaphysics," "new age," "self-help," and so forth. Most of the volumes found on such shelves are of a practical nature, some loosely related to religious traditions and focused on experiences of one sort or another. They might offer guidance in prayer or meditation, suggest how readers can cultivate a deeper awareness of the interior life, or explore psychological insights borrowed from religious practices, traditions, or sources. Such books are often shaped by story and anecdote and only rarely delve into the area of critical reflection and analysis. Scholars laboring in the emerging field devoted to spirituality as an academic discipline might find such volumes interesting and perhaps even important as illustrative of cultural or religious trends, but rarely do these books offer much help in understanding spirituality from a critical point of view.

The essays collected in this opening section have helped to shape the definitions and methodologies used and adapted by scholars of this discipline, and they exemplify three noticeable features of the field. First, they share the view that the study of spirituality as an academic discipline generally goes on within existing fields, such as history and theology, while also creating its own methodological distinctiveness through the interdisciplinarity of this work. As a result, the emerging literature of this discipline borrows and adapts the methods, questions, and problems integral to established fields within the theological curriculum, developing a hybrid nature that mirrors wider trends in the intellectual scene of the late modern academy. Many contributors to this work have been trained as historians, theologians, or biblical scholars, but they bring to this inquiry a blending of methods and approaches in their commitment to understanding the lived experience and expression of Christian faith and life.

Second, exploration of questions of definition and method has established a close and complex relationship between scholars and practitioners of Christianity. The emergence of this field in academe reflects a deepening interest in spirituality within the wider society. Scholars are not the only voices in this conversation, and because the *critical* study of Christian spirituality is developing within such a lively context of cultural exchange, it is laden with the promises and perils inherent in broadly popular impulses. One hopes that this volume will find a place in the very bookstores mentioned above that cater to a general audience, because the explorations offered here are of importance not only for experts in the academy but also for those eager to deepen their own appreciation of the faith they have inherited.

Third, this new field has already begun to change the classical disciplines of the theological curriculum by bringing a different set of questions, assumptions, and approaches to bear on the study of Christianity. This emerging discipline is not only derivative from but is also exerting a formative influence upon the very departments and institutions within which those traditional scholarly pursuits are found. Whether this work is accomplished within existing fields in the academy or in emerging departments and programs devoted primarily to the study of Christian spirituality, the very presence of such integrative study shapes the ethos of the theological conversation conducted in the academy.

Questions of definition and method occupy scholarship in any emerging field, and the study of spirituality is no exception. In the lead essay of this section, Sandra Schneiders explores what she calls the contours and dynamics of this newly emergent plot in the academic landscape. She suggests that the formal object of this study, the "lived experience of the faith," defines the nature and shape of the discipline, which is intentionally driven by experience and self-consciously shaped by praxis. As such, it is deliberately and unavoidably interdisciplinary, and for this reason it resists an expertise understood as a commanding control of the material under scrutiny. Her discussion concludes with a long excursus on Christian spirituality as a self-implicating enterprise, a theme that occupies the entire second section of this volume. Here, she emphasizes the positive role of what she calls "constructive postmodernism" in this field of inquiry.

Approaching the question of methodology from a historical vantage point, Bernard McGinn explores the origin and development of the word "spirituality," from its original Latin forms to its various modern usages. McGinn suggests that we might speak of three expressions of spirituality: a dogmatic definition "from above"; an anthropological understanding "from below"; and a historical-contextual approach. It is this last approach that most occupies his discussion. He goes on to explore whether spirituality should be taught within the academy and how these various approaches influence it as an academic pursuit. His essay concludes with the assertion that such study need not be done from *within* a particular religious tradition—that is, as an expression of a defined confessional approach—but that it does require "a desire to try to appreciate how religious people actually live their beliefs." Its critical character is of vital concern to McGinn, since what he calls the "first-order definition" of spirituality as a formative discipline or practice has no place in academia but rather within "the traditions of spiritual training, which academics need to study but which they too often imitate at their own peril." He worries about adding a "practical" element to this study, a theme to which we return in Part II.

Within any religious community or tradition, texts are easily misread or "under-read" if studied in isolation from the broader context of religious practices and cultural sensibilities. Walter Principe's essay asserts that context is a necessary corrective lens in reading sources for the study (or practice) of spirituality. Texts alone, he insists, cannot provide a sufficient understanding of spiritual themes, traditions, or styles. He suggests that we locate the spirituality discerned in a given text or tradition within the particularity of its own time and place, arguing that historical and cultural context is decisive in properly understanding and appreciating any source. The proper reading and appropriation of such sources requires an *academic* and not merely a *personal* approach, since meaning is itself conditioned by context. Principe reminds us that a proper engagement with such sources is always a quest dependent upon hermeneutical issues, and thus he argues for what he calls a "microscopic view focused on the writings." Such an approach measures a text's meaning within its own horizon, first of all, and only on this basis suggests how meaning might be retrieved for later readers. Principe suggests that we develop and apply "a continually growing list of leading questions to think about" as we read any text in terms of its spirituality. Careful judgments based upon such an approach must come *before* assimilation. The critical study of texts is not one task among others but a necessary and unavoidable prerequisite for an accurate understanding of the spirituality studied.

In the final essay of this section, Sandra Schneiders offers a hermeneutical approach to the study of Christian spirituality. This piece directly responds to the questions and cautions posed in the preceding two contributions. In conversation with McGinn's criticism, Schneiders clarifies what she means in her emphasis on an anthropological approach to spirituality, exploring the significance of "an interdisciplinary hermeneutical approach which entertains a certain tensive openness toward the praxis issue even while eschewing any explicit formational agenda." This study, in other words, must honor the engaged, experiential dimensions of spirituality, even while resisting the temptation to conduct its work solely from the perspective of experience alone. She goes on to explore "the material and formal object" of this study and, in such terms, considers appropriate critical methods. Here again, experience emerges as a crucial and problematic element, requiring that we move beyond the traditional fields of historical and theological studies to include the social and natural sciences, comparative religion, aesthetics, literature and the arts, "and whatever other disciplines might be required by the character of the phenomenon" studied. Her essay concludes by examining praxis in the study of Christian spirituality, a theme that awaits more extensive probing in the second section of this volume.

The Study of Christian Spirituality

Contours and Dynamics of a Discipline

SANDRA M. SCHNEIDERS, I.H.M.

*T*he post-Enlightenment assumption that academic disciplines are self-evident and self-contained specializations, each adequately distinct from all others by reason of its object and method of study, is increasingly recognized as an illusion. As A. K. M. Adam, a biblical scholar, put it,

> . . . the disciplinary boundaries that seem "natural" to academic life are not defined by natural law or by some Platonic ideal toward which we are evolving. On the contrary, we define disciplines much more by such pragmatic considerations as whether there are numerous scholars investigating a particular set of questions, or whether enough students are likely to enroll in courses.[1]

This is not a cynical observation about the mercenary functioning of the academy, but a recognition of how academic disciplines actually do come into existence. Most of us in the field of spirituality started out as, and indeed remain, biblical scholars, historians, theologians, pastoral counselors, religious psychologists, or literary critics. We found ourselves increasingly interested in something that did not yet have a name in the academy but in which a number of our colleagues were also interested, and for which students were asking. The name "spirituality" emerged, was argued over, and seems to have gained general acceptance as an appropriate designation of this new discipline.[2] As discussion, writing, and teaching in this new area began to develop, the theoretical issues about the disciplinary nature of the new field arose.[3] It is these issues that I want to engage and advance in this essay.

DEFINING SPIRITUALITY

Traditionally, academic disciplines have been distinguished by their material object or *what* they study, their formal object or the *particular aspect* under which they study it, and their method or *how* they study it. Most scholars would agree that the *material object* of the discipline, i.e., *what* we study, is lived Christian faith. This designation is, however, a bit too vague and inclusive. I would, therefore, propose to specify this general formulation by a slightly modified version of a definition I proposed some years ago, namely, that spirituality as the subject matter or material object of the discipline is "the experience of conscious involvement in the project of life-integration through self-transcendence toward the ultimate value one perceives."[4] In Christian spirituality these formal categories are specified by Christian content: the horizon of ultimate value is the triune God revealed in Jesus Christ, and the project involves the living of his paschal mystery in the context of the Church community through the gift of the Holy Spirit. Living within this horizon of ultimate value, one relates in a particular way to all of reality and it is this relationship to the whole of reality and to reality as a whole in a specifically Christian way which constitutes Christian spirituality.

The *formal object* of the discipline, that is, the particular aspect under which this lived experience of the faith is studied, specifies the discipline. I would propose that the distinguishing formality of spirituality is its focus on "experience." Spirituality as a discipline does not seek to deduce from revelation what Christian spirituality must be, or to prescribe theologically its shape, character, or functioning, or even necessarily to promote pastorally its exercise.[5] It seeks to understand it as it actually occurs, as it actually transforms its subject toward fullness of life in Christ, that is, toward self-transcending life-integration within the Christian community of faith.

This formal object, the focus on Christian experience as experience, demands the interdisciplinarity of *method* that characterizes the study of spirituality. In effect, spirituality as a discipline does not have *a* method. I would argue that it has an approach which is characteristically hermeneutical in that it seeks to interpret the experience it studies in order to make it understandable and meaningful in the present without violating its historical reality. And there seems to be a characteristic three-phase procedure in many research projects undertaken in the field, namely, "thick" description of the aspect of experience being studied, critical analysis of the phenomenon under scrutiny, and constructive interpretation. But there is no one method or even one type of method which is peculiar to studies in this field. The study of spirituality is interdisciplinary by nature, a point to which I will return momentarily.

Another less classical approach to defining the study of spirituality which might throw some light on where or how to situate the academic enterprise is to ask whether spirituality is a discourse, a field, or a discipline. Under different aspects, it is all three and that is part of the reason for the linguistic confusion around the topic.

A *discourse* might be defined as an ongoing conversation about a common interest. For example, economics is a discourse in which many people, specialists and lay people, participate even though they may disagree vehemently about the topics discussed. Spirituality is a discourse in which diverse sets of people, practitioners of all manner of spiritual disciplines, pastors and preachers, parents and teachers, professionals in the field of spirituality and specialists in related fields, and many others participate. Indeed, the discourse on spirituality has become so widespread in our culture that it risks becoming a catch-all term for whatever anyone takes seriously.[6] Articles in the popular press about spirituality range from Marian piety at Lourdes to marathon aerobics and body piercing, from crystal rubbing and channeling to millennialism, from ecology to relations with extraterrestrials.[7] In 2002, at the annual meeting of the Society for the Study of Christian Spirituality, Meredith McGuire gave a sociological map of this phenomenon and Peter Van Ness critiqued it from a philosophical perspective.[8]

A *field*, in contrast to discourse, is an open space in which activities which have something in common take place. On an athletic field, for example, one might find a soccer match, a pageant, or Tai Chi exercises occurring at different times. Many people from doctors to medical secretaries could describe themselves as being in the medical field. In the field of spirituality we find not only researchers and teachers but also ministers, practitioners, popular writers, publishers, and others carrying on a variety of activities that could be described as "spiritual" or concerned with the spiritual.

When we speak of the *discipline* of spirituality, however, we are talking about teaching and learning, including research and writing, on subjects specified by the material and formal objects of Christian spirituality in the context of the academy. It is here that the questions with which I am concerned in this essay, interdisciplinarity, Christian specificity, and self-implication, become relevant and important.

SPIRITUALITY AS AN INTERDISCIPLINARY ACADEMIC DISCIPLINE

Spirituality as an academic discipline is intrinsically and irreducibly interdisciplinary because the object it studies, transformative Christian experience as such, is multi-faceted. Every topic of study in this field requires that several disciplines be used together in a reciprocally interactive and not merely juxtaposed way throughout the process of investigation.

It seems to me that there are two layers of interdisciplinarity active in any research, writing, or teaching project in the area of spirituality. First there are two *constitutive disciplines* which necessarily function in relation to the subject matter precisely because they supply the positive data of Christian religious experience as well as its norm and hermeneutical context, namely Scripture and the history of Christianity.

The second layer of interdisciplinarity comprises what I will call *problematic disciplines* because they are called into play and integrated into the methodology of a particular study because of the problematic of the phenomenon being studied. Sometimes the leading problematic discipline will be Scripture or Christian history, one of the constitutive disciplines, but often the leading problematic discipline will be psychology, sociology, literature, science, or some other discipline which allows better access to the experiential aspect of the object under investigation. In other words, as Scripture and history of Christianity come into play because the experience being studied is *Christian*, the problematic disciplines come into play because the object of study is *experience as such*.

Finally, the interdisciplinarity of spirituality involves *theology* which is related to both the constitutive and the problematic areas. On the one hand, the Church's reflection on both Scripture and Christian experience, that is, its theology, will function in some way, explicitly or implicitly, in any research project in the field of spirituality. In this respect, theology belongs to the constitutive disciplines. On the other hand, because theology is not the positive datum of either "pole" of the spirituality relationship, i.e., divine self-revelation or lived human response to revelation, but is rather second order reflection on one or both or the relationship between them, it is primarily an analytical and critical tool, among other tools, for the understanding and criticism of spirituality phenomena. In this respect, theology belongs functionally to what I am calling the problematic disciplines. Because of this double situation as well as several other peculiarities of theology in relation to spirituality, I will return to the consideration of theology after talking about the two layers of interdisciplinarity, namely, the constitutive and the problematic.

The Constitutive Disciplines

Scripture, which mediates the foundational and normative access of the Christian to revelation, supplies not only the positive data of the earliest Christian experience and its Jewish matrix, but also both the basic symbol system of Christianity and the meta-story into which each individual and communal Christian story is integrated and by which it is patterned. The scholar of Christian spirituality, therefore, needs a functional knowledge of the Christian Scriptures, that is, a deep familiarity with the content and dynamics of this literature and a methodological competence that will allow her or him to handle biblical material responsibly.

The spirituality scholar, unless specializing in biblical spirituality as such, need not have the professional knowledge of biblical languages, the detailed historical and archaeological expertise, and the command of a plurality of exegetical and critical methods that a biblical scholar would have. The scholar of spirituality is not an exegete or even, usually, an original independent biblical interpreter. But the mind and imagination of the scholar of Christian spirituality must be shaped by the great biblical motifs. Not only must he or she be deeply imbued with the content of Scripture but also have an understanding of the inner dynamics of the sacred story, its developmental patterns from Old Testament to New Testament, and its characteristic literary features. And because they most often will deal with biblical material through secondary texts, spirituality scholars must have sufficient methodological sophistication to be able to judge the reliability of writing in the field of biblical studies.

Sometimes, when investigating spirituality phenomena that are explicitly biblical, for example, the spirituality of Mark's gospel, the researcher will use biblical methods and content extensively. In this case, biblical study becomes also the leading problematic discipline and the scholar must become much more competent in the biblical field than would otherwise be the case. At other times scripture will function as part of the background for understanding how a particular phenomenon is or is not related to the Christian tradition. For example, if one were investigating the role of the Higher Power in the spirituality of Alcoholics Anonymous the biblical God image would be an important point of reference but other disciplines such as psychology, sociology, or the physiology of addiction would be the leading problematic disciplines.

The second constitutive discipline is the history of Christianity. This field supplies the positive data of Christian religious experience throughout the 2000 years of its existence and is the basic or general hermeneutical framework for the interpretation of every phenomenon of Christian experience, past or present. Again, the spirituality scholar is not usually a specialist in church history. The development of doctrine and of the ecclesiastical institution are not the primary concerns of the scholar of spirituality. The historical focus of spirituality is the quest for holiness throughout the ages. This quest cannot be extracted or abstracted from its historical context but the ingress of the spirituality scholar into church history will usually be more through the writings of and about the giants of the spiritual life, the development of schools of spirituality, or specific themes and topics such as asceticism or spiritual friendship. Again, broad familiarity with the story of Christian religious experience, and enough methodological competence to treat historical materials responsibly will be the aim.

As is the case with Scripture, history may become not simply the hermeneutical context of a research project in spirituality but the leading problematic discipline as well. For example, if someone were studying the development of cloister for women's religious communities up to the twelfth century, history would be the primary discipline in operation and the scholar would have to become much more competent in historical method than would someone studying the role of the body in post–Vatican II Catholic ascetical practice. The latter would require some familiarity with the approach to the body in Catholic theology and practice throughout history in order to appreciate the specificity and originality of the post-conciliar approach as well as its continuity with past theory and practice. But this use of historical data would be quite different from that of someone studying, specifically, the history of bodily asceticism in Christianity from the tenth to the sixteenth century.

The Problematic Disciplines

The second layer of interdisciplinarity is what I am calling the "problematic disciplines," that is, those which are called into play by the problematic of the particular object of research. This is perhaps best illustrated by an example. Suppose the researcher has focused on the spirituality of the sixteenth-century Carmelite mystic and reformer, Teresa of Avila. If the research problem is finally defined as the role of the humanity of Jesus in Teresa's spirituality, theology, which from another standpoint is one of the constitutive disciplines, would be the primary problematic discipline as well. But if the focus of study is the functioning of the metaphor of water in Teresa's spirituality, literary studies might be the leading problematic discipline. If the issue is the role of achievement and self-esteem in Teresa's spirituality, developmental psychology and/or feminist theory might be the problematic discipline(s). This does not exhaust the possible foci of study in Teresa's spirituality which might call for the use of different disciplines, but it illustrates the point of how the problematic disciplines function in research.

Theology

Theology is, from one perspective, a constitutive discipline of Christian spirituality as Christian. Unlike Scripture and history of Christianity, it does not supply the foundational normative and positive data of the tradition. Rather, it is second-order reflection on that data. However, that reflection has produced several bodies of discourse which are part of the history of Christianity. It is scarcely conceivable that there would be a research project in Christian spirituality that would not involve theological data in some way. Therefore, some competence in theological content and method is necessary for the spirituality scholar.

Furthermore, like biblical studies or history, theology may become the leading problematic discipline in some research projects. If, for example, one is studying Eucharistic spirituality in the thirteenth century, theology would undoubtedly be a primary ingredient in the methodology. However, in other projects it might be much less salient, for example, if one were investigating the effect of frontier experience on the spirituality of a religious congregation founded in the United States in the 1900s.

Thus far, theology is implicated in the study of spirituality, as are Scripture and history. But the peculiarity of theology in relation to spirituality arises from two factors it does not share with biblical studies and church history. One is the complicated historical relationship between theology and spirituality and the second is the fact that theology has three different personae, each of which makes theology function differently in the discipline of spirituality.

There continues to be a tension among, first, those who think that theology is the subject matter of spirituality, that is, that spirituality is the living out of the implications of theology, and therefore that the study of spirituality is the investigation of how theological categories such as grace, sacraments, and morality function in the experience of the Christian; second, those who think that spirituality is part of the subject matter of theology, that is, that theology studies, among other things, the experience of Christian faith life as a locus of revelation; and third, those who think that theology is thinking about the faith, whereas spirituality is living the faith in which thinking about it is one aspect, and that the discipline of spirituality studies that living.

In the *first case*, theology is prescriptive and normative of spirituality which is not considered a research discipline in its own right. Rather it is an applied discipline, the practical application of conclusions from systematic and moral theology. Studying spirituality means learning how to mediate theological theory into religious practice.

In the *second case*, spirituality as a discipline disappears completely into theology which expands its scope to include analysis of Christian religious experience by means of theological methods and through theological categories. What is lost to view in this approach is all the rest of spirituality as lived experience, all that is not susceptible of theological analysis such as the psychological, sociological, artistic, scientific, and so on. Grace, for example, is not theologically different in John of the Cross and Hildegard of Bingen. The difference in their spiritualities arises from such factors as their gender, temperaments, ages, experiential backgrounds, historical settings, and so on. These are features not amenable to theological analysis and are thus factored out in a purely theological study of these spiritualities.

In the *third case*, in which spirituality is understood as the experienced, multi-faceted living of faith, and theology as critical reflection on faith, theology and spirituality as disciplines are equal partners in the academy. They each investigate, by their diverse and proper methods, their diverse and sometimes overlapping objects to their mutual enlightenment. Thus, for example, theology might ask what theory of grace would best explain Teresa of Avila's mystical prayer, while spirituality is asking about the mystical experience of Teresa from psychological, psychosomatic, artistic, cultural, and literary, as well as theological angles.

Obviously, where one comes down in this discussion will determine how one views the role of theology in the interdisciplinary configuration of spirituality as an academic discipline. In the first case, there is no such discipline except as an applied field; in the second, the discipline disappears and spirituality becomes a specialized object of theological analysis; in the third, spirituality is a genuine interdisciplinary discipline in which theology is a moment, that is, one of the contributing disciplines.

Theology, in relation to the discipline of spirituality, has three different faces or personae and each of the three relates theology differently to spirituality. First, theology is a *body of discourse* which has become part of the history of Christianity and is therefore integral to the positive data which history supplies to spirituality. For example, an integral part of Luther's spirituality is his theology of justification by faith which no study of Luther's spirituality can ignore, even if its primary focus is some non-theological aspect of Luther's spirituality such as the role in it of spiritual anxiety.

Second, theology is an *analytical and critical discourse* which reflects on revelation through the categories it derives from one or some human science(s), e.g., philosophy. There is no such thing as theology in the singular, but only theologies, depending on which categories are used. All theology is local theology, human reflection on faith. This relativizes the role of theology in spirituality in a way that neither Scripture nor church history is or can be relativized.

Third, Christian theologies are *denominational discourse* and in that sense once again plural. Orthodox, Lutheran, Reformed, Catholic, or Evangelical students of Christian spirituality will each approach the theological aspects of their research projects very differently. In all three of these respects, theology functions in the study of spirituality much more like the problematic disciplines than like the constitutive ones.

By way of summary, then, I would say that in some cases theology functions substantively in the discipline of spirituality. This is the case when theology as historical discourse is under investigation, e.g., in a study of Eucharistic spirituality in the thirteenth century. In other cases, it functions critically, as might be the case, for example, in a study of social justice commitment in the spirituality of Dorothy Day. Students in the field of spirituality have to be methodologically sophisticated in figuring out when, where, which, and how theology functions in their particular projects.

My experience suggests that many of the topics students are interested in studying today demand an interdisciplinary approach in which the problematic discipline(s) are often much more central to the research than the constitutive disciplines which function as a background or frame of reference. This raises the interesting question of whether the field of spirituality is best situated in the religious studies department or the humanities. Although I cannot discuss that question in this context, I am persuaded that, especially for studies in Christian spirituality, the most congenial situation remains the religious studies or theology department.

If the foregoing description and analysis of the interdisciplinary character of the study of Christian spirituality is valid, there are problems to be addressed at three levels: how to initiate non-specialist students into the field of spirituality; how to prepare and mentor doctoral students effectively; and how to organize scholarly research.

In relation to the first, which is faced by teachers in colleges and seminaries who may have the chance to teach only one or two courses in spirituality to their students, we can learn from elective courses designed to introduce students to other fields. The objective is to give students a somewhat inclusive and interesting taste of the discipline. One could do this by a course on spiritual giants of our own time like Dorothy Day or Dag Hammarskjold, by a course on prayer, or by a study of the spirituality of some school, denomination, or period in history.

The challenge for those preparing doctoral students is considerably greater because these students have to achieve sufficient competence in the discipline of spirituality to be equipped for a career in the field as they begin to map out their own area of specialization. Without taking time to develop the suggestion, I would propose that a solid doctoral program in spirituality requires at least three basic elements. First, such a program would have as a *prerequisite*, much like philosophy in relation to systematic theology, an adequate masters level theological preparation within the denominational tradition of the student. Second, the student would need to do *comprehensive* level augmentation of, and refocusing toward, spirituality of his or her biblical and history formation. Thirdly, students need to begin work in a *problematic discipline* appropriate to their eventual research specialization. Mentors have to insure that the interdisciplinary methodology which students develop to pursue their research is sufficiently broad and sufficiently focused that the student will be neither a shallow generalist nor an academic lone ranger.

The third area of challenge is that which faces all of us in our own work. If the field of spirituality is to develop, we need not only to do serious scholarly research but to become more explicit about our interdisciplinary methodology and how our projects relate to those of other scholars in the field. This is the only way that studies can become cumulative rather than simply accretions, and the discussion move forward rather than requiring every scholar to, in a sense, "reinvent the wheel" in the area of spirituality.

The Psychological Fallout of Interdisciplinarity

One implication of this intrinsically interdisciplinary character of the study of spirituality is that the scholar in the field is usually not an "expert" in the traditional sense of one who dominates the subject matter and controls the literature in a particular recognized academic sphere. I venture to affirm that no one is, or ever will be, a universal expert in spirituality. Rather, the scholar becomes a specialist in some area or aspect of spirituality and continues to learn throughout his or her career. However, the panic or sense of generalized incompetence that this can generate in students, and even in established scholars, is probably unfounded. Increasingly it is the case, even in the traditional disciplines, as knowledge explodes in every direction and ways of generating information multiply exponentially, that no one has the kind of comprehensive competence that once seemed possible and was expected of a scholar. Biblical scholars not only specialize in one of the Testaments but usually in one author, tradition, or method; systematic theologians are christologists, ecclesiologists, or sacramental theologians. In other words, this overwhelming knowledge explosion is not peculiar to the field of spirituality.

Not only are disciplines becoming unmanageable from within, forcing specialization, but disciplines as such, despite their continuous expansion are inadequate to many of the topics which scholars are interested in studying. Until relatively recently, methodology dictated what a respectable scholar could study, namely, those questions which the accepted method in one's discipline was designed to answer.[9] Increasingly, scholars are studying topics and problems which overflow the boundaries of a single discipline and demand the use of different kinds of methods from within and outside their own discipline or field. In the nature of the case, a given scholar who uses several disciplines will not be a world-class expert in all of them. As A. K. M. Adam, speaking of interdisciplinary biblical research, put it,

> When interpreters obey the injunctions of the disciplines whose borders they are crossing, we may describe this dimension of postmodern biblical criticism as "interdisciplinary"; when they mix discourses and genres without careful attention to the rules of the realms they invade, their interpretation is called not so much interdisciplinary as "undisciplined."[10]

What we need to avoid in ourselves and prevent in our students is, on the one hand, an "undisciplined" mixing of methods used without sufficient attention to the demands of the disciplines involved and, on the other hand, imprisonment in narrow disciplinary enclaves through fear of being less than expert.

In summary, interdisciplinarity, challenging as it might be, is increasingly the ethos of contemporary research. What is becoming clear is that many crucial research subjects, among them probably the vast majority of subjects in the area of spirituality, do not fit neatly into one area of investigation. The firm, closed boundaries of the classical and modern disciplines are giving way to a postmodern transgressing of academic frontiers and recombining of discourses. Method no longer dictates what can be studied or how. Rather, methods are tools in the service of research that is increasingly dictated by the interests of researchers and the needs of society rather than by the agendas of the academic guilds. Spirituality as a young discipline is not an anomaly in this respect. It is not a grab bag of idiosyncratic interests and vague procedures as was recently suggested by Carlos Eire who described it as an academic "tent city" thrown up on the margins of the well-ordered theological metropolis.[11] It is a typically postmodern discipline that is interdisciplinary in its formulation of research projects and in the methodologies it develops for prosecuting those projects.

A major problem for younger scholars in spirituality is how to situate themselves in the academy. Perhaps for the immediate future, while the traditional disciplines still guard their turf and job openings appear under classical headings such as theology, history, or biblical studies, they will have to translate their credentials into acceptable categories and work out ways to do their research within academic boundaries that do not quite fit, much as psychologists once had to do within philosophy on the one hand or education on the other.

Mature scholars of spirituality are actually organizing their work in terms of foci or specializations according to periods, places, populations, problematic disciplines, themes, subjects, or perspectives which allow them to increase their competence in a particular area while retaining a wide choice of specific research projects. One thing that seems clear is that scholars are increasingly committed to researching, writing on, and teaching about those issues and problems which they see as interesting and/or crucial and that the strict boundaries of the post-Enlightenment disciplines can no longer contain or divide committed scholars.

CHRISTIAN SELF-DEFINITION

The second "hot button" topic that I want to address, much more briefly, is that of Christian specificity. Given the increasingly intercultural and interreligious character of life on our shrinking planet, is it not counterproductive, if not embarrassingly parochial, to attempt to specialize in Christian spirituality? This question can be asked on a number of levels.

At the first level, namely that of *legitimacy*, I do not think we need apologize for our self-identification as scholars of Christian spirituality. If it is legitimate to specialize in western European history or modern abstract art, each of which belongs to a larger universe of inquiry, it is certainly legitimate to specialize in Christian spirituality which belongs to the larger universe of spirituality in general but has been historically the most influential spirituality . in the western hemisphere.

At a second level, namely that of *practicality*, it is probably clear that becoming a scholar of spirituality in general is, *de jure* and *de facto*, impossible. If we take the anthropological approach to the discipline that has become the norm in the last couple decades,[12] rather than a theological approach,[13] spirituality is virtually coextensive with human transformative experience. In-depth research requires that scholars cordon off areas sufficiently focused to allow for the development of some genuine competence and of a community of scholarship.

It is at the third level that the question becomes significant. Given that some specialization is legitimate and necessary, is specifying our area as Christian a *good choice*? Obviously there are many other ways to cut up the spirituality pie, for example, by topic, culture, or gender. Specifying the object by religion calls for examination of the two ways in which the adjective "Christian" determines the field of research.

Vertically, choosing Christian spirituality as the area of specialization involves a choice to deal with a specifically theistic religious spirituality thus distinguishing its object of study from nontheistic spiritualities such as Buddhist or Confucian spirituality, and from secular spiritualities such as ecological or feminist spiritualities. Horizontally, Christian spirituality is distinguished as the study of the spirituality of one of the great world religions. This involves focusing on a coherent tradition as opposed to eclecticism or syncretism, and the constitutive role in the spirituality of a particular religion, i.e., of a particular creed, code, and cult.

It seems to me that there are at least two possible ways to understand self-situation within the field of Christian spirituality, one of which might have more future than the other in an increasingly pluralistic academy. One position, particularly characteristic of scholars who approach spirituality primarily or exclusively through the lens of theology, would maintain that the proper object of Christian spirituality is the expressly Christian, e.g., the writings of Christian saints, Christian liturgy, Christian asceticism, or prayer. There is no doubt that these scholars will not run out of research topics any time in the foreseeable future. But they could gradually exclude themselves from the expanding academic discourse of spirituality and find themselves talking exclusively to each other.

A second position would be more characteristic of those who approach spirituality anthropologically. For these scholars, the Christian spiritual tradition is the vantage point from which they study not only expressly Christian spiritual phenomena, but any topic within the field of spirituality in general. Like the feminist scholar who sees everything as a feminist but does not restrict her research to expressly feminist topics, the scholar of Christian spirituality might be studying whether and how a non-Christian practice of spirituality such as Tai Chi or zazen might be integrated into Christian spirituality as such[14] or be studying some aspect of non-Christian spirituality in and of itself simply to enrich the environment within which he or she studies

Christian spirituality. I suspect that this approach has more potential for allowing both legitimate specialization in Christian spirituality and keeping Christian spirituality scholars in the larger conversation about spirituality which is developing all around us.

If it is legitimate, practical, and coherent to specialize in Christian spirituality, what might be some advantages of doing so? First, within Christian spirituality a community of scholarship can develop, and thus research results can begin to cumulate. The initiation of new journals in the field,[15] major publishing projects such as the Paulist Press series Classics of Western Spirituality and the Crossroad encyclopedia of spirituality, and the development of doctoral level programs in Christian spirituality testify to the beginning of this process of disciplinary development.

Second, Christian spirituality, as it develops, will be able to bring a coherent and specific voice to the vast discourse on spirituality that is swirling around us. Until there are communities of research who bring a cumulative competence to the discussion, there can be only Babel on the one hand or the sharing of idiosyncrasies on the other. Christianity has a tradition of spirituality that is 2000 years old, immensely varied, very rich, and distinct from that of other world religions. The discussion needs this voice as Christian spirituality needs to hear from the experience of other traditions.

Third, spirituality is the aspect of organized religion which is least under the control of the religious institution. Spirituality is much more impervious to institutional scrutiny and much more powerful at times in its appeal to the ordinary membership in the church. A rigorous and responsible discipline of Christian spirituality could play a major role not only in helping to develop healthy Christian spiritualities but also constructively criticizing aberrations which arise.

Finally, Christian spirituality recommends itself as an area of specialization within the mega-discipline of spirituality simply because it is intensely interesting. What, if anything, has been as influential in shaping the western mind, soul, and culture as Christian spirituality? As an area of specialization, Christian spirituality is sufficiently broad to allow us to engage virtually any important topic but sufficiently focused to ground our efforts in a common enterprise that can hope to make some specific contribution to the broader discussion.

CHRISTIAN SPIRITUALITY AS A SELF-IMPLICATING ENTERPRISE

The Meaning of Self-Implication

Our third "hot button" topic is one that has caused scholars in other disciplines to raise questions about the scientific quality of spirituality and led to much soul-searching among scholars in the field, namely, its self-implicating character. This issue arises in a number of unsettling ways. Many of us probably felt drawn into spirituality precisely because our questions about spirituality were not heuristic devices to generate research projects or ways of participating in a scholarly guild. They were real, intensely personal questions that had implications for our own lives.

Self-implication also implies that we care personally and not just academically about the answers to our questions. We are not really neutral or detached about what our research generates. Vital personal interest in the answers to one's questions can lead to skewing one's research, consciously or unconsciously, by a slanted formulation of the question, methodological manipulation, or a selective interpretation of results. Conversely, it can also lead to a passionate honesty in the search for the truth no matter where that might lead.[16]

Self-implication also implies that research in the field of spirituality can be dangerous to the researcher. What if a woman's research on feminist spirituality makes continued Christian self-identification impossible for her? Or what if one's study leads to a conversion that leaves no aspect of one's life untouched? Hidden in the attraction to the study of spirituality is probably, for many people, a deep yearning to see God. Scripture says that no one can see God and live. Studying the human experience of God is not viewing through a telescope a bush burning in a distant desert. It is taking a chance on hearing our name called at close range.

Finally, as we are aware, self-implication can lead to methodological narcissism. Personal anecdotes, no matter how numerous, interesting, or supportive of one's prejudices, do not constitute evidence. It is often difficult to get students past a fixation on their own religious experience and into the public forum of intersubjectively available data, public discourse, and mutual criticism. Somehow, the researcher has to gain methodologically valid access to subjective data without denaturing the experience or getting mired in the purely private and idiosyncratic.

Why Self-Implication Is a Problem

I suspect that the reason the self-implicating character of the study of spirituality is problematic for those of us in the discipline is not that we are uncomfortable with our own concerns and commitments, but that they place us in an ambiguous relationship to three historical periods of western intellectual life, leaving us, in a sense, intellectually homeless. By temperament and sensibility scholars in the field of spirituality have a good deal in common with the medieval, even the monastic, approach to learning in which thinking about God was integral to, indeed directed toward, relating to God, and personal transformation was not merely a by-product of study but its objective.[17] However, we have all been educated in the critical rationality of the Enlightenment which not only distinguishes between thinking about and relating to the object of one's study, but regards them as mutually contaminating. And, finally, although the intellectual commitments of modernity are still largely in control in the academy, we are all nervously aware of the postmodernism that is nibbling at the edges of every discipline. To our medieval holism the academy tends to say, "You're old fashioned." Our own modern training whispers accusingly, "You're not sufficiently critical." And our postmodern contemporaries look at what we are studying and say, "If it exists you can't study it, and if you could, it would be irrelevant."

The characteristics of our discipline which lead to these criticisms, coming from without and within, need to be seriously engaged if spirituality is to find its niche in the academy as a self-respecting and respected partner in the search for knowledge and wisdom. Our affinity for the medieval ideal of holistic study that eschews compartmentalization, that wants to embrace duality without dichotomy and distinction without division, that wants to openly acknowledge the spiritually transformative effects of the intellectual life and the passion for God that feeds the flame of prayer as it feeds the thirst for wisdom, also must acknowledge that any convincing reclaiming of these values within the academy cannot be simply a rejection of the Enlightenment and a return to pre-critical quasi-monastic procedures of inquiry. The exclusive hegemony of the critical revolution certainly can be challenged but it is not reversible. Nor can we simply reintegrate into a kind of modern "lectio divina" the academic disciplines which have, over the course of more than two centuries, been distinguished and developed as specialized arenas of academic discourse.

If spirituality is to be taken seriously in the academy it has to function as a modern critical discipline which respects the protocols of public discourse. Respect does not necessarily entail capitulation on every count, but it does require us to explain what we are doing when it differs significantly from "what is done" in the well-regulated academy. We cannot proceed as serene medievals confident that everyone subscribes to a common faith (or any faith, for that matter), respects the same authorities (or any authorities), and regards probity as the supreme criterion of credibility. How to integrate a holistic approach to research with full accountability to the standards of criticism, personal commitment to what one is studying with appropriate methodological perspective, and practical involvement with theoretical integrity is, in my view, one of the major challenges the discipline of spirituality faces as it develops its identity in the academy.

Other disciplines that have emerged and finally been credentialed in the modern academy have faced similar challenges. The development of psychology and sociology, both of which are less than a century old, are good examples of "upstart" intellectual enterprises which, over time, have established the reality of their seemingly imaginary objects and the effectiveness of their scandalously "inexact" (because non-mathematical) methods. It may well be that as psychology has enriched all intellectual discourse by establishing introspection as a valid path to knowledge, and sociology has taught us not only that relationships are real but that they are more than the sum of their parts, spirituality may help validate what many in the academy suspect, namely, that care and commitment not only do not contaminate thought but enhance it. Becoming more is not inimical to knowing more but should be its organic outcome.

While we affirm the critical ideals of modern scholarship, it is past time to admit that the Enlightenment ideal of scientific objectivity is, and always has been, an illusion. A benefit of the recent explosion of "social location" theory has been to make us all aware that the only kind of knowing available to us as humans is subjective. There is no presuppositionless, non-perspectival knowing mind that conforms to a free-standing object known in its totality and without affecting it. All human inquiry is self-implicating and all knowledge is personal to some degree. The only truly critical approach to the knowing process is self-knowledge and honesty about our social location and presuppositions, and methodological control of their effects.

The challenge to the Enlightenment's subject-object dichotomy, its ideals of methodological purity, and its confidence in the mathematical certitude of research results, is characteristic of the postmodern sensibility emerging in the academy. While critical modernism raises the most vocal challenge to spirituality as a self-implicating discipline, modernity's days are numbered. Spirituality will develop, if indeed it does develop, in the context of postmodernity. Some cultural critics have made a distinction between constructive and deconstructive postmodernism[18] which I think is important for our discipline.

Deconstructive postmodernism is, in my opinion, in principle nihilistic whether or not a given thinker or school of thought has yet come to that explicit position. There is much to be learned from deconstructionist postmodern thought, especially about the glib naïveté with which we have posited foundations and confidently propounded totalizing explanations which have then been used to legitimate all kinds of conclusions that are more mystification than explanation. Postmodernism's refusal to respect boundaries or play by the rules is liberating and exciting. But the infinite deferral of meaning must finally imply the denial of meaning, and if every text, literary or existential, can be and must be read against its own grain, then the "other" can never make real claims on the interpreter and reality becomes not merely intensely personal but totally subjective.

However, deconstructive postmodernism is not the only possible direction in which to go. A number of scholars who have identified and rejected the objectivism, methodolatry, over-compartmentalization, scientistic dogmatism, obsessive anthropocentrism, and catastrophic progressivism of Enlightenment modernity are trying to develop a non-reductive postmodern approach to learning and life.[19] Constructive postmodernism may be the intellectual climate in which spirituality as an academic discipline will finally discover breathable air. Constructive postmodernism is willing to admit, even embrace, the superiority of holistic approaches to the human subject that reject the matter-spirit, nature-culture, subject-object dichotomies in favor of a definition of the human as embodied spirit. It recognizes the transcendent dimension of human experience as constitutive of personhood rather than illusory, and as susceptible of respectful investigation that can be validated even if not proved. It acknowledges the integration of the human into a universe that is not dead matter but living organism. It is comfortable with, even intrigued by, mystery. And its ideal of understanding is less control, prediction, and domination than mutuality and relationship in wholeness.

Such constructive postmodernism is perhaps a context in which Christian spirituality as an academic discipline can find dialogue partners. The conversation will be humbler, no doubt, but perhaps more in tune with reality than either the totalizing discourse of medieval Christendom which knew it was the only game in town, or the inflated rhetoric of the Enlightenment "man" who was the exultant measure of all things, or yet the deconstructivist who makes and unmakes a tinker toy reality as a playful diversion until cosmic bedtime. For the immediate future, spirituality, in the context of the modern academy, will have to march to a different drummer. But the postmodern beat is getting louder. In a constructive postmodern context, spirituality as a self-implicating discipline will be no stranger.

CONCLUSION

I have tried, if not to praise the discipline of Christian spirituality as a fully developed partner in the academy, at least to prevent its premature burial as a spurious academic enterprise. I have tried to carry out this preventive strategy on three fronts by insisting that Christian spirituality is intrinsically interdisciplinary, that it is Christian not merely strategically but programmatically, and that its self-implicating character is not only defensible but, at least potentially, a sign and an instrument of its postmodern character.

The point of insisting on the genuine interdisciplinary character of Christian spirituality was to challenge not only a reduction of spirituality to the human and personal sciences, but also a subsuming of spirituality into one or another of the sacred sciences. Rather it is the interdisciplinary study of Christian religious experience understood as maximally inclusive.[20] Its material object, the experience itself of living the paschal mystery of Jesus Christ in all its ramifications, under the formal object of experience, requires this interdisciplinarity of method.

In arguing for the appropriateness of its self-identification as Christian, I have maintained that it is not only legitimate to specialize in the spirituality of one of the world's great religious traditions, but practically necessary for in-depth research and shared, cumulative results. Furthermore, this need not limit what one studies or with whom one dialogues, but simply establishes a committed and participative perspective from which to do so.

Finally, I have tried to take seriously the problem that self-implication in one's research poses in the modern academy, and to suggest that neither a nostalgic attempt to recreate the medieval approach to learning, nor a surrender to the nihilism of deconstructive postmodernism, seems to be an appropriate response. Rather, on the one hand, we need to recognize that Enlightenment modernity in its positivism and impersonality is losing its stranglehold on the academy and, on the other hand, that the critical ideal is a permanent achievement of the human spirit which must be both respected and integrated into a new constructive postmodernism in the academy. There is reason to hope that Christian spirituality as an academic discipline will not only find itself in its element in a postmodern context, but also be part of the evolution of that element.

When all is said and done, Christian spirituality as an academic discipline is an attempt to realize, by bringing serious and personally transforming study to bear on the ultimate human value of union with God, what is arguably the most cited text in the Christian canon, Jesus' promise, "If you remain in my word you will become my disciples and you will know the truth and the truth will set you free" (Jn. 8.31–33).

NOTES

1. A. K. M. Adam, *What Is Postmodern Biblical Criticism?* (Minneapolis: Fortress, 1995), 62.
2. For a full length monograph on the history of the word spirituality see Lucy Tinsely, *The French Expression for Spirituality and Devotion: A Semantic Study* [Studies in Romance Languages and Literatures 47] (Washington, DC: Catholic University of American, 1953). This study was augmented by Jean Leclercq in his article, "Spiritualitas," *Studi Medievali* 3 (1963), ser. 3: 279–296, which he wrote in response to the study by Italian historian Gustavo Vinay, "'Spiritualità': Invito a una discussione," in *Studi Medievali* 2 (1961): 705–709. Leclercq's study, in turn, has been summarized and augmented by Walter H. Principe in "Toward Defining Spirituality," *Studies in Religion/Sciences Religieuses* 12 (1983): 127–141.

   John A. Coleman, "Exploding Spiritualities: Their Social Causes, Social Locations and Social Divide," *Christian Spirituality Bulletin* 5 (Spring 1997), 9–10, says, "Spirituality is a word secular people can adopt." He notes that many people who do not describe themselves as religious "nevertheless, considered themselves 'spiritual.' Spirituality, thus, has become the more inclusive word."

It should be noted that this was not true even fifteen years ago when academic institutions were still resisting the use of the term because it was perceived to be exclusively Christian and non-academic. The progressive appearance of volumes of scholarly articles in the Crossroads series, *World Spirituality*, on non–Christian traditions, helped to expand the use of the term beyond its original Christian location and to establish the academic seriousness of the study.

3. The first three issues of the *Christian Spirituality Bulletin*, 1 (Spring and Fall, 1993) and 2 (Spring 1994), carried a number of articles by Philip Sheldrake, Rowan Williams, Bernard McGinn, Walter Principe, Bradley Hanson, and Sandra Schneiders, on the subject of the nature of the discipline. Three of these essays appear in this volume as Chapters 2 (McGinn), 3 (Principe), and 4 (Schneiders).

4. In "Theology and Spirituality: Strangers, Rivals or Partners?" *Horizons* 13 (1986), 266, I originally defined it as the "experience of consciously striving to integrate one's life," but a number of colleagues objected to the word "striving" because it seemed to have a Pelagian or "works righteousness" tone or at least to leave inadequate room for the passive dimension of the spiritual life.

Peter Van Ness, in *Spirituality, Diversion and Decadence: The Contemporary Predicament* (Albany, NY: State University of New York Press, 1992), 273–274, talking not about Christian spirituality as such but about spirituality as a dimension of human beings, says: "What is spiritual is a specific aspect of human existence . . . Facing outward, human existence has been deemed spiritual insofar as it intentionally engages reality as a maximally inclusive whole. Facing inward, life has been accorded a spiritual dimension to the extent that it is experience as the project of one's most vital and enduring self. An integration of these inner and outer characterizations is achieved by equating the spiritual dimensions of life with the existential task of discovering one's truest self in the context of reality apprehended as a cosmic totality." The last part of the final sentence, in my judgment, says virtually the same thing that my definition does.

5. This, in my view, is the point of distinction between spirituality as an academic discipline and spirituality as pastoral practice.

6. Coleman, in "Exploding Spiritualities," 9–10, notes that one sociological study of the religion of the Baby Boomer generation "ended up rejecting the term, spirituality, because it seemed that its meaning was so vague and amorphous (at least in popular, non-technical usages) as to be totally non-discriminating."

A very enlightening study of the enormous expansion of the term in the "New Age" phenomenon is Carl A. Raschke, "New Age Spirituality," in *Spirituality and the Secular Quest*, ed., Peter H. Van Ness [*World Spirituality: An Encyclopedic History of the Religious Quest*, vol. 22] (New York: Crossroad, 1996), 203–221.

7. The prestigious Crossroad Series on world spirituality has added a volume *Spirituality and the Secular Quest* to its religious spirituality volumes in recognition of the contemporary phenomenon of individual, idiosyncratic, and religiously non-committed search for personal integration.

8. Meredith B. McGuire, "Mapping Contemporary American Spirituality: A Sociological Perspective," *Christian Spirituality Bulletin* 5 (Spring 1997): 1, 3–8; Peter H. Van Ness, "Philosophy as a Spiritual Catalyst: Spirituality in a Secular Age," *Christian Spirituality Bulletin* 5 (Spring 1997): 16–18.

9. This is the burden of Hans-Georg Gadamer's masterwork, *Truth and Method* [2nd rev. ed.], trans. and rev. by Joel Weinsheimer and Donald G. Marshall (New York: Crossroad, 1989).

10. Adam, *What Is Postmodern Biblical Criticism?*, 62.

11. Carlos M. N. Eire, "Major Problems in the Definition of Spirituality as an Academic Discipline," *Modern Christian Spirituality: Methodological and Historical Essays* [American Academy of Religion Studies in Religion, no. 62] ed., Bradley C. Hanson (Atlanta: Scholar's Press, 1990), 60–61.

23

12. See the article by Jean-Claude Breton, "Retrouver les assises anthropologiques de la vie spirituelle," *Studies in Religion/Science Religieuses* 17 (1988): 97–105, which presents well the arguments for this approach.

13. Writers who represent this approach include Charles-André Bernard, *Traité de théologie spirituelle* (Paris: Cerf, 1985) and Eugene Megyer, "Theological Trends: Spiritual Theology Today," *The Way* 21 (1981): 55–67.

14. See the dissertation written in the Graduate Theological Union doctoral program in Christian spirituality by Peter Feldmeier, *Interrelatedness; A Comparison of the Spiritualities of St. John of the Cross and Buddhaghosa for the Purpose of Examining the Christian Use of Buddhist Practices* (Berkeley, CA: Graduate Theological Union, 1996).

15. For example, *Christian Spirituality Bulletin* in this country and *Studies in Spirituality* in Europe.

16. A very interesting essay by Robert Cummings Neville, "The Emergence of Historical Consciousness," in Van Ness, ed., *Spirituality and the Secular Quest*, 129–156, on "scholarly piety" in the academic scholar of religion takes up this same question from a secular rather than religious viewpoint.

17. The classic study of this characteristic of medieval monastic scholarship is Jean Leclercq's *The Love of Learning and the Desire for God: A Study of Monastic Culture*, 3rd ed. (New York: Fordham University Press, 1982).

18. A good example of constructive postmodern reflection is the Suny Series on Constructive Postmodern Thought in which one volume is entitled *Sacred Interconnections: Postmodern Spirituality, Political Economy and Art*, ed., David Ray Griffin (Albany, New York: State University of New York Press, 1990). See also Charlene Spretnak, *States of Grace: The Recovery of Meaning in the Postmodern Age* (San Francisco: Harper, 1991).

19. Besides the authors mentioned in note 14 above, see Douglas C. Bowman, *Beyond the Modern Mind: The Spiritual and Ethical Challenge of the Environmental Crisis* (New York: Pilgrim, 1990), and *Postmodern Theology: Christian Faith in a Pluralistic World*, ed., Frederic B. Burnham (San Francisco: Harper and Row, 1989).

20. Peter Van Ness defines spirituality in such a way as to include non-religious spiritualities as "the embodied task of realizing one's true self in the context of reality apprehended as a cosmic totality. It is the quest for attaining an optimal relationship between what one truly is and everything that is . . . " This definition would aptly include Christian spirituality. "Introduction: Spirituality and the Secular Quest," in *Spirituality and the Secular Quest*, ed. Peter H. Van Ness, 5.

2

The Letter and the Spirit

Spirituality as an Academic Discipline

BERNARD McGINN

*T*he late Justice Potter Stewart was the source of the noted remark, "I don't know how to define obscenity, but I sure know it when I see it." Much the same can be said for spirituality. Obscenity, despite endless debates and not a few court decisions, still lies mostly in the eye of the beholder. Spirituality, which cannot profit from legal decisions about community standards for its possible identity, usually has to rely on the fickleness of academics to try to speak its name, though this fact has never prevented people from just doing it and not bothering about defining it. Academics, unfortunately, do need to be attentive to issues of description and definition.

Both spirituality and obscenity are also linked by a common semantic explosion—everybody seems to be talking about them, though often at cross-purposes. The debate over obscenity, of course, gets into the news more frequently, but the documentation on the prolific growth of the term "spirituality" in recent American culture is substantial, and it involves not only those interested in religion. I await the moment (perhaps not far off) when a product will be advertised on national television because of the contribution it makes to some form of spirituality.

In 1961 the Italian medievalist Gustavo Vinay referred to spirituality as "a necessary pseudoconcept we don't know how to replace."[1] It is certainly the kind of pseudoconcept which seems to have a life of its own, whether academics oppose it or attempt to profit from its ubiquity. Given the relative novelty of "spirituality" to many, as well as the ambiguity that allows it to be used so variously (often in contradictory fashion) a case could certainly be made that the term should be dropped from the contemporary study of religion. But I am convinced that despite the ambiguities of the word, there are important issues at stake in spirituality's recent popularity, as well as considerable contributions that the study of spirituality can bring to religion in the decades ahead. Trying to present this case is not easy, because it requires a survey of the history of the term followed by reflections on definition and methodology in religious studies—issues that make all but the most academic eyes glaze over.

HISTORY OF THE TERM SPIRITUALITY

Spirituality is not a new word in English. As used in the fifteenth century, it generally meant either an episcopal gathering (i.e., a spirituality of bishops, the equivalent of a pride of lions), or ecclesiastical possessions or revenues. These are not the meanings most of us have in mind when we talk of spirituality today, however much we hope bishops may be spiritual people. But as early as the fourteenth century "spirituality" (or "spiritualty") was to be found in the more ancient sense of the quality or condition of being spiritual, as can be seen in *Piers Plowman* (Passus 5 of the B text) where Wrath relates how he delights in setting friars against parish priests:

> I, Wrath, walke with hem and wisse hem of my bokes,
> Thus they speken of spiritualte, that either despitheth oother
> Til they be bothe beggars and by my spiritualte libben,
> Or ellis al riche and ridden aboute.
>
> (*lines 146–48*)

It is noteworthy that Langland's view of spirituality is already particularized into special forms, and is also capable of being twisted to the devil's purpose by Wrath. The problems of spirituality and its perversions seem to go back to its earliest English appearances.

Where then did the term originate and what is its history? The role of the spirit (*ruah*) of God in the Old Testament was the foundation for the New Testament emphasis on the importance of the "spirit" (*pneuma*) and the qualifier "spiritual" (*pneumatikos*) in the foundational Christian documents. In Luke–Acts the Spirit is in Jesus in the act of establishing the community (e.g., Lk. 4:14, Ac. 2:32–33). Paul identifies the Risen Lord with the *pneuma* (e.g., 2 Cor. 3:17, 1 Cor. 6:17), and John emphasizes the rebirth in the Spirit and in truth (e.g., Jn. 3:3–8, 4:23, and the Last Discourses). As is well known, the Christian opposition between "flesh" (*sarx*) and "spirit" originally had nothing to do with a dualistic anthropology contrasting body and soul, but rather addressed the concrete human choices between life lived according to egoistic satisfaction and that conducted according to God's purpose. Despite popular accounts to the contrary, few patristic and medieval theologians missed this point, though they often had difficulties harmonizing it with the dualistic Platonic anthropology they adopted from Hellenistic sources.[2]

Spiritualis, the Latin translation of *pneumatikos*, appears 22 times in the Vulgate of St. Jerome, but it was not until the fifth century that we find the noun *spiritualitas*, appearing in a letter anciently ascribed to St. Jerome: "Age ut in spiritualitate proficias," that is, "Act in order to grow in spirituality."[3] It is clear that in this text, the term still bears the meaning that *pneumatikos* had from the origins of Christianity—increase your hold on the Spirit of Jesus, the source of the Christian life. This is the way in which the substantive was used in its rare appearances in the early Middle Ages.[4] In the twelfth century, however, *spiritualitas* was employed more frequently and more diversely. Not only was it used in the traditional sense of the power animating Christian life, but it began to be used by Scholastic theologians, Gilbert of Poitiers for example, in a naturalistic and philosophical way, as what pertains to the soul as contrasted with the body. The perhaps unavoidable mingling of these two meanings in later Christian history has been one of the less happy consequences of Scholasticism—the root of those conceptions of spirituality which willy-nilly used it as the reason for giving the physical world and especially the human body a largely negative role in what they conceived of as authentic Christian life. Thomas Aquinas forms an interesting example of a bridge figure. According to the *Index Thomisticus*, the term appears about seventy times, and Thomas seems usually to think of *spiritualitas* in the traditional sense of integral Christian perfection, as when he says that "Sanctificatio gratiae pertinet ad spiritualitatem," or "Sanctification by grace belongs to spirituality." But he is not above using the newer philosophical mode in which spirituality means what belongs to the soul as soul. It was also in the thirteenth century that *spiritualitas* found a juridical use, being applied to ecclesiastical offices and goods.

The later Middle Ages was the era of the great migration of Latin terminology into the vernaculars of Europe whose descendents we still use in our theological constructions. According to Lucy Tinsely's study, the first émigré of *spiritualitas* appears in the Old French *espiritualité* of the mid-thirteenth century, though this word was most often employed in the jurisdictional sense. The fourteenth- and fifteenth-century Middle English examples cited above are indicative of the spread of the term throughout the late medieval vernaculars. At the beginning of the sixteenth century, in Johannes Altenstaig's *Vocabulary of Theology*, the Latin adjective *spirituale* still kept its biblical meaning as referring to the whole person's way of acting,[5] but during the course of the sixteenth and seventeenth centuries there seems to have been a gradual shift of "spirituality," both in Latin and in the vernaculars, toward signifying only the inner dispositions, the interior states of the soul. This is the way we find it used in John of the Cross, for example, in the words, "And if, now that the spirit has achieved spirituality [espiritualidad] in this way . . . " In seventeenth-century France "spirituality" was widely used in the sense of "everything connected with the interior exercises of the soul free of the senses which seeks only to be perfected in the eyes of God," as one dictionary puts it.[6]

But the crisis of mysticism caused by the condemnation of Quietism at the end of the seventeenth century had its effect on the popularity of "spirituality," as we can see in Voltaire's ironic references to "la nouvelle spiritualité" of

Madame Guyon and François Fénélon.[7] In the eighteenth and nineteenth centuries the terms "devotion" and "piety" became far more popular among both Catholics and Protestants. Jon Alexander, for example, points out that "spirituality" was used in the nineteenth century mostly by free religious groups, the same groups who kept alive interest in such suspect figures as Madame Guyon.[8] On the academic side, the dogmatic categories of ascetical and mystical theology favored by the Italian Jesuit Giovanni Battista Scaramelli (1687–1752) won the day. Up to the middle of the twentieth century, among Roman Catholics at least, ascetical and mystical theology was still the preferred term for what is now almost universally referred to as either spiritual theology or spirituality.

The reasons for the revival of the term "spirituality" in France around the beginning of the last century remain something of a mystery. Auguste Saudreau, who was using the term in 1900, issued his *Manuel de spiritualité* in 1916, and Pierre Pourrat's very successful four-volume *La spiritualité catholique* was published between 1918 and 1928. The Jesuit Joseph de Guibert also began employing the term extensively, and in 1932 the first fascicule of the great *Dictionnaire de spiritualité* appeared. By 1943 when Étienne Gilson gave the inaugural lecture for the establishment of the chair of the history of spirituality at the Institût Catholique in Paris, spirituality had definitely arrived.[9]

Spirituality became popular more gradually in English, being first introduced among Catholics in dependence on the French, and, according to Principe, appears first in twentieth-century English in the 1922 translation of Pourrat.[10] Alexander's survey of the *Catholic Periodical Index* turned up only 11 uses in titles of articles between 1930 and 1964 and no fewer than 146 uses between 1965 and 1976.[11] By the 1970s the all-powerful gravitational pull of spirituality was as evident in America as it was in France. One sign was the capitulation of the journals. The French Jesuit periodical which had started out "Scaramellianly" as the *Révue d'ascétique et de mystique* in 1920 changed its name to the *Révue d'histoire de la spiritualité* in 1972, and in 1977 the American journal *Cross and Crown* became *Spirituality Today*.

God alone probably knows how many appearances of "spirituality" can be found in journal articles of the past fifteen years. On the American scene, these same fifteen years have witnessed the publication of the *Classics of Western Spirituality* series (seventy-seven volumes since 1978), and the commencement of *World Spirituality: An Encyclopedic History of the Religious Quest*, of which eleven volumes have appeared since 1985. A number of single-volume dictionaries of spirituality have also become available, as well as countless books, academic and popular, with "spirituality" in the title. It is now possible to take a Ph.D. degree in spirituality in at least four American universities (Fordham, Catholic University, Duquesne, and the Berkeley GTU). Perhaps most surprising has been the willingness not only of non-Catholic Christians but even non-Christians to embrace the term spirituality, as has been demonstrated by the *World Spirituality* project (though, to be sure, this was not without its conflicts and difficulties). One may think of the growth of the term "spirituality" in the past generation as either a good or a bad thing, but it is certainly a major new factor on the map of American religion.

For this reason, I would like to consider the question of the role of spirituality, whatever it may be, primarily in terms of religious academia, that is, the teaching of religion in all its aspects. I will pursue this question under three headings. First, what is spirituality and how are we to relate it to other disciplines that concern the study of religion? Second, should it be taught? And, third, how should it be taught?

WHAT IS SPIRITUALITY?

Without by any means making an exhaustive search, I recently turned up some thirty-five different definitions of spirituality, both "first-order" definitions, that is, ones concerned with the phenomenon itself, and "second-order" definitions treating of the study of spirituality. Most of the second-order definitions are of the theological variety. (Second-order definitions of an anthropological and historical-contextual type usually add nothing to the first-order definition except the qualification of "the study of.") It would be, of course, possible to add qualifications about the perspective used in such study, though in the case of defining mysticism, this appears to have been rarely done, at least in the sense of entering into the definition itself. Walter Principe makes an interesting distinction between three levels of spirituality: (a) the real or existential level; (b) the level of a formulation of a teaching about the lived reality, as in Ignatian spirituality; and (c) the study by scholars of the first and especially the second levels.[12]

At first glance, this might seem to indicate total semantic chaos, but things are not quite that dismal. These descriptions and definitions tend to fall into broad groups exhibiting common features, however much they differ in details. At this stage in the evolution of the discipline (if such it be), semantic confusion and vigorous debate is probably not a bad thing, especially insofar as it tends to clarify the current state of the question. I also think that it is possible for scholars to disagree about what is primary in the notion of spirituality and still work together in productive fashion because they are convinced that there is something primary about spirituality itself, however conceived.

Sandra Schneiders in her important 1989 article "Spirituality in the Academy" suggests two kinds of approaches to the study of spirituality—"a dogmatic position supplying a 'definition from above' and an anthropological position supplying a 'definition from below.'"[13] I think that the picture is actually more complicated than that, because there is a third option, an historical-contextual one. I would like to suggest that rather than the model of above-and-below (which is not a very nuanced view of how much contemporary theology deals with the problem of relating God and world), it would be better to think of recent views of spirituality as trying to relate various theological, anthropological and historical-contextual ways of conceiving the connection between limited and unlimited value systems. It is also important to note that a number of investigators provide both general definitions of spirituality, as well as scientific definitions of Christian spirituality, a process that often enables them to combine two or all three approaches.

Be not afraid. I do not intend to discuss thirty-five different definitions of spirituality, any more than I would as many legal definitions of obscenity. But I do need to provide some key examples of important definitions and to reflect on what camps they fall into in order to frame my own understanding of the state of the field. I apologize for the way in which often subtle and extensive presentations will be summarized here—few of the authors cited will probably be happy with my brief characterizations of their position in the paragraphs that follow.

(a) Theological Approach. Older examples of definitions of spirituality, largely Catholic in provenance, were often second-order definitions emphasizing the theological character of the discipline to the exclusion, at least by implication, of anthropology, history, and the human sciences as having any constructive role. Pierre Pourret was more resolute than most of his followers when he affirmed early in the twentieth century that "[s]pirituality is that part of theology which deals with Christian perfection and the ways that lead to it," but this view has not been absent from recent Catholic thought either. For example, one can cite C. A. Bernard, who sees spirituality as "a theological discipline studying Christian existence by describing its progressive development and elucidating its structures and laws,"[14] as well as Eugene Megyer.[15] Those who take this approach often prefer the term "spiritual theology" to spirituality itself; James A. Wiseman, for example, describes spiritual theology in Lonerganian terms.[16] Non-Catholic scholars, such as Bradley C. Hanson, take a similar line, arguing that spiritual theology involves not only "a rigor of reflection" but also "a strongly existential relation to the subject matter."[17] The Anglican writer Kenneth Leech is another example of someone who understands spirituality primarily as spiritual theology. Leech's preface to *Experiencing God: Theology as Spirituality* describes his book as "[a]n exploration in spiritual theology, that is, in the search for a transforming knowledge of God."[18] However, many recent discussions of spirituality, even by Catholics, have hesitated over the term "spiritual theology," perhaps because of their fear that this may involve the reduction of spirituality to a mere appendage of dogmatic or moral theology. For example, more than thirty years ago, Louis Bouyer, although he spoke of spirituality as based on dogmatic theology, insisted that "Christian spirituality (or any other spirituality) is distinguished from dogma by the fact that, instead of studying or describing the objects of belief as it were in the abstract, it studies the reactions which these objects arouse in the religious consciousness." Thus he saw the discipline, which he, however, also spoke of as "spiritual theology," as being intimately connected to both human psychology and history.[19] I find something of the same in Josef Sudbrack's article on "Spirituality" in *Sacramentum Mundi*, though he avoids any definition.[20] The problem is this: Is spirituality a theological discipline or a separate field of the study of religion? And, if it is a theological discipline or specialization, how does it relate to the other aspects of the study of theology, whether conceived in traditional or non-traditional ways?

31

A significant option, argued by some of the most weighty twentieth-century Catholic theological voices, is built upon a distinction between a generic notion of spirituality based upon human hunger for transcendence and specifically Christian spirituality which is to be measured by the norm of revelation (which does not necessarily have to mean that Christian spirituality is just a specialization of dogmatics). Perhaps the most interesting spokesman of this view has been the Swiss theologian Hans Urs von Balthasar, who, in three typically dense and powerful papers distinguished between spirituality as a "basic practical or existential attitude which is the expression of how one understands ethically committed existence,"[21] and the properly Christian spirituality which is nothing other than "the subjective aspect of dogmatic theology."[22] Another example can be found in the Dominican Jordan Aumann who says that " . . . spirituality refers to any religious or ethical value that is concretized as an attitude or spirit from which one's actions flow." For Aumann, spirituality is not restricted to any particular religion; it pertains to the field of religious psychology. It becomes the basis for spiritual theology when the spirit in question is understood as the Holy Spirit, so that properly Christian spirituality is "a participation in the mystery of Christ through the interior life of grace."[23] Principe also appears to follow this line, explicitly appealing to von Balthasar, but creating his own definitions of general spirituality and specifically Christian spirituality. General spirituality is "the way in which a person understands and lives within his or her historical context that aspect of his or her religion, philosophy or ethic that is viewed as the loftiest, the noblest, the most calculated to lead to the fullness of the ideal or perfection being sought."[24] Note the important anthropological and historical elements here. The definition of Christian spirituality is "life in the Spirit as brothers and sisters of Jesus Christ and daughters and sons of the Father."[25] Finally, although Karl Rahner was not at pains to give a definition of spirituality, on the basis of his distinction between transcendental experience and supernatural experience (and how he applied this to mysticism), one can think that a position along these lines would not be foreign to him.[26]

(b) Anthropological Approach. Despite these nuanced theological options, the majority of definitions today can be described as variants of "anthropological" understandings (taken in both a philosophical and social scientific sense), that is, ones that put the greatest stress on spirituality as an element in human nature and experience. Many scholars see spirituality primarily as a "depth-dimension" of human existence. These definitions involve, implicitly or explicitly, a notion of human authenticity, and often also of transcendence, or at least of self-transcendence. Let me cite some examples to give you the flavor. Spirituality involves "the inner dimension of the person . . . [where] ultimate reality is experienced"[27] or it concerns "the constituent of human nature which seeks relations with the ground or purpose of existence,"[28] or it is seen as "a capacity for self-transcendence."[29] Shifting from attempts to characterize the inner ground itself to characterizations of our experience of it, we find an even larger number of definitions/descriptions. Spirituality has to do "with becoming a person in the fullest sense,"[30] or is "one typical way of handling the human condition."[31] For J.-C. Breton, it is a way of engaging anthropological questions in order to arrive at a richer and more authentically human life, something which does not seem much different from Jon Alexander's view that it concerns those aspects of human life which are seen by their subjects as intentionally related to what holds unrestricted value.[32] Sandra Schneiders praises the basic line taken by Breton, but tries to be more precise by defining spirituality as "the experience of consciously striving to integrate one's life in terms not of isolation and self-absorption but of self-transcendence toward the ultimate value one perceives."[33] This position leaves open the possibility for forms of non-religious, or secular, spirituality, as does Edward Kinerk who thinks of spirituality as the expression of a dialectical personal growth from the inauthentic to the authentic.[34] Michael Downey, on the other hand, would seem to exclude this because, in his preface to *The New Dictionary of Catholic Spirituality*, he sees spirituality as concerned with the relational and personal dimensions of the human person's relation to the divine.[35] Perhaps the vaguest expression of the anthropological approach known to me occurs in an article by Rachel Hosmer, who begins her piece with the observation: "Spirituality in the broadest sense defies definition. It refers to whatever in human experience is alive and intentional, conscious of itself and responsive to others." However, like the theological positions cited above, Hosmer goes on to talk about specifically Christian spirituality, which she describes as "focused in Christ and his Body the Church as the community of believers and the locus of the encounter between the human and the divine."[36]

The advantages of the anthropological approach are many, as Sandra Schneiders among others, has pointed out.[37] First, this option seems to be that adopted by the majority of recent investigators (though the argument from numbers should not be decisive). Second, this approach allows for ecumenical Christian and wider inter-religious use of the term, and even, in most cases, for the possibility of a secular spirituality (which many today argue is an important option). A third advantage, at least from the academic point of view, is that it encourages the study of spirituality from the viewpoint of the human sciences and thus gives it entry into academia on as broad a base as possible. The disadvantages, however, are equally evident. Many of the definitions or descriptions cited above are so vague that they make any definition of spirituality as a field of study impossible—if spirituality is everything that is good and positive about what is human then all it needs is a round of applause rather than cultivation and study. Even those definitions, like that of Sandra Schneiders, which clarify more precisely exactly what aspect of human behavior is the subject matter of spirituality, as well as the perspective from which it is to be studied, run into the difficulty of distinguishing that subject matter and perspective from what it is that religion is supposed to study, or from the object of ethics broadly conceived.[38] In trying to determine what spirituality is by taking the anthropological route alone, it may well be that all we have come up with is another name for religion. More careful distinctions between religion, ethics, and spirituality are certainly in order at the present time—their creation would seem to be important to the academic future of the discipline.

(c) Historical-Contextual Approach. There is a third approach to defining spirituality, one less often found in a pure form perhaps, but still worthy of note. I refer to this as the historical-contextual approach because it emphasizes spirituality as an experience rooted in a particular community's history rather than as a dimension of human existence as such (not that it excludes this). I myself had something like this view in mind in the "Introduction" to *Christian Spirituality I,* when I spoke of Christian spirituality as "the lived experience of Christian belief in both its general and more specialized forms," and later termed it "the effort to appropriate Christ's saving work in our lives."[39] This quasi-definition has been criticized with some justice, in particular by Carlos M. N. Eire, for being vague and difficult to distinguish from moral theology, though I did try to make such a distinction by restricting spirituality to "those acts in which the relation to God is immediate and explicit."[40] However, I have no interest in unyielding defense of this particular formulation in an essay whose point is that there is no fully adequate definition.

Several other recent students of spirituality have emphasized the contextual element in helpful ways. In his *Christian Spirituality,* Rowan Williams says, "And if spirituality can be given any coherent meaning, perhaps it is to be understood in terms of this task: each believer making his or her own that engagement with the questioning at the heart of faith which is so evident in the classical documents of Christian belief."[41] Urban T. Holmes also adopted an historical-contextual approach, defining his task as answering the question "How has Christian humanity throughout its history understood what it is to seek God and to know him?"[42] A good example of a description of spirituality that emphasizes the historical dimension while being able to include the other two elements can be found in the French historian André Vauchez, who speaks of spirituality as "the dynamic unity of the content of faith and the way in which it is viewed by historically determined human beings."[43] Recently, Philip Sheldrake's *Spirituality and History* has also emphasized the importance of history in the study of spirituality.[44]

The emphasis on the historical rootedness of spirituality in a particular community, of course, would seem to cast doubt on the possibility of a secular spirituality, unless we think of certain secular traditions (e.g., Marxism) as taking on the aspects of a quasi-religious community. It is also clear that a historical-contextual approach alone, since it rests primarily on the witness of adherents who say they have a spirituality, cannot, of itself, address normative questions.[45] Therefore, the historical-contextual approach, of its very nature, has the advantage of implying the other two, that is, it must have a relation to the beliefs of the community, the theology that formalizes these, and eventually, if not in every instance, to the truth claims of those beliefs. And it also must take into account what the study of the practice of beliefs within historical human communities has to say about human nature as such, that is, it must be open to anthropology, conceived of from both philosophical and social-scientific perspectives. The mutual implication of all three approaches to understanding the meaning of spirituality hinted at here provides, I believe, an important insight into the current situation regarding the status of the term.

What may seem like helpless confusion, or open warfare between different approaches, may, if we turn it on its head, actually be an advantage. I do not believe that we have any really adequate definition of spirituality at the present time—and we may never have (just as we will probably never have a fully adequate definition of religion). Theologically speaking at least, Hans Urs von Balthasar provides us with a reason for this when he reminds us: "No mission, no spirituality, is capable of being defined in its living center. They all come from the infinite variety of the divine life, which always exceeds the compass of the human."[46] If it is indeed the case that spirituality is one of those terms where exploration will never yield a clear and universally acceptable definition, then it is primarily in the ongoing discussion among the three approaches outlined above, that we will, if only in some asymptotic fashion, approach a more adequate understanding of what spirituality is in itself, as well as possibly work out better ways to study it. What I would insist on at the present is that all three options remain in the conversation, though this conversation will doubtless take different forms depending on the context, that is, whether it takes place as a part of the humanistic study of religion or in specifically religious educational institutions.

SHOULD SPIRITUALITY BE TAUGHT?

This brings me to the second question, this is, should spirituality be taught? There are those who think that spirituality cannot be taught, at least in the way in which other subjects can be. To these we may respond that it has always been taught. As Ewert Cousins has reminded us, "The transmission of spiritual wisdom may be the oldest discipline in human history."[47] The question is rather the relation of this ancient tradition of handing on spiritual wisdom to the highly developed ways in which modern society trains the next generation, especially through its formalized academic institutions.

35

To my mind, the transmission of spirituality in the first-order definition will, and should, take place primarily outside academia within the traditions of spiritual training which academics need to study but which they too often imitate at their own peril. I am frankly hesitant about how much of a "practical" element can and should be incorporated into the academic study of spirituality, both within religious schools and in secular academic settings, though I am convinced that for committed Christian academics teaching itself is a spiritual discipline. A number of the current projects concerning the study of spirituality seem to involve confusions about the relation between intellectual appropriation and personal commitment that would be impossible to implement in non-religious institutions and possibly unwise even in religiously-affiliated institutions of higher learning. Something of this seems to me present in Schneiders' insistence on the "participative" dimension of the study of spirituality.[48]

These dangers kept in mind, however, it seems clear that there is considerable consensus today among those involved in the study of religion, concerning the necessity of incorporating spirituality, in some way, into the curriculum. This is particularly evident among those who view spirituality as spiritual theology. Numerous modern theologians have reflected on the sad history of the separation of theology and spirituality, that "diastase" that Hans Urs von Balthasar traced back to the incipient distinction of polemical and inner-churchly theologies in the patristic period and which grew immeasurably worse in the late Middle Ages due to the separation between the rational theology of the Scholastics and the affective theology of some mystics.[49] For the Swiss theologian, the very structure of the covenant between God and humanity witnessed to in the Hebrew Bible requires the reintegration of

McGinn | The Letter and the Spirit: Spirituality as an Academic Discipline

spirituality and theology. Reflection on Scripture, especially the unity of dogmatic and paranetic teaching in the Pauline letters, leads him to conclude: "On this basis one can already ask oneself the question whether it makes sense in the future to distinguish any longer between theology and spirituality."[50] We need not accept the whole of von Balthasar's program for overcoming the disjunction between spirituality and theology to use him as a spokesman for agreement among contemporary theologians concerning the need to bring theology and spirituality back together.[51] If theology finds its ultimate purpose in the conversion of the subject, as my teacher Bernard Lonergan argued, it seems impossible to exclude spirituality from the task of religious self-appropriation which Lonergan saw as theology's goal. As Regina Bechtle noted, for Lonergan "knowing oneself in relation to God and giving oneself over to the discipline of transformation emerge as prerequisites and not just frills for one who would do theology."[52] Even those who do not wish to take a primarily theological route into the study of religion, both in religiously-affiliated and non-affiliated schools, have begun to argue that spirituality should take a place in the curriculum. Every religious tradition needs to understand its past, and there is something that answers to the broad description of spirituality in all religions, at least in the sense that beliefs have always been practiced and were always intended to be appropriated on a deep personal level. This history of appropriation has often been neglected in narrowly rational models of the study of religious traditions that concentrated only on doctrines and institutions. Spirituality may not be the only way to correct this myopia, but it is certainly one way that should not be neglected. From the perspective of the study of religion in non-religious higher education, this historical-contextual approach to spirituality makes a particularly strong case for the need to include spirituality, in some way, in the curriculum.

To be sure, there are those, even among believers, who doubt the wisdom of this. Bradley Hanson, for example, questions whether spirituality can be taught within a religiously-neutral academic environment because of the degree of existential involvement spirituality always entails.[53] Precisely this issue of subjective interest, as well as the admitted vagueness of the term, would lead many non-religious educators to rule spirituality out as a fit subject of study. But I want to argue against these positions, claiming, as Walter Principe and others have done, that spirituality can and should be an integral part of the curriculum both within theological education and in the humanistic study of religion.

To those who say that the "existential orientation" entailed in spirituality is incompatible with the objectivity that is at least the ideal of the humanistic education, I reply that we need more adequate distinctions among various kinds of existential orientations. In the religiously-related school, existential orientation will mean one thing; it will mean something rather different in a department of religious studies or a non-church-related divinity school like the one where I teach. Here the existential orientation entailed in the study of spirituality need not be directed either immediately or mediately to the student's own religious life, but should at least include the student's willingness to investigate a particular spirituality as one way of expressing the central concerns of living the human condition, however foreign that may be to him or her on a personal level. Put more existentially, the study of spirituality requires a desire to try to appreciate how religious people actually live their beliefs.

HOW IS SPIRITUALITY TO BE TAUGHT?

In some ways I think the final question I wish to address, that is, how spirituality is to be taught, is the most difficult and the one on which there may well be the most disagreement. There have been a number of recent articles that have set out programs for the incorporation of spirituality into academic curricula. In 1981, Edward Kinerk, using insights from Bernard Lonergan, suggested that a curriculum for the study of spirituality could be constructed by the application of questions for analysis that would allow one to find the form of a spirituality, followed by questions for comparison and contrast among spiritualities that would eventually lead to questions for evaluation.[54] In 1989, James A. Wiseman advanced another Lonerganian plan. Treating spiritual theology as a "subject specialization" in terms of Lonergan's *Method of Theology*, he tried to show how the subject matter can be specified by the use of the five categories of symbolic expression that P. Joseph Cahill, in his book *Mended Speech*, identifies as the core of any religious tradition. The five symbolic expressions are: (1) a body of normative literature, such as the Bible; (2) theological formulations, broadly taken; (3) visual art forms; (4) aural art forms; and (5) popular devotions and the like.[55] This subject matter would then be approached through the mediation of Lonergan's eight functional specializations (research, interpretation, history, dialectic, foundations, doctrines, systematics, communications).[56] Walter Principe's article also contains brief reflections on the teaching of spirituality both from the theological perspective and the history of religious point of view. More recently, Sandra Schneiders has provided a rather detailed picture, basically Ricouerian in inspiration, which treats spirituality as an interdisciplinary "field-encompassing field" which should be descriptive-critical, ecumenical, holistic, and participative. Each of these four programs has merits. Read individually, each seems convincing, at least in part; taken together, their considerable differences demonstrate the problems of curricular development in an area still so unsure of itself.

This is not the occasion for a detailed evaluation of these plans and exactly why I would not want to implement any one of them myself. This is not to deny the important contribution they represent, nor to put a stop to the discussion of exactly how to implement the teaching of spirituality into the curriculum. However, I do want to go on record with what may seem a rather anomalous statement after my insistence on the importance of spirituality for the teaching of religion, that is, I am not at all sure that spirituality needs a separate niche in the curriculum in order to be adequately assimilated. The creation of programs of spirituality is an important part of the process of giving spirituality the voice it deserves, but need not be taken as the only way to achieve the goal.

Speaking as a Christian theologian, I believe that it is quite possible to teach spirituality effectively in and through traditional disciplines such as theology, both historical and constructive, ethics, and also the history of Christianity. In saying this I do not mean to exclude other disciplines, or the necessity of being open to non-Christian forms of spirituality, especially because so much good theology today is theology that is being done in dialogue with other traditions. The reason for this has been well put by von Balthasar when he says, "Nothing in the Church is mere abstract principle: everything that is valid for all rests on concrete persons, or better, on concrete tasks entrusted to concrete persons."[57] This attention to the concrete person and the concrete task in the study of religion necessarily implies what I understand as spirituality. As long as we do not treat this hunger for the concrete in an elitist fashion that would narrow the scope of spirituality to the thought of a few great masters, the incorporation of this perspective in our teaching will help us be attentive to what we seem unable not to call spirituality.

We may ask in closing how the efforts of believing teachers and educators relate to first-order spirituality, that is, to the personal appropriation of Christian faith. Each teacher must have her or his answers to this question. Generalization is particularly difficult here, perhaps impossible. So let me instead tell two stories. The first involves a vision of sorts, but a contemporary vision that might have been given to anyone concerned with the teaching and dissemination of spirituality.

A Long Island commuter stands on a platform watching trains speeding past each other east and west in their rush towards what seem to be opposite goals. This particular commuter happens to be a religious editor who suddenly grasps this as an image of the mutual ignorance and lack of connection between Eastern and Western spiritual traditions. If only something could be done to get the trains to slow down, he thinks, to stop, to converse window-to-window, might they not realize that their opposition is not as great as it seems? This sudden illumination, a kind of modern analogy to Augustine's third kind of vision (the intellectual vision discussed in the twelfth book of the *Literal Commentary on Genesis*), was the actual beginning of the *Classics of Western*

Spirituality series, which was originally designed to be one-half of a joint enterprise called the *Classics of Eastern and Western Spirituality*.

I doubt if the recipient of this commuter-vision would want to describe himself as a mystic, despite his interest in spiritual traditions. The astute among you will have noticed that the moment of illumination he was given did not refer directly to God, but to the contemporary audience of spiritual seekers. However, this moment of enlightenment and the work that has gone into making it at least partly real surely is not without relation to the personal appropriation of belief on the part of the hundreds of thousands who have profited from better access to classical spiritual teaching, Jewish, Christian, and Muslim. To hand on what we have been given, even imperfectly, is to play a role.

Reflecting on this role reminds me of the story that some of you may remember from the end of Gershom Scholem's great book, *Major Trends in Jewish Mysticism*. Scholem says he heard it from the Hebrew novelist S. J. Agnon. I conclude by quoting it in full:

> When the Baal Shem had a difficult task before him, he would go to a certain place in the woods, light a fire and meditate in prayer—and what he had set out to perform was done. When a generation later the "Maggid" of Meseritz was faced with the same task he would go to the same place in the woods and say: We can no longer light the fire, but we can still speak the prayers—and what he wanted done became reality. Again a generation later Rabbi Moshe Leib of Sassov had to perform this task. And he too went into the woods and said: We can no longer light the fire, nor do we know the secret meditations belonging to the prayer, but we do know the place in the woods to which it all belongs—and that must be sufficient; and sufficient it was. But when another generation had passed and Rabbi Israel of Rashin was called upon to perform the task, he sat down on his golden chair in his castle [obviously, he was an academic] and said: We cannot light the fire, we cannot speak the prayers, we do not know the place, but we can tell the story of how it was done. And, the story-teller adds, the story which he told had the same effect as the actions of the other three.[58]

NOTES

Reprinted, with permission, from *The Cresset* (Valparaiso University). The original address, given at Valparaiso University in Fall, 1992, was part of a conference, "Spirituality and Higher Education" sponsored by the Lilly Fellows Program in Humanities and the Arts.

1. Gustavo Vinay, "'Spiritualità': Invito a una discussione," *Studia Medievali*, 3a series 2 (1961), 706.
2. For more information regarding the term's history, see Jean Leclerq, "'Spiritualitas.'" *Studia Medievali*. 3a series 2 (1961); Jon Alexander, "What Do Recent Writers Mean By Spirituality?" *Spirituality Today* 32 (1980): 247–56; Walter Principe, "Toward Defining Spirituality." *Sciences Réligieuses* 12 (1983). For New Testament study, see Albert Schweitzer, s.v. "Pneuma," in *Theological Dictionary of the New Testament*, edited by Gerhard Friedrich (Grand Rapids: Eerdmans, 1968), 6:332–455.

3. This fifth-century text, found in *Patrologia Latina* 30:115A, has been doubtfully ascribed to both Pelagius and to Faustus of Riez.

4. Leclercq, "Spiritualitas," 281–84.

5. Jill Raitt, "Saints and Sinners: Roman Catholic and Protestant Spirituality in the Sixteenth Century." In *Christian Spirituality II: High Middle Ages and Reformation*, edited by Jill Raitt, et al., (New York: Crossroad, 1987), 454–56.

6. Leclercq, "Spiritualitas," 293–94.

7. Walter Principe, "Toward Defining Spirituality," 132.

8. Ibid., 148.

9. Étienne Gilson, *Théologie et histoire de la spiritualité* (Paris: Vrin, 1943).

10. Principe, "Toward Defining Spirituality,"134.

11. Ibid., 149.

12. Ibid., 135–36.

13. Sandra M. Schneiders, "Spirituality in the Academy." *Theological Studies* 50 (1989), 682.

14. C. A. Bernard, *Compendio di Teologia Spirituale* (Rome: Gregorian University, 1976), 37.

15. Eugene Megyer, "Theological Trends: Spiritual Theology Today." *The Way* 21 (1981): 55–67.

16. James A. Wiseman, "Teaching Spiritual Theology: Methodological Reflections." *Spirituality Today* 41 (1989), 143–59.

17. B. C. Hanson, "Spirituality as Spiritual Theology." In *Modern Christian Spirituality: Methodological and Historical Essays*, edited by Bradley C. Hanson (Atlanta: Scholars Press, 1990), 49.

18. Kenneth Leech, *Experiencing God: Theology as Spirituality* (San Francisco: Harper and Row, 1985).

19. Louis Bouyer, *The Spirituality of the New Testament and the Fathers* (New York-Tournai: Desclee, 1961), viii–ix.

20. Josef Sudbrack, "Spirituality I. Concept," in *Sacramentum Mundi: An Encyclopedia of Theology*, edited by Karl Rahner, et al., vol. 6 (New York and London: Herder and Herder, 1970).

21. Hans Urs von Balthasar, "The Gospel as Norm and Test of All Spirituality of the Church." *Spirituality in Church and World*, Concilium Vol. 9 (New York: Paulist Press, 1965).

22. Hans Urs von Balthasar, "Spirituality," in *Explorations in Theology I. The Word Made Flesh* (San Francisco: Ignatius Press, 1989), 211. He defines *theologia spiritualis* as "the Church's objective teaching on how revelation is to be realized in practice," 212.

23. Jordan Aumann, *Spiritual Theology* (New York: Sheed and Ward, 1980), 17–18.

24. Walter Principe, "Toward Defining Spirituality," 136.

25. Ibid., 135.

26. Bernard McGinn, *Foundations of Mysticism: Origins to the Fifth Century* (New York: Crossroad, 1992), 286–89.

27. Ewert Cousins, *Christian Spirituality*, I, xiii.

28. G. Wakefield, *The Westminster Dictionary of Christian Spirituality* (Philadelphia: Westminster, 1983), v.

29. Joann Wolski Conn, *Women's Spirituality: Resources for Christian Development* (New York: Paulist Press, 1986), 3.

30. John Macquarrie, *Paths in Spirituality* (New York: Harper and Row, 1972), 40, 47.

31. Raymundo Panikkar, *The Trinity and the Religious Experience of Mankind: Icon-Person-Mystery* (Maryknoll, New.York: Orbis, 1973), 9.

32. Jean-Claude Breton, "Retrouver les assises anthropologiques de la vie spirituelle." *Studies in Religion/Sciences réligieuses* 17 (1988), 97–105.

33. Sandra Schneiders, "Spirituality in the Academy," 684.

34. Edward Kinerk, "Toward a Method for the Study of Spirituality." *Review for Religious* 40 (1981), 6.

35. Michael Downey, "Editor's Preface." *The New Dictionary of Catholic Spirituality.* Michael Glazier Books (Collegeville, MN: Liturgical Press, 1993), 425.

36. R. Hosmer, "Review Article: Current Literature in Christian Spirituality," *Anglican Theological Review* 66 (1984), 425.

37. Sandra Schneiders, "Spirituality in the Academy," 683.

38. See Bradley Hanson, "Spirituality as Spiritual Theology," 48–49.

39. "Introduction," in *World Spirituality,* vol. 16, *Christian Spirituality: Origins to the Twelfth Century,* ed. Bernard McGinn and John Meyerdorff (New York: Crossroad, 1985), xv.

40. Ibid., xvi.

41. Rowan Williams, *Christian Spirituality* (Atlanta: John Knox, 1979), 1.

42. Urban T. Holmes, *Spirituality for Ministry* (San Francisco: Harper and Row, 1982), 3.

43. André Vauchez, *La spiritualité du moyen âge occidental: VIIIe-XIIe siècles* (Paris: Presses Universitaires, 1975), 7.

44. Philip Sheldrake, *Spirituality and History: Questions of Interpretation and Method* (New York: Crossroad, 1992).

45. In the discussion following the oral version of this paper, the interesting question of the possibility of a "Satanic spirituality," or a "Nazi spirituality" was raised. I would argue against seeing these as authentic spiritualities, but it would be difficult to do so on a historical-contextual approach alone, since significant communities would assert that these represented their "authentic," and even "transcendent" values.

46. Von Balthasar, "Spirituality," 226.

47. Ewert Cousins, *Christian Spirituality,* I, xiii.

48. Sandra Schneiders, "Spirituality in the Academy," 693–95.

49. See Hans Urs von Balthasar, "Theologie und Spiritualität," *Gregorianum* 50 (1969): 571–87.

50. Ibid., 586.

51. See Regina Bechtle, "Theological Trends: Convergences in Theology and Spirituality," *The Way* 23 (1985), 305–14.

52. Ibid., 308.

53. Bradley Hanson, "Spirituality as Spiritual Theology," 49–50.

54. Edward Kinerk, "Toward a Method," 7–19.

55. P. Joseph Cahill, *Mended Speech: The Crisis of Religious Studies and Theology* (New York: Crossroad, 1982).

56. James A. Wiseman, "Teaching Spiritual Theology," 147–57.

57. Von Balthasar, "The Gospel as Norm," 20.

58. Gershom G. Scholem, *Major Trends in Jewish Mysticism* (Jerusalem: Schocken, 1941). I am grateful to my colleague Wendy Doniger for bringing this story to my attention.

3

Broadening the Focus

Context as a Corrective Lens in Reading Historical

Works in Spirituality

WALTER H. PRINCIPE, C.S.B.

When I reflect on studying the spirituality of historical persons through their writings, the image that comes to my mind is that of a microscope or opera glass. These instruments focus on one narrow aspect of the object without giving a view of the whole. A microscope shows you the cells of a frog but not the whole frog; the opera glasses spotlight the vivacious Carmen but leave out her lover Don José and the chorus of cigarette girls or gypsies. Something similar can happen when we read some historical person's text on spirituality. We can indeed get a partial insight but we can also experience considerable distortion if we study such a person's spirituality by fixing our attention exclusively on the writings of that person or only on what the person says explicitly.

There is reason for this distortion in human psychology. I take it as both axiomatic and verifiable by experience that writers, preachers, speakers, spiritual assistants, etc., chiefly write or speak about what they perceive as a need or a lack they think should be addressed. It might be the elementary needs of a beginner in the life of the Spirit; it might be the particular ways of dealing with difficulties; it might be, especially, bringing into sharp focus some element of that life they think is lacking or insufficiently stressed. Thus Teresa of Avila tries to convince her sisters not to be afraid to leave vocal prayer for mental prayer, and she describes the way that life in Christ can develop by greater interiority. John of the Cross has special problems to examine: he rails against attachments to visions, locutions, and feelings; he is severe with spiritual directors who refuse to allow passive contemplation to those invited to this kind of prayer when they observe the signs of invitation to it that John himself gives. These were real concerns for these spiritual authors. But do they—and indeed the whole corpus of their writings—give us a full picture of the spirituality of either of these two great saints? Read their works and you will find practically no mention of their liturgical prayer; yet they spent considerable time reciting or singing the divine office, including the Eucharist. This part of their lives must have been very important for their spirituality but Teresa and John do not mention it because they seem to have found no problem in that part of their lives or in the lives of those for whom they wrote.

Further, what does it mean that Teresa speaks so often of "honor" (an important trait of Spanish culture in her time) and that she likes to speak of God as "His Majesty"? Or that John of the Cross could use the artistic canons of his contemporary poetry, including its love-imagery, when composing his outpourings of love for God; and that then he could adopt stilted sixteenth-century theological vocabulary to explain them? What I mean is that there is a lot more to get at than the explicit writings of an author if we want to grasp the full spirituality of a historical person. Of course, the person's writings are the important first approach, but it is my conviction that we must bring to our research many questions that can tease out much more than is evident from a simple reading of the texts.

As a hermeneutical principle, I am taking it for granted that it is important in these and in all writings to go beyond the text itself. Reader-response theory stresses the existential response we make to a text as it stands and as it is read by us today: indeed, I presume that such a response is the correct ultimate goal of reading such texts unless, of course, one is merely a detached scholar studying spirituality without any commitment to personal spiritual development. But, as with biblical and other texts, we avoid misleading judgments and erratic responses if we first examine the various contexts that lie behind the text. Thérèse of Lisieux's *Life of a Soul* did indeed inspire many readers who had only her text to respond to, but how much deeper and inspiring is the work when scholars discovered the following facts: (a) her sister edited and changed her text in order to have Thérèse look like her own idea of what a nineteenth-century saint should be (this is not an uncommon practice in hagiography); (b) the details of her family situation both within and outside the convent (think of what it meant that out of 25 cloistered sisters living so closely together, 4 were blood sisters of the Martin family and another was a cousin; 19 were old enough to be her mother); (c) the intense rivalry between her sister, Mother Agnes, and the powerful and eccentric Mother Mary of Gonzaga; (d) her psychological problems in her early years as examined by the study of Jean-François Six;[1] (e) her daring repudiation of some current views of spirituality, and her strong adherence to basic gospel values often played down in her times.

And so, as I see it, we need to ask a number of questions about any author's spirituality. These questions, of course, will vary according to what we mean by spirituality. Here a distinction is in order. A person's spirituality may refer to what is most basic—the person's *lived experience*, the real, existential level, that is, how that person lived in the Spirit. Or it can refer to the person's *teaching* on spirituality. Let us examine some, at least, of the contexts that must be examined in the two cases, contexts to be kept in mind when reading an author or studying writings about a person.

LOCATING SPIRITUALITY IN TIME AND PLACE

To discover fully the lived, existential spirituality of another person, past or present, is of course impossible. One would always be dealing with approximations. The task of an ordinary biographer, dealing so often with external events, is difficult enough; how much more difficult it is to penetrate the way a person lived or lives in the Spirit. One way of access would be through writings of such persons if they speak of their lives and spiritual experiences (St. Paul, St. Augustine, Teresa of Avila come to mind) or who, through letters or treatises, reveal something of their outlook and spiritual journey. But here too the microscope or opera glass factor would come into play. We should have to correct the narrowness of the vision provided by these writings by trying to situate such persons in their history by using such methods as social-psychological history, and by examining the mentalities of the time. In what culture did the person live? What was popular religion like at the time? What were the social and religious movements and ideals of the person's time, and how did the person reflect these and react to them? Ignatius of Antioch's letters on his way to martyrdom and Ignatius of Loyola's *Spiritual Exercises* are not only different literary genres, but also reflect vastly different social and religious situations and different psychological temperaments. Bernard of Clairvaux, Mechtilde, and Thomas Merton were all Cistercians, similar in their ideals, but how different the social and religious contexts in which they wrote! For each author we have to go even further beyond these questions: What was the whole secular context of the person—political, economic, sociological, sociopsychological, philosophical, artistic, scientific?

For example, was the society in which the person lived a static, well-structured society or one going through important changes? Again, compare these persons: Bernard preaching the Crusades against Islamic penetration of Europe; Catherine of Siena encouraging a weak pope to return from exile in France and seeking peace among the warring Italian city-states; the sixteenth-century Spanish saints influenced both by the politics of the Reformation and the exploration and conquest of the Americas; Mary Ward trying to serve the educational needs of persecuted English Catholics by founding a non-cloistered community despite opposition from Roman canonists and others; Vincent de Paul and Louise de Marillac circumventing canon law to establish the non-cloistered Filles de la Charité to go out and serve the poor; Thomas Merton as a withdrawn monk wrestling with his literary talents and at the same time active in the peace movement; Dorothy Day working as an intensely dedicated lay woman often misunderstood by Church authorities, by religious, and by other laity in her service of the poor.

The spirituality of Dorothy Day calls to mind a special problem now being investigated more intensively. This is the position and role of women authors, especially their situation in their culture and in the Church. Despite the silence of historians so often obscuring these contexts in the case of women, much recent study is shedding more light in this area. Yet there are special problems. It is helpful to know that the lives and spirituality of a number of women in the past have often been brought to our knowledge through the writings of men, often their confessors or spiritual assistants who in ancient and medieval times could write more easily (there were exceptions of course: Hildegard of Bingen, Eloise, more recently the two Teresas, Edith Stein, etc.), but how many of these portraits were filtered through the outlook and judgments of these men, with their ideals of spirituality? In a reading course I did with a talented student, we examined the letters of direction written by men for a number of different women from the twelfth to the fourteenth century. In some cases, at least, it was clear that the male authors were using their own male-oriented models of spirituality; further, the ideals and the practices they urged upon these women reflected either their partial experience of women or their prejudices about women, or both. For example, they warn anchoresses living in their small rooms by the cathedral to keep their windows closed, to avoid chattering and gossip, and to lead an excessively strict style of life by rules that no man would submit to.

The situation of women in the past is one—obviously an important one—of many areas that should be considered. A meeting at the State University of New York at Binghamton in 1993 chose as its general topic the marginalized in medieval society, and this suggests, as Philip Sheldrake has pointed out, our need to be aware of many levels of society and spiritual life that have been neglected, as well as of the control over the history of spirituality exercised by those in present-day control.[2] A hermeneutics of suspicion should accompany a lot of our study of spirituality.

Other questions to be put, in more detail: What was the personal history of the one being studied, to the extent that this can be known? What were the family background and childhood experiences? (Compare Catherine of Siena, Teresa of Avila, and Thérèse of Lisieux.) What was the person's vocation and to what kind of life—to life in the world or religious life or the priesthood? What kind of education in general and what particular spiritual training did the person receive? (My brother Charles has done a lot of work on the kind of theology studied by the first Jesuit missionaries to the Indians in North America and how it influenced their view of the apostolate.) What were the person's achievements and difficulties experienced? And so forth. (In this respect, I am impressed by the massive 1993 biography of Pope Paul VI by Peter Hebblethwaite—through all his description of Montini's life [using of course many of his letters and speeches] you get quite an insight into his lived spirituality, even if this is not the main focus of the work.)

The witness of others who knew the person is another important context for getting at the lived spirituality of someone. Here, of course, one has to proceed with caution if the person in question is a highly revered person, e.g., the founder of a religious community. One community I know has got both its foundress and her successor canonized and is now working on the third in line; and the recent controversy over the beatification of the founder of Opus Dei might be a case in point! (It raises the issue of who gets canonized. Why have Jean Gerson or Bossuet or Newman, or single or married lay persons been passed over while a Canadian foundress of an order of sisters to be priests' housekeepers is beatified?) It is only in recent years that the old style of hagiography has been modified and we begin to see presentations of holy persons, warts and all—something that reflects a whole new idea of what holiness really means, and how grace and nature are intertwined in spiritual growth. The different theologies of holiness, by the way, are themselves important contexts to be kept in mind when we examine the accounts of the life of a person being studied.

BROADENING THE THEOLOGICAL CONTEXT

The second aspect of an author's spirituality—the *doctrine* or *teaching* contained in the person's writings—likewise calls for a broader and deeper analysis of context than is often done in practice. If, as frequently happens, we confine our notion of spirituality to an author's views on prayer and various methods and stages of prayer, the overcoming of sin and temptation, the practice of virtues, descriptions of stages of development in life of the Spirit, our questions would relate to these topics and go little further. It is interesting in this regard to see what kind of textual choices some editors of historical authors make in presenting the spirituality of the author each is editing. (Having conducted seminars on the full theological spirituality of Thomas Aquinas, I was disappointed to see the narrow focus of the texts chosen by Simon Tugwell for the *Classics of Western Spirituality*—mainly texts on prayer, active and contemplative life, and a few aspects of religious life. True, he had to include Albert as well, but these texts hardly begin to tap the rich spirituality of Aquinas.)

To concentrate too narrowly on these themes is unconsciously to continue the split between spirituality and theology that began in the fourteenth century and was intensified with the breakdown of theology itself into distinct and even isolated disciplines: dogmatic and moral theology, moral theology and spiritual theology (how can Christian morality not be spiritual or Christian spirituality not be moral?), ascetic and mystical theology, speculative and practical theology. For the great *patristic* and *medieval* authors up to the end of the thirteenth century, the study and teaching of life in the Spirit was inseparable from the theology of God's graciousness and call to a graced life, the missions and indwelling of the Trinitarian Persons reflecting the inner life of the Father, Son, and Holy Spirit, the gifts and fruits of the Holy Spirit, the doctrine of creation and created realities with the attendant problems of good and evil in creation, the image of the Trinity in human persons, the vocation and destiny of intellectual creatures, doctrines of free will, the nature and effects of original and actual sin and the way of conversion, the sacramental life, final beatitude, and other areas of theology.

In my opinion, this entire theological context needs to be drawn out from any author who is being examined for spiritual doctrine. Often, as I have suggested, one has to heighten the power of microscopic view focused on the writings to go even deeper, penetrating as it were to the DNA theological structures out of which the statements and teachings of the author grow. Or, to use another method, one has to put aside the too narrow focus of the writings and look at the broader theological context. This broader and deeper theological context is often implicitly assumed and must be made explicit. On the other hand, an author's silence about some issues is itself indicative of the partiality of the author's spiritual teaching. For example, if an author neglects the role of the Holy Spirit or overly emphasizes human effort to the neglect of God's gracious assistance, this should be observed and carefully questioned. Other theological positions important to spirituality that should be sought out are the author's views about both the person and saving activity of Jesus Christ, the author's ecclesiology, and her or his views on human history, the place of created realities, and of human involvement in human history through work, leisure, and zeal for social as well as individual justice.

Beyond the theological areas, one should examine other implications that may be found in the text or that should be asked about: the psychological traits of the author or the psychological views implicit in the work, e.g., regarding vice and virtue or the way of personal growth in the Spirit; the author's hermeneutics concerning Scripture, church teaching, other literature; the type of writing itself (didactic, poetic, scientific, rhetorical, etc.).

All this may seem a very tall order, and indeed it is. But I have found that one can begin to train students—and oneself—to take such a contextual view of an author's works by developing and applying a continually growing list of leading questions to think about as we read a work. As an example, my students, prompted by the question concerning the place of the Holy Spirit in an author's teaching, found on reading Bonaventure's *Itinerarium mentis in Deum* that this treatise describing the way of the mind into God scarcely mentioned the Holy Spirit. On the other hand, with this question and fact about the *Itinerarium* in mind, they were able to appreciate Bonaventure's excellent placement of the role of the Holy Spirit in his *Breviloquium*, where the gift of the Spirit and the Spirit's gifts and fruits follow upon the death and resurrection of Christ. And, by contrast, they saw that in Thomas Aquinas's *Summa theologiae*, although the Holy Spirit figures prominently elsewhere, the role of the Holy Spirit within the governing power of the risen Christ in history is not mentioned. To help myself and the students in this regard, we drew up a large number of questions, many of which are listed in an article in *The Way* concerning varieties of spirituality and ways of assessing their Christian authenticity.[3] And when I received and read the new *Bulletin* of our society, I realized that I shall have to go back over the list and add quite a number more.

To conclude: to read a text in all these contexts is to situate an author's spirituality in a way that will lead to critical judgment and assimilation of this spirituality. Only then can there be a sound, fully justified and satisfactory response to the text and the author.

NOTES

1. Jean-François Six, *La Véritable enfance de Thérèse de Lisieux* (Paris: Seuil, 1972). His second volume on the saint, *Thérèse de Lisieux au Carmel* (Paris: Seuil, 1973), is a good example of contextual study illuminating many aspects of her spirituality.
2. Philip Sheldrake, "Spirituality and the Process of History," *Christian Spirituality Bulletin* 1 (Spring 1993) 1, 3: reprinted from his *Spirituality and History: Questions of Interpretation and Method* (New York: Crossroad, 1991).
3. Walter Principe, "Theological Trends: Pluralism in Christian Spirituality," *The Way: Contemporary Christian Spirituality* 32/1 (January 1992), 54–61.

4

A Hermeneutical Approach to the Study of Christian Spirituality

SANDRA M. SCHNEIDERS, I.H.M.

$\mathcal{B}$efore proposing a methodological approach to the study of Christian spirituality, I would like to make three preliminary points. First, I have been challenged by the recent articles of Bernard McGinn[1] and of Walter Principe[2] to re-think the entire issue of "approaches to the study of spirituality" and have been led to re-articulate my own approach as "hermeneutical" rather than "anthropological." This is not because I have fundamentally changed my mind about what we in the field of spirituality are studying and/or how it should be studied, but because, for two reasons, "anthropological" is a misleading, or at least potentially misleading, way of talking about it.

First, to refer to the approach I have favored as anthropological suggests that a single discipline, namely, anthropology (whether cultural or theological), governs the approach, and I have long been convinced that the most adequate approach in this discipline is not only multi-disciplinary but explicitly inter-disciplinary. Also, the use of the term anthropological can easily suggest a basically "history of religions" or "scientific study of religions"[3] approach to spirituality and I am persuaded that spirituality as a discipline must be distin-guished from these fields of study even if both spirituality and religious studies sometimes investigate the same phenomena.

My second preliminary point is that I follow McGinn in affirming that the three approaches to the study of spirituality that he describes, namely, the theological, the historical-contextual, and the hermeneutical, are valid, impor-tant, and mutually complementary and that they should all be kept alive and in conversation with each other especially during the formative years of this new field of study. I remain persuaded, for reasons I will soon propose, that the hermeneutical approach is more adequate to the subject matter, though it might not always be best suited to the academic context, the resources of the institution, and/or the competencies of the researcher.

Apropos of this point, I am beginning to think that academic context has had a great deal to do with the elaboration of particular approaches to this field of study. A single denomination seminary is the logical place for the development of a strictly theological approach which might tend toward some wedding of the research approach to spirituality with a formation agenda that would find the inclusion of some type of spiritual practice within the study program quite congenial. On the other hand, the non-denominational divinity school or the university religious studies department would be more comfortable with an historical/contextual and/or anthropological approach and would probably be very reserved about, if not suspicious of, the introduction of any formational element into the program. The inter-denominational, inter-religious graduate theological institution, such as the one with which I am associated, would be more hospitable to an inter-disciplinary hermeneutical approach that entertains a certain tensive openness toward the praxis issue, even while eschewing any explicit formational agenda at least at the doctoral research level.

My third preliminary point, concerning how disciplines or fields of study have been traditionally delineated, will lead directly into my own proposal of a hermeneutical approach to the field of spirituality. Basically, fields of study are marked off in terms of a specific object of study and a particular method of studying it. The object is specified not only materially, i.e., in terms of the phenomenon to be investigated, but formally, i.e., in terms of the aspect or formality under which the phenomenon is to be investigated. Thus, for example, the material object of psychology is the human subject and the formal object is the psychic structures and functions of that subject. Anthropology also studies the human subject but under the formality of cultural participation. The methods deemed appropriate for a study also help mark the discipline off from related fields. Psychology, for example, uses such methods as critical introspection, experimentation, and clinical observation and treatment, whereas psychobiography might approach the same questions with literary and sociological methods. Two fundamental questions for the field of spirituality—and perhaps they are ones which we are not yet in a position to answer definitively—are: *What is the object, both material and formal, of this study?* and *What is/are the appropriate method(s)?* I would like to float a trial balloon response to these questions as the foundation for my suggestion about the appropriate approach to the field.

THE OBJECT OF THE STUDY OF SPIRITUALITY

I would propose that the object of spirituality as an academic discipline is the spiritual life as experience. In our case, it would be the experience of the spiritual life of Christians or perhaps the experience of the Christian spiritual life. While these two formulations are slightly different and could be the subject of another discussion, I will by-pass that discussion for the time being and take up each term in the definition in order to show how, together, they describe an object of study that is not precisely the same as the object of theology, the history of Christianity, the scientific study of religion, or other related disciplines.

First, spirituality studies the spiritual *life*. This field is not concerned with isolated experiences, whether religious or mystical, or with episodes or epiphenomena or temporary experiments or idiosyncratic dabblings. Nor is it specifically and directly concerned with theological formulations about God, the soul, the Church and so on even though such formulations may enter into the investigation of the life. It is concerned with the spiritual life as existential project which, elsewhere, I have called the project of self-integration through self-transcendence within and toward the horizon of ultimacy which, in the case of the Christian, is God revealed in Jesus Christ who is present as Spirit in and through the community of faith called Church.[4] No matter how particular or limited the research topic of a particular study in the field of spirituality may be, it is studied as integral to Christian spiritual life considered as a life project. The life project may be that of an individual, of a particular group or tradition, or even of the Church as a whole. But we are still concerned with the project of self-integration through self-transcendence rather than with unrelated episodes, aberrant phenomena, or theoretical constructs.

Second, spirituality[5] is concerned with the *spiritual* life which is today understood as the vital, ongoing interaction between the human spirit and the Spirit of God with both poles receiving equal attention and the focus being on the fact, the modality, the process, the effects, the finality of the interaction itself. The human spirit is not simply the "soul" as this was understood in pre-conciliar scholastic theology in distinction from the body, but the radical capacity of the human subject for self-transcendence; thus, the essential role, in the study of spirituality, of anthropology (both cultural and theological), psychology, and sociology as well as the other humanistic disciplines. But spirituality is not simply transpersonal psychology which studies the openness of the human spirit to the transcendent without raising the question of the fact or character of such a transcendent. Spirituality, especially religious spirituality, and *a fortiori* Christian spirituality, is also concerned with the divine Spirit with which the human spirit is engaged—thus the essential role of the theological disciplines in spirituality.

However, because spirituality is concerned with the interaction of the human spirit with the divine Spirit and, at least in its contemporary form, does not conceive of that interaction simply in terms of the submission of the former to the latter, Christian spirituality cannot be reduced without remainder to either the theologically Christian or the exclusively religious. This is evident to anyone who is attentive to the manifestations of Christian spirituality in our own times. For example, the influence of feminism on the spirituality of Christian women is not coming from theology. And the powerful role that psychotherapy plays in the spirituality of many contemporary Christians is not specifically religious in the sense of pertaining directly to creed, code, or cult.

But who would deny that feminist consciousness raising and psychotherapy are integral to the Christian spirituality, that is to the spiritual life project, of many contemporary people, influencing in decisive ways their ongoing interaction with God?

Third, spirituality is concerned with the study of the spiritual life as *experience*, i.e., "in the round." This is the most difficult dimension of the object to explicate because experience is notoriously difficult to define and the problem is exacerbated by the addition of the adjective "spiritual." Nevertheless, this is precisely the point of differentiation between spirituality on the one hand, and theology and historical studies and/or religious studies on the other. Obviously, in the study of the spiritual life as experience the theological element is important, even essential, because the Christian spiritual life is, in some measure at least, a response to, and an appropriation of, divine revelation in Jesus Christ which is somehow transmitted and normed by the ecclesial incarnation of that revelation in creed, code, and cult. Likewise, the historical/contextual dimension is absolutely essential to any investigation in this field because the experience of the spiritual life, precisely as experience, is necessarily concrete. It takes place in some specific historical-cultural setting which, at least to some extent, determines and specifies it.

Nevertheless, on the one hand, the experience of the spiritual life includes more, much more today, than religion, and religion includes much more than theology, and theology includes more than specifically Christian content.[6] On the other hand, the specificity of concrete spiritual experience is not exhausted by the historical context. In other words, while theology has crucially important things to say about the human spirit in terms of theological anthropology, morality, and so on, and equally important things to say about the divine Spirit, there are aspects of both that are important for spirituality which are not within the province of theology strictly speaking, even as theology is more expansively understood today. For example, the embodiment of the human spirit must be studied not only theologically but psychologically, sexually, sociologically, aesthetically, and from the standpoint of gender. And the spirituality of many Christians is deeply influenced by the effect on their God-image of developments in the natural sciences and interaction with non-Christian religious traditions, effects which may go beyond or be outside the purview of theology. Likewise, spiritual experience is not only culturally and historically situated but involves an interiority which can only be partially examined by historical methods. Other methods of study must be brought into play to examine other aspects of that experience.

In short, the study of spirituality as experience requires us to bring into play not only theology and historical studies, but psychology, sociology, the natural sciences, comparative religion, aesthetics, literature and the arts, and whatever other disciplines might be required by the character of the phenomenon to be studied. Spiritual experience includes religious phenomena which are theologically articulated and are always historically situated, but the life project of self-integration through self-transcendence is more inclusive than either or both of these dimensions, and that which it includes, other than and beyond theology and history, is not peripheral or decorative or dispensable. As Rahner said about mysticism, theologically it is indistinguishable from the "ordinary" life of grace but experientially it is very different and the difference can only be explained by some other discipline such as psychology.

Similarly, Thomas Merton recognized that his attempt to articulate his understanding of the contemplative life in theological categories in *The Ascent to Truth* was a relative failure and he turned, quite deliberately and consciously, to literature, poetry, and autobiography as more adequate to his subject matter precisely because experience in the round was his subject and theology could not handle much that was essential to that subject. He said,

> I found in writing *The Ascent to Truth* that technical language…does not convey what is most personal and most vital in religious experience. Since my focus is not upon dogma as such, but only on their repercussions in the life of a soul in which they begin to find a concrete realization, I may be pardoned for using my own words to talk about my own soul.[7]

While we would certainly not talk about theology exclusively in terms of dogma as Merton did, nor of the spiritual life as the repercussion of dogma in the soul, his insight into the fact that systematic theology, however precise and clear it might be, was not adequate to the concrete experience of the spiritual life which, as experience, is far more inclusive, was quite accurate. In other words, the task of spirituality as a discipline is to study Christian spiritual experience which, in our day, cannot be reduced to the exclusively Christian or the exclusively religious even when it is the experience of the committed Christian.

Finally, the object of the discipline of spirituality is, for our purposes, experience of *Christian* spiritual life. When Christian teaching, symbols, rituals, moral expectations, behavioral expressions, in short, the whole complex of Christian life coordinates, form the basic framework or paradigmatic context of the spiritual life, we can speak of Christian spirituality. However, the range of such spirituality is extremely broad today. It extends from the most narrowly confessional Christian spirituality of the fundamentalist to such "borderline" spiritualities as some forms of Goddess-oriented feminist spiritualities, some versions of creation or nature-centered spiritualities, or some types of recovery spiritualities whose relationship to the Christian framework is marginal at best.

53

Schneiders | A Hermeneutical Approach to Christian Spirituality

However, historically, one of the most interesting characteristics of Christian spirituality as lived experience is its capacity to be outside of, or even ahead of, theological developments, and to introduce into the theological and/or religious purview of the Church insights and convictions which stretch the received theological categories and paradigms. One has only to think of the teaching of John of the Cross about the equality of the soul with God, Julian of Norwich's insight into the femininity of Jesus, or Teresa of Avila's convictions about the role of humanity of Jesus in mystical experience, to realize that spirituality is not simply the application in practice of the teachings of theology but a contributor of genuine noetic content to the Christian tradition.[8] Certainly in our own day we have to recognize that the spirituality of liberation in general and of feminism in particular is having radical effects on theology.[9] Something similar must be recognized in regard to the influence of the new cosmology on spirituality[10] and the questions it is raising for theology.[11] Consequently, the premature application of theological criteria of acceptability to phenomena in the field of spirituality can be a serious mistake.

Let me summarize this section of the object of Christian spirituality as an academic discipline. I am suggesting that the object of the discipline is *materially* the spiritual life of the Christian and *formally* the complex and concrete experience of that life in its totality as the interaction of the human spirit with the Spirit of God, an interaction that includes but is not reducible to its theological or religious components or dimensions, nor necessarily exclusively Christian in its sensibilities or content. As such, the object of the contemporary discipline of spirituality must be distinguished from that of its honorable forbears in the field of spiritual theology, namely ascetical and mystical theology, and from that of its honorable academic partners, theology and the history of Christianity.

THE METHOD OF THE DISCIPLINE OF SPIRITUALITY

I will turn now to the issue of method in the field of spirituality, in particular, the appropriate approach to the study of spirituality. As I have said, I think there is a legitimate place, especially at this stage in the development of the field, for a plurality of approaches each of which emphasizes particular dimensions of the spiritual life which it studies. However, I do not think all of the candidates are equally comprehensive.

The theological approach offers evident advantages. First, it puts the emphasis on the Christian character of the spirituality under study. Secondly, it relates spirituality to the standard curriculum of the seminary in ways that can be understood in that academic setting. Thirdly, it insists upon the normative role of the Christian tradition in specifying the object of study and critically examining that object. Fourthly, it justifies the inclusion of an explicitly formative practical element in the study of spirituality and this is precisely the element with which many seminaries and practical masters programs are most concerned.

In my view, however, there are also some problems with the theological approach. The most evident, at least to me, is that the theological approach rules out, or at least prescinds from, the study of some of the most interesting phenomena on the current spirituality scene, such as the integration into Christian spirituality of elements from non-Christian sources, e.g., native spiritualities, the other world religions, or feminism, in a way that goes well beyond classical ecumenical or inter-religious dialogue.

Furthermore, the theological approach has a strong tendency to apply normative criteria of acceptability, which is not equivalent to the deductive and derivative approach of the nineteenth century manuals but which nevertheless does make spirituality subject to dogmatic and moral theology in a way that I consider far too restrictive given the enormous variety and latitude of contemporary Christian spirituality.

The historical/contextual approach also offers important advantages which Bernard McGinn and Walter Principe have elaborated. I am of the opinion that history supplies indispensable positive data for all critical study in the field of spirituality. But strictly speaking, history, if I understand it properly, deals with publicly available data within the time-space continuum and is subject to laws of cause and effect. While this covers an enormous scope of reality there are many realities in the sphere of spirituality which, although they have historical aspects, are essentially transhistorical or outside the proper sphere of the discipline of history. If I am reading him correctly, this is precisely what Bernard McGinn says in the General Introduction to *The Foundations of Mysticism*:

> [T]here can be no direct access to experience for the historian. Experience as such is not a part of the historical record. The only thing directly available to the historian or historical theologian is the evidence, largely in the form of written records, left to us by the Christians of former ages.[12]

One can study the conditions leading up to a conversion experience, the observable conditions of the experience itself, and its publicly available results including first or third person accounts of the experience. But can one study, historically, the conversion experience itself? Or mystical experience as such? Or transformation as religious or spiritual experience? Of course, one can raise the question of whether, in fact, one can by any means, historical or otherwise, study religious or spiritual experience as such and if so how. But, whatever the answer to that question, it seems to me that historical study, while indispensable as a participant in the study of the spiritual life, is not the defining method.

I would, however, agree with McGinn when he suggests that one can study spirituality through the study of Christian history and that this might be the appropriate way to study it in contexts which are not amenable to spirituality as a discipline in its own right.[13] Just as one can study morality through the study of literature, or christology through the study of religious art, or ecclesiology through the study of the political and social history of Europe, one can indeed study spirituality through Christian history or theology, especially as these disciplines are understood today. In my opinion, however, this does not render superfluous the development of the discipline which studies the experience of the spiritual life as its explicit and proper object.

The approach which seems to me the most adequate to the object of the discipline of spirituality is the hermeneutical approach. By this I emphatically do not mean the application of some particular hermeneutical theory, e.g., that of Paul Ricoeur, to the subject matter of spirituality. Nor do I mean the prosecution of some particular hermeneutical agenda, e.g., feminist or deconstructionist hermeneutics, in regard to the subject matter. Rather, I mean that the primary aim of the discipline of spirituality as I understand it, is to *understand* the phenomena of the Christian spiritual life as experience. And since understanding of such phenomena is a function of *interpretation*, the presiding intellectual instrumentality is hermeneutics understood as an articulated and explicit interpretational strategy. The project of interpretation, as I have already suggested, is interdisciplinary because of the complex and multifaceted character of spiritual experience as such. But the hermeneutical procedure, as I see it, involves a triple operation which is only theoretically sequential since, as the hermeneutical circle revolves, the three phases will mutually condition and re-condition each other.

The logically first step is one of description of the phenomenon/a under investigation, for example, the conversion experience of Teresa of Avila when she saw the image of the suffering Christ in the oratory of the convent.[14] The description will be, ideally, as "thick" as possible, taking into account not only the historical facts, the textual witness to the experience, the historical setting of sixteenth-century Spain, the theological and ecclesiological setting, the artistic character of the precipitating object, the psychological pressures on Teresa up to that point and at that point, the possible effect on Teresa's experience of the very similar conversion experience of Augustine which she says she read at just about the same time, and so on.

The logically second step is one of critical analysis. This will surely include theological criticism. But it may also include raising the developmental question about the midlife situation of Teresa, the sociological/feminist question about the inculcation in women of a pathological sense of responsibility for the suffering of men, perhaps questions about the erotic symbolism and imagery characteristic of Teresa's writing in general, the aesthetic question about the art object itself, questions about Teresa's social location and education, and so on.

The logically third step is one of constructive interpretation. The objective of the study of spirituality is not simply to describe or explain the spiritual experience but to understand it in the fullest sense of that word. Understanding involves not only intellectual deciphering of a phenomenon but appropriation that is transformative of the subject, what Ricoeur calls expansion of the being of the subject. A further objective of the study of spirituality is the enlightenment of the current situation, a contribution to the understanding of the spiritual life today. The study of Teresa's conversion experience may be brought into dialogue with current reflection on the process, dynamics, and criteria of religious conversion, the role of art in religious experience, the significance of gender analysis in the study of religious experience, or any number of other contemporary issues in spirituality. The point here is that studies in spirituality are, ideally, neither purely descriptive nor merely critical but also constructive, even though any given study might focus more directly, or even exclusively, on one or another dimension of the project.

THE ISSUE OF PRAXIS

This last point, on the intention of a hermeneutical approach to spirituality to engage the present, brings me to my final topic, namely, the much disputed and troubling issue of the role of practice and/or praxis in the academic study of spirituality. Let me begin with two distinctions. First, there is a distinction to be made between practice which is designed to foster the spiritual life of the student, such as personal daily prayer, the keeping of a spiritual journal, spiritual reading, and so on, and practice which is intended to supply the student with first-hand experience of the spiritual life which will serve as a direct or remote resource in the study of spirituality, such as doing supervised spiritual direction, leading groups in spiritual practice, or assisting people in reflection on social justice involvement. Secondly, I would distinguish between the study of spirituality in the seminary or in a practical masters program, in which part of the explicit aim of the study is the spiritual formation of the student in a particular religious tradition and/or the preparation of the student for ministry in the area of spirituality, and the study of spirituality in the context of a research program such as the doctorate.

In the first sphere, which I will call the formative one, I think the practice of spiritual disciplines and/or guided ministerial experience and reflection on this personal and ministerial experience is appropriate. Such formative study of spirituality is most likely to take place in a setting in which people share the same denominational affiliation or have worked out the appropriate modifications to allow all students to participate in the practices with integrity of conscience. In this sphere, I would hope that the results of the very best research in the area of spirituality would be utilized in the scripture courses of seminarians or in Bible study groups. The purpose of such programs is not research or the production of new knowledge in the field of spirituality; it is personal appropriation, both intellectual and practical, of the tradition.[15]

In the research sphere, however, I would have very serious reservations about the inclusion of any kind of mandatory practice of the direct use of such personal practice in the construction or prosecution of research projects. In the research arena the purpose of the study is, as in any research field, the expansion of knowledge in the field. However, as in some other fields of research such as psychology or art, work in the field of spirituality has a relation to personal involvement which may be more intimate and constitutive than in a field such as chemistry or physics. First, controlled introspection is an appropriate method of investigation when placed in proper relationship to other research methods. I would never permit a student to use his or her own religious experience as the subject of the dissertation. However, there is no question that students' religious experience raises many of the questions they eventually decide to study. And introspection is an indispensable source of understanding in many areas of spirituality. Just as a psychology student who has never been depressed might find it very difficult to understand the research literature on clinical depression, a spirituality student who has never prayed will probably have little understanding of mystical literature. Introspective knowledge must be rigorously criticized. But it is, nevertheless, an important resource in certain fields. Had Jung not used himself as a subject of investigation[16] he would not have been able to develop his theory on midlife transformation through individuation.

A second way in which practice enters the research field of spirituality is through fieldwork or the practicum in which a student works directly with other people's spiritual experience in order to understand the spiritual life in the concrete in a way only available through direct interaction. For example, a student working on midlife religious conversion of first world women might learn a great deal from accompanying some midlife women in their spiritual life by functioning, under supervision, as spiritual director for these women. Or a student investigating the influence of social justice activism on the spiritual life of young people might learn from being involved in the reflection group in which some of these young people process their experience.

A third way in which practice enters the research field is more subtle and perhaps even more powerful. Spirituality, like psychology and art and some other fields, is self-implicating. As the student deepens his or her investigation of the spiritual life, she or he is bound to experience the influence of what is being studied on his or her personal spiritual life. In other words, genuine understanding is transformative. Study, in this sense, is spiritual practice of a special but powerful kind. The transformative effect of understanding is verified in any field. But in the field of spirituality the subject matter is the interaction between the human spirit and God, the ultimate locus of personal transformation. There might be a genuinely qualitative, and not just quantitative, difference between the transformative effect of research in the field of spirituality and research in some other fields which might be more exclusively speculative or less personal by nature.

In any case, I have very serious reservations about the appropriateness of including any kind of personal practice aimed directly at the spiritual formation of the students in the academic field of spirituality at the research level. On the other hand, I recognize the self-implicating nature of the field and I think that we need to continue to reflect on this aspect of the discipline, be aware of the potential for distortion of research that this represents, and struggle to find ways to allow the field to be genuinely transformative of students, but appropriately so, through understanding and not through proselytism or discipling or formation.

CONCLUSION

In summary and conclusion, I would propose that Christian spirituality as an academic discipline is a genuine research field of study whose proper object is the Christian spiritual life as experience and whose proper methodology is a hermeneutically governed interaction of description, critical analysis, and constructive interpretation for the purpose of the fullest possible understanding of the phenomenon. I would distinguish it, without isolating it, from the formative study of spirituality which is aimed at the personal development of the student through the appropriation of Christian theory and practice and/or the preparation of students for ministry to the spiritual life of others. The hermeneutical methodology is necessarily inter-disciplinary, cross-cultural, and inter-religious and, insofar as it is the study of Christian spirituality, necessarily involves, but is not subordinate to, biblical, historical, and theological content and methods. While I think it is possible to study spirituality indirectly through the study of history, theology, art, literature, psychology, or other disciplines, I do not think spirituality is reducible to a subdivision of, or a moment within, any of these fields. The distinct subject matter and appropriate methodology of the field of spirituality justify its place in the academy as a distinct field of research with the potential to contribute to human understanding in a unique and significant way, especially in our own time when religious experience in all its complexity is recognized as an important source of such nightmares as Jonestown and Waco, and such vistas of hope as the signing of the accord between Israel and the Palestinians. The field is indeed young, but all fields were once new, and just as the trivium and quadrivium gave birth to the contemporary spectrum of the liberal arts, so the study of the human spirit in its embodied and social adventure through time and space can profit from more than one type of study. Spirituality is perhaps one of these types.

NOTES

1. Bernard McGinn, "The Letter and the Spirit: Spirituality as an Academic Discipline," was originally published in *The Cresset* of Valparaiso University (June 1993). See Chapter 2 in this volume. Used with permission.
2. Walter Principe, "Christian Spirituality," *The New Dictionary of Catholic Spirituality*, ed., Michael Downey, Michael Glazier Book (Collegeville, MN: Liturgical Press, 1993): 931–938.
3. McGinn, "The Letter and the Spirit," 17–18.
4. Sandra Schneiders, "Spirituality in the Academy." *Theological Studies* 50 (December 1989), 684.
5. Unless otherwise specified I am here using the term "spirituality" to designate the academic discipline which studies spirituality as experience rather than the experience being studied.
6. It should be noted that both the sources and methods of theology have expanded greatly in the past few decades and are no longer limited to the explicitly religious and philosophical.
7. Thomas Merton, *The Sign of Jonah* (New York: Harcourt, Brace, 1953), 8–9.
8. Karl Rahner in "The Theology of Mysticism," *The Practice of Faith: A Handbook of Contemporary Spirituality*, ed., K. Lehmann and L. Raffelt (New York: Crossroad, 1986), 74, makes the point that the mystic supplies data for the theologian which are not available from the traditional theological sources. The same point is made by William Thompson in *Fire and Light: The Saints and Theology: On Consulting the Saints, Mystics, and Martyrs in Theology* (New York/Mahwah, NJ: Paulist, 1987).
9. This is remarkably demonstrated by the thorough reworking of the theology of God by Elizabeth Johnson in *She Who Is: The Mystery of God in Feminist Theological Discourse* (New York: Crossroad, 1992).
10. See, for example, Fritjof Capra and David Steindl-Rast with Thomas Matus, *Belonging to the Universe: Explorations on the Frontiers of Science and Spirituality* (San Francisco: Harper, 1991).
11. Sallie McFague, in her new book, *The Body of God: An Ecological Theology* (Minneapolis: Fortress, 1993), begins to work out some theological implications of what has been essentially a development on the frontiers of science and spirituality.
12. Bernard McGinn, *The Foundations of Mysticism*, vol. 1 of *The Presence of God: A History of Western Christian Mysticism* (New York: Crossroad, 1992), xiv.
13. McGinn, "The Letter and the Spirit," 8–9.
14. The account of this experience is given in Teresa of Avila, *The Life of Teresa of Jesus*, trans. and ed. E. Allison Peers (Garden City, NY: Image Books, 1960), ch. 9.
15. However, my colleague Elizabeth Liebert pointed out to me the importance of recognizing explicitly that research in the field of spirituality is not only a resource for practical theology in the ministerial sphere but also is resourced *by* practical theology.
16. The record of Jung's intensive introspective experience which grounded his later work on individuation in midlife is presented in C. G. Jung, *Memories, Dreams, Reflections*, ed., Aniela Jaffé and Richard Winston, trans., Clara Winston (New York: Random House, 1965).

PART TWO

The Self-Implicating Nature of the Study of Spirituality

$\mathcal{T}$he essays in Part II focus in a more in-depth way on a theme introduced in Part I, that is, the self-implicating nature of the study of spirituality. As we emerge from a post-Enlightenment world in which a narrow, rational empiricism held sway, scholars are again discussing the role of the subject in research and intellectual inquiry. Past endorsements of a pure form of scholarly objectivity are now seen as illusions. This new conversation raises important questions: What is the relationship between the subject studying and the object being studied? How do personal and social locations affect the topics we examine, the ways we frame the questions, and the outcomes of our study? Is there a sliding scale of objectivity when it comes to scholarship, ranging from crass self-interest to a modicum of scholarly distance and freedom? Do we have vested interests that lead us to use our scholarship to defend personal positions or lifestyles? Are we open to the possibility that our study may transform us, change our lives in simple, or perhaps even dramatic, ways?

In the United States, a country with a long and distinguished history of philosophical pragmatism, we often favor the existential and practical over the theoretical. In the field of spirituality this has often led to conflict between the rigors of theory and careful attention to methodology on the one hand and piety or spiritual transformation on the other. For instance, some deem careful analysis, the construction of arguments, and the creation of appropriate categories for spirituality unnecessary because these are deemed extraneous to the heart of the spiritual life. Impatience with scholarship is visible in comments such as "Why do we have to make this so complicated? Why can't we just live the gospel?" as though gospel living were a transparent and simple exercise. In addition, the tendency toward over-simplification has its own dangers, leading to a lack of discernment about how spirituality is or is not faithful to its traditions. It is also important to be able to offer reasons for the authenticity of a particular spirituality. A more benign form of pragmatism agrees to engage in theoretical work if its link to the essence of life's meaning is discernible, or at least promised.

The essays in Part II address these knotty issues. They remind us that spirituality has the potential to affect all aspects of our lives, operating as it does within the messiness, the frustrations, the joys and sufferings of ordinary living. These authors caution against limiting spirituality to some abstract, distant, disembodied sphere. For example, in the context of a global society, spirituality may lead us to learn about the earthy spiritual traditions that the West has marginalized and devalued. Or premodern ritual practices that centered on the body and matter may help us reconnect with the material aspects of spirituality, such as healing, sexuality, and other pragmatic material concerns.

Reflecting on her experience teaching spirituality in a seminary, Mary Frohlich leads us through the Scylla and Charybdis of spiritual experience and systematic thought about it. Building on ideas from Bernard Lonergan and Michel de Certeau, Frohlich names *interiority* as the defining methodological principle in spirituality as an academic discipline. Interiority is not solipsistic introspection but an awareness that opens us to others, the world, and God in compelling ways. Frohlich poses a compelling question when she wonders whether the mission of the academic discipline of spirituality may be to repair the breach between life and knowledge that began in the late Middle Ages and became solidified in the modern period.

Pastoral theologian Elizabeth Liebert also argues that the practice of spirituality is a constitutive dimension of the study of spirituality. She brings clarity to the definitional complexities of the term "experience" and helps us see how spiritual practice enhances the appropriation of class material for both teachers and students by advancing the content of the study itself. She offers fresh insight into how to hold in creative tension our lived experience of the Spirit and the canons of scholarship. Liebert counsels those in both seminaries and secular universities always to be doing what they study and studying what they do. She suggests, "When lived spiritual experience comes into the room, it makes the study of Christian spirituality immediate, transformative, compelling, self-implicating, and life changing."

Turning to the *Sayings* of the fourth-century desert fathers and mothers, Douglas Burton-Christie brings to light the dynamic and costly aspects of the monks' spiritual conversation. Tracing his own journey of being attracted to the desert tradition through loving it, and then subjecting it to historical-critical analysis, Burton-Christie leads us through the tension between personal engagement and scholarly distance. The desert monks' expressions—"Speak to me a word" and "What should I do?"—are instructive for students of spirituality in that they remind us that there is something at stake in the questions we bring to this study. The love of our subject, embedded in our questions, helps bring it to life, and careful critical analysis keeps us honest as we attempt to re-appropriate the tradition for our own time.

The symbol of the spider becomes a touchstone for Belden Lane to explore the symbol-making and symbol-interpreting process that he sees as central to the study of spirituality. For Lane, the spider web is an image that both captures the interdisciplinary character of spirituality and functions to "carry us over" (*meta-phora*) from abstract ideas to concrete lived experience. In particular, Lane explores the use of the spider image in the writings of eigh-teenth-century American Reformed theologian Jonathan Edwards, showing how Edwards encouraged his readers to enter as participant into the spider's performance. Lane advocates the use of myth, symbol, and cultural studies in order to plumb the symbol-making character of a given spirituality. He chal-lenges us to dwell in these symbols, rooted as they are within their distinctive context, and allow them to work in us the transition from knowing to living.

Meredith McGuire takes on the age-old problem of dualism, a worldview that pits the spiritual and the sacred against matter, bodies, and the secular. Contrary to the common understanding that spirituality pertains only to spirits or souls, most religious practice is embodied in ways that activate memory, deeply felt emotion, social connectedness, and spiritual meaning. Viewing spirituality from the perspectives of sociology and anthropology, McGuire focuses our attention on the concrete, everyday patterns through which people make sense of their lives in the world. She argues that all aspects of spirituality involve *real bodies*—arthritic, athletic, pregnant, malnourished, healthy, or suffering bodies. She asks us to reflect on our own spiritual experience, to attend to the nuanced working of all of our senses. How would we set up our physical environment in order to open ourselves to the deep rhythms of holiness? How would we use our bodies? Are others involved, and if so, how? To help engage us in the materiality of spirituality, McGuire explores the examples of music making, both medieval and contemporary, and the ritualization of planting, growing, preparing, and consuming food. Is it possible for us to reclaim our dining room tables as a primary locus of sacred ritual?

In a final essay, Bernard McGinn examines the language that describes a specific type of experience: the inner experience of the mystics. McGinn broadens the horizon of McGuire's discussion of the senses by tracing the historical trajectory of the "spiritual senses" tradition. He notes both the variety and the problematic nature of this tradition in which mystics engage in the impossible but necessary task of naming their transforming encounters with God. He examines the quite different ways in which patristic and medi-eval writers articulated the inner and outer dimensions of their religious experience. Some privileged the inner realm, others the outer, and still others critiqued use of the language of experience altogether in favor of "pure unknowing and forgetting" of self and world.

These essays reveal both the importance and the challenge of attending with reverence and care to transforming experiences of God, and they remind us of the difficulty of finding language to describe the indescribable. While our understanding of experience is obvious in some ways and elusive in others, it is at the heart of the spiritual life and of our study of its content and patterns. Organized reflection on the spiritual life requires that we attend to our existential encounter with the world and with the transcendent-immanent, very far and always near, God.

5

Spiritual Discipline, Discipline of Spirituality

Revisiting Questions of Definition and Method

MARY FROHLICH, R.S.C.J.

As a professor of spirituality in a school of ministry, I am challenged daily by students for whom the idea of spirituality as an "academic discipline" is a hard sell. Why, they ask, should we study spirituality academically when what is really of interest is being spiritually transformed? While not every such complaint needs to be taken seriously, there is a nugget of genuine concern in these questions. Meanwhile, academic specialists in spirituality are far from settled concerning many fundamental questions of the discipline. "Exactly what is it that our discipline studies?" "Under what unique aspect do we study it?" "What methods are uniquely appropriate for this?" In this essay, I describe an approach that is designed to address questions raised by practitioners regarding concerns over the seeming conflict between academic study and spiritual transformation. Ultimately, I believe this approach may have an important contribution to make, not only in academia but on a larger scale as well.[1]

In perhaps the most important recent article reflecting on fundamental questions for this discipline, Sandra Schneiders defines the material object of the study of Christian spirituality (what is studied) as "lived Christian faith" and the formal object (the aspect under which it is studied) as "experience."[2] I both agree and disagree with this definition. I agree that, on a practical level, what we study is lived, experiential spirituality. In this essay, in fact, I will make that assertion even more strongly than Schneiders does. I will also argue, however, that we need to think more carefully about what is involved in navigating between lived experience and disciplined study. An academic discipline that would name its object simply "experience" is in danger of becoming hopelessly mired in a morass of practical and philosophical problems. Since spirituality as an academic discipline *is* rooted in lived experience it cannot totally avoid that morass, but rather must strive all the harder to name its object in a way that makes it possible to navigate intelligently in this rather slippery terrain. To that end, I contend that any disciplined study of spirituality will need to draw on the resources and language of philosophy—despite the fact that, at times, these tools may seem alien to the life-concerns that are spirituality's focus.

As the metaphor of navigation indicates, it is also a question of method. According to Schneiders, the study of spirituality is "interdisciplinary by nature" and does not have a method of its own. What she then goes on to say about the necessity and specific character of interdisciplinary work in the field of spirituality is accurate and helpful. Yet, while there may not be a single "method," I think it is possible to name a "methodological principle" specific to spirituality as a discipline. To preview my most significant conclusion: I will attempt to reclaim the notion of "interiority" as fundamental to both the object and the method of the discipline of spirituality. I will begin by offering a brief account of the path by which I have come to this conclusion.

"WHAT AM I DOING WHEN I TEACH SPIRITUALITY?"

I learned from Bernard Lonergan (who probably learned it from Aristotle) that asking the right question is the motor of progress toward insight. Lonergan's almost childlike yet incredibly productive question was, "What are we doing when we are knowing?" A productive first question for my own search for insight is, "What am I doing when I teach spirituality?" The question is about "teaching" not because I have a purely practical (as opposed to theoretical or research-centered) interest in spirituality, but because, in my context, teaching is the concrete activity that mediates between my own spiritual living, and my academic research and writing within the discipline of spirituality.

I teach at Catholic Theological Union, a school of theology and ministry where essentially every class is "multicultural" in ethnicity, nationality, age, gender, ecclesial vocation, academic program, and more. Within this setting, the situation that particularly challenges me to clarify my positions on the academic study of spirituality is our Doctor of Ministry program. These students typically are in mid life or older, with strong and well-developed ministerial identities and goals. They have chosen to enter on further graduate studies, but they tend to resist the "merely academic" if they cannot see its connection to ministerial reality.

My efforts to introduce these students to the academic discipline of spirituality (in a course entitled "Foundations for the Study of Spirituality") have gone through four stages. My first approach was the standard academic one: I introduced my students to the literature of the field and expected them to gain familiarity with the various positions on such questions as definition and method, so that they could work toward claiming critically nuanced positions of their own. This approach was minimally successful—students fulfilled the requirements but were not really satisfied with the course, and in most cases their appropriation of ideas remained quite superficial.

The following year I took a different tack. I began by assigning Etty Hillesum's *An Interrupted Life*,[3] a text that can always be counted on to shake up students' settled assumptions about spirituality and spiritual writing. I then reflected with the class on the transformative spiritual process that occurred in the midst of Hillesum's unconventional, oppressed, and yet often very mundane life, and also on the various layers of textual and personal interpretation through which we encounter her experience. With this foundation, we then went to the literature on definition and method in the academic study of spirituality. This approach was definitely an improvement, but many students' appropriation of the academic literature still did not reach the desired level.

The third time around, I added another preliminary piece: after the Hillesum assignment, students wrote a short account of a significant spiritual experience of their own. Once again, we then reflected both on the character of the experiences and on the multiple processes of interpretation through which they were encountered, remembered, written down, and finally orally presented in class. The point of this assignment was twofold: first, to get students to connect to and articulate (in more than one genre) what "spiritual experience" was for them; and second, to push them as far as possible in personal discovery of the effects of factors such as tradition, personal history, culture, life stage, genre, and immediate setting on how the experience is named and presented. This approach was clearly a major step forward, as many students made significant strides in insight as they engaged in this way with experiences, texts, and reflections on interpretive processes. With this foundation, it was relatively easy to guide them in making lively connections between this set of reflections and the academic literature on definition and method.

I have taught the "Foundations" course in this form for several years, and it has been a good course. Yet I have continued to have the uneasy feeling that what my students are actually most concerned about as they enter into the academic study of spirituality is not adequately addressed by the available literature on questions of definition and method. I recently discovered a quotation that perhaps applies to our situation: "Now one of the chief errors of thought is to continue to think in one set of forms, categories, ideas, etc. when the object, the content, has moved on, has created or laid premises for an extension, a development of thought."[4] This statement describes something of my experience over these years in the trenches teaching the discipline of spirituality. In view of that, this essay deals with my reflections as I work toward developing the fourth stage of my approach to the foundational course.

Observing the trajectory of the course's development, I note that it traces backward the four levels of spirituality outlined by Michael Downey in his book, *Understanding Christian Spirituality*.[5] My first approach began with texts describing spirituality academically, my second with a text expressing spiritual wisdom, and my third by engaging the students' own "lived spirituality." The emerging fourth approach, finally, involves insight into the foundational character of human "spirit" as a basis for designing methods of study that fully engage all the dimensions of spirituality.

THE PRIMACY AND CHARACTER OF "LIVED SPIRITUALITY"

The fact that my goal of engaging students in the academic discipline of spirituality was only effectively achieved at the third stage is significant. I have become convinced that "lived spirituality" is, and must remain, the key point of engagement for any study of spirituality. In saying this, I am clearly taking a stand for the "self-implicating" character of such study. What we study, how we study, what we learn, is rooted in our own spiritual living. In this context, "spiritual living" does not necessarily mean adherence to a defined religious or spiritual tradition. It does mean, however, that one attends with as much authenticity as one can muster to the truth of one's own experience. Clarifying and affirming this context makes the study of spirituality a tremendously energizing and exciting process for most students. At the same time, it creates significant challenges—as well as opportunities—for the professor whose goals include training students in an academic discipline.

Before further exploring the implications of these assertions, it is important to more fully describe the character of "lived spirituality." Like what Michel de Certeau called "the practice of everyday life,"[6] lived spirituality is an ongoing dynamic activity in which individuals and groups create and recreate meaning, joy, and shared life from whatever materials are at hand. It is always a bricolage (a patching together, a creative reinterpretation, a claiming-as-one's-own) of a somewhat happenstance conglomeration of elements from nature, historical accident, and established traditions.

Using another of de Certeau's ideas, I would suggest that lived spirituality is basically tactical rather than strategic. "A tactic insinuates itself into the other's [i.e., the available traditions'] place, fragmentarily, without taking it over entirely, without being able to keep it at a distance"; whereas, "A strategy assumes a place that can be circumscribed as proper (*propre*) and thus serve as the basis for generating relations with an exterior distinct from it."[7] For de Certeau, in other words, a tactic works creatively with whatever comes to hand, while a strategy claims control over a particular turf. To say that lived spirituality is tactical rather than strategic is to say that it is more a "making do" than a "controlling" or "grasping"; it has more in common with managing to survive in the thick of a wilderness than with flying over that wilderness pointing out the sights.

Essential to the self-implicating character of spirituality, then, is a certain ineradicable messiness and uncontrollability. Even in our academic study, we (as well as our students, colleagues, and readers) are necessarily involved in our own ever-shifting processes of creative bricolage. If we accept this fact, however, we find ourselves with several significant problems. In both the personal and cultural spheres, fragmentation and relativism appear to reign unchecked and we are left with no evident grounds for spiritual integration, discernment, or community. In the academic sphere, meanwhile, we may seem to have lost our purchase on academic respectability. If we stand in the messy reality of lived spirituality, have we fallen all the way down the "slippery slope" to wallow in sheer subjectivity? I don't think so. We do, however, face a major challenge in rethinking fundamental issues for our academic discipline.

CRITICAL REFLECTION ON EXPERIENCE

The problem I have set up for us here is this: We seem to be stranded on the shifting sand of lived experience, perhaps enjoying the dynamism but with no sure ground on which to move toward personal integration, let alone toward the more systematic thinking and communicating appropriate to the academy. To find such ground, we need to reflect more profoundly on the relation between experience and thought.

In a 1992 article, George Schner proposed that there are at least five different ways in which "experience" can be taken up into theological reflection and argument.[8] First, if we were simply to assert that experience is the limited, shifting, radically perspectival viewpoint of our own lived spirituality, we would be limited to some version of what Schner calls the "appeal hermeneutical." This approach refuses all claims of universality or normativeness. There are other possibilities, however. Perhaps most distasteful to the academy is the "appeal confessional," in which the narrative of an experience is straightforwardly presented as authoritative for the community of hearers. Also suspicious to many academicians is the "appeal mystical," in which the experience is asserted to be so radically transcendent as to pass beyond human intentionality and language. The other two approaches, however, have somewhat more respectability within the academy. They are the "appeal constructive," in which the experience engages a transformational dialectic between a transcendent element and derivative, constructed elements; and the "appeal transcendental," which looks away from any specific experiences toward naming general structures and conditions of possibility for all human experience.

What Schner offers us is a reflection on why asserting that we begin from "lived spirituality" does not fully answer our most important questions at either the personal or academic levels. In fact, at both levels we have a variety of choices for what we will do with our own lived experience as well as the lived experiences of others we encounter. In personal life, we often make these choices without reflecting on them, but in our academic work they must be made deliberately. A first methodological principle, then, will be to ask the questions, What are we doing with the experiential dimension? What sort of implicit or explicit appeal are we making on its basis? By what steps do we move from the place of living to the place of speaking, writing, and making claims? Are the form of appeal and the steps we make appropriate to the actual context in which we are living, studying, and/or teaching spirituality?

This is a variation on another Lonerganian injunction that has influenced my own reflections on method, namely, "Know what you are doing when you are doing it!" For Lonergan, this is the basic principle of what he calls "interiority."[9] Interiority is, first of all, presence to oneself. As a conscious stance, it is critical appropriation of one's presence to oneself so that one does, in fact, "know what one is doing when one is doing it." This kind of critical self-presence is pivotal for a disciplined use of the "appeal constructive" as well as the "appeal transcendental."

In fact, the "appeal constructive" is closely related to the kind of work I demand from my students in the "Foundations" course when I call on them to name, recount, and critically reflect on life-changing, "transcendent" spiritual experiences, as well as on the multiple contingent factors that have shaped how these experiences have been taken in by them and articulated. I believe that increasing rigor in this kind of reflection is a crucial skill for anyone whose ministry involves mediating among people's spiritual experience, theological and ecclesial traditions, and the exigencies of life in the real world—that is, just about anyone who works in the area of "spirituality." And, it is this type of work that will be especially important in mediating a much-needed move beyond the syncretistic, bricolage character of "lived spirituality" to the responsible personal and communal re-appropriation of the best potentials of the world's spiritual traditions.

While the "constructive" appeal to experience may be most important for practical work in spirituality, I feel that critical use of an "appeal transcendental" is crucial for the grounding of spirituality as an academic discipline. For Lonergan, interiority (as defined above) is also the existential basis on which one can make the claims of the "appeal transcendental." That is, by noticing what one is actually doing while insights, judgments, decisions, and actions emerge in one's lived experience, one can arrive at insights into the general structures of human subjectivity.[10] We must do this to clarify what Michael Downey called the first meaning of the term "spirituality," as referring to "the reality which is named in speaking of human being as spirit in the world."[11] Also, we must do this in order to accurately define the "material and formal objects" of the study of spirituality.

In the progression of my own teaching/learning experience, I made the common mistake of assuming I had dealt with this issue at the beginning (by employing preformulated philosophical perspectives on the structures of human being). What I learned from experience is that an accurate insight is possible only in the midst of immersion in "lived spirituality," and only after a full acknowledgment of its foundational character. Indeed, to answer the question of the specific character of spirituality, our starting point must be critical reflection on what we are actually doing when we live, study, and teach spirituality. Having traversed that path in earlier sections of the essay, we are finally ready to address this foundational question.

WHAT DEFINES SPIRITUALITY?

Here I will state my conclusions first, and then review more fully the process by which I arrived at them. I would say that the material object—the actual, concrete 71 thing that we study when we study spirituality—consists of *constructed expressions of human meaning*. The trouble, of course, is that it is difficult to define any boundaries; everything human beings have ever made or done potentially fits this definition. This is, in fact, a perennial problem for those of us who claim spirituality as our field—boundaries tend to be porous and ever-expanding. This is why the question of the "formal object" is so crucial for spirituality as an academic discipline. I would propose that the formal object, which names the particular aspect under which the material object is studied, is *the human spirit fully in act*. This language is, admittedly, awkward and archaic, and a more felicitous expression will eventually need to be found. In the meantime, however, perhaps a bit of explication will help. "The human spirit fully in act" means the core dimension of the human person radically engaged with reality (both contingent and transcendent). It refers to human persons being, living, acting according to their fullest intrinsic potential—thus, ultimately, in the fullness of interpersonal, communal, and mystical relationship.

It is important to clarify that the statement that this is the formal object of study does not imply that everything in the study of spirituality must manifest such radical and core-level engagement. Rather, it means that when we study constructed expressions of human meaning under the rubric of the academic discipline of spirituality, the particular aspect under which these are studied is how they do (or do not) tend toward that kind of radical engagement. For example, when studying a potentially dangerous cult, we examine both how that cult's way of constructing human meaning does in some manner engage human persons radically (and thus attracts some individuals to total commitment) and how in other aspects it actually perverts the depth-potential of human persons. In such research, of course, we may also have to study other aspects of these constructed expressions, for example rhetorical structure, psychological and sociological characteristics, or cultural heritage. However, if any of these other aspects becomes the central focus of our study, our research no longer remains directly within the purview of the discipline of spirituality.

The process by which I arrived at these definitions was one of critical reflection on my own practice of living, studying, and teaching spirituality, especially in relation to the development of a particularly challenging course, as described above. In teaching this course, my first insight was this: Everything my students and I were engaged in was a "constructed expression of human meaning"; thus, developing a more critical and sophisticated insight into the processes and dynamics by which we construct meaning is crucial to our study of spirituality. However, this insight only made more acute the nagging question, "Then what makes this a study of spirituality instead of, for example, a literary, psychological, or anthropological study?"

Further reflection produced the insight that even though all constructed expressions of human meaning may be potentially eligible for study under the rubric of spirituality, the ones we are most frequently drawn to study have a specific character—they actually or potentially engage the whole human person to the fullest degree possible. The concept of the "classic," as defined by H.-G. Gadamer[12] and David Tracy, is a way of naming the specific character of such a constructed expression of meaning. The classic has the capacity to awaken and engage us at the deepest and most profound levels of our being. Tracy states that encounter with a classic involves "some disclosure of reality in a moment that must be called 'recognition' which surprises, provokes, challenges, shocks and eventually transforms us."[13]

Originally, I defined classics in a fairly narrow way, as referring to the traditional canon of historical texts that are commonly named "spiritual classics." Further reflection on practice—especially that of my students, who continually press the boundaries of anything appearing to be a "dominant culture"—opened me to the realization that the particular character of the "classic" exists in many expressions, far beyond the boundaries of the traditional canon. My students, given the assignment of studying a classic, have done papers not only on traditional texts but also on buildings, devotions, rituals, persons (some famous, some not), popular and classical musical forms, paintings, frescoes, and prayer forms. Many have done excellent work in showing how the historically located, constructed expression they have chosen is able to engage people at a radical level, across boundaries of culture and time.

And so, at last we come to a complete answer to the original question regarding the formal object: Under what particular aspect does the discipline of spirituality study constructed expressions of human meaning? It was through further reflection on what actually occurs as we engage with a "classic" (as defined above) that I arrived at my definition: The discipline of spirituality is formally focused on interest in "the human spirit fully in act." This, I think, is what really fascinates us. We are fascinated, first, by being persons who live and act according to our most radical potential; thus, we are drawn to the phenomena that promise to engage us at that level. Second, we are fascinated by the challenge of understanding the particular expressions that human beings have constructed that possess this charisma, either for ourselves or others. Third, we may feel a responsibility to critique and unmask those expressions that fall short or even pervert the human spirit. But if this is what engages us, does it have implications for the question of whether there is a method (or a methodological principle) uniquely appropriate to the academic discipline of spirituality?

THE METHOD QUESTION

In reviewing the available literature discussing method for the study of spirituality, the most striking point for me is that the methods proposed have no real specificity to the character of our discipline. Over the years, discussion of method for the study of spirituality has focused on theological, historical, anthropological, hermeneutical, and appropriative methods,[14] with a tendency for many scholars to accept Schneiders's hermeneutical approach and/or Downey's appropriative method[15] as more or less normative. In view of the definitions I have proposed for the material and formal objects of the discipline, each of these methods clearly captures an essential aspect of what we do when we study spirituality. The hermeneutical approach focuses explicitly on the interpretation of humanly constructed expressions of meaning, while the appropriative approach focuses on how both the expressions and the persons who engage with them are transformed by that interaction. However, we need to go another step in order to name something even more crucial to method in the study of spirituality. The somewhat controversial claim I will make is this: To ground spirituality as a discipline in its own right, with a methodological principle specific to it, involves reclaiming both medieval and contemporary insights into "interiority."

As mentioned earlier in this essay, Lonergan spoke of interiority in terms of "knowing what you are doing when you are doing it"—and I have tried to show thus far how this statement plays out in the case of the study of spirituality. What I want to suggest now is that defining the formal object as I have proposed mandates a fundamental methodological move that must be made prior to choosing the specific "methods" appropriate to the study of the material object. We cannot know "the human spirit in act," except *as* the human spirit in act. We cannot recognize the constructed expressions that radically engage the human spirit except on the basis of our own radical engagement. This does not mean, of course, that every time we engage in the study of spirituality we are seized with contemplative ecstasy. Rather, it means that methodologically, we must begin by acknowledging that when we select, claim understanding of, or evaluate something as "having to do with spirituality," we do so based on our own living of spirituality—that is, our own spirits "fully in act." To acknowledge and appropriate this starting point is what Lonergan terms *interiority*.

I will return to discussion of Lonergan's definition of interiority shortly. First, however, that discussion must be placed in the context both of the long, rich history of interiority as a theological term and of the contemporary critique it is undergoing today. To begin with the former: Kenneth L. Schmitz has pointed out that in medieval theology interiority did not have the connotation of private introspection.[16] Rather, interiority meant an engagement and intimacy with God involving the most profound depths of one's being. Schmitz notes that, with this meaning, interiority is the mark of personhood—a person may be defined as one who receives and gives existence in the act of intimate presence. As Catherine LaCugna put it, in her discussion of human and divine persons, "To exist as a person is to be referred to others; the negation and dissolution of personhood is total self-reference."[17] Within a Christian theological framework, then, human interiority is fundamentally a capacity for intimate, self-transcendent communion; ultimately, it is the capacity to dwell in the personal and transcendent God, and to be a place-in-the-world where this God dwells. Transposed into the more philosophical language used earlier in this essay, it is "the human spirit fully in act"; or, in other words, "human persons being, living, acting according to their fullest intrinsic potential."

Now, on to the contemporary critique of interiority. Owen Thomas has recently offered a compelling argument, based largely in Wittgenstein's philosophy, that the focus on interiority is a fundamental mistake on both philosophical and practical levels.[18] The concerns he raises about the implications of an overly interior focus on the practical level of "lived spirituality" are certainly valid. As lived, spirituality cannot be about a personal "inner life" that in any way downplays or denigrates the "outer life" of embodiment, community, tradition, political responsibility, and so on. Rather, lived spirituality is what we do with all these things as we struggle, alone and with others, to construct meaning.

Thomas's philosophical argument is sophisticated, and I cannot address all its facets within the brief scope of this essay; however, it is important to note that Thomas himself acknowledges that the pernicious form of interiority he rejects is fundamentally based in the mistake of dualism. He notes, following Denys Turner's discussion of *The Cloud of Unknowing*, that "[i]t is only for the outer self that the duality of inner and outer persists. The inner self knows that there is no inner as against outer."[19] The understanding of interiority that I am presenting here is fundamentally non-dualistic; it reclaims traditions for which interiority is that dimension or state of the human being capable of a living union between inner and outer, material and transcendent, communal and solitary, eternal and transient. Only by first affirming its non-dualistic nature can we appropriately identify what interiority does have to do, experientially, with "innerness." Affectively experienced as "presence" or "communion," it is manifested in such forms as human love, intuitive knowing, or a sense of group solidarity. It is as important to extroverted forms of spirituality such as commitment to social justice or involvement in a Christian community as it is to traditional forms of interior prayer.

When Lonergan took up the term "interiority," he shifted it into a modern context, trying to do so without losing the theological grounding of its medieval context. For Lonergan, interiority is an appropriation of one's own experience in which intimacy precedes and grounds objectivity. The primary goal of interiority is not self-objectification but self-appropriation—that is, enhancement of the self-presence that is the ground of all presence—with what is other.[20] The fruit of this can be a form of objectivity that, rather than reifying its objects, enjoys a kind of "knowing in the biblical sense"—a living apprehension of the true being of what is known. His distinction between introspection and interiority is perhaps akin to Jean-Luc Marion's distinction between knowing an idol and an icon: An idol freezes one's gaze on itself; an icon guides one's gaze in its intention toward infinite relatedness.[21] In introspection, one makes an idol of oneself; in interiority, one comes to know one's personhood as an icon through which the grounding mystery of existence flows.

SPIRITUAL DISCIPLINE, DISCIPLINE OF SPIRITUALITY

In summary, since there are essentially no intrinsic boundaries to the material object of spirituality, what is unique about the discipline cannot be any of the concrete "things" we study (for example, texts, rituals, historical persons, etc.); nor can it be any of the specific methods we use to study these "things." Rather, what *is* unique must be the formal object and any methodological principles that are necessary for knowing it. By naming interiority the uniquely defining methodological principle of the academic discipline of spirituality, we are basically saying that our primary means of access to knowing "the human spirit fully in act" is through standing inside, and coming to know, the lived reality of our own spirits. This is not simply an introspective activity; rather, it is a matter of full presence with oneself, with others, with the world, with God. On the practical level, this is why our "lived spirituality" is both where we stand and what we look at—and it is why the study of spirituality is necessarily a self-implicating discipline.

In short, I suggest that the actual "object" that spirituality studies cannot be approached except with the attitude like that of one who takes up a spiritual discipline. The term "discipline," when applied to spirituality, is necessarily multivalent. What are we really up to when we study spirituality? Perhaps we could define it thus: We are entering into the personal and communal discipline of discerning and appropriating authentic human interiority as it presents itself in the multiple and changing forms of lived spirituality. This is an activity that, taken seriously, will demand the utmost of us, both in our living and in our scholarship. This perspective implies that if the academic discipline of spirituality is to have any specificity, it must claim and clarify its character as a form of spiritual discipline. Spirituality can be an academic discipline only insofar as it coheres with its deeper character as spiritual discipline. Unless it is understood in clear relation to its real core, the academic study of spirituality will fragment across all other disciplines and lose any specificity.

It will be crucial, of course, to continue to clarify how this "discipline of spirituality" differs from traditional, precritical, spiritual disciplines. On this point, some historical perspective on the evolution of our understanding of the word "discipline" may be helpful. The roots of the word are in the way of life of a disciple, pupil, or apprentice; one takes up such a way of life to imbibe the wisdom carried within it. A spiritual discipline, in this sense, is a structured, committed approach to learning how to live spiritually. Even though such spiritual disciplines necessarily employ constructed forms, the original underlying emphasis is on the transformation of life rather than on mastery of the forms. Pierre Hadot has discussed how, before about the thirteenth century, the pursuit of "philosophy" ("love of wisdom") entailed a form of discipline that was integrally both spiritual and intellectual. With the rise of the medieval universities, however, a gap began to open between the two.[22] Philosophy, which then became the central academic discipline, came to be understood simply as discourse, while spiritual exercises and their fruit—the transformation of life—were relegated to the margins. Today, most academics still are credentialed as "Doctors of Philosophy," and the "discipline" of the academy is typically understood as a set of practices in which mastery of linguistically constructed forms (literature, terminology, methods, skills, etc.) has priority over whatever effect one's involvement may have on one's actual living.

Perhaps, indeed, the "historic mission" of the academic discipline of spirituality will be to help repair the breach between life and knowledge that Hadot has described.[23] In recent decades, the "linguistic turn" has taken the focus on discourse to its limit—and has come face to face with its emptiness. My suggestion is that if constructed expressions of human meaning are not contextualized as the "material object" through which we may come to know (in the biblical sense) something of the human spirit, then they are, indeed, empty. Perhaps the academic discipline of spirituality will play a unique role in moving academia toward a "second naïveté"[24]—a period in which the critical insights of the linguistic turn can be linked again to the life of the spirit.

Such a discipline of spirituality will, to be sure, be of a different character than the spiritual disciplines of former eras. Rather than an obedient immersion in an institutional culture, it will require a high tolerance for aloneness, permanent quest, vulnerability, and "things falling apart."[25] It will presume a willingness to probe, experiment, and accept challenges to every element of one's lived spirituality. It will call for the repeated risk of dialogue with the sometimes unnerving range of interpretations applied to the phenomena of one's own and others' spiritual experiences. And finally, it will demand the usual hard work of any scholarly endeavor—including mastery of the necessary literature, terminology, and methods. Yet in all this, its most fundamental focus will be less on the perfection of critique than on the authenticity of the life of the spirit.

Indeed, such a discipline may have an essential contribution to make, not only in resolving issues facing academicians and practitioners in the field of spirituality but also to some of the broader challenges facing the postmodern world. As Louis Dupré has commented, referring specifically to today's Christian: "I see no alternative but that he or she must now personally integrate what tradition did in the past."[26] The emerging discipline of spirituality speaks to the urgent needs of this new era, which cries out for people prepared to exercise the full rigor of both personal authenticity and critical thought.

NOTES

1. My thanks go to Margaret Benefiel, Douglas Burton-Christie, Michael Downey, Paul Lachance, Bruce Lescher, Michael A. Montoya, Diana Villegas, and the anonymous *Spiritus* reviewers for their graciousness in reading and commenting on this essay in draft form. Their insightful comments have helped to make it much better.
2. Sandra Schneiders, "The Study of Christian Spirituality: Contours and Dynamics of a Discipline," *Christian Spirituality Bulletin* 6/1 (Spring 1998): 1–3. (See Chapter 1 of this volume.) I would note that my reflections are concerned with spirituality in general, rather than only with explicitly Christian spirituality. I also acknowledge, however, that my own commitments and training are thoroughly Christian, and that this horizon profoundly affects my approach.
3. Etty Hillesum, *An Interrupted Life* (New York: Pantheon, 1983). This text is the diary of a young Jewish woman during the Nazi occupation of Holland. She was sexually liberated, intellectually and spiritually syncretistic, and deeply committed to a spirituality of both service and contemplation.
4. C. L. R. James, *Notes on Dialectics: Hegel, Marx, Lenin* (London: Allison and Busby, 1980). Cited in J. T. Klein, *Crossing Boundaries* (Charlottesville, VA: University Press of Virginia, 1996).
5. Michael Downey, *Understanding Christian Spirituality* (Mahwah, NJ: Paulist, 1997), 42.
6. Cf. Michel de Certeau, *The Practice of Everyday Life* (Berkeley: University of California Press, 1988).
7. De Certeau, *The Practice of Everyday Life*, xix.
8. George P. Schner, "The Appeal to Experience," *Theological Studies* 53 (1992): 40–59.

9. For some basic texts on interiority, refer to the index in Bernard Lonergan, *Method in Theology* (London: Darton, Longman and Todd, 1971).

10. For a clearly written and thorough development of this approach, see Terry J. Tekippe, *What Is Lonergan Up To in Insight?* (Collegeville, MN: Liturgical Press, 1996). For a briefer summary, see "Introduction" in *The Lonergan Reader*, eds. Elizabeth A. Morelli and Mark D. Morelli (Toronto: University of Toronto Press, 1997), 3–28.

11. Downey, *Understanding Christian Spirituality,* 42.

12. Cf. Hans-Georg Gadamer, *Truth and Method* (New York: Crossroad, 1984), especially pp. 253–58.

13. David Tracy, *The Analogical Imagination: Christian Theology and the Culture of Pluralism* (New York: Crossroad, 1981), 108.

14. For various views on questions of method for the academic study of spirituality, see *Modern Christian Spirituality: Methodological and Historical Essays*, ed. Bradley C. Hanson (Atlanta, GA: Scholars, 1990); *Christian Spirituality Bulletin*, especially volumes 1–3; and Downey, *Understanding Christian Spirituality,* chap. 6.

15. Downey, *Understanding Christian Spirituality,* 129–31.

16. Kenneth L. Schmitz, "The Geography of the Human Person," *Communio* 13 (Summer 1986): 27–48.

17. Catherine Mowry LaCugna, *God For Us: The Trinity and Christian Life* (San Francisco: Harper Collins, 1991), 289.

18. Owen Thomas, "Interiority and Christian Spirituality," *Journal of Religion* 80 (2000): 41–60.

19. Thomas, "Interiority and Christian Spirituality," 53. He refers to Denys Turner, *The Darkness of God: Negativity in Christian Mysticism* (Cambridge: Cambridge University, 1995), 209–10.

20. On the kind of self-presence that is involved in interiority, see Bernard Lonergan, *Understanding and Being,* 2nd ed. (Toronto: University of Toronto Press, 1990), 14–17.

21. Jean-Luc Marion, *God Without Being* (Chicago: University of Chicago Press, 1991), chap. 1.

22. Pierre Hadot, *Philosophy as a Way of Life* (Cambridge, MA: Blackwell, 1995).

23. Although he is not dealing explicitly with the discipline of spirituality, David Tracy makes a similar connection between interiority and the repair of this breach in "Bernard Lonergan and the Return of Ancient Practice," *Lonergan Workshop*, vol. 10 (Boston: Boston College, 1994), 319–31.

24. Paul Ricoeur spoke of "first naivete" as a stage of the uncritical reception of symbols. It is followed by a period of critical distance, and finally by a "second naivete" in which critique and full reception coexist and enhance one another.

25. The allusion, of course, is to Yeats's well-known line: "Things fall apart, the center cannot hold."

26. "Seeking Christian Interiority: An Interview with Louis Dupré." *Christian Century* 114/21 (1997): 655.

6

The Role of Practice in the Study of Christian Spirituality[1]

ELIZABETH LIEBERT, S.N.J.M.

"'Right (communal) doing' seems in some sense a precondition for right understanding," claims Miroslav Volf.[2] This statement raises a number of intriguing questions about what constitutes real understanding and how we arrive at it, questions that have particular significance for those engaged in scholarly reflection upon spiritual experience. Some of the questions are epistemological: What does it mean to know? Are there different "knowings" for theory and practice? Or might they be figure and ground of the same reality? What particular kind of knowing constitutes "scholarship"? Other questions have to do with perspective: What is the nature of the perspective taken by the scholar vis-à-vis the object of study and between the scholar and the scholar's audience? Where, in fact, is scholarship best pursued? And still other questions are of a pastoral character: How can one come to understand the other, be it the other in the pastor's study or in the neighborhood, the socioeconomic, racial, ethnic, and gendered other, the ecumenical or interfaith other, even the non-human other?

In this essay, I would like to reflect on Volf's first phrase, "right communal doing," and ask what it might look like in a particular case: that of the academic study of Christian spirituality. I propose that a particular kind of doing that I shall call "practice," when employed by the scholar in the study of spirituality, is not merely something useful, but is a *constitutive* dimension of the discipline. Because of this, spirituality offers a useful and necessary perspective to other theological disciplines. Furthermore, when used in conjunction with appropriate scholarly methods, "practice" advances the content of the study itself.

To construct this argument, I will proceed in three interlocking steps: First, by examining the recent history and development of another young discipline, pastoral theology,[3] I will note some comparisons and contrasts between this discipline and the academic study of spirituality. Second, I will address one of the commitments shared by both disciplines, namely, to "experience." Finally, using the notion of "experience" as the launching point, I will propose a constructive suggestion for the academic study of spirituality concerning "practice."

PASTORAL THEOLOGY AND SPIRITUALITY

In their report, "Teaching Christian Spirituality in Seminaries Today,"[4] Arthur Holder and Lisa Dahill noted that theology and history dominate the degrees of specialization among those teaching the introductory course in Christian spirituality (together, fifty percent of their sample). They wondered: "Given the preponderance of historians and theologians among those who teach introductory courses in Christian Spirituality, it is not surprising that these courses tend to stress history and theology, with very little attention to social scientific or aesthetic or practical theological or even biblical perspectives." What would happen if we were to pay attention to the insights and methodologies of these other disciplines?

My graduate study occurred in the program in Religion and Personality at Vanderbilt, and its discipline was the young and fluid one called pastoral theology. In reflecting on my own history, it occurred to me that the vicissitudes in the development of pastoral theology as an academic discipline offer interesting similarities and contrasts to the development of our discipline. This reflection has also led me to a claim based on an aspect of the academic study of spirituality, namely, its intrinsic relationship to that notoriously slippery concept, "experience."

Pastoral theology traces its formation to such psychologists of religion as William James, G. Stanley Hall, and James Leuba in the early years of the twentieth century, Anton Boisen and Russell Dicks in the 1920s and 1930s, and to such systematizers as Seward Hiltner, Carroll Wise, Paul Johnson, Daniel Day Williams, Wayne Oates, and Howard Clinebell in the 1950s, 1960s, and 1970s.[5] These scholar-practitioners employed various biblical, theological, philosophical, and psychological systems to ground their work. In the late 1970s, as I began my study, pastoral theology as an academic discipline was not quite sure if it was supposed to prepare clinicians, pastors, theologians, or a hybrid of all three. Consequently students in various doctoral programs tried on all three personae. But all used, to a greater or lesser degree, a series of practices, both clinical and reflective, to ground the emerging discipline.

In its widest sense, pastoral theology attempts to relate the meanings and requirements of faith to concrete human problems and situations, using human experience to come to a more profound understanding of God. In this endeavor, it deals inescapably in concreteness, with *this* event, *this* relationship, *this* liturgy, *this* life-crisis, asking, What does it mean? What does it ask of me, of others? How does it affect an understanding of and relationship to God? Similarly, the correlation proceeds in the other direction: How does my understanding of and relationship to God affect the interpretation of this particular experience? If God/Christ/Church/world is like this, then what can I make of this child's death, for example?[6]

The dynamic nature of pastoral theology appears in the following illustration. To read this diagram, begin on the lower right side, with the sphere marked "case," then move to the left, to the sphere marked "tradition," and finally to the three fruits emerging from their dialectical interaction.

Pastoral Theology

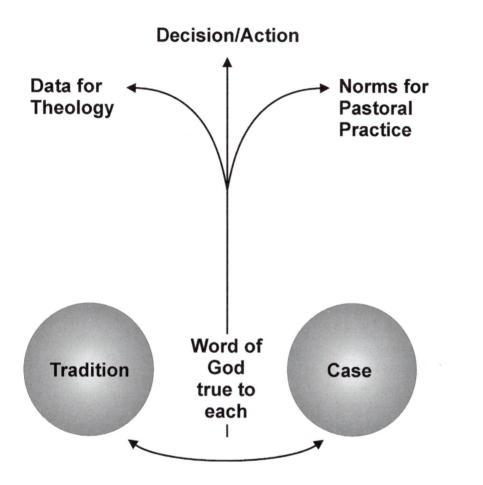

Decision/Action

Data for Theology

Norms for Pastoral Practice

Tradition

Word of God true to each

Case

Pastoral theology, as this illustration reveals, is the task of prayerfully holding in tension the *particular event or case*[7] in all its concreteness (that is, the individual's experience; the minister's experience; the community's experience; the sociological, cultural, psychological, economic, and other dynamic realities) with the *tradition* in all its richness and plurality (that is, the texts of the Christian community, particularly the Scriptures and the foundational documents of the given faith community; the history of the praxis of the community; the *sensus fidelium*) until we can hear the word of God that is true to each simultaneously. Once that word of God has become evident, however provisional and specific to the particular situation, it provides threefold direction: it *suggests appropriate responses* to the situation; it *provides touchstones for evaluating pastoral praxis*, and it *contributes data* to the larger theological enterprise and its development.

This description focuses on the moment of doing of pastoral theology. It leaves assumed the prior step of careful description of the case. So, a more complete illustration might look like this:

Pastoral Theology

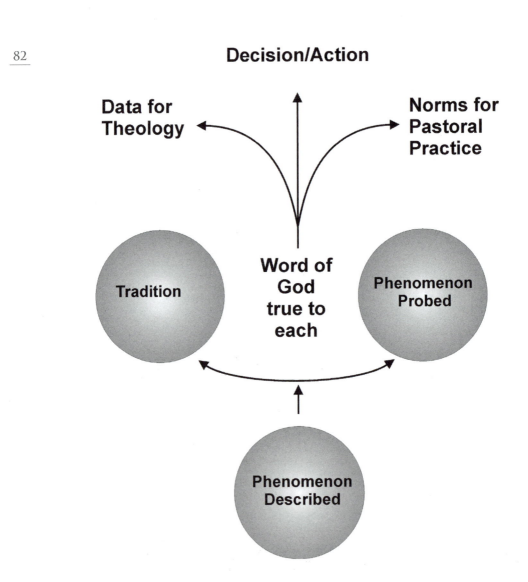

Decision/Action

Data for Theology

Norms for Pastoral Practice

Tradition

Word of God true to each

Phenomenon Probed

Phenomenon Described

By focusing on the process rather than the content, the description begins to look quite like the pastoral circle of liberation theology, which illumines the dynamic, repetitive nature of a process for determining focused intentional action in a given setting:

Pastoral Circle

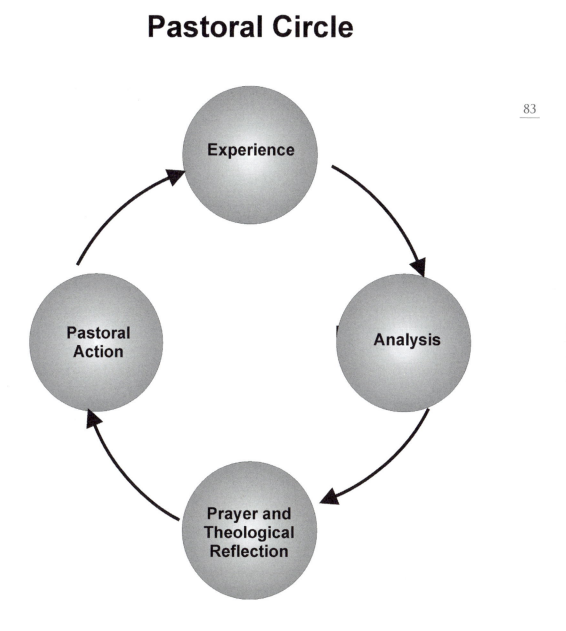

In my experience, systematic theologians often seem not to take pastoral theologians with much seriousness. From their point of view, pastoral theologians deal in soft methodologies, such as case study and verbatim recording of conversations for analysis, and engage in sloppy and fuzzy theological thinking, mucking around as they do in the particularity of human experience. The primary data of pastoral theology is not the second-order systematic thinking about God that developed over the history of Christian thought and was systematically refined in the last several hundred years. The academic discipline of spirituality faces similar kinds of problems of perception and credibility as it establishes itself among other academic disciplines.

Today, in the field of pastoral theology, just as in the academic study of spirituality, there is an explosion of dialogue partners. Groups of scholars from both disciplines are asking, "What are the boundaries of our discipline?" Both disciplines attempt to focus their scope in two ways: by crafting a definition that delimits the discipline, and by selecting appropriate methods with which to address this subject matter. The definitional issues in the field of spirituality have received a great deal of attention lately, so I will not dwell on these here.[8] As for methodological parameters, pastoral theologians are guided by a particular case, or situation, in determining the critical discipline employed; this discipline in turn determines the range of appropriate methodologies by which to correlate theory and practice in a given situation. Analogously, in the academic study of spirituality the particular research question determines the dialogue partners and methodology.[9] But since there are an infinite number of cases and interesting research questions, both disciplines find their boundaries continually exploding and overlapping with other disciplines.

For pastoral theologians, as for scholars of Christian spirituality, the particular case is itself intrinsically challenging and worthy of critical reflection. It is the "stuff"—the contents—that the discipline studies. Likewise, the "problematic disciplines" of both communities of scholars, to use Sandra Schneiders's language,[10] are precisely those that will assist one better to understand the experience (case) at hand with greater knowledge, accuracy, and empathy, and more importantly, to help the persons or group themselves to understand their own experience and that of others more deeply. In these respects, pastoral theology is a close cousin to Christian spirituality.[11] The term "pastoral theology," like the term "Christian spirituality," can refer, at different moments, to the phenomenon (experience/case) in the round, the in-depth reflection on the case (the actual doing of pastoral theology), and to the academic study of the history, methods, and philosophy of the field.[12]

Before proceeding, I do want to point out some obvious inconsistencies between these two realms of discourse. Perhaps because pastoral theology arose primarily in Protestant theological and ecclesial contexts, it has tended to dwell on the human person in crisis and the appropriate helping acts taken by a representative of the church on behalf of and accompanying the person in crisis, including helping him or her to connect with faith where possible. The angle of entry, if you will, and the goal of the enterprise differ from the academic study of spirituality, which focuses more on the experience of the Holy as manifested in various theaters of personal and communal life. But since the focus of pastoral theology is still on a human person, albeit one in crisis, pastoral theologians may make virtually identical theological assumptions as scholars of spirituality do about the self-transcending nature of the human person, though these understandings of personhood often focus more on the negative, determined, and "fallen" aspects. So, while there are significant differences in these disciplines, the common emphasis on experience is important for our purposes.

THE COMMON GROUND: EXPERIENCE

Pastoral theology reveals this shared predilection for critical reflection on experience in its consistent use of the particular event or situation: the case. Christian spirituality shows it in its careful attention to Christian religious experience as such, in the self-implicating nature of the study, and in the insistence of many that the study of Christian spirituality as an academic discipline must be grounded in the lived spiritual discipline of the one studying as well as the person, movement, text, or event studied.[13]

But what exactly do we mean by "experience"? Conversations in the Christian spirituality guild usually assume the meaning is self-evident. In fact, it is a complex issue. Following my disciplinary roots, I will use resources from pastoral theology to tease out the meaning of this slippery term.

Experience, says pastoral theologian Brian Childs, is "participation in or encounter with reality."[14] The term may also refer to "the practical knowledge gained through such participation or encounter." It is "whatever we have undergone and done, and the ways in which we have *learned* something from what we did and underwent."[15] When opposing experience and reflection, an unfortunate dichotomy we would do well to avoid, experience stresses the immediacy of the occurrence as opposed to reflection on that experience. But, Childs insists, experience actually includes reflection as well as the original immediacy.[16] This more holistic sense of experience grounds wisdom and practical knowledge.[17] Furthermore, human experience develops within a web of relationships. These relationships provide the contents, the objects, the environment, and the context of our experience. They provide the material from which our memories, thoughts, images, feelings, and decisions are formed. They comprise the world upon which we act. These "others" can be variously grouped: nature, self, other humans, socio-political structures, and the transcendent.[18] Thus, what enhances and makes conscious the web of relationships in, for example, the doctoral classroom, makes possible enhanced experience.

"PRACTICE" IN THE ACADEMIC STUDY OF SPIRITUALITY

Perhaps because of this disciplinary home in pastoral theology with its foundation in immediate experience, and also perhaps because I spend most of my time teaching ministry students for whom the issue of spiritual formation is both "hot" and hotly debated, I find myself diverging from some of my spirituality colleagues on the issue of the admissibility of "practice" into the academic study of spirituality, and consequently, into the quintessential venue for the academic study of spirituality, the doctoral program classroom.

What is "practice"? How is it related to experience? In general terms, according to theologian Rebecca Chopp, practices are

> socially shared forms of behavior that mediate between what are often called subjective and objective dimensions. A practice is a pattern of meaning and action that is both culturally constructed and individually instantiated. The notion of practice draws us to inquire into the shared activities of groups of persons that provide meaning and orientation to the world, and that guide action.[19]

In terms of Christian spirituality, I propose to use the term "practice" as follows: "Practice" is the intentional and repeated bringing of one's lived spirituality into the various theaters of one's scholarly work and attending to what happens when one does.

I have deliberately chosen the word "practice" because it exists as both a noun and a verb. The word "practice" typically connotes a particular spiritual discipline. But as I am using it, "practice" stands for the activity of continually bringing—practicing—lived spirituality into our scholarship. Lived spirituality, is "attending with as much authenticity as one can muster to the truth of one's own experience,"[20] including the truth of the other that challenges and de-centers us. As we do our scholarship, we attend to this basic experiential level intentionally, repeatedly, publicly, and self-critically toward some goal beyond itself. Lived spirituality, Mary Frohlich insists, remains the focus of engagement for any study of spirituality.[21] Thus, scholars of Christian spirituality practice reflecting together on the truth of our experience until it becomes second nature to us. We practice until our whole way of approaching a text or a figure or an event is informed by it. We practice attending to our lived spirituality in front of students and we give them opportunities to practice in the very learning of the discipline. In short, we develop a particular *habitus* that leads to growth in understanding.[22]

For me, then, "practice" means much more than just importing classic or contemporary spiritual disciplines into the classroom, though that too could be

86

included under certain circumstances. It is a matter of *doing always* what it is that we *study* (as well as studying what we do). This shared and self-critically reflective experience of lived spirituality, is, in shorthand terms, "practice."

I can well imagine the kind of objections to these assertions that will inevitably arise: "*But* how will the necessary scholarly rigor be maintained?" "That might work in a seminary classroom, *but* you can't do it in the university, especially a public university." "That may work with some contemporary or more existential topics, *but* it won't work for ancient or classical texts." "*But* I don't do that kind of work." "*But* . . ."

Sandra Schneiders has stated the problem most cogently in her 1997 presidential address to the Society for the Study of Christian Spirituality:

> How to integrate a holistic approach to research with full accountability to the standards of criticism, personal commitment to what one is studying with appropriate methodological perspective, and practical involvement with theoretical integrity is, in my view, one of the major challenges the discipline of spirituality faces as it develops its identity in the academy.[23]

She has also stated the objections most forcefully in "A Hermeneutical Approach to the Study of Christian Spirituality":

> In the research sphere, however, I would have very serious reservations about the inclusion of any kind of mandatory practice or the direct use of such personal practice in the construction or prosecution of research projects. In the research arena the purpose of the study is, as in any research field, the expansion of knowledge in the field.[24]

While Schneiders does make room for experience in the study of Christian spirituality in several important ways,[25] she also insists on bracketing any form of mandatory practice designed to foster the spiritual life of the student, and to restrict such practice to ministerial formation programs. Leaving aside my reservation about making any given discipline mandatory for all persons, I still wonder if the situation is this clear and distinct.

I contend that in most situations it is *not* clear that one and only one of these realities, namely "mandatory practice intended to foster the spiritual life of students" versus a scholarly investigation of the material at hand, is occurring at a given moment. For example, I teach *lectio divina* to divinity students simultaneously as a form of personal prayer that they may find conducive in their own personal spiritual life, as a means of enhancing and deepening the various ways they access biblical texts in sermon preparation, and as a method of group prayer useful in many congregational settings. But if I were teaching Benedictine spirituality in a strictly academic setting such as a doctoral seminar, I might still invite all of us to immerse ourselves for a time in both *lectio divina* and the Divine Office. My primary intent in this situation is not the personal spiritual formation of the student (though I won't object if that occurs), but helping the students understand more deeply aspects of Benedictine spirituality. Even in the doctoral seminar, one means might be to invite immersion in some of the methods that took root in and were transmitted to the wider church through Benedict and Benedictine spirituality. I actually have a second goal that is straightforwardly pedagogical: to involve the student in a variety of avenues for appropriating the material *as suggested by the material itself*. I want to offer many avenues where students can really grasp and be grasped by the material we are together investigating. That is, I want to create a space where the self-implicating and transformative nature of our discipline can potentially take root. I maintain that when experience "comes into the room," it makes the study of the experience immediate and compelling.

INSIGHTS FROM EDUCATIONAL THEORY

An interesting pedagogical strategy has appeared in religious studies that bears on our topic, namely using service projects as a primary means for the learning of the course to occur. Proponents of service learning see the desire to base the study of religion solely on an objective, scientific approach as both epistemologically and pedagogically unsatisfactory. It is epistemologically unsatisfactory because it distances the topic of study from the subjects, professors, and students in the name of neutrality and objectivity. These advocates of service learning claim, with Parker Palmer,[26] that there is an intricate connection between epistemology, pedagogy, and ethics. The relationship of the knower to the known becomes the basis for the relationship of the actor to the world. Thus, an objective, arm's-length study of religion or spirituality keeps the teachers and students disconnected from what they know and what they want to know, and may also inhibit appropriate action in relation to what they know. Spirituality, like religion, is precisely about the way people generate order and meaning in their lives in relationship to themselves, others, and God. Distancing oneself from the nature of spirituality in order to study it may actually prevent one from fully grasping the essence of various spiritualities and their vitality.[27]

Pedagogically, their argument goes like this: As we have come to realize in this postmodern era, there are no neutral starting points or standing points. What one believes and what one has experienced inevitably influence what one knows (and how one teaches). Better not to try to banish the unbanishable, but to bring it self-consciously but critically into the discussion and dialogue with the study of spirituality in a way that is inclusive, respectful, and productive of greater insight and understanding.[28]

Shifting our attention to educational theory offers further insight about the pedagogical aspects of my thesis that the disciplined reflection on lived spirituality is constitutive of the discipline of Christian spirituality. Howard Gardner's work on multiple intelligences brings home the need for multiple entry points to the same material. In *The Disciplined Mind*,[29] Gardner offers three important general strategies.

1. *Provide multiple points of entry*. How to engage students initially in the topic at hand is an important pedagogical decision. Different students will find various entry points more conducive to involving them in the study, and there is no reason that all students should even engage the same one at the same time. In our class on Benedict and Benedictine spirituality, one person might enter through the practice of *lectio divina*, another through a narrative of the life of Benedict and the spread of Benedictine spirituality throughout Europe, a third through the Benedictine patronage of the arts, and still another through the recent struggle of the Prioress of the Benedictines of Erie (PA) to define the scope of Benedictine obedience in the face of Vatican demands.

2. *Offer apt analogies*. The educator's crucial task consists in conveying the power of the analogy, but, equally important, conveying the limitations as well. The pedagogical challenge consists in figuring out which entry points hold promise for particular understandings, trying them out and evaluating them, and making explicit the assumptions, contexts, possibilities, and limits of the analogies employed. The example of asking doctoral students to engage for some time in *lectio divina* is illuminative. Uncritically appropriated, such a practice can obscure even as it illuminates. Just because we have employed *lectio divina*, do we then know what *lectio divina* was like in Benedict's time? Not necessarily.

Mary Frohlich offers a welcome move beyond the morass we can get ourselves into by bringing experience and practice into the doing of academic spirituality. She recognizes that simply asserting that we begin from "lived spirituality" will not fully answer our most important questions at either the personal or academic levels. She notes:

> A first methodological principle, then, will be to ask the questions, What are we doing with the experiential dimension? What sort of implicit or explicit appeal are we making on its basis? By what steps do we move from the place of living to the place of speaking, writing, and making claims? Are the forms of appeal and the steps we make appropriate to the actual context in which we are living, studying and/or teaching spirituality?[30]

Thus, it is not merely importing lived experience into our scholarship and teaching that by itself constitutes effective "practice." We must also develop skills and nuance and critical awareness about the way in which experience functions in our scholarship and pedagogy. We must "practice our practice," so to speak, in order that it develop into an intentional methodological perspective on the materials with which we engage.

3. *Provide multiple representations of the central or core ideas.* Powerful and effective educators can represent the issue in several sets of language, and can evaluate and teach others to evaluate new attempts to express the same topic. An impressive example from the field of Christian spirituality of both multiple entry points and multiple representations of core ideas is Belden Lane's *The Solace of Fierce Landscapes: Exploring Desert and Mountain Spirituality*. Its power lies, I believe, precisely in his decision to juxtapose three different entry points: his own experiences of loss and grief, his immersion into particular places of desert and mountain, and the spiritual tradition of the *via negativa*, creating a brilliant and evocative treatment of desert spirituality.[31] This kind of multiple-leveled engagement, including "practice," is exactly what I am proposing we continue to develop as a self-conscious strategy in our scholarly writing and teaching.

THE IMPORTANCE OF PRACTICE IN SPIRITUALITY

I have so far argued the notion that studying the human experience of the transcendent while carefully excluding many of the possible avenues for experiencing the transcendent offered by our particular topic of study is pedagogically unwarranted. There is no guarantee that doing so will preserve one from bias, and it may, at least subliminally, perpetuate a seriously truncated notion of spirituality. But my constructive move pushes further than simply useful pedagogy or even pedagogy that takes seriously the nature of spirituality. Let me re-state it in its fullest form. Not only should the practice of spirituality not be banned from the academic study of Christian Spirituality (and therefore from the classroom where such academic study takes place), practice provides one of the constitutive elements of our discipline's approach. Because of it, spirituality offers both a useful and necessary perspective to other theological disciplines, such as systematic theology and history, that may focus on the same content. Practice offers a possible context for access to the immediate experience of the spiritual life, the subject matter of the discipline. When experience "comes into the room," it makes the study of the experience of the Christian life immediate and compelling. But, more importantly for the development of the discipline, it advances the content of the study itself.

Many scholars of Christian spirituality work almost exclusively with texts: biblical texts, texts of various literary forms that have been recognized as part of our Christian heritage, texts left by important Christian thinkers, pastors, and spiritual guides. The key questions our discipline poses to texts of all kinds and eras include, What is the lived spiritual experience of this text? The experience that gave rise to it? The experience that it met in its first hearers or readers, as much as this can be reclaimed, and its experience in me and in my students today? In light of this discussion, we can now further ask, What new experience is created in the act of investigating this text and wrestling with its provenance, interpretation, and existential usefulness? What experiences of my own would help me enter faithfully into the world of this text? What shared practices would help us come to understand this text and its world and ourselves as interpreters?

I *do not* mean that one can simply read one's own self into the text. All the appropriate exegetical moves *must* occur, including establishing the accuracy of the text as it exists, the adequacy of any translation employed, the serious study of the context, the author, the author's community, the literary form, the reason that the author is writing this text as far as it can be ascertained, and the position and frame of reference of those to whom the text was addressed. We must also try to become aware of our own assumptions and biases and attempt to set them aside during the investigative phase of our work with the text. But when that foundational work has been done, what are we faced with? A text that in its otherness is struggling to communicate with us across vast gulfs in cultures, languages, world-views. Do we allow ourselves to be transformed by the disciplined practice of uncovering all the levels of experience present in the encounter, the ones the text brought and the ones we brought? Do we allow the disciplined practice of lived spirituality to help us to rethink the text? What scholars of Christian spirituality do, I believe, is "to interpret the experience [spirituality] studies in order to make it understandable and meaningful in the present without violating its historical reality."[32] Making it meaningful and understandable in the present, that is, by engaging it *in the present* but *on its own terms*.

The careful work of the scholar, Wendy Wright insists, can be both self-implicating and transformative precisely in the way it brings us face to face with the radical otherness of what it is that we study. And in the very wrestling with this otherness, we might even be transformed. That is, not only might our scholarly opinions and conclusions be revised, but also the very way we pray, act, and live might also change.[33]

One of the reasons scholars of Christian spirituality banish practice from the academic study of spirituality is, I suspect, because the immediacy of direct experience can make critical distance more difficult. But I believe it is not impossible. It does require careful attention to the need for and process of holding in tension the experience/case, one's own lived spirituality, and the canons of good scholarship. And the benefits can be substantial for one's scholarly work as well as for one's person.

91

THE PRACTICE OF SPIRITUALITY

What might this notion of practice as the intentional and repeated bringing of one's lived spirituality into one's scholarly work look like concretely? First, let me offer an example of research and writing and then one of teaching.

The process that my two co-authors and I recently concluded as we wrote *The Spiritual Exercises Reclaimed: Uncovering Liberating Possibilities for Women*[34] provides an example of this kind of practice. Let me highlight some of the ways that emerged in our collaboration.

We had several goals for this work: We wanted to advance the scholarship on the *Spiritual Exercises*. We wanted to offer a feminist perspective. We wanted to make the *Exercises* available to contemporary women and thereby advance their practice. One of our first decisions committed us to a way of being together that would support the vocation of scholarship, but we only gradually learned what that meant in practice. For more than a year, we talked, read, reflected. We talked together about our experiences of the *Exercises*, what worked and didn't work for us, and talked to contemporary women who have completed them and who have also served as directors of others who have completed them. We conversed and argued back and forth with the text, trying to let it say what it said, not what we thought it said or wanted it to say. We reviewed the history of interpretation of the *Spiritual Exercises* and of the period and context in which they were written. We talked to the women again and again. We tried to pay attention to the anger, the energy, the disjunction, the frustration, and every other experience that arose in all these conversation partners and in ourselves. We frequently disagreed on substance or emphasis and often had to hold our different perspectives in tension for a long time before the way through appeared. We began writing. All the writing came back to the three of us, often numerous times, for comment, critique, and finally, celebration.

Since we were working with a text that gives directions for prayer, we realized that our appropriation of the text would be incomplete if we stood outside the prayer to which the text invites. We had all completed the *Spiritual Exercises* in the thirty-day retreat form at some point in the past and all had directed and taught the *Exercises* in our various settings. But we needed to engage the *Exercises* together and on their own terms if our collective interpretation process was to move into new ground. So, every day that we worked together, one of us took the responsibility to prepare some kind of common prayer related to the aspect of the *Spiritual Exercises* that we were presently struggling with. Sometimes the struggle resolved itself. Sometimes it didn't. But our *scholarship* advanced through this common prayer. We gleaned perspectives that we might never have seen without this practice as an integral part of our writing.

There are some predictable pitfalls to this kind of work. One is that publishers may not know what to do with the result. It doesn't look quite like the typical scholarly book. We included a contemporary rewriting of the dynamics in the form of a modern morality play. We had to justify not once but several times the presence of the play in the text. For us, it offered not only a way to summarize our insights, but also to draw others into their own experiences of the *Spiritual Exercises* and to enhance that experience through their common experience of "readers' theater."[35] Our experience suggests that it will take a while to learn to write and publish a new kind of scholarship for a developing discipline.

The other venue for our scholarship is the classroom. How can scholars of Christian spirituality practice intentionally and critically bringing lived spirituality into the classroom dedicated to the academic study of spirituality? One of my colleagues has made some interesting discoveries about practice as he taught psalms to various constituencies over time. These discoveries have changed the way he teaches at a basic level.[36]

The impetus for his using practice as an intentional strategy came from students preparing for ministry. "If psalms are sung prayer, can't we sing them in class?" some students asked. Little by little and across introductory and advanced versions of psalms courses, he began to recognize that something different happens when students and other interpreters *perform* a text than if they simply read it.[37] This difference appears on several levels. First, performance helps internalize the text; like *lectio divina*, it draws attention to certain words, motifs, and repetitions that don't get noticed otherwise. Students learn these texts from the inside out, and remember and connect them to other texts as they increase their exegetical range. Second, performance allows an immediate understanding of how different people interpret the same text, and reconfirms the position that there is no absolutely correct interpretation. Third, this approach embodies the belief that both synchronic and diachronic approaches to biblical texts are important and necessary in order for the interpreter to complete the task of interpretation.

Granted, the psalms are a special case, because through them we address God, rather than listen to God's address to us. However, the principles garnered in this special case have wider application. In my colleague's other biblical courses, he now tends to ask, "Does approaching the text inductively, through such practices as singing, listening to or performing musical renditions of a text, looking at artistic interpretations, or allowing movement or dramatic interpretation or response, help to solidify learning about this text?" His criteria for appropriate practices grew out of his commitment to the learning gleaned through performance: "Does the activity we are engaged in help us to become more deeply immersed in the text, to know and understand what is in the text, to grasp various ways to interpret it, and to command something of the history of interpretation?"

Not only are psalms a special case within the biblical canon, but in one sense the biblical canon is a special case within Christian literature; Christians understand it as a record of God's word to humankind. In Christian life and spirituality, the Bible is approached as a living text. But what about other Christian texts? Any text with which one interacts deeply and personally and at a transformative level,[38] as well as intellectually and critically, *becomes* a living text in that very interaction. Thus, any text that offers us contents for the study of Christian spirituality benefits from critical reflection on the lived spirituality of the interpreter. "Practice" is thus constitutive of our discipline.

Before we leave the classroom context, it is worth noting a style of teaching called "phenomenological." Phenomenology involves reflecting on experience and letting conclusions emerge from these reflections. It assumes that experience is accessible to the inquirer and seeks to understand the intentionality of both the experiencing subject and the experienced other.[39] This basic teaching method allows for many variations and contexts,[40] but always takes experience seriously, including the experience of lived spirituality that I have been calling "practice."

Can there be too much practice in the classroom? The question arises naturally when practices are used as a means of enticing students into the material the teacher wishes to communicate. But when practice shifts to the understanding promoted in this essay, namely the critical reflection on lived spirituality, then it becomes intrinsic to the learning process. At this point the question evaporates.

Throughout this essay, I have assumed that the scholar of Christian spirituality is Christian, and works from within this tradition. Is this perspective valid for the scholar who studies Christian spirituality but as an adherent of another spiritual tradition? Likewise, what of the Christian scholar who looks at another spiritual tradition? Can these scholars still employ practices as constitutive of their scholarly work? Although I work from within the Christian tradition, almost exclusively examining aspects of that same tradition, I believe that this understanding of practice as constitutive of the work of scholars of Christian spirituality still extends to these other situations. Both emic and etic perspectives[41] benefit from critical reflection on lived spiritual practice. When one is an outsider to a tradition, however, one must exercise particular sensitivity to the practices selected and the interpretations rendered, giving priority to interpretations from within the tradition where these are available, and taking care not to assume easy correspondences in apparently similar practices from different traditions. Important insights can come from both perspectives.[42]

It is, I believe, time to quit being so timid about practice as a constitutive aspect of our discipline. We "have a tiger by the tail," and are not quite sure what to do with it, how to tame it sufficiently to allow it into the study and the classroom. But we also have something uniquely useful to offer scholars in other disciplines. When lived spiritual experience comes into the room, it makes the study of Christian spirituality immediate, transformative, compelling, self-implicating, and life changing.

NOTES

1. An earlier version of this essay was delivered on the occasion of the Presidential Address, Society for the Study of Christian Spirituality, November 2001. I thank Society for the Study of Christian Spirituality members Maria Bowen, Mary Rose Bumpus, Joseph Driskill, and John Endres, and my other colleagues at the Graduate Theological Union and San Francisco Theological Seminary, especially Sandra Brown, for their conversation on earlier drafts. Lisa Dahill graciously shared early research on practices from a three-year study of theological education being conducted as part of the Lilly-funded Preparation for the Professions.
2. Miroslav Volf, "Theology for a Way of Life," in *Practicing Theology: Beliefs and Practices in Christian Life*, ed. Miroslav Volf and Dorothy C. Bass (Grand Rapids, MI: Eerdmans), 257.
3. By making this comparison, I do not intend to re-open the issue of the relationship of spirituality to theology. See Sandra Schneiders's discussion in "The Study of Christian Spirituality: Contours and Dynamics of a Discipline," *Christian Spirituality Bulletin* 6 (Spring 1998): 1, 3–12 (Chapter 1 of this volume) for a discussion of this issue and for a provisional, though not exactly tidy, resolution of this relationship.
4. *Christian Spirituality Bulletin* 7 (Fall/Winter 1999): 11.
5. G. Stanley Hall, *Adolescence* (1904); William James, *Varieties of Religious Experience* (1908); Anton Boisen, *The Exploration of the Inner World* (1936); Richard Cabot and Russell Dicks, *The Art of Ministering to the Sick* (1936); Russell Dicks, *And Ye Visited Me* (1939); Carroll Wise, *Religion in Illness and Health* (1942) and *Pastoral Counseling: Its Theory and Practice* (1951); Seward Hiltner, *Pastoral Counseling* (1949) and *Preface to Pastoral Theology* (1958); Daniel Day Williams, *The Minister and the Cure of Souls* (1961); Wayne Oates, *Protestant Pastoral Counseling* (1962); Howard Clinebell, *Basic Types of Pastoral Counseling* (1966); and Paul Johnson, *Person and Counselor* (1967).
6. J. R. Burck and R. J. Hunter, "Pastoral Theology, Protestant," *Dictionary of Pastoral Care and Counseling*, ed. Rodney J. Hunter. (Nashville: Abingdon Press, 1990), 867.
7. By "case" I mean a situation, event, dilemma or system that has been abstracted sufficiently from its dynamic flow so that its reality can be described. I also mean a description in the round or "thick description" itself. I am not specifically referring to the method of Robert Evans and Thomas Parker in *Christian Theology: A Case Method Approach* (San Francisco: Harper & Row, 1976), though their approach would fit into my use of the term. For a good summary of the types, benefits, and disadvantages of case as a method, see Mary Elizabeth Mullino Moore, *Teaching from the Heart: Theology and Educational Method* (Harrisburg, PA: Trinity Press International, 1998). Significantly, Moore stresses case study's connection to particularity.
8. See, for example, Bernard McGinn, "The Letter and the Spirit: Spirituality as an Academic Discipline," *Christian Spirituality Bulletin* 1 (Fall 1993): 1, 2–10 (Chapter 2 of this volume); Sandra Schneiders, "Spirituality as an Academic Discipline," *Christian*

Spirituality Bulletin 1 (Fall 1993): 10–15; and the four essays in Bradley Hanson, ed., *Modern Christian Spirituality: Methodological and Historical Essays* (Atlanta, GA: Scholars Press, 1990).

9. Sandra Schneiders, "Spirituality in the Academy," *Modern Christian Spirituality: Methodological and Historical Essays,* ed. Bradley C. Hanson (Atlanta, GA: Scholars Press, 1990), 32 and elsewhere.

10. Schneiders, "The Study of Christian Spirituality," 3–4.

11. Schneiders, "Spirituality in the Academy," 17: ". . . the term *spirituality*, like the term *psychology*, is unavoidably ambiguous, referring to (1) a fundamental dimension of the human being, (2) the lived experience which actualizes that dimension, and (3) the academic discipline which studies that experience." From p. 32: "Spirituality is interested in the experience as experience, i.e. in its phenomenological wholeness, that it must utilize whatever approaches are relevant to the reality being studied . . . spirituality is not the practical application of theoretical principles, theological or other, to concrete life experience. It is the critical study of such experience."

12. Different degrees of abstraction occur when speaking at these levels: one uses first order religious language to describe the initial, immediate experience; second order religious language for the explication and critical evaluation or appropriation of the basic meaning; and third order religious language if the process continues to reflect on the way in which such judgments are made and a critical evaluation of the procedures. See Theodore Jennings, "Pastoral Theological Methodology," *Dictionary of Pastoral Care and Counseling,* ed. Rodney J. Hunter (Nashville: Abingdon Press, 1990), 862.

13. I am following the "anthropological" approach here; this category is suggested by McGinn, "The Letter and the Spirit," 1, 3–10 (Chapter 2). Sandra Schneiders has strongly proposed this perspective as the most adequate to the complex reality to be studied, but see also Mary Frohlich, "Spiritual Discipline, Discipline of Spirituality: Revisiting Questions of Definition and Method," *Spiritus: A Journal of Christian Spirituality* 1:1 (Spring 2001): 65–78 (Chapter 5 of this volume); and Michael Downey, *Understanding Christian Spirituality* (New York: Paulist Press, 1997), especially Chapter 2.

14. Brian Childs, "Experience," *Dictionary of Pastoral Care and Counseling,* ed. Rodney J. Hunter (Nashville: Abingdon Press, 1990), 388.

15. Nicholas Lash, *Easter in Ordinary: Reflections on Human Experience and the Knowledge of God* (Notre Dame, IN: University of Notre Dame Press, 1988), 91.

16. Childs, "Experience," 388.

17. We see this inclusive sense of "experience" in Evan Howard's recent study, *The Affirming Touch of God: A Psychological and Philosophical Exploration of Christian Discernment* (Lanham, MD: University Press of America, 2000), 292–304. Here, Howard does some of the necessary groundwork on the term "experience" using the disciplines of cognitive studies and philosophy. Experience, for Howard, is a process consisting of a number of stages that can be isolated and studied, as do these disciplines. The first level, if you will, the "raw material" out of which all human experience arises, is Being Aware (Howard capitalizes the terms for the levels), or bare consciousness of such variables as range, intensity, energy, and level. The second stage is characterized by Experiencing (stimulus, sensation, perception, initial memory processing, imagery). The third stage is Understanding (cognitive psychology's conceptual processing, general knowledge, and language processing; and emotion research's appraisal and regulation). Fourth, Judging, deals with such questions as "what is the case?" and "is it really the case?" At this point, affective experience completes its appraisal and moves toward emotion formation. Deciding and Acting follow Judging, involving investment of the person in the judgment previously made. In the Judging stage, affections reach the expressive level and give rise to a tendency to act, phenomenal feelings, mental

preoccupation, physiological changes, and the like. The final aspect of the experience process is World-view Adjusting. Every action reinforces or shapes the nature of our developing selves. This, says Howard, is the ordinary progression of experience.

18. Howard, *The Affirming Touch of God*, 298–303. Howard's view of these "others" is similar to the theoretical perspective adopted by San Francisco Theological Seminary's spirituality program under the title of "The Experience Circle." See also Nancy Wiens St. John, "The Definition and Role of Environment in Christian Spiritual Discernment," unpublished paper, Graduate Theological Union, December 14, 1998.

19. Rebecca Chopp, *Saving Work: Feminist Practices in Theological Education* (Louisville: Westminster/John Knox, 1995), 15. A growing conversation around the notion of "practice," in theological education, has taken its impetus from Alasdair MacIntyre's treatment in *After Virtue*, 2nd ed. (Notre Dame, IN: University of Notre Dame Press, 1984), 181–203. For example, in *To Understand God Truly: What's Theological about a Theological School* (Louisville: Westminster/John Knox, 1992), 118, David Kelsey defines "practice" as "any form of socially established cooperative human activity that is complex and internally coherent, is subject to standards of excellence that partly define it, and is done to some end but does not necessarily have a product." As cooperative human behaviors, the actions Kelsey has in mind are bodily, social, interactive, cooperative, and share rule-like regularities. They contain standards of excellence, and thus necessitate self-critical reflection as part of a larger communal discourse. See also Craig Dykstra, "Reconceiving Practice," in *Shifting Boundaries: Contextual Approaches to the Structure of Theological Education*, ed. Barbara Wheeler and Edward Farley (Louisville: Westminster/John Knox, 1991), 35–66; Dorothy C. Bass, ed., *Practicing Our Faith* (San Francisco: Jossey-Bass, 1999); and Miroslav Volf and Dorothy C. Bass, eds., *Practicing Theology: Beliefs and Practices in Christian Theology* (Grand Rapids, MI: Eerdmans, 2002). These works, rooted in McIntyre, focus on larger-scale communal practices over longer periods of time that address fundamental human needs and that together constitute a way of life. This essay, however, follows the alternate usage in the social sciences, in which "practice" can refer to any socially meaningful action, and therefore can include smaller and more discrete actions than would be included, for example, in Dykstra, Bass, and Volf.

20. Frohlich, "Spiritual Discipline," 68.

21. Frohlich, "Spiritual Discipline," 68, 76.

22. Social anthropologist Pierre Bourdieu defines *habitus* as "the durably installed generative principle of regulated improvisations." That is, *habitus* is the unconscious regulator that both reproduces and adjusts our responses to social situations that appear to us to be self-evident. See *Outline of a Theory of Practice*, trans. Richard Nice (Cambridge: Cambridge University Press, 1977), 78. See also Kelsey, *To Understand God Truly*, 126, and Chopp, *Saving Work*, 5–14, 76, 103–4.

23. Schneiders, "The Study of Christian Spirituality," 10. (See above, pp. 19–20.)

24. Sandra M. Schneiders, "A Hermeneutical Approach to the Study of Christian Spirituality," *Christian Spirituality Bulletin* 2 (Spring 1994): 13. (See above, p. 58.)

25. Two are methods, namely controlled introspection to access one's own internal processes, and the practicum wherein students get in touch with the lived spirituality of *other* persons. The third is an awareness: recognizing that our own thoughtful and passionate work in the discipline of spirituality transforms us—our work is inevitably self-implicating, and its disciplined prosecution is itself a form of spiritual practice. See Schneiders, "A Hermeneutical Approach," 13–14. (See above, pp. 58–59.)

26. Parker Palmer, *The Courage to Teach* (San Francisco: Jossey-Bass, 1998), 51.

27. Joseph Favazza and Fred Glennon, "Service Learning and Religious Studies: Propaganda or Pedagogy," *Council of Societies for the Study of Religion Bulletin*, 29 (November 2000): 106.

97

28. Favazza and Glennon, "Service Learning," 106.

29. Howard Gardner, *The Disciplined Mind* (New York: Penguin Books, 2000), 185–99.

30. Frohlich, "Spiritual Discipline," 69. (See above, p. 70.)

31. Belden Lane, *The Solace of Fierce Landscapes: Exploring Desert and Mountain Spirituality* (New York: Oxford University Press, 1998), 4. In his words, "This book makes no claim to be a thoroughgoing historical-critical study of the apophatic tradition. Nor does it offer an ethnographic analysis of specific cultural understandings of desert and mountain environments. What it attempts, instead, is something of a performance (rather than a mere description) of apophatic spirituality. . . . The book therefore invites the reader into several of the pivotal texts (and contexts) out of which such events of vulnerability and union have repeatedly been generated in the history of the tradition. Its purpose is to allow these texts (and this terrain) to engage the reader at a deep level of personal risk, through the intimate involvement of the interpreter's own voice in the process of saying and unsaying what is otherwise wholly unavailable to discourse."

32. Schneiders, "The Study of Christian Spirituality," 3. (See above, p. 6.)

33. Wendy M. Wright, "Keeping One's Distance: Presence and Absence in the History of Christian Spirituality," *Christian Spirituality Bulletin* 4 (Summer 1996): 21.

34. Katherine Dyckman, Mary Garvin and Elizabeth Liebert, *The Spiritual Exercises Reclaimed: Uncovering Liberating Possibilities for Women* (New York: Paulist Press, 2001).

35. Belden Lane, "Spirituality as the Performance of Desire: Calvin on the World as a Theatre of God's Glory," *Spiritus: A Journal of Christian Spirituality* 1:1 (Spring 2001): 23. "Absorbed in the mystery of the making and unmaking of worlds, a theatrical performance forces the audience into multiple and simultaneous levels of perception. Even as it gives pleasure, it also profoundly disturbs, suggesting at times a complete reversal of things previously held certain. . . it is a performance that demands participation."

36. I am indebted to John Endres and the numerous conversations about what goes on in his psalms courses that we have shared during the course of our collaborative writing.

37. In this vein, Belden Lane has recently defined spirituality, following John Calvin, as "the performance of desire." See "Spirituality as the Performance of Desire," 1.

38. Frohlich, "Spiritual Discipline," 71. (See above, p. 71.)

39. Moore, *Teaching from the Heart*, 94. Stated as a method: First, one must identify the experience that is the focal point of the study. Second, one identifies and brackets one's own prejudgments and assumptions about the experience. Next, one observes and describes the experience. As we have seen, both pastoral theology and the academic study of spirituality suggest that one or more appropriate critical disciplines be brought to bear on the description in order to understand the experience from a variety of perspectives. We engage these disciplines prior to or along with theological reflection. The final step involves decision about and implementation of an appropriate action. These actions can be quite varied, from intending to pursue this line of inquiry further, to a decision to write or teach about this reality, to mobilizing a community for a particular behavior—in other words, decisions for action are related to the reality under study, the one studying and the various communities where these realities intersect. See pp. 120–22.

40. Maria Lichtman, "Teaching and the Contemplative Life," *Christian Spirituality Bulletin* 6 (Fall 1998): 21, offers some ways to begin, including free-writing at the beginning or end of class, a time of centering to allow students to put aside their distractions, sharing writing in nonthreatening ways, working collaboratively, cards with questions at the end of class, ritual openings and closings, body movement, sharing food, pauses in either writing or speaking, "ah-ha" papers, and inviting (and welcoming) nonlinear or

nonverbal responses to texts and figures without dispensing with the usual array of scholarly responses. In terms of the meta-structure of the classroom, one might employ case studies or offer entry points, responses, or interpretations through art, literature, drama, music, or film.

41. "Emic" refers to a single, unified system, and "etic" to raw data considered independently from the system as a whole. "Emic" and "etic" can refer to the perspective from which we examine data: the examiner is a part of the whole being examined (emic) or examines data from a perspective outside the whole (etic).

42. Amy Plantinga Pauw, "Attending to the Gaps between Beliefs and Practices," in *Practicing Theology*, ed. Miroslav Volf and Dorothy C. Bass (Grand Rapids, MI: Eerdmans, 2002), 41, 43.

99

7

The Cost of Interpretation

Sacred Texts and Ascetic Practice in Desert Spirituality

DOUGLAS BURTON-CHRISTIE

*T*he *Sayings* of the early desert monks echo with two recurring questions: "Abba, speak to me a word" and "Amma, what should I do?" Taken together, they suggest the dynamism and cost of interpretation within early desert monasticism. The dynamism is inherent in the first question, the plea for a "word." This reflects first of all the character of living encounter that marks the *Sayings*: monastic teaching arose not out of a systematic rendering of accumulated wisdom but out of the back-and-forth conversation between two persons, with all the risk and unpredictability implied by such an encounter. The request for a word also suggests the pervasive sense among the monks that language (including words from Scripture and the words of the elder) had real power; to pose a question to an elder was to risk being bowled over, having one's world come apart, being transformed by the word he or she uttered. Which points to the second question: "What should I do?" This is another way of asking: What should I do with this word? How should I act? In what ways am I to be changed by this encounter? The recurring character of these questions among the desert monks suggests their acute sense of the cost of interpretation. To interpret a word meant striving to somehow realize it in one's life and to be transformed by that realization.

In my own work during the past few years, I have been occupied with trying to understand and describe this process of interpretation, what I have called the desert hermeneutic.[1] I would like to use this as a starting point for reflecting upon some of the challenges we face in doing research in the field of spirituality. In particular I want to raise the question of how we balance the critical and analytical task of interpreting a school, person, or movement in the history of spirituality with the not-always-controllable demands the subject matter makes on us.

It has been argued that one of the characteristic features of the emerging discipline of spirituality is that it is participative or self-implicating. That is, to adequately and fully investigate the subject matter of the discipline, one must be willing to enter into it, even be transformed by it. Leaving aside for the moment the question of whether spirituality has a special claim to such an approach, I want to inquire into the inherent tension between the critical moment in the study of spirituality and the self-implicating moment. Is it true that we must allow ourselves to become existentially or personally implicated in order to really understand the subject matter of spirituality? How far can we allow ourselves to become implicated without skewing or muddying the process of critical reflection? Can these two moments of the interpretive process be brought into a fruitful dialogue with one another? I think they can, though not without considerable difficulty. I would like to illustrate the tensions inherent in trying to maintain a balance between critical distance and participative engagement with examples from my own experience of studying early desert monasticism. First, the participative moment.

INITIAL ENGAGEMENT: LOVING A SUBJECT

"You start by loving a subject." Thus biologist E. O. Wilson, in his book *Biophilia* begins his description of how innovation in science occurs. "Birds, probability theory, explosives, stars, differential equations, storm fronts, sign language, swallowtail butterflies—the odds are that the obsession will have begun in childhood. The subject will be your lodestar and give sanctuary in the shifting mental universe."[2] Surely most of us could compile our own list of persons, figures, issues in the history of spirituality that have engaged our attention—and have kept it engaged. The point I wish to note is Wilson's unabashed insistence on the importance of love, engagement, participation in the ongoing process of understanding. This is, I believe, an important episte-mological statement: we begin to know a subject by loving it. Everything else follows from this, including the hard critical work of deepening our under-standing of it.

I can locate precisely the genesis of my own attraction to desert monasti-cism and its characteristic attention to language: it was a cold, stormy Novem-ber evening almost twenty years ago; some friends had just dropped me off at the gate of a Trappist monastery in Northern California where I was to spend the next four days on retreat. The guestmaster ushered me up the walkway and into the dark silence of the church. Soon compline began. Several things struck me then and throughout the weekend: the aesthetic beauty of the language of scripture set to Gregorian chant; the rhythm of words and silence, words and manual labor, pulsing through each day, each year, through the entire life of each monk; the communal power of shared chanting; the evident desire on the part of the monks to ingest the words at the deepest level of their being (suggested by the monastic practice of rumination, or chewing on the text); the sense of the endless depths of mystery contained in these words.

At least part of the reason this experience had such a profound effect on me was that I was a recovering literalist: I had spent several years under the influence of a literalist-propositional reading of Scripture propounded by a semi-fundamentalist group of which I had been a member in college. This desiccated hermeneutic allowed almost no room for the imaginative power of symbol and metaphor that is present everywhere in Scripture. Thus my exhilaration at discovering an approach to Scripture at once attentive to the beauty and power of language and aimed unabashedly at the religious transformation of the reader/hearer/proclaimer. Prompted by this initial experience, I decided to probe further, and spent the next year living and exploring the monastic life with a variety of communities in this country and abroad—with Cistercians in California, Wales, France, and with Orthodox monks on Mt. Athos and in the Judean desert. This experience only deepened my sense of the value of the monastic tradition of *lectio* and *ruminatio* and contributed markedly to my decision to pursue graduate study, primarily in Scripture.

Imagine my surprise and chagrin when I discovered that my teachers at Oxford were less than sympathetic to the monastic hermeneutical sensibility. The rigorous historical criticism that I learned at Oxford appeared to have almost nothing in common with the prayerful, ruminative, imaginative approach of the monks. While I came to respect the historical complexity of biblical texts, and learned to appreciate the need for the appropriate application of a range of critical methods, I found such an approach to interpretation was (taken on its own) immensely unsatisfying religiously and personally. The cost of interpretation here was quantitative, focusing attention on the multiplication of methods and information necessary for understanding a text, rather than qualitative, as I had found the insistently probing rumination practiced by the monks to be.

Yet this critical approach to Scripture also raised in my mind certain questions about the viability of the monastic practice of interpretation. What was one to make of an interpretive approach that seemingly displayed no historical awareness, that played with the text in an imaginative, allusive manner, that left the question of its meaning maddeningly undetermined? Not much, apparently, at least when judged against the canons of historical criticism. It is no wonder that church historian Hans Lietzmann, commenting on the approach to Scripture found among the early monks, said: "It should of course be understood that this learning by heart was nothing more than a superficial accomplishment, ascetic in character, a kind of weaving and mental matting. . . . The mechanical memorization did not penetrate the heart; it gave indeed only the faintest biblical tinge to the world of ideas in which the monks lived."[3]

My own experience and reading of the early monastic literature told me that such a judgment was mistaken, that there was more to the desert hermeneutic and to the long tradition of monastic *lectio* than this. Yet, I did not know how to articulate the logic of the desert hermeneutic in a critically cogent way. A question began to form in my mind, one that would eventually become the focus for my research on early monasticism: Could the desert approach to interpretation be retrieved, reappropriated in terms that were both faithful to its original spirit and comprehensible to a critically minded contemporary audience?

Putting the question in this way was important. It enabled me to include in the research project both my initial assumptions regarding the power and meaningfulness of the desert hermeneutic ("my love of the subject"), and my growing awareness of how necessary hard, critical analysis was for understanding the complex character of the early monastic world. Should I have suspended those initial assumptions in favor of the subject in the interests of critical objectivity? I think not. In the first place, without these assumptions, I would have had no "entry point" into the study of the early monastic hermeneutic, no real reason for pursuing the study in the first place. But more importantly, as I soon came to recognize, there is no presuppositionless starting point for any work of inquiry. "Prejudices," as Gadamer has noted, are the "biases of our openness to the world."[4]

In this sense, one's love of the subject, far from being a hindrance to careful academic work, constitutes an initial and enduring interpretive key, informing our work at every step along the way. This process has been described as moving from an initial naïveté, where the love of the subject is all, to a more critical perspective, in which the subject "comes apart" as it were into its component elements, to a post-critical "second naïveté" where one is able to reintegrate what has been pulled apart in the critical process, reengage the subject matter deeply and thoughtfully. What does this look like in practical terms? Let me give an example of this from my own research.

CRITICAL DISTANCE AND REENGAGEMENT

In examining the attitudes to language and interpretation among the early desert monks, I discovered a number of critical issues that needed to be addressed before I could assess and retrieve the desert hermeneutic. I needed to understand, among other things, the possible historical sources of monasticism itself (Scripture being only one of these, and often discounted in importance); the social-economic forces impinging on the early monastic experience; the nature and historical reliability of the early monastic texts, especially the *Sayings*; questions of literacy among the early monks and the availability of Scripture in codex or scroll forms; the dynamics of early monastic community, especially the relationship between master and disciple. Even having examined these issues in some detail, I had still not yet come to my main task of describing and assessing the early monastic hermeneutic itself. In order to do this, I was still faced with the daunting task of somehow explaining (to myself and others) the logic of the overall interpretive approach of the monks as well as their often peculiar attitudes toward language. Two contemporary critical approaches—studies of oral culture and hermeneutics—provided particular help in understanding these issues.

Contemporary studies of oral culture by scholars such as Walter Ong, Eric Havelock, Jack Goody, and William Graham helped me to understand a primary reason for the peculiar attitudes to language found among the desert monks: they were rooted in oral culture.[5] Thus the monks' sense of the power of spoken language, the revelatory significance given to the words of the elder, the tremendous importance of the relationship between abba and disciple (like the apprentice relationship in all oral cultures), the process of weaving words together (rhapsodizing) in meditation which came so naturally to them, the interpretive and social tensions which sometimes arose in early monastic communities between those with books and those without books—all this can be accounted for by recognizing the presence of a vibrant oral culture within early monasticism. This also helps to explain why a historian like Lietzmann (who described the monastic practice of *lectio* as "a kind of weaving and mental matting . . . mechanical memorization") saw so little of value in the early monastic hermeneutic: not only was he judging it by the standards of a later critical sensibility; but he was also judging it by the standards of a writing culture. Once the oral character of early monasticism was made clear, its entire interpretive logic could be seen more clearly.

A second critical approach that I found immensely helpful for understanding the early monastic approach to interpretation was hermeneutics. Using insights from contemporary hermeneutics as a heuristic lens, I began to understand more clearly some of the dynamics at work in early monastic attitudes toward Scripture. Let me cite a few examples.

First, the notion of "word event," used so effectively by contemporary theologians like Ebeling and Funk to describe the dynamic character of biblical language, proved immensely helpful for showing how powerful language was—both the words of Scripture and the words of the elder—in the experience of the desert monks. Second, the idea that the meaning of a text is found not in a single univocal understanding, but in the imaginative "world" it projects ahead of itself, which the reader or hearer is called to enter, helped to illuminate two things: the particular power certain biblical texts exerted on the early monastic imagination (texts pertaining to freedom from care, humility, and compassion were especially important); and the ruminative process through which the monks strove to enter the worlds projected by these texts. Third, the recognition of the importance of "prejudice" in the interpretive process helped to explain how the monks' particular interest (e.g., solitude, silence, humility, compassion) influenced their choice of texts and their approach to interpreting them (e.g., their belief in the importance of silence and humility sometimes kept them from commenting on the sacred texts at all). Fourth, the images of "fusion of horizons," conversation, and hermeneutical circle, shed light on the dynamic, concrete process through which most of the work of interpretation in the desert took place (the abba-disciple relationship), and on the seemingly endless possibilities that opened up before the texts. Finally, the notion that *praxis* or *applicatio* is intrinsic to the process of interpretation helped to explain one of the characteristic features of the desert hermeneutic: its practical character. The monks manifested a passion for what George Steiner called execution. "An interpreter," he says ". . . is, in essence, an executioner, one who 'acts out' the material before him so as to give it intelligible life. Interpretation is to the largest possible degree, lived."[6]

How did this show itself in the literature of the desert? Above all through the intense focus in the *Sayings* on the person—the gestures, facial expressions, words, silences of the holy one. This is where one looked to understand the meaning of a text. Thus to learn the meaning of renunciation, detachment, freedom from care, suggested by Mt. 19:21 ("If you would be perfect, go, sell what you possess and give it to the poor"), look at Abba Macarius, who, when he encountered a man plundering his cell, "came up to the thief as if he were a stranger and helped him load the animal and saw him off in great tranquility."[7] To understand the meaning of humility suggested by the first beatitude, one need only consider the power of John Colobos' witness: "Who is this John," one of his contemporaries asked, "who by his humility, has all Scetis hanging by his little finger?"[8]

The call to love? The realization of this gospel commandment among the early monks manifested itself above all in their unwillingness to judge others. Thus, Abba Moses, when asked to participate in a communal judgment of a brother who had committed a sin, picked up a large, leaking jug, hoisted it onto his shoulder, and followed his brothers to the appointed place. Pressed to explain his behavior, he told them, "My sins run out behind me, and I do not see them, and today I am coming to judge another."[9] Or consider Abba Ammonas, who was said "to have advanced to the point where his goodness was so great, he no longer took any notice of evil."[10] If anyone came asking him to judge another, he would "feign madness" to avoid doing so.[11] It was above all in simple gestures of tenderness that the early monks showed their realization of the commandment to love. Consider Abba Poemen's response to some brothers who came to him to express their concern with preserving a minimum level of strictness in monastic observance. They asked him: "When we see brothers who are dozing at the *synaxis*, shall we rouse them so that they will be watchful?" Poemen responded: "For my part, when I see a brother who is dozing, I put his head on my knees and let him rest."[12]

In focusing on such gestures, the monks reflect much the same sensibility one finds throughout the ancient biographies of holy men and women, whose aim, Patricia Cox Miller suggests, "was to evoke, and thus to reveal the interior geography of the hero's life . . . ; when they sought to 'capture the gesture,' they were negotiating the intersection of the human and the divine."[13] This also expresses the aim and purpose of interpretation in the desert: to facilitate transformation.

THE RISKS AND THE RESULTS

This is another way of saying that interpretation is costly. And it brings us back to our original question regarding the study of spirituality. What Steiner calls "execution" is not only an apt description of the dynamism and cost of interpretation among the early desert monks; it also suggests an important dimension of our own interpretive efforts in the study of spirituality. For the monks, the parameters of the interpretive quest were set by their two primary questions, "Speak to me a word," and "What should I do?" These questions determined the participative shape of their quest for God, and the demanding cost of fulfilling that quest. While the kind and range of questions we bring to the study of spirituality are no doubt different from those the early monks put to one another, we would do well, I think, to listen to their questions in formulating our own. They remind us first of all that there is something "at stake" in the issues we engage in the study of spirituality, that it is the "love of the subject" imbedded in our own questions that helps bring it to life. They also remind us that there is real value and purpose to careful critical analysis (analogous to the demanding critical process the monks called discernment of spirits) of the questions under consideration. The process of critical correlation I have described above contributed significantly to my ability to move from an inchoate intuition about monastic *lectio* to a deeper sense of its meaning, in particular to a clearer recognition that the final term of interpretation in early monasticism was a transformed life.

What kind of result does such a critical-participative approach to the desert hermeneutic yield? First, it shows that it is indeed possible to move beyond the narrowly reductionistic attitudes towards early monasticism expressed by scholars such as Hans Lietzmann and others. This means that we can again hear the voices of these desert dwellers on their own terms and intelligently reappropriate what is valuable and enduring in their hermeneutic. On another level, it can help to sharpen our awareness of the transformative, revelatory power of Scripture, especially within the context of solitude and silence. It can challenge us to recognize our own evasive interpretive strategies and prompt us to risk ourselves more deeply in the interpretive process. But the study of spirituality is after all a risky business. Which leads me to suggest, in conclusion, that only by investing ourselves completely—both imaginatively and critically—will the subject we so love yield its secrets in deepened understanding and appreciation.

NOTES

1. D. E. Burton-Christie, *The Word in the Desert: Scripture and the Quest for Holiness in Early Christian Monasticism* (New York: Oxford University Press, 1993).
2. E. O. Wilson, *Biophilia: The Human Bond with Other Species* (Cambridge, MA: Harvard University Press, 1984), 65.
3. Hans Lietzmann, *A History of the Early Church.* Vol. 4: *The Era of the Church Fathers* (London, Lutterworth, 1951), 153.
4. H.-G. Gadamer, *Philosophical Hermeneutics* (Berkeley: University of California Press, 1976), 9.
5. See for example: Walter J. Ong, *Orality and Literacy: The Technologizing of the Word* (London and New York: Methuen, 1982); Eric Havelock, *The Literate Revolution in Greece and Its Cultural Consequences* (Princeton, N. J.: Princeton University Press, 1982); Jack Goody, *The Domestication of the Savage Mind* (Cambridge: Cambridge University Press, 1968); William A. Graham, *Beyond the Written Word: Oral Aspects of Scripture in the History of Religion* (Cambridge: Cambridge University Press, 1987).
6. George Steiner, *Real Presences* (Chicago: University of Chicago Press, 1989), 7.
7. Macarius the Great 18 [PG 65: 269BC].
8. John of Colobos 36 [PG 65:216C].
9. Moses 2 [PG 65: 281D–284A].
10. Ammonas 8 [PG65: 121 BC].
11. Ammonas 9 [PG65: 121C].
12. Poemen 92 [PG65: 344C].
13. P. Cox Miller, *Biography in Late Antiquity: A Quest for the Holy Man* (Berkeley: University of California Press, 1983), xi.

107

Spider as Metaphor

Attending to the Symbol-Making Process in the Academic Discipline of Spirituality

BELDEN C. LANE

Several years ago I had a student leave class one day in an ecstatic state. (That doesn't happen very often!) In an undergraduate class, Nature and Theology, we had just participated in a micro-hike. Everyone had spent the last forty-five minutes on the grass outside the classroom building, paying attention to the two-foot diameter circle formed by a string attached to a tent stake. Thinking the exercise ridiculous, this student had put his tent stake in the middle of a patch of dead grass and decided to go to sleep. But just as he was dozing off, he noticed a spider climbing onto the top of his tent stake. The spider looked around from that vantage point, then shot out a length of web and pulled it back in.

The student had never seen this before and was fascinated. He watched then as the spider shot a length of web over to his hand and began to walk across it toward him, while he lay there perfectly still. Reaching his hand, the spider looked around once again and spun out a line this time to the boy's forehead, walking up it toward him. By now the class was nearly over and the student couldn't wait to tell somebody about what he'd just experienced. He ran up to me, exuberant over the fact that, for the first time in his life, he had watched a spider spin its web . . . *and* he had been still enough for it to spin its web on *him*!

Caught up in the spider's performance of a quiet, methodical, deliberate consciousness, the student was able to see mirrored his own inchoate desire for quiet and deliberate action in his life. The spider as symbol invited a corresponding performance on his part, a mimetic practice allowing him entry into what almost approximated an experience of "Theater." He could briefly imagine living in the subjunctive mode, "as if" the world of his imagination were now one in which he could actively participate as reality. This performative function of a symbol is what makes it particularly important in the task, not only of living out, but also of understanding and analyzing a given spirituality.[1]

I want to use this symbol of the spider, especially as found in the work of Jonathan Edwards, as a way of reflecting on the symbol-making and symbol-interpreting process I believe to be central to the study of spirituality (or "lived religion") as an academic discipline. The metaphor of the spider offers a fine image of the web-spinning, interdisciplinary character of spirituality, as it connects various historical, anthropological, psychological, and myth-and-symbol concerns in exploring the human search for self-transcendence.[2] It also exemplifies how a particular metaphor, especially one drawn from nature, is able to "carry over" (meta-phora) abstract theological ideas into concrete lived experience.[3]

Researchers concerned with the function of symbol in theological dis-course, from Tillich to Ricoeur and Tracy, argue that symbols are the quintes-sential language of theology: they readily invite participation.[4] Ricoeur says it is the "double intentionality" of a symbol, conveying a literal, obvious mean-ing on one level and a deeper, analogical meaning on another, that makes it most effective. The symbol embodies what it also conceals, opening the imagination to multiple layers of meaning. As Maura Campbell says, "a symbol is not merely a concept-bearer, but an experience-bearer."[5]

Nature symbols in particular seem to be the stock in trade of writers throughout the history of Christian spirituality—from Gregory of Nyssa's emphasis on Moses and the mountain of unknowing to Teresa of Avila's insistence that nothing surpasses water imagery in describing the spiritual life. Bernard McGinn reflects on the "ocean" and "desert" as recurring symbols of mystical absorption, while Andrew Louth uses the image of "wilderness" to discuss a variety of spiritual writers in the Christian tradition. From the hexameral literature in the early church to St. Bonaventure's *Tree of Life*, from medieval bestiaries to Puritan typologists such as Milton and Bunyan, Chris-tian spirituality lives and breathes through nature symbols.[6]

The spider is a particular symbol that recurs repeatedly in this history—from Augustine's *Enarrationes* on the Psalms to Horace Bushnell's essay on spiders and pests in his *Moral Uses of Dark Things* (1868).[7] The number of theologians and clergy, in fact, who have played a part in the history of arachnological research is remarkable—from the Rev. Dr. Thomas Muffet (father of "Little Miss Muffet") in sixteenth-century England to Jonathan Edwards in colonial Massachusetts, from Anglican priest Octavius Pickard-Cambridge (one of the fathers of British arachnology) to Princeton-trained theologian Henry McCook, who wrote the definitive nineteenth-century text, *American Spiders and Their Spinning Work*.[8]

Throughout the history of this curious preoccupation with eight-legged arachnids is an awareness that the spider serves as a highly multivalent symbol, admired *and* loathed at the same time. Augustine praised the spider as an exemplar of quiet contemplation, yet also observed that its moral weakness (lying in wait for insects) makes it rightly expelled from paradise.[9] We praise the industry of spiders, the beauty and pattern of their weaving. But we also are repulsed by their venom, their seemingly nefarious ways of trapping their victims.

In mythology, the spider is often very wise, sensitive, and skillful, like Charlotte in E. B. White's children's book *Charlotte's Web*. There is the honored Spider Woman of the Navajo, teaching her people the art of weaving and connecting each of them to her by an invisible thread. But in the classical tales of Ovid, the spider is also Arachne, punished by the goddess Minerva for her stubborn pride. The spider is Anansi the Trickster, the cunning web-spinner of Mary Howitt's poem that invites the fly into her parlor, the enemy-mother in Freudian symbolism who would take us back into the womb, binding us tightly to the impotence of infancy.[10] All these images of delight and horror, creativity and seductiveness, Rudolf Otto's *mysterium tremendum et fascinans*, are contained in this one symbol of the spider.

An analysis of the spider in the writings of Jonathan Edwards offers a case study in spirituality of how thought is transformed into action through the symbol-making process, how doctrine and life are joined in a web of mutual interconnectedness. In Edwards' case, his eighteenth-century Reformed theology of a Sovereign God found metaphorical expression in the delight (and risk) that a spider takes in ballooning out on a filament of web borne by warm air currents on a Fall day.[11]

The symbol of the spider appears most prominently in two different sections of the Edwards corpus.[12] One is a collection of Spider Papers, probably penned in 1720 (when he was 16 years old), written with unfulfilled hopes of being published in England. They reported on his meticulous observations of "flying spiders," including hand-drawn illustrations of how the spider floats on the air, seemingly buoyed up by the lightness of its web. He goes on to draw from these observable facts a powerful symbol of his Calvinist theology, showing how it exemplifies "the exuberant goodness of the Creator, who hath not only provided for all the necessities, but also for the pleasure and recreation of all sorts of creatures, even the insects."[13] Here Edwards invites his reader (Judge Paul Dudley of the Royal Society) to imagine himself in the place of the spider, possessed of that capacity for delight, that interior sense or "taste" for Being that every good Calvinist draws from his contemplation of the world as a *theatrum gloriae Dei*.[14]

Edwards' second use of the spider as symbol is found, of course, in his infamous sermon of 1741, "Sinners in the Hands of an Angry God."[15] Through this one sermon the image of the spider has become virtually a defining metaphor in the history of American spirituality, a shorthand form for characterizing the intensity and grimness of the whole revivalist tradition. Once again, Edwards employs the spider as symbol to encapsulate certain strands of Calvinist theology and motivate his listeners to decisive action. Here the spider is at great risk, held in the fingertips of a Sovereign God over raging flames. The readers (or listeners) are encouraged to imagine themselves in the place of the spider, fully aware of that towering uncertainty, the horrible threat of non-being that forms the human dilemma of all who have failed to exercise that delight which God had meant for their highest existence.

In both the earlier and later uses of this spider image, the observer is encouraged to enter as participant into the spider's performance, imagining him- or herself in its place, as it symbolically mirrors the observer's *own* performance of delight and horror, respectively. In the first case, the multifaceted symbol suggests, for the subsequent reader of the Spider Letter, an interior shift from the mere intellectual "concept" of conversion to an intimate sharing in that aesthetic sense of delight that Edwards would later define as the clearest mark of a conversion experience. In the second case of the "Sinners" sermon of 1741, the listener is drawn into a vicarious identification with the spider dangling over the flames, evoking the interior transmutation of an abstract doctrine of hell into a deep Kierkegaardian sense of the human condition at risk before God, without refuge, forced at last to decide.[16]

The analysis of Edwards' spirituality, in these two instances, becomes a study of human participation in symbols, asking how theological constructs are creatively turned into motivating energies. Spirituality as an academic discipline, I want to argue, has much to learn from the work of myth and symbol studies in analyzing the dominant narratives and images by which a given community repeatedly structures meaning for its common life.[17]

Indeed, there may be important parallels between American studies and spirituality as two still-relatively-young disciplines searching for adequate methodologies in doing research. Both are "field-encompassing fields," viewed with some suspicion by scholars in traditional disciplines because of their interdisciplinarity.

American studies began in the '50s and '60s as a body of scholarship concerned with interpreting the principal symbols that capture the energy of American cultural experience. Henry Nash Smith, Leo Marx, and Alan Trachtenberg analyzed symbols of the garden, the frontier, even the Brooklyn Bridge, for example, showing their role in the construction of American identity.[18] This myth and symbol school in American studies was initially very influential, but it had serious limits, too. It tended toward sweeping generalizations based on a few elite literary texts. It tended to celebrate free-floating ideas without rooting them enough in specific social and historical contexts. It was prone to emphasizing American exceptionalism and lacked the discipline of a critical theory of culture.[19] As a result, American studies has gradually turned its attention to cultural studies as a corrective to earlier patterns of research.

Similar criticisms might be made of Christian spirituality as a nascent academic discipline. It has attended primarily to mainstream voices in the history of the tradition (largely ignoring what R. Laurence Moore describes as the "outsiders"). Its tendency has been to focus on disembodied ideas apart from the complexity and ambiguity of their cultural settings. It has granted privileged status to Christianity in a way that both minimizes the importance of comparative studies and fails to deal critically enough with Christian practice itself. If the field expects to be taken seriously as an academic discipline, these are concerns it will continue to address.

I would argue, to this end, that myth and symbol studies can be useful in examining the way a particular spirituality moves from symbolic meaning to communal practice. But the critical perspective of cultural studies will also be necessary in observing how this simultaneously emerges as a social construction of reality. It is important to ask about the *interiority* of the symbol, as it engages the participation of those shaped by the myth, and *also* how this symbolic process of identification is played out in particular cultural settings with their own privileged centers, circulations of power, and ways of constructing human subjectivity. Highly prominent symbols and "master narratives" not only give shape to a community's spirituality. They also channel and solidify its power, imposing silences and constraints on those excluded from the symbolic order.[20]

In looking at Edwards's use of the spider in his 1741 sermon, for example, one must ask not only how the symbol is employed to invite participation in a Calvinist theology of the human dilemma, but also how various social and political tensions are subtly being addressed at the same time.[21] Edwards may be weaving a webwork of his own, in other words, trying to catch a variety of flies in the web of his mid-eighteenth-century, western Massachusetts sermon. Unspeaking, but nonetheless present in this text are dissident church members with whom Edwards had been in conflict since the completion of a new church building three years earlier.[22] Also present are the parents of young people unhappy over his practice of publicly addressing their children's "dating" behavior.[23] Even beyond the walls of the church, unseen but pervasive, are Quabaug and Narragansett Indians threatening from the northwest, hinted at by Edwards' reference to "the bow of God's wrath [being] bent, the arrow made ready on the string."[24]

Given the highly precarious position of the spider in this sermon, one has to ask whom the spider represents? Which voices are being empowered to speak and which ones are being silenced by the use of the same symbol? That is a question that cultural studies demands of us. We can never assume, in some naïvely pious way, that the operation of symbols within a spirituality is simply a reflection of theological categories. They are inextricably bound up with specific social and historical contexts, even with questions of contest and exchanges of power, sexuality and the body. Spirituality as an academic discipline, therefore, has to combine an imaginative sensitivity to the symbol-making process along with the hard-nosed task of cultural criticism.[25] It has to remember the caution of Roland Barthes that myth and symbol often serve to legitimize as "universal" what may only be local, as "transcendent" or "natural" what is actually socially determined, as "value neutral" what is laden with political interest.[26] Spiritualities are unquestionably involved in masking various forms of hegemony and ideology, their disguised agendas often hidden under the surface of theological description.

Scholars attentive to these questions in the study of American spirituality, for example, include Robert Orsi, Ann Taves, Ann Braude, Leigh Eric Schmidt, Jenny Franchot, and others. They anchor their investigation of Catholic devotionalism or nineteenth-century spiritualism or Easter piety in a disciplined cultural analysis. That *has* to be done, and it *can* be done without falling into a cultural reductionism that excludes theological questions as irrelevant. Bob Orsi could not write about the construction of women's identity in connection with the Shrine of St. Jude in Chicago, for instance, without also exploring the Catholic American theology of suffering. The two are inseparable. Cultural studies does not have to push God out of the analysis. It can provide instead an important way of rooting (or, if one prefers, "incarnating") spiritual experience into the warp and woof of culture.

In focusing, then, on the symbol-making character of a given spirituality—asking how it operates in facilitating the transition from theology to cultural expression—I am arguing that we have to do both: attend to the interior operations of the symbolic life *and* to the larger cultural web by which that life is always and inevitably formed and reformed.

Spirituality as an academic discipline is the study of a community's mode of engagement with life, the way it makes the transition from "knowing" to "living" in its appropriation of the truth it practices. This necessarily includes the symbols that the community uses to embody its deepest convictions, as well as the ritual performances which subsequently express that symbolic reality in mimetic action. Understanding the symbol-making process requires the most disciplined skills of observation and analysis, the careful work of poet and critic alike.

A. R. Ammons, the American poet, touches the heart of the matter when he writes of the mysterious way of a spider with its web. "It is/ wonderful/ how things work" he says, "I will tell you/ about it/ because/ it is interesting/

and because whatever *is/* moves in weeds/ and stars and spider webs/ and [if] known . . . is loved."[27] That, finally, is the goal of Christian spirituality (if not other spiritualities as well)—to make the transition from knowing to loving, from conceptualization to engagement. The goal of spirituality as an academic discipline is to analyze the process by which all this occurs, bringing to the task as much imaginative reflection *and* critical insight as possible.

NOTES

1. On the relevance of performance theory to these questions, see Victor Turner, *From Ritual to Theatre* (New York: Performing Arts Journal Publications, 1982); Erving Goffman's work on "frame analysis" in Charles Lemert and Ann Branaman, eds., *The Goffman Reader* (Malden, Mass.: Blackwell Publishers, 1997); and David George, "On Ambiguity: Towards a Post-Modern Performance Theory," *Theatre Research International*, 14:1 (1989), 71–85.

2. See Sandra Schneiders, "Spirituality in the Academy," *Theological Studies* 50:4 (December, 1989), 691.

3. On the importance of metaphor in the study of spirituality, see Belden Lane, "Language, Metaphor, and Pastoral Theology," *Theology Today* 43:4 (January, 1987), 169–77.

4. Paul Ricoeur, *The Symbolism of Evil* (Boston: Beacon Press, 1967), 15, 161. Tillich argued that "a symbol, as opposed to a sign, *participates* in the truth to which it points." *Theology of Culture* (London: Oxford University Press, 1959), 54–55. James W. Heisig, in his article on "Symbolism" in *The Encyclopedia of Religion*, ed., Mircea Eliade (New York: Macmillan, 1986), vol. 14, p. 204, says "The nature of the symbolic process consists in the fact that one thing, usually concrete and particular, stands for something else, usually abstract and generalized, and becomes a focal point for thoughts and emotions associated with that referent, or a trigger for a set of habits associated with it." Cf. David Tracy, *The Analogical Imagination* (New York: Crossroad, 1981), 205–6, 281–87.

5. Maura Campbell, "Symbol and Reality: Water, Life, Death and Christian Baptism," *Dialogue and Alliance* 4:1 (Spring, 1990), 49. The term "myth," as used in this paper, refers to a sacred story so basic to a community's identity that its truth is assumed without question. A "symbol" is a shorthand form used in signifying the myth, participating in its power. "Ritual" is the means by which the myth is mimed or gestured as representative practice.

6. See Bernard McGinn, "Ocean and Desert as Symbols of Mystical Absorption in the Christian Tradition," *Journal of Religion* 74:2 (April, 1994), 155–81. Andrew Louth, *The Wilderness of God* (Nashville: Abingdon Press, 1997). Conrad Cherry plots the development of an American expression of this impulse in his study of nature symbolism from Jonathan Edwards to Horace Bushnell: *Nature and the Religious Imagination* (Philadelphia: Fortress Press, 1980).

7. For Augustine's Exposition of the Psalms, see *Sancti Aurelii Augustine, Enarrationes in Psalmos*, in Corpus Christianorum, Series Latina (Turnholti: Typographi Brepols Editores Pontificii, 1956), vols. 38–40. Bushnell's essay "Of the Animal Infestations" is found in *Horace Bushnell: Sermons*, ed., Conrad Cherry (New York: Paulist Press, 1985), 175–88.

8. Henry C. McCook, *American Spiders and Their Spinning Work: A Natural History of the Orbweaving Spiders of the United States* (Philadelphia: Academy of Natural Sciences, 1889–1893), 3 vols. McCook also penned an article, "Jonathan Edwards as a

Naturalist," for the *Presbyterian and Reformed Review* (July, 1890), 393–402. For a brief history of spider research and spiders in folklore, myth, and literature, see Paul Hillyard, *The Book of the Spider* (New York: Random House, 1994).

9. Augustine of Hippo, *Enarrationes in Psalmos*, Psalm 89, par. 9, line 3 (Corpus Christianorum, vol. XXXIX, 1248); and Psalm 122, par. 6, lines 32–33 (Corpus Christianorum, vol. XL, 1819).

10. In medieval bestiaries, "the hideous spider" was often presented as the antithesis of the pious and graceful "praying mantis." See Louis Charbonneau-Lassay, *The Bestiary of Christ*, trans. D. M. Dooling (New York: Arkana, 1992), 356–61. See also the entry on "Spider" in J. E. Cirlot, *A Dictionary of Symbols* (New York: Philosophical Library, 1971), 304.

11. Edwards' fascination with nature symbolism—making use of the image of fruit trees and grafting to describe the corporate character of human nature, for example—is examined in David Weddle, "Jonathan Edwards on Men and Trees, and the Problem of Solidarity," *Harvard Theological Review* 67:2 (1974), 155–75. Clyde Holbrook emphasizes the centrality of nature imagery for Edwards, showing how the Connecticut River Valley served as stimulus to his imagination, in *Jonathan Edwards, the Valley and Nature* (Lewisburg: Bucknell University Press, 1987), 15–32.

12. Beside these two, there are several brief references in the manuscript notebooks that made up Edwards' *Images of Divine Things* (compiled between 1728 and 1757). There, for example, he speaks of spiders as "poisonous and hurtful animals . . . [who] incline for the most part to hide themselves or lurk in secret places. Herein they are types of devils and the lusts of men." See *The Works of Jonathan Edwards*, vol. 11: *Typological Writings*, ed. Wallace E. Anderson (New Haven: Yale University Press, 1993), 97.

13. "The Spider Letter," October 31, 1723, in *The Works of Jonathan Edwards*, vol. 6: *Scientific and Philosophical Writings*, ed. Wallace E. Anderson (New Haven: Yale University Press, 1980), 167. This letter drew upon a slightly earlier essay by young Edwards, "On Insects." His stress on the spider's "pleasure" in web-spinning is thoroughly Calvinist. The first question of the Westminster Catechism had insisted that "the chief end of man [and woman] is to glorify God and enjoy him forever."

14. See John Calvin, *Institutes of the Christian Religion*, trans. Ford Lewis Battles (Philadelphia: Westminster Press, 1960), I: vi, 2, 72. Cf. p. 61n. Edwards writes of this "sixth sense" received by the Christian as a "true distinguishing sign" of conversion in his sermon "A Divine and Supernatural Light" (1734) and his *Treatise Concerning the Religious Affections* (1746) in *The Works of Jonathan Edwards*, vol. 2, ed. John E. Smith (New Haven: Yale University Press, 1959), 205–7 and 271–75.

15. Preached at Enfield, July 8, 1741, in *The Works of President Edwards* (New York: S. Converse, 1829), vol. VII, 163–77. The sermon was first preached earlier that summer in Northampton.

16. Perry Miller suggests that with the 1741 Enfield sermon, "Edwards's preaching was America's sudden leap into modernity." *Jonathan Edwards* (Amherst: University of Massachusetts Press, 1981), 147. Cf. J. A. Leo Lemay, "Rhetorical Strategies in *Sinners in the hands of an Angry God* and *Narrative of the Late massacres in Lancaster County*," in Barbara Oberg and Harry Stout, eds., *Benjamin Franklin, Jonathan Edwards, and the Representation of American Culture* (New York: Oxford University Press, 1993), 186–192.

17. Ernst Cassirer, in his *Philosophy of Symbolic Forms* (Berlin, 1923–29), defined the human species as *homo symbolicus*, incurably given to symbol making. Anthropologist Clifford Geertz defines culture itself as "an historically transmitted pattern of meanings embodied in symbols, a system of inherited conceptions expressed in symbolic forms by means of which men [and women] communicate, perpetuate and develop their knowledge about and attitudes toward life." *The Interpretation of Cultures* (New York: Basic Books, 1973), 89. While he seeks to locate symbols within their specific historical

115

contexts, Claude Levi-Strauss looks for a universal structure of the mind that undergirds the symbol-making process. See his *Structural Anthropology* (New York: Basic Books, 1963–76). Mircea Eliade's attention to the pre- and post-verbal character of archetypes, rituals, myths, and symbols in the study of religion remains profoundly important for the study of spirituality. See *Myths, Rites, Symbols: A Mircea Eliade Reader*, ed. Wendell C. Beane and William G. Doty (New York: Harper, 1975), 2 vols.

18. See Henry Nash Smith, *Virgin Land* (Cambridge, Mass.: Harvard University Press, 1950); Leo Marx, *The Machine and the Garden* (London: Oxford University Press, 1964); Alan Trachtenberg, *Brooklyn Bridge: Fact and Symbol* (New York: Oxford University Press, 1965). Cf. Cecil F. Tate, *The Search for a Method in American Studies* (Minneapolis: University of Minnesota Press, 1973).

19. See Giles Gunn, "American Studies as Cultural Criticism," in *The Culture of Criticism and the Criticism of Culture* (New York: Oxford University Press, 1987), 147–72. For a critique of the myth and symbol school, see Bruce Kuklick, "Myth and Symbol in American Studies," *American Quarterly* 24 (October, 1972), 435–50.

20. See George Lipsitz, "Listening to Learn and Learning to Listen: Popular Culture, Cultural Theory, and American Studies," *American Quarterly* 42:4 (December, 1990), 615–36.

    Recent studies that incorporate a cultural studies approach to aspects of American spirituality include Ann Taves, *The Household of Faith: Roman Catholic Devotions in Mid 19th-Century America* (University of Notre Dame Press, 1986), Ann Braude, *Radical Spirits: Spiritualism and Women's Rights in 19th-Century America* (Boston: Beacon Press, 1989), James T. Fisher, *The Catholic Counterculture in America, 1933–1962* (University of North Carolina Press, 1989), Jenny Franchot, *Roads to Rome* (Berkeley: University of California Press, 1994), Patrick Allitt, *Catholic Converts: British and American Intellectuals Turn to Rome* (Ithaca: Cornell University Press, 1997), and Leigh Eric Schmidt, "The Easter Parade: Piety, Fashion, and Display," *Religion and American Culture* 4:2 (Summer, 1994), 135–164.

    William L. Portier offers a critique of cultural studies as applied to the study of spirituality, fearing that its tendency to cultural reductionism may too easily leave God out of the analysis. See his article, "'Catholics in the Promised Land of the Saints' Revisited: Cultural History and Its Irony," *U.S. Catholic Historian* 14 (Fall 1996), 141–154.

21. Similar questions could be asked about Edwards's early Spider Papers as well. The October 31, 1723, date given by Edwards to the finished text of his letter, only recently discovered in the manuscript collection of the New York Historical Society, would indicate that the work was not written (as earlier thought) at the age of twelve, but after Edwards had completed both bachelor's and master's degrees at Harvard. This would mean that the young theologian (and amateur naturalist) was writing about the "delight" he observed in flying spiders about the same time that he met the attractive Sarah Pierpont, beginning to notice the "exceeding sweet delight" that she took in the glories of God while "walking in the fields and groves" around New Haven. See Edwards' notes on Sarah Pierpont, penned in the front of his Greek grammar, in *Jonathan Edwards: Representative Selections* (New York: Hill & Wang, 1962), 56.

22. A major contention over seating in the new church sanctuary had arisen in Northampton in 1738. Contrary to Edwards' wishes, the new pattern of seating ranked members of the congregation according to wealth, giving deference no doubt to those who had contributed most to the new building. Edwards began preaching against "contention and a party spirit," attacking those "seated high in a place that is looked upon hungrily by those that sit round about." See Patricia J. Tracy, *Jonathan Edwards, Pastor: Religion and Society in Eighteenth-Century Northampton* (New York: Hill & Wang, 1980), 129. In that same year, 1738, a separate town house had also been built

in Northampton for secular meetings, indicating still further the extent to which civic concerns were being separated from clerical power.

23. Edwards had been attacking the practice of "bundling," for example. His eventual dismissal from the Northampton Church would occur a decade later in connection with another case of "sexual irregularity" concerning young people secretly reading a mid-wife's manual.

24. "Sinners in the Hands of an Angry God," *The Works of President Edwards*, vol. VII, 170. A major fortification of the town in response to Indian attack had been made in 1690. The nearby village of Southampton would have to be abandoned over the winter of 1748 because of Indian raids. Tracy, Jonathan Edwards, Pastor, 94. The captivity narrative of Mrs. Mary Rowlandson, one of the most widely-read works of this genre in eighteenth-century New England, recounted the experience of a Puritan woman in western Massachusetts who had been captured by Quabaug Indians in 1675 and taken up the Connecticut River Valley. See *The Narrative of the Captivity of Mrs. Mary Rowlandson* (Boston: Houghton Mifflin, 1930), 14 n17.

25. An excellent example of this work can be found in Rowan Williams, *Teresa of Avila* (Harrisburg, PA: Morehouse, 1991). In analyzing Teresa's spirituality, he attends naturally to questions of power that arise from her Jewish background and the investigations of the Inquisition. He considers questions of sexuality and the body, the construction of subjectivity within the cultural milieu of sixteenth-century Spain, the manner in which voices are heard and suppressed, and the polysemous way by which meanings are exchanged from different points of view—all of this without any explicit reference to the methodological paraphernalia of cultural studies as such. He asks these questions intuitively as they arise from the subject he studies.

26. Roland Barthes, *Mythologies* (London: Jonathan Cape, 1972).

27. A. R. Ammons, "Identity," in *The Selected Poems* (New York: W. W. Norton, 1986), 27–28.

9

Why Bodies Matter

A Sociological Reflection on Spirituality and Materiality[1]

MEREDITH B. McGUIRE

*M*any of us were brought up thinking that the spiritual realm is completely set apart from the mundane material realm. Perhaps even opposed to it. Western societies, in recent centuries, have tended to view spirituality and materiality as dichotomous, in tidy binary opposition. Accordingly, those individuals who wanted to enhance their spirituality would have to overcome the burden of their materiality, deny their material urges and concerns, and transcend the limitations (perhaps, even the pollution) of the material body.

I argue, to the contrary, that spirituality fully involves people's material bodies, not just their minds or spirits. The key connection here is not ideas about the body, nor simply moral control of the body and its impulses. Rather, spirituality is closely linked with material human bodies—and not merely in the abstract. I mean *real bodies*—arthritic bodies, athletic bodies, pregnant bodies, malnourished bodies, healthy bodies, and suffering bodies. I mean human bodies that labor and rest, bodies that create and destroy, bodies that nurse babies and bodies that torture the bodies of others, bodies that eat, drink, fart, and sweat. With our real material bodies, we also touch, hear, see, and taste our material worlds.

So why do these real bodies matter? What do they have to do with spirituality or spiritual concerns? As a sociologist, my research has emphasized *lived* religion (i.e., religion as practiced and experienced by ordinary people in the context of their everyday lives). Religion, in this broad sociological sense, consists of how people make sense of their world—the stories out of which they live. Lived religion includes the myriad individual ways by which people put these stories into practice.

Sometimes an individual's lived religion is closely linked with the teachings and practices of an official religion, such as a Christian denomination; that individual uses his or her church's stories and rituals to shape individual experience. There is no necessary connection with official religion, however, because lived religion consists of the actual practices and salient beliefs of people as they live their lives. Thus, many individuals choose to believe and practice elements selected from several different religious "packages," and they often use church-prescribed practices in ways completely unforeseen by the official religion. We must remember that humans are creative agents, not merely over-socialized automatons.

I am using the term "spirituality" to describe the everyday ways those ordinary people attend to their spiritual lives. Some people describe themselves as deeply spiritual, and some devote considerable energy and discipline to their spiritual development. Others consider themselves not very spiritual and not very interested in their spiritual lives. Some find spiritual development and support as committed members of a congregation; others see no connection between their spiritual lives and any organized religious group. Some consciously choose practices to enhance their spirituality; others notice their spiritual practices only retrospectively or when asked to think consciously of them (for instance, in response to a sociologist-interviewer).

Lived religion is constituted by the practices by which people remember, share, enact, adapt, create, and combine the stories out of which they live. And it comes into being through the often-mundane practices by which people transform these meaningful interpretations into everyday action.[2] *Human bodies matter, because those practices*—even interior ones, such as contemplation—*involve people's bodies*, as well as their minds and spirits.

SPIRITUALITY AND EMBODIED PRACTICE

If our conception of religion is too narrow, we fail to comprehend how central our material bodies are in the very practice and experience of religion. All religions engage individuals through concrete practices that involve bodies, as well as minds and spirits. It is easy for us to recognize those bodily practices when we think of, for example, Native American religious experience.[3] In that cultural context, intense bodily involvement in practices of drumming, dancing, vision quests, smoking, feasting, sweating, and chanting is completely consistent with a high level of spiritual development.

Our religious practices and experiences in contemporary American society are similarly linked with our bodies. For instance, think about how you would arrange your physical environment if you wanted to reach a deeply spiritual state of being. Where do you imagine you would be? In a corner of a peaceful garden? In your own room? In an empty chapel? In a processional throng? What postures and gestures do you find conducive to spiritual experience? Kneeling? Standing? Sitting on a chair? Lying prostrate? Sitting in a lotus position? Eyes closed or open? Head bowed or upright? Hands clapping? Folded on your lap? Uplifted? Holding the hands of others? Arms swaying? Body rocking? Body twirling? Breath slow and drawn out? Breath rhythmic, in time with a drum beat or music? What physical connection to others do you imagine? Does a human touch promote your spiritual depth or does it get in the way? Do you need to be alone or in a group? And so on.

My point is that, like the Native American, most of us also experience certain body practices (e.g., postures, movements, ways of focusing our attention) as more conducive to our spiritual experiences than others. Certain visual images, sounds, and smells heighten our spiritual focus and evoke meaningful religious experiences. And our sense of connection with our spiritual community—the others with whom we share collective memories and experiences—is also promoted by concrete body practices, such as a deeply felt embrace. Our sense of connection—our identification with a family, community, or other group—is based on a myriad of remembering practices, involving our bodies and emotions, as well as our thoughts.

Where is memory located? In Western ways of thinking, we tend to identify the memory as an operation solely of the brain. But biological evidence suggests that memory resides in the whole body, such as in nerve connections and in the cells of the immune system.[4] Traveling in Norway a couple of years ago, I smelled fresh-baked brown bread, and it kindled a memory of a wonderful loaf I had bought thirty years earlier in Monnickendam, Holland. The olfactory memory was so vivid that, unbidden, it instantly awoke dozens of related memories—sights, sounds, and tastes of my first experiences in Europe.

Anthropologist Pierre Bourdieu[5] suggests that *all* our senses—not just our physical senses, but also our social senses[6]—are involved in remembering and embodying practices. Thus, our bodies have embedded in them certain learned senses such as a sense of justice, sense of good taste, moral sense, sense of disgust, and common sense. For instance, our sense of disgust is learned (i.e., it is not the same in all cultures, and babies have not yet acquired it). Yet, once learned, that sense causes us to react to a disgusting scene viscerally, for example needing to vomit if we witness torture. If we accept Bourdieu's thesis about embodiment and social practices, then we can understand how senses—not only moral senses but also religious senses—can be acquired and embedded in our bodily experience.

Some sociologists have described religion as a community of memory.[7] Spiritual practices are ways by which individuals engage their socialized senses in the activation of such embodied memory. Bodies matter very much, both in the individual's spiritual life and in the development of a spiritual community. Further in this essay, I develop two examples to show why bodies matter for both individual and collective spirituality.

Religious ritual consists of chains of such embodied practices, each link having the potential to activate deep emotion and social connectedness, as well as spiritual meanings. Because the practices for engaging in ritual are embodied—embedded in the participant's mind/body itself—each "link" in the chain has the potential to evoke social senses related to other links. Through embodied practices, thus, we confirm the reality—not just the symbolic idea—of the ritual act. In this sense, ritual really produces an effect—sometimes privately for the individual practicing it, sometimes for a whole social group engaged in ritual practice.[8] When some people describe ritual as "dead" or "lifeless" or "meaningless," they refer to ritual practices that have been severed from the emotions, social ties, and spiritual experiences for those who merely "go through the motions." But an utterly *dis*embodied religious expression is likely to be equally "lifeless," because it may be relevant only in the believer's thoughts.

Perhaps it is a modern conceit to think that our religious practices are more "civilized" because they are less linked than were pre-modern practices with our human bodies. But any religion that speaks only to the cognitive aspect of adherents' experience (i.e., limited to their beliefs and thoughts) cannot address their emotional needs, their everyday experiences, their whole person. Human embodiment—the quality of having and being intimately identified with our human bodies—is a defining part of our humanity. Thus, all religions address embodiment in some way, as they speak to human concerns about bodily health, suffering, birth, and death. In theory, Christian religions should be particularly aware of human embodiment, because of their central idea of Christ's incarnation and, thus, Christ's humanity. But, due to several different historical developments, many Christian groups today are uncomfortable with any emphasis on human embodiment—especially with religious practices that call attention to the material body or treat it as anything but profane.

Likewise, human material concerns, such as bodily sickness and pain, childbearing and fertility, and need of adequate food, shelter, and protection from adversity, have come to be denigrated as somehow less appropriate matters for religious attention than "purely spiritual" concerns. For example, why did my students and some colleagues laugh when I read them some of the *ex-votos* from a South Texas popular religious shrine: "Thanks for your help in obtaining my truck driver's license," ". . . for my daughter's rapid recovery from surgery," ". . . for getting me a winning lottery ticket," ". . . for the washing machine a neighbor left behind when she moved," and so on. Is it because we consider these material concerns less worthy than some "purely spiritual" requests?

THE HISTORICAL MARGINALIZATION OF EMBODIED PRACTICE

Our tidy dichotomy between sacred and profane (and its corollary, between spiritual and material) is a social construction with a history.[9] Thus, it is amenable to sociological analysis. Unfortunately, most sociological studies of religion have been limited by an overly institutional conception of religion.[10]

Our ways of thinking about religion limit our ability to perceive and to interpret the meaningful social practices which ordinary people use in their religious lives. Many scholars have uncritically accepted, as a given, the definitions of religion's boundaries established in early modern times by official Western religious organizations—specifically, Christian churches. Many surveys, for example, try to tap how individuals practice their religions in the twenty-first century, but the researchers construct their indices from responses to questions about such practices as church attendance, reading scripture, and tithing. Studies limited by such narrow definitional boundaries simply cannot tap the many possible ways that individuals practice their religions outside of the realm of churches, official religious teachings, and church-sanctioned devotions.

Those boundaries are social constructions. Thus, what we think of as "religious" is not inherent in nature and is certainly not an object that we can point to for easy empirical examination. Rather, the definitional boundaries are a human product; they are also clearly ethnocentric. They use Western official religions as a baseline for comparison with other religious expressions, encountered as "Other." Definitional boundaries around what was considered properly "religious" were hotly contested throughout much of Western history, especially during what some historians call the Long Reformation.[11] During those roughly three centuries from late medieval through early modern times, both Catholic and Protestant churches were engaged in intense movements for internal reform and for firm boundaries between themselves and all others. Others were considered highly dangerous—heretics, infidels, witches, pagans.

The outcome of the contest in Western societies defined as marginal and impure most of the ordinary religious practices which previously had linked the spiritual realm with people's pragmatic, quotidian needs, such as healing, fertility, protection from adverse fortune, and obtaining desired material goods. After the definitional boundaries around religion were recast, most Western religions came to privilege belief over practice. This definitional bias is now so taken for granted that we often refer to religions as "creeds" or "faiths."

Historian Peter Burke has likened the contest over religion's boundaries to the images in Bruegel's sixteenth-century painting "The Fight between Carnival and Lent."[12] The painting depicts a busy town square full of people engaged in practices associated with para-liturgical celebrations of these two seasons. In the foreground is a mock jousting match between a sledge-borne figure representing Carnival and a cart-borne figure representing Lent. Carnival is depicted as a fat man, astride a wine barrel and bearing a cooking skewer with remains of a roast pig. He is propelled by a troupe of jesters, musicians, and costumed merrymakers. The opposing figure represents Lent, gaunt and pale, with flatbread and fish, and armed with a baker's paddle. His cart is pulled by a monk and dour old lady with a following of children eating the flatbread. Other contrasts are between the Lenten somber dress, sobriety, and almsgiving, on the one side, and Carnival games, contests, dancing, and mockery, on the other.

According to Burke, before the reformation movements, Carnival and Lent were complementary aspects of the ritual year. The ritual expression of abstinence, sorrow, bodily mortification, and thoughts of death was balanced by periods of ritual practices of consumption, joy, bodily pleasure, and affirmation of life. Carnival and Lent were major moments in a complex series of calendrical rituals that structured people's everyday lives. People participated with their very bodies in the ritual expression of these emotion-laden religious seasons. This structure of time resulted in a diffuseness of the sacred and its interpenetration with the profane.[13] As another historian, Eamon Duffy, exclaimed: "To fifteenth- and early sixteenth-century sensibilities, the liturgical year was spread over twelve months, not six, and *none of it was secular.*"[14]

Pre-modern Christianity was characteristically a material religion. Not only was it closely tied to people's material concerns, such as healing, fertility, and nourishment, but also it was grounded in the material reality of the human body. Thus, before "the Long Reformation" movements, the dramatic binary oppositions between spirit and body, as well as between sacred and profane, simply did not pertain in popular religious belief and practice. Drawing firm boundaries (and, thus, creating the dichotomies that came to be treated as paradigmatic) was a central project of the reformation efforts in both Catholic and Protestant churches.

After a long period of contest, lasting into the eighteenth century in developed parts of Europe and the Americas, Lent essentially won the "fight." Religion came to exclude, as improper, impure, or downright sinful, the entire range of ritual practices that previously addressed people's material concerns and everyday lives. Churches downplayed or eliminated many ritual practices involving the human body, especially the myriad religious practices by which laypersons had tapped religious power for their bodily well-being and material needs.

The churches treated the material world in which the body is, by definition, situated as oppositional—as profane. These dichotomous boundaries between sacred and profane, material and spiritual, were historically constructed. There are compelling reasons why today we should not uncritically accept them in our own definitions of religion and religiosity. I argue that, if we want to better understand the location of religion and religiosity in contemporary society, we should carefully re-examine those areas of life that were defined out—as not pertaining to religion—during that important phase in

Western religious history. This is particularly true of everyday ritual practices, for such practices historically linked people's spiritual lives with their mundane material lives. I hypothesize that, for many individuals in contemporary times, such practices continue to contribute to spirituality, albeit in different patterns from those of late medieval and early modern individuals.

RITUAL PRACTICE: BODILY GROUNDING OF RELIGION

Because people readily thought in bodily images (rather than trying to repress them as many nineteenth- and twentieth-century sensibilities were socialized to do), medieval spirituality actively used images of the divine body.[15] Even the era's mystical spirituality, which attempted to transcend the material world, was remarkable for its physicality.[16] Medieval ritual practice was particularly rich in visual sensations. Sounds, smells, touch, and taste were also used to promote everyday religious experience. Physically sensing the smell of burning beeswax candles, the sound of a church bell, the touch of a fingered cross, could create a desired religious experience. Performing religiously meaningful postures, gestures, and ritual acts, could also produce—physically as well as spiritually—a religious sense of awe and worshipfulness. Bodily sensations produce a confirmation that what one is experiencing is real, not just imaginary. Especially in such an intensely visual cultural setting as medieval society, visual sensations made spiritual experiences vividly real. Sight was linked with insight.

Let me illustrate this characterization of embodied religious practice with my own experience of a few years ago. I need to preface the story by mentioning that I am a practicing Quaker. Although they value mystical experience at least as much as did medieval Catholicism, Quakers nowadays do not promote many body practices—except, perhaps, the use of silence for practicing the presence of God. So, for me, the intensely physical, sensual practices of medieval Christians were a little hard to fathom, until I experienced a few occasions for physically imagining them.

I was living in Salzburg, Austria, during a sabbatical leave, and I was immersed in reading historians' analyses of late medieval religion, especially the religious practices of ordinary people. It was a bitterly cold March night, when I walked across the high hills overlooking the old city of Salzburg to the tenth-century Benedictine abbey to hear an American quartet of women singing the medieval chants of Hildegard of Bingen. Even wearing wool socks and slacks, winter boots and down coat, I never got warm inside the church. The sanctuary was dark, the wooden seats hard, and the stone walls stark. As the singing began, the only sounds were the rise and fall of the chant and an occasional creak of a pew as someone shifted weight. I tried to imagine the nuns of Hildegard's time praying the early morning Hours in such an abbey.

Their voices would not have been so beautiful or studied as those of the performers, but their minds, bodies, and spirits were probably more focused on the ritual act. Their spirituality would have incorporated the sensations they were experiencing, including the numb cold of their fingers, the soaring sounds of the chants punctuated by deep church-bells tolling the hours, the smells of the beeswax candles by which the choir was dimly lit, and the captivating visual image of a brilliant medieval altar triptych—the only brightly lit object in the cavernous church. As the luminous altar painting riveted my attention, I recalled depictions of medieval religious sensibilities that I had read earlier that very week: sight linked with insight; sensual experience linked with spiritual reality; emotions evoked, expressed, and ritually transformed. The result could be an entire mind/body/self engaged in a meaning-filled, deeply *felt* experience.

Medieval religious practice also involved bodily performance and dramatic enactment. People participated in public religious displays (such as processions), not only by watching but also by engaging themselves in enactments of religious meanings. Mystery plays, Passion plays, dramatic enactments of biblical or other religious stories, dances and musical performances, and ritual spectacles (such as the penitential processions of Holy Week) were significant parts of lay religiosity. These regular performances involved participants and spectators in the ritual action through their bodily experiences, making divine power tangibly present. People encountered religious meaning less as thought, and more as sensed, or experienced, in their bodies and emotions. In other words, people encountered religious meaning physically as well as spiritually.

What would sociologists of religion notice or understand differently if we were to re-examine contemporary religious expression with an eye to religious practice (not just belief)? What would we see if, rather than indicators of official religiosity, we looked for ordinary, mundane ritual practices and other everyday lived religious experiences? Specifically, how might we comprehend embodied practices in today's patterns of spirituality? Elsewhere, I have examined how contemporary patterns of spirituality are linked with embodied practices pertaining to health and healing, gender and sexuality, and pragmatic material concerns.[17] Here, I draw two different examples of how contemporary patterns of spirituality involve embodied practices to produce both individual and communal spiritual experience.

EMBODIED PRACTICE AND CONTESTED BOUNDARIES: FOOD AND EATING

One important material aspect that was defined out (as not properly religious) was food—obtaining it, preparing it, serving it, eating it. According to their post-Reformation boundaries delimiting "religion," official religions allowed only spiritual food in their truncated ritual practices.[18] For Catholics and some

Protestants, spiritual food meant Communion elements, while for other Protestants, the only true spiritual food was the Word of God. Other food and eating, even done in the company of the congregation, was denigrated as merely profane or became outright forbidden as licentious. In the battle of Carnival versus Lent, Carnival's feasts became suspect as occasions for sinful excess (e.g., gluttony), while Lent's meals were transformed into "mere" sustenance. Wakes and weddings—previously occasions of considerable community feasting and entertainment, often in the church building itself— were reduced to private and more moderate, sober, and decorous practices. Those few religious meanings of food that were retained were treated as symbols, as metaphors; the ritual practices surrounding food—obtaining it, preparing it, serving it, eating it—no longer counted as "religious" practices.

Thus, when the churches effectively changed the definition of religion, they simultaneously eliminated or greatly truncated most of the ways by which people previously had involved their bodies in spiritual practices and experiences. Food and eating retained only minor vestigial significance as metaphors for spiritual nourishment. The material world, with which human bodies were identified, came to be distinguished dramatically from the spiritual realm. Defined out of official religious practice, festive eating continued to be a part of popular religious expression, for example among ethnic communities celebrating the feast-days of their particular old country patron saints.[19] Unfortunately, sociologists have often viewed popular religious practice as merely vestigial of peasant folkways, doomed to extinction in modern urban life. They have thus failed to observe the fact that many fully acculturated, well-educated, economically comfortable, "modern" persons have found the preparation and eating of special foods and celebration of meaningful feasts to be highly spiritual practices.

Many persons interviewed in my researches have described spiritual practices that valorized mundane domestic materiality, such as the processes of growing, cooking, and eating food. For example, two couples, who incorporated Buddhist meditative practices into their Christian spirituality, described their cooking and eating as "mindful," and as "being fully present."[20] Others described gardening, especially organic gardening, as a spiritual practice.[21] Late modern capitalist societies promote the commodification of time and time-saving body practices, such as buying processed foods to heat-and-serve or consuming "fast" food.[22] It takes considerable effort to buck this tide. For example, what would you have to change in your everyday routine in order simply to eat your meals as a "mindful" practice?

And what about the physical experience of preparing food? Can you imagine cooking as a spiritual practice? My husband and I became aware of what a difference mindful food preparation can make when we visited

Tassajara Zen Center (a remote retreat in the mountains near Carmel, California).[23] Without electricity and labor-saving appliances, the Zen monks made from scratch the hearty soups, hot fresh breads, and tangy salads served to guests, and all was an integral part of their spirituality. The mindful experience also transformed the serving and eating process. Those who were serving the food related to those who were eating with a mutual respect and sense of honor conspicuously lacking, not only in most commercial restaurants, but also in many homes. Those who were eating the food were drawn into the meditative atmosphere. The room was full of quiet conversations, laughter and smiles, but it would have seemed a sacrilege to bolt the food down and race out or to consume it while raucously recounting bad jokes.

When we allow that food preparation and eating can be highly meaningful spiritual practices, we can have a different appreciation of women's religious roles. Elsewhere, I have argued that the same process of reformation boundary creation also effectively marginalized much of women's religious contribution, especially their domestic religious practices.[24] Women's spiritual practices came to be viewed as, at best, unimportant, and at worst, downright dangerous.

Today, however, as church-oriented religious practices seem to be waning, we should not lose sight of the fact that some important everyday practices take place in the home, in the realm of domestic materiality. For example, although Latina Catholics have a lower rate of Mass attendance than Anglo women, they often devote considerable attention to maintaining a home altar and to preparing home rituals and feast-day meals.[25] Similarly we would better understand women's roles in African-American churches if we allowed that the preparation, serving, and eating of church suppers may be as much a religious practice as singing in the choir or preaching. Preparing a church supper is considered to be not just service but ministry.[26] Anthropologist Peter Goldsmith noted the centrality of food as religious expression in a black Pentecostal church on the Georgia coast. He emphasized that it was not only the experience of eating together that produced a sense of community, but indeed the work of preparing food was an important form of religious production and self-definition.[27] In order to fully understand women's lived religion, we need to appreciate their ritual practices centered around the private, domestic, familial sphere (where their roles are likely to be more active and expressive). These private sphere rituals are at least as important as participation in the public, organizational sphere (where women's ritual roles have traditionally been more passive).

Challenging the Western philosophical tradition that valorizes "knowing work," while denigrating "hand work" or practical work, philosopher Lisa Heldke argues that growing, cooking, and eating food should be understood as forms of "bodily knowledge."[28] She explains:

> The knowing involved in making a cake is "contained" not simply "in my head" but in my hands, my wrists, my eyes and nose as well. The phrase "bodily knowledge" is not a metaphor. It is an acknowledgment of the fact that I *know* things literally with my body, that I, "as" my hands, know when the bread dough is sufficiently kneaded.

Heldke suggests that growing and preparing food are thoughtful practices that both use and generate emotional and erotic energy—not merely as incidentals, but as vital parts of the process.[29] Although such embodied practices are not necessarily understood as "spiritual" by all who engage in them, their potential to involve integrally a person's knowing body, knowing mind, sensations, memory, emotions, and spirit is evident.

MAKING MUSIC TOGETHER: SPIRITUAL PRACTICE AND INTERSUBJECTIVITY

The phenomenologist Alfred Schutz used "making music together" as a metaphor for the ways by which people relate deeply with each other, sharing subjective experiences.[30] Although this metaphor could apply equally to a jazz combo as to a religious choir, it gives us a clue about how an embodied spiritual practice (especially singing) can produce religious experience and a sense of community.

I described above my experience of hearing a group of musicians (called the Anonymous Four) singing, *a capella*, the medieval chants written by Hildegard of Bingen. These hymns require considerable vocal interdependence, even though there is no harmony line, because each part is lyrically interwoven such that each singer must come in at the right moment. But there is no conductor, no obvious beat or percussion instrument setting a tempo to coordinate the interdependence. It was fascinating to watch how the singers nonverbally communicated to accomplish this coordination. I noticed how the intonation of a chant was rotated among the four, with the use of rocking and bowing to each other as cues for timing. A clear norm was that no one singer should seem to stand out, either by her volume or virtuosity or badge of leadership. How much more so would this interdependence have been a spiritual value in medieval cloisters!

Perhaps because of my own experience of choral singing, I could easily imagine how such singing together could become a moving spiritual experience that literally effected community. Also, my childhood experiences of my family of seven heartily singing together in the car, around the campfire, beside the piano, are deeply embedded (and profoundly embodied) memories of how singing together both reflects and produces unity and harmony. The physical sensations of producing song, of resonance in one's head, of breathing deeply to sustain long notes, of hearing one's own voice meld in harmony with others'—all deeply sensual, yet potentially also spiritual, experiences.

The uses of time in making music together also produce an experiential sense of togetherness—perhaps even inter-subjective experience. To sing together, we must adjust our timing to fit with others'. Often this means bodily timing, such as our breathing or rhythmic motions like toe-tapping or rocking. Breathing is the epitome of an embodied practice.[31] Although all living persons must breathe and do so automatically, our breathing patterns can be profoundly affected by our social, psychological, and religious practices. Pranayama yoga, for instance, is a physical/spiritual discipline that uses control of the breath to effect other changes in the mind/body/spirit as a whole. Practitioners hold that one pranayama practice involving regular, rhythmic, slow breathing through alternate nostrils literally accomplishes physical, emotional, spiritual, and social balance.

Communal religious settings can produce a resonance of several individuals' experiences and thus an even deeper sense of sharing "inner time."[32] A good example of such intersubjective experience is the several days—and nights—long Navajo chant for healing, through which participants attune their individual experiences toward the culturally valued sense of harmony between the individual, social group, and environment.[33] Thus, such intense intersubjective experience and shared time can accomplish the needed harmony that constitutes healing.

In Western cultures, the very notion of singing in harmony is likewise highly social. If a group is to produce what we have learned culturally to hear as harmony, individual members cannot wildly improvise or deviate from the group's designated chord. Indeed, some groups interpret the accomplishment of musical harmony as a divine approval of their group's social and spiritual harmony. For example, some charismatic prayer groups especially value "singing in tongues" for the sense of harmony that emerges. Because, for them, the actual words (i.e., *glossolalia*) recede in importance (except that they generally believe that the words are God-given), the prayer group collectively attends only to an expressive chord of praise.[34]

A dramatically different spiritual use of making music together is the U. S. revival of Sacred Harp (or "shape note") hymn singing. Unlike most choral singing, a director is not really necessary after singers learn their parts (facilitated by the simple "shape notes" and predictable rhythms). People typically sing every song at the top of their lungs, regardless of the beauty of their voices or the accuracy of their pitch. Singing at the top of one's lungs, sometimes for three or four hours at a time, is a profoundly embodied practice, affecting breathing, hearing, consciousness, and sense of connectedness with other participants. Interestingly, the revival of Sacred Harp singing appears to be occurring outside of church organizations per se, even though it is clearly still a religious expression. Singers at a day-long "sing" may come from a wide range of denominational backgrounds and, thus, experience a kind of temporary community. My impression, however, is that they are bound together by the *practice* of Sacred Harp singing, far more than by *beliefs* held in common. Indeed, several participants have told me that before they could enjoy the singing of these early American hymns, they had to overcome their personal theological objections to the religious ideas that the words expressed.

The temporary community of a Sacred Harp "sing," although real, is far looser than the community expressed by an Appalachian congregation of Primitive Baptists singing together. Consonant with their extreme form of congregational polity, each Primitive Baptist congregation expresses its unique identity, tradition, and localistic sense of community in its very practice of singing together.[35] Congregational singing, which often lasts up to an hour before the official beginning of each worship service, is a central ritual practice in these churches. Each congregation has developed its unique way of singing hymns, and members feel at home only with their own local community's song style. One traditional style that highlights the communal quality of the practice of singing together is "lining out," involving the song-leaders' calling out the words of the next line of a song as the congregation is singing the last of the previous line. For those who identify with it, the practice creates an experiential sense of spiritually elevated community. One church elder whose congregation kept this tradition explained:

> Now when a song is sung with great movement [of the spirit] . . . it will be lined in the same way . . . . *When a song is really sung together, and I'm saying now all of the people in unity and putting forth their voices, being magnified together* . . . it really causes the man who's [lining] it to be as magnified as the people are in singing. And you'll find a difference.[36]

A completely different communal singing together is "The Gospel Hour," a two-hour-long gospel hymn performance and sing-along in an Atlanta (Georgia) gay bar. The performing trio, the Gospel Girls, includes two gay men in drag (wearing sequined gowns, wigs, and makeup), and many of the mostly gay audience sing together enthusiastically in the weekly hymn service. Many (perhaps most) participants in The Gospel Hour experience genuine religious feeling and community. One participant said, "My friends and I call it 'coming to services.'" The simultaneous ritual performance of evangelical Christian gospel hymns and of high drag serves to assert an alternative Christian message for gay worshippers and to symbolically erase gender boundaries exaggerated by the dominant society.[37] Singing gospel hymns together both expresses and partially resolves the dissonance experienced by gays whose religious memory is based on Southern evangelical tradition.

Each of these kinds of spiritual "making music together" reflects and reproduces a different kind of spiritual experience. Such experiences clearly involve the body integrally. Embodied practices, such as singing, tap emotions and memories. Collective embodied practices, such as singing or dancing together, can produce an experiential sense of community and connectedness. Without the full involvement of the material body, religion is likely to be relegated to the realm of cognitions (i.e., beliefs, opinions, theological ideas). Embodied practices—including mundane and seemingly unexceptional activities like singing and preparing a meal—link our materiality as humans and our spirituality.

CONCLUSION

Lived religion is constituted by the practices by which people remember, share, enact, adapt, and create the stories out of which they live. And it is constituted through the practices by which people turn these stories into everyday action. Ordinary material existence—especially the human body—is the very stuff of these meaningful practices. Human bodies matter, because those practices—even interior ones, such as contemplation—involve people's bodies, as well as their minds and spirits. Here I have used, as examples of material embodiment, the spiritual practices of preparing and eating food and of singing together. Material bodies are also linked to spirituality through healing, sexuality and gender, through fertility, childbirth, and nursing, and a myriad other ways.

Our material bodies come to be linked with spirituality through social senses and through the ritual restructuring of our sense of space and time. Bodies matter, because humans are not disembodied spirits. Individuals' religions become *lived* only through involving their bodies, as well as minds, and their emotions, as well as their cognitions. Spirituality is developed by just such embodied practices.

NOTES

1. This essay is adapted from a lecture by the same title, presented on October 8, 2002, as part of the Cassassa Lecture Series at Loyola Marymount University, Los Angeles, California. Thanks to Douglas Burton-Christie, John Coleman, and Jim Spickard for their helpful comments.
2. Robert A. Orsi, "Everyday Miracles: The Study of Lived Religion," in *Lived Religion in America*, ed. D. Hall (Princeton, NJ: Princeton University Press, 1997), 3–21.
3. See James V. Spickard, "Experiencing Religious Rituals: A Schutzian Analysis of Navajo Ceremonies," *Sociological Analysis* 52:2 (1991): 191–204.
4. Bill Moyers' 1993, made-for-television series, "Healing and the Mind," illustrated some of the biophysical bases for these ideas of mind-body linkages. Moyers himself struggles to comprehend and find a language to express the notion of a mind-body unity described by the cellular biologist he was interviewing.

5. Pierre Bourdieu, *Outline of a Theory of Practice* (London: Cambridge University Press, 1977).

6. Following early Christian thinkers, Origen and Gregory of Nyssa, theologian Sarah Coakley posits a parallel, "spiritual senses," in *Powers and Submissions: Spirituality, Philosophy and Gender* (Oxford: Blackwell, 2002).

7. See Danièle Hervieu-Léger, *Religion as a Chain of Memory*, trans. Simon Lee (New Brunswick, NJ: Rutgers University Press, 2000).

8. Catherine Bell, *Ritual Theory, Ritual Practice* (New York: Oxford University Press, 1992).

9. Meredith B. McGuire, "Contested Meanings and Definitional Boundaries: Historicizing the Sociology of Religion," in *Defining Religion: Investigating Boundaries between the Sacred and Secular*, ed. Alfred Greil and David Bromley, Religion and the Social Order, vol. 10 (Amsterdam: JAI, 2002).

10. Virtually all social surveys use institutional notions of religion for ease in pre-coding responses (e.g., the large survey by Barry A. Kosmin and Seymour P. Lachman, *One Nation under God: Religion in Contemporary American Society* [New York: Harmony Books, 1993]). Sociologists who rely heavily upon these and other quantifiable "measures" of religion for their analysis are, similarly, limited; the most flawed of these is Rodney Stark (for example, in *Acts of Faith: Explaining the Human Side of Religion*, written with Roger Finke [Berkeley: University of California Press, 2000]).

11. Edward Muir, *Ritual in Early Modern Europe* (Cambridge: Cambridge University Press, 1997), 6.

12. Peter Burke, *Popular Culture in Early Modern Europe* (London: Temple Smith, 1978).

13. Robert W. Scribner, "Cosmic Order and Daily Life: Sacred and Secular in Pre-Industrial German Society," in *Religion and Society in Early Modern Europe, 1500–1800*, ed. K. von Greyerz (London: George Allen & Unwin, 1984), 17–32; Robert W. Scribner, "Ritual and Popular Religion in Catholic Germany at the Time of the Reformation," *Journal of Ecclesiastical History* 35:1 (1984): 47–77.

14. Eamon Duffy, *The Stripping of the Altars: Traditional Religion in England, c.1400–c.1580* (New Haven: Yale University Press, 1992).

15. Muir, *Ritual in Early Modern Europe*, 149–159.

16. See especially Caroline Walker Bynum, "Women Mystics and Eucharistic Devotion in the Thirteenth Century," *Women's Studies* 11 (1984): 179–214.

17. For spirituality linked to health and healing, see Meredith B. McGuire, "Religion and Healing the Mind/Body/Self," *Social Compass* 43:1 (1996): 101–16. For issues of gender and sexuality, see Meredith B. McGuire, "Gendered Spiritualities," in *Challenging Religion*, eds. James A. Beckford and James T. Richardson (London: Routledge, 2003), and Meredith B. McGuire, "Gendered Spirituality and Quasi-Religious Ritual," *Religion and the Social Order* 4 (1994): 273–87. For further discussion of material concerns, see Meredith B. McGuire, "Toward a Sociology of Spirituality," *Tidsskrift for Kirke, Religion, og Samfunn* 13:2 (2000): 99–111.

18. See Muir, *Ritual in Early Modern Europe* and Caroline Walker Bynum, *Fragmentation and Redemption: Essays on Gender and the Human Body in Medieval Religion* (New York: Zone Books, 1991).

19. Robert Anthony Orsi, *The Madonna of 115th Street: Faith and Community in Italian Harlem, 1880–1950* (New Haven: Yale University Press, 1985).

20. Meredith B. McGuire, *Ritual Healing in Suburban America* (New Brunswick, NJ: Rutgers University Press, 1988).

21. Several religious and quasi-religious groups have made food growing an important religious practice. The Findhorn community in Scotland is a good illustration; U.S. examples include some "back-to-the-land" movements in the twentieth century and some communitarian movements in the eighteenth and nineteenth centuries; Rebecca Gould, "Getting (not Too) Close to Nature: Modern Homesteading as Lived Religion in

America," in *Lived Religion in America: Toward a History of Practice*, ed. David D. Hall (Princeton, NJ: Princeton University Press, 1997), 217–42.

22. Social theorist George Ritzer, a co-founder of the Slow Food movement (see www.slowfood.com), has criticized the advertising and fast food industries for this commodification of time involved in food preparation and eating, the extreme rationalization of food preparation (e.g., standardization of each portion and each ingredient to the point that "fries" are exactly the same in each restaurant of the McDonald's chain), and the resulting destruction of cultural diversity, enjoyment of cooking, and pleasures of tasting well-prepared food; George Ritzer, *The McDonaldization of Society* (Thousand Oaks, CA: Pine Forge Press, 1996).

23. Our reflections on that experience were presented in our paper: Meredith B. McGuire and James V. Spickard, "Feeding Religiosity: Food Preparation and Eating as Religious Practice," presented at the Society for the Scientific Study of Religion (1998).

24. Meredith B. McGuire, "Contested Meanings and Definitional Boundaries: Historicizing the Sociology of Religion," in *Defining Religion: Critical Approaches to Drawing Boundaries Between Sacred and Secular*, eds. Alfred Greil and David Bromley, Religion and the Social Order, vol. 12 (Association for the Sociology of Religion/JAI, 2002).

25. Richard Flores, "Para el Niño Dios: Sociability and Commemorative Sentiment in Popular Religious Practice," in *An Enduring Flame: Studies on Latino Popular Religiosity*, eds. Anthony M. Stevens-Arroyo and Ana María Díaz-Stevens (New York: Bildner Center for Western Hemispheric Studies, 1994), 171–90; Richard Flores, "Gender and the Politics of Location in Popular Religion," unpublished paper presented to a conference of the Program for the Analysis of Religion among Latinos (PARAL), 1996. See also Ana María Díaz-Stevens, "Latino Popular Religiosity and Communitarian Spirituality," unpublished paper presented to a conference of PARAL, 1996.

26. Jualynne E. Dodson and Cheryl Townsend Gilkes, "'There's Nothing Like Church Food': Food and the U.S. Afro-Christian Tradition: Re-Membering Community and Feeding the Embodied S/Spirit(s)," *Journal of the American Academy of Religion* 63:3 (1995): 519–38.

27. Peter Goldsmith, *When I Rise Cryin' Holy: African-American Denominationalism on the Georgia Coast* (New York: AMS Press, 1989).

28. Lisa M. Heldke, "Foodmaking as a Thoughtful Practice," in *Cooking, Eating, Thinking: Transformative Philosophies of Food*, eds. D. W. Curtin and L. M. Heldke (Bloomington, IN: Indiana University Press, 1992), 204–29. Note also the parallels between this concept of bodily knowledge in growing and cooking food and the notion of "somatic modes of attention" which anthropologist Thomas Csordas suggests as a phenomenological understanding of how healing works; Thomas J. Csordas, "Somatic Modes of Attention," *Cultural Anthropology* 8 (1993): 135–56.

29. The transformative power of such energy is linked directly with cooking and eating in the magical realism of Laura Esquival's novel, *Like Water for Chocolate*; the protagonist's emotional and erotic state while cooking a meal is "consumed" and subsequently experienced by all who eat the meal. A very different emotional energy is embodied in the congregation's eating of *Babette's Feast* (film based on a short story by Isak Dinesen). The cook's sacrifice, gratitude, and love transform the dour, ascetic sect's eating into an experience of honest pleasure, communal affection, hope, and joy.

30. Alfred Schutz, "Making Music Together: A Study in Social Relationship," in *Collected Papers II: Studies in Social Theory*, ed. Arvid Brodersen (The Hague: Martinus Nijhoff 1964), 159–78.

31. Marcel Mauss, "Techniques of the Body," *Economy and Society* 2 ([1934] 1973): 70–88.

32. Mary Jo Neitz and James V. Spickard, "Steps Toward a Sociology of Religious Experience: The Theories of Mihaly Czikszentmihalyi and Alfred Schutz," *Sociological Analysis* 51:1 (1990): 15–33.

133

33. James V. Spickard, "Experiencing Religious Rituals: A Schutzian Analysis of Navajo Ceremonies," *Sociological Analysis* 52:2 (1991): 191–204.
34. See Meredith B. McGuire, *Pentecostal Catholics: Power, Charisma, and Order in a Religious Movement* (Philadelphia: Temple University Press, 1982).
35. Beverly Bush Patterson, *The Sound of the Dove: Singing in Appalachian Primitive Baptist Churches* (Urbana: University of Illinois Press, 1995).
36. Quoted in Patterson, *The Sound of the Dove: Singing in Appalachian Primitive Baptist Churches*, 53 (emphasis added).
37. Edward R. Gray and Scott L. Thumma, "The Gospel Hour: Liminality, Identity and Religion in a Gay Bar," in *Contemporary American Religion: An Ethnographic Reader*, ed. P. E. Becker and N. L. Eiesland (Walnut Creek, CA: Altamira, 1997), 79–98.

134

10

The Language of Inner Experience in Christian Mysticism

BERNARD McGINN

"*Inner* experience" at first sounds like a simple enough term, but the more we think about it, the more complex the linguistic and philosophical problems it raises.[1] Anyone who thinks that "experience" has a commonly agreed-on definition should take a look at the way the word has been used in the study of mysticism, let alone in wider philosophical discourse. When we talk about *inner* experience, furthermore, we refer not only to how something is perceived by a subject, but we also seem to suggest that this perception takes place in the absence of observable external sensations or testable stimuli. Recent philosophical and theological reflection on the nature of experience, especially experience of God, emphasizes how important, yet problematic, the issue remains.[2]

The nature of inner experience, specifically the kind of experience many mystics describe, is not what I want to analyze here—if, indeed, it would be possible to say anything meaningful on such a topic in a short compass. What I want to investigate, if only in summary fashion, are the modes of communicating what the verbal marker "inner experience" points to, that is, the ways in which mystics have presented their teachings about God's action in the transformation of consciousness, whether they put it in autobiographical or in more objective forms. Briefly, I want to sketch how mystics' accounts of inner "experience" of God (in itself an abstraction) become concrete and communicable by being fixed within modes of symbolic discourse that are presented as forms of affective intentionality. In other words, insofar as mystical self-consciousness seeks to constitute itself as communicable, if always imperfectly, to others, it often does so by utilizing language that tries to fuse feeling and knowing—*amor ipse intellectus est*, as a well-known expression of medieval Latin Christian mysticism puts it.[3]

There are many particular forms of such discourse created by Christian mystics, in the manner of individual languages like English, German, or Yiddish. But there are also language families and branches, that is, broader groups such as the Indo-European family, and the Germanic branch of this. In the history of Christian mysticism, one of the most important branches of discourse about inner transformation has been the language of the spiritual senses. The purpose of this essay is to investigate aspects of how this language came to be used, modified, and criticized.[4]

ORIGEN AND GREGORY OF NYSSA

At the beginning of his homilies on the Song of Songs, one of the masterpieces of patristic mysticism, Gregory of Nyssa gives advice to the soul seeking God that seems paradoxical to say the least.[5] According to Gregory, in order to master the Song of Songs, the textbook of mysticism, the soul must undergo three inner transformations. The first, moral transformation through following the teaching laid down in the Bible and epitomized in the book of Proverbs, is preliminary. Reading the Song, however, effects two stranger changes. The soul who is addressed as "son" in Proverbs must become the female bride of the Song, just as the feminine Divine Wisdom of Proverbs 8 transmutes into the male Bridegroom, that is, Jesus, the Incarnate Word. This gender reversal is accompanied by a mutation in the language of passion found in the Song. Unrestrained desire is reprehensible in human eros, Gregory holds, but "passion for bodiless things is passionless," so we should love as strongly and as madly as possible in this arena. Gregory explains:

> The most acute physical pleasure (I mean erotic passion) is used as a symbol in the exposition of these teachings [i.e., in the Song]. It teaches us the need for the soul to reach out to the divine nature's invisible beauty and to love it as much as the body is inclined to love what is akin to itself. The soul must transform passion into passionlessness so that when every corporeal affection has been quenched, our mind may seethe with passion for the spirit alone.[6]

What can it mean to "seethe with passionless passion"? Is this merely an example of the kind of obfuscation mystics have often been accused of, or can it be given real significance, at least on the level of affective intentionality? To be sure, "passionless passion" is a good example of the paradoxical language typical of mysticism, but it is not just another paradox.[7] Rather, it is a key to understanding how Christian mystics used the language of the spiritual senses to communicate inner transformation.

Gregory's passionless passion is what we can call a master metaphor for unlocking his understanding of the spiritual senses, which is based upon a "perception of God" (*aisthêsis theou*) as a paradoxical state in which every enjoyment of God is also at one and the same time the kindling of a more intense and unfulfilled desire, and in which every knowing of God is also a grasping of his transcendental unknowability.[8] But the "analogy between the activities of the soul and the sense organs of the body" that Gregory finds in the Song did not originate with him.[9] It was Origen, writing in the mid-third century, who put the spiritual senses at the center of Christian mystical discourse.[10]

The very notion of spiritual senses probably seems as bizarre to us as it was necessary for Origen. We may suppose that Origen and those who followed him created their new language primarily to underline the difference between ordinary affective intentionality and the hidden, mystical consciousness of God's action. This is true, but it is equally important to note that Origen did not think he was creating the language of spiritual senses, but rather that he was finding it—it had been given him in the Bible. Scripture was a book that used human language about God, and in the case of the Song of Songs very physical erotic language—"May he kiss me with the kisses of the mouth" (Sg. 1:1); "Let me see your form, let me hear your voice" (2:14); "The curves of your hips are like jewels, the work of the hands of an artist" (7:1). If the book is to be interpreted as a love song between God and his people, or between God and the individual, as was the case in traditional Jewish and Christian exegesis, what was one to do with such forms of discourse?

For Origen the Bible was nothing less than the divine *Logos* present in the world and offering salvation to fallen souls. Just as a scribe writes down letters that only have meaning to someone who has learned how to read, so too the *Logos* uses the letter of the biblical text to convey the inner message of his saving action. The believer must place him/herself within the text, inscribing its spiritual, mystical meaning on the soul in order to taste its fruit.[11] Hence, for Origen, mystical contact with God (inner experience, if you will), by definition, is achieved in and through the Bible—the text of the Song of Songs becomes the text of the soul's progress toward God. All of Scripture's references to ordinary, external, sense language—most especially the erotic descriptions of the Song of Songs—need to be translated into the language of interior sensation, where the soul comes to feel and to know God the Word. According to Origen, although the spiritual senses were created as the sensorium for each soul in the first (or spiritual) creation, after the fall into the second (or material) world all souls lie dormant, untrained, unable to feel or to know in the true sense. Like newborns, they have to learn how to use their inner senses through the *paideia* of Christian biblical education.

We moderns would be inclined to think that Origen read his division between the inner and the outer senses into Scripture in a form of "eisegesis," but he was convinced that the distinction was right there in the text. Had not Paul spoken about the inner and outer man (e.g., 2 Cor. 4:16)? And didn't Genesis describe a double creation of humanity—once in the image of God (Gen. 1:26), and then as formed "out of the slime of the earth" (Gen. 2:7)? It was on this basis that Origen laid down the fundamental principles for his understanding of what Karl Rahner called "the organs of mystical knowledge."[12] In his *Commentary on the Song of Songs*, Origen put it this way: "The divine scriptures make use of homonyms, that is to say, they use identical terms for describing different things . . . so that you will find the names of the members of the body transferred to those of the soul; or rather the faculties and powers of the soul are to be called its members."[13] Hence, the potent sense language of the Song of Songs, when rightly read, reveals the even more powerful language of inner experience of God—"a sensuality which has nothing sensual in it," as Origen put it.[14]

The spiritual senses as employed by Origen, Gregory of Nyssa, and other patristic and medieval Christian mystics, can be seen as forms of affective intentionality that display their analogical relation to outer sensation through a variety of linguistic transformations. There are, to be sure, many passages in which a more or less direct allegorical translation is at work; that is, a sensory image in the Bible is immediately read as a theological affirmation of some kind. For example, Song 1:2 ("For your breasts are better than wine" LXX and Vg) for Gregory means that the teaching (= milk) of Christ's breasts is superior to all human knowledge (= wine).[15] But the complexity of the transformation process is more evident in the frequent appearance of synesthesia; that is, descriptions within which different or opposing sense perceptions are combined, exchanged, or fused with one another to present a message that is both cognitional and affective. Such presentations are often used as a way to challenge the limits of all language about God.[16] Synesthesia can also employ what can be called "inter-imaginality" (an analogue to inter-textuality), a process by which an image or sense description found in one scriptural text is explained, qualified, and enriched by related images and sensations from another text. A brief example will illustrate the point.

Song of Songs 2:5 in the LXX and the Old Latin version (2:4 in MT) reads, "Strengthen me with perfumes, surround me with apples, for I am *wounded* with love" (italics added).[17] What does it mean to be wounded with love? Origen explains the wound of love first by invoking biblical images of instruments of wounding—arrows and swords—specifically: "He set me as a chosen arrow" (Is. 49:2 LXX), and "Receive God's word from the Spirit to use as a sword" (Eph. 6:17). Both texts emphasize the Christological meaning of the wound—Christ the Word is both arrow and sword, wounding the soul within. To explain what the soul experiences in being wounded in this way, he appeals to the ancient trope of love's bittersweet piercing, so that the text speaks of "the sweet wound of him who is the chosen dart."[18] Origen then explains the emotional effect of the wound by rhetorically inviting the reader to imagine a rich panoply of sensations, cognitions, and unfulfilled longings:

> If there is anyone who has been pierced with the loving spear of his knowledge so that he yearns and longs for him by day and night, can speak of nothing but him, can hear of nothing but him, can think of nothing else, and cannot desire nor long nor hope for anything save him, that soul then truly says, "I have been wounded by charity."[19]

Origen rarely speaks in such passionate terms.

Gregory of Nyssa builds on Origen's reading, but develops it within the framework of his program of "passionless passion." Like Origen, he ties the Song's "wound of love" to Isaiah's "chosen arrow," namely Christ, but he then explores new intellectual and affective dimensions suggested by the image. Doctrinally, Gregory gives it a trinitarian meaning. God the Father, Divine Love, sends his Arrow, the Only-Begotten Son, whose triple point of faith, hope, and charity has been dipped in the Holy Spirit to strike the Bride with "the beautiful wound and sweet blow by which Life penetrates within."[20] To explain further this life-giving wound, he joins verse 5 with its active imagery of wounding to verse 6, a picture of the Bride at rest ("His left hand is under my head and his right hand shall embrace me"). This enables him to fuse the contrary sensations of being in motion and being at rest (something impossible for external sensation), thus illustrating the paradoxical nature of the spiritual sensation in which the loving soul is both at rest in the arms of the Divine Lover and flying forward toward the infinite goal that always eludes her. "Simultaneously," he says, "I am carried away by his act of shooting and I am at rest in the hands of the Bowman."[21]

AUGUSTINE AND GREGORY THE GREAT

Although there were other forms of language used to communicate inner transformation, the appeal to the spiritual senses was a fundamental mode of expression in patristic and medieval mysticism. Most richly developed in the Song of Songs, the spiritual senses, with their many affective and cognitive nuances, were applied across the Bible, that is, throughout the spiritual exegesis that was the central practice of Christian mysticism up to the twelfth century. Augustine of Hippo, who was not interested in a mystical reading of the Song, used the spiritual senses extensively in the *Homilies on the Psalms*, his most important mystical text. The rich language of the Psalms provided Augustine with a gold mine of sense descriptions that, like Origen, he insisted were really about inner experience of God.

Augustine recognized the impossibility of directly speaking about experiencing God. In his *Homily on Psalm 99*, he states that when we begin "to become fully conscious of God" (*pertinescere Deum*) we will experience what to say and what not to say as love grows in us. "Before you had the experience," he continues, "you used to think that you could speak of God. You begin to have the experience, and there you experience that you cannot say what you experience."[22] But Augustine the preacher can use the words of God's Eternal Word, as found in Scripture, in order to invite his hearers to go within themselves and to learn to participate in such experience. As a good Platonist, at least in part, Augustine can employ the language of spiritual vision in his teaching, but he also mingles vision-language with that of the other senses, especially touching, in what often seems to be a confusing way, precisely to underscore the impossibility of really describing inner contact with God. For instance, one often hears the experience of God that he and Monica shared at Ostia recounted in book 9 of the *Confessions* described as the "Vision of Ostia." But if you read the text, you will discover that they *see* nothing of God. Rather, the account is pervaded with the language of affective intentionality, and uses the polarity of hearing and silence, and the tactile images of touching and being struck to convey its message.[23] In his commentary on Psalm 41, a favorite mystical psalm, Augustine employs the image of the deer thirsting for water to construct a mini-treatise on mystical desire. He begins with vision. We seek God in order "to see, if possible, something of him." But that seeing is not external vision; it is first interior, moving within, and then transcendent, moving above. As Augustine begins to interpret the movement above revealed in the Psalm, the inner senses of hearing, smell, and touch emerge ever more strongly. For example, describing how the soul ascends from the tabernacle of the church to the heavenly house of God (Ps. 41:4), he states, "The soul . . . is led to the house of God by following a certain sweetness, an indescribable interior hidden pleasure. It is as if a musical instrument sweetly sounded from the house of God, and while walking in the tabernacle she heard the interior sound, and, led by its sweetness, followed it."[24] The goal, however, is described in terms of pure intellectual vision: "With the fine point of the mind we are able to gaze upon something that is unchangeable, though hastily and in part."[25] Gregory the Great, the other major mystical writer of the Latin patristic tradition, also employed the language of the spiritual senses.[26] Gregory is important to note here, if only because he shows us that negative spiritual sensation, as well as the positive perceptions and emotions emphasized thus far, play a role in the communication of mystical transformation. Gregory's mysticism is primarily conveyed in his sprawling *Moral Commentary on Job*, a book that modern critics unfamiliar with spiritual exegesis have sometimes dismissed as being about everything except Job. The many descriptions in the biblical text of the anguish and alienation that Job suffered allow Gregory to emphasize that inner sensations of dread and terror are integral to mysticism. In commenting on the texts (e.g., 4:13 and 33:15) in which Job encounters God in a "night vision" (*visio nocturna*),[27] Gregory shows how the dread of the sinful soul who meets the uncircumscribable divine light in the dark of night is a necessary part of what the pope called "the mystical understanding of intimate contemplation."[28]

Origen, Gregory of Nyssa, Augustine, and Gregory the Great all felt the need, to a greater or lesser degree, to emphasize the distinction between outer sensory experience and the inner workings of the spiritual senses dynamized in Bible study. When we look at many later medieval mystics, however, we begin to see the sharp distinction between the two sensoria, the outer and the inner, lessen and sometimes even vanish, so that transformational consciousness of God, although still a mystery beyond human comprehension, is described as being directly felt in what Bernard of Clairvaux called "the book of experience" (*liber experientiae*). In other words, there is a movement from mystical language of the spiritual senses to mystical language of embodied sensation.

BERNARD OF CLAIRVAUX

The parallel between the *liber naturae* and the *liber scripturae* was an ancient topos known to both Jews and Christians, as was the motif of the *liber vitae* cited in Psalm 69:29 and Apocalypse 20:12. Bernard was the first, to my knowledge, to use the expression *liber experientiae*.[29] This coinage reveals a significant shift in Christian mysticism that became evident in the twelfth century and grew ever stronger in the late Middle Ages—an emphasis on the need for experiential confirmation of the message found in the *liber scripturae* and a heightened concern for the analysis of states of inner experience. In his *Sermons on the Song of Songs*, after prefacing two homilies explaining the title of the book, Bernard gets down to work in Sermon 3, beginning his analysis of the personal meaning of the Song with the announcement, "*Hodie legimus in libro experientiae*" ("Today we read in the book of experience").[30] Later, in Sermon 22, he insists, "In matters of this kind [i.e., mystical teaching], understanding can only follow where experience leads."[31]

Bernard's repeated appeal to the "book of experience" is not meant to lessen the role of the book of Scripture. What Bernard is doing is asking his hearers/readers to place themselves in a new intertextual situation in which the book of Scripture and the book of inner experience are meant to illuminate each other, leading the soul (i.e., the Bride of the Song) into an ever-deeper love bond with the Divine Bridegroom.[32] Bernard would have been horrified if someone interpreted him as valuing the book of experience over the Bible, or as giving personal experience independent status. As he puts it in a Lenten sermon: "Follow the judgment of faith and not your own experience, because faith is true but experience is false."[33] Nevertheless, guided by the meaning of the love relation with God revealed in the Song of Songs, the soul's inner life gradually comes to be formed not by its own fallen interiority (*cupiditas*), but by the communication of divine *caritas*. The Bride's progress toward God is a journey that is both personal (i.e., the story of developing experience of the individual) and exegetical (achieved through ever deeper appropriation of the meaning of the Song).[34]

In describing how inner experience is reformed and transformed by *caritas* Bernard makes ample use of the spiritual senses, though he rarely theorizes about their nature.[35] Rather, Bernard portrays how the inner senses function as forms of affective intentionality through a lush rhetorical style that often synesthetically mingles and melds different sense descriptions. Like most Christian mystics, contemplative seeing with "the eyes that are the internal senses and affections" is important for him, but Bernard rarely paints pictures for the inner eye, because he insists that true vision will come only in heaven. More frequently, he invokes hearing, smelling, tasting, and touching to describe the soul's relation to God. In our fallen condition, we must begin by hearing the word of God, both without and within.[36] We can also be attracted to deeper experience of God by smell, as Bernard shows by his odd interpretation of Psalm 44:2 ("My heart belched forth a good word") as our smelling of the "good odor" sent forth from the mouths of the scriptural authors who have tasted deeply of God, such as Moses, David, and Paul.[37] Bernard prefers the language of tasting and touching to describe the ultimate contact with God, even visionary contact, possible in this life. For example, in Sermon 28, he uses Mary Magdalene, who was forbidden to physically touch the Risen Christ (Jn. 20:17), as a model for the mystical soul who can only touch him "by desire not by hand, by wish not by eye, by faith not by senses." Christ promises that a soul who has grown beautiful in the life of faith will be able to touch Christ's "deep and mystical breast." "You will touch," he writes, "with the hand of faith, the finger of desire, the embrace of devotion; you will touch with the eye of the mind." He concludes with a typical alliterative flourish that is meant to reverentially hide the inner experience of God found in the Song at the very moment that it seems to reveal it through alliterative expressivity. Bernard states, *"Talem talis taliterque tange et dic: Dilectus meus candidus et rubicundus, electus e millibus"* (Sg. 5:10); that is, "Let such a Bride touch such a Groom in such a way and say: 'My Beloved is fair and ruddy, chosen from thousands.'"[38]

Though Bernard adhered in principle to the traditional distinction between inner and outer sensation, his emphasis on the importance of the book of experience, the emotive power of his rhetoric, and even the core of his Christology, all served to undermine the separation that Origen, Gregory of Nyssa, Augustine, and others had created between inner and outer sensation. These authors taught that one must turn away from the outer person and external sensation in order to cultivate the inner self and the dormant spiritual senses. Bernard, on the other hand, daringly affirmed that the way back to God from the depths of our fallen "land of unlikeness" (*regio dissimilitudinis*) has to begin with what he called *amor carnalis Christi* ("carnal love of Christ"). As he put it in the fifty-sixth of the *Sermons on the Song of Songs*: "It is our sins, not our bodies, that stand in the way" of experiencing God.[39]

According to Bernard, we humans were created so that we could know and worship God, pure Spirit, through the use of our fleshly senses. But due to

Adam's fall we became trapped in the flesh so we can no longer use the body and its senses as a means to God. The Incarnate Word, therefore, needed to take on flesh in order to save creatures who no longer could use flesh to attain spirit. "He offered his flesh to those who knew flesh so that through it they might come to know spirit too," as Bernard put it.[40] Thus, grace begins the way back to God by inspiring us with "carnal love of Christ," that is, the fleshly emotion that draws us to the figure of Jesus of Nazareth, who was born, lived, and died for his fellow humans—"the man for others," in the description of some modern theologians. Bernard's mystical itinerary, at least in theory, ends in the higher levels of purely spiritual love, where the spiritual senses are active, but it must begin on the carnal level. Suppose, however, that it were possible to fuse the carnal and the spiritual levels?

THE LATER MEDIEVAL TRADITION: HADEWIJCH OF ANTWERP

This is precisely what seems to have been the case for a number of late medieval mystics, especially women, who do not make use of the distinction between inner and outer sensation and who present their consciousness of contact with God in a fully embodied, if also transformative, manner. This shift in the description of mystical experience is a complex phenomenon. The fact that it is characteristic of women (though also found in some men) invites gender analysis—and this has not been lacking.[41] It is important, however, not to forget the role of the changing relation between the book of Scripture and the book of experience, though this too has gender implications. If Bernard of Clairvaux stressed the mutuality of the two books within an overarching strategy of the ultimate authority of the Bible, the *liber experientiae* takes on a larger and larger role in the accounts of many thirteenth- and fourteenth-century mystics. That is to say, that personal accounts of visions and ecstasies, quasi-autobiographical or not, come to predominate over exegesis of Scripture, especially among women. No woman mystic, to my knowledge, ever denied the authority of Scripture, but since women could not be scriptural commentators *ex officio* the way that monks and friars could, they use the *liber scripturae* in a different way—by way of illustration and secondary confirmation, not as the essential context of their presentation of mystical consciousness. However, some male mystics, for example, the Dominican Henry Suso (1295–1366), although they were trained as theologians and exegetes, also used the Bible in a similar fashion. This is evident in Suso's mystical treatises, and especially in his auto-hagiographical *Life of the Servant*.

Here I can offer only one example of this new embodied mystical language in which experiencing the Divine Lover is no longer portrayed in a way that stresses the separation between the outer and inner organs of affective intentionality. Hadewijch of Antwerp, a Dutch beguine generally thought to have flourished around the mid-thirteenth century,[42] has left us a wide-range of mystical texts—poems, visions, and letters.[43] These are cast in direct experiential language, both when she speaks of the ecstatic fruition (*ghebruken*) and delight (*ghenoegen*) of love, and also when she addresses the negative side of the encounter with God: what she describes as madness (*orewoet*), unfaith (*ontrouwe*), despair (*onthope*), and sense of estrangement that is the lot of those who pursue divine *minne* with absolute dedication—unrestrained, excessive, totally uncompromising.[44] "More multitudinous than the stars of heaven are the griefs of *minne*," as she put it in one of her *Poems in Stanzas*.[45]

A noted example of Hadewijch's presentation of mystical consciousness occurs in her seventh vision which took place at dawn one Pentecost.[46] It is no accident that this vision is eucharistic in content, since the physical reception of Christ's Body and Blood in communion often plays a central role in the new embodied language of sensation. In this showing, Hadewijch describes herself as waiting in a state of extreme physical disturbance. "My heart and veins," she writes, "and all my limbs trembled and quivered with eager desire, and, as often occurred with me, such madness and fear beset my mind that it seemed to me I did not content my Beloved, and that my Beloved did not fulfill my desire, so that dying I must go mad, and going mad I must die." Her desire for "full fruition" of the Beloved comes in a vision in which Christ first appears as a child giving her communion. But as she receives the Body and Blood, he transmutes into the form of "a human being and a man, wonderful, and beautiful, with a glorious face." The text continues with a powerful, to some even shocking, account of physical uniting: "After that he came himself to me, took me entirely in his arms, and pressed me to him; and all my members felt his in full felicity, in accordance with the desire of my heart and my humanity. So I was outwardly satisfied and fully transported." It is important to note that this corporeal uniting leads on to an even higher form of interior uniting in which Hadewijch states, "It was to me as if we were one without difference," but she closes by emphasizing the importance of the physical union in which the Bridegroom and Bride "each wholly receive the other in all full satisfaction of the sight, the hearing, and the passing away of the one in the other."

Such language, which might seem nothing more than humanly erotic to us, need not have had the same connotations for Hadewijch and her audience. But it is certainly different from what we have seen in Origen, Gregory, and the other adherents of the classic doctrine of the spiritual senses. As Gordon Rudy puts it in discussing Hadewijch, "She talks about the body in order to talk about God."[47] Hadewijch of Antwerp and the other late medieval mystics who used such direct, "untranslated," erotic language to describe their encounter with God would have agreed with Simone Weil, who once wrote, "To reproach mystics with loving God by means of the faculty of sexual love is as though one were to reproach a painter with making pictures by means of colors composed of material substances. We haven't anything else with which to love."[48] My point is that the Origenist tradition of spiritual senses thought that we did.

This new form of embodied language about God was controversial. Among its opponents was David of Augsburg, a Franciscan active in the mid-thirteenth century, the author of a treatise whose title testifies to his adherence to the traditional distinction between the inner and the outer in Christian mysticism—*The Composition of the Interior and Exterior Man according to the Triple State of Beginners, Proficient and Perfect*.[49] This popular work, a handbook on the states of prayer and the ascetical and mystical life, expresses a marked reserve about visions, revelations, and ecstasies. "The less we meddle in such things," David asserts, "the less opportunity there will be for deception." What David was particularly worried about was visions involving embracing, kissing, and, as he puts it, "being caressed by other less decent deeds and acts, so that just as the interior spirit is consoled by Christ or Mary, so too the exterior flesh is caressed in a physical way and carnally consoled by a sensation of delight fitted to it."[50] Even those who favored the new embodied sensation of God sometimes felt uncomfortable with it. Several generations after David, the Dominican visionary Margaret Ebner (c. 1291–1351) became concerned that the visitations of her Divine Lover were so strong that her senses would be overpowered or destroyed. Christ reassured her by telling her, "I am no robber of the senses; I am the enlightener of the senses" (i.e., the outer senses).[51]

This is not the place to pursue the implications and development of the new embodied presentation of mystical consciousness.[52] What I want to look at before concluding this overview is a reaction against all mystical language involving the senses, both the traditional discourse of the spiritual senses and the new embodied form.

MEISTER ECKHART

Meister Eckhart, as is well known, had little interest in visions, auditions, and ecstasies, though he never denied they could have a role in the path to God. What he was concerned about was that these special states of consciousness could come to be considered "ways to God." According to the German Dominican, "Whoever is seeking God in ways is finding ways and losing God, who in ways is hidden."[53] Eckhart does not use the language of the spiritual senses to describe contact with the hidden divinity. Rather, as Denys Turner put it, Eckhart is "relentlessly anti-experientialist,"[54] that is, he believes that the desire for any kind of mystical "experience," either exterior or interior, is misleading. To attain God, we must free ourselves from ourselves, that is, from the self insofar as it is a created particularity, through the process of dispossession of all cognition and affection, exterior and interior, that he calls "detaching" or "cutting-off" (*abscheiden*), "letting-go" (*sich lassen*), "dis-imaging" (*entbilden*), and "un-becoming" (*entwerden*).[55]

Eckhart mounts a concerted attack not only on all forms of psychologizing (i.e., describing and/or analyzing experiences of inwardness), but also on the use of the language of sensation itself. He is not only speculatively apophatic in his approach to God, but also pragmatically so—for him there is no distinction between the two aspects. The truly poor, or detached, person knows nothing, wants nothing, has nothing—"He should be so free of all knowing," Eckhart states, "that he does not know, or experience, or grasp that God lives in him."[56] Such detachment is not the psychological condition of being without desire; it is negation of all psychology.[57] Eckhart's mysticism is one of resolute interiority, but an interiority that negates experience rather than seeking to transform it.

Eckhart's attack on the language of experience is evident in a cycle of four sermons he preached during the Christmas season on the theme of the Birth of the Word in the soul. These sermons, which appear to date from the first years of the fourteenth century, are a systematic presentation of the essence of his teaching.[58] The cycle explores three basic themes: where the birth of the Word takes place; what our response should be to this birth; and the profit that comes from the birth. Under the second category Eckhart returns again and again to his insistence that one must go within, "shunning and freeing oneself from all thoughts, words, and deeds . . . , maintaining a God-receptive attitude," as the only "way" to prepare the soul for the birth that comes from God's action, not ours.[59] He recognizes that the ecstasies and states of absorption described both in the Bible and tradition may be helpful in reaching the total interiority and passivity that he counsels, but attaining the fused identity of the *grunt*, or ground, in which there is no distinction between God and soul, the place from whence the Word is born, is independent of ecstasy and non-ecstasy insofar as these are characteristics of created reality and imply a difference between God's ground and the soul's ground. For Eckhart the state of existing "without a why" is a "not-knowing that draws the soul into amazement and keeps her on the hunt."[60] Later in the first sermon he summarizes: "Though it may be called an unknowing, an uncomprehending, it still has more within it than in all knowing and comprehending outside it, for this unknowing lures and draws you from all that is known, and from yourself."[61]

In the third sermon Eckhart discusses this passive unknowing in detail, responding to objections. He recognizes, of course, that it is possible to have what would be called inner experiences of God. "Your being aware of him," he states, "is not in your power, but in his. When it suits him he shows himself, and he can hide when he wishes."[62] But it is obvious that these experiences are unessential and secondary to the "pure unknowing and forgetting of self and creatures" that is the core of his mysticism.[63]

CONCLUSION

Eckhart's critique of the language of experience is found in a different form in the mysticism of his contemporary, Marguerite Porete (d. 1310). It was also taken up by later Christian mystics, including the author of the *Cloud of Unknowing* (c. 1380), and John of the Cross in the sixteenth century. This powerful tradition of anti-experientialism demonstrates that the language of inner experience, whether conceived of according to the topos of the spiritual senses, or of the embodied sensorium combining outer and inner feeling, while a major trajectory in the history of Christian mysticism, was also one fraught with problems. This can serve to remind us that to speak of inner experience of God is just another example of the impossible but necessary task of all speaking about the unknowable God—an inherently contradictory activity, as mystics of many traditions have insisted. Nevertheless, mystics continue to strive to communicate how God has come to them, changed them, and commissioned them to invite others to a similar transformation. It is in the critical interplay among the various forms of mystical expression that a good part of its message about God begins to reveal itself to those willing to listen.

NOTES

1. This essay was prepared for the conference, "The Religious Experience: Inner and Outer Forms," held at the Mishkenot Sha'ananim Center in Jerusalem in June 2001. I wish to thank the conference organizers for the opportunity to present my thoughts and the participants for their helpful comments and suggestions.
2. See, for example, William J. Hoye, *Gotteserfahrung? Klärung eines Grundbegriffes der gegenwärtigen Theologie* (Zürich: Benziger, 1993); Caroline Franks Davis, *The Evidential Force of Religious Experience* (Oxford: Clarendon Press, 1999); and Louis Roy, *Transcendent Experiences: Phenomenology and Critique* (Toronto: University of Toronto Press, 2001).
3. This essay will not attempt to lay out a theory of affective intentionality, either in historical terms (e.g., by reflection on the meaning of a phrase like *amor ipse intellectus est*) or in a contemporary vein. Several recent contributions, however, have explored the usefulness of the category for the study of mysticism; see, for example, Andrew Tallon, "The Heart in Rahner's Philosophy of Mysticism," *Theological Studies* 53(1992):700–728; and David B. Perrin, "Mysticism and Art. The Importance of Affective Reception," *Église et théologie* 27(1996):47–70. These essays appeal to the thought of Paul Ricoeur, *Fallible Man* (Chicago: Regnery, 1965), specifically chap. 4, "Affective Fragility."
4. Though much has been written on the spiritual senses, especially with regard to individual figures, there is no in-depth account of this central thread in the history of Christian mysticism. For a survey, see Mariette Canévet, "Sens spirituel," *Dictionnaire de spiritualité* 14 (Paris: Beauchesne, 1989):598–617. A classic essay is that of Karl Rahner, "Le doctrine des 'sens spirituels' au Moyen Age, en particulier chez saint

Bonaventure," *Revue d'ascétique et de mystique* 14 (1933):263–99, available in an abridged form in Karl Rahner, *Theological Investigations*, vol. 16 (New York: Seabury, 1979), 104–34. A rather different perspective was presented by Hans Urs von Balthasar, *The Glory of the Lord. A Theological Aesthetics. Vol. I: Seeing the Form* (San Francisco-New York: Ignatius-Crossroad, 1982), 365–80. For a comparison, see Stephen Fields, "Balthasar and Rahner on the Spiritual Senses," *Theological Studies* 57 (1996):224–41. An original treatment covering the period through the mid-fourteenth century can be found in Gordon Rudy, *Mystical Language of Sensation in the Later Middle Ages* published in the series Studies in Medieval History and Culture (Routledge, 2002).

5. The Greek text can be found in *Gregorii Nysseni In Canticum Canticorum*, ed. Hermann Langerbeck (Leiden: Brill, 1960). For the passage discussed here, see Homily 1 (ed., 14–42). There is an English translation by Casimir McCambley, OCSO, *Saint Gregory of Nyssa. Commentary on the Song of Songs* (Brookline: Hellenic College Press, 1987).

6. *In Canticum Canticorum*, Hom. 1 (ed. Langerbeck, 27.5–15; trans., 49).

7. On the role of paradox in mystical discourse, see Steven T. Katz, "Mysticism and the Interpretation of Sacred Scripture," in *Mysticism and Sacred Scripture*, ed. Steven T. Katz (Oxford: Oxford University Press, 2000), 41–51.

8. Gregory's emphasis on the "endless pursuit" (*epektasis*) of God has been much studied. A foundational work remains that of Jean Daniélou, *Platonisme et théologie mystique. Doctrine spirituelle de Saint Grégoire de Nysse* (Paris: Aubier, 1944).

9. On the analogy and Gregory's preliminary illustrations of how to read the physical language of the Song of Songs in terms of the spiritual senses, see *In Canticum Canticorum*, Hom. 1.3 (ed. Langerbeck, 34–36; trans., 52–54).

10. Karl Rahner was the first to emphasize the importance of Origen's role in the history of the spiritual senses in his article, "Le début d'une doctrine des cinq sens spirituels chez Origène," *Revue d'ascetique et de mystique* 13 (1932):112–45. A shorter version of this essay is available in English, "The 'Spiritual Senses' according to Origen," in Karl Rahner, *Theological Investigations*, vol. 16 (New York: Seabury, 1979), 81–103. For a recent account of Origen's views, see Rudy, *Mystical Language of Sensation*, chap. 2. On Origen's mysticism in general, Bernard McGinn, *The Foundations of Mysticism. Origins to the Fifth Century* (New York: Crossroad, 1991), 108–30.

11. This point has been emphasized by Karen Jo Torjesen, *Hermeneutical Procedure and Theological Method in Origen's Exegesis* (Berlin: De Gruyter, 1986), 39–41, and 130–38.

12. Rahner, "The 'Spiritual Senses' according to Origen," 97.

13. Origen, *Commentarium in Canticum Canticorum*, ed. W. A. Baehrens, in vol. VIII of *Origenes Werke. Die griechischen christlichen Schriftsteller* (Leipzig: Hinrichs, 1925), prologus, 64.16–65.19. I will use the translation of R. P. Lawson, *Origen. The Song of Songs. Commentary and Homilies* (Westminster, MD: Newman, 1957), 26–27.

14. Origen, *Contra Celsum* 1.48, in *Origenes Werke*, vol. 1, 98.20–22.

15. *In Canticum Canticorum*, Hom. 1.3 (ed. Langerbeck, 35; trans., 52).

16. Rudy, *Mystical Language of Sensation*, chap. 1, has useful reflections on the apophatic character of such synesthetic language.

17. For a comparison of the interpretation of this verse across four commentators (Origen, Gregory, Bernard of Clairvaux, and William of Saint Thierry), see Bernard McGinn, "Tropics of Desire: Mystical Interpretations of the Song of Songs," in *That Others May Know and Love. Essays in Honor of Zachary Hayes, OFM*, ed. Michael F. Cusato and F. Edward Coughlin (St. Bonaventure: Franciscan Institute Publications, 1997), 133–58.

18. On the history of this theme in Greek literature and philosophy, see Anne Carson, *EROS the Bittersweet. An Essay* (Princeton: Princeton University Press, 1986).

19. Origen, *Comment. in Cant. Cant.* (ed. Baehrens, 194.6–13; trans., 198).

20. Gregory of Nyssa, *In Canticum Canticorum*, Hom. 4 (ed. Langerbeck, 128; trans., 103–4).

21. Gregory, *In Canticum Canticorum*, Hom. 4 (ed. Langerbeck, 129; trans., 104).

22. Augustine, *Enarratio in Psalmum* (hereafter *En. in Ps.*) 99.6, in *Patrologia Latina* (hereafter *PL*), ed. J.-P. Migne (Paris, 1844–64), Vol. 37:1274.

23. See *Confessiones* 9.10 (*PL* 32:773–75), and the discussion in McGinn, *The Foundations of Mysticism*, 234–35, and the literature cited there.

24. *En. in Ps.* 41.9 (*PL* 36:470).

25. *En. in Ps.* 41.10 (*PL* 36:471).

26. For brief remarks on Gregory on the spiritual senses, see Bernard McGinn, *The Growth of Mysticism. Gregory the Great through the Twelfth Century* (New York: Crossroad, 1994), 64–65.

27. On these passages from Job, see Gregory the Great, *Moralia in Iob* 5.30.53, and 23.20.37–21.43, as found in *Sancti Gregorii Magni: Moralia in Iob*, ed. Marcus Adriaen, 3 vols. (Turnholt: Brepols, 1979–86; CC 143, 143A, and 143B) 1:254–55, and 3:1171–76.

28. *Sancti Gregorii Magni. Homiliae in Hiezechihelem Prophetam*, ed. Marcus Adriaen (Turnholt: Brepols, 1971; CC 142), Hom. 2.3.18 (ed., 250).

29. On Bernard's mysticism and the role of experience, see McGinn, *The Growth of Mysticism*, chap. 5. For the book topos in the Middle Ages, see Ernst Robert Curtius, *European Literature and the Latin Middle Ages* (New York: Harper & Row, 1963), chap. 16; and Eric Jager, *The Book of the Heart* (Chicago: University of Chicago Press, 2000), who discusses the *liber experientiae* on pp. 60–64. For more on the *liber experientiae*, see Jean Leclercq, "Aspects spirituels de la symbolique du livre au XII siècle," *L'Homme devant Dieu. Mélanges offerts au Père Henri de Lubac*, 3 vols. (Paris: Aubier, 1964) 2:63–72.

30. See *Sermones super Cantica* 3.1 (hereafter *SC*), in *Sancti Bernardi Opera*, ed. Jean Leclercq et al. (Rome: Editiones Cistercienses, 1957–77) 1:14.

31. *SC* 22.2 (*Opera* 1:130). For some other appeals to the necessity of *experientia/experimentum*, see, for example, *SC* 4.1, 9.3–7, 21.4–5, 31.4, 50.6, 52.1–2, 69.6–7, 84.6–7.

32. See McGinn, *The Growth of Mysticism*, 185–90.

33. *Sermones in Quadragesima* 5.5 (*Opera* 4:374).

34. A good illustration of this can be found in *SC* 23, in which the topography of three locations of the encounter with the Divine Lover (*hortus* of Sg. 5:1; *cellaria* of Sg. 1:3, and the *cubiculum* of Sg. 3:4) is read both as the three senses of the biblical text and the stages of the introvertive journey (see *Opera* 1:140–49).

35. There are three brief theoretical discussions; see *Sermones de diversis* 10.2–4, and 116 (*Opera* 6.1:122–24, and 393–94), and *Sententia* 3.73 (*Opera* 6.2:108–12). For a fuller account of Bernard's teaching on the spiritual senses, see Rudy, *Mystical Language of Sensation*, chap. 3.

36. For example, *SC* 28.7, and 53.2 (*Opera* 1:197, and 2:96–97).

37. See *SC* 67.4–7 (*Opera* 2:190–93).

38. *SC* 28.9–10 (*Opera* 1:198–99).

39. *SC* 56.3 (*Opera* 2:116).

40. *SC* 6.3 (*Opera* 1:27).

41. See, for example, Caroline Walker Bynum, *Holy Feast and Holy Fast: The Religious Significance of Food to Medieval Women* (Berkeley: University of California Press, 1987); and John Giles Milhaven, *Hadewijch and Her Sisters: Other Ways of Knowing and Loving* (Albany: State University of New York Press, 1993).

42. A case for dating Hadewijch in the early fourteenth century has recently been put forward by Wybren Scheepsma, "Hadewijch und die 'Limburgse sermoenen.' Überlegungen zu Datierung, Identität und Authentizität," *Deutsche Mystik im*

149

abendländischen Zusammenhang. Neu erscholossene Texte, neue methodische Anszätze, neue theoretische Konzepte, ed. Walter Haug and Wolfram Schneider-Lastin (Tübingen: Niemeyer, 2000), 653–82.

43. For introductions to Hadewijch's mysticism, see Kurt Ruh, *Geschichte der abendländische Mystik. Band II. Frauenmystik und Franziskanische Mystik der Frühzeit* (Munich: Beck, 1993), 160–232; and Bernard McGinn, *The Flowering of Mysticism. Men and Women in the New Mysticism (1200–1350)* (New York: Crossroad, 1998), 200–222.

44. On Hadewijch's embodied form of spiritual sensation, see especially Rudy, *Mystical Language of Sensation*, chap. 4.

45. The most recent edition of *Poems in Stanzas* is that of Edward Robauts and Norbert de Paepe, *Hadewijch, Strophische Gedichten: Middelnederlandse tekst en modern bewerking met enn inleidung* (Zwole: Willink, 1961). I will use the translations found in *Hadewijch. The Complete Works*, translated and introduced by Mother Columba Hart (New York: Paulist Press, 1980); see *Poems in Stanzas* 17.17–18 (p. 172).

46. Hadewijch, Vision 7, as translated in *Hadewijch. The Complete Works*, 280–82. The most recent edition of the visions is Frank Willaert, *Hadewijch: Visioenen* (Amsterdam: Uitgeverij Promotheus, 1996), 78–83 for Vis. 7.

47. Rudy, *Mystical Language of Sensation*, 151.

48. Simone Weil, *The Notebooks of Simone Weil*, trans. Arthur Willis, 2 vols. (London: Routledge & Kegan Paul, 1976) 2:472.

49. On David of Augsburg, see McGinn, *The Flowering of Mysticism*, 113–16.

50. *Fr. David ab Augusta: De exterioris et interioris hominis compositione secundum triplicem statum incipientium, proficientium et perfectorum* (Quarrachi: Collegium S. Bonaventurae, 1899) 3.66.1–5.

51. On Margaret Ebner, see McGinn, *The Flowering of Mysticism*, 308–14.

52. For more on thirteenth- and fourteenth-century developments, see Rudy, *Mystical Language of Sensation*, chap. 5.

53. The standard edition of Eckhart's writings is *Meister Eckhart. Die deutschen und lateinischen Werke herausgegeben im Auftrag der deutschen Forschungsgemeinschaft* (Stuttgart and Berlin: Kohlhammer, 1936–), using the abbreviations *DW* for the German works and *LW* for the Latin. The passage cited here is from Eckhart's German Sermon (Pr.) 5b, as translated in *Meister Eckhart. The Essential Sermons, Commentaries, Treatises, and Defense*, translation and introduction by Edmund Colledge, and Bernard McGinn (New York: Paulist Press, 1981), 183.

54. Denys Turner, *The Darkness of God. Negativity in Christian Mysticism* (Cambridge: Cambridge University Press, 1995), 174.

55. Turner puts it well: "Eckhart's detachment is not a mechanism whereby space is *made* for God to occupy; it is rather, the process whereby space is recovered from the infilling of attachments" (*The Darkness of God*, 176). For a survey of the role of detachment and its consequences in Eckhart, see Bernard McGinn, *The Mystical Thought of Meister Eckhart. The Man from Whom God Hid Nothing* (New York: Crossroad, 2001), 131–47.

56. Pr. 52, as translated in *Meister Eckhart: The Essential Sermons*, 201.

57. According to Turner (*The Darkness of God*, 183): "The strategy of detachment is the strategy of dispossessing desire of its desire to possess its objects, and so to destroy them. . . . Detachment, for Eckhart, is not the severing of desire's relation to its object, but the restoration of desire to a proper relation of objectivity; as we might say, of reverence for its object."

58. Pr. 101–104 are forthcoming in a new edition by Prof. Georg Steer in *DW* 4. I wish to thank Prof. Steer for allowing me access to the new text prior to its publication. For a study of the sermon cycle, see McGinn, *The Mystical Thought of Meister Eckhart*, chap. 4.

59. Pr. 101, lines 28–30.
60. Pr. 101, lines 155–60. Eckhart's terms here (*unwizzen/unbekante bekantnisse*) appear to be the earliest vernacular uses of the term *docta ignorantia* that goes back to Augustine (see Ep. 130.14.28 [*PL* 33:505]).
61. Pr. 101, lines 209–12.
62. Pr. 103, lines 108–109. Later, in Pr. 104A, lines 75–79, Eckhart even speaks of the soul "seeing and experiencing" God.
63. See Pr. 103, line 39.

151

PART THREE

Interpreting the Tradition

Historical and Theological Perspectives

$\mathcal{F}$rom the earliest sources of the first Christian communities, the importance of memory emerges as a prominent theme. "For the tradition I received from the Lord," writes Paul, "I handed on to you" (1 Cor. 11.23). The metaphor of "handing on" the faith has rooted itself in Christian theology through the ages. It is enacted each time communities gather for worship to hear ancient biblical texts, to speak or sing prayers both ancient and new, to recite creeds or confessions of faith shaped by these memories, and so forth. Worship is a vast repository of this memory. It is the fundamental context in which memory becomes identity through the retrieval of the ancient witness of God's acts, from creation, through the historical narrative of Israel, to the emergence of Jesus and the communities gathered in his name. Such memory, of course, is a complex reality, since it is not simply a backward-looking movement meant to recover in an unchanging way a primal story. It is at the same time a forward-looking movement that is being constantly revised in terms of the ideals held by a later culture. Thus, for example, when Paul concludes his witness to "the supper" by claiming that in this act Christians "are proclaiming the Lord's death until he comes" (1 Cor. 11.27), we see that his understanding of this event is in its form embraced by the trajectories of memory and hope. One might say that the church's—or churches'—tradition is always a dynamic memory shaped by present circumstances and future hopes. Any properly Christian theology involves a reckoning with this tradition in a full sense. A spirituality claiming to be Christian must also express something of this tension.

An authentically Christian spirituality is also grounded in theology, here understood as the reflection upon the church's inherited tradition as well as its present experience of God. This uniting of memory and experience is one measure of the necessity of relating spirituality and the sources and methods of theology. Such a union calls us not to an unswerving obedience to the past but to an ever attentive listening to the tradition in a posture at once critical and creative, discriminating and constructive. It has meant that remembering is something done "in the Spirit," just as spirituality is done within the dynamic stream of tradition. Such a posture of conversation must face the lingering suspicions of modernity, since the Enlightenment, toward the continuing relevance of authoritative sources from the past, whether scripture or tradition. In the late modern period, this methodological instinct has denied any singular view of tradition in deference to the honoring of *traditions*—communities of memory, styles of culture, race, gender, and so forth. Such is the context in which Christians in our time face the ancient responsibility to *re-member* the story that grounds the faith. In the postmodern situation, this mandate to remember requires that the personal be joined to the communal, the latter constructed not only in space but in time. We confess, in the words of the ancient creed, that we believe "in the communion of saints," a testimony that joins our lives to others' as a means of knowing God's faithfulness in places and times other than our own. A spirituality shaped only or even primarily by the present betrays the dynamic historicity of the Christian faith and either ignores or dismisses the theological claim about God's historicity in past periods and cultures and the import of this conviction for contemporary experience.

The call to take tradition seriously requires that the church's theological work be grounded within the practices and disciplines, the memories and yearnings, of real Christian communities of both the past and the present. In his essay asking about a "turn to spirituality," Matthew Ashley reminds us that this turn calls us into conversation not only with "the broader, dynamic, and unfinished Great Tradition" but with the particular diversities of race and culture, of ethnicity and nationality, as a means of "walking according to the Spirit." He speaks of spirituality not only as a classic constellation of practices "which forms a mystagogy into a life of Christian discipleship" but also as "particular ways of speaking and thinking" about God that we discern in song and poetry, in sermon and theological argument. His essay offers a rich exploration of how theology, as a "second step" discourse, arises from, and in turn shapes and changes, the practices and intuitions that are best described as spirituality. His conclusion, that spirituality and theology are inevitable partners in the conversation necessary for shaping and guiding Christian life, advocates a turn to spirituality not as an ironclad methodology but rather as "a fruitful locus for posing questions correctly and interrelating them productively."

The question of distinguishing "the great tradition" from "traditions" lies at the heart of Lawrence Cunningham's essay. The criteria of an authentically Christian spirituality, he argues, should be shaped in terms of how we apprehend the tradition as "a dynamic process rather than a finished edifice." This requires seeing tradition as including both continuity and change, retaining an essential identity in the midst of developments. He suggests, citing Gordon Laycock, that the church's task in this discernment call upon us is to "make the center strong, the symbols large, the words of Christ clear . . . that center accessible, the circle large, the periphery permeable." Tradition is unfinished, in other words; the orthodoxy it conveys arises from a tension between a historical inheritance and our experience as historical persons. It is a past that always has a future, one that includes our own experience as well as that of those coming after us. Cunningham suggests that this requires of us a commitment to broadening our memory to include neglected, forgotten, or excluded dimensions of the story. Tradition is not only about this discernment; it is the very process of such discernment.

This lively discussion relating theology and spirituality has as one of its driving interests a desire to understand more adequately not only the doctrinal but also the experiential aspects of tradition. One way to ask about this relationship is to explore the language and imagery accorded to the Spirit by theologians in the tradition. Elizabeth Dreyer turns our attention to this question in terms of Augustine's theology. She suggests that a proper understanding of Augustine's view of the Holy Spirit requires that we consider not only his theological treatises, such as *De trinitate,* but a wider range of sources, including prayers, hymns, sermons, and catechetical materials. She also suggests that we read historical sources not simply as inert artifacts but as living voices that might well interrogate us, "expanding our horizons in both constructive and deconstructive directions, exposing us to fresh ways of seeing and thinking about God." Approaching Augustine's texts in such a way opens us to making deeper connections than contemporary theologians often do between pneumatology and ecclesiology, between the expression of the Holy Spirit and the manner in which the experience of the Spirit shapes communities of faith. The Spirit, according to Augustine, is "the Gift that makes possible communion with God and with each other." Dreyer points out that if we appreciate the Spirit as an "existential force," as Augustine argues we must, and not merely as a metaphysical topic of the theological curriculum, we might begin to understand that spirituality is not a possible partner in, but an indispensable dimension of, the theological conversation.

Some historical periods offer particular windows of perception into the spiritual life. Barbara Newman turns our attention to one such episode, exploring the mystical outpouring of the twelfth century as what she calls a "Mozartian moment." On the formal level, her piece offers a thoughtful review of Bernard McGinn's *The Growth of Mysticism,* the second in his multivolume series, *The Presence of God,* exploring the Christian mystical tradition from its origins to modernity. She explores the adequacy of defining mysticism *only* in terms of "the immediate presence of God," as McGinn contends we should, since many of the spiritual traditions from the late Middle Ages—including many of the female visionaries whose importance dominates this period—related to *mediated* forms of such presence. It is a period of an almost unbounded optimism about love, both divine *and* human. Its dominant voices from the Cistercian and Victorine traditions, which she describes as the "undaunted doctors of desire," teach us that desire is finally rational, even though it transcends reason; that desire begins and ends with the body as a locus of struggle and triumph; and that desire is insatiable, since it is a union of "endless yearning and utmost fulfillment in the love of an inexhaustible object." This emphasis upon desire arises from the conviction, widely shared during this period, that "the yearning heart has its own economy, and when it becomes disordered, the Desired One himself will set it aright." This is a Mozartian moment, to be sure, an era that continues to inspire with its playful melodies and erotic harmonies even—and perhaps especially—in an age like ours, marked by a less optimistic and daring spirit.

A theme that has acquired considerable interest in recent years is that of apophatic theology, a "negative" theology that reminds us that every affirmation about the divine is at best partial and incomplete. In a chapter that draws heavily on modern poetics, Mark Burrows explores this theological tradition by turning our attention to the hermeneutical demands of properly theological language. Here, it is important that we recognize what such language can, and what it should not, claim; we must learn not to misread apophatic texts "by applying the tools of discursive reasoning and scholastic analysis to texts that follow the wisdom of a different genre." Engaging Michael Sells's study of this theme, *Mystical Languages of Unsaying* (Chicago and London, 1994), Burrows suggests that the approach to such texts cannot follow the Kantian dictates of practical reason, nor should we assume that *apophasis* as a linguistic strategy is sufficient of itself to discern a presumed core hiding within the "husk" of meaning. Perhaps, he suggests, a mystical text—and, more broadly, spiritual themes or traditions—must always be understood in terms of the positive assertions and practices, personal and communal, within which such sources function.

In the final essay, Mark McIntosh continues this discussion, asking in a sober tone whether "it is in fact possible for academic theology to recover its relationship to spirituality," since it has largely "forgotten how different this communion [i.e., that of "its occasional visits with spirituality"] is from what it usually enjoys with philosophy, hermeneutics, sociology, and psychology." McIntosh turns to the doctrine of Christology to suggest that the necessary conversation between spirituality and theology might well lead to what he calls "a mystically informed theology," one that does not assume that rational argument can sustain constructive theological work. He borrows the language of paradox to make some sense of the Christian testimony about God, and, drawing heavily upon the Cappadocian fathers, insists that a theology informed by the dialogue with spirituality, far from being "anti-noetic," actually enlivens the quest for God through "an awareness that the source of one's desire is beyond the grasp of intellect."

Throughout the essays collected in this section, the theme of integration stands out: the need to understand tradition as a dynamic force grounded in the experience of and yearning for the divine presence, the urgency in understanding spirituality as the context for theological reflection, the importance of broadening the scope of theological sources to include those reflective of spiritual experience, the role of desire in Christian spirituality, and the significance of tradition and desire in holding our present attention in the polarities of past and future, of memory and hope. What is clear across the range of approaches included in these pieces is the conviction that theology is a spiritual discipline and that spirituality is unavoidably theological. This unity is most fruitfully grasped when we remember that desire is the essential shape of Christian memory, and the energizing source of Christian hope. Read together, these voices call us to discern in spiritual experiences the very heart of the theological task and to seek expressions of this *novum* appropriate to our vocation as both inheritors and bearers of the tradition.

11

The Turn to Spirituality?

The Relationship between Theology and Spirituality

J. MATTHEW ASHLEY

*W*hat? Another "turn" in theology? Have we not already had more than enough? In the past few decades we theologians have been advised that we need to make the critical turn (the turn to praxis), the linguistic turn, the interpretive (or hermeneutical) turn, the turn to the subject, and the turn to human experience. Furthermore, we have also been advised that we need to return to Scripture, and, in some postmodern atheologies, to turn to turning itself. I admit that I am thoroughly turned around. How much more complex does the situation become if the study of spiritualities, past and present, is added to the list of theological prerequisites? Theologians end up with another, and potentially even more sweeping, realm of literature which they must take into account. For their part, scholars of spirituality (just like philosophers or Scripture scholars before them) often look with a jaundiced eye on the theologians, worrying (not entirely without justice) that they come to the field only with the intention of subalterning it to their own tidy systems.

Nonetheless, I will suggest here that such a turn is not only unavoidable for a theologian today, but potentially at least as fruitful as the other possible turns on the theological *itinerarium*. Unavoidable because, whether we like it or not, the wide ditch between spirituality and theology has already been bridged, and is being bridged more and more often today. As we negotiate the transition from a more or less monocultural, Eurocentric church, to a multicultural, polycentric global church,[1] we have witnessed the birth of many theologies which not only admit but insist upon a constitutive relationship with particular spiritualities.[2]

James Cone, for example, asserts that it was only when he reflected upon the spirituality of his African-American forebears—articulated in the spirituals and the blues—that he was able to overcome the conceptual limitations of the white, North Atlantic theologies in which he was trained and craft theologies adequate to the experience of his community.[3] Similarly, Gustavo Gutiérrez has insisted from the beginning that the articulation of a liberation spirituality "from below" is an essential prerequisite of a liberation theology. His second major work, *We Drink from Our Own Wells*, attempted to fill this need.[4] Hispanic theology in the United States has insisted on the importance of the often disparaged "popular religiosity" for its theology.[5] The same can be said of feminist theologians, as well as African and Asian theologians. All insist that the received European theologies cannot adequately speak for and to their communities, that theological concepts, categories, and methods need to be reconfigured in the light of the spiritualities articulated by these new, or previously unheeded, voices.

This development certainly obliges theologians to cultivate in ourselves and others a healthy respect for the diversity and particularity of the many ways we "walk according to the Spirit," and to be aware of the ways that we can misjudge or distort a given spirituality by applying our theological categories to it prematurely. On the other hand, insofar as theology serves not only its local community and its tradition, but is accountable to the broader, dynamic, and unfinished Great Tradition, theologians also need to develop the conceptual tools to manifest the truth—or perhaps better to *make* the truth (Jn 3:21)—that there are many gifts, but they are inspired by the same Spirit. This way we can ensure that, in our diverse and particular spiritualities, we all still walk together, in a solidarity of common worship, conversation, and action.[6]

That this necessity can also be a virtue is my claim here. But, at the outset of the argument, the problem of definition looms large. An attempt to bring spirituality and theology into creative relationship with one another requires clear definitions of the two phenomena. However, it is a commonplace that the definition of spirituality in general and the self-definition of spirituality as a field of study within the academy, are tangled and controversial issues. Theology is not unfamiliar with this problem, since both the delineation of its subject matter and its legitimacy within the academy have been up for grabs at least since the time of the Enlightenment. Scholars more qualified than I have essayed the difficult task of defining spirituality (or explaining the limits of definition).[7] Here I will heed Bernard McGinn's observation that there is not at present, and perhaps in principle cannot be, an exhaustive and omni-competent definition of spirituality, but that the resultant ambiguity can be a productive one.[8] The same could very well be said of theology.

Thus I offer the following as a heuristic definition of spirituality which is, I hope, at least plausible, and whose value will emerge from its ability to keep lines of communication open between different approaches to the study of spirituality, on the one hand, and the theological endeavor, on the other. As I understand it here, a spirituality is comprised by two complementary aspects.

First, a spirituality is a classic constellation of practices which forms a mystagogy into a life of Christian discipleship. This aspect emphasizes the particularity of spiritual traditions within the history of Christianity, and so draws heavily on what has been called the historical-contextual approach to studying spirituality.[9] By defining a spirituality as a constellation of practices, I am focusing on the fact that a spirituality is something that one does. For example, whatever else Ignatian spirituality is, at its heart lies a set of Spiritual Exercises and a regimen of daily practices (like the Examen of Conscience). Benedictine spirituality has at its heart a rule of life that sets down a specific set of practices. Dominican spirituality is built upon a set of practices that revolves around teaching and preaching and renounces the monastic practice of stability. First embodied and formulated by a founding figure (or small circle of such), a constellation of practices becomes a classic over time when it proves its ability to transcend the particular historical and social context of its birth and continues to offer a rich and animating mystagogy into a life of disciple-ship in contexts that present different resources and challenges to such a life. This view allows one to recognize that a given spirituality admits of various degrees of participation, depending on the extent to which the entire constella-tion of practices is embraced (not everyone is ready to kiss leprous sores), and the degree to which they are integrated into and transform the person's broader life.

Thus far my definition is primarily descriptive. Including the term "mystagogy" in the definition adds a normative-critical dimension to the definition. This term is used in different ways with varying degrees of theologi-cal ramification. My primary analogue is the period in the liturgical year, between Easter and Pentecost, when the newly initiated are invited to deepen their appropriation of the life of *imitatio Christi* which they have just received in the sacraments of initiation. This is done by individual and communal prayer, reflection on Scripture, and particularly through participation in the Liturgy. This period is also a time for the wider church to recommit itself to this process of putting on Christ, drawing inspiration from the newly initiated. In calling spirituality a mystagogy, then, I am making at least the following theological claims about what spirituality should be. First, whatever else it is or does, ultimately a spirituality is instrumental to an encounter with God, an encounter which is consummated to the degree that it becomes incarnate as a life of discipleship. Second, a spirituality should incorporate one more deeply into the body of Christ. A spirituality is, or should be, a communal, indeed, an ecclesial reality. Just as for the liturgical period of mystagogy, spirituality is for the adherent of the particular spirituality, helping him or her to enter more deeply into the mystery of Christian discipleship by becoming more fully incorporated into the body of Christ. But it is also for the wider Church, inspiring all of its members (to be sure, often enough by prophetic challenge) to a deeper appropriation of the same mystery.

The second and complementary aspect is the particular way of speaking and thinking—in song, poetry, sermon, and even in theological and doctrinal assertions—about God, about the ultimate meaning of human life that both nurtures and is nurtured by the set of practices that make up the spirituality. Again, various adherents of a spirituality will embrace this broader vision, with its symbols, narratives, metaphysical speculation, and so forth, in different ways and to different degrees. How many of us have met deeply spiritual persons who have embraced and integrated a given set of practices into the rest of their life in a way that suffuses the whole with the light of Christ, and yet are relatively inarticulate when it comes to the vision that underlies these practices? This leads me to suspect that the practice of spirituality is a more primary dimension. It is true that a new spirituality can emerge when an existing set of practices (like the practice of evangelical poverty) receives a new interpretation, but I think that this could be explained in terms of the interaction of this set of practices with a new set of broader cultural practices.[10] Still, this is not the place to try to untie, much less cut, the Gordian knot between *praxis* and theory.

By theology I mean here the disciplined and self-critical attempt to construe all of reality—God, the human person, society, human history, and the natural cosmos, individually and in their inter-relations—in the light of the symbols and narratives of the Christian tradition, and in dialogue with other disciplines in the academy that attempt to understand and interpret reality.[11] It may very well be that I have already decided my argument by these definitions, since by them theology already bears some affinity to the second dimension of spirituality. So, in one sense, the rest of my argument will consist in elaborating on the relationship that is implicit in these definitions. I will do this by making use of the admittedly permeable division between systematic and fundamental theology. From the perspective of systematic theology, classics of spirituality can offer new, creative, often provocative formulations of the symbols, doctrines, and practices of Christian faith. From the perspective of fundamental theology, a given spirituality can define the horizon, or perhaps better, the atmosphere within which theology is undertaken and which permeates its methods and results. Careful work in the history of Christian spirituality provides us with "test cases" for how this has happened in the past. These "test cases" can in turn yield paradigms for the present: both for how these processes are already at work, and for how theologians can discern the spirits, moving beyond description to evaluation and interpretation. Let me elaborate on these two avenues along which the turn to spirituality can enrich theology.

The first avenue—the relationship between systematic theology and spirituality—has already been richly explored, and I will have less to say about it than of the second.[12] It considers the use of images, symbols, and narratives from the classics of spirituality to illuminate specific issues and problems in systematic theology. As I have said, spiritual teachers give expression in various ways to a vision of reality, the world, human existence, human history, society, and God that recommends and nourishes, but also legitimates their particular spirituality. They do this in creative, often provocative or even scandalous ways, selectively using, stretching (to some, abusing) the religious symbols handed down within the Christian community. This is certainly true for the daring images of God and the Trinity found in the Rhineland mystics, which have borne theological fruit even into this century in, for example, Karl Rahner's elaboration of his theology of God as absolute, holy Mystery. In a similar way, Hans Urs von Balthasar has creatively juxtaposed imagery of the dark night with scriptural and doctrinal reflections on the passion of Christ. The experience and portrayal of Jesus as mother in many medieval women mystics has served a similarly illuminating function for feminist theologians.[13]

As these examples show, such daring articulations of the experience of God arising from within the history of Christian spirituality can breathe new life into theological systems that have become too closed in on themselves and too obsessed with the drive to logical consistency and technical articulation. Furthermore, they can serve as correctives to narrowly conceived theological constructs, when, for instance, they emphasize only the distance and kingship of God, and not also God's nearness and tenderness. Karl Rahner recognized this role of the spiritual classic when he described it as a "'creative,' original assimilation of God's revelation in Christo, . . . a new gift by God's Spirit of the ancient Christianity to a new age."[14]

But, lest this way of speaking of the relationship between spirituality and theology create the impression that theology is the discipline which receives and reflects upon the models, images, and practices of spirituality "from the outside," let me move on to a second and complementary dimension of the relationship. Marie-Dominique Chenu articulated this dimension of the relationship over fifty years ago in these words:

> The fact is that in the final analysis theological systems are simply the expressions of a spirituality. It is this that gives them their interest and their grandeur. . . . One does not get to the heart of a system via the logical coherence of its structure or the plausibility of its conclusions. One gets to that heart by grasping it in its origins via that fundamental intuition that serves to guide a spiritual life and provides the intellectual regimen proper to that life.[15]

Most theologians are now comfortable with the recognition that theology is a "second step," that it does not generate results out of its own resources and cannot authorize them simply on the basis of logical coherence and argumentative precision, but rather, relies on the experience of the Church (both present, and as retrieved from the past). Indeed, the complexity of this reliance is one of the reasons for all of the various "turns" which are pressed upon the theologian today. Chenu seems to be pointing to a similar sort of derivative character for theology. But how should we understand Chenu's reference to a "spiritual life" and the "intellectual regimen proper to that life" as comprising the heart of a theological system? I think we need to consider how the constellation of practices that makes up a given spirituality also influences those of its adherents who are theologians to be attentive to the world in a certain way, such that when they attempt to articulate this presence in systematic theological language they draw on the store of religious symbols, concepts and theologies handed down to them in correspondingly selective ways.

An analogy with developments in the philosophy of science might help me make my point. At least since the debate incited by Thomas Kuhn's controversial book, *The Structure of Scientific Revolutions*, philosophers of science have by and large come to recognize that there is no fully neutral, purely raw and uninterpreted data (experience) to which one can appeal in order to authorize scientific theories or adjudicate disputes between rival theories. Scientific arguments and results cannot be legitimated solely in terms of logical coherence or by appeal to some interpretation-free facts independent of the scientific systems under consideration. Rather, they are justified against the broader background of the life-world of the scientific community: its often tacit beliefs, attitudes, convictions, aversions, and practices, into which scientists are initiated by lengthy and arduous *exercises*, which are intended to actualize and/or transform their ways of being present to the world and constituting it as an object of investigation. Even a practice as seemingly trivial as the way scientific results are recorded and reported is significant for eliciting and sustaining a particular way of perceiving the world, as Frederick Ferré notes:

> There is a ritual way of writing up experimental reports. . . . The ritual is to write everything in the passive voice, with all references eliminated if possible, but if not, at least transformed into the third person. . . . The ritual of scientific writing style systematically impersonalizes. Why? I suspect that neither clarity nor precision would need to be sacrificed in a laboratory report that used first-person active language; but the mood, the tone, the subliminal feel would be very different. And so would the symbolism, which now works to cultivate a consciousness in which the peculiarities of individual subjectivities count not at all. The persons who do or see or measure don't matter; what matters, as symbolized and reinforced by the ritual language, are the objective events, the recorded observations, the performed measurements.[16]

The point is that the scientific mode of perceiving the world is not an unproblematic, "natural" way of being present to the world; rather, it is laboriously elicited, sustained and reinforced by a specific constellation of practices and assumptions to which a scientist commits him or herself when he or she commits to the scientific community. One necessary element (to be sure, not the only one) of the structure of scientific revolutions is the development of a coherent set of practices for sustaining a new way of being attentive to the world, as well as the sociological mechanisms necessary to initiate new adherents into those practices. In this context it is suggestive to recall that the origins of modern science in the late Middle Ages have much to do with the origins and growth of a new spirituality: Franciscan spirituality, with its practices revolving around and sustaining what Ewert Cousins has called "the mysticism of the historical event."[17]

Analogously, theological arguments and results cannot be legitimated solely in terms of logical coherence or by appeal to facts (be they facts of experience, of tradition, or of Scripture). Rather, it is the broader world of the Christian community—constituted by the relationship to God through Christ that is discipleship—to which the theologian belongs that allows the world to show up the way it does. Theologians are formed and initiated into this lifeworld by academic *and* spiritual exercises (and let us not forget that, at least at the origins of the University, these were not strictly distinguished). In the process they are transformed, become attentive to self and world in a new way, allow reality to be present to them in a new way. This presence lies at the heart of the theology by means of which they try to articulate and justify their understanding of God, self, and others, and of the physical world. This is, I believe, what Chenu was getting at. Any theology of any breadth and depth has, either explicitly or implicitly, a constitutive relationship to a spirituality, and it cannot fully be understood without taking this into account.

Disagreements between theologians and theological schools are often due, at least in part, to the different ways that they are attuned to the world—these in turn arising from the different spiritualities that incarnate over time their response to God. Thus, for example, the differences between Bonaventure and Thomas Aquinas certainly include distinctive argumentative strategies, choices of philosophical conceptuality, and so on. But I am convinced that one cannot get to the root of their distinctive theological approaches without understanding their commitment to and grounding in the Franciscan and Dominican traditions—the former with its practices fostering devotion to the concrete particularity of the crucified one, and its focus on love; the latter with its center on preaching and teaching the Word, and its concomitant emphasis on truth as *the* central transcendental for articulating the presence of God, and knowledge as the central descriptor for human beatitude.[18] Such differences cannot be overcome or even fully comprehended by purely conceptual considerations. We need a transformative shift of attention in our thinking (not illogical or absurd, but perhaps alogical, indebted to imagination and empathy), analogous perhaps to what Thomas Kuhn had in mind when he talked about paradigm shifts in science.

My claim here is that a theologian's grasp of his or her system is incomplete until and unless he or she has grappled with the particular spirituality of which his or her theology is an expression, and which gives this theology its "interest and grandeur." Does this mean that a theologian must have a spiritual life, must embrace a spirituality? On the one hand, this assertion really only amounts to saying that a theologian must be a believer, with the added proviso that being a believer and following Christ never occur in the abstract, but always in the concrete as a specific set of practices by means of which one grows into the inexhaustible riches of discipleship (viz., a spirituality). On the other hand, it would be misleading to suggest that one needs to be a Dominican to appreciate the theology of Aquinas, or a Jesuit to appreciate Rahner. There are, after all, many degrees and ways of embracing or appreciating a spirituality. Indeed, my argument for a "turn" to spirituality is a recognition of this fact, and appreciation of the specific results and methodologies that the study of spirituality can offer to help the theologian find ways to enter into other spiritual traditions, short of actually becoming a disciple.

Nor does this claim necessarily imply that theologies are only valid within the horizon of the spirituality which gave birth to them. Theological concepts and arguments may (and quite often do) not only slip free of the particular spirituality out of which they arose, but may break free entirely from any appeal to spirituality. An extreme, but far-reaching, instance of this is found in Heidegger's relationship to Eckhart.[19] What does seem evident at this point is that theologies will mean and function differently when correlated with different spiritualities.[20] This can be a fruitful encounter, a way in which theology can enrich a spirituality by deepening its own self-understanding, relating it to a cross-section of the Great Tradition that is different from the one which it might adopt on its own accord, and by relating it to other sorts of practices in which we engage and other fields of knowledge.

In short, theology can enrich spirituality as well. The above analysis will make a theologian wary of imposing theological concepts forged within one spiritual tradition upon another. But a given spirituality may nonetheless be enriched by considering it anew, and differently, using theological concepts that arise from a different mystagogy into the inexhaustible riches and mystery of God. Clearly, our history is replete with the ways that theologies and spiritualities have interacted productively. This was certainly the case for the relationship between Meister Eckhart's mastery of scholastic theology and his powerful advocacy of a particular way of living the mystical life found in his sermons and exhortations.[21] A similar relationship held true of Bonaventure's commitment to the spirituality of his master Francis and his mastery of the Neoplatonic tradition, as well as of scholastic argumentation. For a more recent case, think of the fascinating interplay between phenomenology and mysticism—Husserl and Teresa of Avila—in Edith Stein's life and work. Or consider (moving farther afield), the intriguing—at times baffling—interplay between Kabbalistic mysticism and Marxist philosophy in Walter Benjamin, a figure who, while most emphatically not a Christian, has had a signal impact on the development of political and liberation theologies.

Such cases demonstrate the permeability of the boundaries between spirituality, theology, and philosophy. Our understanding of this permeability can be aided by the sort of careful "thick descriptions" offered by the historical-contextual approach to the study of spirituality, as well as by the insights arising from psychology, cultural anthropology, sociology, and so on, offered by the anthropological approach. On the other hand, the theologians can help to remind us that spiritualities are at their origins not (or not only) ways to achieve purified states of consciousness, a more peaceful, integrated life, care of the soul, and so on, although these all may result. They arise in response to the call of the Spirit and they are taken up in order to live more deeply the mystery of discipleship. This should affect how we study and interpret them.[22] Furthermore, theology can remind us that even the most self-avowedly secular descriptions of the human condition which we then apply to spiritualities, may very well have a theological history worth attending to.[23] For example, many definitions of spirituality use terms like self-transcendence, ultimate value and meaning, which seem theologically and spiritually neutral at first blush. I do not intend to deny the legitimacy of these sorts of definitions, but it is important to note that these terms are themselves part of an intellectual (often overtly theological) tradition that takes its inspiration from one spirituality: Christian Neoplatonism in general, more specifically, the Eckhartian tradition.[24]

This raises the question of what happens when one uses terms that bear an affinity to one particular spiritual tradition as a heuristic guide for recognizing and studying other traditions. My suspicion is that they will do quite well with some spiritualities, provide interesting insights or even fruitful misreadings of others, but fail to recognize or adequately interpret others. Again, my intention here is not to proscribe definitions (my own included) or even to deny the need for definitions and methodologies that are as "theologically neutral" as we can make them. Rather, it is to point out the limitations of these strategies, with the hope that this growing body of research can help us map out these limitations and use our definitions fruitfully within those limits. Those familiar with the disciplines of history and philosophy of science will recognize in these thorny issues strong affinities with the still-living "commensurability debate" that followed upon Kuhn's book. Has not the problem of theological pluralism become virtually insoluble once one concedes, as I do, that different theologies are ultimately grounded in different spiritualities? I do not think so. This

167

realization need not lead to historicism, relativism, or radical skepticism in theology, or any more than the parallel insight in the case of the history and philosophy of science.[25] It does mean, however, that just as an alliance between careful historical work, sociological and anthropological investigation, and philosophical probing has brought to light a more complex but fruitful understanding of how the arguments and results of science are related to "lived scientific experience," so too does an alliance between different approaches to spirituality, philosophy, and theology promise a deeper comprehension of how theologies are born and develop, as well as of the relationship between the practice of spirituality and the various ways of articulating and understanding it, be they overtly theological or not.

168

In conclusion, the various turns of our century have made life difficult for the theologian. They have raised almost intractable problems concerning the possibility and legitimacy of theology as an academic discipline. The "turn to spirituality" offers neither easy answers to these problems nor an edifying excuse for avoiding them. All of the problems highlighted by the other turns will show up again in this one, and the various methodologies developed to make those other turns will no doubt prove useful in this one as well. What the turn to spirituality *does* provide is a fruitful locus for posing the questions correctly and interrelating them productively. The history of spirituality is, furthermore, a rich historical "data base" such that discussions at this locus have a better chance of avoiding the enervating ambiguity and abstractness that often attend debates over "experience," "praxis," or "language."[26] Finally, this turn puts theologians in contact with a new discipline that has already been hard at work there. Certainly there will be difficulties in working out disciplinary boundaries, and definitional ambiguities will continue to frustrate. But I am convinced that in the long run this cross-disciplinary work can help both disciplines as they attempt to chart a course into the next millennium, and aid them in their continuing service to the Great Tradition.

NOTES

1. This is Johann-Baptist Metz's formulation, which was inspired in part by his teacher, Karl Rahner. Not coincidentally, Metz has insisted on the mystical or spiritual turn to theology for at least two decades. See, for instance, "Unity and Diversity: Problems and Prospects for Inculturation," in Johann-Baptist Metz and Jürgen Moltmann, *Faith and the Future: Essays on Theology, Solidarity, and Modernity* (Maryknoll, New York: Orbis, 1995), 57–65. From Rahner, see his classic, *The Shape of the Church to Come*, trans. and ed. Edward Quinn (New York: Crossroad, 1983).
2. Of course, I would by no means assert that the best European theologians were not aware of this. To speak only of the Catholic theologians with whom I am familiar, I need name only M.-D. Chenu, Friedrich von Hügel, Yves Congar, Hans Urs von Balthasar, and Karl Rahner to make the point that this move was not only anticipated by these masters of theology *and* spirituality, but that, insofar as they prepared the

ground for the Second Vatican Council and the openness to pluralism and inculturation that it initiated, however tentatively, they helped make the present dialogue possible.

3. See his *The Spirituals and the Blues* (Maryknoll, New York: Orbis, 1991). On the theological purpose and underpinnings of Cone's turn to the spirituals, see ibid., 6; also, *My Soul Looks Back* (Maryknoll, N.Y.: Orbis, 1986), 60–61.

4. See *A Theology of Liberation*, rev. ed. (Maryknoll, NewYork: Orbis, 1988), xxii, 74; *We Drink from Our Own Wells*, trans. Matthew O'Connell (Maryknoll, New York: Orbis, 1984), 35–38 and *passim*. While *The Power of the Poor in History* appeared between *A Theology of Liberation* and *Wells*, it is not a single work but a collection of essays.

5. Virtually every book by Hispanic-Latino/a theologians insists on this point, beginning with Virgil Elizondo's ground-breaking *The Future Is Mestizo: Life Where Cultures Meet* (New York: Crossroad, 1988). For a methodological essay see Orlando Espín, "Tradition and Popular Religion: An Understanding of the *Sensus Fidelium*," in *Frontiers of Hispanic Theology in the United States*, ed., Alan Figueroa Deck (Maryknoll, New York: Orbis, 1992), 62–87. For a concrete application of the principle, see Jeanette Rodriguez, *Our Lady of Guadalupe: Faith and Empowerment among Mexican-American Women* (Austin, Texas: University of Texas Press, 1994).

6. On the "Great Tradition" as the context within which to understand, interpret, and evaluate Christian spiritualities, see Lawrence Cunningham, "*Extra Arcam Noe*: Criteria for Christian Spirituality," *Christian Spirituality Bulletin* 3:1 (Spring, 1995), 6–9. This essay appears as Chapter 12 in this volume.

7. See essays by Bernard McGinn, "The Letter and the Spirit: Spirituality as an Academic Discipline" (Chapter 2 in this volume), and Sandra Schneiders, "Spirituality as an Academic Discipline: Reflections from Experience," and the literature cited therein, *Christian Spirituality Bulletin* 1:2 (Fall, 1993), 1–15.

8. McGinn, "The Letter and the Spirit," 7.

9. For descriptions of the historical-contextual, as well as the anthropological and theological approaches to the study of spirituality, see McGinn, "The Letter and the Spirit," 4–7. It is also true that, insofar as my definition insists that a spirituality is a mystagogy into discipleship it is also a theological definition, and is restricted to Christianity.

10. Thus, a new interpretation of poverty emerged in the Middle Ages because of the need to integrate the practice of poverty with a changing set of social and economic practices. See Lester K. Little, *Religious Poverty and the Profit Economy in Medieval Europe* (Ithaca, New York: Cornell University Press, 1978).

11. This is an amended version of the definition offered by Roger Haight in *Dynamics of Theology* (Mahwah, New Jersey: Paulist Press, 1990), 1.

12. For a fuller treatment see William Thompson's books, *Fire & Light: The Saints and Theology* (Mahwah, New Jersey: Paulist Press, 1987) and *Christology and Spirituality* (New York: Crossroad, 1991).

13. The classic here is Caroline Walker Bynum, "Jesus as Mother and Abbot as Mother," in *Jesus as Mother: Studies in the Spirituality of the High Middle Ages* (Berkeley, California: University of California Press, 1982), 110–169. On the general issue of the significance of this kind of imagery for Christology, see Elizabeth Johnson, *She Who Is: The Mystery of God in Feminist Theological Discourse* (New York: Crossroad, 1992), 101–102, 150–154. For a theological study related to one key figure, see Joan Nuth, *Wisdom's Daughter: The Theology of Julian of Norwich* (New York: Crossroad, 1991), 65–69, 92–94, and *passim*.

14. Karl Rahner, *The Dynamic Element in the Church*, trans., W. J. O'Hara (London: Burns & Oates, 1964), 86.

15. From *Une École de Théologie: Le Saulchoir* (1937). Cited in Gutiérrez, *We Drink from Our Own Wells*, 147 n. 2.

16. Frederick Ferré, *Hellfire and Lightning Rods: Liberating Science, Technology and Religion* (Maryknoll, New York: Orbis, 1993), 13f.

17. On this novel form of spirituality and its impact on medieval theology, see Ewert Cousins, "Francis of Assisi: Christian Mysticism at the Crossroads," in Stephen Katz, ed., *Mysticism and Religious Traditions*, (New York: Oxford, 1983), 175–188, and "The Humanity and Passion of Christ" in Jill Raitt, ed., *Christian Spirituality II: The High Middle Ages and Reformation* (Crossroad, 1989), 375–391. For Francis' role in the shift from the classical topos of "cosmos" to the modern scientific topos of "nature," see Louis Dupré, *Passage to Modernity* (New Haven, CT: Yale University Press, 1993), 36–41. Note here that what Francis and his first followers introduced was not a new theology or cosmology, but the *practices* which fostered a form of devotion to the concrete individuality and physicality of Jesus. It was up to later disciples (Bonaventure in particular) to articulate the vision that corresponded to this new spirituality and which (as Dupré notes) was of decisive importance for the development of the modern, scientific worldview.

18. I owe this insight to lectures given by David Tracy at the University of Chicago Divinity School during the Fall of 1991.

19. See John Caputo's wonderful book, *The Mystical Element in Heidegger's Thought* (New York: Fordham University Press, 1978). Here Caputo is very careful to note that Heidegger's thought is not mystical per se, but has a mystical *element*, and further suggest that the abstraction of the mystical terminology from its own spiritual horizon shifts that terminology in significant, indeed, dangerous, ways (xvii–xviii, 245–254).

20. They may shift meaning so much that they break down or even backfire. For instance, Michael Buckley has demonstrated that when theology attempted to mount arguments for the existence of God without reference to religious experience (in my terms, without reference to specific spiritualities), it ironically (to say the least) generated its own antithesis in atheism. See Michael Buckley, *At the Origins of Modern Atheism* (New Haven: Yale University Press, 1987).

21. See Bernard McGinn, "The God beyond God: Theology and Mysticism in the Thought of Meister Eckhart," in *The Journal of Religion* 61 (1981): 1–19.

22. Here the situation is analogous to one found in that other difficult relationship: between theologians and Scripture scholars. Paraphrasing Sandra Schneiders' formulation, we have come to the paradoxical state that while we study and interpret the texts because they are "the Word of God," that fact makes almost no difference at all for the interpretation of the texts themselves. See Sandra Schneiders, *The Revelatory Text: Interpreting the New Testament as Sacred Scripture* (San Francisco: HarperCollins, 1991), 2.

23. This much at least is demonstrated in John Milbank's contentious book, *Theology and Social Theory: Beyond Secular Reason* (Cambridge, MA: Blackwell, 1990), whether or not one agrees with the particular construal of that history that Milbank presents.

24. Certainly the language is Rahnerian. But even in its secular usage—in Heidegger and the existential and hermeneutical tradition—it does not escape this influence. Again, see Caputo, *The Mystical Element in Heidegger's Thought*.

25. See also David Hiley, James Bohman, and Richard Shusterman, eds., *The Interpretive Turn: Philosophy, Science and Culture* (Ithaca, New York: Cornell University Press, 1991), particularly the articles by Shusterman and Bohman, which argue persuasively against those (like Richard Rorty or Paul Feyerabend) who draw radically skeptical conclusions from the hermeneutical turn in the epistemology of science.

26. To give just one example, George Schner has mapped out the ambiguities in the "turn to experience" in contemporary theology: "The Appeal to Experience," *Theological Studies* 53 (1992): 40–59.

12

Extra Arcam Noe

Criteria for Christian Spirituality

LAWRENCE S. CUNNINGHAM

*T*he little Latin tag in the title of this essay comes from Cyprian of Carthage's *On the Unity of the Church*. The ark, of course, in patristic usage, is the church. The issues before us are: who is called to the ark, what is the price of admission, and who actually stays on board? That is, what are the criteria for judging authentic Christian spirituality?

This essay assumes an understanding of Christian spirituality that means, roughly, life in the Spirit as lived out in fidelity to the Risen Christ.[1] It further presumes that this life exists within an ecclesial context broadly conceived. I will, at times, use the term "church" and "tradition" interchangeably without being too precise about how those terms are used. Roughly, what is meant by Tradition is the essential Spirit-inspired *paradosis* of the saving acts of Jesus Christ as remembered, recalled, and re-enacted in time and space. Finally, the essay uses, on occasion, the word "catholic" but understands it in its creedal (which is to say, theological) sense and not as a denominational term. Understood in this fashion we can assert, using Luke Timothy Johnson's recent formulation, that a "classical spirituality" is one which sets its limits within the parameters of the biblical canon, the historical creeds (especially the Nicene, which all Christians accepted up to the modern period until the emergence of what Johnson calls the "pure biblicists") and the *lex orandi*.[2]

Within a "classical spirituality" it is not hard to see what the primary criterion for an authentic spirituality would be. It would be spirituality which lives within what has been called the "Great Tradition." There is no need to rehearse here the history of how that tradition marginalized and/or condemned those ways of being Christian which did not fit within the consensus. That story is well known. The very word *orthodoxy* ("right worship"—with its opposite: heterodoxy/heresy) gives us a clue. Thus, this way of understanding tradition "reads" the marginalization of Marcion or the defection of Tertullian to the Montanists in the third century, or the condemnation(s) of the Origenists in the later patristic period, or the problems of the Fratecelli, Beghards, etc. in the medieval period, or the Quietists in the period after the Catholic Reformation, as an inevitable result of their straying beyond the bounds of "orthodoxy." One could add many other names to this list. In all of these cases, the Great Tradition judged these movements or persons to be outside the acceptable canon of belief and practice; they were "heterodox." I note this simply as a fact and not a justification of the fact.

At this level, then, this essay could be very short: the criterion for an authentic spirituality would be simply to invoke the principle that Irenaeus, in the second century, used in the *Adversus Haereses*: is what you do or who you purport to be in conformity with the community of Faith founded by the apostles? This principle, of course, did not solidify overnight as Jaroslav Pelikan has magisterially shown.[3] Further, as history tells us, it has been applied mechanically at times to the very embarrassment of the tradition. Thus, for example, many theologians who were condemned, at least by implication, in *Humani Generis* (1950) were later to be vindicated during the Second Vatican Council. Nonetheless, one should not underestimate the persuasive power of the criterion of apostolicity and catholicity. Who, for example, can forget the great set piece in Newman's *Apologia Pro Vita Sua* when the words of Augustine (*securus judicat orbis terrarum*) hurled at the Donatists drove a stake through his idea of the *Via Media* and led him, finally, (and implausibly, given the times) to Rome?

Still, the matter is not as simple as that. What constitutes that Great Tradition, after all, is not made of an impermeable fence with precise delimitations. While the broad contours of that tradition are clear enough, it is almost a banality to note that that Tradition is a dynamic process rather than a finished edifice. To borrow from a classic title of Yves Congar: there is Tradition and there are traditions, and the relationship between the two is not always transparent.[4] As Sandra Schneiders, citing among others Elizabeth Schussler-Fiorenza, has noted, the concept of "heresy" demands this query: are we dealing with historical winners and losers? Are we dealing with real deviation? Or are we sensing an ideological agenda?[5] Finally, has there been enough awareness of how the Great Tradition has, in fact, accommodated, at different levels, elements which seem deviant or peripheral? Wayne Meeks has made the intelligent point that after the canon of the New Testament had been fixed in the patristic period, the non-canonical gospels still were sources of inspiration and edification right through the period of the medieval and Renaissance era.[6] Any observer of many of the great late medieval or Renaissance cycles of narrative paintings (e.g., Giotto's Arena Chapel at Padua) on the infancy of Christ, or reader of Jacobus de Voragine's influential *Golden Legend* recognizes this.

It can be argued that the criterion of the received tradition can still be invoked to judge authentic Christian spirituality only if we understand that the invocation of that tradition itself is always a process. That is, the tradition itself enlarges, deepens, and even, at times, corrects itself. In this regard,

Gordon Laycock has a precise description of this point: "The task of the assembly is a task of polarity: make the center strong, the symbols large, the words of Christ clear, and make that center accessible, the circle large, the periphery permeable."[7]

Examples of the need for such flexibility are not hard to discover. Luke Johnson, for example, wisely says that any adequate contemporary model of spirituality must go beyond the "care of the soul" (which is a kind of Gnosticism against which the tradition struggles) just as it must have a social dimension both with respect to the world and our social relations with others without turning that tradition into pious social work.[8] That affirmation is a perfectly justified contemporary correction to one stream of spirituality deeply embedded in the Great Tradition which saw the spiritual search as a kind of Christianized variation of the Plotinian *Solus cum Solo*. The tradition, in short, is "in progress" and that progress does not always proceed in a straight line.

The essential note of catholicity, understood as a theological category, is, according to Avery Dulles, to reconcile opposites (*coincidentia oppositorum*) after the manner of our understanding of Christology itself.[9] Authentic spirituality must do honor to the conjunction of the bodiliness (humanity) and the transcendence (divinity) of the human person without dissolving the coincidence into either one of its poles. In other words, the tradition is in a constant state of balancing the poles without letting go of the tension between them. It is only when the tension is maintained that we have something which approximates "catholic" spirituality.

Thus, to cite some examples, Christian spirituality will insist that liturgical prayer does justice both to the sense of community and the need for worship. Likewise, it will not turn prayer simply into a form of therapy just as it will not make prayer into a bloodless exercise of abstraction. Authentic spirituality will resist the docetic temptation in the following of Christ just as it will resist the impulse to turn him, as Matthew Arnold once caricatured the liberal concept of God, into an "infinitely magnified and improved Lord Shaftesbury."

It does not seem necessary that we explicitly invoke the "Tradition" against every seemingly new experiment or approach in Christian living. It is true that some of the greatest saints have invoked the received tradition emphatically. Cassian tells of a monk weaned away from the *anthropomorphite* heresy who, after years, "was drawn back to the faith of the catholic tradition" after hearing how the "Catholic churches of the East" expounded the meaning of Genesis 1:26.[10] Saint Francis wished the followers of his way of life to be faithful adherents of the Catholic faith.[11] Among the fourteenth-century English mystics, fidelity to the Catholic faith is reiterated even in *The Cloud of Unknowing* when one would hardly expect ecclesial

173

deviation to be rampant among the Carthusians.[12] The most conspicuous example of such an admonition may be found in the *Spiritual Exercises* of Ignatius of Loyola where, in the "Rules for Thinking, Judging and Feeling with the Church" one finds this extraordinary statement: "What I see as white, I will believe to be black if the hierarchical church thus determines it."[13]

What we need to note, of course, is that such protestations must be contextualized. Cassian, after all, was an admirer and one-time delegate of the vigorously orthodox St. John Chrysostom before his sojourn in the West. Francis lived at a time when deviant groups also attempted to live as Poor Men of Christ. The *Cloud* author and the other English mystics wrote, we think, when Lollardy was abroad in England. And Ignatius, of course, wrote after the Protestant Reformation (hence: the adjective "hierarchical" describing the church). In more recent times, protestations of orthodoxy were reinforced by way of the ecclesiastical censors. My point, however, is that overly protective measures with respect to orthodoxy must always be read against the background of crisis, conspicuous deviance, or the perception of such. Historical circumstances both contextualize and relativize such exercises. From the privileged stance of history, we now know that the Poor Men of Lyon, the Lollards, and the Reformers had enormously important and prophetic things to say about living a Christian life. Recent examples of "orthodox" interventions (e.g., the *monita* of the Vatican about the dangers of Eastern mysticism) must be read in a similar contextualized background.

However much the power to define orthodoxy might have been misused in the past or used too prematurely, it is still fair to say, I think, that there needs to be some way for the believing community to assess what is and what is not compatible with the following of Jesus. How one exercises those criteria is an issue which follows on the first, but the two must be kept at least conceptually distinct. If it is correct to say with Philip Sheldrake that Christian spirituality must hold in tension both the common Christian tradition and our experience as actual historical persons without losing the tension between the two,[14] then it follows that any assessment of a Christian spirituality must answer two questions: does this conform to the gospel as it has been received and does this ring true to what I experience as a free human person "in Christ"?

The issue becomes all the more urgent in our own time when the term spirituality has come to be a descriptive buzzword for a whole range of movements, some of which are only tangentially connected to Christian faith, others of which are merely silly, and a few of which, indeed, are militantly opposed to the historical faith and need to be named as such. Who, for example, would resist passing judgment on the racist ideology of the Aryan Church movement or the (mis)use of the Exodus paradigm by fundamentalist Afrikaaners to justify the apartheid system?

Sometimes, of course, we can only reach a consensus in response to those questions through historical retrospection. From the privileged spot in the future we can look on the development of the Patarines or the Beguines and Beghards in the Middle Ages and say: these were authentic attempts to develop a new ecclesiology suited to the new reality of an emerging urban life and as a reaction to the increasingly clericalized culture of both the monastic, canonical, and emerging mendicant experiments of the post-Gregorian reform. Attempts to either control the shape of this movement by "clericalizing" or "regularizing" it were anachronistic and their suppression unfortunate. Every historical re-assessment is a cautionary tale for the Tradition. The contemporary search for new forms of community, from *communidades di base* to various experiments with intentional communities, fits a pattern that has a long history within the Great Tradition.[15] From the communal memory of the tradition we should learn cautionary tales and detect models that might be helpful.

By contrast, we can look back to that same period just before the emergence of the Beguines and render negative judgments from the vantage point of historical hindsight on what were then judged acceptable forms of spirituality (some highly articulated) but which, from the same vantage point of later experience, seem deviant and incompatible with the gospel. Who, for instance, would wish to reinvigorate a monastic *religio* which wedded the ascetical life to the bearing of arms? Not only was such a *religio* founded (and sanctioned at the Council of Troyes in 1128), but no less a personage than Bernard of Clairvaux wrote a *Book in Praise of the New Militia* (finished 1136) to justify the need of the Knights Templar to kill enemies. What the subsequent tradition teaches is that there emerged a spiritual shift in which the actual knightly ideal becomes, in time, spiritualized and turned into a new paradigm. While Joan of Arc led an army, she would not herself shed blood. Later, the concept of the knight becomes elevated into the "Christian Knight" by the pacifist Erasmus, or the "soldier of Christ" by the ex-soldier, Ignatius of Loyola. What happens in this strain of history is a learning experience for the tradition.

The historical tradition of Christianity, shaped by creed, ethos, and worship, is both circumscribed and elastic. It has a definite shape, but it is a shape that is in process and not finished. There is no Golden Age when a synthetic harmony existed, and there will be none short of the *eschaton*. The great tradition is, and should be, polyphonic. The tradition, in short, is complex and it *learns*.

But how do we sort out, within that tradition, what is risible, dangerous, or destructive of the Gospel? First, through a capacious sense of our common history, tradition, story telling, and lore. That sense involves not only grasping what we have at the fore but also recalling what we have forgotten or what we have repressed. Without that grasp of history we have no story, or at best, one which is truncated. The Great Church was right to say "no" to Marcion because Marcion would have cut off our common beginning by eliminating the Hebrew Scriptures, and in so doing would have detached our anchor-hold on the goodness and grace of creation to say nothing of our roots in Judaism.

We who stand within (or at the margins of!) the tradition are negligent, however, to the degree that we fail to foster the forgotten stories in the tradition. The recent salutary drive to recover the story of women in the tradition is a case in point. That re-calling and re-naming exerts a powerful influence on the way we understand our tradition today even when it has failed as yet to percolate up into the narrower expressions of the church.[16] The first practical axiom that derives from this fact is that we must constantly turn back to the sources of our common heritage both for admonition and for instruction.

The other side of this appeal to the inherited tradition is its power to aid us in our resistance to the limitations or short-sightedness about the relevance of the present. There is a persistent danger in absolutizing present experience as normative. In that sense, at least, a sense of the tradition acts as a check against a too hasty impulse to sacralize the present. A perfectly ghastly example might be in order here. Early in the twentieth century many Jews in Western Europe abhorred the nascent Zionism preached by Theodor Herzl. To show their disdain for the Zionists, these largely assimilated Jews modified one element of the Passover ritual; instead of the traditional "Next year in Jerusalem!" they raised their wineglasses and intoned, "Next year in Berlin!"

Michael Buckley quite rightly notes the vital importance of our own experience as crucial for understanding spirituality, both individually and socially. However, our experience becomes temptation "under the persuasion that the intensity of experience absolves one from discretion, critical reflection, and the doctrinal content of Christian faith, giving experience a priority over the unspeakable Mystery that approaches human beings through experience and transferring the religious guidance of a single person or of an entire community to an unchallengeable subjectivity, to sentimentality or superstition or excited enthusiasms."[17]

We live "between the times." As followers of the Spirit we must stand with the "cloud of witnesses" with the firm realization that we are not yet there. Our never-ending task is to exercise what the tradition calls *discernment*. Paul tells us that we must not quench the Spirit but we also must "test everything" (I Thess 5:19–22; see: I Jn 4:1). Crucial to that test is the witness of that church which is both catholic and seeks to become catholic until we inherit the fullness of time.

NOTES

1. Some representative descriptions of Christian spirituality:

   Philip Sheldrake, *Spirituality and History* (New York: Crossroad, 1992), 37. "I would suggest that what the word 'spirituality' seeks to express is the conscious human response to God that is both personal and ecclesial. In short: 'life in the Spirit.'"

   Sandra Schneiders, "Scripture and Spirituality," in *Christian Spirituality: Origins to the Twelfth Century*, edited by Bernard McGinn et al. (New York: Crossroad, 1985), 2: "Christian spirituality, then, is personal participation in the mystery of Christ begun in faith, sealed by baptism into the death and resurrection of Jesus Christ, nourished by the sharing of the Lord's Supper, which the community celebrated regularly in memory of Him who was truly present wherever his followers gathered, and was expressed by a simple life of universal love that bore witness to life in the Spirit and attracted others to faith."

   Gustavo Gutiérrez, *We Drink from Our Own Wells* (Maryknoll, NY: Orbis, 1984), 70: ". . . A way of being a Christian, that has as its foundation an advance through death, sin, and slavery, in accordance with the Spirit, who is the life-giving power that sets the human person free . . . Christian spirituality consists in embracing the liberated body and thus being able to say 'Abba – Father!' and to enter into comradely communion with others."

2. Luke Timothy Johnson, *Faith's Freedom: A Classic Spirituality for Contemporary Christians* (Minneapolis: Augsburg, 1990), 4. John Macquarrie sets Christian spirituality into the complex interplay of doctrine, worship, and deeds, arguing that lack of attention to any part of this tripod brings aberrations: *Paths in Spirituality*, 2nd edition (Harrisburg, PA: Barlow, 1992). For a more nuanced view of Tradition, see Sandra Schneiders, *The Revelatory Text: Interpreting the New Testament as Scripture* (San Francisco, CA: Harper/Collins, 1991), 65 and *passim*.

3. Jaroslav Pelikan, *The Christian Tradition: The Emergence of the Catholic Tradition*, vol. 1 (Chicago: University of Chicago Press, 1971), esp. 332ff. on the emergence of what Pelikan calls the "orthodox consensus."

4. Yves Congar, *Tradition and Traditions* (New York: Macmillan, 1967).

5. "The Bible and Feminism," in *Freeing Theology*, edited by Catherine Mowry LaCugna (San Francisco, CA: Harper/Collins, 1993), 42. It does seem arguable, however, that "winners and losers" is a non-encompassing lens through which to see the tension between orthodoxy/heresy.

6. Wayne A. Meeks, *The Origins of Christian Morality* (New Haven: Yale University Press, 1993), 192. Meeks says that such works were a kind of "penumbra around the canon."

7. Gordon Laycock, *Holy Things: A Liturgical Theology* (Minneapolis, MN: Fortress/Augsburg, 1993), 132.

8. Johnson, *Faith's Freedom*, 9–10.

9. Avery Dulles, *The Catholicity of the Church* (Oxford: Clarendon, 1981). John Milbank puts it in a similar fashion: "Christianity is therefore (in aspiration and faintly traceable actuality) something like the 'peaceful transmission of difference' or 'differences in a continuous harmony.'" *Theology and Social Theory: Beyond Secular Reason* (Cambridge, MA: Blackwell, 1990), 417.

10. *Conferences* X.3. Note Cassian's insistence on the Catholic reception of reading scripture, a subject to which Augustine would turn in the *De Doctrina Christiana*.

11. Cajetanus Esser's edition of the *Opuscula Sancti Patris Francisci Assiensis* (Grottaferrata: Ad Claras Aquas, 1979) cites at least ten instances of this in the glossary of terms. Typical is the injunction in the *Regula Non-Bullata* that all the brethren are to be Catholics and should live and speak in a Catholic manner (*Omnes fratres sint catholici, vivant et loquantur catholice*).

12. The *Cloud* author even insists that his contemplative exercises should not be entered into until all of the church's ordinary means of purification (e.g., sacramental confession) be observed; see *The Cloud of Unknowing*, edited by James Walsh (New York: Paulist, 1981), 179. Similar cautions are found in Julian and Walter Hilton. Julian, for example, writes: "I am hungry and thirsty and needy and sinful and frail and willingly submit myself among all my fellow Christians to the teachings of Holy Church to the end of my life." *Showings*, Edmund Colledge, O.S.A. and James Walsh, S. J., trans. (New York: Paulist Press, 1978), 148.

13. *Ignatius of Loyola: Spiritual Exercises*, edited by George Ganss, S.J. (New York: Paulist, 1991), 213; for the background of these rules, see John O'Malley, *The First Jesuits* (Cambridge, MA: Harvard University Press, 1993), 49–50.

14. Philip Sheldrake, *Images of Holiness: Explorations in Contemporary Spirituality* (Notre Dame, IN: Ave Maria Press, 1988), 2.

15. The medieval attempt, after the time of Gregory VII, to articulate the *vita apostolica* is a case in point. The various moves to develop a renewed Gospel life provide a necessary background for the emergence of everything from the Mendicants to lay movements such as the Patarines or Beguines. See Duane V. Lapsanski, *Evangelical Perfection* (St. Bonaventure, NY: Franciscan Institute, 1977), 6–51.

16. In the *Catechism of the Catholic Church* there are sixty-two authors quoted (apart from popes); six are women and two of them are biographical allusions to works by their (male) hagiographers.

17. "Discernment of Spirits," in *The New Dictionary of Catholic Spirituality*, edited by Michael Downey (Collegeville, MN: Liturgical Press, 1993), 274–75.

13

Spirituality as a Resource for Theology

The Holy Spirit in Augustine

ELIZABETH A. DREYER

In a 1995 issue of the *Christian Spirituality Bulletin*, a number of theologians discussed the relationship between spirituality and theology.[1] What is behind the interest in reconnecting these two central aspects of the Christian story? In part, it is a response to a fresh and rather widespread desire on the part of many Christians to live a more lively and intentional spiritual life. Spirituality has become important, thus demanding inclusion in the wider theological conversation. This existential development has also made demands on theologies that had become divorced from the lived faith experience of the community.

As Philip Endean notes in speaking about the theology of Karl Rahner, a disjunction between experience and doctrine is misguided in several ways. It is obvious that theology and doctrine cannot exist without a prior "spirituality" or experience of God. But it is also true that the language of theology and doctrine are intrinsic to and ground Christian experience. Spirituality and theology are brought into an even more intimate relationship if one holds, as Rahner did, that "the reality of God's self-gift in grace is identical with its presence in our experience, our spirituality."[2] Within this framework, theoretical and practical disciplines in theology are ultimately the same reality and therefore cannot be disjoined. God's self-gift, our experience of it, and both our poetic and systematic expressions through which we speak and think about this experience are not separate entities, but different aspects of the same reality.

Awareness of the need to reconnect spirituality with theology in our present circumstances has become obvious. But in the study of the tradition, there has been a tendency for theologians to focus almost exclusively on the theological and/or doctrinal expressions of grace and to lose sight of the truth that Christians in every age experienced God in the daily workings of their lives and struggled with both how to love God and others, and how to fight the demons that prevented this love from flowering. We have been diligent in studying the more formal, theological aspects of the tradition. We have now begun to examine spiritualities as well. One task ahead of us is to discover legitimate and creative ways to relate them. Granted, gaining access to the more experiential aspects of our ancestors in the faith has its challenges distinct from those of analyzing more systematic theological treatises. But it is not impossible, and the rewards include a fuller, more lively, and truer portrait of Christians throughout the tradition.

My more specific goal is to ask how our forefathers and foremothers spoke about the Holy Spirit. One way to approach this query is to locate and reflect on the language, imagery, and concepts of select, neglected texts on the Holy Spirit in a way that takes seriously the faith experience of the community and its social, ecclesial context.[3] Why did our ancestors in the faith speak of the Spirit the way they did? What needs and questions did a given approach attempt to answer? What didn't they say about the Holy Spirit and why? What problems were glossed over? What enemies silenced?

This task presents a further challenge inasmuch as the East has always been seen as the shining star in the preservation and celebration of the Spirit's presence. Criticisms of the Western tradition's theologies of the Holy Spirit are numerous.[4] Theologians complain that insufficient attention has been paid to the distinctiveness of the persons in the Trinity. Indeed, now familiar descriptors of the Spirit include: personally amorphous, faceless, forgotten, upstaged, ethereal and vacant, unclear and invisible.[5] Descriptors of pneumatology include ambiguous, reticent, obscure, neglected, groping, abstract.[6] Karl Rahner's lament that in their practical life, Christians are "almost mere monotheists" has attained the status of a mantra in the literature.[7] So, at first glance, the situation does not appear promising. Must one therefore conclude that indeed, the trinitarian persons have been seriously neglected in the West, and that in particular, the Holy Spirit is aptly described as Cinderella, i.e., the neglected member of a trio, consigned to invisible drudgery in the cellar?[8]

How might we account for this tendency to undervalue the tradition's treatment of the distinctive role of the persons and in particular, of the Holy Spirit? One problem is the tendency to attend to only a very narrow range of texts—usually more systematic theological works. Another is the failure to appreciate adequately the language and imagery of these texts and the ways they may have functioned in specific historical contexts. What was the setting in which speech about the Holy Spirit took place? Is there a discernible purpose behind specific ways of invoking the Spirit? Is an individual author influenced by movements that gave a key role to the Holy Spirit and that were judged to have been on the fringes of established doctrine, or even heterodox in some or all of their ideas and practices?

These issues are the topic of a recent analysis of the treatment of Augustine in contemporary Trinitarian theology by Michel René Barnes. Barnes calls attention—as many others have before him—to the continuing and unhelpful use of Théodore de Régnon's late-nineteenth-century categories contrasting Greek and Latin approaches to trinitarian theology.[9] Barnes criticizes what he perceives as systematic theologians' preference for what he calls grand, architectonic, and idealistic styles of writing. In this approach, details matter less than perspective, and historical facts become epiphenomena, often reduced to an "expression or symptom of a hermeneutic or ideology." History is treated as the material enstructuring of those themes which are constitutive of contemporary systematics.[10]

German theologian Michael Welker is interested in establishing a better connection between systematic theology and the biblical tradition for similar reasons. He notes that biblical material is more creative and complex than one might think, given the thrust of systematic statements. Theological talk about law and gospel and creation has reduced these concepts, denuding them of their diverse, complex, and creative biblical expressions. He describes his approach as "looking at abstractions, misleading abstractions, and trying to correct them."[11] My thesis is that the same approach needs to be used in the study of historical texts.

Yet another way to express this tension is to call attention to the need to explore the creative possibilities between what Langdon Gilkey calls particularity, or the language of story, and universality, or the language of ontology—both essential to Christian theology. While narrative is the primary language of theology, since the encounter between God and humans is essentially dramatic, one must then proceed to the task of *thinking* about the divine-human relation.[12] The ideal is to take both moments of this single reality seriously and to keep them in dialogue with each other. Some of the criticisms of past pneumatologies are valid; but others reflect inadequate attention to the *particular*, to the dramatic, to the narrative dimension of earlier communities' experiences of the Holy Spirit in the scriptures, in liturgy, in religious experience.[13] In this regard, one might ask why in her careful study of the Trinity, *God for Us*, Catherine Mowry LaCugna criticizes Augustine on the basis of a hypothetical separation of his systematic from his exegetical and pastoral works:

> Even if Augustine himself intended nothing of the sort, his legacy to Western theology was an approach to the Trinity largely cut off from the economy of salvation. . . . When the *De Trinitate* is read in parts, or read apart from its overall context and in light of Augustine's full career, it is both possible and common to see no real connection between the self-enclosed Trinity of divine persons and the sphere of creation and redemption.[14]

For a more adequate perspective, one needs to consult the vast collection of scripture commentaries that often provide the backdrop for disputed questions and *summae*. Many medieval theologians engaged in this task throughout their lifetimes. The Holy Spirit is often treated in sections on the annunciation, the baptism of Jesus, Pentecost, other references to the Holy

181

Spirit in the synoptics, and the all-important passages in John and Paul. Narratives of the Spirit were consistently shaped by this biblical language and imagery. Contemporary theology could benefit from an examination of prayers, sermons, liturgical resources, catechetical material, and accounts of mystical experience in order to arrive at a "thicker description" of how earlier communities experienced the Spirit's presence.[15] Sermons and catechetical materials are explicitly oriented to communication and praxis in a pastoral setting. Lives of the saints and mystical texts often reveal the God met in intense experiences—usually of individuals—and by extension, of the communities and societies in which they lived.[16] These genres have the potential to provide a window onto the life of the communities to which they were addressed in a way that formal, systematic treatises simply do not. And each genre offers a distinctive perspective and reveals different aspects of a community's interpretation of its experience of God. They complement one another and provide a more adequate account of the ways in which a community experienced, thought about, imaged, and spoke of the Holy Spirit.[17] We might even ask whether the Holy Spirit is more prominent in certain genres, and if so, how might it be explained?

A constricted vision in systematic theology is not the only problem. Historians also contribute to muting the tradition when they relegate the past to the past, refusing to engage in a dialectic that connects the past to the present in critical and meaningful ways. Is it not just as legitimate to allow the past to "read us," as it is for us to "read" the past?[18] One can allow the tradition to call us to account, not by judging us and finding us wanting according to archaic and fossilized criteria, but by expanding our horizons in both constructive and deconstructive directions, exposing us to fresh ways of seeing and thinking about God.

One can explore these questions in the lives and work of theologians, mystics, prophets, and saints. The roles of the Spirit present in these texts are many. A sampling of the most prevalent themes includes: imaging the Holy Spirit as agent of reconciliation and unity; as the one who offers comfort and confidence to those who suffer; as messenger of God the gift-giver; as the one who empowers the believer to act, especially in the realms of virtue and love of neighbor; and as the one who renews the face of the earth. The Spirit is seen as the wind or breath that blows where it will, bringing freedom; as an aid to contemplation; as the fire of Love that transforms the affections; as the gift of insight, leading to an intelligent grasp of the faith, and the ability to live it maturely; as courage to witness to the gospel and to prophesy.

It is instructive to take Augustine as a starting point, since he set the agenda for trinitarian theology in the West perhaps more than any other theologian. In this essay I propose to ask whether there are narratives of the

Spirit in Augustine's corpus that have been obscured or forgotten.[19] If so, can these texts be interpreted in an imaginative and historically responsible way that will allow them to be useful to contemporary pneumatology (and by extension christology, trinitarian theology, spirituality, ecclesiology, etc.) and to the faith life of our communities by evoking a more lively and relevant way to encounter the mystery of the Spirit in everyday life?

I begin with a word about Augustine's attention to the distinctiveness of the trinitarian persons. Following this I will explore four ways in which Augustine emphasized the action of the Spirit: the Spirit is active principle of church unity and agent of reconciliation; the Spirit inspires the faithful with courage to witness to the gospel; the Spirit enables one to live the Christian life intelligently; the Spirit is love, empowering us to love God and one another, to abide in God, and to enkindle desire that will lead us home.

THE HOLY SPIRIT AS A DISTINCT PERSON

In terms of Augustine's approach to the unity and plurality in God, two things are true: he had great difficulty explaining plurality in God, and he portrayed the distinctive roles of the persons in creative and lively ways. Let us explore this tension.

Augustine's sense of accountability to the scriptures led him to use language and imagery that point to three persons with quasi-distinct operations, mitigating his preoccupation with establishing the unity of God and God's operations. Augustine called the scriptures the "countenance of God,"[20] and Peter Brown writes that Augustine "had come to believe that the understanding and exposition of the Scriptures was the heart of a bishop's life."[21] But Augustine does not easily come to terms with biblical allusions to three persons in God, for example in Luke's account of Jesus' baptism (3.22), where the Father has a voice, the Son is seen in the human nature he assumed, and the Holy Spirit is portrayed as a dove. In Augustine's world—in which supreme value was given to unity—it would be impossible, except for an explicit revelation, to arrive at a triune God. For Augustine, this revelatory language functions to teach us that, though the persons are "inseparable trinity, yet they are a trinity." And just as we cannot pronounce all three names at the same time—even though their existence is inseparable—"so in some places of Scripture also, they are by certain created things presented to us distinctively and in mutual relation to each other."[22] For Augustine, the Trinity is not something separate from the God who is revealed. It *is* the God who is revealed.

The scriptures also use speech about distinct persons because of the need to accommodate our human weakness. In true neo-Platonic fashion, Augustine seems embarrassed by our fall into variety. In a letter written in 389 in response to a question from his friend Nebridius about why the incarnation is ascribed only to the Son, when belief states that all operations in the Trinity are common, Augustine offers a rather "pale" explanation. The human fall from unity to plurality explains why we cannot grasp the unity of operations and thus requires that they be presented in distinct ways.[23] Four years later, in *On Faith and the Creed*, Augustine also acknowledged that the lack of previous discussion on the Holy Spirit by learned and distinguished investigators of the scriptures, makes it difficult to "obtain an intelligent conception of what also constitutes his special individuality (*proprium*): in virtue of which special individuality it comes to be the case that we cannot call Him either the Son or the Father, but only the Holy Spirit; excepting that they predicate Him to be the Gift of God, so that we may believe God not to give a gift inferior to Himself."[24]

On the other hand, Augustine is credited with being the first in Christian history to formulate a theology of the Holy Spirit as Love within the Trinity and therefore as properly Gift to the church.[25] Augustine's pneumatology thus portrays the Spirit as connected to the community of the faithful in an integral, experiential way. The same is true for the Son. For example, in *On the Trinity*, speaking of the missions of the persons, he says of the Son: "And He is then sent to each one, when He is apprehended and perceived by each," in so far as the human soul is capable.[26] One can also call attention to Augustine's intense search for analogies within human experience (e.g., memory, understanding, and will) that would make the trinitarian persons better known to human understanding. And this understanding of intra-Trinitarian life leads naturally to the missions of the persons as Word and Love.

In *On the Trinity*, Augustine also speaks of the special, distinctive nature of the second sending of the Spirit at Pentecost. He says, "But that He was given twice was certainly a significant *economy*, which we will discuss in its place."[27] Augustine explicitly links the Spirit to both the divine and human realms: "and so the Holy Spirit is not only the Spirit of the Father and of the Son who gave Him, but He is also called ours, who have received him. . . . Therefore the Spirit is both the Spirit of God who gave Him, and *ours* who have received Him."[28] This Spirit is not the spirit by which we are human beings but the Spirit by which we are made holy: "the Spirit is ours in another mode, *viz.* that in which we also say, 'Give us this day our bread.'"[29]

I suggest that Augustine's drive toward precise metaphysical speculation did not obliterate his ability to speak of the individual persons as active in the life and struggles of the community. His obvious skepticism about plurality in God led him to emphasize the unity in God and God's operations. But might it also have fueled his not insignificant efforts to lead the community to knowledge of God specifically as triune? Augustine's skepticism about plurality in God can only be understood fully when juxtaposed with texts in which Augustine speaks of the persons' distinctive activities in language that reveals existential liveliness, warmth, and engagement. Let us turn to select texts on the Holy Spirit.[30]

THE SPIRIT AS AGENT OF UNITY AND RECONCILIATION

Augustine struggled in the midst of a failing empire to combat forces that he judged inimical to orthodoxy and the church's integrity. The fourth century witnessed the Arian controversy and debate about the Spirit's identity. And at every turn, Augustine invoked the Holy Spirit to support his idea of church against that of the Donatists.[31] The Donatists held out for a church that was pure and holy in contrast to the society around it. Peter Brown describes how the imagination of African Christians had become riveted on the idea of the church, thought of as a preserve of safety and cleanliness in a world ruled by demonic powers. Africans came to church, he says, not because they were thirsty and burdened but to survive in a battlefield.[32] Both the Donatists and Augustine compare the church to Noah's ark (Gen 6. 6,9), but to different ends. W. H. C. Frend notes the presence among the Donatists of Cyprian's popular metaphor of the church as the ark—"within the saved, outside the drowning multitudes." Images of an ark and a dove on a sculptured pillar of a Donatist church in central Numidia portray the church of the saints watched over by the Holy Spirit.[33] For Augustine, on the other hand, the church lived out of a confidence that it could absorb the world around it without losing its identity—an identity that was not dependent on the holiness of its members, but on the power of Christ and the Spirit.[34] In *On the Gospel of John,* Augustine says, "if the ark was a figure of the church, you see indeed that in the present deluge of the world, the church must of necessity contain both kinds, as well the ravens as the dove. Who are the ravens? They who seek their own. Who are the doves? They who seek the things that are Christ's."[35]

But in an effort to calm the fears and doubts of those wondering about the identity of the true church (and also to threaten them a bit?), Augustine calls on the Spirit to support his portrayal of a church with clear boundaries for insiders and outsiders. He says, "whoever has the Holy Spirit is in the church . . . whoever is outside this Church hasn't got the Holy Spirit."[36] Those can be sure of having the Holy Spirit who "consent through sincere charity firmly to attach their minds to the unity."[37] Within the church, Augustine warns those members who belong insincerely by deceit and dissimulation.[38] Those outside the church (the Donatists) who "hate the grace of peace and who do not hold on to the fellowship of unity" have "absolutely no share in this gift of the Holy Spirit."[39] Outside the church the Holy Spirit gives life to no one. Outside the church the enemies of unity are blocked from partaking of divine love.

For Augustine, the sending of the Holy Spirit revealed a trustworthy God who fulfills all promises.[40] But he warned his congregation that just as the soul departs from a severed limb, so the Spirit departs from those who cut themselves off from the church.[41] In a Pentecost sermon, he further develops the body metaphor.

> It can happen in the human body—or rather from the body—that one part is cut off, a hand, a finger, a foot; does the soul follow the amputated part? When it was in the body, it was alive, cut off, it loses life. In the same way too Christian men and women are Catholics, while they are alive in the body; cut off, they have become heretics, the Spirit doesn't follow the amputated part. So if you wish to be alive with the Holy Spirit, hold on to loving-kindness, love truthfulness, long for oneness, that you may attain to everlastingness. Amen.[42]

And in his commentary on John, Augustine says "there is nothing that a Christian ought to dread so much as to be separated from Christ's body."[43]

But Augustine's sometimes harsh language about the Spirit's presence or absence to ecclesial insiders and outsiders must be juxtaposed with his struggle for reconciliation. Against the Donatists, Augustine underlined the importance of the forgiveness that can be offered only within the church and only through the power of God. The Holy Spirit is the Gift that makes possible communion with God and with each other. For Augustine, the remission of sins is the first blessing of God's goodness in the Holy Spirit. And in his commentary on Psalm 8, he locates the bowels of the mercy of God in the Holy Spirit.[44] Against this gratuitous gift, the impenitent heart stands as an affront of enormous proportion.

In a number of texts, sermons, and letters, Augustine comments on Matthew 12.31–32: "Therefore I tell you, every sin and blasphemy will be forgiven, but the blasphemy against the Spirit will not be forgiven."[45] Part of the context for Augustine's interest in, and understanding of, the sin against the Holy Spirit was the fierce debate going on about the contrast between the ideal unity and holiness of the church and the often unedifying behavior of its members. In Sermon 21, Augustine excoriates the recalcitrant individual who remains impassive in the "persevering hardness of an impenitent heart." Such a heart is the "blasphemy of the Spirit which shall not be forgiven, neither in this world, nor in the world to come."[46]

Augustine also spoke of the effects of the remission of sin. In his exposition on the Apostles Creed, written for the bishops of Hippo-Regius in 393 when Augustine was still a presbyter, he elaborated on the sources and fruits of reconciliation, all of which are founded in the love poured forth into hearts by the Holy Spirit (Rom 5.5)—perhaps Augustine's favorite biblical reference to the Spirit. Reconciliation in love, he says, makes us sons and daughters of God (1Jn 4.18); casts out fear (Rom 8.15); fills us with the spirit of liberty by which we cry, "Abba, Father" (Rom 8.15); calls us back into friendship and acquaints us with all the secret things of God (John 16.13).[47]

Almost twenty-five years later, in his *Treatise Concerning the Correction of the Donatists*, written to the tribune Boniface in 417, Augustine characterizes the fruits of pardon in this way: "The prince of sin, the spirit who is divided against himself, should no more reign in us . . . we should thenceforward be made the temple of the Holy Spirit, and receive Him, by whom we are cleansed through receiving pardon, to dwell in us, to work, increase, and perfect righteousness."[48] One is reminded here of Paul's interior struggle in Romans: "For I do not do what I want, but I do the very thing I hate" (Romans 7.15). John Cavadini speaks of the articulation of the ambiguous, "mixed" character of life as we know it, as one of Augustine's most characteristic and enduring accomplishments.[49] Augustine links this freedom from inner division to the work of the Spirit, visible in those community members who are no longer slaves to the war within.

But in addition to defining the church over against its enemies, Augustine wanted to establish the Spirit's on-going presence and function in the church as well. In a Pentecost sermon delivered in 412, he lays down the challenge to those who suggest that the Spirit no longer visits the community. He asks rhetorically, "Isn't the Holy Spirit being given nowadays, then, brothers and sisters? Anyone who thinks that, isn't worthy to receive it. It certainly is given nowadays."[50] Evidently, one of the arguments used to suggest the Spirit's absence was the disappearance of the gift of tongues. As part of his response to this complaint, Augustine alters the Pentecost account in Acts 2.3–4, positing that *each* individual spoke in *all* tongues. The reason Christians no longer spoke in tongues was because the promise of Pentecost had been fulfilled. At Pentecost one person speaking in the tongues of all nations pointed to the unity of the Catholic church.[51] The sign of the Spirit's presence in Augustine's time was the unity of a world church that embraced all languages.[52]

> Among you, after all, is being fulfilled what was being prefigured in those days, when the Holy Spirit came. Because just as then, whoever received the Holy Spirit, even as one person, started speaking all languages; so too now the unity itself is speaking all languages through all nations; and it is by being established in this unity that you have the Holy Spirit, you that do not break away in any schism from the Church of Christ which speaks all languages.[53]

The variety of tongues given by the Spirit pointed to the unity of the world church that Augustine envisioned, contrary to what he perceived as the narrow, parochial vision of the Donatists.[54]

The Holy Spirit is also the Gift that makes possible communion with God and with each other. In Sermon 71, Augustine linked the bond of love that is the Holy Spirit within the Trinity, with its effects in the community of faith. He says, "The Father and the Son have willed that we enter into communion among ourselves and with them through That which is common to them, and to bind us into one by this Gift which the two possess together, that is by the Holy Spirit, God and gift of God. It is in him in fact, that we are reconciled with the Divinity and take our delight in it."[55]

Augustine's intense drive toward unity and his desire for communion among the faithful was grounded, in part, in the decidedly mixed character of the church's members and the daily, life-and-death struggle with the Donatists. Using the scriptures as a launching pad, he turns to the Holy Spirit as a force for unity and reconciliation within each individual and within a divided community. He persuades, cajoles, threatens, and anathematizes in the interest of preserving what he sees as the life, integrity, and future of the Catholic church. Augustine's talk about the Spirit gives the reader a clear sense that the Spirit is not an abstract principle, but rather a present and compelling force, engaged in the struggle to preserve the church.

PREACHING WITHOUT FEAR

At Pentecost, a prominent effect of the Holy Spirit's descent took the form of wiping out fear and instilling courage in the hearts of the apostles, allowing them to bear witness to the risen Lord (unfortunately at the expense of the Jews, and of women whose witness remains largely invisible).[56] In several instances, Augustine focuses on Peter as an embodiment of this courage. I cite at some length a stirring description from his commentary on the gospel of John:

> And then that Spirit, pervading him thus with the fullness of richer grace, kindled his hitherto frigid heart to such a witness-bearing for Christ, and unlocked those lips that in their previous tremor had suppressed the truth, that, when all on whom the Holy Spirit had descended were speaking in the tongues of all nations to the crowds of Jews collected around, he alone broke forth before the others in the promptitude of his testimony in behalf of Christ. . . . And if any one would enjoy the pleasure of gazing on a sight so charming in its holiness, let him read the Acts of the Apostles: (2.5) and there let him be filled with amazement at the preaching of the blessed Peter, over whose denial of this Master he had just been mourning; there let him behold that tongue, itself translated from diffidence to confidence, from bondage to liberty, converting to the confession of Christ the tongues of so many of His enemies, not one of which he could bear when lapsing himself into denial. And what shall I say more? In him there shone forth such an effulgence of grace, and such a fullness of the Holy Spirit, and such a weight of most precious truth poured from the lips of the preacher, that he transformed that vast multitude of Jews.[57]

In this rhetorically powerful passage, we glimpse how Augustine envisioned the working of the Spirit, and possibly his own identification with Peter's effective eloquence. One can conjecture that Augustine identified with Peter and desired that the Spirit function in him as it did in Peter at Pentecost.

The elements of commonality are several. To begin, the *Confessions* reveal a kind of betrayal on Augustine's part prior to his conversion, after which he spent his life proclaiming the truth of the one true God he had encountered in Christianity. As a rhetor, Augustine also seemed to have high expectations of his preaching skills. In his response to a request from a Carthaginian deacon, brother Deogratias, for some help in catechizing the uninstructed Augustine says,

> Indeed with me, too, it is almost always the fact that my speech displeases myself. For I am covetous of something better . . . when my capacities of expression prove inferior to my inner apprehensions, I grieve over the inability which my tongue has betrayed in answering to my heart. For it is my wish that he who hears me should have the same complete understanding of the subject which I have myself; and I perceive that I fail to speak in a manner calculated to effect that.[58]

189

Augustine perceived the decadence of his society and the forces of personal and social evil to be daunting, requiring a superhuman love and intelligence—gifts with which he describes the Spirit-filled Peter.

For Augustine, the Spirit's distinctive role is as an agent of visible change and renewal. Frigid hearts, locked lips, diffidence, fear of speaking the truth, bondage, and mourning for sin—all are transformed in the power of the Holy Spirit. The Spirit's presence is described as a fuller effulgence of grace, a presence that compelled Peter to witness to Christ with astonishing ease. Through Peter's words and actions, the truth and power of Christ, given through the Spirit, were visible and effective, leading to the conversion and renewal of those who were once Christ's enemies. One can imagine other churches—Augustine's and many others down through the ages—that needed the Spirit's gifts visible in those who could preach and witness to the truth of Christ's redeeming love.

THE HOLY SPIRIT AS SOURCE OF INTELLIGENT CHRISTIAN LIVING

For Augustine, the Spirit also fosters understanding.[59] It is not that Augustine does not connect knowledge and understanding with the Word. But in the gospel and letters of John, we witness a reversal of the standard associations of Word and Spirit. The Spirit is linked with truth (Jn 14.17) and the Word with love. In his commentary on John 16.13—the Holy Spirit leads us into all truth—Augustine compares the knowledge that comes from our own spirit with the knowledge of God that is the Holy Spirit. He says,

> So also the things of God knoweth no man, but the Spirit of God. We with our spirit, God with His: so, however, that God with His Spirit know also what goes on within us; but we are not able, without His Spirit, to know what takes place in God.[60]

In other words, the Holy Spirit is the power, in both God and humans, that makes it possible for us to know one another.

Augustine understands this function of the Holy Spirit to be a completion, a fulfillment, a more mature stage in the experience of faith in which the believer not only has faith, but knows it. Commenting on the role of the dove at Jesus' baptism (John 1.32–33), Augustine argues that at Christ's baptism, John the Baptist *learned* something—not that Christ is God, not that he baptizes with the Holy Spirit, but, against the Donatists—that the effectiveness of baptism rests in Christ, not in good or bad ministers![61] Augustine also puzzles over the passage in John 14.15–17, in which the Lord says that if the apostles keep the commandments, God will send another Paraclete to abide with them. How can the Spirit be sent a second time, when the prerequisite for the Paraclete's coming—loving and keeping the commandments—demands that the Spirit be already present? Augustine's solution is to understand Pentecost as a fuller possession of the Spirit. Augustine distinguishes between possessing the gift of Love which is the Holy Spirit and the further stage of being conscious that one has the gift. He says,

> We are therefore to understand that he who loves has already the Holy Spirit, and by what he has, becomes worthy of a fuller possession, that by having the more he may love the more. . . . They had Him in a hidden way, they were yet to receive Him in a way that was manifest; for this present possession had also a bearing on that fuller gift of the Holy Spirit, that they might come to a conscious knowledge of what they had.[62]

A further instance in which Augustine connects the Holy Spirit with understanding is in his treatise on the Sermon on the Mount. Commenting on 1Cor. 12.3, "No one can say that Jesus is Lord except by the Holy Spirit," Augustine describes what must obtain in order to make this statement of faith properly. It requires that the speaker be engaged "with the deliberate consent of the will. . . . But truly and properly those parties say it whose utterance in speech really represents their will and intention."[63] Belief is not intended to be a mindless, empty "going-along," but rather an integral part of one's whole being—mind, heart, speech, and behavior.

One might inquire how Augustine's plea for an intelligent Christianity squares with his commitment to an inclusive church. We know that Augustine fought mightily for an inclusive church—one that had room for sinners as well as for the virtuous. And against the Donatists, he rejected a church of the pure, of an intellectual or spiritual elite. He drives this point home in a letter to Bishop Evodius, who asks if the text of 1Cor. 14.38, "He that is ignorant shall be ignored," refers to those who cannot comprehend the unity of the Trinity. Augustine responds,

For if Christ died for those only who with clear intelligence can discern these things, our labour in the Church is almost spent in vain. But if, as is the fact, crowds of common people, possessing no great strength of intellect, run to the Physician in the exercise of faith, with the result of being healed by Christ, and Him crucified, that "where sin has abounded, grace may much more abound" (Rom. 5.20) . . . many glorying in the cross of Christ, and not withdrawing from that same path, attain, notwithstanding their ignorance of those things, which some with most profound subtlety investigate, unto that eternity, truth, and love,— that is, unto enduring, clear, and full felicity,—in which to those who abide, and see, and love, all things are plain.[64]

And yet on another level, Augustine was a philosopher and scholar, committed to the "highest peak of human reason" within the realm of faith.[65] He admits that, in the end, the Spirit infuses us who are infirm with a "certain learned ignorance,"[66] but in the heat of daily life in the church, he combated the fundamentalism and anti-intellectualism around him: "Far be it from us to think that God would hate in us that which distinguishes us from the beasts. . . . Love understands wholeheartedly."[67] The Holy Spirit played a key role in this loving understanding. Not only was Augustine committed to speculative thought, so brilliantly displayed in his *On the Trinity*, but he was also intent on inviting others to understand the faith, so that they might open themselves to the Spirit's power and become intelligent Christians in their own right.[68]

Thus, without the Spirit's presence, individuals may hear about the Good News of salvation, but they would be unable to know the truth about God's life; or that God dwells within (1Jn 3.24; 4.13) or to proclaim that "Jesus is Lord."[69] For Augustine, the Christian life is a longing for home that admits of growth and development. It's as if he says, Don't be a stupid believer, but rather, live in the Spirit, that is, seek understanding, vision, wisdom, and the joy that accompanies ease in being good. The presence of love and the gifts and fruits are signs of the Holy Spirit's presence. But being conscious of that love is a fuller gift. In a suggestive rather than explicit way, Augustine connects the fullness of the Spirit's truth with a mature faith. By so doing, he reminds ministers of every age that the Spirit not only empowers belief but also enables Christians to come to maturity, that is, to know, to will, and to rejoice in, that belief.

THE HOLY SPIRIT AND LOVE

I highlight two points on the fourth and final topic, that is, Augustine's original contribution that envisions the Holy Spirit as the bond of love,[70] linking the first and second persons of the Trinity and linking us with God.[71] In *On the Trinity*, Augustine writes, "Therefore the Holy Spirit, of whom God has given us, makes us to abide in God and God in us; and this it is that love does. . . . Therefore God the Holy Spirit, who proceeds from the Father, when He has been given to humans, inflames them to the love of God and of neighbor and is Himself love."[72] And in Sermon 21, Augustine again emphasizes the love of communion. "The Father and the Son have willed that we enter into communion among ourselves and with them through the One who is common to them, and to bind us into one by this Gift which the two possess together, that is by the Holy Spirit, God and gift of God. It is in Him in fact, that we are reconciled with the Divinity and take our delight in it."[73] Biblically this connection is anchored in Rom. 5.5, a passage that runs like a leitmotif throughout Augustine's corpus. As we have seen, in his struggle to maintain the orthodoxy and integrity of the church against what he sees as false competing positions, Augustine literally hammers away at the ways in which the Holy Spirit gathers the church into a unity, reflecting the Holy Spirit's unifying role within the Trinity.[74] At Pentecost, the apostles speak in all tongues because they are members of the church whose unity of members is of one mind through charity.[75] And in what today may seem a quaint, yet provocative exegesis of Isaiah's description of the Holy Spirit as the finger of God (53.7), Augustine says,

> But inasmuch as it is through the Holy Spirit that God's gifts are divided to His saints, in order that, although they vary in their capacities, they may nevertheless not lapse from the concord of charity, and inasmuch as it is especially in the fingers that there appears a certain kind of division, while nevertheless there is no separation from unity, this may be the explanation of the phrase.[76]

Further, this unifying love bears fruit. In the midst of the struggle of life, the Holy Spirit's love enables believers to love their neighbors as themselves (Gal 5.14). God the Holy Spirit, who is Love, is given to us and inflames us to the love of God and neighbor.[77] Augustine concludes the *Enchiridion* by emphasizing that the aim of all commandments is love, a love that embraces love of God and love of neighbor, on which hang the law, the prophets, the gospel, and the apostles.[78] But there is more. The Spirit at Pentecost allows Christians to fulfill the law in loving God and neighbor, "not only without the sense of its being burdensome, but even with a joyful mind."[79] No doubt, Augustine intends this message for himself as well as for his hearers. The weight of his responsibilities must have indeed at times seemed burdensome. But the Spirit's important role as "keeper of the joy," as it were, offers the hope that the command to take up the Lord's easy burden in love (Mt 11.20) can be fulfilled and even extended to one's enemies.[80] For Augustine, the unity that joins believers together as members of one body can be effected only by the love that is "poured out" by the Holy Spirit, a love that "quickens" and "enlivens" both individual members of the church and the body as a whole.

Faith unites. Understanding quickens. As a result, "there is nothing that a Christian ought to dread so much as to be separated from Christ's body."[81]

As an extension of Augustine's understanding of the Spirit as bond of love, he speaks of the Holy Spirit's link with human desire. Following on the Spirit's gift of repentance, the gift of baptism in the Holy Spirit and fire brings fervor to love.[82] Augustine speaks of the drive that compels us to migrate home, a place of peace symbolized by the dove. The tongues at Pentecost caused the dead to be "pricked in their hearts and converted."[83] "Therefore, that you may love God, let God dwell in you, and love Himself in you, that is, to His love let Him move you, enkindle, enlighten, arouse you."[84]

For Augustine, the Spirit of desire is connected with prayer. Paul assures the Romans (8.26) that in their weakness and inability to pray, the Holy Spirit comes to their assistance. Augustine comments that it is not within the Trinity that the Holy Spirit groans, but rather the Spirit groans so that we may groan. He goes on, "Nor is it little matter that the Holy Spirit teaches us to groan, for He gives us to know that we are sojourners in a foreign land, and He teaches us to sigh after our native country: and through that very longing do we groan."[85]

Letter CXXX to Proba, a widow from a noble and wealthy Roman family, is really a little treatise on prayer.[86] Proba sought Augustine's opinion about Paul's statement in Romans that we know not for what we should pray (8.26). His response is a reflection on the good and bad desires of the heart. Since Proba is a woman of wealth and position, Augustine attributes the power to extinguish a desire for riches to the Holy Spirit and urges her to thirst and long for God alone (Ps 63.1): "a person lives in those things which he loves, which he greatly desires, and in which he believes himself to be blessed."[87] The image of the Holy Spirit groaning within us comes to life in the following:

> To use much speaking in prayer is to employ a superfluity of words in asking a necessary thing; but to prolong prayer is to have the heart throbbing with continued pious emotion towards Him whom we pray. For in most cases prayer consists more in groaning than in speaking, in tears rather than in words. But He sets our tears in His sight, and our groaning is not hidden from Him who made all things by the word, and does not need human words.[88]

For Augustine, then, the Holy Spirit had a number of important and practical roles in the believer's journey to God. As we have seen, the Spirit has not been relegated to a place in the wings, but is an existential force in the life of the individual believer and of the ecclesial community. Augustine sees the Spirit as a force, leading believers to a full and mature knowledge of the things of God. The Spirit also calls and empowers the church to the very difficult tasks of living in unity, loving, and forgiving one another. It is the Spirit, he says, who teaches us the way of charity, bends the knee to God for us so that we may know the supereminent knowledge of the love of Christ; and finally brings us to rest.[89] In his exegesis on Genesis at the end of the *Confessions*, Augustine discusses why the Holy Spirit alone was said to be "borne over the waters" (Gen 1.2). He says,

> In your Gift we rest; there we enjoy you . . . By your Gift we are inflamed, and are borne upwards; we wax hot inwardly, and go forwards. We ascend your ways that be in our heart (Ps 84.5), and sing a song of degrees; we glow inwardly with your fire, with your good fire, and we go, because we go upwards to the peace of Jerusalem; for glad was I when they said to me, "Let us go into the house of the Lord" (Ps 122.1). There hath your good pleasure placed us, that we may desire no other thing than to dwell there for ever.[90]

NOTES

1. Philip Endean, "Theology out of Spirituality: The Approach of Karl Rahner"; Mark McIntosh, "Lover Without a Name: Spirituality and Constructive Christology Today"; J. Matthew Ashley, "The Turn to Spirituality? The Relationship Between Theology and Spirituality"; Anne M. Clifford, "Re-membering the Spiritual Core of Theology: A Response." *Christian Spirituality Bulletin* 3/2(Fall 1995): 6–21. The Ashley essay is Chapter 11 and the McIntosh essay is Chapter 16 in this volume.
2. Endean, "Theology out of Spirituality," 6.
3. See Roger Haight, "The Case For Spirit Christology," *Theological Studies* 53(1992), 260. In concluding comments of the second volume of the multi-volume work *The Presence of God: A History of Western Christian Mysticism*, Bernard McGinn describes his method as one that does not criticize by measuring the gap between ideals and reality or by judging the legitimacy of the ideals. Rather he seeks to identify the spiritual values various mystical authors said they were trying to inculcate in their lives and societies. That they no doubt often failed or deluded themselves about their intentions does not necessarily falsify the values at which they aimed. I take a similar approach in this essay. *The Growth of Mysticism: Gregory the Great through the 12th Century* (New York: Crossroad, 1994), 420.
4. Critical statements about early pneumatology are not limited to Roman Catholic theologians, e.g., Protestant process theologian David Griffin laments the loss of Paul's awareness of the Spirit's presence. "But it was not long before the experience of being guided by the Spirit waned. A Christian was increasingly defined in terms of certain doctrinal beliefs, and these were beliefs that did not concern the relation of God's Spirit to the actual experiences of daily life. . . . The sense of a present experience of God that characterized Jesus and the early Church was largely gone." "Holy Spirit: Compassion and Reverence for Being," in *Religious Experience and Process Theology: The Pastoral Implications of a Major Modern Movement* (New York: Paulist Press, 1976), 109.
5. See Elizabeth Johnson, *She Who Is: The Mystery of God in Feminist Discourse* (New York: Crossroad, 1992), 50; Sallie McFague, *Models of God: Theology for an Ecological, Nuclear Age* (Philadelphia: Fortress, 1987), 169–71; 157–80; Walter Kasper, *God of Jesus Christ*, trans. V. Green (New York: Paulist, 1976), 223; Frederick Crowe, *The Doctrine of the Most Holy Trinity* (Willowdale, Ont.: Regis College, 1970), 18, 69.
6. Kilian McDonnell summarizes highlights of this discussion in "A Trinitarian Theology of the Holy Spirit?" *Theological Studies* 46(1985): 191–227. Ralph Del Colle focuses

on Orthodox criticism in *Christ and the Spirit: Spirit-Christology in Trinitarian Perspective* (New York: Oxford University Press, 1994) 8–33. McDonnell notes that Wolf-Dieter Hauschild has questioned assessments that pneumatology was lacking in the early theologians. *Gottes Geist und der Mensch: Studien zur fruhchristlichen Pneumatologie* (Munich: Kaiser, 1972), 11.

7. Karl Rahner, *The Trinity*, trans., Joseph Donceel (New York: Herder and Herder, 1970), 10. Rahner offered an early invitation to present the doctrine of the Trinity in such a way that it becomes a reality in the concrete lives of the faithful. He asks, practically, "How can the contemplation of any reality, even of the loftiest reality, beatify us if intrinsically it is absolutely *unrelated* to us in any way?" Ibid., 14–15, 39.

8. See G. J. Sirks, "The Cinderella of Theology: The Doctrine of the Holy Spirit" *Harvard Theological Review* 50/2 (1957): 77–89.

9. Michel René Barnes, "Augustine in Contemporary Trinitarian Theology," *Theological Studies* 56/2 (June 1995): 237–250. Théodore de Régnon, *Études de théologie positive sur la Sainte Trinité*, 2 vols. (Paris: V. Retaux, 1892).

10. Barnes, "Augustine in Contemporary Trinitarian Theology," 241.

11. "'Why are you so interested in the wandering people of God?' Michael Welker on Theology and Common Sense." *Soundings* 79/1–2 (Spring/Summer 1996), 132–133.

12. Langdon Gilkey, *Catholicism Confronts Modernity: A Protestant View* (New York: Seabury Press, 1975), 91–92.

13. Underlying this approach is the conviction that the theological task is located in the discovery of the presence of the triune God in history, what Killian McDonnell calls the "contact point" where God and humankind "touch" one another. One starts with the individual and collective experience of the Spirit, what he calls the obverse side of the Spirit's mission. "A Trinitarian Theology of the Holy Spirit?" *Theological Studies* 46(1985), 206, 208. Another presupposition is the conviction that theological and spiritual texts bear witness to religious experience. In her book *From Virile Woman to WomanChrist*, Barbara Newman expands on this conviction in three points. First, the subjects of religious experience are persons with developed interiority—conscious and unconscious wishes, anxieties, projects, and beliefs regarding key human concerns such as life, love, and death that are often expressed through religion. Second, religious experience takes place in complex, dynamic cultures characterized always at some level by struggle. Third, religious experience reveals mysterious, multivalent, often opaque traces of a real and transcendent object (Philadelphia: University of Pennsylvania Press, 1995), 16.

14. *God for Us: The Trinity and Christian Life* (San Francisco: HarperSanFrancisco, 1991), 102–103. LaCugna also suggests that Augustine's obvious love of metaphysical speculation caused him to neglect the scriptures. Peter Brown comments to the contrary, "He [Augustine] had come to believe that the understanding and exposition of the Scriptures was the heart of a bishop's life. His relations with the Scriptures, therefore, come to form a constant theme throughout the *Confessions*." *Augustine of Hippo: A Biography* (Berkeley, CA: University of California Press, 1967), 162. Brown also cites A. M. LaBonnardière, "Car si Saint Augustine est un théologien, il est un théologien de la Bible; son enseignement sourde directement de l'Écriture," *Recherches de chronologie augustin* (1965), 180. In Sermon XXII.7, Augustine calls the scriptures the "countenance of God" (Ergo pro facie Dei, tibi pone interim scripturam Dei), *Patrologia latina* (hereafter PL) 38, 152. Cited in Brown, 262. See also *Confessions*, XI.ii.2. *Nicene and Post-Nicene Fathers* (hereafter NPNF) I, 163/PL 32, 809. James O'Donnell offers a fine analysis of the use of scripture in the *Confessions* in *Confessions, By Augustine* (Oxford: Clarendon Press, 1992). However, LaCugna also acknowledges the need to keep narrative and doctrine linked: "The doxological mode of theology keeps together primary and secondary theology, reaffirming both the centrality of the narratives of

Christian experience for Christian theology, and the appropriateness of theological reflection on the divine 'actor' in the narratives." *God for Us*, 358.

15. Joan Nuth comments, for example, that scholarly consideration of texts by doctors of the church Catherine of Siena and Teresa of Avila fall under the rubric of spirituality since they are not considered theologians. As a result, "any doctrinal insights born of their experience of God are neither noticed nor studied as such, because one does not expect to find them." *Wisdom's Daughter: The Theology of Julian of Norwich* (New York: Crossroad, 1991), 1.

16. In an article entitled "Towards a Theology of the Holy Spirit," Edmund J. Dobbin situates trinitarian language within the context of religious experience. He argues that since the Christian experience of the presence of God in our inmost depths (*intimissimum*) has been symbolically expressed primarily through the symbol of the Spirit, we need to attend to the accounts of that experience. He suggests that the symbol "Father" evokes the transcendent dimension of the numinous as *dissimilis nobis*; the "Son" is Jesus as *Realsymbol* of God; the Holy Spirit is donative of the immanent dimension of the numinous presence, the *similis nobis*. For Dobbin, the Spirit represents the deep abyss within the inmost self whence the power of action emanates, the numinous ground of the unrestricted *eros* of the human spirit. He suggests that such in-depth experiences of God are most visible in mystical literature. He suggests, therefore, that any comprehensive pneumatology must address this part of the tradition, since these accounts offer the most focused, detailed accounts of the experience of the immanent presence of the Spirit. Edmund J. Dobbin. "Towards a Theology of the Holy Spirit," *Heythrop Journal* I:17/1 (1976): 5–19; II:17/2 (1976): 129–49.

17. For an example of how audiences played a role in the genesis of a work see Katherine Gill, "Women and the Production of Religious Literature in the Vernacular, 1300–1500," in *Creative Women in Medieval and Early Modern Italy: A Religious and Artistic Renaissance,* ed. E. Ann Matter and John Coakley (Philadelphia: University of Pennsylvania Press, 1994), 63–104; and Aron Guervich, *Medieval Popular Culture: Problems of Belief and Perception*. Cambridge Studies in Oral and Literate Culture, 14. Trans. Janos M. Baak and Paul A. Hollingsworth (Cambridge: Cambridge University Press, 1988), 3–8.

18. David Tracy calls attention to this perspective: "If the text is a genuinely classic one, my present horizon of understanding should always be provoked, challenged, transformed." *The Analogical Imagination: Christian Theology and the Culture of Pluralism* (New York: Crossroad, 1981), 102.

19. Dieter Hauschild, *Gottes Geist und der Mensch*, 11.

20. Sermon XXII.7/PL 38, 152–153. Cited in Peter Brown, *Augustine of Hippo*, 262.

21. Peter Brown, ibid., 162. See *Confessions* XI.ii.2. NPNF I, 163/PL 32, 809.

22. Letter CLXIX.2.5 written to Bishop Evodius in 415. NPNF I, 540/PL 33, 744. See also *On the Trinity* IV.21.30, NPNF III, 85–86/PL 42, 909, and Sermon XXI. NPNF VI, 324/PL 38, 142–148.

23. Letter XI.4 to Nebridius written in 389. NPNF I, 230/PL 33, 76.

24. *On Faith and the Creed*, IX.19. NPNF III, 329/PL 40, 191.

25. *On the Trinity* V.9.10. NPNF I, 92/PL 42, 918; V.11.12. NPNF III, 93/PL 42, 919.

26. *On the Trinity* IV.20.28. NPNF III, 84/PL 42, 907: "Filius mittitur cum a quoquam cognoscitur atque percipitur."

27. Ibid., IV.20.29. NPNF I, 84–85/PL 42, 908.

28. Ibid., V.14.15. NPNF I, 94–95/PL 42, 921.

29. Ibid.

30. Yves Congar notes that from 393 onwards, "Augustine became intensely interested in the theology of the Holy Spirit." *I Believe in the Holy Spirit*, 3 vols. (New York and London: Seabury Press and Geoffrey Chapman, 1979–80), I: 77. Patout Burns also

suggests that "Augustine moves from a mysticism of the second person of the Trinity in his early writings to a mysticism of the third person in the later writings." William J. Collinge cites this sentence from a lecture given by Patout Burns at Yale University in 1973. "John Dunne's Journey of the Mind, Heart, and Soul," *Horizons* 16/1(1989), 35.

31. The Donatists also called on the Spirit. W. H. C. Frend suggests that part of the Donatists' ability to survive was due to their ability to combine a hierarchically governed church with a non-hierarchical community devoted to the Spirit. Readers in their liturgies were thought to be transmitting the Spirit to the congregation. *The Donatist Church: A Movement of Protest in Roman North Africa* (Oxford: Clarendon Press, 1971 [1952]), 319–320.
32. Peter Brown, *Augustine of Hippo*, 212–214.
33. W.H.C. Frend, *The Donatist Church*, 238.
34. Peter Brown, *Augustine of Hippo*, 212–214.
35. *On the Gospel of John*, Tractate VI.2. NPNF VII, 40/PL 35, 1425.
36. Ser. 268.2; 269.2/PL 38, 1232 and 1235.
37. Ser. 269.4/PL 38, 1237.
38. Letter CLXXXV.50, NPNF IV, 651/PL 33, 815.
39. Ser. 271/PL 38, 1246.
40. Ser. 266.2/PL 38, 1225.
41. Ser. 267.3/PL 38, 1230–31; Ser. 268.2/PL 38, 1232.
42. Ser. 267.4/PL 38, 1231.
43. "Haec dicuntur ut amemus unitatem, et timeamus separationem. Nihil enim sic debet formidare Christianus, quam separari a corpore Christi." *On the Gospel of St. John*, Tractate XXVII.6. NPNF VII, 176/PL 35, 1618.
44. *Expositions on the Book of the Psalms*, Ps VIII.8. NPNF VIII, 30/PL 36, 112.
45. Sermon XXI. NPNF VI, 318–332/(Ser. LXXI) PL 38, 445–467; Letter CLXXXV. 49–50, NPNF IV, 650–651/PL 33, 814–815.
46. Sermon XXI.20. NPNF VI, 325/(Ser. LXXI) PL 38, 455.
47. *On Faith and the Creed*, 9.19. NPNF III, 330/PL 40, 191–192.
48. Letter CLXXXV.50. NPNF, IV, 651/PL 33, 815.
49. John Cavadini, unpublished response given at CTSA Seminar. Annual Convention (New York: June, 1995), 4.
50. "Cur donum linguarum non modo conceditur numquid modo, fratres, non datur Spiritus sanctus? Quisquis hoc putat, non est dignus accipere. Datur et modo." Ser. 267.3/PL 38, 1230. And in Sermon 269.1 we read: "Can they [Donatists] possibly deny that even now the Holy Spirit comes upon Christians?" PL 38, 1235.
51. Ser. 268.1; 268.4; 269.1/PL 38, 1232, 1233, 1234. "The reason, after all, why the Holy Spirit was prepared to demonstrate his presence in the tongues of all nations, was so that those who are included in the unity of the Church which speaks all languages might understand that they have the Holy Spirit." Ser. 268.2/PL 38, 1232.
52. Ser. 269.1, 2; 270.6; 271/PL 38, 1234–35, 1243, 1245.
53. Ser. 271/PL 38, 1245.
54. Ser. 266.2; 269.1/ PL 38, 1225, 1234.
55. Ser. 71.12.18/PL 38, 454.
56. *On the Gospel of John*, Tractate XCII.2. NPNF, VII, 363/PL 35, 1863. See also *Expositions on the Book of Psalms*, Ps XCI.16. NPNF VIII, 451/Ps XC.8. PL 37, 1167. The root of our boldness and confidence is also attributed to Christ in Ephesians 3.11–13.
57. *On the Gospel of John*, ibid.
58. *On the Catechizing of the Uninstructed* 2.3. NPNF III, 284/PL 40, 311.
59. The link between knowledge and the Holy Spirit runs throughout the tradition. In an article on the significance of Jesus' baptism in the early church, Killian McDonnell

speaks of ways in which the Spirit affects knowledge. The Spirit's testimony allows the community to know the hidden cosmic vocation of the son (218) and that Jesus was the true Son of God (227). "To those who follow him down into the waters, Jesus imparts his quiet and the rest of the Spirit, a new way of knowing" (236). "Jesus' Baptism in the Jordan," *Theological Studies* 56(June 1995), 209–236.

60. *On the Gospel of John*, Tractate XXXII.5. NPNF, VII, 194/PL 35, 1614.

61. Ibid., Tractate VI.7. NPNF VII, 41/PL 35, 1428.

62. Ibid., Tractate LXXIV.2. NPNF VII, 334/PL 35, 1827.

63. *Our Lord's Sermon on the Mount*, II.xxv.83. NPNF VI, 62/PL 34, 1307.

64. Letter CLXIX.1.4. NPNF I, 540/PL 33, 744.

65. Letter CXVIII.5.32–33. NPNF I, 449–450/PL 33, 447–449. Cited in Brown, *Augustine of Hippo*, 276.

66. Letter CXXX.15.28. NPNF I, 468/PL 33, 506.

67. Letter CXX.3 and CXX.13. PL 33, 453. Cited in Brown, *Augustine of Hippo*, 277.

68. A good example of this drive to lead his congregation to understanding is Sermon LXXVI on the ways in which faith allows us to see what is unseen in those things that we do see: "God has made you a rational animal, set you over the cattle, formed you after His Own image. . . . Don't be like a horse and mule, which have no understanding" (Ps. xxxii.9). In the end, Augustine counsels meditation as perhaps a superior or supplemental route to understanding: "Let this suffice, Brethren; I know that I have said that which perhaps, if meditated upon, may develop itself to many, which oftentimes when expressed in words may chance to be obscured." Sermon LXXVI.4, 15. NPNF VI, 482, 486/PL 38, 699 (CXXVI.3.4) and PL 38, 705 (CXXVI.11.15).

69. Killian McDonnell traces the connection between knowledge and the Holy Spirit in parts of the tradition in "A Trinitarian Theology of the Holy Spirit?" 219–226.

70. For mention of Holy Spirit as "gift"—an idea closely connected for Augustine with love—see *On the Trinity*, V.15.16. NPNF III, 95/PL 42, 921; and XV.10.17–19, NPNF III, 215–220/PL 42, 1069–1071. On Holy Spirit as "breath" see *The City of God*, XIII.24. NPNF II, 259–61/PL 41, 398–404; *Confessions*, XIII.VI.6–X.10. NPNF I, 191–93/PL 32, 827–830.

71. *On the Trinity*, VI.5.7; X.8.11; XV.10.17–19. NPNF III, 100, 140, 208–209/ PL 42, 928, 979, 1069–1071. See William Hill, *The Three-Personed God* (Washington, DC: Catholic University of America Press, 1982), 56, n. 12 and Bertrand de Margerie, *The Christian Trinity in History* (Still River, MA: St. Bede's Publications, 1982 [1975]), 110–121.

72. *On the Trinity*, XV.19.37. NPNF III, 219/PL 42, 1071.

73. Sermon XXI.18. NPNF VI, 324/(Ser. LXXI) PL 38, 454.

74. "Whence he says again, 'If any man have not the Spirit of Christ, he is none of His'(Rom 8.9). To which Person then in the Trinity could the communion of this fellowship peculiarly appertain, but to that Spirit which is common to Father and the Son?" Sermon XXI.29. NPNF VI, 328/PL 38, 461 (LXXI.18.29. See also *On the Gospel of John*, Tractate XCIX.4–9. NPNF VII, 382–84/PL 35, 1887–1890; *On the Trinity*, V.10.11. NPNF III, 93/PL 42, 918; Letter CLXXXV.50. NPNF IV, 651/PL 33, 815.

75. *On the Gospel of John*, Tractate XXXII.7. NPNF VII, 195/PL 35, 1615.

76. *On Catechising of the Uninstructed*, 20.35. NPNF III, 305/PL 40, 356. See also Letter LV.16.29. NPNF I, 313/PL 33, 219; *Expositions on the Book of Psalms*, Ps VIII.8. NPNF VIII, 29/PL 36, 112.

77. *On the Trinity*, XV.10. 17, 19. NPNF III, 217/PL 42, 1069–1071. The Holy Spirit is given once upon earth (John 20.22) on account of the love of our neighbor and a second time from heaven, on account of the love of God (Acts 2.4). Ibid., XV.16.26. NPNF III, 224/PL 42, 1079.

78. *Enchiridion*, 121. NPNF III, 275–76/PL 40, 288.
79. *On the Catechising of the Uninstructed*, 23.41. NPNF III, 308/PL 40, 340.
80. Letter CXXX.6.13. NPNF I, 463/PL 33, 499.
81. *On the Gospel of John*, Tractate XXVI.6. NPNF VII, 176/PL 35, 1609.
82. Sermon XXI.19, NPNF VI, 324–325/PL 38, 147–148. See also *On the Gospel of John*, Tractate VI.2. NPNF VII, 40/PL 35, 1425.
83. *On the Gospel of John*, Tractate XCII.1. NPNF VII, 363/PL 35, 1862.
84. Sermon LXXVIII.ii.4. NPNF VI, 492/PL 38, 715 (CXXVII.ii.4).
85. *On the Gospel of John*, Tractate VI.2. NPNF VII, 39/PL 35, 1425. Those who groan for heavenly things are doves. Those who "clamor" for earthly things are ravens. There must be room in the church for both.
86. Letter CXXX. NPNF I, 459–469/PL 33, 494–507.
87. Letter CXXX.i.2, ii.5 and iii.7. NPNF I, 460–61/PL 33, 494–497.
88. Letter CXXX.x.20. NPNF I, 465/PL 33, 502.
89. *Confessions*, XIII.vii.8. NPNF I, 192/PL 32, 847.
90. *Confessions*, XIII.ix.10. NPNF I, 193/PL 32, 848–849.

14

The Mozartian Moment

Reflections on Medieval Mysticism

BARBARA NEWMAN

In a memorable scene from Mark Helprin's novel, *A Soldier of the Great War*, the protagonist Alessandro learns that he has just failed his orals and will not receive his degree. His examiners explain that they failed him for being insufficiently clever, but Alessandro replies, "I was clever when I was a child. I could do all kinds of tricks; I could memorize, analyze, and argue until my opponents were paralyzed, but whenever I did these things I felt shame." This remark makes the professors furious: "Shame? For what?" they ask. It does not help our hero's academic career when he responds, "It was easy to be clever, but hard to look into the face of God, who is found not so much by cleverness as by stillness." Moreover, "anyone can analyze . . . but to describe something so as to approach its essence is like singing."[1]

Bernard McGinn's magnum opus, *The Growth of Mysticism*,[2] is not a clever book. It is a respectful, even a reverent book, which he has dared to write in an age that sees "irreverent" as a term of praise. With great and attentive clarity, our premier historian of mysticism has described for us the descriptions of those who have looked into the face of God. If he has not given us the "essence" of mysticism, to use a now-suspect term, he has done something far more constructive, laying the vast historical foundations for any future speculation about what that term might usefully mean within the Christian tradition. He has cleared the field of many stifling and outworn conceits, such as the old gender-biased distinction between "intellectual" and "affective" mystics; and by focusing on texts rather than experiences, he has freed us from the futile endeavor to classify mystical writers on the basis of judgments about their level of spiritual attainment.

McGinn's four-volume series, *The Presence of God*, will be to the history of mysticism what Jaroslav Pelikan's *Christian Tradition* is to the history of doctrine. Both of these masters have given us histories of the tradition from within; both combine astonishing erudition with lucid expository prose; both take ideas and their truth-claims seriously, leaving the concerns of biography and social history to other hands. There is one major difference, however. Pelikan set out deliberately and almost polemically to write an *ecclesiastical* history, subordinating the quirks of individual theologians to forge a composite account of "what the church believed, taught, and confessed on the basis of the word of God." Perhaps inevitably given the nature of his subject, McGinn has done the opposite, bringing out commonalities only in the course of his searching and detailed exegesis of individual authors. Nevertheless, the degree of commonality remains impressive as he proceeds toward the year 1200. In Volume III, we can expect to see far more variety, even conflict, as alternative streams within the tradition emerge and diverge.

The story McGinn tells in Volume II will hold no surprises for those familiar with the period. Aside from his welcome attention to Gregory the Great and Eriugena, what he presents is chiefly the mysticism of the twelfth century, dominated by the Cistercians and Victorines. The towering figure is clearly Bernard of Clairvaux, as Augustine was in Volume I. Benedictines and Carthusians put in much briefer appearances. Most strikingly, Volume II—unlike Volumes III and IV to come—is the history entirely of men, except for the four pages (out of 600) devoted to Hildegard of Bingen and Elisabeth of Schönau. The overwhelming female silence speaks for itself, and of course it is not the author's fault. Nevertheless, the small space allotted to these women raises a question about the core problem of definition that any book of this kind must confront. What is a "mystic," anyway, and how do we decide who counts and who doesn't?

Perhaps McGinn's most controversial argument lies in his assertion that visionaries (such as the two nuns, Rupert of Deutz, and Joachim of Fiore) *may* be but are not *necessarily* to be considered "mystics." The crucial distinction, for McGinn, is whether a given visionary claimed either to experience the immediate presence of God or to guide others toward that presence.[3] By this criterion, Elisabeth of Schönau and Joachim of Fiore are excluded, while Hildegard and Rupert are seen to be "mystics" but not "mystical authors." Thus McGinn includes a narrative of their personal encounters with God—Rupert's erotic dream visions, Hildegard's "living light"—while omitting any discussion of their exegetical and theological works. There is actually much to be said for this distinction, and I am in no position to quarrel with it, since I have argued myself that it is downright misleading to read Hildegard as a mystic. Yet McGinn does treat Hugh of St. Victor's *Didascalicon* and *On the Sacraments*, texts that are surely no more "mystical" than Hildegard's *Scivias* and *Book of Divine Works*.

I raise the point not so much to quibble as to suggest another way of looking at the border zone where McGinn locates these figures—on the penumbra of "mysticism proper," so to speak. He defines the mystic as one concerned with "the immediate presence of God"—not just a fleeting experience, but "the practice of the presence of God," in Brother Lawrence's happy phrase, which includes the whole range of transformative disciplines flowing toward and from such experience. But one might ask, is there not also a mysticism of the *mediated* presence of God? What about the symbolic cosmologies, the schemes of sacred history, the tables of correspondences, even the world of the bestiaries, in which God does not so much embrace the naked soul as go forth to meet it in every nook and cranny of creation? What M.-D. Chenu christened "the symbolist mentality," so typical of twelfth-century thought in all spheres, is not itself mysticism, yet forms a preparation and backdrop for it by situating the believer within a cosmos already suffused through and through with divine presence. This "mysticism of the mediated presence" has lately been recreated for us in the rhapsodic meditations of Adso, Umberto Eco's monk-narrator in *The Name of the Rose*. One might well ask when and where the tenet of God's immanence passes from doctrinal faith into theophany, as it does for Adso, and, I believe, also for Hildegard—and as it certainly does for St. Francis.

Such a broadened definition would make a history of twelfth-century mysticism almost impossible to write, since one would have to include virtually every major religious author—even scholastics like Alan of Lille, who are hardly mystics in any traditional sense. Yet to my mind one of the most significant differences between twelfth- and thirteenth-century mysticism is the profound *loss of interest* (if not yet belief) in this symbolic cosmos, or more precisely, in the divine presence immanent in any creature other than the human soul. What I mean is not simply the apophatic turn around 1200, the new preference for negative language or metaphors of desert and abyss, or the emphasis on the radical unknowability of God. It is also a relentless inward turn, an exclusive concentration on the drama of God and the soul, a degree of introversion that makes even Augustine and Bernard look like men of the most variegated interests (as indeed they were). Certainly neither Mechthild of Magdeburg nor Meister Eckhart nor Marguerite Porete would have wasted their time devising cosmic mandalas like those we find in Hildegard and Hugh of St. Victor, or geometries of sacred history like Joachim's. But whether or not we decide to call these visionary and apocalyptic writers "mystics," some more serious problems of definition and exclusion may come later, with the Renaissance Platonists' revival of interest in the twelfth-century symbolic cosmos. What are we to make of Marsilio Ficino, for example? Or Jakob Boehme? If Boehme is to be considered a mystic, is it on the ground only of his intense Christocentric piety, or do we also include his elaborate cosmological thought?

The strain of twelfth-century symbolic cosmology so richly explored by Chenu, M.-M. Davy, Marie-Thérèse d'Alverny, and others, branches out in many directions. One of these leads to esotericism, a kind of spirituality that seeks the Divine through study of the intricate harmonies and correspondences of the created world, as epitomized by Boehme and his disciples. Another bears fruit in the tradition of panentheist or nature-mysticism, running all the way through the Romantics to modern figures like Teilhard de Chardin. (I would use the term "creation-centered" if Matthew Fox had not made it tantamount to "New Age.") Yet another current is the intense sacramentalism of many later medieval mystics—if we view their eucharistic visions and ecstasies as a Western answer to the liturgical mysticism of the Eastern church. Let me tentatively suggest that in the twelfth century, alongside the schools of contemplation represented by writers like Bernard of Clairvaux and William of St. Thierry, we see also the flowering of a complementary spirituality. Above I called it a mysticism of the mediated presence; another term might be "extraverted mysticism," or contemplation of the theophanies of God in creatures. Richard of St. Victor recognizes this type in his two lowest levels of contemplation, those characterized by imagination rather than reason or intellect, for in any neo-Platonic scheme of things, such contemplation must perforce be inferior to the contemplation of God in himself or in the soul. Nevertheless, this kind of mysticism has its own rich history. Whether or not we accept Richard's hierarchical scheme, its relation to the more familiar, introverted types of mysticism is among the most keenly debated questions in contemporary Christian spirituality.

But let us return to the twelfth century as McGinn presents it. I do not know how anyone could read these luminous pages—much less Bernard's *Sermons on the Song of Songs* or William's *Golden Epistle*—without concluding that Western thought in these twelfth-century mystics soared to a height of optimism it had never scaled before and—it seems all too obvious—may never attain again. It is not that they denied or neglected the mystery of evil, as did some of the sillier Victorians or American pragmatists. Nor is it just that they had a seemingly boundless faith in God's power and love. In the monastic writings of this age, as Caroline Bynum once put it, "both predestination and free will are used to convince readers that God is a goal toward which they are in fact moving."[4] And it is no coincidence that in the twelfth century, the theme of heaven emerges as a favorite topos of mystical writing.

But the breathtaking confidence of these texts stems above all, I think, from their unparalleled optimism about *human* love. We have learned much in recent years about the history of sexuality, that intriguing field that borders so closely on the history of mysticism. We all know the dark underside of this twelfth-century optimism: the lingering Augustinian distrust of all sexuality; the taboos that canon law brought to bear even on marital sex; the campaign for clerical celibacy, with its enormous cost in human misery for priests and their wives faced with compulsory separation; the renewed blasts of misogynist propaganda and antifeminist satire; the sexual tragedies of Abelard and Heloise, of the anonymous nun of Watton, and untold others. Yet in spite of all, a palpably new attitude toward eros can be scented, and not only in the troubadours and romance poets. Sexuality may be suspect, yet eros has entered its golden age: here is sublimation in all its glory. For these undaunted doctors of desire, eros is to be neither playfully expressed nor serenely transcended nor tragically endured. We are equally far from the civilized hedonism of Ovid and the animal passion of D. H. Lawrence; from Stoic *apatheia* and Buddhist tranquility; from the frantic obsession of Jerome and the mournful resignation of Freud. Sublimation is often praised, but I doubt that it has ever been more brilliantly theorized or more triumphantly practiced.

For the twelfth-century mystics, considered as theorists of human subjectivity, three paradoxical assertions meet in one. First, the deepest human desire is ultimately rational even when it transcends reason: *amor ipse notitia est*, to use the Gregorian axiom these authors so often cited. Love and knowledge are not merely compatible or complementary: at their endpoint they converge. This core belief distinguishes virtually all twelfth-century mystics from a significant number of later ones like Marguerite Porete and the *Cloud of Unknowing* author, who made no secret of their contempt for reason. Second, desire begins with the body—our own and Christ's—and in the end it comes full circle to the body risen, although it must climb a steep Platonic ladder in between. The discipline of eros is hardly new in the twelfth century: without Plato's *Symposium* and Augustine's *Confessions*, none of these authors would be thinkable. Just as the Platonists taught, love must be snared at its starting point and retrained, reoriented toward its true and infinite goal. But Plato did not have the Song of Songs at his disposal, and Augustine did not read it as the twelfth century did. Neither adopted the language of bodily love with the intimate passion of a Bernard or even a Rupert of Deutz—not to mention the remarkable gender inversion to which the Song committed monks who used it in this fashion.

Finally and perhaps most important, desire is insatiable, yet for that very reason it is destined—and destines us—for an eternal and inconceivable satisfaction. This is the theme of *epektasis* so richly developed by William of St. Thierry and others: the coincidence of endless yearning and utmost fulfillment in the love of an inexhaustible object. It is this that makes the mystics such astonishing optimists where their contemporaries, the doctors of earthly desire, fall into tragic sublimity. Compare Bernard or William with Tristan or Lancelot—as I am sure Richard of St. Victor did when he wrote the *Four Degrees of Violent Charity*, that brilliant little treatise with which McGinn's volume ends. Richard was not only one of the most subtle psychologists of his age, but also its best clandestine critic of courtly literature.

In the preface to Volume II, McGinn highlights two phrases that capture the most distinctive innovations of the twelfth-century mystics: *ordinatio caritatis, liber experientiae.* To take the last first, no one will have forgotten Bernard's famous etymology: *intellegere*, "to understand," derives from *in te legere*, "to read in yourself." The most private experience, for Bernard and his audience, is not chaotic or random but legible. It is indeed a book—a text, we would now say—that if rightly interpreted, coincides perfectly with the book of Scripture—and not just any scripture, but the textbook of Love revealed. Bernard and his compeers thus pioneered the "method of correlation" for which Paul Tillich would be celebrated in our own age, but no one has ever surpassed the early Cistercians in correlating revelation with the realm of erotic experience. For what we read in the "book of experience" is the "ordering of charity": *introduxit me [rex] in cellam vinariam, ordinavit in me caritatem.* If experience is legible, emotion is ordered: the yearning heart has its own economy, and when it becomes disordered, the Desired One himself will set it right. Thus the two master-themes of twelfth-century thought—the "blessed rage for order" and the anatomy of love—meet in this quintessentially hopeful doctrine that asserts the ultimate (if not the empirical) accord of wisdom and longing, authority and experience, ascetic denial and erotic delight.

It is a moment rare even within the history of ideals—a moment of high classicism, of passionate equilibrium that cannot long be sustained. For an instant, for a small elite, the heart's pendulum stands dead center, vibrant at the midpoint of its arc, while all things seem possible. But soon it will swing again, and the arcs will become not smaller but wider than before. The weight of the pendulum is of course desire—*pondus meum amor meus*—and the non-elites of the medieval world, especially women, will set it to vibrate anew with a powerful momentum. On the one hand, new extremes of rhetoric and doctrine—more dizzying raptures, more desolate abysses, more flamboyant and mind-bending assertions—will clothe the ancient quest in the exotic colors of mannerism. On the other hand, new extremes of suspicion and repression will reunite the mystic with the martyr.

Having begun with a novel, I cannot forbear ending with one, for Umberto Eco has told it all. The last page of *The Name of the Rose* is a history of medieval mysticism *in toto*—though of course, one must already know the history to understand that page. In the end, as the great darkness descends, Adso tells us:

> All I can do now is be silent. *O quam salubre, quam iucundum et suave est sedere in solitudine et tacere et loqui cum Deo!* Soon I shall be joined with my beginning, and I no longer believe that it is the God of glory of whom the abbots of my order spoke to me, or of joy, as the Minorites believed in those days, perhaps not even of piety. *Gott ist ein lauter Nichts, ihn rührt kein Nun noch Hier.* . . . I shall be in the simple foundation, in the silent desert where diversity is never seen, in the privacy

where no one finds himself in his proper place. I shall fall into the silent and uninhabited divinity where there is no work and no image.[5]

That is the next, if not the final chapter; we are awaiting developments. But for now, let us savor the twelfth century, the Mozartian moment, while it lasts.

NOTES

1. Mark Helprin, *A Soldier of the Great War* (New York: Avon, 1992), 428–9.
2. Bernard McGinn, *The Growth of Mysticism: Gregory the Great through the 12th Century* (New York: Crossroad, 1994).
3. Ibid., 327.
4. Caroline Walker Bynum, *Jesus as Mother: Studies in the Spirituality of the High Middle Ages* (Berkeley: University of California Press, 1982), 160.
5. Umberto Eco, *The Name of the Rose*, trans. William Weaver (New York: Harcourt Brace Jovanovich, 1983), 501.

15

Words That Reach into the Silence

Mystical Languages of Unsaying

MARK S. BURROWS

And what you thought you came for
Is only a shell, a husk of meaning
From which the purpose breaks only when it is fulfilled
If at all.
—T. S. Eliot, "Little Gidding"

What is it that we "came for" when we attempt to read texts from ancient and medieval mystical traditions? Can we at least hope to apprehend what lies beyond knowledge, to experience through the medium of ordinary language a reality which (as such texts remind us) exceeds its grasp? How is it that we penetrate that "husk" of meaning, as Eliot put it, when apophatic writings call us to "possess what [we] do not possess" and "arrive at where [we] are not" (in "East Coker," recalling John of the Cross, *The Ascent of Mount Carmel* I. 13.11)? What are the strategic "retractions" in these texts which serve to create a "propositionally unstable and dynamic discourse in which no single statement can rest on its own as true or false, or even as meaningful?"[1] And how is it that such patterns of unsaying usher us into the peculiar landscape called "mystery," which lives in the "interstices of the text" (3, 8)?

Such questions lie at the heart of Michael Sells' impressive recent study, *Mystical Languages of Unsaying.* They will be familiar to students of spirituality, even those whose acquaintance with the wide range of primary sources Sells explores might not be direct or detailed. For Sells' project, an exploration of varied examples of that form of discourse known as "negative theology," leads us deeply into the question of divine ineffability. But these are also questions with a wider reach, affecting all who attempt to "speak" of the divine, or to address God through the fractured vessels of human language. As C. S. Lewis put it in one of his poems:

He whom I bow to only knows to whom I bow
When I attempt the ineffable Name, murmuring *Thou*,
And dream of Pheidian fancies and embrace in heart
Symbols (I know) which cannot be the thing thou art.

The subject of Sells' study, mystical texts that articulate an apophatic grammar of discourse, touches on the broader question of how all language functions in bridging the abyss separating humans from the divine. This is *in nuce* the hermeneutical question.

On the surface Sells' work presents us with a fascinating study not of apophaticism as a genre but of various "languages" of unsaying in texts from diverse religious traditions. Through a series of "readings" of key apophatic texts, Sells explores these languages as they find expression in the writings of Plotinus, John the Scot Eriugena, Ibn Arabi, Marguerite Porete, and Meister Eckhart, though he casts side glances throughout toward a broader horizon of Muslim, Jewish, and Christian texts. By examining the logic of the language found in this sampling of voices, he intends to discern what he calls the "meaning event" that lies "just beneath the semantic surface" of such texts. As such, the study gains strength and depth as the chapters unfold, precisely because of the accumulating comparisons inherent in his approach.

Sells opens this provocative study with a ringing indictment familiar to those working in the field of spirituality, the warning that apophatic texts "have suffered in an acute manner from the urge to paraphrase the meaning in non-apophatic language or to fill in the open referent—to say what the text really meant to say, but didn't" (4). Unlike Schumann, who when asked to explain a difficult étude sat down and played it another time, we often in our roles as interpreters of such texts move too easily to explain and define what is, strictly speaking, inexplicable and indefinable. But Sells' concern is not with analysis per se, since texts such as these require careful reading. Rather, he directs his warning to those who misread apophatic texts by applying the tools of discursive reasoning and scholastic analysis to texts that follow the wisdom of a different genre. Such a mistaking of voice and intent is akin to reading poetry as if it were technical prose—i.e., without imagination and a capacity for the surprising inventiveness of language. To recall Bernard McGinn's poignant analogy, misreadings of this sort handle such texts like "phone books or airline schedules," seeking in them "handy sources for confirming what we already expect."[2]

Sells' study offers another approach by illumining the subversive linguistic strategies employed by masters of apophasis, a task he accomplishes not by entering directly into the margins of darkness and silence that envelop such texts, but through the intermediate path of semantic analysis. It is, in this sense, a prolonged examination of method and the functional texture of apophatic language, which Sells describes as "a discourse of double propositions, in which meaning is generated through the tension between the saying and the unsaying" (12). Yet his hermeneutical approach avoids for the most part what George Steiner has called the "Saturn of explication" which devours what it adopts.[3] His slow and astute "rumination" of these texts enlivens their semantic power, often by interpreting with painstaking care the detailed structure of particular images, tropes, and arguments. Sells' approach thus accepts these texts on their own authority, resisting a diversion of his (and our) attention to anachronistic modern questions of verifiability or authenticity. His several readings serve as a critical propaedeutic, an invitation to readers who hope to encounter these texts by an analysis leading towards a postcritical or "second" naïveté.

The author concludes his study with a striking comparison between poetry and the apophatic language of mystical texts. The parallel seems fitting since poetry is perhaps the last genre of a secularized culture such as ours which echoes the paradoxical strategies of apophatic texts. As Sells himself points out in the waning pages of his study:

209

> In trying to understand how the poetry works, we are led more deeply into the event of reading the poem . . . [W]hat has been commonly accepted for poetic discourse—a resistance to semantic reduction—is frequently viewed as a form of mystification in apophasis. (216)

Like poets, authors of apophatic texts know that we must be "undeceived/ Of that which, deceiving, could no longer harm" (T. S. Eliot, "East Coker"). These texts are indeed dangerous, as Sells argues, because they expose the shallowness of the distractions by which we ordinarily think and live.

His analysis offers a particularly astute reading of Marguerite Porete and Meister Eckhart, both of whose writings offer a deliberate subversion of the condemnations they faced. As Sells suggests, these "boundary" voices accomplished this purpose by directly inverting—often with the playful seriousness of double entendre—the meaning of the official judgments leveled against them. This is not to say that Sells reduces their thought to veiled political arguments. He does not. But he succeeds in leading us more deeply "into the event of reading the [mystical] text" by grasping how such writings functioned in the wider context of theological discourse—in the case of Porete, for example, by bringing forceful criticism to bear upon "holy Church the little," which condemned her thought. This is the critical accomplishment of the final chapters in particular, since Sells here suggests that the apparent conflict between such paradoxical voices and the orthodoxy their thought challenged reflects "not a difference in doctrine but a difference in discourse" (154). It is at least this, though one wonders whether the exclusive contrast Sells assumes accounts adequately for the "thick texture" (pretext?) of such conflicts.

As an attempt to explore mystical texts as "a cross-cultural mode of discourse emerging out of a variety of religious and cultural traditions," this study concentrates on locating certain "key semantic features" of apophatic discourse. Sells is thus less interested in the specific content than in the functional character of such discourse, though he recognizes how inseparable these often are. As Wallace Stevens once put it (in "From an Ordinary Evening in New Haven"),

> The poem is the cry of its occasion,
> Part of the res itself and not about it.

Just so with apophatic texts, as Sells reads them here: these are themselves the cry of their occasion, part of the *res* itself and not just "about" it. One must read them in order to embark on a dialectical journey of saying and unsaying, often in deliberate defiance of what he refers to as the "reifying tendencies" of scholastic discourse. Sells insists that this will require of us not simply an acquiescence to silence itself but the use of a linguistic-analytical approach, a method that attends to the dialectic structure of semantic strategies. If we would arrive at such "meaning events" by these means, we must accept the inversions of this paradoxical thought-world, embracing the logical contradictions that structure the heart of such texts—i.e., the "double sentence or dual proposition" which Sells identifies as a key tactic in these texts. Thus, for instance, he points to what he calls the "disontology" of Plotinus' writings, a subversive strategy that bends logical assertions back upon themselves (e.g., "It is neither X nor not X").

The impossible, unreasonable, and even absurd logic of such thinking, including the anti-theo-logical arguments inherent in such texts, must become an unknowing and perhaps an unthinking, if thought remains captured by what Heidegger calls the "calculative reasoning" of the marketplace. Only in this manner do we break the "husk of meaning" for which we *thought* we came to such texts. At stake is not Tertullian's familiar question, "What has Athens to do with Jerusalem?" but rather a quite different query: viz., whether modern descendants of the Enlightenment can make sense of the precritical and even anti-critical "non-sense" of Athens and its mystic heirs. It is small wonder, therefore, that apophatic texts have not fared well in official and academic circles with the dawning of modern consciousness. They are, after all, unmanageable according to the dictates of practical reason.

The crucial question which lingers in my mind upon completing this impressive study moves in another direction altogether from that which Sells himself offers in the closing pages. In the epilogue, he asks whether "one has to be a mystic to understand mystical language" (215), an important question to be sure. But my wondering leads in a quite different direction, toward what might well be a prior question: namely, whether it is possible to follow the unsaying of a tradition where one has not yet participated in the pattern of saying (kataphasis) itself. To ask such a question is to be somewhat at odds with the guiding assumption of Sells' project, for he labors to find "a cross-cultural mode of discourse" in such texts without "belaboring [their] obvious doctrinal contrasts" (206). Surely apophasis is in some sense a linguistic strategy based upon a perception common to diverse religious traditions, but do we find the depth of its resonance without first entering the particular thought-world within which such texts do their work of deconstruction? Is the unsaying of mystical apophasis detachable from "doctrine" and thus capable of being extracted as a style of argument from the forms of expression familiar to particular religious communities and their traditions? Or, to ask this question not from a philosophical but from an historical perspective: What happens when we approach such texts as acknowledged outsiders, as those who do not know something of what Stephen Crites aptly termed the "musicality" of a religious community? Can we grasp the often veiled shape of unsaying in such texts without first giving ourselves over to the saying of invocation, of lament and praise? Can we unsay what we have not first said?

This is not to gainsay the importance of Sells' study. In point of fact, his treatment of such texts offers a reading that does locate them in this wider context. But it is to wonder about the living grammar of apophasis, and whether it is possible or desirable to probe such texts without regard for the wider context of prayer and act, of intention and invention, in which their unsaying is at home. This is not a small question for those of us who read such texts as voices that come not from some common core of human experience but from a living religious tradition in which we find ourselves residing. Sells is probably correct when he asserts that "the central moment in the act of reading is the meaning event, the mimetic reenactment at the semantic level of subject and object[,] of the fusions of self and other that occur in mystical union" (215). But is the "meaning event" the last plateau, the highest state of consciousness "beyond" knowing and understanding and experience? And, at a more elementary level, is mystical union in any recognizable sense a "meaning-event"? What relationship does such "unsaying" have to the traditions of prayer in a given community, since these are both a saying and unsaying?

To cite but one example: Dionysius' treatise, *The Mystical Theology*, opens not with discursive argument but with a hymnic prayer, not with the unsaying that is a semantic strategy addressed to the reader but with an unsaying directed to the deity—even if, as he insists, he is calling upon the one who is "higher than any being, any divinity, any goodness" (i.e., the God beyond God/god, to recall Sells' usage). Does the intentionality of this address as prayer matter for our appreciation of Dionysius' treatise? Can we interpret the full range of the apophatic voice heard in *The Mystical Theology* without first familiarizing ourselves with the labyrinthine score of *The Divine Names*? Can we speak intelligently of union without the categories of self and a real "other," even given the proviso that one is not attempting to speak of a subject/object but of a subject/subject encounter? And is the variance when one moves from one tradition of unsaying to another merely the repetition or approximation of a similar semantic appeal, without significant regard to the positive assertions implied in the "saying" of doctrine and *Weltanschauung*?

These are important questions, and the virtue of Sells' volume is that it brings them into central focus even if his own premises follow another approach. Sells assumes that a comparativist approach can search for "a literary mode" by which such texts can be read, and the strength of his analysis is to attempt this feat without seeking to discover "a common religious . . . or . . . mystical experience" (216). This might well be a disputable hypothesis, though the approach does offer an informed analytical reflection upon common strategies in the "unsaying" of these texts. The deliberate inertia of this approach—and this is a peculiar virtue of his work—takes us along a more circuitous road than the direct and pragmatic question, "But *what* do such texts mean?" to wonder *how* it is that they mean. As he rightly points out along the way, apophatic voices, by speaking through deliberate inversions, avoid altogether the modern quest for "experience" that all too often tempts readers to hunger for the "shell," the "husk of meaning." We can, after all, focus our attention so excessively upon what Bernard McGinn has rightly called "the highly ambiguous notion of mystical experience" that we lose sight altogether of the "special hermeneutics" of mystical texts.[4] This book does much to rectify this imbalance.

Sells' hermeneutical approach thus offers a purposeful detour to those who would otherwise read these texts for some immediate gain, often by seeking in them a meaning or experience that imposes a pattern of our own design. The growing literature on "spirituality" abounds with such examples, many of which offer little more than violent, anachronistic (mis)readings that violate cultural boundaries and ignore the distance separating such texts from the modern reader. Sells is quite aware of these tendencies and helps us to avoid their seduction by analyzing how apophatic language functions—namely, as an "aporia [which] keeps the mind in incessant activity, never allowing it a fixed referent" (3), as a "vision of a nonentified divinity" (58), etc. The effect of his comparativist approach also identifies, even if he refuses to speculate about, the causes for semantic parallels occurring across religious and cultural boundaries (as, for example, his recognition that "Sufism and European Christian mysticism were part of a larger multireligious cultural entity" [134]).

A distinct humility of ambition also characterizes Sells' epilogue, where he concedes that the question "whether or not the meaning event, as a mimetic reduplication of mystical union, is in some sense itself mystical is not a decision for the critic to make" (216). Fair enough, at least for the critic. But this disclaimer may seem restrictive to readers who find themselves reading these texts as participants within the particular religious tradition from which they emerged. This is not to say that we should expect Sells to settle a question in which these texts themselves are generally not interested—i.e., the modern concern about verification ("Is it *true*?"). But it is to ask what is lost in comparisons across religious traditions when the inquiry disregards the point that religious faith has both a grammar *and* a vocabulary—and both must presumably be mastered before the mystic (as with the poet) gains the license of her trade. As Eliot reminds us, "Words, after speech, reach/Into the silence" ("Burnt Norton"). But does the silence sound differently by becoming peculiarly resonant on the other side of religious affirmations? Must we not first know the words, the positive vocabulary of saying, before we are able to follow them into the "negative" edges of silent apprehension? Are the words of religious traditions simply interchangeable units in a linguistic vocation common to all transcendent experience? Or is the silence itself intelligible in large measure because of the linguistic terrain one must first learn to traverse by light of day before leaving it behind in a dark cloud of unknowing?

The density and richness of Sells' study brings questions of this sort into acute focus, and this is itself an accomplishment rendering his work worthy of a close reading. As an analysis of apophatic style, *Mystical Languages of Unsaying* reminds us that answers to such questions must themselves come not in criticism of the text (the "secondary discourse" George Steiner opposes in *Real Presences*) but in the "performance" of reading, that moment when the mystical text becomes the occasion for a "merging of the way of knowledge and the way of love" (115). "The best readings of art are art," as Steiner has reminded us. Can any other assumption guide our reading of mystical treatises? Such texts call for an exegesis that moves us beyond mere "referential strategies" to something approximating the *theoria* of the *Enneads* (see Sells, 21), since, as Sells recognizes with penetrating force, the treatises he explores are and remain more than the relics of an obsolete culture. When approached in this spirit they become guides not only for (un)knowing but for conversion—for the death (un-living?) that necessarily precedes resurrection. To be properly read, we must approach them "neither demanding a special gnosis . . . nor high intellectual rank" (115), but rather through the posture of vulnerability (217) to what lies beyond the reaches of "conventional rationality" (Sells' phrase).

Reading in this way opens us to the *coincidentia oppositorum* by which such texts awaken us to what Sells calls "the original aporia of ineffability" (211). By "risking enchantment" (Eliot, "East Coker") on this journey into what Sells aptly characterizes as the bewilderment of aporia, we find ourselves grasped by a "learned ignorance" (the phrase is Nicholas of Cusa's) which invites us to speak of what remains unspeakable, to know by unknowing, to bring the transcendent into the immanence of speech. But what is this but an adventure of surprising semantic twists and turns, one that reminds us that "[t]he only wisdom we can hope to acquire/ Is the wisdom of humility: humility is endless" (Eliot, from "East Coker"). For those embarking on this journey of undeceiving, Sells' study will serve as an articulate companion and an eminently useful exegetical guide.

NOTES

1. Michael Sells, *Mystical Languages of Unsaying* (Chicago and London: University of Chicago Press, 1994), 3. Future references to this volume are in parentheses in the text.
2. Bernard McGinn, *The Foundations of Mysticism: Origins to the Fifth Century* (New York: Crossroad, 1991), xiv.
3. George Steiner, *Real Presences* (Chicago: University of Chicago Press, 1989), 38.
4. McGinn, *Foundations*, xiv.

16

Lover without a Name

Spirituality and Constructive Christology Today

MARK McINTOSH

Therefore, the virgins say [to the Bride], "How can we know him who cannot be known by any name? He does not answer if you call, nor is he found when you seek him."
—Gregory of Nyssa, *Commentary on the Song of Songs*, Homily 13.

$\mathcal{R}$ecovering slowly from a nasty abandonment by her lover Rudolphe, Emma Bovary slips into a languorously "religious" mood. Flaubert writes that she even "fancied herself seized with the finest Catholic melancholy ever conceived by an ethereal soul."[1] Unhappily for poor Madame Bovary, the new divine object of her desire seems quite as elusive as all the others.

> When she knelt on her Gothic prie-Dieu, she addressed to the Lord the same suave words that she had murmured formerly to her lover in the outpourings of adultery. She was searching for faith; but no delights descended from the heavens, and she arose with aching limbs and the vague feeling that she was being cheated.[2]

Without wishing to draw unflattering parallels, is there, I wonder, in the inconstant heart of Emma Bovary a lesson for theology today? Does theology sometimes settle in at the old prie-Dieu, content to pour out the same suave words it usually murmurs to its more familiar suitors in the academy? If theology gets up from its occasional visits with spirituality with a vague feeling of being cheated perhaps it's because theology has forgotten how different this kind of communion is from what it usually enjoys with philosophy, hermeneutics, sociology, and psychology. Is it in fact possible for academic theology to recover its relationship to spirituality? Is it willing to let its own speech, its own questions, be themselves questioned and even stripped away by the Reality which is not simply one among all the others, the Reality who cannot be named?

In his continuing reflections on naming and thinking God today, David Tracy has noted how the peculiarly modern genre for theological reflection has been the rational argument. And the ensuing concepts of God have been formulated, most ingeniously in some cases, as one or another –ism —theism, pantheism, panentheism, etc. To be taken seriously in the modern academic study of theology, God has, above all, become that which is thinkable. But as Tracy has also suggested, this may well underexpose theology to that most radical insight of the Christian mystics, namely that God is in fact the very One who is incomprehensible, the One "who cannot be known by any name," in Gregory of Nyssa's phrase.[3] I mean to suggest by all this that as we explore the possibilities of renewed dialogue between theology and spirituality, it might be prudent *not* to suppose at the outset that theology should consult and interact with spirituality as it might with simply any other academic discipline.

What *would* this kind of dialogue be like? How would theology be influenced by mystical texts that speak of God by saying God cannot be spoken of, texts that evoke the presence of God precisely by the virtuoso excess of their rhetoric of God's absence? Michel de Certeau points out that mystical texts, unlike theological treatises, are always straining, undoing themselves, in the attempt to express their object. But since that object is really infinite,

> [s]uch a mystical text is never anything but the unstable metaphor for what is inaccessible. Every "object" of mystical discourse becomes inverted into the trace of an ever-passing Subject. Therefore, *mystics* [the discipline] only assembles and orders its practices in the name of something that it cannot make into an object . . . something that never ceases judging *mystics* at the same time that it eludes it.[4]

Perhaps a theological "turn to spirituality" would at the very least remind us of Aquinas' conviction that the "object" of Christian doctrine is never really an object among others in the universe.[5] As Rowan Williams has suggested: "Language about God is kept honest in the degree to which it turns on itself in the name of God: it is in this way that it becomes possible to see how it is still *God* that is being spoken of . . . to show the novum of God's action in respect of any pre-existing human idiom."[6] There are of course many ways that such a mystically-informed theology might set to work today. It might for example look for insights in classical mystical texts whose freshness and creativity directly address contemporary perplexities in theology. In what remains of this essay, however, I would like to illustrate the possible use of an even more indirect and yet more widely dispersed resource. Rather than focusing only on mystical texts that directly address issues in christology or trinitarian theology or some other doctrinal locus—something that certainly can bear much fruit— there is also the chance that one might find in broader mystical themes—the role of eros in the union with God, the stance of *apatheia* or self-abandonment in the spiritual journey, etc.—certain very suggestive analogies that might be brought to bear on contemporary problems in theology. As an example, let me take up the case of early developments in Christian apophaticism as a resource for a particular contemporary christological problem, the self-consciousness of Jesus.

The range of argument against Chalcedon's incarnational christology is fairly wide today. Yet there does seem to be a fundamental consensus among the critics that, simply put, we would not today understand our experience of Jesus in terms of a literal incarnation because a literal incarnation is simply unintelligible today, i.e., we don't understand the world or the human self in ways that could make sense of it.[7]

This argument usually points to a dilemma. If Jesus is the Word incarnate it would seem likely that he would have some consciousness of his identity, but would such knowledge really be coherent with a truly human existence? On the other hand if Jesus is not humanly conscious of his identity, in what sense can we coherently speak of a literal incarnation of the divine Word in this human life? Of course this critique acknowledges the attempts of other eras to answer these questions, but on the basis of new biblical research and modern understandings of God and the human self, these earlier answers are seen to be unworkable. Generally speaking, it is argued further that the doctrine of the Incarnation inherently leads to severely vitiated or inconsequential renderings of Christ's humanity. However much the Chalcedonian definition may declare that Jesus is fully human, in every respect sharing our human nature, it seems that accepted orthodox christologies are unable to accord much significance to the real human struggle of Jesus' historical existence. Can a human being be a divine Person and really still be human?[8]

I would like to suggest that in apophatic mystical traditions within Christianity one can find some habits of thought, so to speak, which might prove to be useful tools in trying to answer these critical questions. I will focus here only on Gregory of Nyssa, whose reconstrual of the Origenian mystical itinerary in light of a new emphasis on the divine infinity is so important for Christian spirituality.[9] The generating hypothesis I want to explore is this: Gregory (and so many others of apophatic perspective) describes the highest levels of divine presence to the soul as a luminous darkness, an unknowing, and an unsatiated desire; this insight provides a mystical analogy that can help us understand the manner of Jesus' consciousness of his own identity. In other words, we might be able to find in this analogy a way to do justice both to incarnational christology and to a realistically human interpretation of Jesus' historical self-consciousness. Let me now offer at least the preliminary outline of such an argument.

Vladimir Lossky among others has pointed out that for Origen and Evagrius, darkness remained a sign of all that separates the soul from the light of God; but for Gregory of Nyssa the dark cloud of Sinai and the shimmering night of the Song of Songs represent a far more perfect "mode of communion with God."

> If God appears first as light and then as darkness, this means for Gregory that of the divine essence there is no vision, and that union with God is a way surpassing

vision or *theoria*, going beyond intelligence to where knowledge vanishes and only love remains. . . . Desiring God more and more, the soul grows without ceasing, going beyond herself; and in the measure in which she unites herself more and more to God, her love becomes more ardent and insatiable.[10]

Lossky summarizes all our themes here, but for the moment note the sense that this powerful yearning for God, which draws the soul beyond the self, is not a diminution of the self but the means of its growth: the human self is drawn into fuller and fuller existence by the lure of God.[11]

In his treatment of the Song of Songs, Gregory describes the divine Lover as wooing the bride into true beauty, from a kind of provisional existence into the concreteness of actual reality. "The bride says, 'My beloved is mine and I am his who feeds among the lilies,' the same one who has transformed human life from shadowy phantasms to the supreme truth."[12] The bride recognizes herself as one who is given identity precisely by her delight in the bridegroom, and Gregory clearly sees this as a mystical paradox, an ecstatic passing beyond the self to the other which is in fact the constitution of the self, the drawing of the self from phantasm into truth. Suppose we allow these perceptions to serve as a matrix within which we interpret the historical existence of Jesus: his human existence is literally drawn into being by union with the Word, and this need not be seen as a static ontological fixity but as something perpetually achieved anew—the human being Jesus coming to fuller and fuller self-expression precisely as Jesus hungers and thirsts with an ever more fateful urgency "to do the will of the Father."

If we turn to the much vexed question of Jesus' (self?) knowledge of God, it will be salutary to ask ourselves what kind of genuinely human "knowledge" one can have of God in any case. Since God is not among the items of the universe, one would surely not expect God to be an "object" of knowledge per se. As Herbert McCabe has put it with his characteristic trenchancy: "If we are to enter into the mystery of God it is not information that we need, and in principle we could not have information—our language and concepts break down in the presence of God. What we need is to be taken up by God himself, to share in his knowledge of himself, a sharing that to *us* must just look like darkness."[13] Whatever it could mean to "know" God would seem to be connected to a sense of spiritual darkness and perhaps of being grasped by a yearning necessity beyond one's understanding (Gethsemane?). "We can say that it is an intellectual experience of the mind's failure when confronted with something beyond the conceivable."[14]

Daniélou has catalogued the various ways in which Gregory of Nyssa depicts this experience of God's infinity: darkening of the intelligence, the images of inebriation, vertigo, dizziness, all point to "the soul's complete confusion in the presence of a reality for which there is no common measure."[15] The bride's restless search for the absent beloved causes her to realize "that her sought after love is known only in her impossibility to comprehend his essence" (CSS, 131). So in Gregory's view, a sense of unknowing and unclarity are the veritable hallmarks of authentic knowledge of God. And beyond this there is perhaps an authentic unknowing knowledge of God that is distilled as a new sense of self. This knowledge of God is, in other words, embodied not as information in the mind but as a sharpening sense of mission and identity—the soul comes to define its own existence more and more in terms of its yearning for the absent One and its desire to fulfill the wishes of this One.

This suggests, then, that in speaking of Jesus' human consciousness of God we would hardly expect a series of metaphysical propositions but rather an intensifying sense of personal urgency, of calling, of willingness to abandon himself into the hands of one who seems ever more absent and unavailable— all features of many historical constructions of the gospel narratives. Gregory describes the bride as saying: "I have sought him [the bridegroom] by my soul's capacities of reflection and understanding; he completely transcended them, and escaped my mind when it drew near to him" (CSS, 220). The soul's experience is not anti-noetic in the sense of implying that the quest for God demands an infamous sacrifice of the intellect, rather it is an awareness (with a very definite intellectual component) that the source of one's desire is beyond the grasp of the intellect.

This is not, therefore, a humanly diminishing mindlessness but a kind of amazement that is exhilarating and liberating for the whole person; drawn closer to God in this way, Gregory implies, the human self is invited into a realm of possibilities it would never have imagined. We might note the simple analogy of a truly overwhelming work of art: the beholder stands mutely riveted in delighted wonder before an expression of unutterable depth; while one clearly will never begin to fathom the work, one is marvelously engaged by a world of meaning whose existence one had never even dreamt of. This experience is by all accounts among the most life-giving and ennobling one can have. For Jesus to feel himself drawn towards God, indeed constituted by this desire to respond to God, in ways that far outstrip the power of his own understanding—this is in the apophatic mystical tradition both a momentum toward greater fulfillment as a human being *and* also an authentic sign of the infinite intimacy of God's presence to Jesus.[16] Indeed Daniélou, commenting on this insight from the apophatic tradition, has proposed that the greater the sense of wonder and incomprehension, the more definitive the presence of God to the soul.

> The knowledge of God in the darkness is not merely negative. It is truly an
> experience of the presence of God as He is in Himself, in such wise that this

awareness is completely blinding for the mind, and all the more so the closer it is to Him. In fact, one might also say that the darkness expresses the divine presence, and that the closer He comes to the soul, the more intense is the darkness.[17]

And of course this deepening darkness is experienced by the soul not only in intellectual but broadly existential terms. Jesus' experience of abandonment and isolation in the final stages of his life could thus be read in terms of the unfathomable presence of God drawing Jesus into an intimacy so infinite that our world can only experience it as absence, forsakenness.

Let me now go on to propose that the themes of desire and ecstasy present in the very roots of the apophatic mystical tradition also afford illuminating christological correlates. Just as the soul enters into knowledge of God by the way of darkness or unknowing, so the soul embraces God by an endless eros that is never satiated but rather draws the soul beyond itself. In fact Gregory speaks of the soul being continually led from her "place" by desire for God (CSS, 218–220).[18] The point of construing Christ's ever greater momentum of self-giving in terms of a spirituality of continual *ekstasis* like Gregory's is not to suggest that Jesus was some kind of ecstatic in the technical sense but rather to offer this theme of being-drawn-beyond-oneself as a way of interpreting Jesus' existence. The deepening sense of necessity, even of fateful self-surrender, implicit in the gospels might be read in this way as pointing to the intensity of desire being aroused in Jesus, and thus to the intimate presence of the One who stimulates such desire. Summarizing this theme as it appears in *The Life of Moses*, Lossky writes: "Filled with an ever-increasing desire the soul grows without ceasing, goes beyond itself, and, in so doing, is filled with yet greater longings. Thus the ascent becomes infinite, the desire insatiable."[19] We note that in this apophatic tradition there is absolutely no sense in which a full divine presence diminishes or subverts the fully authentic humanity of the individual. Quite the reverse. The ever-fuller intimacy of the divine presence to the soul draws the soul beyond the usual limits, stretches it to the fullest and highest extent of human existence.

Yet this yearning extension of the self beyond all limits, even while it so to speak "grows" the soul, might well be experienced in terms of anguish or sorrow, a painful lack: "The bride is perplexed and distressed because she does not have the object of her desire, and she makes known her soul's anxiety" (CSS, 130). ("My soul is very sorrowful, even to death" [Mk 14:34], "I thirst" [Jn 19:28]). The point of the apophatic construal is to see this desperate thirst as paradoxically indicative of an infinite presence quite beyond human sensibility; that is, the definitiveness of the divine presence is indicated precisely by the extremity of the sorrow/thirst. In one place Gregory implies that perhaps the best indicator of God's presence is exactly the arousal of this painful desire in the soul. So the daughters of Jerusalem ask the bride, "Teach us by what signs this unseen lover can be found, that we may know him by the shaft of love which wounded your heart and intensified your desire for him through a sweet pain" (*CSS*, 232). It is because of the divine infinity that the soul's desire must ever remain frustrated and this, says Gregory, casts the soul into a kind of "despair" which is only alleviated as the soul comes to understand that there is a profound satisfaction in an ever-progressing search for the beloved; for then "the bride is enflamed by a more vehement longing and makes known her heart's affliction" (*CSS*, 225).

None of this is to suggest that the bitter historical realities of Christ's crucifixion are only a kind of dumbshow of the more real interior drama of his soul. Rather the point is to see that these viciously mundane details of Christ's suffering might be construed as the concrete manifestation for him of the unattainability of an infinitely loving God in our world. That is, Jesus' sorrowfulness and his thirst are not merely a kind of "spiritual" desolation somehow quite other than the actual brute facts of his existence in the world; no, the desperate thirst of his soul is fully and really lived out in his *ekstasis* from Jerusalem to Golgotha, in his self-abandonment into the hands of the other, both human and divine. By reading this desolation in terms of the apophatic traditions, we begin to see how entirely his dereliction might be the fullest sign of his union with God. In the language of mystical paradox, then, one might even say that Jesus is most divine and the incarnation is most fully consummated exactly at Golgotha, when the aching physicality of his humanity is unlimited and the unknowing of himself and God is entire. At the very least, the usual criticism that incarnational christology is unintelligible for moderns seems unconvincing. The fullest, most intense expressions of Jesus' human existence, when construed in correlation to apophatic traditions, are seen as the most coherent signs of his infinite intimacy with God.

In the end, then, perhaps Emma Bovary's sense that her newly sought-for divine lover had eluded her ought not to have discouraged her so quickly. To experience divine presence precisely as a long and harrowing form of divine absence would undoubtedly have been too much for Madame Bovary, but perhaps the experience would be profitable for academic theology. This would mean not only, as I have fleetingly attempted here, to search for thematic clues to contemporary puzzles. It would also mean for theology a renewed attentiveness to the kind of spiritual exercises that could prepare one to think and write and speak about the one who, in Gregory's words, "does not answer if you call, nor is he found if you seek him."

NOTES

1. Gustave Flaubert, *Madame Bovary*, trans., Paul De Man (New York: W.W. Norton & Co., 1965), 155.
2. Ibid.

3. Gregory of Nyssa, *Commentary on the Song of Songs*, trans., Casimir McCambley (Brookline, Massachusetts: Hellenic College Press, 1987), 232.

4. Michel de Certeau, *The Mystic Fable*, vol. 1, *The Sixteenth and Seventeenth Centuries*, trans., Michael B. Smith (Chicago: University of Chicago Press, 1992), 77. De Certeau, whose rich if baffling complexity on this quality of mystical texts is often noted, remarks that such texts can only speak truly of the Infinite as they "lose themselves in what they show, like those landscapes by Turner that disappear into air and light. Modulated by pain, enjoyment, or 'letting be' (the Eckhartian *Gelâzenheit*), an absolute (unfettered) inhabit the torture, the ecstasy, or the sacri-fice of the language that can only *say* it by effacing itself. That absolute owes nothing to the language it haunts" (p. 15).

5. "The revelation of God in Jesus in no way, for Aquinas, changes this situation. By the revelation of grace, he says, we are joined to God as to an unknown, *ei quasi ignoto coniungamur* (*ST* Ia, 12, 13, ad 1). God remains a mystery which could only be known by God himself, or by our being taken up to share in his own knowledge of himself, a sharing which for us in this world is not knowledge but the darkness of faith." Herbert McCabe, O.P., *God Matters* (London: Geoffrey Chapman, 1987), 41–42.

6. Rowan Williams, "Theological Integrity," *New Blackfriars* 72 (March 1991): 144, 146.

7. For some of the strongest contemporary cases against incarnational christology one might consider: Schubert Ogden, *The Point of Christology* (New York: Harper & Row, 1982); Karl-Josef Kuschel, *Born Before All Time? The Dispute over Christ's Origin* (New York: Crossroad, 1992); John Hick, *The Metaphor of God Incarnate: Christology in a Pluralistic Age* (London: SCM Press Ltd, 1993). Kuschel's argument is by far the most nuanced and interesting and comes in the end, I would judge, closer to a sympathetic restatement of incarnational christology than a rejection of it as a hopeless blunder: e.g., "the person, cause, and fate of Jesus Christ belong definitively to the determination of the eternal being of God . . . God himself has determined himself as the Father of this Son, so that the event of Jesus Christ itself comes to have decisive, essentially real consequences for the determination of God's very being" (Kuschel, 495).

8. "Jesus cannot be a *real* man and also unique in a sense different from that in which each one of us is a unique individual. A literal incarnation doctrine, expressed in however sophisticated a form, cannot avoid some elements of docetism, and involves the believer in claims for uniqueness [of Christ] which seem straightforwardly incredible to the majority of our contemporaries." Frances Young, "A Cloud of Witnesses," chap. in *The Myth of God Incarnate*, ed., John Hick (Philadelphia: The Westminster Press, 1977), 32.

9. See the helpful placement of Gregory in Bernard McGinn, *The Presence of God: A History of Western Christian Mysticism*, vol. 1, *The Foundations of Mysticism* (New York: Crossroad, 1991), 139–142. See also the very useful survey by Anthony Meredith, "The Idea of God in Gregory of Nyssa," in *Studien zu Gregor von Nyssa und der christlichen spätantike*, ed. Hubertus R. Drobner and Christoph Klock (Leiden: E.J. Brill, 1990), 127–147 (pp. 138–144 analyze the concept of God in the *In Canticum Canticorum* and in the *De Vita Moysis*).

10. Vladimir Lossky, *In the Image and Likeness of God*, ed., John H. Erickson and Thomas E. Bird (Crestwood, New York: St. Vladimir's Seminary Press, 1985), 37.

11. "The essential element of any ecstasy as I. Hausherr has rightly said, is 'a going out of oneself, not by an unconsciousness involving the suspension of sense activity, but by a kind of projection of the soul beyond the laws of reason under the impulse of love.'" Jean Daniélou, Introduction to *From Glory to Glory: Texts from Gregory of Nyssa's Mystical Writings*, trans. and ed., Herbert Musurillo (Crestwood, New York: St. Vladimir's Seminary Press, 1979), 33.

12. Gregory of Nyssa, *Commentary on the Song of Songs*, 130. Hereafter references to this source will be given in the text as *CSS* and page number.

13. McCabe, *God Matters*, 20.
14. Lossky, *Image and Likeness,* 13.
15. Daniélou, *From Glory to Glory,* 41.
16. I am grateful to my colleague, John Haughey S.J., who suggested to me the apt phrase "infinite intimacy" for describing this definitive characteristic of Jesus' life.
17. Daniélou, *From Glory to Glory*, Introduction, 31–32.
18. Or as Daniélou puts it, "As God's adorable presence becomes more and more intense, the soul is, as it were, forced to go out of itself by a kind of infatuation." *From Glory to Glory*, 43.
19. Vladimir Lossky, *The Mystical Theology of the Eastern Church* (Crestwood, New York: St. Vladimir's Seminary Press, 1976), 35.

223

PART FOUR

Spirituality and Healing

*T*his section gathers together a series of essays on various aspects of spiritualities of healing. We encounter a range of practical and concrete concerns related to everyday life, especially experiences of suffering and injustice. The Christian tradition is examined in both positive and critical ways as it responds to the need for healing in five areas: oppression, abuse of planet Earth, ignoring the particularity of context, illness, and exclusive preoccupation with interiority at the expense of the communal and public dimensions of spirituality.

Among the many functions spirituality serves, the need for healing is prominent. In suffering, caused by anything from illness to the wounding attitudes, words, and acts of others, human beings come face to face with their fragility and vulnerability, and their personal ecosystems falter. In these moments, Christians find themselves turning to a God who calls each person by name, who is full of compassionate love for the least among us, and who, in the person of Jesus Christ, chose to enter into his own agony to show the kind of love God has for the world. As part of this turn to God, the Christian community is perennially engaged in reflection about ways in which spiritualities help or hinder the health and welfare of people and of the universe, which is both precious in its own right and makes human life possible.

Jon Sobrino characterizes the spirituality of El Salvadoran martyr, Monseñor Oscar Romero, as touched by the realism of the struggle for justice and human rights in Latin America. Protesting a spirituality that eschews the material and the historical in favor of the invisible and eternal, Romero saw a spirituality incarnate in the very agony of El Salvador's people. In place of oppressive political power, Romero welcomed the power and energy of the Holy Spirit. Because this spirituality is based on the life of Jesus, Sobrino describes it in terms of incarnation, mission, cross, and resurrection. In the face of pain, poverty, suffering, oppression, and violence, Romero led a church that was not afraid to become an advocate of the people. Through his commitment to honor and be responsible for his people, he entered into conflict, raised a prophetic voice, and, like Jesus on the cross, died for it.

A life-long, faithful advocate of planet Earth, Thomas Berry blames our inability to create a significant rapport with the natural world for our present ecological devastation. He examines what he calls the limitations of the biblical worldview held by the European settlers of North America that prevented them from appreciating and benefiting from the nature spirituality of native peoples. Berry challenges us to create an ecological spirituality that leads to a more humble stance toward nature and a realization that human life will fail or prosper in tandem with the earth's fortunes. His is a spirituality of universal harmony that confronts the deep cultural pathology that celebrates the human at the expense of the non-human. Berry prods us to notice the importance of the physical world and to include the earth as an indispensable part of all Christian spiritualities. For without love, reverence, and care of the outer world, our inner world will never flourish.

Lisa Dahill echoes Sobrino's emphasis on context as a crucial element in our understanding and practice of the spiritual life. On the one hand, Dahill celebrates the particular context of Bonhoeffer's life and the ways in which it shaped his personal spirituality. She describes his comfortable family setting, the development of his considerable intellectual powers, and the courage he showed in confronting Nazism and ultimately facing martyrdom. But examining Bonhoeffer's spirituality from a feminist perspective, Dahill concludes that his understanding of the self and its need to surrender in order to move from aggression to intimacy does not fit well when the subject is an abused woman. Given Bonhoeffer's personal context, he rightly advocated submission of an inflated sense of self, but for women with little or no sense of self, such a spiritual path is both inappropriate and even dangerous. Dahill offers an alternative journey that includes self-awareness, self-defense, and self-investment. We are reminded that while we can appreciate and benefit from many aspects of Bonhoeffer's spirituality, we are wise not to universalize his understanding of the growth of the self in contexts that are dramatically different from his own.

E. Ann Matter, a convert to Catholicism, provides a vivid eyewitness account of her pilgrimage to Lourdes, undertaken after a year of cancer treatment. A trained academician, Matter never imagined herself at Lourdes except, perhaps, to study it. But, changed by her illness and healing, she opened herself to the graces and possibilities of becoming a pilgrim. Her detailed, sympathetic, and touchingly humorous description of God's presence in her journey, in the other pilgrims, in their less-than-perfect guide, and in the prayer and pageantry of Lourdes speaks for itself. She returns each year to renew her bonds and enter more deeply into this particular form of healing spirituality.

In the final essay, Philip Sheldrake returns to the theme of the relationship between the inner and the outer life. Overemphasis on what he calls a rhetoric of interiority has had serious moral and cultural consequences inasmuch as it envisions a spirituality that excludes the public aspects of living in cities and urban centers. He examines urban living as a spiritual practice. According to Sheldrake, spiritualities that extend to the public realm must be based on a dialectic of mystical-contemplative and prophetic-transformative practice. He argues that the mystical-contemplative dimension of spirituality, while over-emphasized in the past, remains a vital ingredient in our engagement with transformative practice in the outer, public world. He offers a more nuanced reading of Augustine's concept of the "city of God" and turns to twentieth-century scholar of mysticism Michel de Certeau to support his contention that urban Christians must develop a contemplative awareness of the city and its life. For many Christians, encounter with God is in and through the daily experience of city life. This urban spirituality incorporates both prophetic voice and overt action against any force in society that diminishes the human spirit.

There is a prominent common thread in these essays. Each confronts any type of dualism that stigmatizes material reality as second-class or irrelevant to the spiritual life. We no longer see body and spirit, heart and head, external and internal, public and private, city and country, woman and man as oppos-ing forces; we no longer understand the spiritual path to be one that leads us away from the first entity in each of those pairs toward the second. Rather, these authors recommend the recovery of the material aspects of existence in order to place them at the center of our spiritual lives. Crucifying political conflict, the vulnerability of planet Earth, battered women, diseased bodies, and the confusion and cacophony of the city: these are the realities through which these authors invite us to imagine the spiritual life. Authentic spirituality must both confront the evils of the marketplace with courage and fidelity, and embrace and celebrate once-banished things as potentially godly and full of Spirit.

17

Monseñor Romero, a Salvadoran and a Christian

JON SOBRINO, S.J.

$\mathcal{T}$he most essential thing about the life, faith, praxis, and destiny of Monseñor Romero was this: he was a real human being, in a real world and a real church, with a real faith, real hope, and real commitment.[1] This is what I wish to affirm when I say that Monseñor was, simply and above all else, a Salvadoran and a Christian. I want to recall this clearly so that Monseñor Romero will not be relegated to the void—to *la nada*. This is what many of those who, in his day, hated him and killed him would like. Many of those who even today do not know what to do about him would like this, too. I want to recall his realism, above all, in order that Monseñor not be relegated to a kind of unreality, to appearance or to Docetism, or turned into a figure on a pedestal who offends no one. It is the profound realism of Monseñor Romero's spirituality that has affected me the most. But before reflecting on that spirituality, I want to say something first about the problems I have with using this word, and why.

I must confess that the word "spirituality" makes me uncomfortable and even scares me somewhat. The reason for this is that spirituality comes from Spirit, and the Spirit is something that is not visible and is often contrasted with what is material and historical. For this reason, to speak of spirituality can and often does carry us, one way or another, off to an invisible world, or even to an unreal one. This danger is clearly present whenever we speak about spirituality, but it is especially tragic that it becomes manifest when one is speaking about Monseñor Romero's spirituality, because if there is one thing that Monseñor did not do, it was to live in an unreal world or insulate himself from the reality of El Salvador. Quite the contrary. Without a doubt Monseñor maintained an intimate relationship with God, the great Invisible, but that did not lead him to confuse the world of spirituality with the world of the invisible. Rather, it led him to incarnate spirituality extremely deeply and radically in the reality of El Salvador. He was, ever increasingly, a "real" archbishop, Christian, and Salvadoran. Spirituality never carried him off into an unreal world.

In the final section I will return to Monseñor's relationship with God. But at this point I simply want to emphasize that he did not fall into this danger and trap—typical of many spiritual persons—as we often see in the history of the

Church. Many years ago a French author observed, in denouncing this error, "Because they are not of this world, they think that they are heavenly beings. Because they don't love human beings, they think they love God." Perhaps these are harsh words, but they are useful and necessary, because they put us on our guard against a spirituality that is false.

What am I saying, then, about Monseñor Romero's spirituality, if this spirituality did not carry him off to an invisible or an unreal world? Basically, I would like to say that Monseñor lived his life in the sight of God and of human beings, and that his work, suffering, and dreams were characterized by power and energy. This is quite proper, because power and energy are both signified by the word "spirit." Monseñor Romero was a spiritual person because he was filled with the power of God, with the Spirit of God. But once again, to avoid falling into the error of attaching wings to the Spirit, let us remember that this Spirit is the Spirit of Jesus, and none other. The Spirit molded Monseñor Romero into a likeness of Jesus.

If we ask ourselves, before beginning our reflection, where Monseñor Romero got this power and energy, and how he was able to bring his life into harmony with the Spirit of Jesus, several things may be said. Without any doubt prayer, and reading and hearing the Word of God, were important "places" where he immersed himself in that Spirit. But prayer and meditation can be done in many places and in many ways. I believe that what was unique about Monseñor was that the special place from which he prayed and meditated was the reality of El Salvador, filled as it is with both sin and grace, with both injustice and hope. To put it in the most human terms, reality for him was the poor of Salvadoran society. It was there, amongst the poor, that he made contact with God and immersed himself in the Spirit, in the power of God.

Monseñor opened himself up to the Spirit of God and let himself be carried along by his compassion for this Salvadoran reality—the terrible suffering, the heroic solidarity, and the poor people's incredible sense of hope. Love for God and the Gospel did not cause him to distance himself from what was real; they did not become some kind of drug he took to help him drift off to sleep. Quite the opposite. Love of God and the Gospel turned him back to face the reality of his people, and from there he drew light so that he might know God better, and he drew power and energy from that place to put the Gospel into practice. Monseñor Romero was a *real* Salvadoran and a *real* Christian, and this, I believe, was the most essential thing about his spirituality.

With regard to Monseñor's spirituality I will reflect on four elements that follow the outline of the life of Jesus: incarnation, mission, cross, and resurrection. Spirituality, for Monseñor Romero, consisted in living out—in reality—these four critical moments in the life of Jesus.

MONSEÑOR ROMERO WAS, LIKE JESUS, "REAL" IN HIS INCARNATION WITHIN THE TRUE REALITY OF EL SALVADOR

I think we all remember a time when, if you wanted to praise someone, it was common to say they were very "human" or "Christian" or "authentic." However, I do not think such words are sufficient in this case. Nor do I think it is enough to say that "he was a saint" or "he was very spiritual." Someone might be all these things and still not be real—in our case, not be Salvadoran. For example, in a country where there have been persecutions, if these do not bespatter us with any dirt, then people might say all the beautiful things about us mentioned above, but we are not real. Indeed, we have become unreal.

Let us recall Monseñor Romero now and ask ourselves, what was the reality of his time? Actually, things have not changed much since then. There were *anawim* in El Salvador then, those "bent beneath the weight of heavy burdens," as the Scriptures say. There were poor people, for whom to be of service was the greatest ambition, and whose most likely fate was often death from hunger or from violence at the hands of the state. There were—and still are—those who had no dignity, who had no significance, those who did not count, those who were excluded. There were those who were silenced, those who had no voice. There were those who were powerless, who did not have the ability to defend their most basic rights. There were also those considered to be of no account because they did not follow the cultural dictates imposed on us.

That was the reality then, and all these groups of persons (Neoliberalism would today add to the list those "who do not exist"—those who cannot even be considered cheap hand labor—because they are unemployed, and it is impossible that they will ever be employed) were oppressed by that reality. Additionally, we are more aware of the oppression, hidden for centuries, of women, of children, and of whole races of people. In the days of Monseñor Romero there also was cruel and inhuman oppression—today it no longer takes the abhorrent forms it did then. As he would say, "Hacking people down with machetes, torture, exile, throwing people into the air (from a helicopter) . . . . That is a Satanic empire."

The question we must ask about Monseñor Romero's spirituality then, is what did he, as a man and as a Christian, do within that reality? Let us begin by remembering what he did *not* do. Although it might seem obvious, one thing that Monseñor Romero never did was to distance himself from that terrible reality. To elucidate this, we might begin by recognizing his limitations, including things he did that may have been mistakes. Still, one thing Monseñor never did was to distance himself from the reality in which he lived—and that is the first step of what Christians call incarnation. When we speak of the flesh that Christ assumed in the Incarnation, the Gospel does not speak simply of "flesh," but of *sarx*, which is to say, "the debilities of the flesh." Monseñor Romero did the same thing: he did not simply incarnate himself within Salvadoran reality; he also took on the debilities of that reality: the pain, poverty, suffering, and oppression of the poor, and the violence directed against them by the state.

I begin my analysis of Monseñor Romero's spirituality in this way because, in my opinion, one of the greatest dangers in the Church today, especially in the Salvadoran Church, is the absence of true incarnation in reality. The danger we face is that of falling into unreality, and thus we end up living outside this world, and never making the real life of the poor of this country our own. The Church might say that its reality has other parameters, which is obviously true—it has its evangelization parameters, liturgical parameters, doctrinal parameters, and canonical parameters. The Church accepts that it can play a role only in the social sphere, not in the political sphere. It reiterates that its true purpose is bringing God's salvation. But what worries me is that by appealing to these arguments—which are of questionable validity—or others like them, the Church ends up distancing itself from the reality of El Salvador.

Let us consider a relatively recent example, which I mention with all respect due such matters, but I mention it because of the way it illuminates the theme of incarnation. In 1996, we were visited by the Holy Father. If we look beyond what was an understandable and inevitable mixture of devotion and euphoria, of Christian message and folk expression, the question becomes, how and where was the reality of this country made visible within the context of that visit? In other words, where were the poor? Of course, they could be seen on the sidewalks all along the route taken by the papal procession, but they were there more as part of the background than as something that is central to our reality. The most "real" aspect of that reality—their poverty and suffering, as well as their hopes and pleasures—was not made a central theme. It would seem that, according to the organizers of the Holy Father's visit, making that reality visible was not truly important. It was certainly not the most central issue. So, in this way, the Church, without meaning to do so, created the appearance of many things at once: of being well organized, and of being close to the leadership of the country and to the media. It did not, however, give the image of being a Salvadoran Church, or a Church of the poor, or a Church that is "real."

With Monseñor Romero, things were not like that. The reality of the poor moved him passionately and he let that passion absorb him, not for superficial sentimental reasons, but because he saw in it the endpoint of pain and of hope, and the endpoint of his own faith: the presence of God and of Jesus. I often say, because it impressed me so deeply, that many things could be said about

Monseñor Romero's Church. You can say that his Church had limitations, that it made many mistakes and committed many sins. But what you cannot say about Monseñor Romero's Church is that it was not Salvadoran. I do not mean this in a populist sense. Nor can you say that the Church was not "real." The majority of the poor, the peasants and the workers, did not feel that this Church was alien to them. They did not see it as separate from themselves. They saw it as Salvadoran, as real, and as theirs.

Monseñor Romero expressed this, above all, in his daily routine. But every once in a while he would let slip some audacious and beautiful remark that captured his great dream, which was that the Church might be Salvadoran. For example, Monseñor Romero would make statements that still amaze us today, such as, "I am glad, brothers and sisters, that the Church is being persecuted." Someone might think that these are the words of a mystic, or a saint, but that would be a mistake. These are simply the words of a Christian and a Salvadoran. He explained the reason he felt this paradoxical gladness: the Church was persecuted "because it tried to become incarnate in the interests of the poor." Monseñor Romero was pleased that the Church was persecuted not because of some precipitant mysticism, but because this made the Church a Salvadoran Church, a Church that was real. Using even stronger words, he sometimes said, "It would be sad that in a country in which there are so many horrible assassinations there were no priests counted among the victims."

These are the words of a great Christian. I would even go so far as to say that they should be sufficient to canonize him and make him a doctor of the Church. But the important thing is not the inspiration or the genius of the formulation, but the depth of the conviction of Monseñor Romero, and of his passion to "be real." Certainly the priests who were assassinated are a testimony to a Church that is incarnate in the problems of the people. They were not perfect; Monseñor recognized this. They had their faults, but they were assassinated for living in and trying to create a Salvadoran Church, a Church that was real.

It is also important to emphasize, not only to correct any suggestion of masochism but also to understand Monseñor Romero's passion for a Church that was real, that he wanted this Church to express the positive aspects of Salvadoran reality, the pleasures and hopes of the poor, as the beginning of *Gaudium et Spes* says to do—but he wanted this to be taken seriously. When he witnessed the tenacity and long-suffering of the people, he would say, speaking to Christians, "If someday they take the radio away from us and shut down the newspaper, if they refuse to let us speak, if they kill all the priests and even the bishop, and you are left alone, if only the people remain, without any priests, then each one of you must become God's microphone. Each one of you must become a messenger. Each one of you must become a prophet."

Sobrino | Monseñor Romero, a Salvadoran and a Christian

These words spoken by Monseñor Romero about his Church reflect what he himself was: a man possessed by the spirit of incarnation, a spirit of solidarity with reality and with its poor. I imagine that if there was one thing that would have made Monseñor ashamed, it would have been a Church that was not bespattered by the dirt of Salvadoran reality. Likewise, he would never have suggested, even within his own heart, that the Church should be exempt from the dangers of our reality. This error, so often accepted without a thought, he would have denounced as Docetism, which is what it ends up being. This type of thinking goes something like this: "Although unjust and regrettable, it is understandable that the labor unions have their microphones confiscated or their buildings bombed, or that the peasants be oppressed and attacked. What is not acceptable is that the Church be treated in this way, because we are not like everyone else." Monseñor Romero would say just the opposite: "I am glad that they confiscated our microphones! We are like everyone else, and we are going to show the same tenacity and long-suffering as everyone else."

I come to the end of this reflection. The Church of Monseñor Romero, with him as its head, was a Church that was real. By way of contrast, a Church that in a time of poverty is not poor; that in a time of persecution is not persecuted; that in a time of assassinations is not subject to assassination; that in a time of solidarity does not manifest solidarity nor dares to do so in times of indifference; that has no hope in a hopeful time nor dares to hope in a time of hopelessness, simply is not a Church that is real. Perhaps it might be considered "spiritual" by other measurements, if you permit me this irony, but it would not have the "spirit of reality" Monseñor Romero had—and which Jesus of Nazareth had, too.

MONSEÑOR ROMERO, LIKE JESUS, FULFILLED HIS MISSION, WHICH WAS THE EVANGELIZATION OF AN ENTIRE NATION, OF ALL OF REALITY

Monseñor Romero evangelized through the Word, announcing the good news of God's love to the poor, denouncing the oppressor, and writing pastoral letters to bring light to the nation. He also evangelized through his deeds: by seeking through dialogue to bring about peace, by supporting the work of Judicial Aid and the Social Secretariat, and by opening the first shelters when the war began. He also evangelized through his person; his way of acting was itself gospel, good news, for the majority of people in the country and for many others beyond our borders. All this is well known. What needs restating, in terms of spirituality, is, in the first place, that Monseñor did all these things in a spirit of mercifulness. In the second place—and this I want to emphasize—this was a mercifulness that was extended to an entire people. Monseñor Romero sought the salvation of an entire nation.

I want to recall this because today there are all kinds of ecclesial movements that seek to bring salvation to married couples, to young people, to university students—we also try to do the same things here at the University of Central America—and we all know how necessary this work is. But we must be clear that the reality of our situation is greater than these things. Reality, of course, includes these things, and it tells how important they are. For example, in our countries the youth issue is decisive. However, we must not forget that reality includes the entire people. Perhaps this sort of language seems outmoded or naïve, because there have been many changes in the Church since the days of Monseñor Romero. But if we wish to recall Monseñor, then we must also remember the popular majorities. We must remember the people.

Ignacio Ellacuría, who is very knowledgeable regarding Monseñor Romero and is anything but naïve, was asked, shortly after Monseñor's death, to write an article about him. He began it with these words: "Monseñor Romero, the man sent by God to save his people." With regard to the mission of the Church, this reminds us that Monseñor's desire was to work out the salvation of the people. With regard to spirituality, it reminds us that he was inspired to include everyone, the whole nation. "I want these homilies," he would say, "to become the voice of those who have no voice," that is to say, of the majority, of the common people. When he witnessed violations, horrors, and the countless occasions of suffering in the country, he would say, "Upon these ruins will shine the glory of the Lord."

When, in compassion, he would look on the people, he said, like Jesus said, "They are like sheep without a shepherd." What am I trying to say by this? That in following Jesus and carrying out the mission of the Church, Monseñor Romero kept the majority of the people and a complete view of reality ever before him. He could not bring salvation all by himself, of course. The Church cannot do that, either. However, he never fell into what I regard as the "triple error." The first error is to place boundaries on the scope of the Church's evangelization, taking care to not overstep the limits of normal ecclesial concerns, and making oneself smaller to stay within those limits, thus reducing the scope of the Church's mission, saying, "This is political, this is *not* political." It is as if, by determining what is and what is not reality through the use of definitions, the primary responsibility of the Church and of all human beings, which is to bring salvation to all of reality, might be made to disappear. The second error is to lower and hold down the horizons of the Church's mission; by satisfying itself with the doing of good deeds the Church is thus absolved of its responsibility. The third error is to agree to an "abridged version," in which the totality of situations is not recounted, such as whole peoples crucified, hopes dashed, and the laborious task it is to try to take them down from the cross. In this regard, Monseñor Romero breathed the spirit of the epic narratives.

Monseñor Romero was not mean-spirited, not a man of pettiness, not the "save what you can" type. In the professional sense, as an archbishop, he was well aware of what his duty was and was not. However, the horizons of his mission were clear: salvation must reach everything and everyone. In this regard, Monseñor Romero was a man with a largeness of spirit, a man of strength when the hour came for decisions to be made. His pastoral letters—and here it must be noted that in the intervening years since his time no pastoral letters of importance have been written regarding this country—his letters considered how problems would impact the entire population. His denunciations, as we all know, were heard around the world. And this happened even though he mentioned, in fact *because* he mentioned, all the cases of human rights violations. His dominical homilies were unparalleled and exemplary; they amounted to a massive pastoral pronouncement on everything, and they reached everyone. This did not happen by accident; rather, it was what he desired and then brought to fulfillment in the light of conditions that made such a massive pastoral pronouncement necessary. It proceeded from serious biblical reflection in preparation for giving a homily that would truly bring light to shine on the country's reality. It was reflected in the credibility of his words, the decision to continue "forever" despite the slander, the many types of interference, or the destruction of the bearer of the Word.

Monseñor Romero's hope was to evangelize the structure of society—something seldom even considered these days. He wanted to change the economic and political infrastructure, as well as the legal institutions, the health care institutions, and the media. He also wanted to change—to evangelize—the ecclesial infrastructure, with its curia, parishes, religious congregations, educational institutions, and internal politics. When he saw serious problems in the country—the violence, the problems faced by grass-roots organizations, and, toward the end of his life, the imminence of war—he tackled these in a responsible fashion. He always acted in the country's best interests. Sometimes he uttered threats of punishment, like the prophets of ancient Israel, but never against this or that person, but rather against an entire class of people guilty of oppression. "You rich, remove your rings, because, if you don't, your hands will be cut off" (quoting, of course, from Paul VI).

Monseñor Romero also perceived that, within the errors I have mentioned above, there are other errors of the opposite sort, too, such as becoming involved in politics as an entity with political power, or trying to do so much that you end up accomplishing nothing. However, he did not regard these as major issues. He did not allow himself to be walled up in a sacristy, or in a pastoral letter, or in a mission with limited horizons.

He accomplished all this with an exceptional creativity that combined real closeness with people in their communities. In making his pastoral visits, he dealt with the reality of the entire archdiocese, and he did not lose the perspective of the country as a whole. If Monseñor Romero went to a specific town or a village, this act would have larger implications. If he spoke on the radio, many communities were able to participate and hear what he was saying. When he opened a shelter—with great symbolism, in the building that housed the seminary—he did much more than to simply open "one" shelter; he started a whole shelter movement.

What am I trying to say? I believe that Monseñor Romero undoubtedly had an idea what evangelism meant—in 1977, he organized a conference for priests on Paul VI's *Evangelii nuntiandi*. The most innovative aspect of this for me was that he wanted to evangelize the country in its totality—everyone: individuals, social groups, and infrastructures—and to evangelize a country in which there was terrible oppression and state-sponsored violence, kidnappings, disappearances, and killings; where there was poverty and injustice but also hope, solidarity, strength, faithfulness, and martyrdom. I repeat, Monseñor was a man of courage, of Pauline *parresía*. "Evangelize" meant, "to bring salvation to a people." There is a deficit of such thinking in the Church these days.

MONSEÑOR ROMERO BORE THE BURDEN OF REALITY: LIKE JESUS, HE DIED ON THE CROSS

This is a well-known fact and it need not detain us. I merely want to make clear that Monseñor's spirituality was not a spirituality of suffering, to be understood either ascetically or mystically, but rather a spirituality of honor in the face of reality, and thus, necessarily, a spirituality of bearing the burden of reality. Monseñor could easily have toned down his denunciations; he could easily have reached an understanding with certain authorities, or left the country—and done so with ample justification. But his sense of honor led him to bear the heavy burden of reality and not seek to escape from it. Above all, it must be said that he never invoked God or the Gospel as an excuse for fleeing from his obligations.

Bearing the cross is not some sublime experience. Rather, it is the most absolutely obvious task if one wishes to behave honorably in the face of reality. I say this because this conviction has become eroded lately. There is a deficit in this country generally, both among politicians and within the Church, of this sense of honor and readiness to bear the burden of reality.

It is commonly said today that things have changed, and it is true that there have been important innovations. But in this country there has been no change in the fundamental reality of poverty and injustice—although they may take on different forms—nor has violence been curbed to any major extent. At the level of world statistics, the annual United Nations reports show that the planet has remained mired in violence to a horrendous extent; there has been no substantive change in the amount of social conflict or the need for its unmasking and resolution. There has been no change in the need to engage in this conflict. What has changed, in many places and also in this country, is the willingness and resoluteness to see and say the truth, as well as to engage in the conflict.

In the days of Monseñor Romero, the Church came into conflict with the powers of oppression when it defended the majority of the people against oppression and state-sponsored violence. We know that this stance created great suffering and, in the long term, that this stance is hard to maintain—and, of course, not all situations in the long term of history are equally serious. However, it would seem that today one tries to avoid anything involving conflict as if on principle, as if some better way has been discovered, some way of being Church and remaining on good terms with other powerful entities in this world, even when these entities continue to create victims.

When this is the case, reality is neither a burden nor something onerous, and there is no need to bear its burden. But then one hears the quiet echo of Monseñor Romero's words: "A Church which does not suffer persecution, but in fact enjoys the privileges and the support of the world, is a Church which should be afraid, because it is not the true Church of Jesus Christ." He said such things at a time when the persecution of the Church and of grass-roots organizations was harsh and pitiless, and today that is no longer the case. However, to think that not suffering persecution is more Christian, or that the most desirable arrangement is for the Church to be on good terms with the powers of this world is an error, if considered in light of the Gospel—and in light of Monseñor Romero.

In society there are many real conflicts, and the Church will find itself facing many other potential conflicts if it is truly fulfilling its mission of prophetic denunciation and maintaining a preferential option for the poor. To face such conflicts, the Church must have a spirit like Monseñor Romero had, a spirit of integrity with regard to reality, a spirit of strength to join in the conflict and a spirit of resolve to bear the burden of that reality. This is what it means to carry the cross today.

MONSEÑOR ROMERO ACCEPTED THE BURDEN OF REALITY AND EXPERIENCED THE GRACE OF LIVING AS IF ALREADY PARTICIPATING IN THE RESURRECTION

Shortly before he died, Monseñor Romero said these well-known words: "If I am killed I will resurrect in the people of El Salvador." And one can say that this has come to pass in many ways: Monseñor lives on in our sense of hope, in the celebrations of individuals and of communities. He lives on, above all, in many Salvadoran hearts, as in the hearts of people all over the world, whenever anyone decides to live as he did, and as Jesus did.

Since we are speaking about the spirituality of Monseñor Romero, I would like to conclude with some reflections that are normally not included. It is true that reality is harsh and one must bear with that harsh reality, but reality also bears with us and helps us to walk within history. In Christian terms, we can say that in reality there is both gift and grace, that there is something we receive. If I were to use even more audacious language, I would say that we can live within reality like persons who already participate in the resurrection. When history no longer binds us down and we are able to triumph over those elements within it that enslave us, then we reflect in some way the triumph of the resurrection of Jesus. What is expressed is a fullness, and it shows forth when, through following Jesus—and remaining focused on love—liberty, joy, and hope appear. That is what showed forth in Monseñor Romero.

239

Reality—that is, the people, with their example of solidarity and generosity—made Monseñor Romero act freely, and made him a man of freedom. This was not the freedom of the liberals, which comes from selfishness. Rather, for Monseñor Romero, as for Jesus, freedom meant that no obstacle could stand in the way of the need to do good. This is what it means to be a free man. And this freedom came to him from the people. The suffering he saw in his people and the love that his people showed him caused him to lower all his defenses. It made him free. It was for that reason that he was able to say, like Jesus, "No one takes my life from me, because I give my life up freely."

Reality—which means, again, simple people and their love—taught him also to rejoice in living and serving. Monseñor was a nervous type of person by temperament, and was sometimes weak and restless. However, I believe that, paradoxically and in the midst of so many difficulties, he lived in peace and joy. Sometimes you glimpsed this in the smile on his face, especially when he was surrounded by children, by peasants, or by simple people. Once, he expressed it in these beautiful words: "With people such as this, it is not hard to be a good shepherd." In truth, being a good shepherd did cost him a great deal. In accepting the burdens of the people, he took on the burdens of the cross as well. And yet, the people also accepted his burdens. For this reason Monseñor Romero had to suffer, but he was not overcome by sadness. Like Jesus, he felt the profound joy of realizing that it is the little ones who understand the kingdom of God.

And finally, there was hope. His well-known denunciations of the country's abominations would have driven anyone to a feeling of impotence or resignation. Nevertheless, Monseñor Romero was a man of hope: "Many times I have been asked, 'is there any way out of this?' And I, feeling full of faith, not just a divine faith, but also a faith in humanity, say, 'yes, there is a way out of this!'" Monseñor was triumphant over resignation, lack of faith, and disillusionment.

From that Salvadoran reality, before which he lived with honor, and all the while being immersed in it, desiring to completely change it, and bearing its burden, there also sprang grace, freedom, joy, and hope. In that regard Monseñor lived like someone who was already resurrected, although still living within history. This is vital to recall today, when there is no such abundance of freedom, joy, or hope in the churches. The key here is having a spirituality of grace, which requires the opening up of oneself to grace.

These I believe to be the main points of Monseñor Romero's spirituality. What I have tried to emphasize is that these points are attitudes, convictions, and practices that were taken up by him in response to reality.

Perhaps this way of interpreting spirituality seems strange, because it is not an analysis of his relationship to God. At this point all I can say is that for Monseñor Romero, God was very real. In the depths of his heart—in the inner "cells of the heart," as he would say—God was present. I have absolutely no doubt about that. I would only like to add that being able to discern God's presence in the heart of another person is, on the one hand, a mystery. But, on the other hand, God's presence can be seen in the way a person conducts himself in reality, in what he does with it, in his willingness to bear its burden and let it bear his burdens. When that exterior self is like that of Jesus, then within the interior self of the person the God of Jesus must be present, too.

Monseñor Romero, a Salvadoran and a Christian. I hope we can continue to regard him in these terms. And I hope that we do not put asunder what God has joined: that which was Salvadoran and that which was Christian, that which was best in the country and that which was best in the Church were united and spoke to us in the person of Monseñor. These parts were joined together not by any jealousy of one part for another, but by *bringing* one part over to *meet together* with that other part.

NOTE

1. This essay originally appeared, in a slightly different form, in *Revista Latinoamericana de Teología* 17 (January/April 2000). The editors of *Spiritus* wish to thank Jon Sobrino and the editors of *Revista* for permission to translate and publish the essay in English. We also wish to thank the translator, Michael O'Laughlin. *Ed.*

18

An Ecologically Sensitive Spirituality

THOMAS BERRY

*H*ere we are in Umbria, on the western slope of the Apennines, bathed in the soft summer light of this region such as was experienced by Giotto and the Umbrian school of painters. What we see now is of course only a remnant of the scene experienced by St. Francis and his early companions. The quiet lanes have been replaced by paved roads, the donkey-drawn carts of earlier times have been replaced by automobiles. We feel an intimacy with these earlier times. But we also breathe an atmosphere less refreshing. A crowded world has emerged on the scene. The beginning of the modern commercial world that St. Francis perceived with a certain foreboding in the opening years of the thirteenth century has developed into the industrial centers of the late twentieth century. The consequent assault on the natural world is leading to a certain anxiety concerning the future course of human affairs.

It is appropriate then for us to come here for a few days of thoughtful brooding over the decisions we must make in these terminal years of the twentieth century and the opening years of the twenty-first century; for the period of St. Francis, the opening years of the thirteenth century, was the period when our present world began to take shape. This time of high spiritual accomplishment of the European world was precisely the time when the commercial spirit entered into the Western soul. The cities of Europe were reborn in these years after their long period of decline following the dissolution of Roman order in the sixth century. The Hanseatic League of commercial cities in central Europe was formed in the thirteenth century. Venice had begun its commercial empire during the period of the crusades from 1095 until 1292.

All of this culminated in the fifteenth- and sixteenth-century overseas ventures of the seacoast peoples of Europe, ventures leading to the discovery of America. With this discovery, the European dominance of the entire planet was begun. It seems appropriate then to speak somewhat concerning the European occupation of the North American continent, for this was in some sense the most momentous deed carried out in these years of discovery.

The historical role of America is especially significant as something of a parable of the larger human process; for when that first tiny mast of a European ship appeared over the Atlantic horizon, every living being on the American continent might have shuddered with foreboding at what awaited it. These peoples from across the sea might have come to join the great community of life on this distant continent. They might have responded to the spiritual grandeur of the forest, the rivers, and the woodland creatures, to the mountains and valleys, with the reverence and wonder that were appropriate. They might have learned something of the spirituality appropriate to this land from the native peoples here.

The difficulty was that these people from across the sea thought they already knew everything they needed to know. They brought with them a Book as their primary reference as regards reality and value. This Book, I would say, while recognizing its vast spiritual significance, has caused endless difficulty not only in America but eventually in the larger community of all the living and non-living components of the great community that constitute the planet Earth; for validly or invalidly, it has served to block the spiritual understanding communicated to humans in the world of natural phenomena.

The North American continent was ready to communicate a profound spirituality to the incoming peoples. In the magnificence of its natural splendor, in the grandeur of its forest, in the beauty of its rivers, in the abundance and variety of its wildlife, this continent still had something of its primordial vigor, something of the innocence that older civilizations had lost long ago. In all these ways it was a more immediate manifestation of the divine than the incoming peoples had experienced for centuries.

Yet to have responded in any worthy manner to this all-pervasive presence of the spiritual world would have been considered as heretical, as unworthy of a people accustomed to experience the spiritual order of things in terms of the biblical world. This incapacity to enter into any significant rapport with the primordial, we might consider as the deep source of our present problems of spirituality and sustainability. Because the spiritual dimension of this continent could not be responded to in any adequate manner, there was no proper reverence for the continent to mitigate the exploitation of the immense wealth that was available here.

This alienation was further strengthened by the humanistic formation of Western civilization which fostered the exaltation of the human throughout its education program. Both the spiritual and the humanist dimensions of the Western tradition had only minimal concern for the natural world. Education that should be oriented toward deepening the intimacy of the human inhabitants with the larger earth community and the comprehensive universe community, was turned away toward the self-appreciation of the human and the exploitation of the non-human.

This attitude was even further confirmed by the Newtonian cosmology set forth in 1687. After the material explanation of the universe given there, the natural world could no longer carry any significant spiritual significance. Everything was explained as a world of objects to be manipulated for the benefit of the human. Already in the first part of the seventeenth century, Descartes had effectively killed the life systems of the planet by his division of the universe into mind and matter. What was not mind was mechanism.

With this background it is little wonder then that when they arrived in America the incoming peoples had no deep feeling for the natural world; they had none of the reverence or even aesthetic appreciation due to the continent. Above all they had no awareness that humans form a single integral community with the other components of the continent, with the planet Earth and ultimately with the universe.

The non-human world could be seen only as a collection of objects to be exploited, not as subjects to be communed with. This exploitation we have carried out in these past four centuries with such a passion that the devastation has flowed over into the larger dimensions of the planet, until now we are at a planetwide impasse as regards human consumption and Earth limits. These two are on a collision course. What is not limited is our understanding, aesthetic appreciation, and spiritual celebration of the Earth. We do need endless progress; not however in material development. Only such trans-material advance in aesthetic appreciation and spiritual experience can be without limits. Advance in material possession and use is severely limited.

Our universal need at the present time is a reorientation of the human venture toward such intimate experience of the world around us. If we would go back to our primary experience of any natural phenomena, we would recognize that immediately on seeing the stars splashed across the heavens at night, on looking out over the ocean at dawn, on seeing the brilliant autumn colors of the oaks and maples and poplars in autumn, on hearing a mocking-bird sing in the evening, or breathing the fragrance of the honeysuckle while journeying through a southern lowland; our immediate response to any of these experiences or parallel experiences on other continents, is a moment of something akin to ecstasy. There is wonder and reverence and inner fulfillment in some overwhelming mystery. We experience a vast new dimension to our own existence.

A return to a mystique of the Earth is, I would say, a primary requirement if we are ever going to establish a viable rapport between humans and the Earth. Only in this context will we overcome the arrogance that sets us apart from all other components of the planet and establishes a mood of conquest rather than of admiration. To assume that conquest and use is our primary relation with the natural world is ultimate disaster.

We have an absolute need of the natural world for activation of our inner world. To lessen the grandeur of the outer world is to limit the fulfillment available to our inner world. For the stars in the night sky over our cities to be so blocked from view by the particle and light pollution is not simply a loss of a passing visual experience, it is a loss of soul. This is a special loss for children. For it is from the stars, the planets, and the moon in the heavens as well as from the flowers and birds and forests and woodland creatures of earth that some of the more profound inner experiences take place in children. To devastate any aspect of the natural world is to distort the more sublime experiences that provide ultimate fulfillment to the human mode of being.

We need to move from a spirituality of alienation from the natural world to a spirituality of intimacy with the natural world; from a spirituality of the divine as revealed in verbal revelation to a spirituality of the divine as revealed in the visible world about us; from a spirituality concerned with justice merely to humans to a spirituality of justice to the devastated Earth community; from the spirituality of the prophet to the spirituality of the shaman. The sacred community must now be considered the integral community of the entire universe, more immediately the integral community of the planet Earth.

Our Western Christian-humanist world has come to a period of the reversal of values. We live in a time when the saving of humans can only be achieved by saving the natural world upon which humans depend for both their psychic and physical survival. While we have already outlined the basic psychic need that we have for the natural world, we need also to mention our need for water, air, nourishment, shelter, and a sense of security in the presence of the grand complex of living and non-living forces that make up the integral community of life.

The pervasive flaw in Western civilization is the attitude that only the human is capable of moral and legal rights. The attitude is that the non-human world has its primary purpose and its primary value in its use by the human. This attitude more than any other single cause has brought about the devastation of the natural world by its human component.

In reality every being has three basic rights. These might be designated as ontological rights which are prior to and more fundamental than any moral or legal rights asserted by humans. These are the right to be, the right to habitat, and the right to fulfill its role in the great community of existence. Negatively every being has rights not to be abused by humans, not to be despoiled of its primary dignity whereby it gives some manner of expression to the great mystery of existence, the right not to be used for trivial purposes.

To bring about a recognition of this new sense of our human role in relation to the natural world, we need a radical transformation throughout the entire human venture. The dynamics of the industrial-commercial-financial empires of these times is driving the Earth into a termination of the Cenozoic period in the geo-biological story of the planet. This period, the Cenozoic, the last 65 million years of life development, has been the culmination of the most brilliant phase of life expansion on the planet. Only at the end of this period, when the planet was at its most gorgeous expression, was the time appropriate for humans to appear. For only in a world of such magnificence could the human mode of being be fully developed, only then could the divine be properly manifested, only in such a world could the burden of human sensitivity and responsibility be sustained, the human condition be endured, and the constant healing needed by the human soul be communicated.

This magnificence was rejected by the settlers of the North American continent and later, throughout the planet, with all the industrial development that has taken place. During this time the spiritual and intellectual guides of our Western tradition have shown themselves to be inadequate to their task, however adequate they have been in the past. A new type of spiritual guide is needed. At one time it was the Benedictine monks who by their patterns of cultivating the soil and by their intellectual work in copying and explaining the great intellectual works of the past established themselves as the guides for our Western endeavor. Later in the medieval period when the cities of Europe were reestablished after the Dark Ages, it was the new spirituality of the cathedral builders, the universities, the mendicant friars who guided the course of human affairs. Then in the eighteenth century came the political and social reformers who brought about a new sense of nation identity and also a new sense of the people as competent to determine their own destiny.

Toward the end of the nineteenth century the research scientists, the technologists, the engineers, but above all the corporations, took over as the controlling persons and institutions guiding the course of human affairs. These last mentioned are the persons and the institutions determined to lead humans into a new golden age through technological exploitation of the planet and its resources. The corporations, supported by the dominant political forces, were determined to take control of the planet in its every aspect. This effort at control has led to our present impasse in human-earth relations. But especially it has led to the radical dysfunction of the planet in all its major life systems.

Throughout this modern period the earlier spiritual types have themselves been incompetent in providing guidance. They failed to recognize that the basic issue is not simply divine-human or inter-human relations but our human relations with the larger community of the planet Earth, and beyond that, with the comprehensive community of the entire universe, the ultimate sacred community. This failure has led to the plundering of the planet by good persons, even deeply religious persons, for the supposed temporal and spiritual benefit of the human. This plundering of the planet to serve human purposes is what must change. The industrial movement with its ideal of subjection of the planet must give way to the ecological movement toward supporting the integral functioning of both the human and non-human components of the planet in a single integral community.

245

This we might say requires a new spirituality. No longer can we identify the guiding person of our society primarily with the prophet or priest or saint, with the guru, the yogi, the Buddhist monk, the Chinese sage, the Greek philosopher, or the modern scientist. Each of these types and their teachings are immensely important in their own proper field of functioning. Yet they might all be considered deficient as guides to the human process in its rapport with the natural life systems of the planet in these times. We now have a new understanding of the universe, how it came into being and the sequence of transformations through which it has passed. This new story of the universe is now our sacred story. None of the traditional spiritual guides seem able to accept this new understanding as a revelatory experience. Only an ecologically sensitive personality can do this. The traditional spiritualities in all their various cultural manifestations seem to have reverted back to neo-fundamentalist attitudes.

An ecologically sensitive spirituality seems to be indicated. The integral ecologist is the type of spiritual guide that is needed. While we can expect this type to be realized in only a partial and inadequate manner in any individual, we can say that this is the spiritual type that is needed. We can also say that just as the spiritual ideal of former ages was realized in an unlimited variety of individual realizations, and rarely in any striking manner sufficient to become a reference for imitation by others, so too with the ecologist as a guiding personality for these times, it is the type that establishes the basic referent. For the great spiritual mission of the present is a renewal of the entire Western religious-spiritual tradition in relation to the integral functioning of the biosystems of the planet.

Until recently there has been a feeling in the spiritual formation of the Western personality that spiritual persons were not concerned with any detailed understanding of the biological order of the Earth. The spiritual person was in some manner abstracted from concern with the physical order of reality in favor of the interior life of the soul. If attention was given to the physical order this was simply in the service of the inner world. The natural world had no inherent spiritual dimension; it was not an integral part of the larger spiritual reality.

This neglect of attention to the natural world permitted those concerned with the more material things of life to take possession of the land and the wealth of the planet. It permitted the exploitation of the entire natural world of human gain and the ultimate ruin of the planet. The integral ecologist, as the type needed, can now be considered as the normative guiding personality of our times. The saint of former times would be spiritually deficient in these times. The integral ecologist would understand the spiritual aspect of an emergent universe from the beginning. The sequence of transformation moments of the universe would be understood as cosmological moments of grace to be celebrated religiously with special rituals. But above all, these moments would appear as revelatory of the ultimate mystery of the universe itself.

The ecologist is the spokesperson for the planet in both its spiritual and its physical meaning, just as the prophet was the spokesperson for deity, as the yogi is the spokesperson for the interior spirit, as the saint is the spokesperson for Christian faith. In the ecologist our scientific understanding of the universe becomes a wisdom. For we can finally appreciate that our new understanding of an emergent universe that comes into being through a sequence of irreversible transformation has a revelatory dimension. This new understanding of the universe establishes a new horizon under which all the traditions will henceforth need to function in their integral mode of self-understanding.

This issue of our human disturbance of the most basic life systems of the planet Earth is such that from here on, for an indefinite period, the main difference between human beings will not be the difference of conservative or liberal, based on social or cultural orientation as has been a primary difference of humans in the Western world throughout the twentieth century. It will rather be the difference between the entrepreneur and the ecologist, the difference between those who exploit the planet in a deleterious manner and those who sustain the planet in its integral functioning. This difference will provide not only the public identity of individuals, it will also be a primary designation in all the professions; in law, in medicine, education, religion, politics, or whatever. The prefix "eco" will occur in a multitude of words that will refer to the coherence of any thought or deed or institution with the integral life systems on the planet.

The seriousness of the situation we are discussing here can hardly be exaggerated for it is the issue of life and death, not for human individuals, or for the human community; it is rather the issue of survival of the most gorgeous expression that the ultimate mystery of the universe has given of itself, so far as we know. In designing a program that can adequately deal with the issue we need to be concerned with principles, strategy, and tactics.

Tactics involve ten thousand things such as recycling materials, limiting our use of energy, composting, conserving water supplies, insulating our buildings, and a multitude of adaptations of a similar nature.

Then there is the question of strategies. This would involve teaching children about the natural world and how living systems function and how humans fit into these systems. This might also involve dealing with corporation enterprises to have them control their emissions from industrial production. It might also involve city planning boards that determine the use of land in a given territory. One of the most significant strategies would be concerned with the universities. The universities need to understand that ecology is not a

247

course, it is not a program; it is rather the foundation of all courses, all programs, all professions—because ecology is a functional cosmology and the universe or the cosmos is the only self-referent mode of being in the phenomenal world. Every other being is universe-referent. Cosmology or the universe story is the implicit basis of every particular course or program.

Beyond these is the question of principles governing the course of human actions. This is what we have been dealing with here in this presentation. We are involved in a deep cultural pathology. What is most needed in addition to the new technologies for integrating our human needs with solar energy and with the organic functioning of the life systems of the planet, is a deep cultural therapy that will identify the sources of our pathology and provide a way of returning to the jubilant life expression that should characterize any human mode of being.

I am proposing in this paper that the most fundamental source of our pathology is our commitment to a discontinuity between the non-human and the human and giving all the inherent values and all the rights to the human. The only inherent value recognized in the non-human is its use by the human. By this discontinuity between the human and the non-human we break the great covenant of the universe, the covenant whereby every being exists and has its value in relation to the great universe community. Nothing bestows existence on itself. Nothing survives by itself. Nothing is fulfilled in itself. Nothing has existence or meaning or fulfillment except in union with the larger community of existence.

As St. Thomas saw so clearly: The integrity of the universe is the ultimate and noblest perfection in things (*Summa Contra Gentiles*, II, 46). In the phenomenal world only the universe is self-referent. Every being in the universe is universe-referent. Only the universe is a text without a context. Every other being has the universe for context. To challenge this basic principle by trying to establish the human as self-referent and other beings as human-referent in their primary value subverts the most basic principle of the universe.

Once we accept that we exist as a component member of this larger community of existence then we can begin to act in a more appropriate human way. We might even enter once again into that great celebration, the universe itself.

NOTE

This paper was originally presented in Assisi, Italy, in the summer of 1996 as part of the Conference on Sustainability, sponsored by the Center for Respect of Life and Environment (Washington, D.C.).

19

Reading from the Underside of Selfhood

Dietrich Bonhoeffer and Spiritual Formation

LISA E. DAHILL

Shirley is a bright, charming woman in her early sixties. She is a member of the congregation I attend in San Francisco and is faithful and active in the life of the church. As chair of adult education, she seeks out opportunities for her own ongoing learning to nourish her leadership and teaching, and so she enrolled two years ago in a week-long summer course on Dietrich Bonhoeffer at the Graduate Theological Union in Berkeley. She told me of her experience in that class the day the professor lectured on Bonhoeffer's view of how one is to relate to the neighbor, the other, the enemy. The lecture moved through Bonhoeffer's early writings on the necessity of giving up one's self in favor of the claims of the other, and loving the other instead of the self, and culminated in a reflection on the utterly central Christian stance of loving the enemy, letting the enemy "grasp" a person in a radical claim on one's time and priorities and even one's life.

Shirley had an unsettling, painful reaction to this lecture, and she was assertive enough to go up to the professor afterward and tell him, "If I had been hearing this theology thirty years ago, I would be dead right now." She went on to recount how her alcoholic and abusive husband had come home one night extremely drunk, and had gone on a rampage, finally pinning her against the wall with his hands around her throat, strangling her. She recalled how she had struggled and realized he was truly trying to kill her. In the brief moments of clarity between this terrifying realization and her imminent loss of consciousness, she had a decision to make. Raised in a conservative Christian home and taught to obey the male authorities in her life, she was lucky, she said, that her pastor at that time was not preaching Bonhoeffer's theology, that these words were not filling her head that night. For in that moment, with his hands around her neck, Shirley chose *not* to let the enemy "grasp" her, and surrender her own claims to his absolute demands. She summoned all her strength and was somehow able to claw him off her, and run for her life.

Shirley's story continues to move me deeply, and it crystallizes in dramatic form some of the uneasiness I too have experienced in trying to come to terms with certain aspects of Bonhoeffer's legacy. I have been reading Bonhoeffer for seventeen years, since my introduction to him in Tübingen, Germany, in 1983–

1984. During seminary and my years in Lutheran parish ministry, I continued to draw nourishment from his compelling vision of a deeply nourishing and thoroughly this-worldly spirituality. In the doctoral program in Christian Spirituality at the Graduate Theological Union, I have studied and taught on Bonhoeffer, and have also had the privilege of serving as translator for volume 16 of the new critical edition of his works.[1] In all my work on Bonhoeffer, he never fails to move me with the clarity and subtlety of his insight, the human texture of his faithfulness and courage. In recent years, however, I have increasingly found his insistence on selflessness, his lifelong assertion that holiness, redemption, and the very presence of God are found in turning decisively away from oneself and toward the claims of others, particularly problematic. Like Shirley, I have experienced aspects of Bonhoeffer's conception of the self and its appropriate spiritual formation to be at odds with the directions my own prayer and Christian discernment were leading me.

This is not, of course, the first time women have noticed a disjunction between their experience and the teachings of respected theologians. Since 1960, an impressive line of feminist critiques has challenged normative Christian understandings of sin and self, as these understandings have developed in highly androcentric ways. To date, however, this sort of critical application of gender analysis, within a larger social location critique, has not taken place for Bonhoeffer's writings. Interpreters continue to follow Bonhoeffer himself in speaking of "the" person, or of "human" sin, as if these could be understood monolithically. Because most interpreters share Bonhoeffer's general social location as educated white Western males, it is not surprising that they find his analysis intuitively compelling and take for granted its similar applicability to others.

Yet Shirley's story reminds us that, far from being somehow universally relevant, as is often assumed even to this day, Bonhoeffer's theology of selfhood and spiritual formation depend for their life-giving power on an accurate grasp of the ways in which his own social location shaped his experience and writings, and how these may be appropriated by people in social and psychological contexts different from his. Such critical contextualization is consistent with Bonhoeffer's own lifelong insistence that truth is never abstract, absolute, or fixed, but requires prayerful, concrete discernment in every new context within the flow of highly complex social-historical circumstances. A reading of Bonhoeffer, therefore, which wittingly or unwittingly universalizes his experience and conception of the self, that is, which fails to take account of the enormous contextual factors shaping these realities, risks missing the heart of his own Christian vision and can have devastating consequences. Far from empowering resistance to entrenched evil, as his writings themselves intend, such uncritical, universal application of Bonhoeffer's thought to contexts beyond his own can actually condone and reinforce the patterns of (so-called)

Christian submission that play right into the hands of evil in abuse. Nor are these merely academic questions; as Shirley's story demonstrates, "lives are at stake."[2]

In this essay I examine Bonhoeffer's writings on questions of selfhood and spiritual formation from the perspective of women in abusive relationships, like Shirley. I have chosen this particular audience partly because its perspectives have so long been completely invisible to mainstream theology, with disastrous results, and partly because these women (who are present at every level of church and society) represent a pole of human experience profoundly different from Bonhoeffer's own. Furthermore, it is specifically around questions of selfhood and its gendered formation that the experience of abused women differs most strongly from Bonhoeffer's and thus offers the greatest possibility of critique. For all his astute and far-sighted sensitivity to issues of race, culture, class, nationality, and privilege as they shape the Christian spiritual life, Bonhoeffer was apparently quite blind to gender oppression as a systemic reality.[3] That is, the experience of those whose bodies and spirits bear the devastating brunt of violently enforced systems of male domination was outside Bonhoeffer's theological awareness.[4] Thus the experience of these women provides an excellent test case for the wider applicability of Bonhoeffer's thinking, and a critical and appreciative reading of him from this perspective can provide a glimpse of strategies by which Bonhoeffer's spirituality might be retrievable also for other marginalized groups.[5]

I situate this analysis of Bonhoeffer's work within the discipline of Christian spirituality. Sandra Schneiders has defined spirituality broadly as "the experience of conscious involvement in the project of life-integration through self-transcendence toward the ultimate value one perceives."[6] Within a Christian context, this "horizon of ultimate value is the triune God revealed in Jesus Christ, and the project involves the living of his paschal mystery in the context of the Church community through the gift of the Holy Spirit."[7] In this essay, therefore, I explore how Bonhoeffer's experience of this Christian mystery and community took shape within the contours of his own concrete particularity, and how his legacy may continue to be revelatory of Jesus Christ for Christians of very different social locations from Bonhoeffer's own, namely for those who struggle with sins of submission. My method is self-consciously interdisciplinary. In addition to engaging in an analysis of Bonhoeffer's writings, and both biographical and historical materials, I draw on feminist psychology to gain access to the complexity of the experience under examination: both Bonhoeffer's own and that of the women through whose eyes I am attempting to read him.[8]

I will look first at Bonhoeffer's articulation of the shape of human selfhood, as that derives from his own experience in powerful and formative ways. Next, I will briefly examine an alternative version and experience of

251

human selfhood, namely that of women suffering in abusive relationships, drawing on the feminist psychological work of Jessica Benjamin and Judith Herman. Finally, I will place into mutual conversation these two very different conceptions of the human self and its appropriate movement toward greater maturity or wholeness, seeking especially to point to resources Bonhoeffer provides for the spiritual formation of submissive selves. My ultimate goal is greater appreciation of Bonhoeffer's insights on spiritual formation for the fuller range of humanity spanning the poles of dominance and submission, based on an awareness of his own concreteness and particularity rather than on the assertion of his universal applicability.[9]

BONHOEFFER AND SELFHOOD

Born into a culture and family that prized male autonomy and intellectual achievement, Bonhoeffer excelled. Clifford Green, a prominent Bonhoeffer scholar, has persuasively demonstrated the ways in which the highly cultured Bonhoeffer family fostered critical thinking and ego strength among its members, as well as illumining those aspects of family life that especially spurred Dietrich toward the driving intellectual ambition that marked his early years.[10]

As a gifted—indeed, brilliant—young thinker groomed throughout his upbringing for a life of public leadership, Bonhoeffer early on garnered himself a great deal of attention and praise for his ground-breaking theological work. He used the considerable power of his gifts, especially his mind, in an attempt to master reality itself, and to prove the supremacy of his insights in academic debate with others.[11] Yet his experience of this drive of ambition and ego was an extremely alienating one. Precisely in this masterful ego, in its relentless attempt to establish itself as the center of the world, Bonhoeffer perceived himself as cut off from God and others in their genuine alterity; instead, he came to realize that the dominating self distorts all of reality into a mere projection of itself.

> The individual has torn himself out of the community with God, and thus also with other people, and now he stands alone, which is in untruth. Because he is alone the world is "his" world, the neighbor has sunk into the world of things . . . , and God has become a religious object; but he himself has become his own creator, his own master and property. . . . [But] in the cold silence of his eternal solitude, he becomes anxious about himself and begins to dread. . . . the cry of conscience only disguises the mute loneliness of a bleak isolation and sounds without echo in the self-dominated and self-interpreted world.[12]

Earlier, Bonhoeffer describes the "self-confinement and isolation of the very loneliest solitude with its tormenting desolation and sterility."[13] Green locates numerous passages throughout Bonhoeffer's early writings that echo this description of the painfully isolated ego whose confinement to a self-projected and distorted world is hell itself. These passages use almost identical language and metaphors to describe this alienated reality: "cold" solitude, the dead "echo" of an utterly isolated cry, the objectification of God and neighbor into projections of the ego, the self at the "center" of this empty world. Green asserts that the striking convergence of these passages is not accidental: "it is . . . to a large degree a self-portrait of the theologian himself, whose urgent existential concern is expressed in this theology."[14]

Indeed, Bonhoeffer's direct and indirect descriptions of his own inner experience are replete with the violence inflicted on reality by an isolated ego intent on maintaining dominance. He employs several variants of the German *Gewalt*, or "force," showing the heightening intensification of such violence: the *Bewältigung* (overpowering)[15] of another person or of reality itself with sheer *Gewalt*,[16] issuing ultimately in the *Vergewaltigung* (rape, violation)[17] of that other. No translator or scholar I have seen has commented on the significance of this latter word choice (*Vergewaltigung*). It and its verbal and adjectival cognates are universally translated in English with terms of "violation" or "doing violence to." Of course, these are not inaccurate translations, and they convey an element of the brutal force denoted here. Nevertheless, the word *Vergewaltigung* simply *is* the German word for "rape" as well, investing the word with a shocking horror beyond the less graphic "doing violence to." Any reader of the German would hear this double meaning: Bonhoeffer chooses language that not only connotes but also actually denotes the violent rape of others, of God, and of reality itself on the part of the sinful "man's" ego.[18] And the fact that (as Green has gone to such lengths to demonstrate) such passages are not merely theoretical for Bonhoeffer, but highly revelatory of his own inner life, suggests that Bonhoeffer chose the term *Vergewaltigung* because it accurately described the ravaging violence within his own self.

Not surprisingly, then, the liberation he discerns corresponds to the shape of this inner bondage experienced as domination, violence, and painful isolation from others. Already in his dissertation, *Sanctorum Communio*, he describes the process by which a person is truly formed: namely, by ethical encounter with an other, a You whose very alterity, reflecting God's own otherness, is what creates the individual as an ethical *Person*.[19] The barrier (*Schranke*) or boundary (*Grenze*) of another person's concrete and separate being confronts the individual with a reality alien to his or her own, thus drawing the person into what Bonhoeffer calls the state of "responsibility," or of ethical demand for some response.[20] The You meets the I in this encounter as "demand" on the I. That is, the I as a "whole person, who is totally claimless, is claimed by this absolute demand."[21] For Bonhoeffer, the only way out of the sterile and lonely wasteland his "dominating ego"[22] had created was to experience himself as "totally claimless" in the face of the "absolute demand" of the other. The language of surrender (*Hingabe*) to this concrete other expresses the longing of the aggressive self to enter a place of actual intimacy, which he finds to be transformative, indeed person-forming. He himself experienced this surrender and the intimacy it opened for him to be utterly life-changing; his conversion to Jesus Christ in prayer and Scripture in the early 1930s was a gradual but powerful breakthrough of love that drew him into increasingly trustful, risky, and disclosive human friendships as well to the end of his life. Emerging from the incessant struggle for domination, Bonhoeffer frames this development as a move into submission, of surrendering at last to reality in the form of the concrete divine or human other. Throughout his life, then, he writes for those whose formation in selfhood is similarly one of alienated isolation and dominance; this is what he clearly means when he speaks of the self, and it has everything to do with his gendered social location.

To claim that Bonhoeffer is writing a highly self-implicating spirituality from a perspective of patriarchal dominance is in no way to disparage him as a human being or a Christian. Indeed, by all accounts he was a warm, sensitive, and conscientious human being.[23] On the whole, he appears not to have acted out the tendencies toward violent egotism with which he struggled but to have worked hard in cultivating virtues of humility, receptivity, and patience. His very sensitivity to the dynamics inherent in his strict patriarchal upbringing may have helped to make him such a perceptive lifelong observer and reporter of their destructive inner reality. Yet this essay's more precise naming of Bonhoeffer's social location within patriarchy opens up space for a feminist reading that will both mark those aspects of his spirituality inappropriate for the abused, and also retrieve the liberating elements he explores. I suggest that this is preferable to the usual uncritical reading that attempts to force all of human experience into his, with potentially disastrous results. To proclaim Bonhoeffer's theology of selfhood as if it were true of everyone simply does not correspond with reality.

WOMEN IN ABUSE: FEMINIST PSYCHOLOGICAL PERSPECTIVES

The work of Jessica Benjamin, a contemporary psychoanalytic theorist, is particularly helpful in understanding the extraordinarily complex dynamics that shape people into patterns of domination and submission.[24] Benjamin develops a feminist intersubjective theory that helps make sense of how traditionally socialized boys come to take on elements of a dominating personality. Many of her descriptions of this personality and the experience it engenders (empty isolation, bubble of the self, mastery of reality) read like citations from Bonhoeffer.[25] Given Bonhoeffer's own articulations of this experience, and Green's comprehensive mapping of them in term of the "dominating ego," it is no stretch to place Bonhoeffer squarely within the realm of those whom Benjamin studies as dominators, that is, a particular and not at all universal dimension of human experience.

Shirley's experience and that of millions of other women is very different. Socialized from birth in patriarchal families and cultures, according to extremely pervasive explicit and implicit gender codes and roles, girls have by and large grown up with a different sense of who they are, who they are allowed to be, and what their tasks and goals in life are to be, than their brothers have done. Thankfully, this is changing for both boys and girls, as shifts in parenting patterns and women's work create new options for them. But the fact that brutal and subtle forms of abuse still fill homes, just as violence fills the news and popular media, means that patterns of domination and submission are still well entrenched, still need naming and challenging. Of course, women can be abusers, and boys and men victims of trauma and abuse. But Benjamin is tracing the continuities between gender socialization and the psychological problems of domination and submission, which in the overwhelming majority of cases still means male abusers and female victims.[26] For this reason, I will risk speaking broadly of the experience of women who suffer abuse.

For those girls and women who live with abuse, then, Benjamin's description of the submissive self reads as accurately as the dominating self described by Bonhoeffer. These human beings live in a world in which their own presence and subjectivity is as thoroughly effaced as Bonhoeffer's was overblown. The victim of abuse realizes that she "is to lose all subjectivity, all possibility of using her body for action; she is to be merely a thing. Second, she is to be continually violated, even when she is not actually being used. The main transgression of her boundaries consists of her having to be always available and open."[27] Far from bringing her pleasure, as Freud suggested in his studies of masochism, Benjamin notes that "intense pain causes the rupture of the self, a profound experience of fragmentation and chaos."[28] And indeed this is found to be true in innumerable studies of survivors of abuse.[29]

Judith Herman, a psychiatrist who has worked extensively with survivors of trauma and abuse, writes,

> People subjected to prolonged, repeated trauma develop an insidious, progressive form of post-traumatic stress disorder that invades and erodes the personality. While the victim of a single acute trauma may feel after the event that she is "not herself," the victim of chronic [abuse] may feel herself to be changed irrevocably, or she may lose the sense that she has any self at all.[30]

Persons subjected to chronic torture and abuse in the home manifest symptoms of deep psychological damage, compounded greatly of course in cases where abuse had begun in childhood. Those whose homes are places of coercive torment and violation develop exhausting forms of hypervigilance, constantly scanning the environment and the abuser for signals of imminent outburst, and expending enormous amounts of energy warding off these explosions, placating the abuser, walking on eggshells, anticipating his every whim. His demands and moods shape every waking moment, and his rages make sleep impossible, due to endless tirades or coercive sexual demands and because of the nightmares filled with terror that shatter sleep.

The abuser's voice comes to fill the victim's whole reality, crowding out any needs or feelings or perceptions of her own; these get beaten out of her if she ever dares to defy him. His rages, insults, surveillance, lies, and threats to herself and/or her children undermine her sense of reality, isolate her, and are backed up with violence should she cross him, even in tiny ways, or threaten to leave. Her autonomy and human capacity for initiative and freedom are relentlessly and pervasively degraded, from the chaos of living for years or even decades in a hell of unpredictable tyranny. The more degraded her sense of self becomes, the more incapable she feels of survival on her own. This is a cycle which leads to death: death of the psyche, death of the self or soul, and very often also physical death: thousands of women are murdered every year at the hands of an intimate other.[31]

This is manifestly *not* a path to holiness, freedom, and fullness of life in Jesus Christ. Yet it is a real-life form of Bonhoeffer's insistence that the self, "who is totally claimless, [be] claimed by [the] absolute demand" of the other. Interpreters of Bonhoeffer need to be extremely careful in interpreting these words to *any* audience, since patterns of abuse and submission are so pervasive, often so hidden to the observer, and so extraordinarily deeply entrenched. Such words mean one thing, indeed life itself, to Bonhoeffer; they mean something completely different to a victim of abuse, for this is the very shape and voice of evil itself in her life. Bonhoeffer's destructive illusion is that the self is omnipotent; for the victim of abuse, it is that the self is "nullipotent," effaced, while the abuser is omnipotent. Thus Bonhoeffer's form of escape will be extremely different from one who suffers abuse, at times nearly its opposite.

MUTUAL INTERROGATION

In contrast to Bonhoeffer, who needed to turn down the volume of the self in order to hear the other, the person living with abuse needs to turn down the volume of the other (specifically, the abuser) in order to attend to herself. Bonhoeffer needed to submit his overbearing self to others' differing reality; the abuse victim needs to defy the abuser's consuming reality in order to claim space for her self.[32] There is a whole universe within her, the uniquely created humanity God brought to life, which has been relentlessly attacked, often since childhood, and never had space to develop. To a greater or lesser extent, her very self has been suffocated.[33] Such selflessness is not holy and not to be naïvely praised. It is a mark of chronic terror and suffering, and cries out for appropriate and courageous naming, remedy, and healing, for the abundance of life intended for every person, every self. Authentic Christian spiritual formation demands nothing less than this. I find three particular areas of significance for the spiritual formation of abused women—self-awareness, self-defense, and self-investment—in which Bonhoeffer can be helpful.[34]

Self-Awareness: The victim of abuse is often so overwhelmed by others' demands as to have very little if any awareness of her own different needs, feelings, or perceptions of reality. A primary and indispensable need for the entire process of healing, and any Christian spiritual formation, is the gift of holy ground in which such self-awareness can begin to grow, perhaps for the first time in her life. Such holy ground is made possible in the space that opens up in a safe and trusting relationship. Benjamin (following Winnicott) speaks of the safe psychoanalysis relationship as just such a "holding space," the transitional space of trust and care that allows a vulnerable self to develop.[35] In addition, spiritual direction, worship, and prayer are arenas in which the Christian experiences holy ground, a space of embrace in which the unconditional love of God is tangibly and personally felt, allowing the pray-er to experience her own self and its movements and desires as well. This provides the sheer novelty of a nonattacking other, a gaze that is profoundly loving rather than accusatory or punishing, a space for nascent self-awareness that evokes neither retaliation nor dismissal by the other.

I find three significant expressions in Bonhoeffer's work of such holy or holding space. The first is the experience of friendship, which for him was transforming and world-opening, particularly in the practice of mutual confession, a revelation of embracing self-disclosure.[36] This is a place of safe noncondemning acceptance that makes possible the life-changing self-awareness abuse victims so need. A second expression comes through the sensory imagery (visual, aural, and tactile metaphors) pervading Bonhoeffer's descriptions of the believer's relationship with Jesus Christ, particularly through meditation on the Gospels. In *Discipleship*, for instance, he consistently uses the metaphor of gaze: living within the gaze of Jesus, keeping one's eyes focused on Jesus, with no sidelong glances at other realities.[37]

> The image of Jesus Christ, which is always before the disciples' eyes, and before which all other images fade away, enters, permeates, and transforms them. . . . Those who behold Christ are being drawn into Christ's image, changed into the likeness of Christ's form. . . . This is the indwelling of Jesus Christ in our hearts.[38]

He makes similar use of "voice" and "touch/attachment" metaphors; the primary image by which voice metaphors are expressed for Bonhoeffer is that of the call (*Ruf*) of Jesus, the powerful and personal Word by which disciples are drawn to the Lord.[39] The metaphor of touch comes through Bonhoeffer's repeated use of the language of *Bindung*, variously translated as "attachment," "allegiance," "commitment," or "bond," and referring to an exclusive devotion that is the only content of discipleship, a life of being "in touch" with Jesus.[40] This sort of sensory imagery in spiritual direction and prayer can be very important for victims of abuse, who are violently conditioned to watch the *abuser's* face for cues of imminent outbursts, to let the *abuser's* voice fill her soul and body. In contrast, the gaze, voice, and touch of Jesus provide a healing and utterly trustworthy alternative, drawing the survivor out of the world controlled by the abuser's voice and hateful glare, and into a world in which Jesus' gaze allows her to see herself and reality anew. Through prayer with the Gospels, Bonhoeffer invites survivors into a holding space, an open space with no other agenda than liberation, healing, and love.

Third, Bonhoeffer's Eucharistic piety and his insistence on Jesus as the servant, the one "for others," can provide resources to help break the gender dynamics sustaining abusive patterns and nourish those who experience physical violation.[41] Here I am developing a sacramental reading of Bonhoeffer's work that runs against the grain of his own sense of the relative locations of self and other. Bonhoeffer insists that Jesus, as "the one for others," models our own "being there for others," which is our encounter with redemptive transcendence.[42] But for those who are *already* "other," whose lives are already poured out for many, Jesus as the one for "others" provides tangible access to a God who is thus "for *me*."[43] To state this in slightly different terms, those like Bonhoeffer, whose powerful selves tend to obscure others' reality, learn from Jesus to attend to the other, to be a "person for others" like Jesus. For those, however, who perceive themselves as no-selves, or for the submerged aspects of any human being, this same Jesus appears as the "one for *me*"; from him these persons learn to experience themselves as worthy of care and love.

This has important gender dimensions as well, particularly in the arena of bodily life. The perception of women as selfless giver and embodied food source is deeply rooted in psyche and culture.[44] Yet Jesus, the One who is present for all who are "other," as Bonhoeffer reminds us, subverts this equation by inviting women to be *receivers* of divine life through his flesh, nourishing their own flesh rather than being givers only, consumed by the demands of family, society, or self-hatred. This redeemer breaks conventionally gendered notions of who is self and who is other. Counter to traditions the world over, in which the female cooks and serves and does not eat (is in fact the "eaten") while the male reclines and consumes (is the "eater"), here a male breaks this pattern to give himself as food for women to bless, break, receive, and eat. And this physical participation in Jesus' bodily life not only draws into healing contact abuse victims' own wounds and crucifixion with his, but reveals as holy even their wounded flesh, allowing a person gradually to perceive her own body as a locus for Jesus' self-revelation. Paying attention to one's body becomes a form of prayer, a means of attending to the One whose body and blood fully saturate the very cells of the disciple's physical being. Experiencing and meeting one's physical needs for food, play, sleep, or love become ways of coming face to face with the One for others, the One whose flesh feeds all selves, all "others."

This Eucharistic reflection is an extrapolation from Bonhoeffer, who does not develop these themes explicitly. But it is a development much in line with his emphases on the physical communion of Jesus Christ and his disciples, and on Jesus' unending devotion to those most in need. It is an example of ways in which Bonhoeffer's spirituality can nourish those who have been violated—here, by locating them among those "others" for whom Christ is really present. Thus in these various ways—in human friendship and searching self-disclosure, and in prayerfully attending to Jesus Christ in Word, sacrament, and one's own body—Bonhoeffer's writings provide significant invitations to growth in transformative self-awareness, a key building block of his spirituality. In his *Ethics*, he later makes explicit the necessity of such self-awareness for mature Christian life, grounding the discernment at the heart of his spirituality.[45]

Self-defense: The ability to defend oneself is a primary capacity of a healthy body and spirit, yet in abuse victims this capacity has been relentlessly attacked. Physical problems, often quite serious and exacerbated by the incapacity to care for oneself, mirror the ways in which verbal and emotional abuse destroys the person's capacity for self-defense. Herman writes,

> Many survivors have such profound deficiencies in self-protection that. . . the idea
> of saying no to the emotional demands of a parent, spouse, lover, or authority
> figure may be practically inconceivable. . . . [They] continue to permit major
> intrusions without boundaries or limits.[46]

There are many forms of self-defense needed, from this capacity to say no at any level to various demands, to asserting the power of anger in making needed change, to ending relationships destructive of one's humanity. All these forms of self-defense depend on healthy psychological boundaries; in abusive relationships, however, these boundaries are overpermeable, enmeshed. This is where Bonhoeffer's emphasis on the centrality of clear boundaries for Christian communities is so helpful. Most explicitly in *Life Together*, but discernible throughout his published writings, his insistence on the necessity of boundaries in all relationships, especially Christian ones, is a gift of protection for those whose attackers know no bounds.[47] Jesus Christ *is* for Bonhoeffer the boundary between persons, so that I cannot relate to another except through Christ. Thus I cannot exploit or attack another except by coming face to face with the One who protects the selfhood of every other, and who protects my selfhood from all would-be attackers as well. Furthermore, this Jesus Christ who protects the vulnerable has the power to call a person out of an abusive situation. His voice draws people from the nets that entangle them and into a costly, joyful life of astonishing freedom in following him.

Bonhoeffer's presentation in *Discipleship* of a God who invites persons into a radical break with the old life may seem impossible or overblown to those whose lives are filled with contentment, but it is good news indeed for those who need to get out of abuse.[48] This is a far cry from traditional Christian pastoral care of the abused, which counsels that suffering under another's attack is "just your cross to bear." In Bonhoeffer's world, both the abused and abuser are called out of that old life for good and set into a world in which boundaries are clear, in which each person's life, at every turn, runs up against the reality of Jesus Christ who alone leads persons into life-giving relationships with others. And finally, Bonhoeffer's participation in the conspiracy against Hitler shows his courageous capacity to say *no* to evil: whether the tyrant is Adolf Hitler or the domestic abuser, Bonhoeffer's witness provides resources for real resistance, including even an ethics of tyrannicide should life itself be at stake.[49]

Self-investment: Finally, the victim or survivor of abuse has great problems with self-investment, understood both as investment *in* the self in self-care, and investment *of* the self in the world in free and creative ways. Bonhoeffer, too, had theological problems with self-investment in the first sense, that is, self-care and self-attention. For him, as for much of the dominant Christian tradition, the self is something to be repudiated, not invested in. Yet for those who live on the underside of selfhood, real investment in the self may be the most radical and audacious aspect of all in following Jesus. Those of the "wrong" gender, race, class, or sexual orientation who have been taught all their lives that their selves are defective, ugly, and inferior do not need to become more selfless but more defiant in claiming the selves they are given. Even those like Bonhoeffer who are socialized into dominance find as they progress in the spiritual life that their own sense of self begins to shift from a false self of mastery, which they have attempted to flee, into a truer and more authentic self able to love and be loved, to act, and to rest.[50] It is no coincidence that Bonhoeffer hesitantly gropes toward a way to include the self in love only toward the end of his life. At the height of his resistance activity, with its unimaginable pressures and looming threat to his and his friends' very lives, that is, he begins to speak positively of self-love for the first time. In a 1941 letter to his close friend Eberhard Bethge, who he feared was in danger of collapse under all the strain, he quotes approvingly a term he had recently read, namely "selfless self-love."[51] Reflected within the context of an abiding friendship, his genuine care for Eberhard, he was learning to see the dangers of the uncompromising selflessness he had been endorsing for so long. Also, he and Eberhard as conspiracy members were now no longer located among the privileged but among the threatened and marginalized—a shift in perspective that may well have allowed him to recognize the subversive importance of claiming self-care more explicitly. This move to the underside, what he names in 1942 the "incomparable. . . view from below," is one he comes to cherish, and it transforms his thinking in crucial ways.[52]

The term "self-investment" includes attention to both self and other, in a way that traditional language about "self-offering" or "pouring out the self" does not. Investing *in* oneself and investing *of* oneself are inseparable, but for victims of abuse it is the first that is the creative growing edge, the risky new venture of faith. Can Bonhoeffer's witness and spirituality help abuse victims recognize, name, and resist the intimate enemy who terrorizes them—can they help them see *self*-investment as, in and of itself, a form of radical discipleship? I hope so. These brief reflections suggest glimpses of a concretely liberating reading of Bonhoeffer for many who are violently oppressed; perhaps they reflect directions he himself might have developed, had he survived his own journey through the underside of history.

CONCLUSION

Clearly, Bonhoeffer was a commanding personality all his life. Despite cease-less attempts in his writings and prayer to foster utter self-surrender to others, he never remotely modeled the passive acquiescence this might seem to en-dorse. From his university days, when he pulled out of voluntary military training exercises because he could not stand to submit to someone else's orders, to the end of his life, when under intense Nazi interrogation he first experienced forced submission, his nature was consistently that of the author-ity.[53] Had he taken completely to heart his own writings on the necessity of absolute surrender to the other, it seems doubtful he would ever have been able to mobilize organized public ecclesial resistance to the Nazis in the face of tremendous antagonism; help found the Confessing Church; serve as a leader in broader international circles galvanizing ecumenical support; push through a structured, monastic rule of life for a Protestant seminary; or muster the creative energy necessary to audaciously re-think fundamental categories of theology, spirituality, and ethics in a time of desperate struggle.

We see, therefore, that Bonhoeffer's professed theology of radical personal surrender to the claims of the other is in fact set within a life whose actual contours look very different. His experience of Jesus Christ liberated him from the sterile isolation of his commanding ego as its own god and allowed him to taste the sweetness of divine and human intimacy for the first time in his life—indeed, even to humble himself emotionally and spiritually in the deep honesty required in a life of confession, prayer, and discernment. This, not the force of his personality, was the only way to life for him. Yet it is clear that the depth of his spiritual vision and the power of his witness derive also from just this capacity for authoritative self-presentation in the world. To preach his theology of the transcendence of the Other to those whose posture is already one of self-abnegation does a grave disservice to his spiritual vision as a whole.

Bonhoeffer's writings disclose a spirituality profoundly and concretely Christian: rich in prayer, friendship, and gratitude, and courageously, incarnationally engaged in the struggles and needs of the world. As a Christian who resisted evil in a time of tremendous ambiguity and complexity, Bonhoeffer reminds all who suffer abuse of the need for a well-discerned perception of reality, of the importance of courage in taking risky action according to the call of God, and of the necessity of rooting this-worldly faith in prayer and community. This examination of his work from the perspective of abused women also serves to caution us all against the tendency to oversimplify the relative place of self and other in the Christian spiritual life, especially regarding the careless use of undifferentiated language of "selflessness," "self-renunciation," or "self-transcendence." Shirley's story invites us to consider carefully the concrete social location/s of our likely audiences as well. Ultimately our consideration of these issues draws us into the mysteries of human relationality, social configurations, and the very structure of the psyche itself, whose extraordinarily complex dynamics of domination and submission, resistance and surrender, make these questions unendingly provocative.[54] We are reminded again of the gift of listening carefully to long-silenced voices in ourselves and others, and of the transformations that can result when they are well heard, transformations of dominant notions of self, other, sin, power, and the actual redeeming work of Jesus Christ in real human lives.

NOTES

1. *Dietrich Bonhoeffer Werke* (hereafter *DBW*), ed. Eberhard Bethge et al. (Munich: Christian Kaiser Verlag, 1986–98). In English, they are in the process of being translated, appearing as *Dietrich Bonhoeffer Works* (hereafter *DBWE*), gen. ed. Wayne Whitson Floyd, Jr. (Minneapolis: Fortress Press, 1996–). The volume I am translating is *Konspiration und Haft: 1940–1945* (*DBW* 16), ed. Jørgen Glenthøj, Ulrich Kabitz, and Wolf Krötke (1996).
2. Christie Cozad Neuger, "Narratives of Harm: Setting the Developmental Context for Intimate Violence," in *In Her Own Time: Women and Developmental Issues in Pastoral Care*, ed. Jeanne Stevenson-Moessner (Minneapolis: Fortress Press, 2000), 86.
3. Several short studies trace Bonhoeffer's attitudes toward women. See Leonore Siegele-Wenschkewitz, "'Die Ehre der Frau, dem Manne zu dienen': Zum Frauenbild Dietrich Bonhoeffers," in *Wie Theologen Frauen sehen*, ed. Renate Jost and Ursula Kubera

(Freiburg im Breisgau: Herder Verlag, 1993), 98–126; Renate Bethge, "Bonhoeffer and the Role of Women," *Church and Society* 85 (July/August 1995): 34–52; René van Eyden, "Dietrich Bonhoeffer's Understanding of Male and Female," in *Bonhoeffer's Ethics: Old Europe and New Frontiers*, ed. Guy Carter et al. (Kampen, The Netherlands: Kok Pharos Publishing House, 1991), 200–207.

4. Throughout his life, he explicitly defends patriarchy (which he terms "patriarchalism") as belonging to the very creation itself, prior to the fall. He distinguishes "patriarchalism understood as punishment" (after the fall) from the "good and necessary" patriarchalism of the primal creation: *Sanctorum Communio*, ed. Clifford Green, trans. Reinhard Krauss and Nancy Lukens, *DBWE* 1 (1998), 97; see also 205, 207, 263. Thus for him it is not women's subordination itself that is the mark of human sin but precisely women's chafing at this God-ordained hierarchy, that is, their seeing it as a punishment!

5. The significance of this reading, therefore, is not limited simply to its applicability to abuse victims and survivors. Rather, those who suffer abuse represent an extreme instance of patterns of submissive selfhood found in various configurations throughout traditional Western female socialization, as well as in the subjugation of nondominant males. Thus many women who never endure physical assault, or men who do, may find elements of this analysis pertinent to their own experience as well, to the extent that their socialization or subsequent relationships have participated in the same dynamics of silencing and submission.

6. Sandra Schneiders, "The Study of Christian Spirituality: Contours and Dynamics of a Discipline," *Christian Spirituality Bulletin* 6 (Spring 1998): 1, 3 (Chapter 1 of this volume).

7. Schneiders, "The Study of Christian Spirituality," 3.

8. Regarding the study of spirituality, Schneiders notes, "Spirituality as an academic discipline is intrinsically and irreducibly interdisciplinary because the object it studies, transformative Christian experience as such, is multi-faceted." Schneiders, "The Study of Christian Spirituality," 3.

9. This emphasis on the particular in Christian experience is of primary importance for the discipline of Christian spirituality. See, for example, Schneiders, "A Hermeneutical Approach to the Study of Christian Spirituality," *Christian Spirituality Bulletin* 2 (Spring 1994): 10f. (Chapter 4 of this volume); and Michael Downey, *Understanding Christian Spirituality* (Mahwah, NJ: Paulist Press, 1997), 119ff. It is also one of the key contributions of Bonhoeffer himself, whose entire life work reflects a highly incarnational and closely reasoned preference for the actual over the ideal, correspondence with concrete reality just as it is, and rejection of systems of abstraction or universalization. He develops this idea most fully in his *Ethik*, ed. Ilse Tödt et al., *DBW* 6 (1992), 260–269. Thus this essay's Christian spirituality approach is uniquely "Bonhoefferean" also, in its attempts in both critique and constructive retrieval to try to do justice to the complexity of concrete human experience around these questions of selfhood, gender, and spiritual formation.

10. Clifford J. Green, *Bonhoeffer: A Theology of Sociality*, rev. ed. (Grand Rapids, MI: Wm. B. Eerdmans Publishing Co., 1999).

11. See, for example, Green, *Bonhoeffer*, 78. Here Green writes, "The man with the 'autonomous self-understanding' who considers himself capable, by his own knowing, of finding the truth about human existence and placing himself in that truth . . . subjects everything to his own authority and power, dominating and violating reality; he 'masters' other people, nature, and even God."

12. Dietrich Bonhoeffer, *Act and Being* (hereafter *AB*), trans. H. Martin Rumscheidt, ed. Wayne Whitson Floyd, Jr., *DBWE* 2 (1996), 137–41. I am deliberately citing this text in the version used by Green, who alters the newly published, inclusive-language translation of *Act and Being* in order to revert to the masculine-language pronouns of the

German original. He does this to emphasize his thesis that Bonhoeffer's writing here is self-referential; that is, that the experience referred to is that of Bonhoeffer himself (Green, *Bonhoeffer*, 92; see also note 36 on page 78).

13. *AB* 42.

14. Green, *Bonhoeffer*, 79. In reference to *Act and Being*, from which these passages are taken, Bonhoeffer's closest friend Eberhard Bethge writes in his biography, "This highly abstract discourse, which the uninitiated are hardly able to follow, concealed a passionate personal involvement. Bonhoeffer's deepest feelings were involved" (Eberhard Bethge, *Dietrich Bonhoeffer: A Biography* [hereafter *DB*], trans. Eric Mosbacher et al., rev. and ed. Victoria J. Barnett [Minneapolis: Fortress Press, 2000], 134).

15. *Akt und Sein*, ed. Hans-Richard Reuter, *DBW* 2 (1988), 36, 58, 61.

16. *Akt und Sein*, 144f, 149.

17. *Akt und Sein*, 89f, 136, 152.

18. Note that in his *Ethik*, Bonhoeffer himself uses the term in both senses: that is, both in reference to bodily rape (179, 212f., 296) and in its metaphorical sense of extreme violation (among others, see 107, 134, 168, 178, 217, 258, 268, 342); p. 168 refers also to the *Vergewaltiger*, the rapist/violator. *Ethik* 168, 178, and especially 134, including also note 37, are examples in which the literal and metaphorical meanings are very nearly indistinguishable. All page citations from *Ethik*, *DBW* 6 (1992).

19. *Sanctorum Communio*, 45ff., 49ff., 54–57.

20. *Sanctorum Communio*, 45, 47, and passim.

21. *Sanctorum Communio*, 54.

22. Green, *Bonhoeffer*, 111 and passim.

23. In the portrait that opens his biography, Bethge writes, "Dietrich's smile was very friendly and warm. . . . In conversation, he was an attentive listener, asking questions in a manner that gave his partner confidence and led him to say more than he thought he could. Bonhoeffer was incapable of treating anyone in a cursory fashion. He preferred small gatherings to large parties, because he devoted himself entirely to the person he was with. . . . [His ability to work with great focus] was accompanied by a willingness to be interrupted, and even a craving for company when playing music. . . . He liked talking to children and took them seriously" (*DB* xvii–xviii). Many of the anecdotes related in *I Knew Dietrich Bonhoeffer*, ed. Wolf-Dieter Zimmermann and Ronald Gregor Smith, trans. Käthe Gregor Smith (London: Collins, 1966), confirm these statements in reminiscences about Bonhoeffer's gifts for friendship and warmth.

24. Jessica Benjamin, *The Bonds of Love: Psychoanalysis, Feminism, and the Problem of Domination* (New York: Pantheon Books, 1988).

25. This sort of language occurs throughout Benjamin's book in reference to the dominating or aggressive form of selfhood traditionally formed in boys. Cf. Benjamin, 64ff., 67f., 70f., 83f., 163, 190f. Here are characteristic phrases and images with clear resonance to Bonhoeffer's descriptions of the human person: the experience of "the self encapsulated in a closed system—the omnipotent mind" (67), "unable to make 'live' contact with outside reality" (68) from within "the bubble of the self" (195). The "omnipotent self [is] imprisoned in his mind, reflecting on the world from behind a wall of glass" (190). The deepest wish of such a person is "to get outside the self into a shared reality" (73), "to break the encasement of the isolated self" (83). This sort of dominating self is marked by "grandiosity and self-absorption . . . flying off into space [with] . . . no limits, no otherness. The world now seems empty of all human life, there is no one to connect with, 'the world is all me'" (70f.). Later in the book, she notes that the "damage . . . [inflicted] on the male psyche . . . [is] disguised as mastery and invulnerability" (161).

26. Statistics repeatedly indicate that "95 to 98 percent of battered spouses are women." Pamela Cooper-White, *The Cry of Tamar: Violence Against Women and the Church's Response* (Minneapolis: Fortress Press, 1995), 108.

27. Benjamin, *The Bonds of Love*, 56f.

264

28. Benjamin, *The Bonds of Love,* 61. For Freud, see "The Economic Problem of Masoch-ism (1924)," *The Standard Edition of the Complete Psychological Works* 19 (London: Hogarth Press, 1953–), 155–72. Benjamin cites also Leo Bersani, *Baudelaire and Freud* (Berkeley: University of California Press, 1977) at this point.

29. The characteristic effects of domestic violence as described in the following paragraphs are drawn from various sources, especially Judith Herman, *Trauma and Recovery: The Aftermath of Violence—from Domestic Abuse to Political Terror* (New York: Basic Books, 1997), 74–95. For additional psychological research, see, for example, Jana L. Jasinski and Linda Williams, eds., *Partner Violence* (Wellesley, MA: Stone Center: 1998). For theological and pastoral considerations on the subject of domestic violence, see among others Neuger (cited in note 2); Cooper-White, *The Cry of Tamar,* 100–125; and Carol Adams and Marie M. Fortune, eds., *Violence Against Women and Children: A Christian Theological Sourcebook* (New York: Continuum, 1995).

30. Herman, *Trauma and Recovery,* 86.

31. Cooper-White, *The Cry of Tamar,* 102.

32. To use the language of *Sanctorum Communio,* the abuser needs to grow in the direction of the "openness" of the self toward others, while the abuse victim needs to learn to recognize and protect her own "closedness." Cf. *Sanctorum Communio,* 65–80.

33. Bernice Martin, "Whose Soul Is It Anyway? Domestic Tyranny and the Suffocated Soul," in *On Losing the Soul: Essays in the Social Psychology of Religion,* ed. Richard K. Fenn and Donald Capps (Albany, NY: SUNY Press, 1995), 69–96. Another theorist uses the image of the "silencing" of the self to describe the effacing which occurs in depression: Dana Crowley Jack, *Silencing the Self: Women and Depression* (Cambridge, MA: Harvard University Press, 1991). Finally, Janet Jacobs explores the "endangered" self with particular attention to women suffering violence: "The Endangered Female Self and the Search for Identity," in *The Endangered Self,* ed. Richard K. Fenn and Donald Capps (Princeton, NJ: Center for Religion, Self, and Society, 1992), 37–46.

34. For material concerning spiritual formation of victims of violence, see in addition to those texts already cited Mary Jo Barrett, "Healing from Trauma: The Quest for Spirituality," in *Spiritual Resources in Family Therapy,* ed. Froma Walsh (New York: Guilford Press, 1999), 193–208; and Mary John Mananzan et al., eds., *Women Resisting Violence: Spirituality for Life* (Maryknoll, NY: Orbis Books, 1996).

35. Benjamin, *The Bonds of Love,* 41ff., 46 (footnote), 126ff. This language of the safe "holding space" was developed by D. W. Winnicott; see for instance "The Capacity to Be Alone," in *The Maturational Process and the Facilitating Environment* (New York: International Universities Press, 1965).

36. See *Theologie und Freundschaft: Wechselwirkungen: Eberhard Bethge und Dietrich Bonhoeffer,* ed. Christian Gremmels and Wolfgang Huber (Gütersloh: Gütersloher Verlagshaus, 1994). For Bonhoeffer's understanding of the transformative power of confession, which for him took place within the context of this friendship, see *Life Together/Prayerbook of the Bible,* trans. Daniel W. Bloesch and James H. Burtness, ed. Geffrey B. Kelly, *DBWE* 5 (1996), 108–18.

37. Dietrich Bonhoeffer, *Discipleship,* ed. Geffrey B. Kelly and John D. Godsey, trans. Barbara Green and Reinhard Krauss, *DBWE* 4 (2001), 58, 72, 86, 92, 107f., 149f., 281ff., 286 and passim.

38. Bonhoeffer, *Discipleship,* 281, 286.

39. Bonhoeffer, *Discipleship,* 57–76, 199ff., and passim.

40. Bonhoeffer, *Discipleship,* 59, 62, 74, 85–87, 89, 116, 118, 125, 127, 133f., 150, 153, 170.

41. Bonhoeffer does not develop a sacramental spirituality as explicitly as his focus on the living Word, but he does cherish the Lord's Supper and in particular its physicality in uniting Christians' flesh with Jesus' own and that of one another. See, for example, *Life Together,* 29, 117f. On his sense of Jesus as the one "for others," see *DBW* 8:558.

265

42. This is Bonhoeffer's view, and his interpreters develop it as well. See, for example, Tiemo Peters, "Der andere ist unendlich wichtig," in *Die Präsenz des verdrängten Gottes: Glaube, Religionslosigkeit und Weltverantwortung nach Dietrich Bonhoeffer*, ed. Christian Gremmels and Ilse Tödt (Munich: Christian Kaiser Verlag, 1987), 166–84.

43. Simone de Beauvoir, *The Second Sex* (New York: Knopf, 1952), was the first to posit woman as the primordial "other."

44. Caroline Walker Bynum has written of the Middle Ages' fertile interweavings of these themes with Christian imagery. See her *Holy Feast and Holy Fast: The Religious Significance of Food to Medieval Women* (Berkeley: University of California Press, 1987). The association continues in contemporary American culture as well, as victims of eating disorders, for instance, testify in wrenching and complex ways.

45. *DBW* 6: 267, 294f., 323–29.

46. Herman, *Trauma and Recovery,* 112.

47. Bonhoeffer, *Life Together,* 41, 43ff.

48. Bonhoeffer, *Discipleship,* 58, 61ff., 78ff., 92–99.

49. *DBW* 6:272ff. Bonhoeffer's reflections on tyrannicide are never, in any way, intended to justify the terrible sin of murder but rather to provide ethical tools to help those embroiled in inescapable guilt to discern the leading of God in responsibility for the coming generation. See Green's analysis of this material in his section entitled "Christian Ethics, Coup d'Etat, and Tyrannicide," *Bonhoeffer,* 304ff.

50. The terminology of true and false self emerged first in the work of psychologist Karen Horney. D.W. Winnicott developed it further, as did Thomas Merton in the area of spiritual formation. See Karen Horney, *The Neurotic Personality of Our Time* (New York: Norton, 1937), 119–20, and *Neurosis and Human Growth* (New York: Norton, 1950), 168; D.W. Winnicott, "Ego Distortion in Terms of True and False Self," in *The Maturational Process and the Facilitating Environment* (New York: International Universities Press, 1965); on Merton, see Anne Carr, *A Search for Wisdom and Spirit: Thomas Merton's Theology of the Self* (Notre Dame, IN: University of Notre Dame Press, 1988).

51. *DBW* 16:65, also 71; Bonhoeffer is citing Josef Pieper, *Zucht und Maß: Über die vierte Kardinaltugend* (Munich: Kösel, 1939), 16f. See also *DBW* 8:417f., letter of May 6, 1944.

52. "After Ten Years," *Letters and Papers from Prison,* enlarged edition, ed. Eberhard Bethge, trans. Reginald Fuller et al. (New York: Macmillan Publishing Co., 1971), 17. The German text is found in *DBW* 8:38.

53. Green, *Bonhoeffer,* 177f., especially notes 201 and 202.

54. *Widerstand und Ergebung* ("Resistance and Surrender") is the German title given by Eberhard Bethge to Bonhoeffer's prison writings. In English this book is entitled *Letters and Papers from Prison*.

20

Lourdes

A Pilgrim After All

E. ANN MATTER

In March of 1997, following almost a year of treatment for cancer, I went to Lourdes for the first time. I consider myself a devout, if sometimes uneasy, Catholic. I think it is fair to say that I never seriously thought I would go to a healing shrine like Lourdes, at least not seriously. Perhaps I could imagine going to see the kitsch, but not as a pilgrim.

But beyond a doubt, my experience of illness and healing changed me; I felt strangely drawn to Lourdes, and I wanted to go—as much as I could—on pilgrimage. So, an Italian friend and I enrolled with a group sponsored by the Paolini, a lay ministry specializing in hospitality and pilgrimage, centered in Milan, where I was spending several months.

At Lourdes, I found something that I really needed and that I have replenished by yearly visits since, both in groups and as a solitary pilgrim. These are my reflections, written all at once in two days, in a pouring forth of words, after my return to Italy from that first trip.[1]

NIGHT IN THE GROTTO

*T*he comet of 1997—named Hale-Bopp—blazed across the sky. It was mountain cold and dark full of stars. The cave is wonderfully secret and dark. The rock is worn smooth by the touch of pilgrims. The spring is paved around and sealed over with Plexiglas. There is a marble lady in the rock shelf—"the least bad" one, Bernadette said. It is still a beautiful place, full of mystery. It is Easter night. Praying people, sick and well. Dark. Banks of candles blaze and smoke.

MORNING IN THE GROTTO

There were five priests behind the altar in the Grotto at this morning's mass, led by a French cardinal. They want so much to take this place back and make it "theirs." Bernadette wasn't one of them, though. Rows and rows of pilgrims in wheelchairs, all wrapped up in knitted shawls against the cold. Most of them are old. They are attended by volunteers, many women with white cloths on their heads, and a few men without white cloths on their heads. I keep imagining a friend from Como who once came to Lourdes accompanying a group of sick people. She had been before, but said that the experience of being with the sick at Lourdes was unlike anything she had known. This group is from Brescia; they all wear blue and purple kerchiefs tied around their necks with the name of their pilgrimage on them. The cardinal keeps talking about "this, the last day of our pilgrimage" (it's our first day, of course). After mass, this group from Brescia is going to the baths. At communion, the priests fan out; each has a layperson next to him, carrying an umbrella—"Body of God here!" I almost get run over by one of the ladies in our group as I go up to communion.

DON SERGIO ON THE *VIA CRUCIS*

Our chaplain talks all the time. Talks about himself all the time. Breaks into the litanies printed in the Paolini booklet: "*se mi permittette . . .* " "if you will allow me . . . " Are we free to say "No!" Not really, so . . . he talks, we listen. He seems to do a lot of these chaplain to pilgrimage group gigs—last night when he met us at the airport he said: "Welcome to Fatima! Oops—Lourdes!" I don't think it was a joke. Sometimes he behaves badly. During the Way of the Cross, he ridicules one of the women who doesn't read the passage very well, breaks in right while she is reading to correct her. I carry the cross for one station, so does Carla. At least he makes me want to assert my presence!

Before we set out to climb the hill of the *Via Crucis*, Don Sergio tells us something he had been promising since the night before when he met us at the airport: exactly why the Virgin Mary appeared here in Lourdes in 1858. "You don't think the Blessed Mother just does things by chance, do you?" he asks us. "She just doesn't have a fight with St. Joseph and decided to go for a walk, and appear on earth! No—there's a very good reason why she appeared in 1858—three of them, in fact." The three reasons are: Charles Darwin's *The Origin of Species*, Karl Marx's *Das Kapital*, and John Stuart Mill's essay *On Liberty*—evolution, materialism, freedom—very dangerous ideas which by 1858 were flourishing. And behind them, an earlier one lurking: Jean-Jacques Rousseau and the idea of the goodness of humanity. So *that*'s why the Virgin Mary came to Lourdes in 1858. Makes me wonder why she didn't appear to John Stuart Mill, Charles Darwin, or Karl Marx! Or at least to the Pope, who knew who these guys were.

Don Sergio acts like we are all here on vacation, and only his presence can make our pilgrimage real. He ridicules the baths and the candles, and tells us to light candles in our parishes instead: "There are already too many candles at Lourdes." As for donations, we should give them to the Paolini rather than to the shrine here. Right. I wonder if he thinks we came here to talk to him? He doesn't seem to know even the little we are learning or can guess about the health of our fellow pilgrims. It seems like everyone is here because of some tragedy. But he doesn't ask, he doesn't want to know.

Coming down from the hill of the *Via Crucis*, Don Sergio starts a rosary, saying, in his always slightly accusatory way: "Would you rather go down the hill chatting or praying?" At the road he goes into a meeting hall where he will be hearing confessions. "Don't you want to go to confession?" says one of the group leaders, a bit surprised. But we go instead into the Upper Basilica, a marvel of nineteenth-century Gothic stone, and finish the rosary surrounded by votives and banners left by the thousands of people who had already come to Lourdes before the end of the nineteenth century. It is the people who are so powerful here. I am so overwhelmed I forget the words.

THE HOTEL ROOM

Tall and narrow and sunny, our room looks out on the town and the river. Across the river is the hill with the stations of the cross. The Grotto is just beyond it, but you can't see it because of the hotels built up on both sides of the river. One has a big neon sign that reads "Hotel la Solitude"—but solitude is the most precious commodity here, with more strangers (and hotel rooms) than any place in France except Paris. But it is quiet here in the room—except for the ruckus of the drunken English at 1:30 a.m.—quiet and private. This is where I felt most vulnerable, away from the cheerful hordes.

A sign in the room says in five languages "Do not deposit needles in the trash—put them *only* in the special containers in the hall." There is a "sharps" container on the wall across from the elevator on every floor. This is Lourdes, after all, not Miramare da Rimini.

THE ILL

I remember thinking—and probably saying out loud and cheerfully—that I probably wouldn't want to go to Lourdes because of all the sick people there. But now, of course, I am one of the sick people, and here I am. There are many grievously ill people here, in wheelchairs, on crutches. Nurses and volunteer aids accompany them. The nurses from Spain are particularly dashing in their white and light blue uniforms and dark blue capes with perky little hats on their heads. They laugh and joke as they swish along—very Cherry Ames. There's a huge pilgrimage of kids from all over England, Ireland, Scotland, Wales—the Handicapped Children's Pilgrimage Trust (HCPT). Each group has its own distinctive dress: T-shirt, funny hat, scarf—in bright colors, polka dots, or stripes. Some have their names written on their backs. They remind me of camp groups—campers and counselors—roaming in bands, singing and chanting. "We are from Cambridge, Sunny, Sunny Cambridge, and everywhere we go, people want to know who we are, so we tell 'em . . . " Many of the children are in wheelchairs. Some are obviously retarded. They are all bouncing around having a lot more fun than we are. It is hard to feel the same about "being sick" in an atmosphere like this. Who are the sick people?

THE BATH

I had a feeling when Don Sergio tried to dissuade us from taking the baths that *this* would be a thing to do without fail. It was the most intensely female experience I had at Lourdes. Men control the flow of bathers into the halls beyond the striped curtain, and, as a group of English teenagers played hymns on a collection of instruments, an English priest intoned Hail Marys in a very funny Latin accent over a creaky sound system. But once inside, it's all girls. We were among the first people there. We sat on the bench waiting with two ladies from England, an elderly Bavarian woman in a dirndl, and a woman from the French Caribbean who now lives in France. We managed to talk in three languages: "How many times have you been to Lourdes? How many times have you done the bath?" The answers astonished me: "five times, three baths—twelve times—every year." We were the only neophytes.

Beyond the curtain is a hallway with a number of little rooms further curtained off. We were led into one where there were six chairs. The assistants were from England, Italy, and a French Basque lady—everyone wore a tag with their language on it. The English language lady, Betty, was in charge in that room. They helped us undress and draped a blue cotton cloak with NDL embroidered into it. We sat on the chairs naked except for the cloak. I looked at my feet on the cold marble floor. Most weird. A young girl from England, one of the HCPT, obviously a kid with Down's, was taken in before us. Betty asked her, "Are you Catholic?" She said no. "Are you Christian?" "Yes." "Then step down into the pool and kiss the lady." "It's cold!" I sat on the other side of the curtain and looked at my feet. When it was my turn, Betty put her arms around me and whispered into my ear, "Now we are going to wrap a sheet around you for modesty's sake—but the bad news is, the sheet is wet!" I stepped back behind the curtain and saw a small pool like a bathtub. Three steps led down into the water. On the wall at the end of the pool was a replica of the statue of Bernadette's lady. One of the assistants was swishing a white linen sheet through the water. They took my cloak off and wrapped the sheet around me from under my arms down. It was cold. The women had told me not to take off my watch; now one of them covered it with her hand. The other took my other arm. Betty stood behind me and said, "Think of your intention. Make the sign of the cross to show us you are ready. Now step down into the water. Now go over and kiss the lady. Now lean back . . . " and they lowered me into the water. BRRRRR . . . . As soon as I came up out of the water, they began "Our Lady of Lourdes, pray for us, Saint Bernadette, pray for us." Welcome invocations at that point! It's true that you don't really need to dry off—maybe it's the cold water ("some sort of thermal inversion," someone suggested later), maybe it's the sheet, but I went back to my chair and got dressed, no fuss, no muss. The Italian lady had to inspect me and show me to Betty before I was allowed to leave. "Betty is very strict," she said, "she wants everyone to be perfect when they go out."

Afterwards, we went to the fountains next to the Grotto and drank and washed our faces in the water and splashed it on our heads. The water is very cold and fresh—it is really a powerful thing. In the Grotto is the place where Bernadette dug and drank. Now it is all paved around and covered with Plexiglas—illuminated, but out of reach. The water is channeled from there to the baths and to the wall of fountains. The people come to wash and drink and take the water away. The water is not for sale, but you can buy containers in the hustle of the town away from the Grotto. The shops in town sell all manner of plastic bottles, some shaped like Mary with a little blue crown-top (even though Bernadette's lady didn't have a crown). The sizes vary from tiny, through family-sized, to industrial strength; and people come collect water at the fountains in any containers they happen to have. I saw a Spanish nurse fill a huge jar labeled "San Vincente."

A neighbor in Milan told us that she had gone to Lourdes with her mother "in the days when you could take so many of those baths." She took seven in one day! Now it's rationed and well people are cautioned that the sick have priority. In fact, sometimes people just sitting there with the sick get swept up in the flow and, before they know it, find themselves naked but for a wet sheet in the pool! I thought about how I would think and talk about the role that Lourdes played in keeping me well, and thought that if I continued to be well, I would certainly acknowledge that part of the reason why is because I came to Lourdes; but even if I get sick again, I will feel that the bath was a moment of healing.

I would have liked to spend more time by the baths, watching the people go in and out. Who knows, maybe I would have seen a miracle. Thousands and thousands of people come to Lourdes every year, most of them looking for a miracle. There have only been sixty-six "real, authentic" miracles in all these years, but there have been over 2,000 "cures." I think I first started thinking about going to Lourdes when a friend was dying and her mother asked me, "Do you believe in miracles?" "Yes," I said, "I believe in miracles." But I didn't think my friend would get well. I thought about the girl with Down's who went in the bath before me—what if she had a miracle happen to her? What does a miracle look like?

PROCESSIONS

On all of the ramparts leading down from the Upper Basilica, the walk through the arches, over the bridge, back through the meadow, there are thousands of candles, a stream of light. The nightly candlelight procession is one of the most moving experiences of Lourdes. When we arrived the first night and went down into the Grotto, we saw pilgrims returning with torches in their hands. The torches are candles with paper lanterns on the top. They sell them in the shops, or, if you buy something from the shop that has the special arrangement with the Paolini, you can get one for free, especially for the procession. Instead, I carried the candle a friend had given me before I left Milan on Easter Sunday—it was the candle she had held in the Easter Vigil. Without the lantern, it dripped all over my hand and made great wax sculptures. The paper lanterns have prayers and pictures on them—the words are in Italian or the other languages of Lourdes: French, English, Spanish, German, Dutch. Everyone has a candle. As we walked past the Grotto, the stream of lights had already filled the meadow on the other side of the river, coming back—a complete circle of light. From the loudspeaker, voices led prayers in Latin, French, Spanish, Italian, German, Dutch, and Gaelic—the entire rosary of the Joyful Mysteries. A group of Irish people next to us answered all of the prayers in Gaelic.

In between the decades of the rosary, we sang hymns. The Lourdes Hymn was wonderful—at the refrain "Ave, Ave, Ave Maria," everyone raised their candles. It is where that hymn belongs, no doubt about it, that hymn that had been the thing I most mocked about Lourdes. I remember hearing the Lourdes Hymn in Finland, at church one Sunday morning in Tampere with the thirty-odd Catholics of the city. The entire service was in Finnish, and the only words I understood at all were the Latin words of the refrain of the Lourdes Hymn. It is incredibly, universally Catholic.

The daytime procession is in honor of the Eucharist. It is led by a group of pilgrims in national costume—today it is of Santander, Spain. Then hundreds and hundreds of sick people in wheelchairs. Then a group of priests (several on crutches or in wheelchairs) including one carrying a monstrance with the Host under a huge yellow canopy. Then there are the groups of pilgrims behind their banners. We march behind flags of the Paolini and banners from Lombardy, Puglia, Veneto, Campagnia, Lazio—a taste of Italy. We are near the end. Again, prayers in the series of Lourdes languages are read over the loud-speaker. Again we amuse ourselves by replying as best we can in the various languages. This procession started across the river in the meadow next to the new Church of Saint Bernadette, and wound all around the oval in front of the basilicas. As we passed the statue of Saint Bernadette with her sheep, a little paraplegic girl in our group, carried on her father's shoulders, cried out "*Voglio toccare le peccore!*"—"I want to pet the sheep!"

The procession ended up in front of the basilicas for benediction and a solemn blessing of objects. We had rosaries and holy cards to be blessed—but what is the protocol? Do you need to hold them up? Are they blessed if they are in your pocket? In your bag? What about the little metal image of the

River Goddess, Godavari, that a student sent me from India? I hope Godavari was blessed too. Earlier that afternoon I had opened the little package that had come with the image on the bridge over the Gave. I poured the red ash in the river, ate the sugar crystals, and freed Godavari from her plastic wrap. I thought about leaving her somewhere along the Grotto, where she could keep company with *Aquéro*, "That One," as Bernadette called her Lady. But I was afraid she would be discovered and thrown away by a scandalized priest, so I took her along in the procession and had her blessed.

During the Eucharistic procession, my friend said to me, "I bet you've never made so many processions in your life!" Actually, I have done a lot of processions, all things considered, including, of course, the almost-yearly academic procession. The only time professors are willing to dress up, and then, in what costumes! I know all about the power of processions. At Oberlin we used to have long, complex Eucharistic processions for Corpus Christi. One year, we had it filmed and then we ran it backwards: the priest walked backwards into the church, the smoke went back into the censers. We thought it was wonderfully funny, in part because the procession had been so solemn. Processions have festivity and human comedy about them. They are the most joyous occasions at Lourdes—*Aquéro* was smart to ask for them.

ROSARIES

By the middle of the first day, when we said a rosary coming down from the *Via Crucis*, and another in the Grotto, I realized that I had never said so many Hail Marys in my life! My Italian friend had spent her entire childhood sitting in churches saying long litanies of prayers. "My parents must have had sex every Sunday afternoon," she said, "because we got sent to Vespers and Benediction with my grandmother. And then, my grandmother would say, 'Nina! Come here and say a rosary!' And Angela and I would moan and do it. For special occasions, we would even say three whole rosaries at a time: Sorrowful, Joyful, Glorious Mysteries. My grandmother said, 'Now you're little, one rosary a day will be enough.' She would often do three in a day." Lots o' Hail Marys.

The first time I ever remember anyone saying a rosary antiphonally was when I was 19—I was visiting in El Salvador, where I had lived as a child, and staying with the family who lived right next door to where I had lived. I was in the back seat of a car with the Colonel and the Señora when suddenly they started the prayer—he would start:

> Dios te salve, Maria, llena eres de gracia, el Señor es contigo.
> Bendita tu eres entre todas las mujeres
> y bendito el fruto del vientre tuyo, Jesús.

and she would reply:

Santa Maria, Madre de Dios,
ruega por nosotros pecadores
ahora y en la hora de nuestra muerte, amen.

I was stunned. When they had finished I asked them what they were doing. "We usually pray a rosary together every day," Señora Gutierrez answered, "today we didn't quite finish it, so we finished it in the car." I had never seen anything like that before.

This was the strangest part of Lourdes for me, saying so many rosaries. Even odder is how, after I left Lourdes, I realized that I had grown into the habit of the prayers of the place, and that I missed it. There it made sense—but it's hard to transfer it, to say rosaries like that anywhere else—"here?" I have always thought there is nothing very easy about saying the rosary. The spiritual discipline of meditation on the Mysteries is no slight task—even keeping count of the beads while repeating the prayers is a challenge. It is a multi-layered act of consciousness. I believe it does induce a meditative state. I believe in the holiness of the old ladies who say so many. I aspire to be one.

When I was in the hospital last year, I amazed a Catholic friend by rattling off the fifteen Mysteries of the rosary—the names that is—even though I had never said all fifteen in a row like she had. Saying the rosary is especially meaningful to me because my rosary was given to me by my Methodist grandmother when I became a Catholic. It's made of white pearl beads with silver crowns and crucifix and a silver medal with Mary's bust on it. Not real pearls and silver, of course, but very handsome—very modern too; the Virgin is a rather abstract, post–Vatican II type of religious art, nothing as sweet as the statues of the Virgin at Lourdes. When my grandmother gave it to me I was not enormously grateful. "Oh—thanks—but, you know, I'm not the kind of Catholic who says a lot of *rosaries*!" "Well, I thought that's what Catholics do!" I have another rosary, blue plastic in a little case, that a friend in Philadelphia gave me just before she died—I carry that one in my purse sometimes. But the white rosary, the one my grandmother gave me, went to Lourdes, so it is the one that has been prayed on. It makes a difference.

CANDLES

In the "Pilgrim's Guide" I picked up at Lourdes there is a photo of burning candles that really evokes the most wonderful part of the experience, the Grotto at night. I thought about my sister so often. She is the candle freak—she would love the experience of seeing so many burning at once. Candles everywhere.

In front of the niche in the Grotto where the statue of the Virgin is, there stands a large wrought-iron candelabrum with a gradation of circles, like a tree of lights. To burn a candle there, you leave it in the bin and the attendants of the Grotto change the candles when they burn down. It's an orderly burning here. Alongside the rock as you approach the Grotto there are bins of candles of different sizes for sale. The very largest are grouped by weight: 10K, 25K, some took two men to carry them. They are all white with blue bottoms, but the big ones have also been decorated with pictures or names or ribbons or photos of the people offering them. The group of sick people from Brescia who were in the mass in the Grotto the first morning left a huge candle all decorated with their colors of blue and purple. It was placed behind one of the first racks to the left of the Grotto, where the huge candles burn, where the pilgrims going into the Grotto pass by. I saw it there both days, but it still hadn't been lit when we left.

Of course, if you *really* want to light a candle, you take it yourself to the metal racks on the right side of the Grotto, towards the baths. They are wrought iron, fashioned for different sizes of candles. The biggest are much smaller than the huge decorated candles on the other side of the Grotto, but still a good size, maybe three or four inches in diameter and three feet long. Since I was there just after Easter, when there are not so many people there, a determined pilgrim could find a place to leave a candle. I left my friend's votive from the Easter Vigil burning there, stuck on the iron frame by its own wax since it was too slender to fit in the holders. It found a place, still burning from the procession, to be consumed.

Some of the larger candles had gone out. I re-lit one and tried but was unable to restart another. In one rack, some of the thick candles had burned together, melting into one another. Are these answered prayers, becoming one? The banks of flame, the side of the cliff, the fantastic shapes of the melted wax are all very powerful.

PILGRIMS

I look at the group photo taken in front of the basilicas and I realize that what was most amazing was the feeling of camaraderie, almost of complicity, with the other pilgrims. We were only together with those people for two days—Sunday night to Tuesday night. It was not a very long time—really insufficient to become close to anyone. Yet by the end of the trip, we knew some stories. Nearly everyone had a need—this was Lourdes, after all, not Rimini. That is what made the priest's dismissal of our desire to be there and to participate in the things there so painful—we *needed* those baths and candles.

The family we ate with: mother, father, teenage son, and the twenty-two-year-old daughter who was the fair-haired child of the priest—she read the Italian at the processions, and was very good at it. The boy mostly stayed in his room—he had a flu and a fever. But there was obviously some crisis here. Only at the end did it become clear, when we learned that the father has lung cancer.

The young woman from Emilia-Romagnia, there with her boyfriend. She weighed nothing. If she turned sideways, she disappeared. In the prayers at mass in the Upper Basilica on Tuesday she said she had not been well and was grateful to be better. I later found out she had a stomach cancer and has had most of her stomach removed. She's fine, but she needs to eat a little at a time, all day long.

Davide, the little nine-year-old boy with the crew-cut and the bomber jacket, became our buddy. We taught him to say outrageous things in English, to read the U.S. license plates embroidered on the back of his jacket: "South Carolina, Illinois, New Hampshire, Nevada—let's hear it again!" He's a sweet boy, kind to the smaller children, patient with adults. His mother takes him into the women's baths—he is unhappy about this, but he doesn't resist too much. His mother tells us he is not doing at all well at school—we ask him about it and he says he can't concentrate very well. Davide has a brain tumor. It is probably benign—he will be operated on later this spring.

Two young couples have small children. One has twin girls, two years old. Chiara is the soul of vivacity—her sister is paraplegic. Her parents were told three months into the pregnancy that one child was not developing properly and would probably be paraplegic. They were offered an abortion, but turned it down. Chiara's sister can't walk, but she wants to pet Bernadette's sheep. The other little girl, about the same age, is mentally retarded. She sits up in her stroller with difficulty—there are obvious developmental problems. Three little girls, but only Chiara can operate on her own. She plays with Davide. In the middle of mass in the Upper Basilica, she suddenly roams down the aisle and starts talking to the priest. He stops, opens his arms, and says, "Suffer the little children to come unto me." Chiara runs back to her sister and her parents.

The director of the group for the Paolini turns out to be a professed lay nun. She teaches *lettere* at a liceo in Milan—formerly in the prestigious Liceo Classico Beccaria, now in a prison. Her friend and fellow sister has had a valve in her heart collapse. She had a heartbeat so fast it was off the charts. She had the most modern microsurgery to correct the valve, but it was not altogether successful. No one knows what will happen now. She is a sweet, quiet woman, who says to me, "May God bless you!" Her friend says about her, "This is love."

The old man we sat next to in the airport waiting for the plane home. While the pilgrims ransacked the duty-free shop, he told us that he has been to Lourdes fourteen times. "Yes, if you live as long as I have, that isn't so many times. This is the last time, though." "Oh, come on," we said, "you'll be back." "No—this is my last time. Now when I say the Hail Mary, I say 'pray for us sinners *now* in the hour of our death.'"

And then there were the five hundred handicapped children brought to Lourdes from the British Isles by the Handicapped Children's Pilgrimage

Trust—young people in bright shirts and funny hats with HCPT and their group number prominently displayed.

And then I was there too.

THE LADY—*AQUÉRO*

She's the reason all the pilgrims go to Lourdes. If she had not appeared to Bernadette in the Grotto there would not be any reason for all these people to troop to Lourdes, France.

Years ago I was told about a man who spent some time driving in France. He was amazed to see so many signs reading "Lourdes" (referring to heavy trucks and directing them to exit at weighing stations). He didn't know what they meant and thought that there were signs to Lourdes, the shrine, every few kilometers along the French highways. He came back to Italy and asked "But do all roads in France lead to Lourdes?"

The Lady. *Aquéro*. The statue in the Grotto did not please Bernadette, but she chose it as the least bad: "It's her and it's not her." It was carved by a sculptor named Fabisch (he carved his name in the pedestal big enough to read standing down in the Grotto) out of Carrara marble, in 1864, six years after the apparitions. In an old photograph of the Grotto, there is a fence in front of the cave and a ribbon of marble under the feet of *Aquéro*. I can't see what it says, but I think it must be the Lady's last message to Bernadette in French: "*Je suis l'Immaculée Conception.*" Now instead there is a slab of marble under her feet with the message as she said it, in the local dialect: "*Que soy era Immaculada Councepciou.*" The statue is all white, white, except for a blue sash at the waist, hanging down in front, and the dark cross of the rosary which she holds draped over her right arm, and golden roses on the toes of her bare feet. She wears a long, collarless white dress with long sleeves, and a white mantle over her head that flows down over her shoulders and over the dress, almost to her feet. No hair is visible under the mantle. Her head is turned slightly to the right. Her hands are held in front of her breast, loosely clasped together, fingers pointed up.

"It's her and it's not her."

In front of the basilicas, in the middle of the huge esplanade, is a huge statue of the Virgin Mary wearing a golden crown. Bernadette's Lady did not wear a crown, but now "*l'Incoronata*" is a central meeting point for groups, where you can pick up a "Pilgrimage for one day" in one of the five languages of Lourdes. But the Lady in the Grotto is utterly simple.

She appeared to Bernadette eighteen times from February 11 to July 16, 1858. All but the last of the apparitions were in the Grotto of Massabielle, at the foot of the cliffs just outside of Lourdes, where a channel of the River Gave lapped the cliff. The river (then as now) winds through the valley of Lourdes, so twisted that you keep crossing it flowing in different directions as you walk through the lower town. The Grotto of Massabielle in 1858 was the town garbage dump, a spot where medical waste from the hospital was taken to be burned. And yet the Grotto is a mysterious place—its holiness is ancient.

Aquéro, "That one," as Bernadette referred to her, spoke for the first time at the third apparition to Bernadette on February 18, 1858. Bernadette had reported her visions to the parish priest and had been given paper and a pencil for the lady to write down her name. But *Aquéro* smiled when Bernadette held them out to her and said, "That is not necessary." Then, very seriously, she added, "Will you do me the favor of coming here for fifteen days?" Bernadette said yes. *Aquéro* continued, "I do not promise to make you happy in this world, but in the next." Bernadette, reporting this conversation, noted that this was the first time anyone had ever spoken to her in the formal "*vous*."

At the eighth apparition, in the middle of the requested fifteen days, the Lady said, "Penitence, penitence. Pray to God for the conversion of sinners."

At the ninth apparition, she said, "Go and drink and wash at the fountain. Eat the grass there. Kiss the ground as penance for sinners." Bernadette saw no fountain, but when she dug into the earth where the Lady had indicated, water welled up under her fingers. The spring was later dug out and has often been channeled and controlled, but it is there now, flowing from the taps along the wall, and into the baths, still flowing.

At the thirteenth apparition, the Lady said, "Go and tell the priests to come here in procession, and to build a chapel here."

At the sixteenth apparition, March 25, Feast of the Annunciation, Bernadette, following orders, pressed the Lady about her identity: "Would you do me the grace to tell me who you are?" and the Lady answered in dialect "*Que soy era Immaculada Councepciou*." Bernadette repeated the words over and over to herself all the way back to town. She had no idea what they meant. But the priest went wild—the doctrine of the Immaculate Conception of Mary had just been declared dogma in 1854, four years earlier, it wasn't even taught yet! Certainly not to an ignorant girl who had not even received her first communion yet! More than anything else, those words made the priests believe Bernadette.

The Lady appeared again twice—once after Easter, and finally on July 16. On this last day the Grotto had been closed off, but Bernadette saw her from the meadow. She did not speak again.

"That is not necessary. Will you do me the favor of coming here for fifteen days? I do not promise to make you happy in this world, but in the next. Penitence, penitence! Pray to God for the conversion of sinners. Go and drink and wash at the fountain. Eat the grass there. Kiss the earth as penance for sinners. Go and tell the priests to come here in procession, and to build a chapel here. I am the Immaculate Conception."

278

These words are spelled out in little heart-shaped votives around the top of the soaring columns of the Upper Basilica. Here and there they have fallen off, leaving some spaces in the letters, but the words are still legible, made up of votives, surrounded by more, larger votives, each one a thank-you for a favor done by the Lady of Lourdes. Those dusty, incomplete words are more impressive than the towering statue of the Crowned Queen. I wonder what happened to the votives that fell from the words. I wonder if they ended up in a classy antique store in Paris. I wish I had one.

BERNADETTE

The first miracle of Lourdes is the fact that the Lady appeared to Bernadette Soubirous, the least of the least. This is the pattern of modern apparitional events—Guadalupe, Fatima, Medjugorje are all like that too. But the story of Bernadette is the tension between her lowliness and the ambitions of her keepers.

What did Bernadette make of her? She certainly did not think of this vision in complex theological terms, she did not come to the conclusions that ultimately the priests reached. Those sorts of things were not in her vocabulary. Bernadette said she saw *Aquéro*, "That one," and that she was simple and shining and beautiful. She said she was the first person to ever give her the "*vous*." That must have been an incredible experience—this beautiful woman who spoke to the young girl in the polite, formal mode. Bernadette was only fourteen years old when this happened. The parish priest thought she was so slow that he had not yet given her First Communion. And she was from a desperately poor family. These are two good reasons why she had never been called anything but "*tu*" before the Lady spoke to her.

I am thinking about a friend's child in Como who is almost fourteen. In the past year and a half, when I was sick and did not go to Italy and so did not see her, she changed from a little girl into a young woman. She has red, red hair and clear blue eyes and white, white skin. For much of her life, she has been oppressed by her red hair—being *rossa* in a culture that considers it bad luck. Now she has a lot more self-confidence; she is a touching mixture of gracefulness and shyness, fawnlike. Compared to Bernadette Soubirous, she is a very privileged girl. What if she had seen a vision of a lady all in white? What would people think? Would anyone believe her? She has many more advantages than Bernadette had—she is from a comfortable, respected Catholic family. She had her First Communion and Confirmation years ago, having been carefully prepared for both; there was never any sense that she would be left out of anything, that she was not good enough for the mysteries of the church. Except for being *rossa*, she has never been marginalized in any way. Yet this young girl, too, has probably never been addressed by the Italian formal "*Lei*" by anyone—her family, friends, teachers all call her "*tu*," and so would anybody on the street asking directions. She's just a child; she's not worthy of respect. If she saw the Lady would anyone believe her? I wonder.

I am looking at four pictures of Bernadette, postcards I bought in the shops of Lourdes. Each of the first three is marked "*Photo authentique de Bernadette.*" The earliest of these is dated October 3, 1863, five years after the apparitions. At this time she was living with the nuns in the Hospice, and it was clear that she would become a nun. She had been given some more religious training, and had had her First Communion and Confirmation. This is "Bernadette the nun-to-be," her head is covered with a white veil, her hands clasped before her, her face is solemn, wary as she looks off to the right of the picture. The second was taken just a few days later, October 12, 1863. It is a headshot taken from the side. Bernadette has a striped kerchief tied up on her head, her eyes are cast down, a slight smile lingers on her lips. This is "Hollywood Bernadette"—rather glamorous, very touching.

The last "authentic" photo is a full-length shot from February of 1864. Bernadette sits in a chair. She is wearing a print dress that comes all the way down to the floor and covers her feet, and a black shawl over her shoulders—it looks to be the same black shawl she is wearing in the other photographs. Her hair is tied up in the same striped kerchief. Her hands are clasped in her lap, holding a rosary that spills down over her shawl. She looks right into the camera, formal and serious. This one reminds me of the way my grandmother and aunts used to sit for photos—dignified and stiff. This is "Peasant Woman Bernadette." In these photos she is nineteen years old and has been a spiritual celebrity for over five years.

Finally there is the horrific card of Bernadette's corpse, in her glass coffin at Nevers. Her body is incorrupt—that's one reason she was canonized. She wears the habit of the Sisters of Charity, black and white, and has a rosary in her hands. Her head rests on a satin, embroidered pillow. This is, obviously, "Saint Bernadette."

The story of the woman Bernadette Soubirous is all about how the awkward, marginalized girl in the garbage dump became the dead saint on a satin pillow. After the visions of 1858, after the spring was uncovered and thousands of people came to the shrine and they built churches there—then they had to do something with the young visionary. Could Bernadette Soubirous get married and be a normal woman of Lourdes? Of course not. So she was sent to the nuns, prepared for a religious life, and sent off to Nevers, closer to Paris than to Lourdes, to the motherhouse. She had to be controlled. Her life as a nun was not very happy; some of her congregation were suspicious and jealous of her and treated her harshly. The mother superior was even scornful of her limp and accused her of trying to play for attention. But it turned out that

Bernadette limped because she had a tubercular tumor on her knee. By the time a doctor looked at her, tuberculosis had consumed her lungs. Bernadette died in 1879 at the age of thirty-five. Even though the waters of Lourdes have cured more people with tuberculosis than anything else, they did not cure Bernadette.

HOME AGAIN

Back in Milan, we were sitting around the dinner table, talking about the trip, about Bernadette. I passed around the pictures of Bernadette and told her story with some excitement. One friend, a German Lutheran, was very quiet. Another, a young noblewoman from the Val Camonica, had a lot to say about Bernadette. "My aunt used to tell me that story," she said, "I know it well. It's very sad, how she had to become a nun, how she had to be protected and controlled. She was just this young girl, and then this thing happened to her, and it became much larger than she was, and so they had to shape her to fit the event. It's a sad story." She sighed and summed it up: "The need to control the sacred—it's a big problem."

I think she got it exactly right. But the wonder of Lourdes is the sacred, not the control; the power of healing that shines from the gloom of the Grotto, from the faces of the pilgrims. Perhaps Bernadette Soubirous was an outsider; perhaps her life was a sacrifice. That sacrifice, though, made it possible for others, even other outsiders like me, to be drawn into a special hierophany, the healing power of *Aquéro*, the Lady of Bernadette's visions.

NOTE

1. For those interested in the history of the shrine at Lourdes, I strongly recommend the study by Ruth Harris, *Lourdes: Body and Spirit in the Secular Age* (New York: Penguin Viking, 1999).

21

Christian Spirituality as a Way of Living Publicly

A Dialectic of the Mystical and Prophetic

PHILIP F. SHELDRAKE

For many people, the word "spirituality" immediately implies interiority in the sense of a quest for personal spiritual experience away from everyday life. The sharp contrast between inner and outer life was prevalent in most books about Christian spirituality until the last part of the twentieth century and has still not disappeared entirely. However, the idea that spirituality is merely the pursuit of individual inwardness has also been criticized in Christian circles. As far back as the 1930s, the idiosyncratic book on prayer by Friedrich Heiler distinguished sharply between mystical-interior forms of Christian religion and active-prophetic forms (of which he approved). According to Heiler the mystical-interior forms arose from a denial of the impulse of life whereas the active-prophetic manifested the energetic will to live.[1] More recently, in an overly polarized essay, Owen Thomas argued that Christian spirituality has been marred by an emphasis on privatized interiority and needs to be radically reformulated in terms of outer life.[2]

A theologically more nuanced critique of the split between inner and outer is made by Rowan Williams who notes:

> Common to a good deal of contemporary philosophical reflection on human identity is the conviction that we are systematically misled, even corrupted, by a picture of the human agent as divided into an outside and an inside—a "true self," hidden, buried, to be excavated by one or another kind of therapy.'[3]

For Williams, this "self" is a morally problematic fiction. It suggests that my deepest interests are individual and preordained and undermines any notion that the human situation fundamentally embodies a common task. Such a view privileges the search for an authentic inner identity "unsullied by the body or history."[4] For Williams there is no complete, *a priori* identity to be unearthed by peeling away various layers of outer existence; rather, the real self is found or made from the very beginning in human communication and interaction. Williams does not deny interiority—believing that it emerges from the hard task of human engagement—but he does suggest that a *rhetoric* of interiority has had serious moral and cultural consequences.

So where does this rhetoric of interiority come from? Richard Sennett, the American social historian, blames Christian theology for the deep division between interiority and exteriority that he believes pollutes Western culture: "It is a divide between subjective experience and worldly experience, self and city."[5] Augustine's *City of God* is, suggests Sennett, the classic expression of the triumph of an inner spiritual world over a human, outer, one.[6] Augustine's legacy, he claims, drove Christian culture to view social, public life with suspicion. Sennett further suggests that modern urbanism is infected with this legacy—what he calls "a Protestant ethic of space" that sees the public world as sterile wilderness.

Are these criticisms of interiority fair? In the first part of this essay, I will suggest that "interiority" is not a straightforward concept. For Augustine and other classic spiritual teachers, the concept did not mean the same thing as it has come to mean for us. I agree with Williams that a dangerous *rhetoric* of interiority, creating a dichotomy between inner and outer life, gradually affected approaches to spirituality over the last hundred years or so. This resulted from the combined influence of some aspects of Enlightenment thinking and late-nineteenth-century psychology. However, we are in danger of getting things the wrong way round if we begin with an *a priori* definition of interiority as inherently private, individualistic, and detached and then interpret spirituality from that fixed standpoint. I believe that, if we survey the Western spiritual tradition as a whole, "interiority" can be redeemed. I also believe that the concepts of interiority and exteriority need to be held in creative tension. The heart of Christian spirituality may indeed be expressed in terms of this tension—a dialectic of the mystical-contemplative and transformative practice (the prophetic). I will go on to suggest that this dialectic is a necessary foundation for conceiving spirituality as a way of living publicly. In the second part of the essay I will illustrate the nature of public spirituality by reflecting briefly on the meaning of cities and on urban living as a form of spiritual practice.

INTERIORITY IN THE WESTERN TRADITION

We need to remind ourselves that the concept of spirituality stems from the Greek words *pneuma* and *pneumatikos* as employed in the Pauline letters. Spirituality here fundamentally means a way of life, or life in the Spirit, in contrast to living in ways opposed to the Spirit of God. It is founded on the practice of a common human everyday life rather than on private experiences or on purely devotional or ascetical exercises.

In his contribution to *A History of Private Life* Peter Brown reminds us that the earliest approaches to the Christian life inherited an intense sense of a vital solidarity between the individual and the community from late classical Judaism. Individual human existence (the self) was intrinsically related to the common good. The perceived danger was that people would retreat into privacy rather than give themselves wholeheartedly to the task of serving their neighbors. Hence, Jewish writers turned their attention to the thoughts of the heart—the supposed core of motivation and intention. Human destiny was a state of solidarity with others, expressed in the image of the undivided heart.[7]

Following this tradition, Augustine among others adopted the symbol of the heart as a way of expressing the self. As Augustine so often takes the blame for pushing Christian spirituality in the direction of a protected inner world, it is worth examining briefly how he actually understands interiority. In Book 10 of his *Confessions*, Augustine refers to "my heart, where I am whatever it is that I am."[8] The heart suggests that the Christian journey takes us towards the interior self, the true self, where God dwells. This is away from what Paul refers to as the outer man: "Even though our outer nature is wasting away, our inner nature is being renewed day by day" (2 Cor. 4:16). Here, the notion of outer refers to our temptation to live on the surface, mistaking what is transitory for what is fundamental.

For Augustine, God created humans with the divine image in their heart. This *imago Dei* is the true self and sin disconnects us from that truth. In his *Tractates on the Gospel of John* Augustine invites us to reconnect with this real self: "Return to your heart! See there what perhaps you perceive about God because the image of God is there. In the inner man Christ dwells; in the inner man you are renewed according to the image of God" (18.10). Earlier in the same section, Augustine suggests that in leaving the heart we leave ourselves: "Why do you go away from yourselves and perish from yourselves? Why do you go the ways of solitude? You go astray by wandering about. . . . You are wandering without, an exile from yourself." It is not the journey into the heart that is solipsistic, but leaving the true self where we engage with God and with all others in God.

To put matters in another way: the outer world is not the problem. The problem is living exteriorly—that is, out of our skins. The language of the heart is not evidence of a necessarily privatized spirituality. What is interior to me is, for Augustine, where I am also united with the whole human family. The *imago Dei* in which we are created and which is imprinted on the heart must be read alongside Augustine's doctrine of creation. In his *Commentary on Genesis*, Adam's sin was pleasing himself and living for himself (*secundum se vivere, sibi placere*). In other words, sin is a withdrawal into privacy, which is distinctly different from interiority. Self-seeking pride is the archetypal sin (*De Gen ad litt* XI.15.19–20). Original Eden, the monastic life, the ideal City of God are all based on "the love that promotes the common good for the sake of the heavenly society" (*De Gen ad litt* XI.15.20). In fact, the most insidious sin was privacy or self-enclosure. The private is seen as the opposite of common or public. For Augustine, the Heavenly City was the community in which there would be the fullness of sharing.[9] Within Augustine there is a tension that should not be resolved between a striking sense of the personal self and an equally striking sense of the fundamentally social nature of human existence.

What of the subsequent Augustinian spiritual tradition? The monastic rule that bears Augustine's name emphasizes love and community as the spiritual ideal rather than withdrawal, asceticism, or even contemplation. "To teach by word and example" (*docere verbo et exemplo*) is their motto, thus emphasizing that monastic life in the Augustinian tradition is not an act of disengagement but of communication with others. An explicitly outward-looking intention contrasts with forms of asceticism that did not have an educative function. The medieval *Exposition of the Rule of St. Augustine* discusses a journey from the exterior to the interior in the classic Pauline-Augustinian manner.[10] This journey is in order that the community should attend deeply to matters of the heart where we are first drawn towards God. This is not detached or disengaged from outward action: "It is necessary that our interior self as an equitable judge preside over ourselves and what we do exteriorly."[11] In other words, exterior living is resourced by interiority. Indeed, medieval Augustinians understood the purpose of interiority to be external action rather than the cultivation of an inner universe of private experience.

According to Caroline Walker Bynum, who has examined spiritual treatises associated with new forms of community life emerging from the twelfth century onwards and based on the Augustinian tradition, edification or teaching by word and example is the key to their spirituality.[12] The purpose of conduct as a whole is to have an effect on others rather than to be primarily ascetical. Nowhere is this clearer that in the motivation for silence. In Augustinian spirituality this is not merely a matter of self-discipline but a necessary preparation for useful speech.[13]

We need to question the assumption that the medieval turn to interiority implied the privatization of spirituality.[14] A growing interest in inwardness during this period has been interpreted as the progressive loss of a sense of community and its replacement by a preoccupation with individual self-expression. However, this is contradicted by the burgeoning of many new forms of community life and the articulation of new collective values from the twelfth century onwards. "If the religious writing, the religious practice, and the religious orders of the twelfth century are characterized by a new concern for the 'inner man,'" Bynum claims, "it is *because* of a new concern for the group, . . . for the 'outer man.'"[15] In other words, an increased awareness of self was both stimulated by the community, and in turn stimulated an awareness of community.

Bynum questions the supposed twelfth-century discovery of the individual in our modern sense. True, writers subsequently placed more emphasis on

285

inner motivation and subjective intention—for example, in Abelard's *Ethics,* value is associated with intention, not with outward actions in themselves. However, others of his contemporaries were more preoccupied with the task of making sense of moral virtue in secular society at a time when new socio-political communities began to appear.[16] Bynum rightly cautions that medieval culture did not possess our concept of the individual personality. In my estimation, this was the product of much later Enlightenment thinking combined with late-nineteenth-century psychological analysis. Like Augustine, the medieval quest for the soul, or inner self, did not imply a unique, particular, autonomous self. Rather, the *homo interior* was a shared human nature, made in the image of God.

René Descartes's *Cogito, ergo sum* (I think, therefore I am) is perhaps the best-known philosophical dictum of all time and, until recently, had a profound influence on Western theology and spirituality. The philosophy of Descartes (1596–1650) has often been linked to Augustine (although Descartes himself was not so convinced of his Augustinian roots). Whatever the case, what emerged from Cartesian thinking has been identified as the modern self. Descartes sought to establish what could be trusted as being absolutely certain. To this end, he peeled everything away until he reached what he saw as the foundational bedrock—individual consciousness. This gave birth to an essentially egocentric perspective. From this arises the dominant Western intellectual understanding of a person as self-conscious, self-reliant, self-transparent, and all-responsible. The self comes first and communication comes second. We fully possess ourselves before we leap into action!

In *Theology after Wittgenstein* Fergus Kerr criticizes much twentieth-century theology for remaining a prisoner of this Cartesian first-person perspective.[17] Central to this approach to theology is the possibility of having a standpoint outside the bodily, historical world. There is also an inclination to conceive of spiritual experience as something radically private and existing solely in our heads. However, while some versions of spirituality display a split between mind and body, between interior and exterior, and strongly privilege subjective interiority in so doing, this cannot be blamed on Augustine. He would not have understood such a dichotomized, lonely self.

To sum up: I do not believe that we need to discard interiority in favor of radical exteriority. This merely perpetuates an unhelpful dichotomy in another guise. Interiority and exteriority express complementary dimensions of human life that should be held in dialectical tension. Denys Turner in his provocative *The Darkness of God: Negativity in Christian Mysticism*[18] points out that while interiority has occupied a central role in descriptions of Christian spirituality, it is ultimately more a theological metaphor than anything else. The modern link between inwardness and spiritual experiences is the real problem. Most of the great contemplative writers either do not mention experiences or attach little importance to them, whereas contemporary aficionados of spirituality frequently link inwardness to the achievement of certain kinds of experience. As Turner puts it, since the nineteenth century we have effectively psychologized the theological metaphor of interiority. By contrast, the earlier language of interiority is self-subverting. For Augustine, inwardness paradoxically leads beyond distinctions of inner and outer towards the eternal boundlessness of God. This self-subverting quality of interiority is present in later spiritual classics as well, notably Meister Eckhart, in a way that is not always noted by the numerous New Age spiritual writings that cite him. Eckhart suggests that only the self-centered person is trapped in a polarization of inner and outer by seeking a God within *as opposed to* without. The truly detached person transcends such distinctions. This is why Eckhart resisted the conventional medieval polarization of the active and contemplative life expressed symbolically by contrasting the way of Martha and the way of Mary.[19]

287

MYSTICISM AND PUBLIC ENGAGEMENT

Mysticism has often been interpreted as the most radically inward form of Christian spirituality, yet the classic mystical texts, properly understood, do not support the viewpoint that mysticism is a "tropical luxuriance" with no role in public, political life.[20] As Evelyn Underhill suggests in her classic book *Mysticism*,[21] a defining characteristic of Christian mysticism is that union with God impels a person towards an active, outward, rather than purely passive, inward life.[22] The most substantial representatives of Western mysticism were opposed to private experience. Underhill's favorite, the fourteenth-century Flemish writer John Ruusbroec, conceived the contemplative life as the life common to all. This common life joined created beings to each other in mutual service and thus harmonized the initially distinct moments of action and contemplation. Thus the spiritually elevated person is also the common person:

> A person who has been sent down by God from these heights is full of truth and rich in all the virtues. . . . He will therefore always flow forth to all who need him, for the living spring of the Holy Spirit is so rich that it can never be drained dry. . . . He therefore leads a common life, for he is equally ready for contemplation or for action and is perfect in both.[23]

Ruusbroec was quite clear that people who practiced the attainment of peaceful inwardness as the goal of prayer and disregarded charity or ethics were guilty of spiritual wickedness.[24]

A number of recent theological writers suggest that the mystical-contemplative way is closely related to the public world or to politics. Both the late

Michel de Certeau and David Tracy write that mystics, like the mad, represent a kind of otherness on the social and religious margins. This otherness has the capacity to challenge traditional centers of power and privilege. In this sense, mystics are socially, theologically, and politically subversive.[25] The Jesuit theologian Robert Egan argues that in Christian terms all sanctification, all inner transformation, is ultimately for the sake of transformative action and redemptive practice in society.[26]

Within liberation theology, the Chilean Segundo Galilea and the Brazilian Leonardo Boff have written powerfully concerning the mystical-contemplative dimension of political and social responses to injustice. Galilea questions the notion that such responses are purely structural. Humans are not able to be truly compassionate, or genuinely transform structures, he claims, without becoming part of Jesus' own compassion. In the context of social action, only contemplative-mystical practice is capable of bringing about the inner transformation needed for lasting solidarity—particularly a solidarity that is capable of embracing the oppressor as well as the oppressed.[27]

Boff sharply criticizes the traditional spiritual formula of prayer and work (*ora et labora*) on the grounds that it espouses a kind of parallelism: it presupposes that contemplation alone is the source of value. Practice does not directly mediate God but has value to the extent that it is fed by contemplation. This conceptual framework implies that the uniquely spiritual nature of prayer redeems the natural profaneness of action.[28] In some contemporary thinking, dominated by social or political theory, this parallelism continues to exist but in reverse. Thus, practice takes precedence over contemplation, which becomes merely another, subsidiary, form of practice. Boff argues for an equal, dialectical relationship, and even coins a new phrase for this—*contemplativus in liberatione*, a unity of prayer-liberation based on a living faith in God existing in all things.[29] Thus the mystical-contemplative life "is not carried out only in the sacred space of prayer, nor in the sacred precinct of the church; purified, sustained, and nurtured by living faith, it also finds its place in political and social practice."[30]

Jürgen Moltmann is his book *Experiences of God* also writes of the ethical dimension of mystical knowledge: "As long as we do not think that dying with Christ spiritually is a substitute for dying with him in reality, mysticism does not mean estrangement from action; it is a preparation for public, political discipleship."[31] For Moltmann, contemplative union with God points beyond itself. At the heart of God is the cross; thus union involves a deeper identification with the crucified Jesus who loses himself in self-giving love. Mystical union therefore becomes a new point of departure for a renewed practice of everyday discipleship.

WHAT IS "LIVING PUBLICLY?"

From this perspective, the mystical-contemplative dimension of spirituality—often described in terms of interiority—is a vital ingredient in our engagement with transformative practice in the outer, public world. Unfortunately, however, Western culture remains deeply polarized. The private sphere (inwardness, family, and close friends) is privileged as the backstage where the individual is truly him/herself, relaxing unobserved before putting on various personae which the self needs in order to play out different roles on the stage of social life.[32] But, from a Christian point of view, is living in public a matter of a role that it is possible to shed or opt not to play? If there is a pre-existent self prior to all roles, then public life becomes detached from identity. However, the Christian theological tradition suggests that there is, strictly speaking, no absolutely private life. Human existence and Christian discipleship inherently embody a common task. "The public" is thus better thought of as a dimension of identity, an aspect of the individual self. There will be different emphases depending on circumstances, but the public element of identity is inherent to Christian discipleship rather than merely contingent.

It is important also to recall the intimate link between Christian discipleship, including the association between public, social life and human identity, and Trinitarian theology. The core of the Christian life is to be united with God in Jesus Christ through a Spirit-led communion with one another. God's own relational nature is fundamental to this life. God *is* persons-in-communion, a mutuality of self-giving love. Communion underpins existence. Nothing *is* without communion, including human life.[33] The *missio Dei* (mission of God) is the divine activity of self-disclosure in creation, salvation history, and Incarnation, drawing all things into the limitless embrace of God's unifying love. The life of discipleship is to participate ever more deeply in this *missio Dei* through a faithful following of the way of Jesus, the bearer and expression of God's mission. For this reason, the biblical notions of mission and discipleship are at the core of the Christian life and are vitally important as we reflect on the public, social nature of spirituality.[34]

I prefer to define "living publicly" more broadly than what José Casanova refers to as "the arena of moral and political contestation."[35] The public is fundamentally our social existence, including what is often referred to as civic life or civil society.[36] The public is the arena where diverse people establish some kind of common life. This includes the relatively anonymous sociability of such contexts as local neighborhoods and less anonymous (yet not necessarily intimate) situations such as church. In other words, living publicly goes beyond an incidental sharing of space with others where the individual self is still primary and demands protection. Richard Sennett suggests that the Western emphasis on inwardness is based on *fear*—the fear of exposure and of the diversity and difference so characteristic of an outer, public world.[37] Michel de Certeau, in his writings on spatial practices, also refers to the fear of mixing and of the disintegration of social boundaries that motivates spatial purification in modernist urban discourse.[38]

In contrast, to live publicly means letting go of a life focused on the survival of the autonomous self. It involves engaging the other in ways that embrace diversity as part of the process of establishing and reinforcing the self. Living publicly implies real encounters, learning how to be truly hospitable to what is different and unfamiliar, and establishing and experiencing a common life. Living publicly excludes social or political quietism, it excludes existing passively in the midst of the world. Interaction, participation, and active citizenship thus should be seen as forms of spiritual practice.

THE MEANING OF CITIES

In our contemporary world, cities are arguably where issues of living publicly are most sharply exposed. In 1965 36% of the world population lived in urban environments; by 1990 about 50% did; and, if predictions are correct, by 2025 this will rise to between 60% and 75%.[39] Thus, the meaning of cities themselves and what it means to live in the city are two of the most pressing questions of our time. In exploring spirituality as a way of living publicly, it is useful to begin with some reflections on the meaning of cities. How can the city itself be a sacred place? How may living in the city be a spiritual practice?

At a basic level, environments shape the human spirit, and our understanding of what enhances the human spirit shapes the environments we create. In particular, the city has always been a powerful symbol of how we understand community—the overall value we place on it and the degree to which our communities succeed in being inclusive. It is vital that cities reinforce a sense that life itself is centered rather than fragmented. We need to ask whether we are physically building an environment that holds what is precious to us. In other words, does architecture and urban design enhance spirituality, and reflect a vision of the human spirit?

There are four aspects of cities that we need to bear in mind. First, we must avoid separating the two Latin concepts of "the city": *urbs* (the physical place, the buildings) and *civitas* (people and their life together). Second, the issues surrounding cities are never purely practical; for example, transportation involves more than matters of engineering, management, investment, and strategy. How we balance private and public transport underlines how we understand the common good versus individual choice. Third, the notion of a city is complex: we cannot separate architecture from urban planning, technology from people, local from global. Finally, cities must embrace their symbolic, historical, and physical past if hopes for the future are to be fully grounded.

For many people the city is a symbol of social and economic opportunity, where one can become anything one chooses. Equally, what might be called "city experience" dominates the culture and thinking of governments, commerce, and the media. This dominant culture insures that groups who do not qualify as urban do not merit the best services—transport, schools, stores, banking, or a post office—because they are not deemed viable. For these and other reasons, the question "what is a city?" becomes a philosophical, theological, and spiritual one as well as an architectural or economic one.

Modern cities built or reconstructed during the last fifty years frequently lack a proper center or multiple centers that embrace the whole life of a multifaceted community. A major part of the problem was the cellular view of urban planning that dominated the immediate post-war era and divided cities into separate areas for living, working, leisure, and shopping. The consequence was often the demise of richly serviced neighborhoods and a fragmentation of diverse communities. This fragmented city emptied sections at night, especially the centers and commercial districts, making them dead and dangerous. Finally, cellular design separated areas of human life by distance and clear boundaries. This substantially increased the need for travel and consequently pollution. Arguably, differentiation into discrete areas reflected a growing secularization of Western culture. We lost a centered—not least spiritually centered—meaning for the city as it became a commodity fragmented into multiple activities, multiple ways of organizing time and space, matched by multiple roles for the inhabitants.[40] Overall, cellular urban design did not draw people into public, humanizing places of encounter.

The modernist city was constructed primarily with a sense of order and efficiency. Yet a harmonious arrangement of our human environment implies more than mechanical order. Part of the aesthetics of a healthy city, beyond the merely efficient mechanics, is the way it facilitates movement and change as opposed to static order. Space theories that are imposed on city environments by urban planners in order to make sense of them are actually totalitarian. The French polymath, the late Michel de Certeau, was most unusual in writing with great power and originality about both the Christian spiritual-mystical tradition and the meaning of contemporary cities. In one essay on urban space, "Walking in the City," he expressed the theme—present throughout his writings—of resistance to systems that leave no room for otherness and transgression.[41] The weak (in this case, those who actually live in the city rather than stand to the side and plan it) find ways to make space for themselves and to express their self-determination. What de Certeau calls "the urbanistic system" attempts to define a literal meaning of geometrical space that is similar to the proper meanings in language constructed by grammarians rather than by usage!

De Certeau's essay speaks of an almost erotic pleasure and temptation of seeing the whole, of looking down upon the city and absorbing its almost abstracted completeness. He describes standing at the top of the World Trade Center and being lifted out of Manhattan's grasp to become *voyeurs* not walkers. We read the city as if it were a single text. But this is an illusion: "The fiction of this kind of knowledge is related to a lust to be a viewpoint and nothing more." Meanwhile the ordinary practitioners of the city live down below. Static urban theory was overcome by "the microbe-like, singular and plural practices which an urbanistic system was supposed to control or suppress."[42] These everyday human practices are what make the city a lived space. Such urban practices, because inherently plural, defy the imposition of social divisions and hierarchies. De Certeau calls this dimension of the city the noise, the difference, the otherness that is a city's lifeblood without which it will die or become an empty shell. That is why, for de Certeau, the role of indeterminacy is so important: "Thus to eliminate the unforeseen or expel it from calculations as an illegitimate accident and an obstacle to rationality is to interdict the possibility of a living and 'mythical' practice of the city."[43]

De Certeau strongly emphasizes the power of narrative to shape and transform human environments. Indeed, in terms of everyday life in the city, it is human narrative as much as architecture or urban planning that shapes identity and enables people to use the city as a means of creative or effective living. De Certeau also stressed the importance of narrative to the practical articulation of everyday actions. As we shall see, this idea of a living narrative expresses something of the nature of Christian discipleship. Stories are more than descriptions, they take ownership of spaces and are therefore culturally, socially, and religiously creative. Because human stories create bridges between individuals and groups, narrative is a vital factor in the creation of the city as a community rather than as an impersonal pattern of buildings. The narrative structure of such communities enables people to shape the world that surrounds them, rather than be passively controlled by it. Narrative also creates ways of mapping and orienting the city, thus establishing paths for moving around it effectively.[44]

In the future, the city is likely to be conceived less in terms of economic organization or production and more in terms of the wider requirements of human culture. There will need to be greater reflection on the civilizing possibilities of cities and the opportunity they offer for community, or social humanization. Cities have a unique capacity to focus a range of physical, intellectual, and creative energies; they create new sets of cultural relationships simply because cities bring into regular contact a uniquely diverse range of people and activities. Cities have an unparalleled ability to combine diversities of age, ethnicity, culture, and religion. Because of their relatively large size and the diversity of their spaces, cities are also able to balance community and anonymity. As human environments, cities can undermine the defensive human instinct for closed assumptions and foregone conclusions.[45] Some European thinkers are struggling to find a middle way between multiculturalism, which sometimes merely strengthens separate cultural identities, and a kind of homogenized melting pot that can merely subsume distinct identities into a more colorful version of the dominant culture. This middle way is tentatively referred to as *interculturalism* in which social life is enhanced by a rich communication between cultures that maintains distinctiveness yet encourages cultural crossovers.[46]

This highlights a central question: what is a humane city? Theologically speaking, if the human city is merely an unavoidable environment for human transit to somewhere else beyond time and space (the eternal city of God), its purpose is merely pragmatic. An excessively eschatological theology of human history leaves us with the sense that life in the city does not describe anything essential about human existence, it is simply an ephemeral shell for our nomadic pilgrimage through life. By contrast, in the humane city people would not only dwell but also belong—that is to say, be joined in attachments of affection and fulfillment as the medium of transcendence. The humane city offers the necessary space for individual personality to be balanced with healthy collectivism. It would enable human aspirations to be productive rather than either repressed or diminished into self-indulgence. It would facilitate a proper connection to the natural world such that environment or ecology would not be distanced, or placed in opposition to, but be continuous with and integrated with people and their buildings. If cities are to have a meaningful future, we must replace alienation, isolation, crime, congestion, and pollution by community, participation, human energy, aesthetics, and joy.

The humane city is person-centered rather than design-centered. In Europe, there is a growing preoccupation with definitions of civic life and the common good, as witnessed by the documentation coming out of Demos, the influential independent British think tank. Notable among these papers is Charles Leadbeater's "Civic Spirit: The Big Idea for a New Political Era."[47] In the quest for a sufficient principle to organize society, his key concept is mutuality, which he argues is based on articulation (the individuality of all members), understanding (recognition of diversity), reconciliation (here understood as reconciling competing claims), action (cooperative effective choices), belonging (trust, goodwill, shared identity), and learning (adaptation). However, when Leadbeater comes to the critical question of how to improve mutuality in a society that has lost touch with it, he suggests renunciation. Renunciation, in his argument, means the renunciation of the absolute claims of individual choice in favor of social cohesion. There is a problem.

293

Leadbeater admits that "[p]ersuading people to be self-denying is a delicate and time-consuming process. It requires us to value restraint as a virtue as much as choice—a counterintuitive view in consumer society."[48] In the end he is stuck with the principle of effectiveness—society will work better if we adopt these values.

SPIRITUALITY AND URBAN LIVING

To talk of the city and citizenship as spiritual issues means more than just effectiveness. If we want to move beyond effectiveness, we need a more developed vision of the human spirit and what enhances it. In Christian terms, spirituality is directly concerned not just with values or commitments but with our desire, with what we love most deeply—our desire fundamentally to respond to the holy, to the sacred. When it comes to the specific contribution of Christian spirituality to reflection about the humane city we face a problem. The Christian life was shaped, until recently, by a contrast between raucous cityscapes and a peaceful, contemplative "elsewhere"—countryside, retreat house, or monastery. In other words, contemplation has been viewed as something that requires freedom from everyday concerns. Can Christian spirituality sustain urban dreams?

A spirituality of living publicly in the city has to engage with everyday life as itself a spiritual practice. Spirituality-as-discipleship, an extension of the *missio Dei*, is essentially a way of being in the world, with God, for others, by faithfully following the path of Jesus. The later writings of Michel de Certeau on Christian believing suggest that Christian discipleship is most richly expressed as a journey, a practice that carries us across the human tendency to fix boundaries and set limits. To express this idea of Christianity-as-practice, he used the classic phrase "a way of proceeding," drawn from Ignatian spirituality and his original membership of the Jesuit Order.[49] "Boundaries are the place of the Christian work," he says, "and their displacements are the result of this work." Still discussing the issue of boundaries, he further states:

> In order to pass from one place to another, something must be *done* (not only *said*) that affects the boundary: namely, *praxis*. It is this action which transcends, whereas speeches and institutions circumscribe each place successively occupied.[50]

De Certeau sought to speak in a world in which society and intellectual discourse were no longer dominated by the Church. How can a believing Christian survive in the secular city where simply mouthing ever louder doctrinal or moral statements makes little impression? After examining various models, he settled for the idea of lived practice, a provocative presence-in-the-world expressed in the age-old tension between discipleship (following) and conversion (change). The believer is called to bear witness, to embody belief, by following Jesus faithfully and consequently to be continuously changed.[51] God's transformative self-disclosure in the event of Jesus Christ is continually to be re-expressed in the life of the community of disciples in every time and place. Spirituality as living publicly in the city is essentially to enact the story of Jesus Christ that points to and enables a way of living differently in the world.

De Certeau's dispersal of Christian spirituality into social experience and social tasks expresses a radicalization of his life-long preoccupation with the Ignatian project of finding God in all things and discipleship in the midst of the world. However, simply to spiritualize politics or social life is immensely dangerous, as Nazi Germany vividly reminds us.[52] To embody a way of living differently in the world first of all demands that we cultivate a contemplative awareness of the city and of life in the city so that transformative encounters with God occur precisely in and through our immersion in the everyday and then feed back into transformed responses to people and situations.

Maurice Giuliani, one of the first exponents of the modern theory of retreats in daily life, reminds us that for Ignatius Loyola a "spiritual exercise" meant anything that prepares us to receive the grace of God. If our notion of a spiritual exercise is confined to explicitly religious practices—such as formal prayer—there is a problem for those who desire to remain profoundly engaged with the public world. One possible response is simply to find new methods of maintaining a conventional prayer rhythm in the midst of life. This is, how-ever, like the parallelism that Boff strongly criticized. Without rejecting the need for periods of contemplation, Giuliani considers this approach on its own insufficient and rather illusory. What Giuliani called "attentiveness in faith" should be extended to include a reflective focus on God's self-disclosure in all things. Every moment, every action is a potential context for movements of God's spirit to be experienced, for resistances to be overcome, for discernment to take place, for life-directing choices to be made, for commitment to God to be deepened. In this way our outer, public activities may be transformed into a genuine spiritual exercise.[53]

To my mind, this approach must imply more than simply the internaliza-tion of certain attitudes by individuals. It needs to be externalized by the dispersal of the Church into communities of presence in the midst of the city that visibly embody a different way of being in the world and offer shoppers, passers-by, and office workers a space to learn and experience contemplative practice in the midst of life. I am thinking of the extraordinary success of new forms of city-center monasticism in Europe such as the Fraternité de Jerusalem with creative liturgies and spiritual teaching open to all comers, the creation of "shop-front" centers of spiritual and pastoral care (*foyers*) in some French cities, or simply the availability of regular celebrations of the Eucharist in the

295

very heart of a major hotel-office complex and shopping mall such as Boston's Prudential Center or England's Gateshead Centre—the largest shopping complex in Europe.

Additionally, to live with faithful attention in the midst of the city is also to be drawn into, to join ourselves to, God's dynamic work in history, the *missio Dei*. We should recall that God's work in history is redemptive. In the context of the city, the idea of spirituality as a way of living publicly is not a placid acceptance of things as they are. If the "mission of God" is to reconcile all things to God and all people to each other, authentic Christian practice is necessarily an act of resistance to everything that divides people from each other or seeks to repress diversity and eliminate otherness. That said, we also need to cultivate a public-social version of the Christian virtue of discernment as we struggle with the problem that embracing diversity cannot uncritically endorse any and every viewpoint.

Living in the city as a spiritual practice includes confrontation with everything that diminishes the human spirit. In our current climate this surely embraces the prophetic presence of Christian communities that intentionally embody diversity and actively work for human reconciliation. I cannot help but recall the recent courage of the Church of Scotland minister in a housing estate near Glasgow, Scotland, who confronted local hatreds by throwing open his church day and night as a safe space for Muslim refugees after one of them was assaulted and murdered. Interestingly, there is a genre of medieval Italian literature that promoted this idea of the city as sacred place.[54] But the city's status as sacred place arose precisely from the fact that it embraced diverse people living together in peace and concord—an anticipation of final harmony in the heavenly Jerusalem. The multifaceted, multicultural city of the present and future has an equal capacity to be a diverse community of reconciliation and concord. The public task of Christian spirituality today is to bear continuous witness to this possibility.

NOTES

1. Friedrich Heiler, *Prayer: A Study in the History and Psychology of Religion* (Rockport, ME: One World, reprint 1997).
2. Owen Thomas, "Interiority and Christian Spirituality," *The Journal of Religion* (January 2000), 41–60.
3. See Rowan Williams, *On Christian Theology* (Oxford and Malden, MA: Blackwell, 2000): Chapter 16, "Interiority and Epiphany: A Reading in New Testament Ethics."
4. Williams, *On Christian Theology*, 259.
5. Richard Sennett, *The Conscience of the Eye: The Design and Social Life of Cities* (London: Faber & Faber, 1993), xii.
6. Sennett, *Conscience of the Eye*, 6–10.
7. See Peter Brown, "Late Antiquity" in *A History of Private Life: Volume 1, From Pagan Rome to Byzantium*, ed. Paul Vayne (Cambridge: Harvard University Press, 1996).

8. Augustine, *Confessions and Enchiridion*, ed. Albert Outler, The Library of Christian Classics series (London: SCM Press, 1955), Book 10, Chapter 3, section 4.

9. On this point see R. A. Markus, *The End of Ancient Christianity* (Cambridge: Cambridge University Press, 1998), 78.

10. *Expositio in Regulam Beati Augustini*, in Migne, *Patrologia Latina* (PL), 176, cols 881–924.

11. *Expositio*, 896

12. Caroline Walker Bynum, *Jesus as Mother: Studies in the Spirituality of the High Middle Ages* (Berkeley: University of California Press, 1982), Chapter 1: "The Spirituality of the Regular Canons in the Twelfth Century."

13. For example Peter of Porto, *Regula clericorum*, Book 1, chapters 32–36 in PL, 163, cols. 720–22, cited in Bynum, *Jesus as Mother*, 45.

14. See Bynum's critical analysis of the theory that the discovery of "the individual" should be back-dated from the fifteenth-century Renaissance to the twelfth-century: *Jesus as Mother*, Chapter 3: "Did the Twelfth Century Discover the Individual?"

15. Bynum, *Jesus as Mother*, 85.

16. See Alasdair MacIntyre, *After Virtue: A Study in Moral Theory*, 2nd ed. (Notre Dame: University of Notre Dame Press, 1984), 167–71 passim.

17. See Fergus Kerr, *Theology after Wittgenstein* (London: SPCK, 1997), Chapter 1: "The Modern Philosophy of the Self," especially "The Turn to the Subject," 3–5.

18. Denys Turner, *The Darkness of God: Negativity in Christian Mysticism* (Cambridge: Cambridge University Press, 1995).

19. Meister Eckhart, *Meister Eckhart: Teacher and Preacher*, ed. Bernard McGinn et al. (New York: Paulist Press, 1988), Sermon 86, 338–44.

20. A view sadly perpetuated by Nicholas Lash in his "The Church in the State We're In," *Spirituality and Social Embodiment*, ed. L. Gregory Jones and James J. Buckley (Oxford: Blackwell, 1997), 126.

21. Evelyn Underhill, *Mysticism: The Nature and Development of Spiritual Consciousness* (Oxford: One World Publications, 1993).

22. Underhill, *Mysticism*, 172.

23. John Ruusbroec, "The Sparkling Stone," in *John Ruusbroec: The Spiritual Espousals and Other Works*, ed. James Wiseman (New York: Paulist Press, 1985), 184.

24. Ruusbroec, *The Spiritual Espousals*, 136–43.

25. Michel de Certeau, *The Mystic Fable* (Chicago: University of Chicago Press, 1992) and David Tracy, *On Naming the Present: God, Hermeneutics and Church* (New York: Orbis Books, 1994), 3–6.

26. Robert Egan, Foreword, *Mysticism and Social Transformation*, ed. Janet Ruffing (Syracuse: Syracuse University Press, 2001); and "The Mystical and the Prophetic: Dimensions of Christian Existence," *The Way* (Supplement, 2002), 92–106.

27. Segundo Galilea, "The Spirituality of Liberation," *The Way* (July, 1985), 186–94.

28. Leonardo Boff, "The Need for Political Saints: From a Spirituality of Liberation to the Practice of Liberation," *Cross Currents* 30:4 (Winter 1980/81), 371.

29. Boff, "Political Saints," 372–73.

30. Boff, "Political Saints," 374.

31. Jürgen Moltmann, *Experiences of God* (Philadelphia: Fortress Press, 1980), 73.

32. José Casanova, *Public Religion in the Modern World* (Chicago: University of Chicago Press, 1994), 42.

33. See, for example, the work of the Orthodox theologian John Zizioulas, *Being as Communion* (New York: St. Vladimir's Seminary Press, 1985), and a more detailed discussion of the relationship between God-as-Trinity and human identity in Philip Sheldrake, *Spirituality and Theology: Christian Living and the Doctrine of God* (London: Darton, Longman & Todd/New York: Orbis Books, 1998), especially 75–83.

297

34. See Anthony J. Gittins, *Bread for the Journey: The Mission of Transformation and the Transformation of Mission* (New York: Orbis Books, 1993), especially Chapter 1 and pp. 63–64.

35. Casanova, *Public Religion*, 3.

36. See Parker Palmer, *The Company of Strangers: Christians and the Renewal of America's Public Life* (New York: Crossroad Press, 1981).

37. Sennett, *Conscience of the Eye*, 19–31.

38. Michel de Certeau, "Practices of Space," in *On Signs*, ed. M. Blonsky (Oxford: Blackwell; Baltimore: Johns Hopkins University Press, 1985), 122–45.

39. These figures are cited by Sir Crispin Tickell in his Introduction to Richard Rogers, *Cities for a Small Planet* (London: Faber & Faber, 1997), vii.

40. For interesting remarks on the relationship between the fragmentation of intellectual discourse, starting with the medieval separation of theology and spirituality, and the contemporary secularization of the city, see James Matthew Ashley, *Interruptions: Mysticism, Politics and Theology in the work of Johann Baptist Metz* (Notre Dame: University of Notre Dame Press, 1998), 10–12.

41. Michel de Certeau, *The Practice of Everyday Life*, vol. 1 (Berkeley: University of California Press, 1988), 91–110.

42. De Certeau, *Everyday Life*, 1:92, 96.

43. De Certeau, *Everyday Life*, 1:203.

44. De Certeau, *Everyday Life*, 1:122–30.

45. See Rogers, *Cities for a Small Planet*, 15.

46. See for example Charles Landry and Franco Bianchini, *The Creative City* (London: Demos, 1998), 29–30.

47. Charles Leadbeater, "Civic Spirit: The Big Idea for a New Political Era" (London: Demos, 1997), Demos Arguments 14

48. Leadbeater, "Civic Spirit," 30.

49. A point noted by Luce Giard, one of de Certeau's closest collaborators and co-authors, in Michel de Certeau, Luce Giard, and Pierre Mayol, *The Practice of Everyday Life*, vol. 2 (Minneapolis: University of Minneapolis Press , 1998), xxii–xxiii. For "a way of proceeding," see de Certeau, "The Weakness of Believing: From the Body to Writing, a Christian Transit," in *The Certeau Reader,* ed. Graham Ward (Oxford: Blackwell, 2000), 215.

50. Michel de Certeau, "How Is Christianity Thinkable Today?" in *The Postmodern God,* ed. Graham Ward (Oxford: Blackwell, 1997), 151.

51. De Certeau, "The Weakness of Believing," 226.

52. On this point, see Geoffrey Wainwright's typology of spirituality, based on H. Richard Niebuhr's *Christ and Culture*, in his "Types of Spirituality," in *The Study of Spirituality,* ed. Cheslyn Jones et al. (London/New York: Oxford University Press, 1986). Wainwright's second type, "the Christ of culture," tends to affirm social and political systems simply as they are, implicitly identifying the Kingdom of God with the world, and is cripplingly deficient.

53. Maurice Giuliani, "The Ignatian Exercise in Daily Life," *The Way* (Supplement, Spring, 1984), 88–94.

54. See Peter Raedts, "The Medieval City as a Holy Place," in *Omnes Circumadstantes: Contributions towards a History of the Role of the People in the Liturgy,* ed. Charles Caspers and Marc Schneiders (Kampen: Uitgeversmaatschappij J.H. Kok, 1990), 144–54.

PART FIVE

Spirituality and Aesthetics

$\mathcal{T}$here was a time, not so long ago, when the discussion of aesthetics seemed to have certain stable features and undisputed parameters. Jacques Maritain began a justly celebrated series of lectures at the National Gallery of Art in 1952 by citing Dante's conviction that "our human art is . . . the grandchild of God." But in the decades that followed, the arts mirrored the political and social upheavals disrupting the wider society. The once certain foundations of aesthetics were under siege, and the intellectual uncertainties of Maritain's generation seemed to give way to what came to be called "the culture wars" in the latter decades of the twentieth century. Artists, often enough at the vanguard of cultural turmoil, were at the center of these changes. Public protests erupted over exhibitions of Mapplethorpe's photographs during the late 1980s. From angry declamations in the halls of Congress to violent exchanges in the editorial pages of the nation's newspapers, these outcries led eventually to the nation's first obscenity proceeding against an art gallery. Andres Serrano's "Piss Christ" created a similar stir, galvanizing reactions to its allegedly pornographic character and leading to the increased scrutiny of public funding for the arts. Within this embattled horizon, both public and academic discussions of aesthetics have been heated and often acrimonious. Intellectual discourse about beauty has become vigorous and contentious in recent decades, largely on the basis of political opposition to it.

In such an unsteady climate, what shape might the conversation about aesthetics take in relation to spirituality in general, and Christian spirituality specifically? This is no simple question. The issues such a question provokes penetrate to the very heart of what the arts are in society. Antoni Tàpies gave voice to the subversive edge often heard in contemporary artists' assessments of their role in society when he suggested that contemporary aesthetic form should throw the viewer off balance. Adding her voice to this chorus, the writer Jeanette Winterson, in "The Semiotics of Sex," contends that art is difficult and demanding because it "has in it warnings and chances and painful beauty." Beauty may still be "in the eye of the beholder," as the familiar adage has it, but the pluralistic nature of late-modern society resists simplistic approaches to aesthetics. What *is* art supposed to be, and do? How do the arts relate to religious aspiration and experience in general, and to Christian spirituality in particular? What contribution do the arts make to the broader philosophical and moral questions of the day? And in what manner do artists engage the politics of meaning in ways that relate to religious communities and traditions, and vice versa, particularly as outsiders either by choice or by exclusion? The very intensity of this engagement suggests the important and complicated role that the arts continue to play in shaping and interpreting culture—and vice versa—and for this reason, among others, the arts remain of vital interest to the study of Christian spirituality.

The essays included in this section point toward the difficulties and possibilities inherent in conversations about the relationship of art and spirit. The opening essay, by Don Saliers, steers directly into the heart of this debate. He sees beauty and terror as realities of human experience that are of crucial importance for Christian spirituality if it is to draw us toward the depths of human life. Saliers argues for a description of "the beautiful" with a level of nuance not usually assumed in the common use of the word. "[I]f we are to be attentive to the world's beauty—in nature, in art, in persons," he offers, "then we also must be prepared to be subject to the world's affliction both through physical suffering (*la douleur*) and through distress of the spirit (*le malheur*)." He concludes by turning our attention to what he calls "the poetics of transformative rituals," by which he means not grand and heroic acts or activities but the familiar gestures of our common life that "rehearse and practice the emotions so essential to seeing the world in more than its literal surfaces." Such rituals, be they a meal shared by mourners or the liturgical celebration of the Lord's Supper in churches, teach in ways that form community and inform the spiritual life, in word and in the deep and partly unspoken patterns of remembrance and hope.

In the second essay we turn from poetry and the shared rituals of communities to the role of images and the visual arts in the transformations of the spiritual life. Wendy Wright explores the sacred heart of Jesus and its role in shaping Roman Catholic piety in seventeenth-century France. She sees in the cultural fascination with this image a type of "visual midrash" upon scripture, an imaginative meditation upon Jesus' body that implies a mystical "exchange of hearts" between Christ and a devotee. This devotion functioned as a particular form of reading, in this case one meant to "deconstruct habituated imaginative constructs and allow imagery to reconstruct a new imaginative lens through which reality is interpreted and possible worlds perceived." Wright argues that we need to broaden our approach to Christian spirituality by paying greater attention to image and ritual and cultivating "the tender art of contemplative seeing," widening the lens of perception beyond the traditional focus on texts and language that has shaped much of the modern discussion about theology and spirituality.

If reading has been the primary medium of theological meaning in modernity, Don Saliers proposes, in his second contribution to this section, that each of the human senses has played a role in the formation and expression of Christian spirituality across the ages. In this essay, Saliers examines sound and hearing, or what he calls "the acoustical or auditory" domain of human experience, as constitutive for spiritual experience and expression. Focusing on music as "the language of the soul made audible," he explores ways in which music has served as a performative mode of prayer and ritual engagement within Christian communities. Our voices are what he calls the "primary instruments of the collective soul," conveying meaning in a subtler and more complex form than narrower cognitive structures of knowing. We "sound" our faith in the music we make, awakening the deeper dimensions of reality and of the soul as we "come to our senses" about the spiritual depths of existence.

In the final essay of this section, we return to the theme of mysticism discussed in several of the essays in this volume. Mark Burrows explores this question in terms of poetics, asking whether the poet's sense of language as what T. S. Eliot once called a "raid on the inarticulate" might move us beyond the modern fascination with argument toward a more complex notion of reason and a less dogmatic approach to revelation. The spiritual shape of reality, viewed from the vantage of poetics, depends to a great extent upon an aesthetic shaped by an "apophatic eloquence." He explores this in the late-modern context with recourse not to theologians, who have been often wary of the mystical and the poetic, but rather to poets, whose aesthetic sensibilities breathe with a different form of knowing. He wonders, given the cultural crises of modernity, what the emerging "technologies of writing" might be that are adequate to conveying the complexity and depth of spiritual experience. He explores this question in terms of the rubrics of margins, surfaces, and fragments, borrowing from the vision of poets who give voice to a spirituality that sings at the edges of mystery.

The essays gathered in this section do not resolve the public disputes surrounding the arts, nor do they assume that aesthetics offers an easy partner in dialogue for Christian spirituality. What they do point to is the complex and necessary role this inquiry has to play within and beyond the boundaries of religious communities, whether Christian or other. They also assert that artistic form is not an end in itself, insisting, as the poet Theodore Roethke once put it, "There's still a life / Beyond this vision, ardent as it is" (from "All the Semblance, All the Loss"). In this sense, these chapters suggest ways in which the arts generally, and questions of aesthetics more specifically, move us into the restless dynamics of creativity and imagination that belong to the very heart of a wider public conversation about meaning—including, but not limited to, that related to contemporary Christian spirituality and its study.

302

22

Beauty and Terror

DON E. SALIERS

*H*aving heard Benjamin Britten's *War Requiem* performed recently brought me to ponder anew the relations between beauty and terror. Britten musically interweaves Wilfred Owen's World War I poems with texts of the Mass for the Dead. At the point of the offertory, the music retells the story of Abram and Isaac: "So Abram arose, and clave the wood, and went/ And took [Isaac] with him, and a knife." The boy observes the preparations for the sacrifice and asks where the lamb is for this offering: "Then Abram bound the youth with belts and straps/ And builded parapets and trenches there, /And stretched forth the knife to slay his son." The images of parapets and trenches contemporize the biblical account. A musical shift interposes the voice of a divine messenger who bids Abram: "Lay not thy hand upon the lad/ Neither do anything to him. Behold, a ram . . . Offer the Ram of Pride instead of him." A children's choir of innocent trebles joins the baritone and tenor soloists. The children begin to sing the ancient Offertorium prayer text from the Latin Mass: *Hostias et preces tibi / Domine laudis offerimus.* . . . ["Sacrifices and prayers we offer, Lord, to you with praise . . . bring them from death to life"]. Unlike the biblical ending of the narrative, however, a terrifying text is then sung by the soloists: "But the old man would not so, and slew his son—And half the seed of Europe, one by one." Britten musically intensifies the phrase, "one by one," repeated in broken musical lines by both soloists over the children's prayers.

In Britten's art, texts of terror are musically articulated in ways that go beyond what language itself can hold. This silence acknowledges the unspeakable, both denying and permitting access to certain elemental facts of the human experience of war. Yet I am drawn to hear this musical work again, knowing that time will deepen such strange beauty, or as novelist William Maxwell might say, "time will darken it."

Poetry about extremity always approaches this paradox of expressing what is on the edge of unspeakability. Think, for example, of the Holocaust-permeated poetry of Paul Celan, in which readers contemplate drinking the "black milk" of the crematorium's smoke. One thinks of Rilke's line from the First Duino Elegy: "For beauty is nothing but the beginning of terror."[1] How often the terrifying and its aftermath of grieving may lead to surprising but near unbearable beauty. Terror and beauty lie unacknowledged for most of us, until the conditions of perception come around: typically when pain and terror strike by chance, or when we are enraptured by the splendor of something radically "other." Without ritualizing into embodied patterns of knowing, feeling, and acting, intense experiences of terror or beauty can be deceptive. They can "lie"—in the sense of distorting our view of what and how the world is. What is revealed in extremity requires retrospect and recollection in order to illuminate how to live. Christian spirituality has a stake in receiving and interpreting such experiences, and guarding against lies and distortions.

Three interrelated questions follow: first, how do we come to see relations between the beautiful and the terrifying? We shift from nouns to adjectives here—for knowledge is in and through our being affected, in and through *eros* for truth, for what is good. Some of these ritual practices are transformative while others may not be so. Second, how might we speak of the intelligence of human emotions stretched between the extremities of human pathos by which human beings gain a sense of the world? Human emotions such as awe, wonder, grief, compassion, fear, and grateful receptivity are ingredients in a way of being and knowing and intending the world. How do we think "in, with and through" our emotions, and not only about them in self-reflection? The third question asks: can we discover transformative ritual practices that open us to beauty and terror, yet help us hold these together in the maturation of emotional intelligence? How might the imaginative capability intrinsic to such rituals lead us beyond the tyranny of the literally given in experience?

The deepest things we know are found in the form of defining passions. This is what might be called a determinate attunement to the world. A person, a community, or a whole society is better known through what is admired, feared, loved, grieved over, and hoped for than through its propositionally stated ideas and beliefs. I am convinced that there is available to human beings, and particularly to communities of moral and religious practice, a "poetics" necessary for forms of human flourishing. The sense of transcendence in and through the finitude of the world appears precisely amidst the contrasts of terror and beauty. Such a *poiesis* is found especially in certain religious rituals. A key element in spiritual maturation may be found in how such rituals form dispositions to construe everyday life.

This essay speaks from particular religious and moral traditions that have shaped my reasoning. The sense and sensibility of these words is situated within a certain range of the Christian tradition, combining a sacramental conception of the world with indebtedness to biblical prophetic critique of religion. Yet I trust the following discourse to provide analogies, resonances, and convergent traces that may be recognized in other Christian and non-Christian spiritual temperaments.

EVOKING CONDITIONS FOR SEEING THE CONTRASTS

We live in a world of immensely beautiful and wondrous things, but this same world is also terrifying. The rhetoric of terror can itself become tiresome and banal, especially as it is diminished by political discourse about terrorism and plans to manage it. So we live amidst the public banalities of the "war on terrorism." Nevertheless, no one can quite take in yet the sense of psychic, not to mention bodily and economic, trauma of the World Trade towers falling to dust. This was dust of human life incinerated. Even with endless replication of the images of planes and towers and the now ended search and reclamation, Americans and many others still recoil at the residual images. Our thoughts are not, nor could they be, simply rational. We recoil because the events of terror are appraised as a deep violation of common humanity, and bring us to a more internal terror of the soul.

Everyday mail can shock as well. I received an appeal for money that begins: "Soldiers shot Tamba's father. Then, as his father lay dying, they trained their guns on the tearful boy and forced him to clap and cheer. Later, soldiers killed Tamba's mother. Tamba is one of thousands of children who have endured unspeakable trauma in the war-racked West African nation of Sierra Leone." We recoil. Some of our thoughts turn to Jerusalem, the West Bank, and to other places of terror. The word "holocaust," so dominating our perception of the century just past, carries with it enormous import for what we feel, how we think, and for how we must live. To say that the world is not a place of such daily terror is to be deceived.

Public historical events such as the previous litany, and the nightly news-casts of local murder and trauma are not the only terrors, of course. What befalls us may also generate a more personal terror. I think of Gerard Manley Hopkins' "Terrible Sonnets," in which the complex relationship between external and inner psychic trauma are given such poignant expression. The ordinariness of his starting point in "To Seem the Stranger" offers a glimpse into personal darkness.[2] He is ill, away from family, with a deepening sense of exile: "To seem the stranger lies my lot, my life/ Among strangers." In Ireland away from England who is "wife /To my creating thought," the poet is weary. "[D]ark heaven's baffling ban" to any life-giving words "leaves me a lonely began."

This deep estrangement and loneliness deepens into bitter self-contempla-tion. He toys with the idea of death as escape, and is caught in a terrifying resistance against self-destruction.

> I wake and feel the fell of dark, not day,
> What hours, O what black hours we have spent
> This night! What sights you, heart, saw; ways you went!
> And more must, in yet longer light's delay . . .

I am gall, I am heartburn. God's most deep decree
Bitter would have me taste; my taste was me. . . . I see
The lost are like this, and their scourge to be
As I am mine, their sweating selves; but worse.

Here terror is internalized within the self, as the soul's struggle with questions of God and eternal death. The emotions are carried and intensified in physical, bodily images that reveal and evince the tortured thoughts:

O the mind, mind has mountains; cliffs of fall
Frightful, sheer, no-man-fathomed. Hold them cheap
May who ne'er hung there. Nor does long our small
Durance deal with that steep or deep. Here! Creep,
Wretch, under a comfort serves in a whirlwind: all
Life death does end and each day dies with sleep.

These strong lines give us the feel of personal terrors that can indeed accompany and compose everyday life. In the case of Hopkins, religious sensibility intensifies human consciousness. Not comforted, yet strung out by the thought of a "carrion comfort, Despair" the poetry itself becomes a spiritual exercise of willed resistance, even against experience and belief. We can read these "Terrible Sonnets" and sense something of Rilke's idea that "beauty is nothing but the beginning of terror."[3] What strikes terror in the human heart depends upon what is valued, and the value-permeated regard we bring to experience and description. The beauty of Hopkins' lines actually holds the terror in a certain way. The poetry becomes a kind of ritual in language. This marks a difference between remaining overwhelmed and inarticulate, and striving to make sense (the *poiesis*) of the experience.

We live in a terrifying world, shot full of absence and the perishing of what is held dear. But this same world is filled with immensely beautiful and won-drous things. Side-by-side with despair and senseless loss lie the mystery and the beauty of being. The notion of beauty is notoriously contested. Still, we continue to be drawn to things we call beautiful. What is it, for example, about a single jonquil in a glass vase, a luminous melody by Mozart, the painting that reorders seeing, a passage from Mahler that transforms our hearing, or the voice of a young child singing in imitation of her mother's lullaby? What is it about these things that arrests us, that prompts the excla-mation, "How beautiful!"? Or, the stunned silence that follows a first encoun-ter with Van Gogh's "Starry Night"—what is this? We know that not all art requires the term "beautiful." The passage in Britten's *War Requiem* is not, in any ordinary sense of the term, "beautiful."

In *Beauty Restored*, Mary Mothersill argues that beauty is a necessary concept in human life. It is more than a disputed term in the philosophy of art;

we need the concept. What is perceived and said to be "beautiful" may, of course, be inconsequential in some instances and settings, while possessing spiritual range and power in others. "Some things," Mothersill writes,

> . . . like a pebble or a clear and cloudless sky, have simple souls. They please in virtue of their aesthetic properties, but those properties once noted and appreciated, do not invite prolonged critical analysis. Decorative formal designs . . . may be elegant, intricate, admirable, and yet, once understood, easily forgotten. All persons and some works of art—those to which we pay homage—have souls that are complex, multilayered, and partly hidden. They are not to be taken in at a glance, and long study leaves room for fresh discoveries.[4]

These words bring to mind Emmanuel Levinas, who, in speaking of the sheer delight in something outside ourselves, extols the "non-nostalgic nature of desire, the plentitude and joy of the being who experiences it."[5] Wendy Farley's discussion of beauty in *Eros and the Other* makes this even clearer. "[T]he exteriority of beauty," she observes,

> is emphasized by its infinity. The experience of beauty is never exhausted. The expression 'I love you more each day' makes little quantitative sense, but it is a fumbling attempt to evoke the experience of unending freshness that accompanies friendship or romance or motherhood. . . . Beauty is the sort of thing that in and of itself delights the soul.[6]

The concept of beauty is notoriously difficult in theory, yet so persistent in our utterances about what affects us and draws our desires in becoming human beings. The stunned silence before an object that attracts powerfully, as well as the silence in the presence of the traumatic may be related in ways we do not ordinarily consider. The unspeakable can refer to the searingly traumatic terror, and also to stunning revelatory beauty.

Two conditions emerge for seeing terror and beauty. The first is what befalls us, the second is what we attend to. Vulnerability and contingency are counterpointed by attentiveness. Thinking of the second condition brings to mind Simone Weil and what she has taught us out of her own emotional complexities regarding affliction and beauty. Human attentiveness to the presences and absences before us she likens to prayer. This is the crucial element in being and becoming human in the world. So the beauty of the world, precisely in the midst of affliction, is "like a mirror . . . [that] sends us back to our desire for goodness."[7] As one of her biographers remarks, "With the exception of Saint Francis, whose life she looks on as 'perfect poetry in action,' she repeatedly castigates Christianity's lack of emphasis on nature's physical splendor. Our very longing for the beauty of the world, in her view, is God-inspired."[8] But if we are to be attentive to the world's beauty—in nature, in art, in persons—then we also must be prepared to be subject to the world's affliction both through physical suffering (*la douleur*) and through distress of the spirit (*le malheur*).

THE INTELLIGENCE OF EMOTIONS AND A SENSE OF THE WORLD

Without particular capacities for emotion we would not understand ourselves and the world as we do. Grief, gladness, gratitude, hope, sorrow, pity, jealousy, envy, compassion: these describe human responses to the beauty and the terror of being alive. Jonathan Edwards, writing in the eighteenth century, observed:

> Take away all love and hatred, all hope and fear, all anger, zeal and affectionate desire, and the world would be in great measure motionless and dead; there would be no such things as activity amongst mankind, or any earnest pursuit whatsoever. ... And as in worldly things worldly affections are very much the spring of men's motion and action; so in religious matters the spring of their actions is very much religious affection ...[9]

We come to know the deepest and most intimate things through our having and cultivating certain emotions. This, I propose, is also the place of encounter with persistent moral and religious questions. The untutored heart has its story to tell. The heart schooled in the inhumanity of our age is racked with anguish, and often traumatized into silence. The distinctively spiritual dimensions of the intelligence of the emotions can be found in how certain ritual practices try to make sense of the world.

Part of the original sense of "passion" (*passio*—to suffer) is called upon in such practices. Referring to how human beings suffer life, that is, how we undergo our lives through time, we uncover the intelligence of emotions. One of the root meanings of "passion" is also found in the term "emotion." We are "moved" by things in the world. Human beings are affected, for good or for ill, when something acts upon us, whether by accident or by intention. But if we attend only to how we feel or undergo our emotions or passions, we miss a crucial point. The feeling states or inner sensations we may indeed experience, especially at the onset of a strongly felt terror or beauty, do not exhaustively define emotions such as gladness or lament. If sorrow or outrage over human injustice, or joy in the company of a loved one were only our private feeling states, then we could only learn them by introspection. Knowledge of emotions would, in this view, only come from looking inside ourselves. However commonsensical this may appear, this is a false view. We characteristically know the emotions of other persons, and others may even know our emotions and motives better than we know them ourselves. Further, putting all emotional features of life in opposition to reflective and intellectual power leads to untruth. One of the reasons we may not recognize another's grief or anger or joy is that we do not share their appraisals of the world. Sharing the same regard or appraisal of things is part of sharing the same emotions. We cannot divorce such appraisals from the having of emotions such as sorrow over the pain of another, righteous indignation over injustice, or love of God and neighbor. Emotions such as these are far more than feelings. They are dispositions that are practiced and are embedded in social histories and narratives about becoming human.

Human grieving is particularly instructive, though grief is especially complex. Grief may take unto itself anger, jealousy, regret, hope—all of these may be part of the pattern of the felt experience. But deep grieving over the loss of a parent, or of the untimely death of a child—much less the unconscious grieving over terror perpetrated on the innocent—all these involve a powerful set of thoughts, appraisals and value-laden descriptions. Thus we describe the circumstances and the consequences as "unimaginable" or "numbing" or the like. The grieving is deep because it comes to comprehend so much of our field of assessment, thought, and feeling. Deep grieving targets elemental features of human existence.

All of these factors alert us to the difference between immediacy of feeling and depth of emotion over time. Emotions, in contrast to passing states of feeling or moods, are narratives of the soul. They have an onset but also durability. Thus we discern the difference between feeling resentful, angry, or grateful in a moment, and being characteristically full of resentment, anger, or gratitude. We commonly learn and express emotions by how we describe things outside our inner self. This is how poetry and literature work. It is thus no accident that sacred rituals combine physical acts with texts that contain poetry and the powers of heightened speech to describe persons and events as holy. Even more so, we find heightened speech in ascribing attributes of the deity in prayer and liturgy: "Holy God, most merciful and compassionate One." Our emotions and affections can be corrected, altered, and schooled precisely by re-descriptions of the world and ourselves that are persuasive. Spiritual practices and ritual acts that transform thus require a capacity for narrative, metaphor, parable, and other forms of imaginative discourse.

Emotions and affections, because they require thoughts and judgments about the world, can be vague or precise, adequate or inadequate, persuasive or banal. In the face of beauty and terror, emotions can be true or false to how things are. The more deeply an emotion is lived into the more it requires understanding specific things toward which the attention is directed. Maturing in love, for example, involves a growing sense of the social context that sustains or alters the emotional regard for neighbor, for strangers, even for enemies. To live fully in a world of such contrasts involves a range of intelligence that goes beyond simple rationality as such. Hence the thoughts of the heart are often deeper and more comprehensive than the thoughts of rational cognition.[10]

Spiritual reflection must preserve something of the older notion of emotions and affections as motions of the soul. What we are and who we are to become in intention and action are more adequately revealed by naming and ritualizing the hopes and fears of the human heart than merely by applying systems of rules or obligations. To say of a person that she possesses a deep sense of gratitude, or that a community is magnanimous, gracious, or hospitable is to remark about their character over time. Of course, a person or a community can also be full of despair or of vengeance and enmity. The evidences of fear, hope, pity, or compassion will be found in human intentions and actions in the daily world. Part of human spiritual maturity is to learn the difference between the superficial and the deep affections. This in turn requires seeing the extremities of the world.

We must turn then to address how certain human practices, especially ritual practices, help us in negotiating life amidst the terror and the beauty, between affliction and joy. As Martha Nussbaum has argued, "in an ethical and social-political creature, emotions themselves are ethical and social-political, parts of an answer to the questions, What is worth caring about? How should I/we live?[11]

THE POETICS OF TRANSFORMATIVE RITUALS

In a small rural church I once served, one of the respected, but tumultuous, members of the community died a sudden death shoveling grain in a local storage silo. After the church funeral was held, we gathered back at the farmhouse where friends and kinfolk had assembled. Food and drink had been lavishly brought to the place. The polyglot crowd began quietly to eat and drink the gifts of the communal feast. Stories began about the deceased. Laughter and tears came, punctuated with quiet solemnity and utter hilarity. Talk about the fear of death, about what it meant to have him as a friend, about what it now meant for the family to go on—all this in everyday language, drawing upon years of friendship and rivalry, with all the gestures that accompany a reconstruction of a life into a new kind of memory. There I came to realize something of what a sacramental meal contains. In later memory I now see how that ritual occasion itself was the embrace of the terror and the beauty of George's life and indeed of the community's sense of life.

The funeral meal, with its co-mingling of joy, sorrow, laughter, and tears of lament, is one of the practices that requires both the vulnerability of everydayness and the intelligence of emotion. This, well practiced, does not shrink from our humanity at full stretch before the mysteries. Here is a connection with religious ritual that depends on a tradition of communal practices and real humanity, honestly shared. This is why in the ritual of Passover Seder, or of Christian Eucharist, we say that the memory differs from mere empirical recall.

This is why the inscription I saw years ago at the Holocaust Museum in Jerusalem is so arresting: "To remember is the beginning of redemption." So it is that we need those kinds of practices, even against the evidence that there is nothing to hope for, or to give thanks for.

We need them especially to help keep us from pulling away from embodied finite life, something those called to the Christian spiritual life have too often tended to do. There is, as Martha Nussbaum has eloquently stated, a strong element in Western philosophy and religious thinking towards the "repudiation of the everyday."[12] Her picture of ascent toward the elevated and ideal humanity portrays human striving for the transcendent and the good. This heroic spiritual striving is wonderfully subverted by a concluding exposition of James Joyce's *Ulysses*. We see the return of the repressed body in this novel. But much more, Joyce portrays everydayness as the condition for thought and emotional appraisal of spiritual selves. Molly Bloom, Leopold, Poldy, and the entire range of both scatological and eschatological vision is there. In, with, and through the earthiness and particularity of these characters and their plight, Joyce shows us the deception of considering human life only under the ideal ascent toward the "higher" or the intellectually superior or purer. Thus Leopold exhibits a profound sense of the struggle for moral discernment in and through his bodily everydayness.

Romantic and heroic views often make the living of daily life seem to be poor soil for religious aspirations. Yet it is in our ordinariness that we come with vulnerability to those practices that constitute the formation of what may be called religious or spiritual affections and dispositions. Seeing the world and human life as something more than what is literally given to sense experience is crucial to having a sense of life—whether of the grandeur or the misery, or of the banality or the unfathomably mysterious dimensions of life. At the same time, we humans, finite and embodied, live in the world of the everyday.

In his *Tragic Sense of Life*, Miguel de Unamuno speaks of the inner connection between the language of human emotion and religious belief:

> Those who say that they believe in God and yet neither love nor fear [God], do not in fact believe in [God], but in those who have taught them that God exists. . . . Those who believe that they believe in God, but without any passion in their heart, without anguish of mind, without uncertainty, without doubt, without an element of despair even in their consolation, believe only in the God-Idea, not in God.[13]

We should not, I think, regard such human ritual practices of memory and meal as mere coping mechanisms or as vestigial projections of infantilism or as false emotional dependencies. Of course such human practices as Passover or the Christian Eucharist can indeed be interpreted this way (most usefully so when religious practices degenerate into idolatry or empty cliché).

Perhaps the meal of memory which comprehends the terror and the beauty is one of the few revelatory things we do. The shaping of certain dispositions toward life and our world where grief and hope are bound together can be a place of re-configuring persons and communities. We might even speak of liberation back to our full humanity. These are practices in the midst of our bodily everydayness. Here memory is more than mere words, more than simple recalling of a past event. Here the boundaries of our speech and awareness of the terrors of annihilation and the deepest gratitude for life converge. Acknowledging that the same capacity that allows the apprehension of exquisite beauty is that which opens the abyss of the terrifying is itself a human achievement. But the practices of prayer and meal and memory reveal that this is also a gift and a grace.

Humanity at full stretch before God and neighbor—this is not merely the province of the intellectual life, nor is it merely what feels natural to us. It requires a form of life and communities that rehearse and practice the emotions so essential to seeing the world in more than its literal surfaces. This can, of course, move either way: toward the world as a prison, a charnel house, or a "war of all against all," or as a created order in which terror and beauty coexist. Only in the stretch of seeing the world in its fullness, in critical awareness of our moving between the terrifying and the glorious, between the unspeakable and the most desirable, do we come to moral and religious maturity. We do have some access, though often faintly, to truth and to what constitutes the good for human existence in a world not of our devising. We must continually awaken and sustain the emotional intelligence required to attend to the beauty and the terror. The task is to hold both the language and the necessary silences before God. How can we form such capacities and those dispositions that awaken and reveal a world beyond cause and effect, beyond the maps of technical reason? Embodied rituals born of memory in the face of terror and beauty hold a key. "Do this in remembrance of me" in Christian liturgy brings to the present moment a crisis. We are to share in this meal both death's terror and life's beauty, the darkness and the light. This is redemptive remembering.

Beauty can deceive, terror can drive us to despair and self-torture. But where our lives in time and space are actively receptive to mystery and suffering we come to the knowing and the unknowing, to the glory and the fragility of humanity as part of the whole created order of things. In the midst of the terror and the beauty we dare the poetics of prayer and worship, speaking the name and the unspeakable reality of God in praise, thanksgiving, and blessing. Doxology without lament can be snare and a delusion. But practices that form us in a sense of the world that takes into itself suffering and joy are more fitting than is a sense of the world that ignores the suffering, or that coldly assesses the brute facts apart from any human subjectivity. When faith speaks truthfully about joy in the midst of tribulation, we pause. When practices make this palpable over time, we may live daily in awe and wonder. This is to grasp, if but through a glass darkly, the hope of which revelation speaks.

NOTES

1. Rainer Maria Rilke, *Duino Elegies*, trans. Stephen Mitchell (New York: Random House, 1980), 9.
2. Gerard Manley Hopkins, *Poems*, ed. W. H. Gardner (New York and London: Oxford University Press, 1948), 107, 109.
3. Rilke, *Duino Elegies*, 9.
4. Mary Mothersill, *Beauty Restored* (Oxford: The Clarendon Press, 1984), 423.
5. Emmanuel Levinas, *Collected Philosophical Papers*, trans. Alphonso Lingis (Dordrecht: Martinus Nijhoff, 1987), 57.
6. Wendy Farley, *Eros and the Other: Retaining Truth in a Pluralistic World* (University Park: Pennsylvania State University Press, 1996), 81–82.
7. Simone Weil, "Forms of the Implicit Love of God," in *Waiting for God*, trans. Emma Craufurd (New York: Harper and Row, 1951), 171.
8. Francine du Plessix Gray, *Simone Weil* (New York: Viking/Penguin, 2001), 221.
9. Jonathan Edwards, *Treatise Concerning Religious Affections*, ed. John E. Smith (New Haven: Yale University Press, 1959), 101.
10. I have always regarded the "Collect for Purity" (found in the *Book of Common Prayer* and several Protestant liturgical traditions) to contain an essential for the spiritual life (italics mine):

    > Almighty God, unto whom all hearts are open,
    >   all desires known, and from whom no secrets are hid;
    > Cleanse *the thoughts of our hearts* by the inspiration of your Holy Spirit,
    >   that we may perfectly love you, and worthily magnify your Holy Name . . .

11. Martha C. Nussbaum, *Upheavals of Thought: The Intelligence of Emotions* (Cambridge: Cambridge University Press, 2001), 149.
12. Nussbaum, *Upheavals of Thought*, especially Part III, "The Ascents of Love)" 457, ff.
13. Miguel de Unamuno, *The Tragic Sense of Life*, trans. J. E. Crawford Flitch (New York: Dover Publications, 1954), 193.

23

"A Wide and Fleshly Love"

Images, Imagination, and the Study of Christian Spirituality

WENDY M. WRIGHT

*T*hree related issues have long occupied the center of my thinking about the history of Christian spirituality: radical life transformations, the function of the imagination in these transformations, and the role of the arts, particularly visual imagery, in shaping the imagination. Visual imagery is so much a part of our Christian heritage, especially in its Roman Catholic and Orthodox forms. Yet its study among academics, with the exception of art historians, is often neglected. The history of Christian spirituality, which has tended to emphasize texts above all other expressions, has been constructed with relatively little reference to the crucial role images play in the spiritual life. When images *are* included, their presence is often merely illustrative. I want to offer here a modest corrective to this tendency, by focusing attention on a primal image that has enjoyed a long and rich life within the Christian community: the incarnate Divine Heart.[1]

First, I will discuss the history of this image as it has emerged from scripture and developed within the Christian spiritual tradition. This brief historical survey will enable us to see how such a primal image, in a compact, non-discursive manner, carries the developing interpretive layers of the Christian mystery. It will also enable us to consider one key way that scriptural themes are passed on and internalized by believers. Second, I will pause and focus on a particular moment and place in this image's history—late-seventeenth-century France. There the image took on a particular complexity and importance through the dissemination of the visions of Margaret Mary Alacoque, a Visitandine nun of the monastery of Paray-le-Monial. Using Margaret Mary as a case study, I suggest some ways in which visual images (both as visual artifacts and as visions) facilitate the process of radical personal and communal transformation. In this discussion I reflect on the dialectic roles of images and the imagination. Finally, I make several observations that these considerations about images and imagination raise in my mind for the academic study of Christian spirituality.

I trust that your interest may be piqued and questions provoked. I trust as well that those whose interests lie in areas of spirituality that make less use of visual imagery than seventeenth-century Roman Catholicism will not see this approach as irrelevant. Recent studies of visual piety in America have revealed the prevalence and significance of images in Protestant as well as Catholic circles.[2] Further, although much of what I present concerns visual images and the practices surrounding them, these observations might well be applied to verbal images as well as visual ones: for example, to hymn texts and the musical practices associated with their use.

THE HISTORY OF THE HEART OF GOD

Scripture is foundational to the study of Christian spirituality. As Sandra Schneiders has suggested, scripture "supplies not only the positive data of the earliest Christian experience and its Jewish matrix, but also both the basic symbol system of Christianity and the meta-story into which each individual and communal Christian story is integrated and by which it is patterned."[3] Images in Christian history, like the image of the Divine Heart, are not merely illustrations of the scriptural text. This image, which has both verbal and visual expression, has scriptural texts at its core. But it does not stop at the boundaries of the text. From another point of view, one I think closer to the lived experience of generations of Christians, the image is a result of the scriptural text being entered and explored through prayer, worship, and study so that the unfolding layers of meaning hidden in the literal word come to light. Over the course of time, the Christian community engaged in a cumulative communal reflection on a cluster of biblical texts to the extent that a thickly packed primal image—the Heart—emerged and took on a life all its own. The unfolding image of the Heart thus is a type of visual midrash through which the centuries-long process of turning over the Word is recorded. It is also an alchemical image which, when internalized, can initiate a practitioner into the mysteries of the divine life itself.

The Word that has been turned over is very much an incarnated one. The Christian community has been gazing at the Body of God for twenty centuries now. Such gazing is an integral part of the intensely incarnational intuition that lurks so insistently in the Christian imagination. The gazing began by standing at a distance outside of the Body and reflecting upon it allegorically. The communal gaze then gradually moved into closer proximity to the Body by exploring the wounds, especially the side wound, not simply as allegory but as an experiential source of wisdom. Eventually the community, through the medium of its visionaries and mystics, climbed *inside* the Body to plumb the mysterious depths of the incarnate divine life. The Heart was the ultimate goal of that intimate exploration. Finally, this cumulative, penetrating gaze gave rise to a public devotional cult and the Sacred Heart became a focal symbol for the Roman Catholic faith.[4]

The history of the Heart of God began in the patristic era by commentators standing outside the body and reflecting allegorically on paradigmatic scenes from the gospels. The early church fathers' approach to God's body was scriptural, metaphorical, and ecclesial. Two primary patristic ideas were significant for what would later develop into a devotion to the Heart. First, Christ as origin of salvation and the saving church was the *fons vitae*. His pierced side was perceived as the fountain from which springs of living water, the sacraments, flowed. All who approached and drank there would receive eternal life. Christ was the rock from which that water sprang. The fathers enriched the allegory with generative and nuptial allusions. They saw the church, like Eve, born from Christ's side. The church-bride was for them the issue of the bridegroom's heart. Among theologians that included Origen, Augustine, Ambrose, and Jerome, favorite scripture passages (especially John 7:37–38, 19:33, Isaiah 53:5, 1Cor. 10:4, and Song of Songs 2:14) linked together and formed an ongoing collective exegesis that imaged the source of salvation as flowing from the cleft in the rock, the opened body of the crucified.[5]

In similarly associative fashion, the fathers seized on the gospel passage that depicts John the beloved disciple at the Last Supper resting on the breast of Jesus (John 13:23–24). The fathers saw John as the intimate recipient not only of salvation but of contemplative wisdom. In loving intimacy the disciple leaned next to the Heart and was edified with the interior knowledge appropriated there. This reading lent itself to mystical interpretation when passages from the Song of Songs (1:4, 4:9) were conflated with the interpretative tradition. This patristic understanding located the site of human-divine intimacy in the pierced body of the Savior from which flowed innumerable graces and which offered a refuge for, and an embrace to, a beloved disciple.[6]

During the medieval period, these patristic ideas were developed and amplified. Or, to put it another way, the praying community entered more deeply into the body. Allegorical speculation gave way to an intensely personal piety which focused not only on the Lord but on his bodily wounds. The side wound especially became an object of cultic devotion. It became the symbol par excellence of the intimate loving relationship between creator and creatures. It was the portal through which salvation was gained, the nurturant fount of living water. It was the aperture through which the new life gestated in the womb of God was birthed.

During this period, the sacrifice on the Cross more and more came to be understood as an expression of profound love, so that a believer, in praying to the wounds, particularly the side wound which was conceptualized as the entryway to the heart, would have access to Love itself. And as the high Middle Ages developed its sacramental theology, the side of Christ with its flowing blood and water came to be seen almost exclusively in a eucharistic light. The body was thus both the medium and the message. Visually and verbally and through performative action, Christians of the medieval world moved deeper into the body of Christ through the side wound into the divine-human Heart where the mystery of a love that poured itself out in death was explored.[7]

Through the lens of the Song of Songs, that favorite poem of the medieval monastic world, a heightened mystical experience of the body of Christ emerged. The mystic who desired union would drink from the opened side, seek intimacy inside the refuge of the wound, and be incorporated into the body of God through the bleeding portal. The Heart was the lodestone of the mystic's search. The recurring motif of a mystical "exchange of hearts" between Christ and a devotee first emerged in this period. This exchange, variously described as "crushing" and "fiery," symbolized the ultimate identity of the Divine Lover and His beloved.

Evidence of the widespread medieval interest in the Lord and his wounded body is overwhelming. Prayers, litanies, accounts of visions, and treatises on the spiritual life abound which have the wounds as their focal point. In iconography the heart detached itself from the body and became an object of veneration and a catalyst for reflection in its own right. Geographically this interest covered eastern and western Europe and extended far into Spain, Gaul, Ireland, and Syria. Devotion to the wounds and the heart was associated with the great names of the Cistercian renewal, the Benedictines, the mendicant orders, and the Carthusians. By the thirteenth century, women in the circle of the Rhineland monastery of Helfta, like Gertrude the Great and Mechthilde of Hackeborn, were recording visions of Christ appearing to reveal his Heart. Fourteenth-century members of the extended Dominican family, like Henry Suso and Catherine of Siena, gave eloquent theological and mystical expression to their attraction to the Lord's wounded body.[8]

During the fifteenth century the devotion spread beyond cloister walls and the mendicant orders into the emergent tradition of lay piety. It showed itself in multitudes of prayers, poems, artistic representations, and incipient liturgical expressions. By the sixteenth century the Dominicans of the Germanic territories had shaped an entire asceticism around the Sacred Heart. Through the Carthusians in that same century it spread to the young Jesuit order. And through the Jesuits, the works of Ludwig Blosius, the entire medieval corpus of mysticism, and the artistic tradition, it flowed into the confluence of streams that found a common streambed in the spirituality of Francis de Sales, Jane de Chantal, and the community of the Visitation that they founded.[9]

Visitandine spirituality in fact was a spirituality of human and divine hearts. It focused on an inner transformation so that Jesus could "live" in the heart through the acquisition of the virtues of the One who was "gentle and humble of heart." The cross and coat of arms of the Visitation community bore representations of the heart of the wounded Savior that mirrored popular devotional images widely circulated at the time. And the sisters were recorded as considering themselves "imitators of the virtues of the Sacred Heart," as "made by and for the Sacred Heart," or as "daughters of the Heart of Jesus." It was to this community that Margaret Mary Alacoque belonged.[10]

The Visitandines were not alone in their era in embracing the Heart of Jesus as the primary archetype that conveyed the fullness of the Christian truth. The image engaged the attention of the seventeenth-century exponents of the French school of spirituality, especially John Eudes, who composed Sacred Heart prayers for liturgical use and whose society of missionary priests actively encouraged the formation of confraternities dedicated to the sacred hearts of both Jesus and Mary.[11]

A multi-valent image with centuries of richly layered and textured meanings, the Heart of Jesus was Margaret Mary Alacoque's birthright as a Christian of the seventeenth century. She is noteworthy in the history of heart imagery because it was her "great revelations," in which she experienced Christ asking for the institution of specific communal and liturgical observances focused on the Sacred Heart, that gave shape to a liturgical cult that was eventually recognized throughout the Roman church.

In 1785 Pope Clement XIII instituted the feast of the Sacred Heart on the Friday of the Octave following Corpus Christi and raised the devotion from the status of a private to a public one. Between that time and Vatican II in the mid-twentieth century, the Sacred Heart became virtually the defining image of Roman Catholicism. It became a focal symbol of such importance that Leo XIII in the year 1899 consecrated the entire world to the Heart of Jesus. The image was ubiquitous in Europe and the Americas. Latin America especially produced distinctive visual imagery which eventually extended beyond Christian piety to pervade the visual world of Latin culture.[12] Energetic evangelists promoted the Sacred Heart devotion for families and encouraged the consecration of households to the Divine Heart. Widely circulated popular images could be alternately magnificent and sentimental. Concomitantly and from all corners of the Roman church, a generation of thinkers systematized and clarified the meaning of the practical devotion. Moreover, the Sacred Heart image has undergirded the visions of some of the twentieth century's most prominent theologians. Both Teilhard de Chardin and Karl Rahner drew deeply from the wellspring of the Heart image for their thought.[13] The Sacred Heart is still a noticeable component of the Catholic visual landscape. But the seismic theological, liturgical, and spiritual shifts of the post–Vatican II Catholic world have for many people rendered the Heart image a quaint, ineffectual image.

What is at work here in this history of the Heart is a meditative and reflective approach to scripture cultivated over the centuries by practices of contemplative reading such as *lectio divina,* by the exercise of imaginative meditative prayer focused on the mysteries of Christ's life (a tradition exemplified by the Pseudo-Bonaventure's *Meditations on the Life of Christ* and systematized by Ignatius Loyola's *Spiritual Exercises*), and by practices of visual meditation. This midrashic approach to scriptural imagery is a communal undertaking which finds expression in a wide variety of media—theological treatises, liturgical prayer, hymns and ritual, popular devotional images, architecture, painting, scripture, experiences recounted by visionaries, public religious festivals, legends, religious theatre, and so forth. It has as its object imitation, or better, radical participation, in Christ.

A PAUSE IN THE SEVENTEENTH CENTURY

A popular misconception is that the image of God's Heart arrived newly on the scene through the visions of Margaret Mary Alocoque. As we have seen, this is simply not the case. But the image did take on new life and complexity in the late seventeenth century. Let me recount the bare facts.[14] Between 1672 and 1675 this obscure sister of the monastery of Paray-le-Monial was the recipient of three "great revelations." In them, Jesus himself claimed her as his apostle, exchanged his heart for hers, and requested that communion be taken each Friday preceded by a Thursday night hour of adoration, and that a feast in honor of his heart be set aside on Friday after the Octave of Corpus Christi.

The validation of these visions by the Jesuit Claude de la Colombière and their gradual dissemination eventually resulted in the establishment of the formal public cult of devotion to the Sacred Heart of Jesus.[15] The visions themselves, indeed the entire autobiographical narrative of Margaret Mary's *Vie par elle même*, give the reader a glimpse into the rococo inner world of this Visitandine nun. To read the text of this spiritual autobiography is akin to decoding a Hieronymous Bosch landscape, only the heavily overlaid symbolic referents are discovered not in the mind of the artist but in the spiritual tradition that has been so deeply impressed on the imagination of the visionary herself. But let us listen to Margaret Mary's account of the first of her "great revelations," which occurred on December 27, 1673, the feast of John the Evangelist. The cumulative tradition of the Divine Heart is embedded in her narrative.

> Once when I was before the blessed sacrament (I had found a little space of time, though the work I had been given left me little), I was suddenly completely surrounded by the divine presence. It was so intense I lost my sense of who and where I was. I abandoned myself to the Spirit, yielding my heart to the power of

his love. He made me rest for a long time on his divine breast where he showed me the marvels of his love and the unspeakable secrets of his sacred heart that had always been hidden before. He opened them to me there for the first time, in such a real and tangible way. Even though I am always afraid of deceiving myself about what I say happens inside me, I should not doubt what was happening because of the effects that the grace produced in me. This is what seemed to me to happen:

He said to me "My divine heart is so impassioned with love for humanity, and for you especially, it cannot contain the flames of its burning charity inside. It must spread them through you, and show itself to humanity so they may be enriched by the precious treasures that I share with you, treasures which have all the sanctifying and saving graces needed to draw them back from the abyss of destruction. I have chosen you as an abyss of unworthiness and ignorance to accomplish this great work so that everything will be done by me."

Afterwards, he asked for my heart. I begged him to take it and he did, placing it in his own adorable heart. He let me see it there like a little atom consumed in a burning furnace. Then he returned it to me as a burning heart-shaped flame, and placed it where it had been, saying, "Here is a precious token of my love, my beloved. This will enclose a tiny spark of living flame within your side. It will serve as your heart and consume you until your last moment. Its intensity will be so unyielding that you will be unable to find relief, except briefly by bleeding. I will mark it so with the blood of my cross that it will bring you more humiliation and suffering than comfort. That is why I want you to ask for it in all simplicity, so that you can practice what is asked of you and be given the joy of shedding your blood on the cross of humiliation. And to prove that the grace I have just given is not imaginary and is the foundation of all the others I intend to give you, the pain in your side will always remain, even though I have closed the wound. If up until now you have only been called my slave, I now give you the name 'Beloved Disciple of My Sacred Heart.'"[16]

This account draws upon the wealth of devotional exegesis from the past. The location of the encounter is before the Blessed Sacrament, that eucharistic fountain of life. There she is situated to gaze upon the body. In her vision she, like the beloved disciple John before her, lays her head on Jesus' breast, where she learns the secrets of His heart. She, like John, becomes a beloved disciple. Like her medieval forebears her relationship with her Lord is spousal in its tenderness. Yet it is also fierce and annihilating. The motif of a fiery, flaming heart is drawn from the iconographical tradition. Further, Margaret Mary stands in a line of women mystics which includes Catherine of Siena, Mary Magdalene de Pazzi, and Catherine de Ricci whose *imitatio Christi* took the form of an exchange of hearts. And like Juliana of Liège before her, she was the recipient of revelations that called for the institution of a public feast.[17]

Sr. Alacoque may have been an obscure young woman with minimal education and limited access to the elite sources of theology. But she was an acute "reader" of the body of God and she had internalized to a remarkable degree the dense layers of meaning that the cumulative tradition had stored in the primal image of the Divine Heart. Although she lived at the end of the seventeenth century, the way that she received the tradition was closer to the religiosity that flourished in the Western church before the Council of Trent. Pre-Tridentine Christianity was a world of interlocking symbols into which one lived, symbols which shaped one's entire experience and interpretation of that experience.[18] This was a type of religiosity that did not divorce doctrine from lived experience and did not teach doctrine except through other dimensions of Christian living, especially through processions, devotions, visual images, gestures, drama, and performative actions.

So in the seventeenth century, through the visionary experience of this obscure religious, the tradition was summed up. But Sister Alacoque was not only an inheritor of tradition, she contributed to tradition as well. Evident in her writings is the particular spirituality associated with the French or Bérullian School that so dominated the end of the seventeenth century. This spirituality is detected in her powerful sense of human nothingness (*anéantissement*) that contrasts so dramatically with her sense of the majesty of God.[19] It is also seen in her emphasis on the key attitudes of reparation and adoration, attitudes which highlight the reality of human ingratitude in the presence of transcendent mystery. These perspectives are her contribution to the heart tradition, a contribution that definitively characterized the devotion after her time.

IMAGES AND TRANSFORMATION

In recent years art historians have at last directed our attention to the key role visual images have played in the Western Christian spiritual tradition, especially in the late medieval and early modern era. Studies like those done by Jeffrey Hamburger of visual practices in fourteenth-century Dominican convents have illuminated medieval habits of meditative gazing upon images for the purposes of imitation.[20] These practices were part of the wider use of imaginative devotional practices, such as the meditation on the Passion, that was current in those centuries and which encouraged imitation of Christ and Mary. Scholars outside the field of art history are very familiar with this mental meditative tradition. In some circles, like the *Devotio Moderna,* such imaginative reflection on Christ was meant to produce moral transformation. For others, especially in monastic and mendicant circles, the transformation was more theatrical, literal, and somatic. At the core of these distinctive spiritual practices are the axioms: one becomes what one imagines, one becomes what one sees. The Divine Heart is a central image in these highly visual, imaginative centuries.

What I find fascinating is the way in which images shape the imagination and thus transform lives. Following philosopher Mary Warnock, I would describe the imagination as an essential capability inherent in all human perception.[21] We need our imaginations to see what is familiar as well as what is unfamiliar. We do not directly perceive something called "reality," but perception and interpretation occur simultaneously. We image, sort, organize, and see patterns and meanings every moment of our lives. This is an imaginative process.

The very same capacity is utilized when we interpret patterns beyond what we directly encounter. To say it simply: the imagination is the crucial capacity of the human person to create a world—either the familiar world of everyday or a world not yet visible. Our relentless human search for new ways of being and relating, our dreams of beauty, our longings for mercy and justice, these are exercises of the imagination that, in a Christian context, we would say are prompted by the Divine Imagination itself.

Images—visual, verbal, spatial, and so forth—are not only the products of our imagination but they give form and content to our imaginations. Repeated focus, as in practices of meditation or contemplative gazing on religious images, facilitates this transformative process. The visual contemplative or meditative arts cultivated in the great religious traditions are vastly different from ordinary sight. Indeed, they are uniquely designed to deconstruct habituated imaginative constructs and allow visual imagery to reconstruct a new imaginative lens through which reality is interpreted and possible worlds perceived.[22] David Freedberg, student of the powerful potential of images, describes the multitude of responses that images may engender in a beholder:

> People are sexually aroused by pictures and sculptures; they break pictures and sculptures; they mutilate them, kiss them, cry before them, and go on journeys to them; they are calmed by them and incited to revolt. They give thanks by means of them, expect to be elevated by them, and are moved to the highest levels of empathy and fear.[23]

Images engage the whole person. They excite emotions and encourage empathy. They vivify the will by arousing desire and inspiring imitation. They inform the intellect by giving access to realms of being not immediately visible. Thus they tease the viewer into conceptualizing a world that does not yet exist, and into longing for a world that is differently constructed from the one in which he or she lives. Images shape the human imagination as well as reflect it.

This holistic engagement may be an unconscious process or it may be deliberately cultivated, as it was in the medieval visual meditative tradition. Freedberg gives us insight into the transformational dynamics of ancient practices designed to transform the human imagination. These practices, which were buttressed by a comprehensive theory, allowed the meditator, by concentrating on physical images, to check the mind's inclination to wander and to ascend with increasing intensity to the spiritual and emotional essence of that which is represented to the eye in material form. Such practices might involve

> ... vivid and graphic description of events and places ... careful construction of the scene by stages and deliberate intensification, also by stages, of the emotional experience on which successful concentration and meditation depend; empathetic intimacy, encouraging of the free flow of the pictorializing imagination, intimation of the divine, and the drawing of appropriate moral and theological lessons.[24]

By extension, it is possible to see how visual imagery that is the focal point of communal worship and shared performative ritual action may profoundly shape the imaginative world of an entire community.

Images, of course, not only futuristically shape individual and communal imagination, they also reflect the status quo and the preoccupations of the cultures that produce them. As Margaret Miles has ably pointed out in her study of contemporary cinematic images, we can ascertain in these images which concerns are polarizing a culture and what prejudices or attitudes are current.[25] Images are reflections of culture. Further, they may alternately serve to buttress conservative trends or to catalyze avant-garde impulses.

In terms of its developmental life, the Divine Heart has functioned at different times both as a progressive image within the religious culture of Catholicism and as a reactionary one. An example of the latter case is the rallying of French royalist factions under the banner of the Sacred Heart. In fact, the trend to conflate the religious symbol of the heart with political and ideological concerns was begun during Margaret Mary's lifetime. In fact, she received a vision instructing her to write to King Louis XIV and admonish him to establish in his heart the reign of the Sacred Heart, an act she was sure would call down divine protection upon France. Interestingly, this was the era French historians have deemed "the civilization of the heart," an era emblematized by the embalming of the hearts of heroic political leaders.[26]

From the perspective of religio-political polemics, the public emergence of this image and its official promulgation is accurately accessed against the background of continuing struggles between French Huguenots and loyalists as well as against the backdrop of the Jansenist movement. Indeed, the affluent Huguenot middle class had been expelled from the town of Paray-le-Monial a half generation before Margaret Mary received her visions there.[27] Both the Huguenot and Jansenist struggles centered theologically on the Eucharist. The visionary's great revelations make chagrined reference to the neglect that Jesus experiences from human beings. His Heart, which was thought to express God's merciful love as poured forth in the Eucharist, a central focus of orthodox Catholic polemics, was viewed as rejected and ignored. Further, the heart, in the form of heart language which stressed personal encounter with the divine through affective experience, is not during this era exclusively a Roman Catholic preoccupation. The public Catholic Sacred Heart cult emerged in a full blown manner at the crest of an era which evangelical scholar Ted Campbell has deemed the era of "the religion of the heart," a term which embraces Pietism, Hasidism, Moravian piety, and Jansenism.[28]

THE VISITATION AT PARAY-LE-MONIAL

Focusing the lens of these insights, I would underscore the fact that images function dynamically in both large and small cultural arenas as well as in individual lives. To bring attention back to the specificity of the Visitation monastery of Paray-le-Monial at the end of the seventeenth century, it is possible to claim that both Margaret Mary and her community experienced profound transformation as they gazed long and lovingly on the Divine Heart and "read" the messages encoded there.

To read Margaret Mary's spiritual autobiography along with her letters and other fragmentary writings is to discern her transformation from a rather troubled and troubling personality when she entered religious life, to a person who was regarded as responsible and balanced at its end. As a child she had developed an intense interior relationship with Jesus which seems to have provided her a psychic refuge from a traumatic family environment—collapse of her natal family due to her father's death, severe psychological abuse by relatives, personal powerlessness in life choices, the burden of caretaking during her mother's illnesses. This intensely interior relationship took the form of almost constant locutions, visions, and intuitions, communications which were in many ways more real to her than any external communication. This interiority she brought with her into the Visitation monastery. Despite the fact that there was ample precedent for this sort of interior life in the hagiographic tradition with which the girl was familiar, the particular charism of the Visitation community did not encourage such exceptional experiences. Rather, exact fidelity to the rule, strict obedience to superiors (who were, to a woman, leery of their novice's interior life), and personal practices of humility and simplicity were the hallmarks of the order.[29] She found herself often at odds with community members and with those in authority. At one point it was questionable whether she would be allowed to remain.

Her own account of her life in religion, which is cast in the form of a spiritual itinerary and which highlights the constant divine communications she received, shows the struggle between her desire to submit to the conformity demanded by superiors and the intense inner directives which often caused bizarre behavior. She seems to have achieved an equilibrium and was eventually able to conform to the rule and still remain essentially inner-directed, this despite the fact that at one point she felt compelled by Christ to confront her sisters in religion about their failure to live the values they professed. Support for her eventual integration is seen in the fact that toward the end of her life she was respected and seen as balanced enough by the community to be appointed novice mistress.[30]

The key to her transformation was desire, the catalyzing and focusing of all her life energies into a single amorous pursuit. Intimate union with Christ was her passion. This union was effected by an intense and embodied participation with Christ on the Cross. What His body did, hers would do, too. His suffering became the interpretive lens that transformed her own suffering into something larger, something cosmic even, in its redemptive capacity. Quite consciously she focused her desire by formally consecrating herself to the Sacred Heart, a practice she later recommended to others.

This motif of redemptive participatory suffering, of course, is not strange to those familiar with the Christian spiritual tradition. But for Margaret Mary the Heart of God was the symbol par excellence that communicated not just the fact of cruciform suffering but its ultimate meaning. Love was its meaning. Love was the basic fabric of a merciful universe in which pain was transfigured into joy. Love was at once the beginning and end point and the point at which all beings converge. In the most intimate recess of the divine life is discovered this fearful and wonderful secret. Wounds, thorns, and piercing, all was in truth sweetness, as the following account attests.

> Another time, when the Sisters were working in common, picking hemp, I withdrew into a small courtyard, near the Blessed Sacrament, where, doing my work on my knees, I felt myself wholly rapt in interior and exterior recollection, and at the same time, the Adorable Heart of my Jesus appeared to me brighter than the sun. It was surrounded by the flames of Its pure love, and encircled by Seraphim, who sang in marvelous harmony: "Love triumphs, love enjoys, the love of the Sacred Heart rejoices!" These blessed spirits invited me to unite with them in praising this Divine Heart, but I did not dare do so. They reproved me, telling me they had come in order to form an association with me, whereby to render It a perpetual homage of love, adoration and praise, and that, for this purpose, they would take my place before the Blessed Sacrament. Thus I might be able, by their means, to love It continually, and, as they would participate in my love and suffer in my person, I, on my part, should rejoice in and with them. At the same time they wrote this association in the Sacred Heart in letters of gold, and in indelible characters of love. This lasted from two to three hours, and I have felt the effects thereof throughout my life, both by the assistance I received, and by the sweetness which it produced and continued to produce in me, although I felt overwhelmed with confusion.[31]

I want to suggest that through Margaret Mary Alacoque's intense, prolonged encounter with the image of the Divine Heart, a personal integration became possible. She encountered the image in visual form both in visions, of which she had many, and as a visual artifact. The Divine Heart as experienced in her visions was a remarkably labile image. It appeared in various forms, each form carrying a distinct message. Its manifestations included the Heart transpierced and torn with poles, pierced with light and opened by an arrow, closely surrounded by a crown of thorns so that blood flowed out in streams, as a burning furnace, as a lover attracting souls, or as an abyss into which the soul must plunge.[32] Although Margaret Mary had experienced visions throughout her life, it was the Heart that dominated her inner world for the later years of her life (she died in 1690 at the age of forty-three), the period in which she became novice mistress and during which she truly claimed her vocational identity as a beloved disciple of the Sacred Heart.

Twentieth-century readers may not be entirely comfortable with Margaret Mary's late-seventeenth-century language of "annihilation" or submission, nor with her intense focus on suffering as the constitutive mark of imitation (a focus she shared with many of her contemporaries). Insights from the history of art, philosophy, and aesthetics might help us to consider this Visitandine's spirituality of the Sacred Heart within the aesthetic period of the rococo style as well as within the specific sixteenth- and seventeenth-century science of "mysticism" that Michel de Certeau has described, a science which had a unique language all its own.[33] But the fact remains that what this obscure Visitandine saw when she gazed upon the blood-soaked, wounded, thorn-tipped incarnate Heart of God was a heart palpitating with love. This recurring image not only consoled her, it became the encompassing image through which the ultimate integration of her personal story and a luminous, transcendent cosmic story was achieved.

If spirituality is accurately defined as "the experience of conscious involvement in the project of life-integration through self-transcendence toward the value that one perceives,"[34] then Margaret Mary is a case in point. And it was precisely through her intense encounter with the image of the Heart that this self-transcending integration occurred.

The same seems to be true for her monastic community. It is, of course, difficult to ascertain what actually went on in a community from the hindsight of many years. But it does appear true that divisive factions had formed in the Paray Visitation during Margaret Mary's early years there. These factions represented the "old guard" who championed a rigid and punitive observance of the rule, and the "youthful party" who seemed to yearn for a more gentle, forgiving atmosphere. One of the foundational charisms of the order was, in fact, to become a "union of hearts," or a "kingdom of charity."[35] These were not merely pious platitudes mouthed by founders Francis de Sales and Jane de Chantal but tangible goals of the community, to be manifest in the exercise of leadership, spiritual guidance, and personal interaction (the cultivation of the little virtues) and institutionalized in such ways as the governmental structure of the wider order (only the bonds of charity and custom linked houses).

In one of Sr. Alacoque's visions, Jesus instructed her to be the instrument of communal healing by pointing out His displeasure at the sisters' failure to live together in charity. No happy prophetic word to bear! Although she was resisted (predictably) at first, it does appear as though factions were healed, not simply because they had been exposed, but because focus in the community came gradually to rest on the image of the wounded Heart of Christ. As novice mistress, Margaret Mary had been given leave to initiate the visual devotion in the noviciate, despite the fact that this was perceived as novel at first and disallowed.

> The Lord assured me that He takes particular pleasure in being honored under the figure of His Heart of flesh. He wished a picture of it to be publicly exposed so that it might touch insensible hearts; and He promised me that He would amply pour out the treasures of graces with which it is filled on all who honored it. Wherever this image is exposed, it will call down all sorts of blessings.[36]

Soon small drawings of a thorn-topped heart made by Margaret Mary or her sisters in religion were set up for adoration in the house. Significantly, one prominent sister who had been among the "old guard" followed Margaret Mary's example and, publicly prostrating herself, took the vow of consecration to the Sacred Heart. Jesus' heart with its message of unconditional love and, according to the beloved disciple, its sorrow at being rejected and ignored, became an integrating force through which the Paray monastery gained a sense of shared mission and identity.

CONCLUSION

I conclude with three observations about wider implications of this study. The first has to do with the interdisciplinary perspective of this inquiry into the meaning of seventeenth-century devotion to the Sacred Heart of Jesus. Sociology might allow us to see the visionary as a "hinge person" both for the wider Catholic community and for the micro-community in the monastery.[37] Similarly, I find it fascinating to filter the Sacred Heart cult through the lens of cultural anthropology's perspectives on space and explore the analogous "spaces" of the body of God, the mystical body of the Church and the body politic.[38] Likewise, Margaret Mary's story, when set next to cross-cultural descriptions of the practices of shamanism, looks surprisingly like a shamanic initiation.[39] If one trains the lens of women's studies on this seventeenth-century visionary, one is reconfirmed in the impression that, in a religious institution and a culture which had few outlets for women's voices, visionary activity provides that outlet. Finally, in the current cross-disciplinary debates about the nature of mysticism and in the canon of Western mysticism as currently being defined, Margaret Mary's visions of the Sacred Heart might be characterized as "embodied mysticism," a term which aligns previously dichotomous concepts such as apophatic versus kataphatic and visionary versus mystical.[40] The scholarly approaches are seemingly endless and allow us to plumb the rich complexity of religious imagery.

But my observations for our discipline turn most keenly about the question of images and imagination. For the most part the study of Christian spirituality has been undertaken primarily through a consideration of written texts. We tend to look at what people produce in writing rather than in other media. This has become less true in the last decade with the rise of ritual and cultural studies. Still, what we know about both the history and present practice of Christian spirituality has mostly to do with ideas expressed in written words. The study of images has generally been left to the aesthetic consideration of art historians or to students of "popular religion." This myopia of ours may reflect our contemporary prejudices about the nature of art as well as the seeming dichotomy between an elite literary spiritual tradition and the faith of common folks. A look at the spiritual function of images in the past denies that dichotomy. It may also reflect ancient iconoclastic struggles which are still with us, struggles which at root are theological and reflect differing understandings within the Christian community of the way that God is indeed with us. It behooves us, as scholars in an intrinsically interdisciplinary discipline, to give due attention to the role images have and do play in the spiritual life.

Second, Sandra Schneiders has suggested that scripture is a constitutive discipline in the study of Christian spirituality.[41] Her point is well taken. We should also be alert to the variety of ways that the images found in scripture are received and experienced by the community of believers. Images are for the most part not simply illustrations of the biblical narrative but are a parallel means by which Christian core insights have been handed down. Similarly, we need to be attentive to the central role that images, both verbal and visual, play in shaping the imagination of both individual and community. And we need to be aware of the transformative practices that allow for the internalization of images, such as imaginative meditation, non-discursive gazing upon visual artifacts, the contemplative, affective "resting" in God cultivated in *lectio divina*, the deeply affecting practice of hymn singing which allows for a holistic embodied appropriation of a hymn text, the enactment of worshipful gestures, the peregrinations of pilgrimage routes and labyrinths. These and other transforming practices facilitate the deep appropriation of the images that we associate with the biblical narrative. Further, we need to be mindful of both the formal techniques of biblical exegesis carried out by scholars and of the prayerful, ruminative way in which the biblical narrative has been and continues to be incorporated into the hearts and minds of generations of Christians. If spirituality is indeed about the "conscious involvement in the project of life-integration through self-transcendence toward the ultimate value one perceives,"[42] then attention to the processes by which this integration takes place is part of our study.

Third, this concern about images and imagination has importance not only as we unearth the treasures from the past. It has significance in the present. I would suggest that significance is ethical in character. A recent National Public Radio report characterized our present era with the phrase "the rise of the image, the fall of the word." We are all very aware we live in an image-saturated culture. Yet we are often naïve about images and their impact. We seem to have the impression that images are neutral, that they exist outside ourselves and we can take them or leave them, or that images function primarily in the realm of fantasy. Indeed, we tend to equate fantasy and imagination, and to consider the imagination as a delightful but non-essential human capability rather than as the powerful capacity that creates and constructs our world. One segment of society that does not hold this naïve view is the advertising industry. Commercial images are manipulated in a most sophisticated manner to influence our buying habits and to shape our sense of self and our needs. As a spiritual tradition that claims that the human person is created in the image and likeness of God and that has been preoccupied for centuries with the re-formation, reconstitution, repair, or gracious redemption of that original image, one would think Christianity would have a vested interest in the images that shape our imaginations. Many of us in this self-implicating discipline of spirituality have a personal and often a professional investment in the faith community. Thus we would do well to attend to these issues.

If we as scholars have anything to offer the wider community of faith in this regard, we do have the opportunity to explore the way in which images shape the religious imagination. This means we have to draw attention to the fact that as a culture, and this includes Christians, we seem to have lost track of the arts of transformative seeing. If teachers bemoan the fact that students no longer seem to know how to read, the same is true of knowing how to see. Our contemporary modes of seeing appear to have most to do with images used as sensory stimulation, as aesthetic pleasure, or as instruments used to create consumer need. With the exception of a revival of interest in Eastern Orthodox icon gazing, Christian communities have all but lost touch with the tender arts of contemplative seeing, and with the profoundly formative practices that enable images to genuinely shape the imagination. The interdisciplinary study of spirituality allows us to explore these questions so that there can be a meeting between past experience and present need, social constructivist analysis and eternal verities, embodied practice and theory, scholarship and prayer.

NOTES

1. The idea of primal images runs parallel to the idea of primal words suggested by Karl Rahner and David Tracy, words like "grace" and "sin" that are pivotal words, thick with layers of meaning, around which the Christian imagination over the centuries has woven its storied tapestry.

2. David Morgan in his *Visual Piety: A History and Theory of Popular Religious Images* (Berkeley: University of California Press, 1998) posits that many American Protestants find a place in their piety for images when the images invoke the faculty of memory: pictures are commendable when they serve to recall scriptural events or dogma or when they assist an individual in assembling a personal spiritual narrative. Cf. 181ff.

3. Sandra M. Schneiders, "The Study of Christian Spirituality: Contours and Dynamics of a Discipline," *Christian Spirituality Bulletin*, 6:1 (Spring, 1998), 4. This essay appears as Chapter 1 in this volume.

4. A focal symbol is specific to its religion, is obvious in its role as a symbol, and serves as a standard focus for worship and identity within the religious community. The discipline that has been most interested in the heart image has been theology, specifically pre–Vatican II Roman Catholic theology. There exists a large literature dedicated to the theological understanding of the devotion to the Sacred Heart. The underlying concern of most of this literature is to ensure the orthodoxy of devotional practice and to underscore a specifically Roman Catholic perspective on the incarnation, atonement, and redemption, and on ecclesiology. There is much less literature on the Heart of God from other fields.

5. Histories of the Sacred Heart are many; classic among them is Rev. J.V. Bainvel, S.J., *Devotion to the Sacred Heart: The Doctrine and Its History* (London: Burns, Oates and Washbourne, 1924). Helpful modern studies are *Faith in Christ and the Worship of Christ*, ed. Leo Scheffczyk, trans. Graham Harrison (San Francisco: Ignatius Press, 1986); *Heart of the Saviour: A Symposium on Sacred Heart Devotion*, ed. Josef Stierli, trans. Paul Andrews (New York: Herder and Herder, 1958).

6. On the patristic contribution to the Sacred Heart tradition see Hugo Rahner, "The Beginnings of the Devotion in Patristic Times" in *Heart of the Saviour*, 37–57.

7. On the medieval era see Josef Stierli, "Devotion to the Sacred Heart From the End of the Patristic Times Down to Saint Margaret Mary," in *Heart of the Saviour*, 55–108: Walter Baier, "Key Issues in Medieval Sacred Heart Piety" in *Faith in Christ and the Worship of Christ*, 81–99.

8. See Gervais Dumeige, "La découverte du Coeur du Christ: Le culte du Coeur du Christ avant Marguerite-Marie" in *Sainte Marguerite-Marie et le message de Paray-le-Monial*, ed. R. Derricau and B. Peyrous (Paris: Editions Desclée, 1993).

9. Dom Louis Gougoud, *Devotional and Ascetic Practices in the Middle Ages*, trans., G.C. Bateman, (London: Burns, Oates and Washbourne, 1927); *Ancient Devotions to the Sacred Heart of Jesus by Carthusian Monks of the XIV & XVII Centuries* (Westminster, MD: Newman Press, 1954).

10. See André Brix, "Saint François de Sales et le 'Coeur'" in Derricou/Peyrous, 55–74; John A. Abbruzze, *The Theology of Hearts in the Writings of St. Francis de Sales* (Rome: Pontifical University of St. Thomas Aquinas, 1983); Wendy M. Wright, " 'That Is What It Is Made For': The Image of the Heart in the Spirituality of Francis de Sales and Jane de Chantal" in *Spiritualities of the Heart*, ed., Annice Callahan, R.S.C.J. (Mahwah, New Jersey: Paulist Press, 1990), 143–158; Hélène Bordes, "Quelques aspects de la première iconographie de Jésus" in Derricau/Peyrous, 349–374; Henri L'Honoré, "Le culte du Coeur du Christ à la Visitation avant Marguerite-Marie," in Derricau/Peyrous, 119–131.

11. John Eudes' first interest in "heart spirituality" was focused on the Heart of Mary. He wrote liturgical texts in honor of her heart to be used at celebrations that concluded the

mission work in which he was engaged. Later he developed a doctrinal treatise on the Heart of Jesus and composed liturgical texts for its veneration. See Jacques Arragain, "St. Jean Eudes et le Coeur de Christ" in Derricau/Peyrous, and Joseph Caillot, "Saint Christ" in Derricau/Peyrous, and Joseph Caillot, "Saint Jean Eudes: Un itinéraire spirituel vers le coeur de Jesus" in *La Spiritualité du Coeur du Christ* (Paris, 1996), 35–56.

12. Boston, Massachusetts, Institute of Contemporary Art, *El Corazón Sangrante: The Bleeding Heart* (Seattle: University of Washington Press, 1991).

13. Cf. Ursula King, *Spirit of Fire: The Life and Vision of Teilhard de Chardin* (Maryknoll, New York: Orbis Books, 1996) and Annice Callahan, R.S.C.J., *Karl Rahner's Spirituality of the Pierced Heart: A Reinterpretation of the Devotion to the Sacred Heart* (Lanham, MD: University Press of America, 1985).

14. A critical edition of the saint's work has recently emerged. See *Vie et oeuvres de Sainte Marguerite-Marie* (Paris-Fribourg: Editions St. Paul, 1991).

15. Margaret Yeo, *These Three Hearts* (Milwaukee: Bruce Publishing, 1940).

16. *Vie et oeuvres de Sainte Marguerite-Marie,* 82–84.

17. "Coeurs (changement des, échange des)," in *Dictionnaire de spiritualité ascetique et mystique*, Vol. II, col. 1046–51. Cf. Chanoine F. Baix and Dom C. Lambot, O.S.B., *La Dévotion à l'eucharistie et le VIIe centenaire de la Fête-Dieu* (Namur: La Procure, 1946).

18. I would remark parenthetically that this was the same type of Western Christianity that was carried by the conquistadors to Latin America, a part of the Catholic community in which the devotion to the Sacred Heart and other visual symbols has been especially strong.

19. See Raymond Deville, *L'école française de spiritualité* (Paris: Desclée, 1987); *Bérulle and the French School: Selected Writings*, edited by William M. Thompson (Mahwah, N.J.: Paulist Press, 1989).

20. S. Ringborn, "Devotional Images and Imaginative Devotion: Notes on the Place of Art in Late Medieval Piety," in *Gazette des Beaux-Arts*, 6th Series, 73 (1969), 159–70; Jeffrey F. Hamburger, "The Use of Images in the Pastoral Care of Nuns: The Case of Henry Suso and the Dominicans" in *Art Bulletin*, Vol. LXXI, No. 1 (Mar. 1989), 20–46; and "The Visual and the Visionary: The Image in Late Medieval Monastic Devotions" in *Viator*, 20 (1989), 161–82.

21. Mary Warnock, *Imagination* (Berkeley: University of California Press, 1976).

22. Recent neurological studies add to our knowledge of the way in which focused practices such as imaginative meditation give rise to hyperlucid states such as vivid visions, sensorially constellated archetypes, cosmic consciousness and so forth. See Eugene G. d'Aquili and Eugene B. Newberg, "Liminality, Trance, Unitary States in Ritual and Meditation," *Studia Liturgica*, 23 (1993), 2–34.

23. David Freedberg, *The Power of Images* (Chicago: University of Chicago Press, 1989), 1.

24. See Freedberg, *The Power of Images*, 161ff.

25. Margaret R. Miles, *Seeing and Believing: Religion and Values in the Movies* (Boston: Beacon Press, 1996). See also her *Image As Insight: Visual Understanding in Western Christianity and Secular Culture* (Boston: Beacon Press, 1985).

26. Jean Nagle, *La civilisation du coeur: histoire du sentiment politique en France du XIIe au XIXe siècle* (Paris: Librairie Arthème Fayard, 1998).

27. Michel Bouillot, "Paray-le-Monial au temps de Sainte Marguerite-Marie" in Derricau/Peyrous, 23–33.

28. Ted A. Campbell, *The Religion of the Heart: A Study of European Religious Life in the Seventeenth and Eighteenth Centuries* (Columbia, S.C.: University of South Carolina Press, 1991).

29. This despite the fact that the Visitation of the late seventeenth century is remembered as a community upon which the rich springs of mystical life were poured out. See the

classic by Henri Bremond, *Histoire litteraire du sentiment religieux en France depuis la fin des guerres de religion jusqu'à nos jours*, 3 vols. (Paris: Bloud et Gay, 1921).

30. The consecration reads:

> O Sacred Heart of my Lord and Saviour Jesus Christ, to Thee I consecrate and offer up my person and my life, my actions, trials and sufferings, that my entire being may henceforth only be employed in loving, honoring and glorifying Thee. This is my irrevocable will, to belong entirely to Thee, and to do all for Thy love, renouncing with my whole heart all that can displease Thee.
>
> I take Thee, O Sacred Heart, for the sole object of my love, the protection of my life, the pledge of my salvation, the remedy of my frailty and inconstancy, the reparation for all the defects of my life, and my secure refuge at the hour of my death. Be Thou, O most merciful Heart, my justification before God Thy Father, and screen me from His anger which I have so justly merited. I fear all from my own weakness and malice, but placing my entire confidence in Thee, O Heart of Love, I hope all from Thine infinite goodness. Annihilate in me all that can displease or resist Thee. Imprint Thy pure love so deeply in my heart that I may never forget thee or be separated from Thee. I beseech Thee, through Thine infinite goodness, grant that my name be engraved on thee, for in this I place all my happiness and all my glory, to live and to die as one of Thy devoted servants. Amen. (*The Autobiography of Saint Margaret Mary*, translated by the Sisters of the Visitation, West Sussex [Rockford, IL: Tan Publishers, 1986]), 127–28)

31. For another perspective on her spiritual itinerary, consult Chanoine Pierre Blanchard, *Sainte Marguerite-Marie: Éxperience et doctrine* (Paris: Editions Alsatia, 1961) and Jean-Claude Sagne, "La personalité spirituelle de Marguerite-Marie," in Derricau/Peyrous, 175–89.

32. *Autobiography*, 113.

33. For example, the image of the Heart with two poles, one by which enjoyment is had and one by which we suffer, communicated to the visionary that only the second of those poles lasts into eternity, and it is ultimately only that pole by which true enjoyment is obtained.

34. Michel de Certeau, *The Mystic Fable: The Sixteenth and Seventeenth Century*, trans. Michael B. Smith (Chicago: University of Chicago Press, 1992).

35. Schneiders, "The Study of Christian Spirituality," 1, 3.

36. Wendy M. Wright, "The Visitation of Holy Mary: The First Years (1610–1618)" in *Religious Orders of the Catholic Reformation*, edited by Richard DeMolen (New York: Fordham University Press, 1994), 217–252.

37. Quoted in the classic study by Emile Bougaud, *The Life of Saint Margaret Mary Alacoque*, English translation by a Visitandine of Baltimore (Rockford IL: Tan Books and Publishers, 1990), 229.

38. Taking a cue from Peter Brown's seminal work on holy persons as "hinge persons" in their societies (*The Cult of the Saints* [Chicago: University of Chicago Press, 1982]), Margaret Mary might be viewed as the bearer of intense, prophetic messages that transform a society. For her intimate community, she had the not always happy role of bearing Jesus' critique of life in the Visitation. In terms of the wider Catholic community, Margaret Mary, like other visionaries before her, notably Juliana of Liège whose visions instituted the feast of Corpus Christi, seems to have lifted up from the collective imagination of the community an image which could give definition to an emerging group identity.

39. It is interesting to think of the space of Christ's Mystical Body as having an "inside." From this obscure woman, hidden in the inner sanctum of the monastery cloister (an institution responsible for prayer, the inner work of the ecclesial body), comes a message from the inner recesses of God's own body—the Heart of Jesus. A somewhat more focused feminist lens produces interesting pictures of the Heart of Jesus as a specifically "women's space." Margaret Mary Alacoque is one of a line of visionaries, almost all

women, who experienced the mystical "exchange of hearts" with Jesus and thereby achieved special intimacy and identification with Him.

40. Inexplicable illnesses, absolute identification with her "guardian spirit," internal rites of passage, all these and more point to her having a shaman's role. See Piers Vitebsky, *The Shaman: Voyages of the Soul* (Boston: Little, Brown and Co., 1995).

41. The basic question: Is mysticism tradition-specific or is it *sui generis*? See a discussion of this question in Bernard McGinn, *The Foundation of Mysticism*, volume 1 of *The Presence of God* (New York: Crossroad, 1991), 291 ff.

42. Schneiders, "The Study of Christian Spirituality," 3. (See above, p. 7.)

43. Ibid., 1, 3.

24

Sound Spirituality

On the Formative Expressive Power of Music for Christian Spirituality

DON E. SALIERS

*E*ach of the human senses plays a constituent role in the formation and expression of Christian spirituality. In most historic religious traditions, seeing and hearing have a primacy of place in awakening, sustaining, and deepening awareness of the divine-human relationship. In many key disciplines of spiritual practice, tensions between what is seen and not seen, between what is heard and not heard are deliberately heightened. So, for example, in devotional practices before icons, sight may seem primary. But the immediate conditions for the gaze include touch and tactility in the devotional kiss, and the kinetic aspects of bowing and reverencing before the image. The interrelation of these senses in the full-orbed devotional practices with icons forms what we might call a *synesthetic matrix*. Such a matrix is found in nearly all spiritual traditions. This is, as I propose to explore, at the heart of mature liturgical participation.

Traditions of communal spiritual practice employ a variety of sounds to awaken, elicit, and sustain particular states of consciousness. Consider the bell in Hindu temples, Buddhism, shamanism, and Christianity. Drums and cymbals, the shofar and the trumpet sound and signify a range of religious sensibility in Jewish tradition, attested to in the Hebrew psalms. The sense of taste is prominent in all food rituals, from Hindu puja to Jewish Passover to the Christian Eucharist. Yet "tasting" can be the opening to "seeing," as in the psalm refrain, "O taste and see the goodness of the Lord" (Psalm 145.1). Could this be analogous to occasions in which we experience "seeing the divine" in and through sound—especially when music and text combine in ritual context?

These initial points remind us at the outset of the ubiquity of human senses in spiritual practices across a wide spectrum of traditions. Even the most severe of interior and apophatic procedures presuppose the role human sense experience plays in spiritual discipline. At the same time one rarely finds one sensory mode standing alone. Ascetic bodily practices of restraint concerning images, whether visual or acoustical, alter the language of the senses, not only to remove distraction, but also to unveil that which transcends the ordinary content of sense experience. In fact, the discourse of spirituality characteristically speaks of another *kind* of sense—a religious or contemplative "sense" as a way of understanding reality and oneself. Cultivation of such a "spiritual sense" by which the divine glory and grace is perceived is often the aim of practices known as spiritual disciplines.

In this essay I explore one of the primary clusters of sense so crucial to much Christian spirituality: the acoustical or auditory domain. In particular I am interested in how hearing sound as music, both with and without words, is central to liturgical spirituality. How is the hearing of sound itself part of the complex sensorium of any act of worship? More especially, what is it about ordered sound as music that constitutes an *intrinsic* dimension of liturgical participation? Music has been called the "language of the soul made audible." Behind this popular definition is the relationship of hearing to sound as an image of the deepest center of human existence. The human voice is *per*primordial in this domain of the formation and expression of a spiritual sense of being-in-the-world.

St. Augustine of Hippo's ambivalence in his *Confessions* provides a good starting point. He addresses a lover's question to God:

> When I love you, what do I love? Not the body's beauty, nor time's rhythm, nor light's brightness . . . nor song's sweet melodies, nor the fragrance of flowers, lotions and spices, nor mana and honey, nor the feel of flesh embracing flesh—none of these are what I love when I love my God. And yet, it's something like light, sound, smell, food, and touch that I love when I love my God—the light, voice, fragrance, embrace of my inner self, where a light shines for my soul. . . . *That's* what I love when I love my God! (Book X: 6,8)

One cannot fail to sense how deeply intertwined the sensible joy and delight in creaturely things are with Augustine's reflections on what loving God is. He was certainly possessed of a sensibility for the beautiful, rooted here in a Platonic view of reason as eros, but also steeped in the concrete language of doxology nurtured in the sensory rhetoric of the psalms and Christian scriptures. He is driven to cite the sensible stuff of liturgical participation and devotional practice as the appropriate analogical discourse of the soul. To say what loving God is "like" is to appeal to a whole series of senses. These seem to form a matrix of sorts. The seeming denial of the physical and sensual aspects of religious devotion is immediately reforged into the description of interrelated patterns of perception. Loving God requires the interanimation of all the available senses.

Even more to the point here are Augustine's references to the beautiful melodies of psalm settings he heard in Milan. He wept with joy at the liberated "delights of the ear" in praying these psalms. Yet he also wishes at times to banish the melodies because of their sensual sound properties in order to attend solely to the "pure" hearing of God's word (Book X: 33). Christian tradition inherited his ambivalence toward the aesthetic dimensions of religious practices, both liturgical and devotional. Yet I contend that his tears of recognition were part of his "hearing." This ambivalence about music (the ordered sound that articulates and animates the texts of prayer) is not peculiar to Augustine. This is a central aspect of how Christian spirituality is formed. Could it be that, in order to show how sound and music shape the Christian life and sense of the divine, we must attend to the *permanent tensions* between aesthetic sensibility and holiness as transformative receptivity to God?

Perhaps we can formulate the foregoing reflections in thesis form: *Music is the language of the soul made audible, conferring upon human speech addressed to the divine its originating silence and mystery, especially as music is the performative mode of the prayer and ritual engagement of a community.* This implies that ordered sound, particularly when it animates sacred texts, shapes human beings in distinctive forms of affection and receptivity. To this aspect of our inquiry we now turn.

For several years in the late sixties and early seventies my family lived in the inner city of New Haven. Our four daughters, then quite young, were taught a set of ritual songs by neighborhood friends. The children would form a circle with jump ropes. Calling out to one another across the swinging ropes, they were singing. One at a time the children would dance into the circle, hop a few steps, then dance away, all the while singing amid the whirling ropes: "Miss Mary Mack, Mack, Mack . . . all dressed in black, black, black . . . with silver buttons, buttons, buttons . . . all down her back, back, back . . . " This was a narrative ritual game. It was clear that children had to learn to accent the words just so. The movements were unmistakably improvisational—with maturation, they could become quite complex. Yet the rules were clear: don't miss the skips, know the words, and all the children had to perform them both with the right spirit.

The children learned both the words, the singing, and the dance together. Performing led to an ever-deepening dexterity and delight, and to communal solidarity. This image of the singing, dancing children remains for me a wonderful metaphor for the formative and expressive power of authentic liturgical participation. It is an image of vitality and of doxology. This natural language of praise is found in the fusion of ordered sound, ruled kinetic participation, and a communal sense of shared narrative.

The children were formed in a way of being together, and of receiving a world of joy, precisely in the multi-sensory doing of the ritual. The sounds of the whirling rope, the sounds of feet on the earth, the squeals of delight combined with the music in performance. These formed them in a kind of understanding they have not forgotten.

336

The body remembers shared music making long after the mind may be dimmed. Those children participated in this *synesthetic matrix*. Sound, pitch, rhythm, and bodily movement are found in what we human beings do in our work, our festivals, our solemn occasions of grieving, or rejoicing. Whether around campfires, in fields of harvest, or in temples and churches, the communal act of singing has formed and expressed deep human emotions. Such emotions are not simply passing states of feeling or mood; they are capacities to consent to a sense of being in the world. If music is the language of the soul made audible, then human voices conjoined in community are primary instruments of the collective soul—a medium for what transcends the immediately commonsense world. In such cases the hearing and the sound itself encode more than what is heard.

337

Music has the power to encode and convey memory with powerful associations. Anyone who participated or lived through the American Civil Rights movement will always hear the courage, the suffering, the pain, and the promise in "We shall overcome." A whole generation of Americans who lived through World War II cannot forget the sound of Kate Smith singing "God bless America." The African-American spiritual "Sometimes I feel like a motherless child" and the Appalachian song "I'm just a poor wayfarin' stranger" touch something beyond our surface longings and wishes. Words set to music are given greater emotive range and associational power than when we only speak them—much less when we only think about them. We are asked to say some things that we don't truly think we believe until we sing them, or hear them in appropriately complex activities.

Some years ago I studied the singing practices in several Protestant churches. In Bethel United Methodist Church in Charleston, S.C., I interviewed a group of older women. After asking them to identify their favorite hymns (to which they gave a standard list of hymns of the late nineteenth and early twentieth century—many of them gospel songs), I asked them why these hymns and songs were so significant. They spoke of "hearing their grandmother's voice," of "leaning against their mother's breast," or hearing the "squeak of the parlor organ," of weddings, funerals, and Sunday evening gatherings. Thus a marvelous range of life experiences and relationships were evoked by the sounding of those hymns. Especially prominent was the sound of human voices, as though human existence itself was held in paraphrase before the divine, yet with all the ordinariness of non-perfection.

Anyone working with Alzheimer's patients knows that often the last way of bringing a person a present is to sing for them (and with them) songs from their childhood. This itself is a kind of metaphor for the deeper power of music to encode life, and to make it present—even in the face of cognitive diminishment.

The witness of those church women also recalls Suzanne Langer's notion of music as a "non-discursive symbolism." Music itself offers us in the hearing—and I would add, in the singing—a pattern of how we actually experience the world and our lives. It presents to us a morphology of human sentience. In more humble terms, I propose that spirituality has to do with sounding life before God. Because we live through time, music is perhaps our most natural medium for coming to terms with time, and attending to the transcendent elements in making sense of our temporality. Our lives, like music, have pitch, tempo, tone, release, dissonance, harmonic convergence, as we move through times of grief, delight, hope, anger, and joy. In short, music has this deep affinity to our spiritual temperament and desire. Our lives, like music, can only be understood in remembering the passage through time. The order of sound is comprehended as we remember and re-configure the previously heard in light of the yet-to-be-heard. So, too, the deeper desires and yearnings of the human soul are not understood until a larger pattern emerges. Remembering the sound of voices of those we loved and lost to death is perhaps one of the most startling examples of recapitulation and fresh re-understanding of that relationship as we move through time.

The foregoing reflections might be formulated in a second thesis: *Music as ordered sound is intimately related to the narrative quality of human experience, presenting our temporality in symbolic form, but always sensually and bodily perceived. The sound of the human voice is primordial, yet always pointing beyond the sounds to the possibility of our becoming more human. Ritual contexts activate the formative and expressive power of sound with respect to the deep patterning of human affections.*

I now understand new depths of spirituality implied in St. John Chrysostom's remark: "The psalms which occurred just now in the office blended all voices together, and caused one single full harmonious chant to arise; young and old, rich and poor, women and men, slaves and free, all sang one single melody . . . together we make up a single choir in perfect equality of rights and of expression whereby earth imitates heaven" (*Homilies on the Psalms*).

When the Christian assembly gathers to sing in the context of worship, deep memory is required. The act of singing praise, lament, thanksgiving, and intercession to God goes beyond the surface of the words, and beyond the musical score. This event itself is metaphoric, parabolic, symbolic. Singing and hearing music that expresses life before God confers a special dignity on our human desires. If the text and musical form are adequate to mystery, to suffering, and to the deeper range of human emotions, the human soul is made available to the transfiguring grace of the divine life. This is the domain of liturgical spirituality. But such phenomena are also present in devotional and personal attentiveness to musical form—even to each distinctive sound. Gerard

Manley Hopkins testified to this in "God's Grandeur": each thing "tells out that being indoors each one dwells."[1]

Spiritual formation and experience, by definition, take us beyond the obvious surfaces we perceive in hearing with the physical senses. Music is remarkably ephemeral, always passing away from us; yet it does seem to open up "levels of the soul." The question of meaning in music hinges on the interaction, and the interanimation between order, sound, and the range of other senses—visual, kinetic, gestural—it conjoins. The circumstances under which something is first heard and then remembered lead to the deeper power of what music offers Christian life. Music is not therefore simply an ornament of something already understood, for example, a text. Neither is music, in ritual and devotional contexts, an enhancement of something already fully determined by the text. Rather, it mediates senses and the reception of religious significance precisely by crossing over to what is not heard. This begins with the human voice in primordial rituals with mother and child. Sounds convey bodily images, have kinetic powers and evocative efficacy.

Even in hearing instruments or distinctive sounds such as the ringing of bells, we are called to attend to the interaction of all the elements of sound. Listening to another's voice, even in reading, requires vulnerability, acceptance, expectancy. The tension is already there with respect to what is yet to be said and heard, and how this hearing will reconfigure the already sounded and heard. Thus it is no accident that we can "hear" in Bach, or in Mahler, or even in the simple deep folk tune a sense of height, depth, breadth, sharpness, softness, liquidity, marching, persistence, and free imagination. Sound implies spatial and kinesthetic orders. The deeper our hearing with imagination, the more these features emerge. Text, music, and bodily participation are fused together in ritual action. Thus music itself can become a gesture. Human speech is more than sound. Hence music shapes our capacities to envision, to come to a sense of being.

A final thesis emerges: *Synaesthesis is required for spiritual maturation. If we only take in the literal surface of what we hear in text and song, the awakening of the deeper dimensions of reality and of the soul are prevented.* When the singing and the hearing allow us to "taste and see," we come to "hear" more. The soul is awakened to a humanity stretched more deeply before the mystery and the glory of God. Worship forms human beings in a growing maturity into the beauty and the holy fear of this temporal life. When sound in worship is adequate enough to engage the other "senses" in perception of the hidden glory and grace of divine self-giving, spiritual maturation is made possible. Something about "coming to our senses," about the mystery of existence, requires this. Something in us must be "sounded," just as we desire to hear and to speak of the divine-human polyphony.

Music can thus express the inexpressible. For the tension between what we see and have not yet seen, what we hear and have not yet heard is the pattern the Christian life offers.

The love of beautiful things generates a disposition toward the good. The practices of attending to whatever is lovely and gracious are thus required for active receptivity of the divine self-giving. Yet it is not the beautiful alone, for the aesthetic experience of things spiritual must conjoin with the otherness of what is holy. Fear and trembling before what is holy are not exhausted by attraction to the beautiful. But if our practices, liturgical and devotional, listen for the lure to live in benevolence, hospitality, and vulnerability to mystery and to glory, then life deepens in gratitude, hope, truthfulness, and compassion. These are notes sounded in the Christian call to a deeper life with God and neighbor.

NOTE

1. Gerard Manley Hopkins, *Poems of Gerard Manley Hopkins,* ed. Robert Bridges (London: Oxford University Press, 1948), 70.

25

"Raiding the Inarticulate"

Mysticism, Poetics, and the Unlanguageable

MARK S. BURROWS

Poetry is a part of the structure of reality.
—Wallace Stevens[1]

*P*oets have not found an easy welcome among modern theologians. They might be commissioned to write an occasional hymn, or ornament a liturgy, but rarely have they been trusted as partners in the professional guild of theologians, ministers, and priests. What, after all, does the instinct of the poet's eye, the habits of the poet's ear, the music of the poet's tongue, have to do with the demands of theology in the "prose-flattened world" of modernity?[2] Plato long ago worried about their art as an indulgent form of play, banishing them from the republic since their work appealed to the emotions rather than to reason, rendering them untrustworthy for the weighty work of public life.[3] But what if poetry is, as Wallace Stevens suggests, "a part of the structure of reality"? What might it mean, in this case, to inquire about the poet's vocation?

Despite such ancient worries, poets have not been without their champions among the philosophers of the modern academy. Schelling saw in the arts the consummation of philosophy, the entrance into the sanctuary of truth not through reason but through the spirit perfecting itself in the act of creation. In the ecstatic form of his *Zarathustra*, Nietzsche offers not an apology but an expression of an unheralded poetic form, one that sought beauty in an "immaculate perception"—as he puts it, to "desire nothing of things, except . . . [to] lie down before them like a mirror with a hundred eyes," and to speak and write and live not with grave and heavy language but with poetic words that can be sung.[4] Gadamer sees aesthetics as a valid way of knowing, despite its having been structurally dismantled in much of continental philosophy—Nietzsche of course excepted—since Kant. He asks:

> Does not the experience of art contain a claim to truth which is certainly different from that of science, but equally certainly is not inferior to it? And is it not the task of aesthetics precisely to provide a basis for the fact that artistic experience is a mode of knowledge of a unique kind . . . [which is] certainly different from all moral rational knowledge and indeed from all conceptual knowledge, but still knowledge?[5]

More recently, Iris Murdoch suggested that literature is the art "most practically important for our survival and salvation," since words constitute what she calls "the ultimate texture and stuff of our moral being."[6] It may even be, as Frye once suggested, that literature fills the vacancy carved out of the popular imagination left behind by the displacement of myths and symbolic narrative in modern societies.[7]

Perhaps theologians' worry about the poets' place in their republic suggests some measure of their own discomfort with the imagination as a source of insight, a way of thinking in the world without a necessary grounding in reason, ethics, or metaphysics. The poet, called by Stevens the "orator of the imagination,"[8] reminds us that the life of language moves beyond a construction of reality within the limits of reason alone, and that a disenchanted world emptied of the symbolic and denied the traces of transcendence is finally a difficult if not unbearable dwelling place. Poets approach their vocation, as Eliot reminds us, knowing that this is always a struggle

> . . . to learn to use words, and every attempt
> Is a wholly new start, and a different kind of failure
> Because one has only learnt to get the better of words
> For the thing one no longer has to say, or the way in which
> One is no longer disposed to say it. And so each venture
> Is a wholly new beginning, *a raid on the inarticulate*
> With shabby equipment always deteriorating
> In the general mess of imprecision of feeling,
> Undisciplined squads of emotion.[9]

Poets live and work at this margin of the *in*articulate. Their work is visual at the edges of darkness, auditory in the cradle of silence. In this raiding of what we cannot speak, their vocation embodies a longing for, a reaching toward, what we cannot manage with our minds alone, the endless working with words which "after speech, reach/ Into the silence" (Eliot).[10] They are the artists of the imagined, drawn into and through language by that which lies within yet always beyond the grasp of speech. Poets live in the transcending arc of metaphor, which creates something new from the combining of familiar but separated things. Such a semantic understanding of transcendence is not of itself a sufficient measure of mysticism, whatever the word finally means, but without it there is nothing we might properly call mystical. Without the play of poetics, theology may serve a useful intellectual work but its language will be "tempted to make reality more articulate than it is."[11] An unpoetical theology renders the spiritual life as a largely verbal technique, attempting the "conceivability of all being" which Nietzsche already so vigorously decried.[12]

Poetics points through language toward the *in*articulate, toward a transcendence not *beyond* but *within* speech. The play of words and meanings and feelings—this "making" that is the meaning of *poiesis*—is the gift brought by the poetic imagination. Our speaking and our very being are shaped at these margins. Theological thinking oblivious to these edges, which lure us like an ocean's horizon where the immensities of sea and sky mingle and play, becomes little more than a thinking strategy without depth or draw. Against such a specter, which according to Nietzsche "makes of wisdom a poorhouse and hospital for bad poets," he queries: "Have you never seen a sail faring over the sea, rounded and swelling and shuddering before the impetuosity of the wind? Like a sail, shuddering before the impetuosity of the spirit, my wisdom fares over the sea—my untamed wisdom!"[13]

Wallace Stevens spoke of poetry as "a means of redemption." But it is surely not always this. Sometimes it is little more than sentimentality, "a failure of feeling."[14] Stevens gets it right when he suggests that the poet "must put the same degree of intentness into his poetry as, for example, the traveler into his adventure, the painter into his painting."[15] At its truest, it is a journey, an imagining, a daring—which is to say, a making that finds no dwelling place in a world of intellect tamed by manageable language. Modern poets accept banishment from such a republic with some relief, leaning toward the apophatic once sited by the mystical theologians of ancient and medieval cultures where truth still shimmers at the margins of the inarticulate. They refuse to concede, as Jorie Graham puts it ironically, that

> [t]his is an age in which imagination
> is no longer all-powerful. Where if you had
> to write the whole thing down, you could.
> (Imagine: to see the whole thing written down).
> Everything but memory abolished.
> All the necessary explanations also provided.[16]

They turn from the cold logic of such a minor ambition, knowing that a world without some guiding force of the imagination is an uninhabitable place. Theirs is still Hölderlin's brooding question, "What are poets for in a destitute time?" and, despite Heidegger's contention that we hardly understand the question anymore, they follow him in facing what the philosopher called "this world's night as a destiny that takes place this side of pessimism and optimism."[17] It is the question of this destiny, and the poets' refusal of silence in the face of this terrible mystery, that frame these reflections.

THE LOSS OF THE POETIC

> I walked the deserted prospect of the modern mind
> where nothing lived or happened that had not been foreseen . . .
> I walked alone in that desert of unremitting purpose . . .[18]

In an age such as this, the poetics of the so-called mystical writers of the late antique and medieval periods seems strangely quaint, even irrelevant. It may well be, as Denys Turner has argued, that mysticism in the classical sources is essentially an apophatic strategy, and has little if anything to do with the experientialist constructions of modernity with its positivist habits of mind. Leigh Schmidt probes this question from another angle, suggesting that interpreting the modern liberal construction of mysticism reflects a nostalgic yearning for an unattained interiority—a longing that has flowered in the widespread popularity of so-called "spiritualities" of every imaginable sort.[19] These voices belong not to the cultured despisers of religion but the wondering and the questing who have too often turned empty away from the noise of our solemn assemblies. Poets of the search, as Dorothy Sayers called them, speak of this unlanguageable longing; among them is Wallace Stevens, that great voice of ineffability whose language conveys what one critic has called a "transcendence downward."[20] Stevens captures this deep and finally unquenchable yearning when he suggests that

> It would be enough
> If we were ever, just once, at the middle, fixed
> In This Beautiful World Of Ours and not as now,
>
> Helplessly at the edge, enough to be
> Complete, because at the middle, if only in sense,
> And in that enormous sense, merely enjoy.[21]

It would be enough, but we feel with Stevens that this longing remains a thwarted desire for those who live "helplessly at the edge," alienated from this sought-after "middle." Precisely this desire drives him toward what he calls "a mystical aesthetic," a sensibility he does not find among the priests and theologians, too often the voices of an exhausted culture, but discovers with the artists—and, above all, painters and poets. Our predicament, he suggests, is

> . . . to find the real,
> To be stripped of every fiction except one,
> The fiction of an absolute . . .[22]

But why does Stevens search this as a "fiction"? We hear Plato claiming his due that poets are only after an illusory world in metaphor and story—until, that is, we recognize the artist's vocation in "an age in which disbelief is . . . profoundly present," when "poet and painter live and work in the midst of a generation that is experiencing essential poverty in spite of fortune."[23] Only the imaginative power of such fiction, Stevens reasoned, could reach the depths where truth lay buried in an unlanguageable silence beneath the sturdy strata of intellectual argument and ethical demand in a disenchanted world.[24]

"It is at the level of imagination," as Amos Wilder once insisted, "that the fateful issues of our new world-experience must first be mastered."[25] Cultural critics as diverse as Morris Berman, Marcel Gauchet, and theologians such as Tillich, Farley, and Neville, agree in portraying ours as a culture in an unstable transition, one that has lost its way by denying the symbols that once structured mythic memory and thus provided its orienting depths. In a republic of this sort, artists turn from philosophers and theologians, preferring the untamed melodies of a Dionysian chorus to the grave chants of a world come of age:

> And now awake at dreaming's end:
> The world is deep,
> Deeper than day can comprehend.
> Deep is its woe,
> Joy—deeper than heart's agony:
> Woe says: Fade! Go!
> But all joy wants eternity,
> Wants deep, deep, deep eternity.[26]

Seekers of this wisdom are what Stevens calls "the clairvoyant men that need no proof:/ The lover, the believer and the poet" whose "words are chosen out of their desire."[27] With the mystics, they refuse the dream of a shallow world, one emptied of desire for what lies beyond the reach of discursive or analytical language. Poet Richard Wilbur concedes the point, lamenting that

> All that we do
> Is touched with ocean, yet we remain
> On the shore of what we know.[28]

Stevens referred to this longing as "the acute intelligence of the imagination . . . [which] rescues all of us from . . . absolute fact."[29] Eliot gathers this insight into a simple imperative: "Risk enchantment."

THE ARTISTRY OF THE IMAGINATION

> . . . The poet

> Increases the aspects of experience,
> As in an enchantment, analyzed and fixed
> And final. This is the center. The poet is
> The angry day-son clanging at its make:

> The satisfaction underneath the sense,
> The conception sparkling in still obstinate thought.[30]

But what precisely is this "inarticulate" realm that shadows human language as a lure of the imagination, drawing speech toward these margins of the unsayable? Is this little more than a futile quest to defend an illusion (Freud), or might it point toward the widening margins of reality that appear to us as a perceptible if also receding transcendence? What I am suggesting is that the intellectual transitions that have shaped theological expression and religious experience in modernity have brought about an unusual alliance. While we find almost no resonance between the classical theology articulated by the ancient fathers and early medieval doctors and theologies of modernity, this earlier world finds its heirs among the poets of our age. Modern poetics holds aloft, in a non-metaphysical form, the mystical banner of the ancient world largely ignored in the republic of theology, and mysticism understood as the depths of longing in human experience—particularly in its attentiveness to the inarticulate and absent—seems to have been largely banished with the artists from this discourse. But in this exile the poets have borrowed this mystical impulse, at least in their search for traces of transcendence at the edges of perception and through the deep surfaces of language.

The prospect of a theological poetics has a long precedent in the actual practice of theological writing in the pre-modern West. We find it in the monastic tradition of *allegoresis*, the allegorical interpretation of biblical texts which, as Julia Kristeva suggests, is a method of reading "inscribed in the very logic of the imagination."[31] But my interest is not in rehabilitating allegory but in probing poetics to discern whether theologians might learn something important from the poets' raids on the inarticulate.

Charles Winquist approaches what he sees as a crisis in theological writing by calling for a new *form* of literature, one that sees itself creating a "recording surface, the body on which a theological practice will be marked."[32] Such a surface destabilizes the Cartesian dominance of the text as an object—or what de Certeau has described as an *écriture*—by creating writings marked by a "fissured surface . . . that are amenable to an erring consciousness," and "spaces through which one can wander or stray"—that is, surfaces marked by silences and gaps, fissures allowing the reader to journey toward the margin of transcendence. Winquist suggests that we need to discover new "writing technologies" appropriate to the goal of theological inquiry and expression, technologies that inscribe "a state of becoming"—a poetics, in other words— within the text itself. He describes this goal as the making of texts "that highlight their fissured surfaces, their disorder and incompleteness," such that the act of writing "can . . . be likened to an erring and also a bricolage."[33] And, in an insight of crucial importance, he suggests that a theological text with such "thick surfaces" or "surfaces of the deep" move us toward assent only if they carry with it "the intensity of aesthetic satisfaction."[34] What he is describing, without naming it as such, falls under the broad category of poetics.

Winquist's description of this desired theological literature points to the importance of rhetoric and grammar among the siblings of the ancient *trivium*. These are the ancient foundation of poetry, and the basis for all writing—including, let us presume for the moment, theological *écriture*. What is important to note is that the estrangement of theology and aesthetics, at least in terms of the formal expression these took in the literatures of modernity, has roots that reach well behind the Enlightenment to a shift occurring at the centers of theological learning in the Western church during the transitional period of the twelfth and thirteenth centuries. As the discourse and practice of theology moved from a monastic to an academic locus, dialectic (logic) took precedence over rhetoric and grammar, and the historical or grammatical senses of the text began to eclipse the earlier interest in the spiritual.

The pressures of such developments meant that metaphor and imagination, and indeed the focal interest in language itself, came to hold less and less importance in theological thought and expression. De Certeau points to this development in the thirteenth century:

> Since the time when theology became professionalized, spirituals and mystics took up the challenge of the spoken word. In doing so, they were displaced toward the area of "the fable." They formed a solidarity with all the tongues that continued speaking, marked in their discourse by the assimilation to the child, the woman, the illiterate, madness, angels, or the body. Everywhere they insinuate an "extraordinary": they are voices quoted—voices grown more and more separate from the field of meaning that writing had conquered, ever closer to the song or the cry.[35]

Of course, this is only the beginning of profound cultural shifts, changes in the *mentalité* of Western societies with the dawning of modernity. As one expression of this development during early modernity, we begin to discern a phenomenon of central importance: viz., the separation of theological language and literature from the arts—and, particularly, modern literary forms such as fiction and poetry that depend upon the artistry of imagination for vitality of expression and form.

THE RISE OF LITERATURE

>   ... Poetry
> Exceeding music must take the place
> Of empty heaven and its hymns,
>
> Ourselves in poetry must take their place ... [36]

With the emergence of an historical consciousness, or *mentalité*, one of the distinguishing marks of modernity as Troeltsch reminds us,[37] the very meaning of the word "literature" begins to take on a new sense. As early as the eighteenth century, literature as an imaginative form began to emerge as a creative genre distinguished from both history and the sciences in a manner we take for granted today.[38] Literature came to occupy the place once held by what moderns came to call "mythology" in pre-literate societies, except that it understood itself as something invented, or fictional, its metaphors and stories no longer presuming to carry cosmic meanings or transcendent mysteries that once held communities together in a shared imagination of origins and ends. It was conceived as an imaginative genre etched into the consciousness of human experience, and hence different from the supposedly non-fictional discourse of historical or scientific thought.

De Certeau traces the lineage of this imagination from its flowering in the mystical sources of early modernity to its eventual fruition in modern poetics. "The mystic experience [in modernity] often has the guise of a poem that we 'hear' the way we drift into dance," he argues. Poetics carries on, against the controlled methods of theological literature, the distinctive elements he had identified as belonging to the mystical impulse: namely, a deliberate musicality, an interior attentiveness, the "canorous gait" of a rhythmic circularity, and the refusal of univocity.[39] These are the modes, he suggests, capable of sustaining the *form* of mystics in a culture that can no longer ascribe to its *substance*— Stevens' "mystical aesthetic"—which is an argument for a "poetry exceeding music" that comes to occupy "empty heaven and its hymns." Such a poetry moves in its raiding the inarticulate by the rhythms of play, with all its "sacred seriousness"—the phrase is Gadamer's[40]—by calling us beyond the manageable confines of what remains "languageable."

When we now return to the question about the role of poetics in our day and its relevance for theological discourse, the question has a complexity and urgency that resist hasty strategies or simplistic conclusions. Poetics is not a solution to the presumed problems of theological *method* in our context. And yet it might well be said that a poetic approach to epistemology—a poetic dimension of theological thinking or even a theological literature in search of a poetic form and voice—offers an insight into modern construals of reality that remain impoverished without it. What follows is an experiment in method, one construing poetics as a "technology of writing" appropriate for theological literature.

Such a poetics would be characterized by an interest in the "motion" of language, the energy speech holds for both self and "other." It leads us to consider the creation of texts that invite the reader into the writer's practice. The work of poetry raids the inarticulate in diverse ways, among which three bear special mention. First, *poetics affirms the eloquence of margins*, those boundaries surrounding all language and insight and experience as the indefinable and elusive far edge of the horizon where ocean and sky mingle. Let us call this eloquence the recognition of unboundedness, or what the poet Rilke often refers to simply as "the Open" (*das Offene*). Second, *poetics values the surfaces* as not only a limiting of meaning behind which the truth hides, in a Platonic sense, but rather as places of change and growth, discovering the "traces" of meaning referred to by the writer John Berger. And, third, *poetics arises among the fragments* of life, conveying a grammar of desire discovered in separations, in the yearning for the other across the distances that carry at least shadows of a once luminous transcendence. Let us call this passion the music of solidarity, the cradle of the imagination, an aesthetic moving us from the private into the public realm. Fragments elicit the political momentum of poetics, the manner in which the language of poetry expresses a longing for communion in the fractured cultural and religious spaces of our time.

In distinctly non-religious ways each of these dimensions of poetics addresses the alienation of modern life by suggesting how late-modern societies are shaped by the experience of *absence* at the margins, *isolation* on the surfaces, and *loneliness* between the fragments. This approach invites us to consider poetics neither as an illustration of religious themes nor as a matter of a literary *form* but rather as an aesthetic, a way of perceiving the *word* and indwelling the *world*.[41] As Jeanette Winterson puts it, poetics offers "not a version of the facts, but an entirely different way of seeing."[42] It is to these three dimensions of poetics that we now turn, categories borrowed not from the metaphysical but from the physical realm: margins, surfaces, and fragments.

MARGINS

> In the presence of the Word which is nameless,
> > Word which is speechless, enigma, yet gathers all unknowing
>
> In its midst—Center of utterance, but unreachable
> > With voice—compass and goal—Shore towards which all
>
> Telling rows, Word which is Vowelless—brutal,
> > Singular portal of being—but barbed flesh of the tongue—
>
> At time's intersection, in a state of unknowing,
> > When that which is unlanguageable nears to enter the body . . .[43]

What is it that we do when we reach the margins where language reaches for an utterance that finally eludes our voice, leaving us in a silence shaped by the comprehension of unknowing? Poetry brings us as to those "frontiers of consciousness," as Eliot puts it, "beyond which words fail, though meanings still exist."[44] Iris Murdoch says it this way. Human language, she suggests, remains "our most evident and primary experience," but it is "broken and tested and altered all the time in relation to *something else* which certainly *seems* to be 'just sitting there.'"[45] This is true for language, she goes on to argue, because "reality [itself] resists us, it is contingent, it transcends us, it surprises us, language is a *struggle*, we live on a borderline."[46]

Not only language but also reality itself resists us. In its incomprehensibilities, it remains a force eliciting verbal expression, often enough provoked by the pressure of this resistance. Its identity as unlanguageable is not *outside* us, alien to our consciousness, but an internal force invading our silences—as the unlanguageable "nears to enter [our] body." At this margin, the provocation of speech means something other than an embarrassment at the insufficiencies of language or a stumbling before the limits of cognition. This experience points to the meaningful importance of absence, the "tactics of incompleteness" constitutive of poetics, the "reaching" which Aristotle construed as the very nature of knowledge.[47] Without such margins, and the necessary distances and absences they signify, the imagination would lose its power. Indeed, this reaching across the distances constitutes the erotic structure of metaphor, just as metaphor stands at the heart of poetics.[48] Can we find a manner of *thinking* and *writing* theology that claims such an imagination as constitutive of its method? Poetics moves us toward the margins of longing inherent in language itself, reminding us that this attraction is the "place" of our creativity. Desire is our home.

In February 1924, Rilke penned these lines on a copy of his *Duino Elegies* he gave to his Polish translator:

> Happy are those who know:
> Behind all words, the unsayable stands;
> And from that source alone, the infinite
> Crosses over to gladness, and to us—
>
> Free of our bridges,
> Built with the stone of distinctions;
> So that always, within each delight,
> We gaze at what is purely single and joined.[49]

It is in the *Duino Elegies* that we come face to face with the poet's physics of the unsayable, the source of deep meaning that can never be held within language. It is this source whose margins point toward an inarticulate inherent in our experience that draws us toward the finite islands of speech amid the surrounding oceans of silence. Such a poetics, as a mystical aesthetic not dependent upon classical metaphysics, finds the seeds of transcendence within the practices of language itself. This is an aesthetic that offers what Winquist has aptly called an "experiment of desire."[50] The poet knows this in the attractions and resistances of metaphor, in the margins where in our reaching we discover the significations of language dancing beyond our grasp. Ellen Hinsey brings us into this truth through an image of "a word's small shape" which she describes poignantly as

Thatch of marks—Wooden sanctuary for desire—
Thin structure of sounds to reach into the thunderous silence—

Meager house of a Word where to shelter its hunger.[51]

Words as the sanctuary of our desire, metaphor as a shelter for our hungers, language as reaching into "the thunderous silence": such physical insights from poetics steer toward a horizon described in pre-modern discourse by recourse to metaphysics. This expresses an essential trace of mystical insight in late modernity, even if this remains religious in an at best informal or even accidental sense. Words shelter our hunger as forms of our desire for fullness. This desire expresses the margins of presence—or is this an articulated absence, a speaking of a presence that is not finally "here" and hence remains finally unlanguageable? With the classical mystic, the poet refuses to know. In a manner reminiscent of Nietzsche's reserve, the poet discerns in our reaching through language toward this inarticulacy—which Rilke often refers to as "the Open"—the heart of our human consciousness. With a reticence characteristic of poets of the search, Rilke concedes that "it is finally our defenselessness [*Schutzlossein*] that protects us."[52]

What this offers is a sobering realization of the narrowing limits of language and, at the same time, of its unboundedness, of its power to move us toward the margins of the inarticulate where we remain within the Kantian limits of knowledge while also turning ourselves both outward *and* inward toward "the Open." Heidegger follows Rilke's lead, contending that "*all art, as the letting happen of the advent of the truth of what is, is as such essentially poetry.*"[53] All art, in its poetic vitality, is essentially "the setting-into-work of truth."[54] This is a startling approach, quite unlike de Certeau's dismissive characterization of modern writing as what he sees as a coercive "scripture" alienated from practice. It is a mark of vulnerability toward the real presences we intuit at the margins of language, a sense we know primarily as absence. The ancient mystical writers in the tradition of Bernard, the author of the *Cloud*, and John of the Cross knew this as well, discerning that the deepest spiritual posture is that of waiting in the desolations, silences, and absences of the heart. These experiences form the depths of human consciousness, these theologians reminded us, evoking the human longing for a presence that eludes us.

The same yearning marks the poetics of reticence—which I call an "apophatic eloquence"—found in the writings of Rilke, Eliot, and Stevens, to name but three. It is not merely a modern concession to the finitude of knowl-

351

edge. It is, positively stated, a sense of the "reach" of human language, and the necessary dispossession of the constructed idols of a language that refuses these traces of transcendence. "The Open," as Rilke describes this posture of vulnerability, steers us beyond the known toward the depths we yearn for. Poetics, which Heidegger calls the "unfolding of unconcealedness"—ours and, strangely, the world's—honors this margin of the inarticulate not as the *limit* but as the *lure* of language. It calls us to a defenselessness in the face of mystery, a longing that arises in the places of absence, in the consciousness of what is not and cannot be spoken—which de Certeau has called "this immense 'remainder' constituted by the part of human experience that has not been tamed and symbolized in language."[55]

SURFACES

> Praise this world to the angel, not the unutterable one.
> You cannot impress *him* with the splendor you've felt,
> for in the heavens, where he feels so sublimely,
> you're but a beginner. Show him some simple thing, then,
> that's been changed in its passage through human ages
> till it lives in our hands, in the shine of our eyes, as a part
> of ourselves.[56]

Art is first of all a way of seeing, a watchfulness by which we surrender to the transcendence of the world, including our experience of language and its limits. Only then does it take a particular form that we re-present not in argument but in image and metaphor and story. "What is the meaning to be found in the visible?" the poet John Berger asks, answering that it is "[a] form of energy, continually transforming itself"[57]—and *us*, in the process. Poetics finds its pulse in this awareness of surfaces, of visibility as an awakening not only to what *is* but also to what is *becoming*, to the flow of the world that grasps us in its energies. For this reason Schelling posited the work of art as "the absolute revelation of God," since "the objective world is the original, yet unconscious, poetry of the spirit."[58] Mary Oliver comes to the same insight:

> And I am thinking: maybe just looking and listening
> is the real work.
>
> Maybe the world, without us,
> is the real poem.[59]

Poetics is this noticing of the world as poem, this locating of ourselves in a reality that bears *and withholds* its own poetic articulations. Berger puts it this way: "It is very possible that visibility *is* the truth and that what lies outside visibility are only 'traces' of what has been or will become visible."[60] Transcendence is not only *beyond* us, in other words, but also *within* us—measured not as a metaphysical category but in the physics of our creatureliness. Earlier, Rilke had followed the same path of insight:

> And we: spectators, always, everywhere,
> turned toward all this and never beyond it.
> It overfills us. We arrange it. It falls apart.
> We arrange it again, and fall apart ourselves.[61]

Attentiveness to the visible calls us not to look *for* something, but to dwell *in* this world by letting it be *as it is*, by learning to see it in its essential dynamism and to know ourselves as held within the widest orbits (Rilke)—and yet as never contained by it since "it falls apart" as we also do. An insight of this sort recognizes the poem as a means of opening ourselves toward the surfaces of what is real, of grasping that these surfaces are *within* us and as such constitute an interior transcendental. The poem, de Certeau suggests, begins where mystics leave off, providing

353

> a labyrinth that branches out the more we circulate within it and the more we hear its voices. It is a body of journeys. To one who repeats it to himself, it contains and reveals myriad secret analogies, unsuspected languages, similarities and contrasts, surprises and unfoldings.[62]

What is true of the poem reflects the physical reality of our lives: that we are "a body of journeys," with surfaces that are themselves places of discovery, sources of unfoldings, occasions of song.

Few poets have captured this sense as poignantly, and persistently, as Wallace Stevens. In an early piece, "The Poems of Our Climate," he offers a meandering and dense meditation upon a porcelain vase filled with pink and white carnations, concluding:

> There would still remain the never-resting mind,
> So that one would want to escape, come back
> To what had been so long composed.
> The imperfect is our paradise.
> Note that, in this bitterness, delight,
> Since the imperfect is so hot in us,
> Lies in flawed words and stubborn sounds.[63]

Poetics, for Stevens, is a manner of embracing visibility as traces of what we can only begin to know. It was "a means of redemption," not in its power to name or penetrate and thereby control reality but in "coming back to the real" and beckoning us toward what he sees as "the huge, high harmony that sounds/ A little and a little, suddenly,/ By means of a separate sense."[64] And what is this but the startling insight that poet as "maker" of *words* is finally maker of *worlds*. This raid—or is it a yielding, an opening?—on the inarticulate *is* reality, or more aptly, through the poets' concession of what cannot be said, cannot be known, we *become* the reality that is ever within and yet also beyond us. This is the poet's fundamental desire, as Rilke conceives it. In his longing, as this finds visibility in word and image, the poet offers her purest meditation, her truest prayer.

FRAGMENTS

In his Norton Lectures of 1981–82, published as *The Witness of Poetry*, Czeslaw Milosz speaks of poetics in late-modern society as shaped by a widely-felt sense of "the fragility of those things we call civilization": "What surrounds us, here and now, is not guaranteed," he suggests, since "[i]t could just as well not exist—and so man constructs poetry out of the remnants found in ruins."[65] In an elegy lamenting the lost culture of his youth, he describes a young boy—the author, perhaps—gazing out upon the landscape in mid-summer, at the time of the second mowing.

> He sees what I see even now. Oh but he was clever,
> Attentive, as if things were instantly changed by memory.
> Riding in a cart, he looked back to retain as much as possible.
> Which means he knew what was needed for some ultimate moment
> When he would compose from fragments a world perfect at last.[66]

The question is not whether we live among such remnants in societies like ours that refuse this truth, but rather how we are to live with these fragments and whether we find in them occasions for despair or hope. This does not avoid the postmodern concern we hear so poignantly expressed by Lyotard that modernity is a culture that has lost "a master narrative."[67] But what it does is to translate the metaphysical question about being or the mythological question about belonging into the mystical question of becoming.

At the heart of this view of poetics is the discovery of fragments as the occasion of a mystical aesthetic (Stevens), a yearning for communion with the other, a desire to indwell with others a common world and in that act not to *make* a whole from broken parts but to *see* in these parts what de Certeau has called "an itinerary . . . that is the meaning of experience." But this is not to give a structure to experience, to impose a duty upon those living perilously within a fragmented society. In this post-Kantian move, desire itself becomes the *modus vivendi*, no longer requiring the insertion of God as a necessary postulate to stabilize duty. Desire rather than duty establishes the foundations of such a late-modern poetics, postulating a morality that functions on the basis of an erotic solidarity.

In the concluding chapter of a brilliant study of ancient Greek poetics, *Eros the Bittersweet*, Anne Carson suggests that desire begins in the cradle of the imagination where we find ourselves drawn to "reach out of the present condition or beyond what [we] already know."[68] In this reaching, or in the space created by it, eros constructs a story, a fiction. "When the mind reaches out to know," Carson concludes, "the space of desire opens and a necessary fiction transpires." "[B]oth the philosopher and the poet," she suggests, "find themselves describing Eros in images of wings and metaphors of flying, for desire is a movement that carries yearning hearts from over here to over there, launching the mind on a story."[69]

Poetics is about this reaching. It is not a binding what is separated into a meta-narrative, but the making of a fiction. But in this case we are not speaking of the "supreme fiction" that Stevens sought to articulate. And this is precisely the point: such a fiction *cannot* be expressed. It remains itself a boundary, an apophatic limit, necessarily relying upon, but finally also eluding, the grasp of language. It lies within but strangely also beyond us, dwelling in the fragments that become the places of our longing. It is closer to the image described in one of his final poems, when he offers that

> We live in a constellation
> Of patches and of pitches,
> Not in a single world,
> In things said well in music,
> On the piano, and in speech,
> As in a page of poetry—
> Thinkers without final thoughts
> In an always incipient cosmos,
> The way, when we climb a mountain,
> Vermont throws itself together.[70]

There is no final completeness, no single world that we can or should imagine, no final thoughts, no ultimacy capable of resolving the tensions or denying our fragmentary condition. We live in the fragments of fiction, and these are the source both of our limits and of our longing. They bring us to the place of re-membering, where we find our vocation as that of "compos[ing] from fragments a world perfect at last" (Milosz). We construct our poetry "out of the remnants found in ruins," which makes of this a political act of transcendence, an offering of the self to the other and a finding of the other as a self caught in the same loneliness. Such a poetics is instinctively and unavoidably political. It may suggest—as Stevens felt it must—a mystical aesthetic in a culture alienated from a substantive use of the imagination.

But what is the origin of what we might see as a quarrel between theology and poetry, reminiscent of Plato's banishment of the poets from the republic? If it is the poets, in our day, who continue to "safeguard the range of lan-guage"[71]—and keep alive the wide margins of silence—how is it that they seem largely alienated from the theologians and priests? Is this because in our long quest for a respectable place in the academy we have purchased our entrance at the price of our soul?

TO SING REALITY

> Maybe there's a land where you have to sing
> to explain anything . . . [72]

There is such a land, of course. Before the coming of modernity, theology was still sung in the Western churches—in the ancient epic accounts kept alive by the bards, in the monasteries with their repeating cycles of chanted psalms, in the liturgies that voiced the biblical memory as a melody of belief. All this now seems of primarily antiquarian interest to historians. But such a singing place still exists, not only in the memories of antiquity but also in the artistry of the imagination. Poets remind us of these presences. In a haunting short story, "How Old Timofei Died Singing," Rilke laments the loss of stories in modernity. The narrator encounters a lame man, Ewald, with whom he shares the old stories, and one day his friend asks, "Where did you get the story you told me last time? Out of a book?" The narrator replies sadly:

> Yes, the historians have kept it buried there, since it died; that is not so very long ago. Only a hundred years since, it lived—quite carelessly, for sure—on many lips. But the words that people use now, those heavy words one cannot sing, were its enemies and took from it one mouth after another, so that in the end it lived, most withdrawn and impoverished, on one pair of dry lips, as on a miserable widow's portion. And there it died, leaving no heirs, and was, as I have already said, buried with all honors in a book where others of its family already lay.[73]

The image of historians tending the graveyard of forgotten texts is a sobering one, and Rilke exaggerates with poetic license when he suggests that the "heavy words one cannot sing" turn away from stories with their imaginative rhythms and moods. As the story unfolds, we discover that the melody of this remembering, the singing of the imagination, constitutes something essential in the human vocation.

But what can we say of theology? Can it sustain itself in a form bereft of the musicality of language, a prosaic genre no longer edged with strong margins of the inarticulate, a limping literature that is incompatible with song? In an age suspicious of poetics, Wallace Stevens' question, "Is there a poem that never reaches words?" seems a frivolous speculation, out of place in the republic of the declarative voice where the subjunctive mood seems an unwarranted fantasy. How can we speak of a poem in search of language, one that never crosses from the far side of the inarticulate margins toward the concretions of metaphor and image, an unlanguageable transcendence caught in the very web of speech?

Poets remind us that this describes the texture of every language act, the depth of each poem; that silence is the primary condition of our beginning and ending, and language what the Quaker writer Douglas Steere calls "the foreground of reality, its articulate shore . . . back of [which] and clinging to it, when it is real, is the receptive sea of silence."[74] In the beginning, before the word found its first utterance, there was a formless void and darkness covering the face of the deep. In the end, if we can even conceive of this, what word will we know as the wind sweeps the last surfaces? The silence that precedes a musical performance is decidedly different from what falls upon the audience as the last notes drift into the waiting stillness; the first is an absence shaped by anticipation, the other of an absence carrying a remembered plenitude. Both are forms of presence, if only in the margins of our imagining. Can song exist without both of these silences? Can theology risk turning from these margins of the inarticulate in its testimony to the word that is embodied and crucified even as it awaits resurrection from the dead?

In the closing debate of the *Republic*, having explored the "long-standing quarrel between poetry and philosophy," Plato concludes that poets are a danger to the commonwealth by stimulating the growth of passion and encouraging compassion even if this opposes "the sovereignty of law." He does concede, however, that the banished poets, before being allowed to return from their exile, should be allowed to "publish [poetry's] defense in lyric verse or some other measure," and that "her champions who love poetry but are not poets" should be encouraged "to plead for her in prose, that she is no mere source of pleasure but a benefit to society and to human life."[75] The poets of modernity have rarely heard such an invitation, nor have they asked for this privilege. They might well fall into silence, conceding with Auden that "poetry makes nothing happen."[76] And, strangely, they might not dispute the content of Plato's indictment, agreeing that, yes, their intention *is* to stimulate the passions, and refusing to confine their ambitions to the minor vocation Plato conceded for them which was that of "celebrat[ing] the praises of the gods and of good men."

What the poets accomplish points toward what Robert Frost called "a clarification of life—not necessarily a great clarification, such as sects and cults are founded on, but in a momentary stay against confusion."[77] What they offer is a distinct manner of seeing, a different way of being in the world than that of argument and demonstration. What they speak in raiding the inarticulate is an invitation to see what Jeanette Winterson has called "the rebellion of art [as] a daily rebellion against the state of living death routinely called real

357

life."[78] What they privilege is the role of the imagination, which Bachelard calls "the faculty of forming images which go beyond reality, which *sing* reality"— and remind us of the creative vulnerability of human experience.[79] And, yes, what they voice is song—of praise and of lament, of clarities amid confusions, of a music that points toward a passionate way of being in the world and participating in the life of the other.

These songs carry us as readers into what Stevens calls "the imagination of life," offering poems as "a particular of life thought of for so long that one's thought has become an inseparable part of it or a particular of life so intensely felt that the feeling has entered into it."[80] Poetics expresses the human vocation at the margins with their articulate absences, upon the surfaces whose isolation beckons us toward the depths, and among the fragments where loneliness still calls us toward the solidarity of a longed-for communion. Each of these movements answers Eliot's call that we face the modern "dissociation of sensibility."[81] Each is a raid on the inarticulate, each a reaching into the chasms of alienation and loss. None seeks to win an argument, or gain a power, but each kneels before a beauty that is at once intimate and removed, unbearably absent but mysteriously present, fragile and yet somehow ineradicable to our experience. And, kneeling, in speech as in silence, each knows enough to sing our peculiar and singular "Amen."

NOTES

This essay was first delivered as the presidential address for the Society for the Study of Christian Spirituality, at the annual convention of the American Academy of Religion and the Society of Biblical Literature in Atlanta, November 2003. I am grateful to all who read, heard, and commented on this work, particularly Teresa Berger, Roberta Bondi, Elizabeth Dreyer, Karlfried Froehlich, Peter Hawkins, and Philip Sheldrake, as well as my colleagues at Andover Newton Theological School who discussed the essay with me at a faculty forum in March 2004.

1. Wallace Stevens, *The Necessary Angel. Essays on Reality and the Imagination* (New York, 1942), 81.
2. See Walter Brueggemann, *Finally Comes the Poet. Daring Speech for Proclamation* (Minneapolis, 1990).
3. Plato, *The Republic* X.601–605. For a careful discussion of the "long-standing quarrel between poetry and philosophy" in this treatise, see Stanley Rosen, *The Quarrel Between Philosophy and Poetry. Studies in Ancient Thought* (New York and London, 1988), 1–26.
4. Friedrich Nietzsche, *Thus Spoke Zarathustra. A Book for Everyone and No One*, trans. R. J. Hollingdale (London, 1961), 145, 245.
5. Hans-Georg Gadamer, *Truth and Method* (New York, 1986), 87.
6. Iris Murdoch, "Salvation by Words," in *Existentialists and Mystics. Writings on Philosophy and Literature* (New York, 1997), 241.
7. Northrop Frye, *The Educated Imagination* (New York, 1964).
8. Wallace Stevens, *The Necessary Angel*, in *Collected Poetry and Prose* (New York, 1996), 732. Hereafter cited as "CPP."

9. T. S. Eliot, "East Coker," *Four Quartets*, in *The Complete Poems and Plays 1909–1950* (New York, 1971), 128 (my emphasis).

10. Eliot, "Burnt Norton," in *CPP*, 121.

11. Douglas Steere, *Where Words Come From. An Interpretation of the Ground and Practice of Quaker Worship and Ministry* (London, 1955), 48.

12. Nietzsche, *Zarathustra*, 136.

13. Ibid., 128.

14. Stevens, from "Adagia," in *CPP*, 903.

15. Ibid.

16. Jorie Graham, "Covenant," *Never* (New York, 2002), 73.

17. Martin Heidegger, "What Are Poets For?" in *Poetry, Language, Thought*, trans. A. Hofstadter (New York, 1971), 92–3.

18. Wendell Berry, *Sabbaths 1987* (Monterey, Kentucky, 1991), 6.

19. Leigh Schmidt, "The Making of Modern Mysticism," *Journal of the American Academy of Religion* 71 (2003): 273–302.

20. For the first, see Alfred Corn, "Wallace Stevens and the Poetics of Ineffability," in Peter Hawkins and Anne Howland Schotter, eds., *Ineffability. Naming the Unnameable from Dante to Beckett* (New York, 1984), 179–88; for the second, see Nathan A. Scott, Jr., "Stevens's Route—Transcendence Downward," in *The Poetics of Belief. Studies in Coleridge, Arnold, Pater, Santayana, Stevens, and Heidegger* (Chapel Hill, NC, and London, 1985), 115–45.

21. Stevens, "The Ultimate Poem Is Abstract," in *CPP*, 369–70.

22. Stevens, "Notes Toward a Supreme Fiction," in *CPP*, 348.

23. Stevens, "Adagia" and "Relations Between Poetry and Painting," in *CPP*, 914, 748.

24. Paul Tillich speaks of this abandonment of the symbolic as a cultural loss of the depths of human experience. In this critique he extends Max Weber's criticism of modernity for its "disenchantment of the world" (*die Entzauberung der Welt*), a *zweckrational* or pragmatic mindset offering no compensation for the loss of the symbolic. Following Weber and Tillich, Edward Farley points to the "loss of [our] society's powerful deep symbols" as imperiling the very possibility of civil society; see his *Deep Symbols. Their Postmodern Effacement and Reclamation* (Valley Forge, PA, 1996), 5. Morris Berman makes a similar point in his *The Reenchantment of the World* (Ithaca and London, 1981). These critics join in arguing for an "enchantment" of culture as an imaginative reconstituting of civic life, the creating of a generative public discourse through a poetics whose symbols derive from a larger narrative framework.

25. Amos Wilder, *Grace Confounding: Poems* (Philadelphia, 1972), ix.

26. Nietzsche, *Zarathustra*, 333.

27. Stevens, "A Primitive Like an Orb," in *CPP*, 378.

28. Richard Wilbur, "For Dudley," *Walking to Sleep. New Poems and Translations*, reprinted in *New and Collected Poems* (San Diego, New York, and London, 1988), 135.

29. Stevens, *The Necessary Angel*, in *CPP*, 681.

30. Stevens, "Reply to Papini," in *CPP*, 383–4.

31. Julia Kristeva, *Black Sun. Depression and Melancholia*, trans. Leon S. Roudiez (New York, 1989), 102.

32. Charles Winquist, *Desiring Theology* (Chicago and London, 1995), 54.

33. Ibid., 96.

34. Ibid., 63, 87.

35. Michel de Certeau, *The Mystic Fable*, vol. 1, *The Sixteenth and Seventeenth Centuries*, trans. Michael B. Smith (Chicago, 1992), 13.

36. Stevens, "The Man With the Blue Guitar," in *CPP*, 136–7.

37. For a penetrating discussion of this development, see Louis Dupré, "The Birth of the Past," in *Passage to Modernity. An Essay in the Hermeneutics of Nature and Culture* (New Haven and London, 1993), 145–64.

38. On this point, see Lionel Gossman, *Between History and Literature* (Cambridge, MA, and London, 1990), 227–56.
39. See de Certeau, *The Mystic Fable*, 295–99.
40. Ibid., 91.
41. Heidegger explores poetry as a "dwelling place" in an essay entitled "Building Dwelling Thinking," reprinted in *Poetry, Language, Thought*, 143–62.
42. Jeanette Winterson, *Art Objects. Essays on Ecstasy and Effrontery* (New York, 1997), 28.
43. Ellen Hinsey, *The White Fire of Time* (Middletown, Connecticut, 2002), 57.
44. Eliot, "The Music of Poetry," in *On Poetry and Poets* (London and Boston, 1957), 30.
45. Murdoch, "Art and Eros," in *Existentialists and Mystics*, 478. These are thoughts offered by Socrates in her fictional dialogue.
46. Ibid.
47. Aristotle, *Metaphysics* A 1.980a21. Cited in Anne Carson, *Eros the Bittersweet*, 70.
48. Carson, *Eros*, 77.
49. Cited in Jane Hirshfield, *Nine Gates: Entering the Mind of Poetry* (Cambridge, Massachusetts, 1983), 56.
50. See here Charles Winquist, *The Surface of the Deep* (Aurora, CO, 2003), 102.
51. Hinsey, *White Fire*, 58.
52. Rilke, as cited in Martin Heidegger, *Poetry, Language, Thought*, trans., Albert Hofstadter (New York, 1971), 99, 121.
53. Martin Heidegger, "The Origin of the Work of Art," in *Poetry, Language, Thought*, 72.
54. Ibid., 74.
55. Michel de Certeau, *The Practice of Everyday Life*, trans. S. Rendall (Berkeley, CA, 1984), 61.
56. Rilke, "The Ninth Elegy," in William H. Gass, *Reading Rilke. Reflections on the Problems of Translation* (New York, 1999), 214–15.
57. John Berger, *The Sense of Sight* (New York, 1985), 212.
58. F. W. von Schelling, *Philosophie der Kunst* (1802), in *Schellings Werke* (Munich, 1977), 493.
59. Mary Oliver, *The Leaf and the Cloud. A Poem* (Cambridge, Massachusetts, 2000), 17.
60. Berger, *The Sense of Sight*, 219.
61. Rainer Maria Rilke, "The Eighth Elegy," from *The Duino Elegies*, in *The Essential Rilke*, trans. and ed. Galway Kinnell and Hannah Liebmann (Hopewell, New Jersey, 1999), 129.
62. De Certeau, *The Mystic Fable*, 298.
63. Stevens, "The Poems of Our Climate," in *CPP*, 179.
64. Stevens, "A Primitive Like an Orb," in *CPP*, 378.
65. Czeslaw Milosz, *The Witness of Poetry* (Cambridge, Massachusetts, 1983), 97.
66. This poem, untitled, is published as the frontispiece of *The Witness of Poetry*, without pagination.
67. See Farley, *Deep Symbols*, 6.
68. Carson, *Eros*, 169.
69. Ibid., 172–73.
70. Stevens, "July Mountain," in *CPP*, 476.
71. John Coulson, *Religion and Imagination. "In Aid of a Grammar of Assent"* (Oxford, 1981), 11.
72. William Stafford, "A Course in Creative Writing," in *The Way It Is* (St. Paul, MN, 1998), 195.
73. Rilke, *Stories of God*, trans. M. D. Herter Norton (New York, 1932), 47–8.
74. Steere, *Where Words Come From*, 48.
75. *The Republic*, Bk. X, 605–6.

76. W. H. Auden, "In Memory of W. B. Yeats," in *The Collected Poetry of W. H. Auden* (New York, 1945), 50.

77. Robert Frost, "The Figure a Poem Makes," in *Collected Poems, Prose, and Plays* (New York, 1995), 777.

78. Jeanette Winterson, "The Semiotics of Sex," *Art Objects*, 108.

79. Gaston Bachelard, *On Poetic Imagination and Reverie*, trans. Colette Gaudin (Dallas, 1987), 15.

80. Stevens, *The Necessary Angel*, in *CPP*, 684.

81. In an essay Eliot finished in the aftermath of the war, "The Social Function of Poetry" (1948), he suggested, "The trouble of the modern age is not merely the inability to believe certain things about God and [humanity] which our forefathers believed, but the inability to *feel* towards God and [humanity] as they did. A belief in which you no longer believe is something which to some extent you can still understand; but when religious feeling disappears, the words in which [people] have struggled to express it become meaningless." See "The Social Function of Poetry" (1948), in *On Poetry and Poets* (London and Boston, 1957), 25. See also his earlier Clark (1926) and Turnbull (1933) Lectures on poetics, recently published in a collection as T. S. Eliot, *The Varieties of Metaphysical Poetry*, edited and introduced by Ronald Schuchard (New York, San Diego, London, 1993). This had been a longstanding intellectual fascination with Eliot, traced back to early essays dating from 1917 on the metaphysical poets of the seventeenth century, and his later Clark and Turnbull Lectures (1926 in Cambridge, England, and 1933 in Baltimore, respectively),81 in which he developed his notion of a "dissociation of sensibility" among modern poets after Donne—which is to say, of the nineteenth and twentieth centuries. By this he pointed to a shift in consciousness and language across the wide divide leading toward modernity, by which time the poetic object, feeling, and thought once identified in a common *mentalité*, were either separated or estranged.

Emerging Issues and New Trajectories in the Study of Christian Spirituality

The wind blows where it chooses, and you hear the sound of it, but you do not know where it comes from or where it goes. So it is with everyone who is born of the Spirit.
—John 3.8 (NRSV)

For those who live in regions with changeable climates, meteorology is at best an inexact science. Weather patterns follow their own designs, defying the certainties of tools used for prediction. The Spirit is as elusive, as this saying from John's gospel reminds us. We might know something about her comings and goings in our own lives and perhaps even in the church and wider society, but the Spirit follows a logic we cannot manage or ever fully know. She is as free as the winds and as variable as the human spirit. The challenge of the study of Christian spirituality is to honor the Spirit's freedom while remaining faithful to spirituality's long and distinguished intellectual traditions. Thus, the study of spirituality as an emerging discipline depends upon formal disciplines of the academy as well as upon the arts of discernment. It increasingly calls into play a wide range of scholarly approaches and fields, as it maintains a humble and clear eye on the elusiveness of the Spirit's power and presence.

The very term "spirituality" has a venerable history.[1] It has also seen a dramatic broadening of usage in recent decades. Indeed, a search of the World Wide Web for "Christian spirituality" yields almost three million sites, a proliferation of uses that is one of the peculiar cultural phenomena of our times. The specific focus of contributors to this volume moves beyond such general uses, addressing the manner in which Christian spirituality has emerged as an arena of intellectual inquiry and entered the formal discourse of the academy as a field of study in its own right. The contributors to this work explore a variety of expressions of Christian spirituality, in both historical traditions and sources and within the broad horizon of contemporary Christian experience.

Many of the chapters in this volume offer groundbreaking initiatives in this field, applying to the inquiry a variety of methods from various disciplines. These include academic disciplines found in the classical theological curriculum, like biblical studies, theology, history, and ethics, and those of the social sciences, like psychology and the sociology of religion and newer disciplines devoted to identity and culture, such as ritual and gender studies. As these collaborations indicate, interdisciplinarity characterizes much of the work done in this field, and there is every reason to expect this trend to continue.

As inquiries into issues of theory and practice, these essays deepen our appreciation of the complex and shifting horizons of the study of Christian spirituality. Several significant research trajectories are worthy of mention, clustering around key themes and methods that suggest future developments. They address the most basic questions of definition: What *is* spirituality, and how can we delineate what constitutes a properly *Christian* spirituality? What methods are best suited to gain insight into the spiritual life in its historical, personal, and global dimensions? What approaches are sufficiently attuned to present cultural realities that they open new horizons, bringing the tradition forward in helpful and compelling ways?

TRADITION AND EXPERIENCE

Miguel de Unamuno once asserted that "we live in memory and by memory, and our spiritual life is at bottom simply the effort of our memory to persist, to transform itself into hope, the effort of our past to transform itself into our future."[2] Christian spirituality is always, in part, a matter of memory, and thus an *inherited* identity. Since the beginnings of Christianity, tradition has been a determining force in faith and life. We continue to read the Scriptures and other texts, ancient, medieval, and modern, because we discern in them not only authoritative theological content but a wisdom that continues to bring life and insight to our contemporary search for spiritual meaning.

This is not to say that spirituality is exclusively historical in nature or to imply that this tradition is one we are to receive uncritically. Much of the work in the field of spirituality explores the critical reception of this witness and the critical relation of experience to such memory. But a properly Christian spirituality will always have some grounding in the inheritance of the church's historical tradition. Paul's words to the Corinthian Christians establish a pattern traced through the church's life: "I have received from the Lord what I also handed on to you" (*quod et tradidi vobis*, 1 Cor. 11.23). Echoing down the ages, this richly complex message establishes the foundation of Christian spirituality, reminding us that present experience always stands in relation to the authoritative memories of scripture and tradition. The very nature of our spiritual identity as Christians brings us into critical and creative engagement with the past, which by its voices addresses us and holds us accountable to question its anomalies and to make sense of its omissions and even its silences.

Christian spirituality is also shaped by present experience—memory transforming itself into *our future*, in Unamuno's terms. Thus, reading the past in light of our lives today reminds us that tradition is a living reality, shaped by the complex influences of culture and identity upon its practices, texts, and images. In the century since William James's Gifford Lectures, *Varieties of Religious Experience* (1901–2), the sense of what constitutes experience has been at the center of scholarly inquiry and debate. We now take for granted insights from sociology and psychology, as well as phenomenology, cultural anthropology, and semiotics, in approaching this question, leading to discoveries that James could only dimly have anticipated. Such perspectives contribute to our understanding of spirituality as a human dimension of experience and continue to shape the study of Christian spirituality in important ways.

It is also increasingly apparent that the physiological dimensions of experience invite us to include biology and the neurosciences as collaborative partners. We now understand that the nature of the brain itself determines dimensions of human experience and perception—including the spiritual—to an extent we are only beginning to appreciate. Future academic study of Christian spirituality will need to attend to these disciplines and apply their methods and approaches to its own work.

SOURCES

Students of Christian spirituality have critically embraced a range of new sources relevant to their task. The "classics" of theological study no longer seem the sole or even the primary measures of what influences and shapes religious experience. In many cultures, spiritual identity cannot be adequately understood by a literacy defined exclusively in terms of canonical texts and their readers. Referring primarily to medieval culture, one historian suggests that "there is also textuality that works orally."[3] This may be even more true for contemporary cultures, not only in the so-called developing nations but also in terms of the increasingly image-oriented cultures of the globalized world of the Internet. What forms will spirituality take in this age of "virtual reality," and how will we learn to study such developments? Students of spirituality will need to be alert and sensitive to the wondrous array of ways in which religious identity is shaped and conveyed in communities and cultures both at home and around the globe. New sources include the material dimensions of Christianity, and the broadening interest in "popular" religion leads toward sources that are often non-textual. Scholars of spirituality also engage ritual studies, a long-established partner in the exploration of non-Christian religions and now used to interpret the complex nature of Christian spirituality as it is transmitted within faith communities via worship, ceremony, and ritual.

More attention is being paid to the arts and their role in expressing and shaping Christian spirituality. This examination spans the history of Christianity, from traditional religious artifacts and sacred spaces created and used by earlier Christians to the interpretation of contemporary artistic expressions as modes of spiritual knowledge and communication. There is a growing interest within and outside the academy in how the visual arts function in devotional, liturgical, sacramental, and even domestic forms of spirituality and in what these insights suggest about spiritual identity. The same is true of the auditory arts, which perform a crucial function in the development of the spiritual life across a spectrum of Christian communities. The expressive power of music and poetry, as forms of public art, has long exerted a strong influence upon Christian spirituality, primarily through hymnody and its uses in public worship. Further collaborative work between artists and scholars will be necessary to do justice to our understanding of the arts and their complex and rich contribution to Christian spirituality. And, finally, study of the arts will need to consider the wide orbit of cultural influences arising from the global industries of film, music, and entertainment.

Such non-traditional fields of study will render more permeable the once discrete boundaries between "classic" and "popular" sources. Research into Christian spirituality will need to find new ways to document and analyze the creative expressions of such diverse phenomena as "New Age" spiritualities, the growing chasm between those who insist that they are "spiritual but not religious," the role of the institutional matrix of spirituality, the rampant growth of religious fundamentalisms—including Christian ones—around the globe, and the prominence of syncretistic spiritual practices that flourish throughout current cultures and those that existed in earlier periods. Scholars must also learn from and assess the vast growth of Pentecostalism, yet another manifestation of the new and often surprising movements of the Spirit. This panoply of spiritual forms illustrates the dictum that piety and prayer (i.e., *lex orandi*) guide and shape belief (i.e., *lex credendi*).

The study of Christian spirituality will explore familiar texts with new eyes and examine a widening range of sources within the context of pluralism in scholarly methods and approaches. Discovering how the sources—old and new—shape the imagination of Christian communities as well as the religious depth of public discourse is an urgent and complex task that will lead to a more nuanced and convincing assessment of Christian spirituality.

THE IMPORTANCE OF THE PARTICULAR

The attention to social location and particularity has challenged the legitimacy of sweeping generalizations and totalizing stories in descriptions of human identity and spiritual experience. The particular comes into play especially when we consider the self-implicating nature of spirituality, as explored in Part II of this volume, since a genuine diversity of "selves" and "others" is crucial for this study. A wave of liberationist, feminist, womanist, *mujerista,* and *minjung* scholars working since the early 1970s have challenged assumptions about the univocity with which the term "experience" has been used. These critical voices, recognizing in diverse ways what Michael Lerner has identified as "the politics of meaning," have prodded academics who still interpret historical sources and traditions as if they were identity-neutral.[4] These voices remind us of the importance of gender and sexual orientation, race and ethnicity, class and social location, locality and nationality, as crucial factors in understanding culture and experience. The study of spirituality cannot ignore how these factors impinge on our understanding of the spiritual life.

Attention to the particular applies not only to individuals and groups but also to our understanding of "church," and other configurations of Christian community. Contemporary study requires greater recognition of the impact globalization is having on forms of Christian spirituality, as the geographic centers of Christianity move from the former dominance of the Euro-American axis into the "two-thirds world." Increasingly, we will need to attend to the importance of interactions between Christianity and non-Christian religions and cultures, and to identify interreligious experience as a constitutive element of Christian spirituality. The church has long been global, but it is becoming ever more pluralistic in the blending of religious traditions and practices. The contribution of a new generation of missiological studies, many conducted outside the boundaries of North American culture, alerts us to these emerging particularities and how they extend our horizons beyond those that have defined the historical and textual foundations of Christianity in its Eurocentric forms.

Thus, we need to speak of the church's catholicity as referring no longer primarily to the assumed geographic universality of Christianity, as in the age of the early ecumenical councils, but rather to the global nature of Christianity and the blending of cultures, faiths, and traditions which characterizes its identity. We are only beginning to understand these influences on forms and styles of Christian spirituality. This awareness demands that scholars consider cross-cultural and interreligious experience and the ways these traditions and practices mingle religious texts and spiritual practices. The sheer magnitude of the change and of the expansion of horizons suggests that these phenomena of globalization can no longer remain marginal to our work.

These changes, of course, are not happening only "there." Pluralism is an increasingly normal dimension of life in the cities and even the remote rural areas of our own country. The laboratory of global Christianity is among us, and this will have ongoing implications for the study of Christian spirituality. When the first Parliament of Religions gathered representatives and delegates in Chicago in 1893, many of the North American observers came into contact with religious leaders from communities and lands that seemed to them strange, even exotic. At the second such gathering, a century later, it was clear that religious diversity was no longer determined by geographic distance. What all of this means for the study of Christian spirituality is only beginning to become apparent to students and scholars working in this field.

A JUST AND PEACEFUL WORLD ORDER

The critical retrieval of past traditions and the appropriation of the divine in the present are undertaken for the sake of the future. How do Christians envision the mission of their communities in a global context? How do our spiritual orientations support and shape commitments to justice, and what forms of ethical engagement are required of us in a world marked by interdependence on so many levels? Questions of this sort will continue to call us to explore how Christian ethical and political commitments find a grounding in spiritual practices and perceptions.

The North American tradition of pragmatism has prodded academicians to eschew the "ivory tower" in favor of creating links between academic work and the needs of the world. In compelling and distinctive ways, the study of Christian spirituality must continue to address issues of injustice, including the deepening shadows of poverty, war, exploitation, hunger, and oppression. This study must not shrink from the prophetic expressions of Christian faith and life, nor can it separate these from the widespread desire for human meaning and spiritual depth. But the very scale of global economic policies and political machinations, as well as the opposition to such commitments among those who understand spirituality as isolated from the political, often discourage and even paralyze the resolve to address matters of justice and peace. While it is important to honor the canons of scholarship as they have been articulated for our time, it is equally urgent that we continue to push the envelope in terms of creative scholarly approaches that deepen compassion for the poor and the commitment not only to understand but also to alleviate the pain of sisters and brothers.

Already particular groups of scholars have openly declared advocacy as central to their methodologies. The important emphasis emerging from the World Council of Churches' Vancouver Assembly (1983), "Justice, Peace, and the Integrity of Creation," has played a crucial role for many Christians. One also thinks of the diverse liberation theologies mentioned above, approaches that address the struggle of the marginalized on every continent. Gustavo Gutiérrez's *We Drink from Our Own Wells: The Spiritual Journey of a People* (Maryknoll, NY, 1984) has become a classic expression of this perspective, offering a compelling integration of theology and spirituality, of historical and theological analysis and the witness to spiritual experience, for the purposes of justice.

In addition, twenty-first-century students of spirituality will continue to show interest in the ways spirituality can address the medical, legal, corporate, and business communities. Concern for the ethical and spiritual dimensions of these professions and contexts is already visible, in such forms as symposia and graduate programs on spirituality and the workplace. How do scholars of Christian spirituality see their responsibilities to work with, contribute to, and learn from these professions? Since the temptation to link spirituality with crass forms of materialism is all too real, the need for informed, intelligent, and careful discernment becomes increasingly important. Most recently, spirituality has been engaged as a partner in advocacy for the health of our vulnerable ecosystems, which expresses concern for the quality of the air we breathe and the water we drink as well as for the alarming loss of species on our planet. In all these spheres we find ourselves asking how Christian spirituality forms our perceptions, attitudes, and behaviors as global citizens who have enormous powers of creativity and destructiveness.

The Christian tradition boasts a cloud of witnesses who embody the thirst for justice and model ways of compassion. Students of Christian spirituality will continue to explore the lives of Christian saints, prophets, and witnesses committed to following Jesus in his concern for others. We rely on the testimony of those who have offered such moral leadership in the church and in the public arena. One thinks of the sophisticated treatment of such justice-engaging spiritualities in recent biographies of Simone Weil, Dorothy Day, Martin Luther King, Jr., Daniel Berrigan, William Sloan Coffin, and many others. These stories offer a vivid testimony of what early theologians, following Gregory the Great, called an "ambidextrous life" that combines contemplation and action. Even when theological approaches and biblical interpretations have not made these connections clearly, spirituality has often been the thread holding them together.

At the root of a properly Christian spirituality is the love of others—family, friends, neighbors, colleagues, strangers both near and far, and even enemies (Mt. 5.43–45). The demand on our imaginations to envision forms of human solidarity and to bring about a world of justice and peace grounded in love is enormous and daunting. But love breeds creativity, and creativity nourishes a renewing flow of strategies for such healing and witness. Opposing these energies is the steadily increasing hegemony of individualism in the West and the pressures of narcissistic spiritualities, together with the dominance of depersonalized and decentralized corporations that define the global market and wreak havoc upon the world community. Christians seeking spiritual authenticity will need to join their work to the efforts of those committed to embodying justice work and peace-making as constitutive expressions of the gospel. A spirituality shaped by such commitments stands as a living response to Jesus' call to be followers of "the way."

ECUMENISM AND INTERRELIGIOUS DIALOGUE

Acknowledging the importance of the particular leads to ecumenical work and interreligious dialogue. Exchange across both denominational and religious boundaries will become increasingly integral to the study of Christian spirituality. These conversations will straddle older distinctions that once dominated ecumenical work and still structure the major initiatives within the World Council of Churches—namely, faith and order, life and work. Spirituality thrives in all these arenas and is often the common thread woven through such tapestries, particularly along the edges where we find points of exchange between these two ways of conceptualizing and experiencing the religious quest.[5]

Fidelity to doctrine, theology, and creed will be enriched through a convergence among spiritual and religious traditions. It may well be that attending to the specific traditions in one religious community will open a door for engagement with another. This possibility is the methodological heart of the emerging fields of comparative theology and spirituality. The vigorous debate about whether and how we might speak of a common mystical experience among practitioners of diverse religious traditions with different theologies, cosmologies, and rituals is likely to continue and sharpen in the years ahead. Collaboration among both practitioners and scholars is a desideratum that will require opportunity, openness, and engagement. But while further exploration in epistemology and in the labyrinthine ways of experience is one of the most demanding tasks ahead of us, it is also among the most pressing. Opening oneself to the harmony of the spheres is a spiritual prerequisite for peaceful relationships on earth, and mutual knowledge and respect is the key to a unity that honors greater and greater diversity.

CONCLUSION

Is the study of Christian spirituality exclusively or even primarily a professional academic enterprise? Certainly not. The work of the academy is but one voice in a multivocal endeavor. But it is important that the academy turn to the sources of a pluralistic and vital spiritual practice "on the ground" in order to offer support, insight, and guidance. If done well, the work of the academy is likely to stimulate new forms of ecumenical engagement, guided by experiential and theological questions arising from the manifestations of the Spirit across a wide spectrum of cultures in our day. What we have sketched in this concluding chapter points to the most prominent among emerging issues and new trajectories in the study of Christian spirituality, but we concede that the future of this discipline is open-ended. As this young academic field grows in clarity and confidence, it will surely also remain in a state of flux, in part because the very nature of Christian experience is dynamic and unfinished. It is imperative for students of Christian spirituality both to guard the venerable traditions of textual study and to welcome developments that cross disciplinary boundaries, bringing into conversation new sources, communities, and practices long separated or excluded.

It is likely, too, that the flurry of recent scholarly interest in apophatic or negative theology will continue. Postmodern skepticism about universals extends to language itself, pushing the centers of meaning toward the margins of unknowing. As we become more and more inundated with words and images, we reach out to the sacred halls of silence whose value has been a constant in the tradition. These new sensitivities to the God who is beyond word and reason invite us to humility and wonder. We are also invited to regard the difficult experiences that arise from the failures, blindness, arrogance, and violence too often visited on the unsuspecting and undeserving in the name of the Christian God of love. The courage to own and analyze such vulnerabilities in a critically discerning way is a *sine qua non* of a vibrant future for this tradition. The tensions between beauty and ugliness, word and silence, reason and ecstasy, history and eternity must be maintained and studied in ever new and creative forms.

The Spirit, like the wind, "blows where it chooses, and you hear the sound of it, but you do not know where it comes from or where it goes." The study of Christian spirituality must attend to and honor the Spirit's free and unbounded movements, even as this study assumes the sacred responsibility of seeking to affirm the order and meaning found in humanity's encounter with the triune God. We offer these essays, a record of significant contributions to this work during the past decade, with the hope that they might accompany, support, and stimulate a wide range of readers: scholars and teachers of spirituality who dedicate themselves to thoughtful and rigorous study of the Spirit's presence in the human community; students of Christian theology and others who express their interest on the boundary of this research; seekers who pursue the Spirit's lead in the light, as well as those who follow its movements into the darkness; and those who open themselves to the Spirit's breath and those for whom this path is difficult or distant. It is the conviction of the authors included in this volume that understanding the Christian spiritual life can lead us, through intellectual discourse and reflection, toward constructive ways of being human in this sacred and fragile world.

NOTES

1. See Bernard McGinn, "The Letter and the Spirit," Chapter 2 of this volume.
2. Miguel de Unamuno, *The Tragic Sense of Life* (London, 1921), 28.
3. Brian Stock, *Listening for the Text: On the Uses of the Past* (Baltimore and London, 1990), 144.
4. Michael Lerner, *The Politics of Meaning: Restoring Hope and Possibility in an Age of Cynicism* (Oxford, 1997).
5. See for example, A. van der Bent, "The Concern for Spirituality: An Analytical and Bibliographical Survey of the Discussion in the WCC Constituency," in *Ecumenical Review* 38 (1986): 101–14.

FURTHER READING

Part I. Spirituality as an Academic Discipline: Foundations and Methods

Hanson, Bradley, ed. *Modern Christian Spirituality: Methodological and Historical Essays*. Vol. 62 of American Academy of Religion Series in Religion. Atlanta, GA, 1990.

Helminiak, Daniel. *Religion and the Human Sciences: An Approach via Spirituality*. Stony Brook, NY, 1998.

Jones, Cheslyn, Geoffrey Wainwright, and Edward Yarnold, eds. *The Study of Spirituality*. New York and Oxford, 1986.

Kinerk, Edward. "Toward a Method for the Study of Spirituality." *Review for Religious* 40 (1981): 3–19.

Principe, Walter. "Towards Defining Spirituality." *Sciences Religieuses* 12 (1983): 127–41; reprinted in *The New Dictionary of Catholic Spirituality*, edited by Michael Downey. Collegeville, MN, 1993.

Sheldrake, Philip. *Spirituality and History: Questions of Interpretation and Method*. New York, 1992.

Waaijman, Kees. "A Hermeneutic of Spirituality." *Studies in Spirituality* 5 (1995): 5–39.

———. *Spirituality: Forms, Foundations, Methods*, translated by John Vriend. Louvain, Belgium, 2002.

———. "Spirituality as Transformation Demands a Structural, Dynamic Approach." *Studies in Spirituality* 1 (1991): 25–35.

Part II. The Self-Implicating Nature of the Study of Spirituality

Bourdieu, Pierre. *Outline of a Theory of Practice*, translated by Richard Nice. Cambridge, 1977.

Houck, Anita. "Spirituality and Pedagogy: Faith and Reason in the Age of Assessment." *Spiritus* 2 (2002): 50–63.

McGinn, Bernard. "The Language of Inner Experience in Christian Mysticism." *Spiritus* 1 (2001): 156–71.

Saliers, Don E. "Prayer and the Doctrine of God in Contemporary Theology." *Interpretation* (July 1980): 265–78.

Springsted, Eric O. "Theology and Spirituality; or, Why Theology Is Not Critical Reflection on Religious Experience." In *Spirituality and Theology: Essays in Honor of Diogenes Allen*, edited by Eric O. Springsted. Louisville, KY, 1998.

Taves, Ann. "Detachment and Engagement in the Study of 'Lived Experience.'" *Spiritus* 3 (2003): 186–208.

Volf, Miroslav, and Dorothy Bass. *Practicing Theology: Beliefs and Practices in Christian Theology.* Grand Rapids, MI, 2002.

Part III. Interpreting the Tradition: Historical and Theological Perspectives

Allen, Diogenes. *Spiritual Theology: The Theology of Yesterday for Spiritual Help Today.* Boston, 1997.

Aumann, Jordan. *Spiritual Theology.* Huntington, IN, 1980.

Bent, A. van der. "The Concern for Spirituality: An Analytical and Bibliographical Survey of the Discussion within the World Council of Churches Constituency." *Ecumenical Review* 38 (1986): 101–14.

Bouyer, Louis, et al. *A History of Christian Spirituality,* 3 vols. London, 1968.

Brooks, Peter, ed. *Christian Spirituality: Essays in Honour of Gordon Rupp.* London, 1975.

Cognet, Louis. *Post-Reformation Spirituality,* translated by P. Hepburne Scott. New York, 1959.

Cousins, Ewert. "Spirituality: A Resource for Theology." *Proceedings of the Catholic Theological Society of America* 35 (1980): 124–37.

DeGuibert, Joseph. *The Theology of the Spiritual Life.* London, 1954.

Downey, Michael, ed. *The New Dictionary of Catholic Spirituality.* Collegeville, MN, 1993.

Dupré, Louis, and Don Saliers, eds. *Christian Spirituality.* Vol. 3, *Post-Reformation and Modern.* New York, 1989; London, 1990.

Giles, Mary E., ed. *The Feminist Mystic and Other Essays on Women and Spirituality.* New York, 1985.

Gutiérrez, Gustavo. *We Drink from Our Own Wells: The Spiritual Journey of a People.* Maryknoll, NY, 1984.

Jantzen, Grace. *Power, Gender, and Christian Mystics.* Cambridge, 1995.

Johnson, Luke Timothy. *Religious Experience in Earliest Christianity.* Minneapolis, 1998.

Johnston, William. *"Arise, My Love . . .": Mysticism for a New Age.* Maryknoll, NY, 2000.

———. *The Inner Eye of Love.* San Francisco, 1978.

Jones, Cheslyn, Geoffrey Wainwright, and Edward Yarnold, eds. *The Study of Spirituality.* New York and Oxford, 1986.

Kaam, Adrian van. *In Search of Spiritual Identity.* Denville, NJ, 1975.

Kereszty, Roch. "Theology and Spirituality: The Task of Synthesis." *Communio* 10 (1983): 314–31.

Leech, Kenneth. *Experiencing God: Theology as Spirituality.* San Francisco, 1985. Originally published as *True God.* London, 1985.

Louth, Andrew. *Discerning the Mystery: An Essay on the Nature of Theology.* Oxford, 1983.

———. *The Origins of the Christian Mystical Tradition from Plato to Denys.* Oxford, 1981.

———. *Theology and Spirituality.* London, 1978.

McGinn, Bernard. *The Presence of God: A History of Western Christian Mysticism.* Vol. 1, *The Foundations of Mysticism.* New York, 1992. Vol. 2, *The Development of Mysticism.* New York, 1996. Vol. 3, *The Flowering of Mysticism.* New York, 2003.

McGinn, Bernard, and Moshe Idel, eds. *Mystical Union in Judaism, Christianity, and Islam: An Ecumenical Dialogue*. New York, 1996.

McGinn, Bernard, and Patricia McGinn. *Early Christian Mystics: The Divine Vision of the Spiritual Masters*. New York, 2003.

McGinn, Bernard, John Meyendorff, and Jean Leclercq, eds. *Christian Spirituality*. Vol. 1, *Origins to the Twelfth Century*. London, 1986.

McIntosh, Mark. *Mystical Theology*. Oxford, 1998.

Megyer, Eugene. "Theological Trends: Spiritual Theology Today." *The Way* 21 (1981): 55–67.

Mooney, Catherine, ed. *Gendered Voices: Medieval Saints and Their Interpreters*. Philadelphia, 1999.

Newman, Barbara. *From Virile Woman to WomanChrist: Studies in Medieval Religion and Literature*. Philadelphia, 1995.

Pannenberg, Wolfhart. *Christian Spirituality and Sacramental Community*. Philadelphia, 1983.

Perrin, David, ed. *Women Christian Mystics Speak to Our Times*. Franklin, WI, 2001.

Petroff, Elizabeth Alvida, ed. *Body and Soul: Essays on Medieval Women and Mysticism*. New York, 1994.

Rahner, Karl. "Mystical Experience and Mystical Theology." Vol. 17 of *Theological Investigations*. New York, 1981.

Raitt, Jill, ed. *Christian Spirituality*. Vol. 2, *High Middle Ages and Reformation*. London, 1987.

Schneiders, Sandra. "Theology and Spirituality: Strangers, Rivals, or Partners?" *Horizons* 13 (1986): 676–97.

Sheldrake, Philip. *Spirituality and History*. New York, 1992.

———. *Spirituality and Theology: Christian Living and the Doctrine of God*. Maryknoll, NY, 1998.

Springsted, Eric O., ed. *Spirituality and Theology: Essays in Honor of Diogenes Allen*. Louisville, KY, 1998.

Williams, Rowan. *The Wound of Knowledge: A History of Christian Spirituality from the New Testament to John of the Cross*. Boston, 1987.

Part IV. Spirituality and Healing

Baird, M. L. *On the Side of the Angels: Ethics and Post-Holocaust Spirituality*. Paris, and Dudley, MA, 2002.

Bakken, Kenneth L. *The Journey into God: Healing and the Christian Faith*. Minneapolis, MN, 2000.

Battle, Michael. *Blessed Are the Peacemakers: A Christian Spirituality of Nonviolence*. Macon, GA, 2004.

Bringle, Mary Louise, and James Fowler. *Despair or Sin? Hopelessness and Healing in the Christian Life*. Nashville, TN, 1990.

Campbell, Peter A. *Health as Liberation: Medicine, Theology, and the Quest for Justice*. Cleveland, OH, 1995.

Epperly, Bruce. *Spirituality and Health*. Mystic, CT, 1997.

Gesler, Wilbert M. *Healing Places*. Lanham, MD, 2003.

Harris, Ruth. *Lourdes: Body and Spirit in the Secular Age*. London and New York, 1999.

375

Hull, Fritz, ed. *Earth and Spirit: The Spiritual Dimensions of the Environmental Crisis.* New York, 1994.

Imoda, Franco. *Human Development: Psychology and Mystery.* Louvain, Belgium, 1998.

Kelsey, Morton. *Healing and Christianity.* New York, 1973.

Kinsley, David R. *Health, Healing, and Religion: A Cross-Cultural Perspective.* Upper Saddle River, NJ, 1996.

Murchú, Diarmuid. *Reclaiming Spirituality: A New Spirituality for Today's World.* New York, 1998.

Olivera, Dom Bernardo, O.C.S.O. "Maturity and Generation: The Spiritual Formation of Our Young People." *Spiritus* 3 (2003): 38–51.

Paulsell, Stephanie. *Honoring the Body: Meditations on a Christian Practice.* San Francisco, 2002.

Pieris, Aloysius, S.J. "Ecumenism in the Churches and the Unfinished Agenda of the Holy Spirit." *Spiritus* 3 (2003): 53–67.

Sanford, John A. *Healing Body and Soul: The Meaning of Illness in the New Testament and in Psychotherapy.* Louisville, KY, 1992.

Shumna, Joel James, and Keith G. Meador. *Heal Thyself: Spirituality, Medicine, and the Distortion of Christianity.* Oxford, 2003.

Wolski-Conn, Joann. *Spirituality and Personal Maturity.* New York, 1989.

Part V. Spirituality and Aesthetics

Apostolos-Cappadona, Diane, ed. *Art, Creativity, and the Sacred: An Anthology in Religion and Art.* New York, 1995.

Avis, Paul. *God and the Creative Imagination: Metaphor, Symbol and Myth in Religion and Theology.* London and New York, 1999.

Balthasar, Hans Urs von. *The Glory of the Lord: A Theological Aesthetics,* 7 vols. San Francisco, 1982.

Begbie, Jeremy S. *Sounding the Depths: Theology through the Arts.* London, 2003.
———. *Theology, Music and Time.* Cambridge, 2000.

Begbie, Jeremy S., and Colin Gunton, eds. *Voicing Creation's Praise: Towards a Theology of the Arts.* Edinburgh, 1991.

Belting, Hans. *Likeness and Presence: A History of the Image before the Era of Art.* Chicago, 1994.

Brown, Frank Burch. *Good Taste, Bad Taste, and Christian Taste: Aesthetics in Religious Life.* Oxford and New York, 2000.

Dillenberger, Jane D. *Image and Spirit in Sacred and Secular Art.* New York, 2000.

Dillenberger, John. *A Theology of Artistic Sensibilities: The Visual Arts and the Church.* New York, 1986.

Dixon, John W., Jr. *Images of Truth: Religion and the Art of Seeing.* Vol. 3 of Ventures in Religion series. Atlanta, GA, 1996.

Dyrness, William A. *Visual Faith: Art, Theology, and Worship in Dialogue: Engaging Culture.* Grand Rapids, MI, 2001.

Finney, Paul Corby. *The Invisible God: The Earliest Christians on Art.* Oxford, 1997.
———, ed. *Seeing beyond the Word: Visual Arts and the Calvinist Tradition.* Grand Rapids, MI, 1999.

Freedberg, David. *The Power of Images: Studies in the History and Theory of Response.* Chicago, 1989.

García-Rivera, Alex. *A Wounded Innocence: Sketches for a Theology of Art.* Collegeville, MN, 2003.

Hazelton, Roger. *A Theological Approach to Art.* Nashville, TN, 1967.

Hornik, Heidi J., and Mikeal C. Parsons, eds. *Interpreting Christian Art: Reflections on Christian Art.* Macon, GA, 2003.

Laeuchli, Samuel. *Religion and Art in Conflict: Introduction to a Cross-Disciplinary Task.* Philadelphia, 1980.

Miles, Margaret R. *Image as Insight: Visual Understanding in Western Christianity and Secular Culture.* Boston, 1985.

Morgan, David. *Visual Piety: A History and Theory of Popular Religious Images.* Berkeley, 1998.

O'Donohue, John. *Beauty: The Invisible Embrace.* San Francisco, 2004.

Viladesau, Richard. *Theological Aesthetics: God in Imagination, Beauty, and Art.* Oxford, 1999.

Wolterstorff, Nicholas. *Art in Action: Toward a Christian Aesthetic.* Grand Rapids, MI, 1980.

Wuthnow, Robert. *All in Sync: How Music and Art Are Revitalizing American Religion.* Berkeley, 2003.

———. *Creative Spirituality: The Way of the Artist.* Berkeley, 2001.

CONTRIBUTORS

J. MATTHEW ASHLEY is Associate Professor of Systematic Theology at the University of Notre Dame in South Bend, Indiana.

THOMAS BERRY is a former director of the Riverdale Center for Religious Studies in Riverdale, New York, and retired Professor of the History of Religions at Fordham University, New York.

MARK S. BURROWS is Professor of the History of Christianity at Andover Newton Theological School in Newton Centre, Massachusetts.

DOUGLAS BURTON-CHRISTIE is Associate Professor of Theological Studies at Loyola Marymount University in Los Angeles.

LAWRENCE S. CUNNINGHAM is John A. O'Brien Professor of Theology at the University of Notre Dame in South Bend, Indiana.

LISA E. DAHILL is a pastor in the Evangelical Lutheran Church in America and a Research Scholar at the Carnegie Foundation for the Advancement of Teaching in Stanford, California.

ELIZABETH A. DREYER is Professor of Religious Studies at Fairfield University in Fairfield, Connecticut.

MARY FROHLICH, R.S.C.J., is Associate Professor of Spirituality at the Catholic Theological Union in Chicago, Illinois.

BELDEN C. LANE is the Hotfelder Professor in Theological Studies at Saint Louis University, Saint Louis, Missouri.

ELIZABETH LIEBERT, S.N.J.M., is Professor of Spiritual Life at San Francisco Theological Seminary and a member of the Christian Spirituality Faculty at the Graduate Theological Union, Berkeley, California.

E. ANN MATTER is Professor and Chair of Religious Studies at the University of Pennsylvania, Philadelphia.

BERNARD McGINN is Naomi Shenstone Donnelley Professor emeritus at the Divinity School of the University of Chicago.

MEREDITH B. McGUIRE is Professor of Sociology and Anthropology at Trinity University, San Antonio, Texas.

MARK McINTOSH is Associate Professor of Theology at Loyola University of Chicago.

BARBARA NEWMAN is Professor of English and Religion and holds the John Evans Chair of Latin Language and Literature at Northwestern University in Evanston, Illinois.

WALTER H. PRINCIPE, C.S.B. (d. 1996) taught at the Pontifical Institute for Mediæval Studies in Toronto, Ontario.

DON E. SALIERS is the William R. Cannon Distinguished Professor of Theology and Worship at Emory University in Atlanta, Georgia.

SANDRA M. SCHNEIDERS, I.H.M., is Professor of New Testament Studies and Spirituality at the Jesuit School of Theology and Graduate Theological Union, Berkeley, California.

PHILIP F. SHELDRAKE is the William Leech Professor of Applied Theology at the University of Durham, England.

JON SOBRINO, S.J., is Professor of Theology at the Universidad Centroamericana José Simeón Cañas in San Salvador, El Salvador.

WENDY M. WRIGHT is Professor of Theology and holds the John C. Kenefick Faculty Chair in the Humanities at Creighton University in Omaha, Nebraska.

The following essays were previously published in the *Christian Spirituality Bulletin*. They are reprinted by permission.

(Chap. 1) Sandra M. Schneiders, I.H.M., "The Study of Christian Spirituality: Contours and Dynamics of a Discipline" 6/1 (Spring 1998): 1–12.

(Chap. 2) Bernard McGinn, "The Letter and the Spirit: Spirituality as an Academic Discipline" 1/2 (Fall 1993): 1–10.

(Chap. 3) Walter H. Principe, C.S.B., "Broadening the Focus: Context as a Corrective Lens in Reading Historical Works in Spirituality" 2/1 (Spring 1994): 1–5.

(Chap. 4) Sandra M. Schneiders, I.H.M., "A Hermeneutical Approach to the Study of Christian Spirituality" 2/1 (Spring 1994): 9–14.

(Chap. 7) Douglas Burton-Christie, "The Cost of Interpretation: Sacred Texts and Ascetic Practice in Desert Spirituality" 2/1 (Spring 1994): 21–24.

(Chap. 8) Belden C. Lane, "Spider as Metaphor: Attending to the Symbol-Making Process in the Academic Discipline of Spirituality" 6/2 (Fall 1998): 1–7.

(Chap. 11) J. Matthew Ashley, "The Turn to Spirituality? The Relationship between Theology and Spirituality" 3/2 (Fall 1995): 13–18.

(Chap. 12) Lawrence S. Cunningham, "*Extra Arcam Noe:* Criteria for Christian Spirituality" 3/1 (Spring 1995): 6–9.

(Chap. 13) Elizabeth A. Dreyer, "Spirituality as a Resource for Theology: The Holy Spirit in Augustine" 4/2 (Fall 1996): 1–12.

(Chap. 14) Barbara Newman, "The Mozartian Moment: Reflections on Medieval Mysticism" 3/1 (Spring 1995): 1–5.

(Chap. 15) Mark S. Burrows, "Words That Reach into the Silence: Mystical Languages of Unsaying" 3/2 (Fall 1995): 1–5.

(Chap. 16) Mark McIntosh, "Lover without a Name: Spirituality and Constructive Christology Today" 3/2 (Fall 1995): 9–12.

(Chap. 18) Thomas Berry, "An Ecologically Sensitive Spirituality" 5/2 (Fall 1997): 1–6.

(Chap. 23) Wendy M. Wright, "'A Wide and Fleshly Love': Images, Imagination, and the Study of Christian Spirituality" 7/1 (Spring 1999): 1–12.

(Chap. 24) Don E. Saliers, "Sound Spirituality: On the Formative Expressive Power of Music for Christian Spirituality" 8/1 (Spring/Summer 2000): 1–5.

The following essays were previously published in *Spiritus*.

(Chap. 5) Mary Frohlich, R.S.C.J., "Spiritual Discipline, Discipline of Spirituality: Revisiting Questions of Definition and Method" 1/1 (Spring 2001): 65–78.

(Chap. 6) Elizabeth Liebert, S.N.J.M., "The Role of Practice in the Study of Christian Spirituality" 2/1 (Spring 2002): 30–49.

(Chap. 9) Meredith B. McGuire, "Why Bodies Matter: A Sociological Reflection on Spirituality and Materiality" 3/1 (Spring 2003): 1–18.

(Chap. 10) Bernard McGinn, "The Language of Inner Experience in Christian Mysticism" 1/2 (Fall 2001): 156–71.

(Chap. 17) Jon Sobrino, S.J., "Monseñor Romero, a Salvadoran and a Christian" 1/2 (Fall 2001): 143–55.

(Chap. 19) Lisa E. Dahill, "Reading from the Underside of Selfhood: Dietrich Bonhoeffer and Spiritual Formation" 1/2 (Fall 2001): 186–203.

(Chap. 20) E. Ann Matter, "Lourdes: A Pilgrim After All" 3/1 (Spring 2003): 68–85.

(Chap. 21) Philip F. Sheldrake, "Christian Spirituality as a Way of Living Publicly: A Dialectic of the Mystical and Prophetic" 3/1 (Spring 2003): 19–37.

(Chap. 22) Don E. Saliers, "Beauty and Terror" 2/2 (Spring 2002): 181–91.

(Chap. 25) Mark S. Burrows, "'Raiding the Inarticulate': Mysticism, Poetics, and the Unlanguageable" 4/2 (Fall 2004).